Susan S Bean $57.00
reviewed for JAOS 5/86

THE *King* AND THE *Clown*
IN SOUTH INDIAN MYTH
AND POETRY

THE *King* AND THE *Clown* IN SOUTH INDIAN MYTH AND POETRY

David Dean Shulman

PRINCETON UNIVERSITY PRESS

Published by Princeton University Press, 41 William Street,
Princeton, New Jersey 08540
In the United Kingdom: Princeton University Press, Guildford, Surrey

Library of Congress Cataloging in Publication Data will be
found on the last printed page of this book

ISBN 0-691-05457-6

This book has been composed in Linotron Bembo and Cartier

Clothbound editions of Princeton University Press books
are printed on acid-free paper, and binding materials are
chosen for strength and durability

Printed in the United States of America by Princeton University Press
Princeton, New Jersey

Parts of Chapters 3 and 5 are reprinted from my article, "Aśvatthāman and Bṛhannaḍā: Brahmin and Kingly Paradigms in the Sanskrit Epic," in S. N. Eisenstadt, ed., *The Axial Age Civilizations*, by permission of the State University of New York Press.

Parts of Chapter 2 are reprinted from my article, "Kingship and Prestation in South Indian Myth and Epic," *Asian and African Studies* (Journal of the Israel Oriental Society), vol. 19, no. 1.

Parts of Chapter 7 are reprinted from my article, "On South Indian Bandits and Kings," by permission of *Indian Economic and Social History Review* (vol. 17, no. 3).

FOR MY CLOWNS:

Eileen, Eviatar, Mishael, and Edan

Contents

List of Figures

Acknowledgments

This is a book not of answers, but of questions. It represents an attempt to extract from South Indian literary sources the vision or visions of kingship and the political order implicit in the medieval culture. Underlying this attempt is the conviction that the medieval South Indian universe was strikingly different from our own—not so much in external ways as in the concepts and perceptions which its people brought to their reality. This conviction gives rise to one fundamental question, broached but not answered here: how did the inner world or worlds of these people affect, and reflect, the nature and ordering of the political and social structures they created? What follows is an extended essay, in the literal sense of the word, aimed at exploring the background to this problem as expressed in literary images and symbols.

It is not the book I intended to write: I had been working for some time on a monograph about Kampaṉ when, gradually but insistently, this project claimed precedence. The process is reflected in the book's personal character, which I ceased to resist at an early stage of the writing.

The completion of the manuscript was made possible by the award of a fellowship from the John Simon Guggenheim Memorial Foundation, to which I am deeply grateful. I am also indebted to the Israel Academy of Sciences and Humanities for an earlier grant, which supported the purchase of several important texts. Drafts of several sections were read in seminars and lectures at the universities of Mysore, Heidelberg, Chicago, Washington, St. Cloud, Pennsylvania, and California; I am grateful to these learned audiences for many stimulating responses. Parts of the book have appeared, in different form, in *Asian and African Studies, The Indian Economic and Social History Review, Journal of Indian Folkloristics*, the *Proceedings of the Israel Academy of Sciences and Humanities* (in Hebrew), and two collections: S. N. Eisenstadt (ed.), *The Axial Age Civilizations* (Albany: State University of New York Press, 1985), and (in German) W. Schluchter (ed.), *Max Webers Studie über Hinduismus und Buddhismus, Interpretation und Kritik* (Frankfort: Suhrkamp, 1984). I am grateful to these journals and to

Professors Schluchter and Eisenstadt for providing a forum in which to develop and test my ideas, and for permission to reprint passages from the articles.

Among the many who have contributed to the thinking and writing of this book, I wish to thank in particular:

Wendy O'Flaherty, most devoted of readers, who found time to comment on several chapters even while she was immersed in the (shared?) dream-adventure of her own book on *māyā*;

J. S. Paramashivaiah, who kindly arranged for a Killekyāṭa performance in his village, and who instructed me in several delightful conversations;

Don Handelman, for extensive, penetrating comments which were of crucial importance at several stages (especially during the formulation of Chapters IV and VII);

Brenda E. F. Beck, for sharing her photographs of the South Indian village clowns;

Carmel Berkson, who showered me with amazing photographs of Śaiva *gaṇas* and other comic sculpture;

Hermann Kulke, Art Isenberg, Stuart Blackburn, and Diane Coccari, for loaning me books (an act of *tyāga* that surely generates great *puṇya*);

Lee Siegel and Joanne Waghorne, for allowing me to read chapters from their work in progress (on Indian comedy and South Indian kingship, respectively);

Jon GoldbergBelle, for long discussions on the Andhra puppet-theater;

George Hart, for insights into Kampaṉ and South Indian kingship;

V. S. Rajam, for illuminating several textual passages;

Robert E. Frykenberg, Shmuel Eisenstadt, Cynthia Talbot, Nicholas Dirks, Paula Richman, Alf Hiltebeitel, and the late Victor Turner, for many lively, encouraging, enlightening discussions;

Henry Abramovitch and James Ponet, for midnight talks on clowns and tragedy;

Margaret Case, for her dedicated and sympathetic editing;

my students in classes and seminars at the Hebrew University, especially Ronit Shamgar, Debbie Golan, Tamar Reich, Anna Shtutina, and Miri Sharf.

This book, begun in Jerusalem, was completed in the tranquil surroundings of the Department of South Asian Studies, University of Wisconsin, Madison. My debt to the department, and above all to its then chairman, Velcheru Narayana Rao, is beyond measure. If the book offers an occasional glimpse into the still largely unexamined riches of Telugu literary sources—which must someday provide a necessary corrective to the traditional Tamil-centrism of South Indian studies—the credit must go to Narayana Rao, who, with kindness, wisdom, and enthusiasm, opened this world for me.

Abbreviations

Akan.	*Akanāṉūṟu*
ALB	*Adyar Library Bulletin*
ASS	Ānandāśrama Sanskrit Series
AV	*Atharva Veda*
BĀU	*Bṛhadāraṇyaka Upaniṣad*
BEFEO	*Bulletin de l'École Française d'Extrême-Orient*
Bib. Ind.	Bibliotheca Indica (published by the Asiatic Society of Bengal)
BKI	*Bijdragen tot de Taal-, Land- en Volkenkunde*
BMGM	*Bulletin of the Madras Government Museum*
BSOAS	*Bulletin of the School of Oriental and African Studies*
Cil.	*Cilappatikāram*
CIS	*Contributions to Indian Sociology*
DED	T. Burrow and M. B. Emeneau, *A Dravidian Etymological Dictionary*
FEQ	*Far Eastern Quarterly*
HOS	Harvard Oriental Series
HR	*History of Religions*
IESHR	*Indian Economic and Social History Review*
JAOS	*Journal of the American Oriental Society*
JAS	*Journal of Asian Studies*
JB	*Jaiminīya Brāhmaṇa*
JESHO	*Journal of the Economic and Social History of the Orient*
JRAS	*Journal of the Royal Asiatic Society*
JTS	*Journal of Tamil Studies*
MBh	*Mahābhārata*
MBh, SR	*Mahābhārata*, Southern Recension
PP	*Pĕriyapurāṇam* of Cekkiḻār
Puṟan.	*Puṟanāṉūṟu*
Rām.	*Rāmāyaṇa*
RV	*Ṛg Veda*
Śat. Brāh.	*Śatapatha Brāhmaṇa*
SII	*South Indian Inscriptions*
SISS	South Indian Śaiva Siddhānta Works Publishing Company
Skt.	Sanskrit

Tai. Ār.	*Taittirīya Āraṇyaka*
Tam.	Tamil
TAS	*Travancore Archaeological Series*
Tiruviḷai.	*Tiruviḷaiyāṭaṟpurāṇam* of Parañcotimuṉivar
Tŏl.	*Tŏlkāppiyam*
WZKSO	*Wiener Zeitschrift für die Kunde Süd- und Ostasiens*

THE *King* AND THE *Clown*

IN SOUTH INDIAN MYTH

AND POETRY

· I ·

Introduction: Labyrinths and Mirrors

1. *Kolam*: The Reality at the Threshold

One lives with hidden presences. Here is the village street, heavy with sun, hard beneath the feet; on either side, ancient wooden houses, thatched roofs, wide verandas supported by square beams. Before you enter this pyal, you step over a labyrinth fashioned from rice powder at the threshold—*kolam* in Tamil Nadu, *raṅgoli* further north. The mistress of the house, or a daughter, or perhaps a trusted servant, has laid out this pattern upon arising in the morning: she may have selected a traditional design of geometric shapes intertwined, or, if her intentions are more elaborate, two peacocks, perhaps, emerging from a maze (see Figure 1). One cannot enter the house without passing through this man-made focus of auspicious forces, which sets up a protective screen before the home.[1] Of course, one cannot see the screen itself, but only its focal point at the threshold, the point at which it emerges into form—a complex form at that, carefully planned and executed, a reflection of some inner labyrinth externalized here at the boundary, the line dividing the inner and the outer, the pure from the chaotic. The boundary is dangerous: a division in the heart. A wholeness has been shattered so that creation can take place.

The *kolam* is a sign; also both less and more than a sign. As the day progresses, it will be worn away by the many feet entering or leaving the house. The rice powder mingles with the dust of the street; the sign fails to retain its true form. Nor is it intended to do so, any more than are the great stone temples which look so much more stable and

[1] Layard (1937).

Figure 1. *Kolam*

enduring: they too will be abandoned when the moment of their usefulness has passed; they are built not to last but to capture the momentary, unpredictable reality of the unseen. For temple and *kolam* both express a sense of the real as that which is hidden and yet held in external form. Both open up toward invisible but palpably sensed powers. Both hold these powers in partial, always temporary control. Both mark a transition, and suggest a movement. Like any vessel of divinity, they are *tīrthas*—points of crossing.[2] They simultaneously contain and obscure: imbued with power in their own right, they point beyond themselves to the wholeness of the divine.

Why place a labyrinth at the gateway? The inner paths of the mind are no less tortuous and no less permeable by the unknown. Space and consciousness intersect at the threshold of divinity. This is the shared dimension of experience never lacking in South India: the beyond keeps breaking in upon the present; it can never be ignored. This is the land of the unseen: just as the Vedic sacrifice, most practical and earthy of rites—at once grisly and sensuous—is said to produce "unseen fruits" (*adṛṣṭa*), so the South Indian landscape issues into the invisible. Every object is pregnant with possibilities: the most ordinary is the most subject to sudden, emotion-laden transformation.[3] That old cowherd, sitting beside a muddy pool, is the hidden saint Tirumūlar;[4] that Untouchable hunter, jingling the bells on his ankles to warn you away from his polluting presence, is none other than the great god Śiva, playing his never-ending game of hide-and-seek with the world. Indeed, the world *is* this game of his: open your eyes, and you may behold him in a new disguise.[5]

The game is not a simple one: when Śiva is your playmate, you can never play by the rules, or even truly understand them. Your divine opponent is a cheat, the game is rigged against you, your loss and your frustration are expressed in the reality of pain. For all that, it is for the most part a bewitchingly beautiful game, and a highly serious one—replete with emotion, infused with the poetry of divine forms, absorbing to the point of enslavement, dramatic in its turns of fortune, its crossings of the borders. And it never ends: only by a supreme effort of the will could you disengage yourself from it and set off alone on another path, free at last of the game—and at the end of that other way, too, you would still encounter the god. Out or in,

[2] See Kramrisch (1946), 1: 3; and Eck (1981).

[3] Note the contrast with the world of Late Antiquity: "For if the invisible world was as real as the visible, then it could be taken for granted in the same way—no greater emotional pressure was required to relate to a god than to a neighbor." Peter Brown (1978), p. 10. In India, the crossing of this border is always an intense experience of transformation and revelation.

[4] *PP* 6.3.

[5] See below III.3 (Paraśurāma and the Untouchable Śiva).

in myth or in meditation,[6] light or shadow, one moves toward the same hidden, wholly real, unlimited source. In effect, one always stands on a threshold: whichever way one turns, infinity stretches just beyond.

The following pages seek to pursue and to define further this inner world of feeling and ideas as it existed and developed in the minds of men and women in medieval South India. My assumption—for that is what it is[7]—is that this internal world was intimately related, in many important ways, to the outer reality in which it flourished; yet this book will not attempt to analyze these relations per se. At most, I hope to suggest something of the direction such an analysis could take, and to point to certain implications that our study of the symbolic and conceptual orders might have for our understanding of the institutional structures and social dynamics of this civilization. Nevertheless, it remains important to reaffirm the conviction of linkage. Indeed, this is not simply a heuristic assumption projected from the outside on to the culture we are investigating; rather, it appears as a cardinal principle of that very culture. From the time of the ancient "Caṅkam" poetry (the first centuries A.D.), the Tamilians have divided the world into "inner" (*akam*) and "outer" (*puṟam*) categories. The first deals with the more private realm of love, in all its emotional variety and instability, and is always anonymous, that is, expressed through stock symbolic types, lyrical, with a marked propensity for nocturnal images and delicate, often blurring lines; the second sings of the world of action, especially kingly virtues and heroic deeds, which tend to flash through a clearly lit world of daytime, of myth,[8] of objectified realities and specific, named actors. The first springs from the experience of the family and the home, the second from the royal courts and the battlefield. The two divisions form a single poetry, and they share similar structures; some poems—especially those dealing with various marginal types of special interest to us, such as we find in the *Kalittŏkai* collection[9]—deliberately confuse the categories. Moreover, both divisions draw upon conventional "outer" features—landscapes characterized by specific distinguishing elements—to suggest inner states of mind and feeling.[10] In a sense, classic Tamil poetics proceeds from our assumption: the outer and the inner, "fact" and feeling, "reality"

[6] On myth as an "outer" genre (*puṟam*), see Ramanujan (in press).

[7] Though it is not mine alone: I pay tribute to the memory of Max Weber.

[8] See n. 6 above; and Zvelebil (1973a), pp. 90-91.

[9] See below, IV.1 and VII.3.

[10] See discussion in Shulman (1981).

and fantasy, may be distinguished but never finally divorced. One feels or imagines or perceives in direct relation to the reality in which one is nurtured and lives: a reality at once physically concrete (the soil, vegetation, fauna, and climate of the surrounding landscape) and socially compelling (the human environment specific to any given place). There is a boundary here between "out" and "in," but, as with the *kolam*, it is a permeable border. Everything hinges upon the relation. In the more prosaic terms of our modern theories: we construct our reality even as it constructs us.[11]

Yet to state the matter in this way is at once too simple and too narrow. No doubt we must distinguish, within the "inner" domain, a conceptual order from a symbolic order, and—by no means a simple parallel to this division—conscious and articulate from unconscious or only partially conscious layers. But beyond this, we must stress the semantic dimension of social reality, inner and outer, for both realms offer expressions of the culture's search for meaning. This, too—the study of the range of cultural meanings that major texts embody and suggest—will occupy our attention. One can hardly aim for wholeness in such an endeavor; huge areas will remain in shadow, awaiting further studies and hands more skilled than mine. To reduce the task to proportions not wholly daunting—to forge, as it were, a wedge with which to begin—I have concentrated on the symbolism of prominent social types, above all on those directly related to the political order. My hope is that in exploring the political iconography of medieval South India, the following essay will shed light on certain of the fundamental issues, ordering principles, and creative tensions at work in this civilization as a whole.

How, then, are we to proceed? We must, it seems to me, attempt to generalize and abstract from a basis in concrete, expressive features available to us in various areas. Let us return for a moment to our village street: have we learned anything from our reverie? We have sensed, perhaps, a certain dynamism and tension, an urge to transformation; an open-endedness in principle; the presence of permeable and self-conscious boundaries; a gamelike attitude toward life; a fondness for the mysterious and the unseen; a predilection for labyrinthine imagery, for the complex and the fluid. We shall find these features recurring in many contexts. But they need to be far more closely defined, their parameters mapped out systematically, their relative importance and interrelations assessed through an analysis of their repeated occurrence. Searching for such consistent components of the

[11] Berger and Luckmann (1972).

inner universe, I have turned to the symbolism of social types as one area where inner and outer intersect. This choice involves a deliberate turning away from the sources traditionally beloved of all historians of South India, that is, the epigraphic record, the meager chronicles,[12] and the not less meager references in the works of foreign visitors.[13] Above all, it is the inscriptions—invariably dated and appearing in a specific, definable place and context—that have served the great historians who have tried to piece together a "factual" history of South India. But to reconstruct the social universe of this region in medieval times on the basis of the surviving inscriptions is somewhat like attempting to depict the tenor and concerns of modern American life by studying a haphazard collection of clippings from the back pages of the daily newspapers: the information is surely relevant to the culture, but the picture that emerges could be at best only a distorted and highly fragmentary one. This is no attempt to denigrate the enormous importance of the inscriptions for our understanding of this area; and we, too, shall refer to inscriptions in the course of the following pages. But our main sources are of another kind, so far hardly utilized for the study of South Indian history: the copious literary documents of the period, in the classical languages of the South (above all, Tamil and Sanskrit).[14] These sources, be they polished works such as Kampaṉ's Tamil version of the *Rāmāyaṇa* or the *paraṇi* war poems of the Chola court poets, or popular creations such as the literature of ballads and folk epics, may not give us reliable dates or hard "factual" material; they do, however, offer a wealth of invaluable data on all aspects of the social and cultural life of the traditional South, and above all on its world view or views. A close analysis of selected passages linked by our thematic concerns may enable us to draw a new picture of South Indian society in the light of its symbolic and conceptual systems.

Our primary concern will be with the Tamil area, during a period that I have called, with deliberate vagueness, "medieval." This period covers roughly a millennium, from the post-Caṅkam centuries (Pallava times) into the Vijayanagar rule, that is, from approximately the seventh to the seventeenth centuries. Clearly, this is much too long a period to be seen as a single unit, and I have no wish to suggest a nonexistent homogeneity either in historical, structural features or in the related symbolic systems. Nevertheless, there is, I believe, reason

[12] Such as the *Koyilŏḻuku* from the Śrīraṅgam temple.

[13] Such as Marco Polo, the Chinese pilgrims, and so on: see Nilakanta Sastri (1939).

[14] Sources of this nature have been used to good effect in the study of European history: see Huizinga (1924), and the more recent works by Le Goff, Davis, and Duby.

to posit an underlying cultural continuity, perhaps most obvious in the symbolic order articulated by our texts. South Indian social symbolism seems at times to be imbued with an innate conservatism, especially when linked to a crystallized, formally defined ideology. Indeed, the continuities may stretch as far back as the Vedic materials on kingship. I have, therefore, not hesitated to juxtapose texts taken from different periods, and even in some cases from widely separated areas, although the transformations in context, and in the symbolic forms themselves, remain in all such cases a factor for analysis. Even classical texts from the North Indian Sanskrit tradition have been utilized when relevant to our concerns; in particular, the two epics, and later puranic texts, are often crucial to an understanding of the distinctive South Indian developments. Moreover, although our conclusions are limited to the area and period mentioned, they are not, it would seem, irrelevant to the study of other Indian places and times: this author, for his part, sees no great divide between North and South, and the parallels with the ancient, including even Vedic, patterns are often very striking.

This said, the main focus of these pages can nevertheless be further narrowed and defined to the Chola period (mid-ninth century to late thirteenth century) and the Chola heartland of the Kāverī delta (especially present-day Tanjore District). There are several reasons for this emphasis. For one thing, this is the part of South India where I am most at home, and which I most deeply love. The flat, radiantly green terrain of endless paddy fields, dotted here and there by the towering *gopuras* of the shrines—many of them Chola foundations, usually claiming to lie astride an imaginary mountain connecting them to heaven, and beside a subterranean river leading down to the worlds of serpents, demons, and the dead[15]—seems imbued for me with the stuff of my karmic memories, *vāsanās*.

Such considerations aside, it remains true that in symbolic terms the Chola period was a moment of immense significance for South India. The Chola kings are, even now, far more than a faded memory of lost glories: they convey still the living sense, which certainly transcends their peculiar moment in history, of a civilization approaching its own limits, living out to the fullest possible extent the rich interplay of its internal design. Culturally, the period marks a classical apogee in literature, painting, architecture, religious and philosophical speculation.[16] We shall say more in a moment about the great wealth of

[15] On the cosmology of the Tamil shrine, see Shulman (1980b), pp. 40-55.

[16] See the standard work on this period: Nilakanta Sastri (1955).

documentation from this period. But also in other areas, notably those of state building, military campaigns, economic activity, and social integration, the Chola period was clearly a high point of medieval South Indian history. Chola armies ranged over the whole southern part of the subcontinent (one expedition, during the reign of Rājendra I, reached the banks of the Ganges); Chola mariners sailed against Southeast Asian kingdoms. Chola embassies were sent to China; international trade flourished under the Chola aegis.[17] More significantly, in a long-term view, the structural patterns and sociopolitical dynamics which were first solidly established during earlier, especially Pallava times, attained their fullest expression under the Cholas. This applies, for example, to the nature of the king-Brahmin alliance; the related pattern of interdependence between Brahmin and peasant (especially the higher peasant castes such as the Veḷāḷas);[18] the function of endowment (royal gift-giving, *dāna*), as a constituent feature of kingship; the organization of the army and its use in predatory raiding; the intimate association of the political order with the great pilgrimage temples and various networks of local shrines; the functioning of the village communities, with their different kinds of assemblies (the non-Brahmin *ūr*, Brahmin *sabhā*, and, toward the end of the Chola period, the supralocal *pěriyanāṭu* assemblies);[19] the self-definition of an orthodox Hindu community in relation to the heroic figures of *bhakti* devotionalism, on the one hand, and to the clearly excluded communities of Buddhists and Jains, on the other.[20] All of these features, though existing in institutionalized form prior to the great Chola kings, were consolidated and fully developed during their reign.

At the same time, important changes occurred. The historical center of Tamil culture shifted, for these centuries, from the Tŏṇṭai area further north and the Pāṇṭiya realm in the far south, to the Kāverī heartland. A new level of social and cultural integration was attained, as we shall see from its symbolic articulation in major works. The inherent dynamism of South Indian society was liberated in new, far-reaching forms. In the arts, a profound measure of reflexivity, self-awareness, and self-confidence became evident.

The central figures on this vital scene were the Chola kings. They are less important to us as individuals (we know little enough about their personal realities) than as symbolic foci. Around them coalesced the classical structures of sociopolitical and cultural integration that

[17] See Hall (1980) and Stein (1965).

[18] Stein has written cogently on this alliance: (1980), pp. 63-89.

[19] *Ibid.*, pp. 216-53; but see Champakalakshmi (1981).

[20] See below, Chapter III.

we shall seek to define. Around them, too, are clustered the semantic burdens of their society: in a sense, the Chola kings were the bearers of the meaningfulness of life as understood by the people of their time. Those elements of the social order which I shall seek to define as "tragic" and "comic," and which help to delimit the range of meanings with which the medieval Tamil attempted to make sense of his world, were worked out in this culture in relation to these central symbolic carriers.

Our analysis will, however, constantly trespass into other periods and areas. If, as suggested above, the Chola integration reflects the development of Indian kingship over many centuries, beginning in Vedic times in the North and with the early Caṅkam warrior-kingdoms in the South, we can hardly avoid looking backward to earlier sources. These will include, apart from the classical Sanskrit texts mentioned earlier, the Tamil Caṅkam poems and the long pre-Chola *kāvyas*, the *Cilappatikāram* and the *Maṇimekalai*.[21] Moreover, elements of the Chola order endured, in altered fashion, throughout succeeding centuries in the Tamil area, although the symbolic center was lost (or, eventually, moved northward to Vijayanagar). The post-Chola period is marked both by extreme fragmentation—the development of highly localized "little kingdoms"[22]—and by the intrusion of powerful forces from the outside (such as the Muslim armies and, more significantly, the Telugu and, later, Maratha warriors).[23] These developments led to major historical transformations. Nevertheless, the symbolic and conceptual orders that had crystallized under the Cholas survived to a large extent intact. They are, for example, still apparent in a major work such as Villiputtūrār's *Pāratam* (c. 1400, over a century after the Chola fall). Although our study does not extend to an analysis of the important developments of Vijayanagar and Nāyak times, sources from these later periods have been used to supplement the more properly "Chola" materials. In short, the central window opening on to the Chola period is flanked here by partial views—perhaps suggestive in their own right, but not fully lit or described—of adjacent periods. Like the parasol of the Chola king, which is said to give shade to all the world, Chola kingship casts its symbolic shadow over a thousand years of South Indian thought and feeling.

[21] Contrary to common opinion, these are certainly not "epics." Tamil tradition appropriately classes them as *kāppiyam* = *kāvya*, ornate literary creations.

[22] On this concept, see Dirks (1979).

[23] See Appadurai (1978).

2. Note on Sources

Chola times witnessed an efflorescence in literature (as in the other arts), as can be seen from the surviving Chola classics and from a great mass of legendary material about the most famous of the Chola poets (such as Kampan̲, Cekkil̲ār, Ŏṭṭakkūttar, and Cayaṅkŏṇṭār).[24] Only a small sampling of these works is studied in the following pages. Among the texts I have cited, pride of place belongs, perhaps, to Kampan̲'s *Irāmāvatāram*, the main Tamil version of the Sanskrit epic, the *Rāmāyaṇa*. We know very little about Kampan̲ himself; the available scraps of circumstantial evidence seem to point to a date in the twelfth century.[25] This poet clearly lived in the Kāverī heartland, which he praises eloquently in many memorable verses. Kampan̲'s work is far more than a simple adaptation of the Sanskrit original; rather, it is the masterpiece of the great creative genius, who used the Rāma story as a frame for giving South Indian devotional religion one of its most powerful expressions.

The Chola period also saw the crystallization of the Śaiva hagiographic traditions. This is a major stage in the development of southern Śaivism: following the centuries during which the classics of the Tamil Śaiva *bhakti* tradition were composed (by the *Tevāram* poets—Tiruñān̲acampantar, Appar, and Cuntaramūrtti—and by the famous Māṇikkavācakar), there came a period of definition and consolidation. The Tamil Śaiva canon was fixed in its present form by Nampi Āṇṭār Nampi, and official biographies of the sixty-three *nāyan̲mār*, the Śaiva saints, were written.[26] This latter work was carried out by the poet Cekkil̲ār under Kulottuṅga II (1133-1150).[27] The stories which Cekkil̲ār incorporated into his *Tiruttŏṇṭar purāṇam* (popularly referred to as the *Pĕriya purāṇam*, the "great *purāṇa*") are, in many cases, clearly older than the twelfth century;[28] but their final, polished form is an important Chola achievement. The great significance attached to these

[24] See, for example, the stories collected in the *Vinotaracamañcari*; also Rajaruthnam Pillai (1909).

[25] See Shulman (1978), (1979), (1980), and (1981); Zvelebil (1975), pp. 181-84. I am preparing a monograph on Kampan̲'s poem.

[26] On the date of Nampi Āṇṭār Nampi, whose story is told in the *Tirumuṟaikaṇṭa-purāṇam*, see the discussion by Balasubrahmanyam (1975), pp. 77-81.

[27] Zvelebil (1975), pp. 179-80. The dating hinges on verse 8 of the *pāyiram*, where mention is made of an Anapāyan̲ who covered the *perampalam* (at Cidambaram) with gold.

[28] Many are referred to in the *Tevāram* poems, and the entire series of *nāyan̲mār* is enumerated for the first time in *patikam* 39 (known as the *tiruttŏṇṭattŏkai*) of Cuntaramūrtti's *Tevāram* (ninth century?).

stories can also be seen by the fact that they are depicted in painting and stone on Chola temples, notably in the complete *nāyaṉmār* series at Tārācaram (late twelfth century, approximately one generation after Cekkiḻār).[29]

Parallel developments occurred within the Vaiṣṇava *bhakti* tradition. The editing of the Vaiṣṇava Tamil canon is attributed to Nāthamuni (d. 920), the grandfather of the famous Śrīvaiṣṇava philosopher Yāmunācārya. Vaiṣṇava hagiographic traditions were first recorded in full by Garuḍavāhana (late twelfth or early thirteenth century) in a Sanskrit work, the *Divyasūricarita*.[30] I have cited this version rather than the somewhat later *Guruparamparāprabhāvas*. One of the major texts of southern Vaiṣṇavism may belong to the start of the Chola period: the much-loved *Bhāgavatapurāṇa*, which we now know for certain to have been composed in the Tamil country.[31]

Among the poetic works that emerged directly from the life of the Chola courts, the *paraṇi* war poems are of special interest to our study. Ŏṭṭakkūttar's *Takkayākapparaṇi* transposes this subject into the realm of Śaiva myth (the destruction of Dakṣa's sacrifice); Cayaṅkŏṇṭār's *Kaliṅkattupparaṇi* celebrates the historical campaign against Kaliṅga led by the Chola general, Karuṇākarat Tŏṇṭaimāṉ, under the poet's patron, Kulottuṅga I (1070-1122).[32] Cayaṅkŏṇṭār was perhaps the greatest master of this genre, which calls upon very ancient Tamil sources; the semantic value of warfare in the Chola kingdom becomes accessible to our understanding through an analysis of this remarkable, eery classic.[33]

Apart from these strictly Chola materials, I have made extensive use of later literary works which, although they stem from different milieux, nevertheless carry the stamp of the older medieval tradition. Foremost among them is the Tamil version of the *Mahābhārata* by Villiputtūrār (c. 1400). This poet—a Vaiṣṇava Brahmin from Tirumuṉaippāṭināṭu in present-day South Arcot District, the heart of the popular Draupadī cults—created a partial synthesis of three main cultural streams: the "high" learned traditions of both Tamil and Sanskrit poetry (Villi handles a variety of Tamil verse forms with consummate skill; his poetic language is heavily Sanskritized, and his familiarity

29 The Tārācuram frieze has been studied in relation to the *PP* by Marr (1979).

30 On the date, see Hardy (1979), p. 35 and n. 62.

31 Hardy's work has revealed some of the many "Tamilisms" in the language of this text.

32 Zvelebil (1975), p. 186; Meenakshisundaram (1969).

33 On the *paraṇi* in relation to other genres of war poetry in Tamil, see Shulman (1979b), pp. 17-19.

with the Sanskrit epic traditions evident throughout); the specific tradition of Tamil Vaiṣṇava poetry beginning with the Āḻvārs, the Vaiṣṇava *bhakti* saints, whose honorific title he also bears (he is commonly known as Villiputtūr-āḻvār); and the popular elaborations on the epic familiar to every South Arcot villager, who would have witnessed their ritual enactments in the festivals for the village goddess, Turopataiyammaṉ/Draupadī.[34] These three streams do not always flow together smoothly in Villi's poem; one often has the sense that the popular traditions slipped past the guard of an otherwise intently classical poet. Villi's *Pāratam* as a whole is markedly different from Kampaṉ's Tamil *Rāmāyaṇa*, for example, with its overpowering lyricism and profound psychological interest, and there can be no doubt that Kampaṉ's work more closely reflects the Chola synthesis. Nevertheless, Villi is very closely linked to the older period, perhaps most significantly by virtue of his relation to precisely that problematic and intriguing stratum of popular or folk traditions, with their inherently conservative character.[35]

Indeed, certain of the issues that we find present, undeveloped, in Chola sources only fully surface in the folk genres of a much later period. This applies, for example, to Tamil puranic myths, which were often recorded in Tamil literary works only after the fifteenth century, although the stories themselves may be quite ancient.[36] I have used several Tamil *purāṇas* in this study.[37] Even more striking are the archaic features in the fully fledged folk genres such as *paḷḷu*, *kuṟavañci*, and *nŏṇṭināṭakam*, which emerge in the seventeenth and eighteenth centuries. These works belong to a very different time: they were, for the most part, composed by poets who flourished in the "courts" of local landlords, in a fragmented polity and a region that had become something of a backwater. Together, they constitute a literature that deserves to be studied in full against the social background of its period.[38] I have called upon some of these compositions to suggest

[34] Alf Hiltebeitel is presently studying these popular Draupadī traditions in the light of the Sanskrit epic; cf. Hiltebeitel (1980) and (1980a).

[35] On the conservatism of the South Indian folk tradition, see Shulman (1979b); (1980b), pp. 11-12.

[36] Shulman (1980b), pp. 8-10, 32-33.

[37] These include the *Aruṇācalapurāṇam* of Ĕllappanayiṉār (mid-sixteenth century), *Perūrppurāṇam* of Kacciyappamuṉivar, the *Kāñcippurāṇam* of his teacher, Civañāṉayoki (both eighteenth-century works), and the famous *Tiruviḷaiyāṭaṟpurāṇam* of Parañcotimuṉivar (early seventeenth century?). I have also cited Sanskrit puranic sources, as noted earlier.

[38] See Zvelebil (1975), pp. 253-62; Subramania Aiyar (1969), pp. 40-43, 67-71, 77-83, 94-102. David Ludden is investigating the *paḷḷu* literature.

certain of the paths leading away from the "high" medieval times; but there can be no doubt that these poems have preserved and expanded upon a precious inheritance of ideas dating, in some cases, back to the origins of South Indian civilization (*nŏṇṭināṭakam*, the "dramas about a cripple," for example, recall themes from the late Caṅkam collections such as *Kalittŏkai*; the *kuṟavañci* "gypsy ballads" work out elements already present in the earliest *akam* love poetry). A similar case is that of those folk genres that never "graduated" into semiclassical form, for example, folk ballads such as the extremely popular *Maturaivīraṉkatai* (probably originally composed in the eighteenth century, but describing events in the mid-seventeenth). My use of sources such as these may be seen as an experiment in extrapolation backward in time, from the explicit record of the seventeenth century to implicit meanings of an earlier era; the reader must judge whether the experiment can be justified.

Finally, the past never wholly dies: in the central chapters on comedy and kingship I have resorted to experiences of present-day South India, where royal clowns can still be found, in a new form, if one but knows where to look.

3. The Problem: The Elusive King in the Transformational State

At the heart of South Indian social symbolism we find the enticing but enigmatic figure of the king. As in the classical North Indian sources studied by Heesterman,[39] the royal role is seen in medieval southern sources as profoundly problematic; hence the profusion of stories that deal with its endlessly varied aspects. In South India, kingship is less a fact than a concern, a congealed longing always in danger of dissolving back into despair. Why this should have been the case is the central issue of the following pages.

This uneasy vision of kingship emerges clearly the moment one begins to look behind the formulaic royal titles of the inscriptions (*praśasti* and—a Chola innovation—Tamil *mĕykkīrti*).[40] The titles themselves are impressive enough: King of Kings, Jewel of the Solar Dynasty, Incomparable Chola, Great Savior, Lion among Kings.[41] Certain epithets will, of course, reflect the history and achievements of

[39] Heesterman (1971), (1978), and (1979).

[40] See Stein (1980), pp. 355-56; Nilakanta Sastri (1955), pp. 4-5.

[41] These examples are cited from the inscriptions of Rājarāja I: see Balasubrahmanyam (1975), pp. 5-6 (*rājarāja, ravikulamāṇikkam, nikarilicoḻaṉ, uyyakkŏṇṭāṉ, rājendrasiṃha*).

specific kings; but the tendency toward the conventionalized, grandiose phraseology remains constant in the *praśasti* portions of the inscriptions. Reading through these lengthy praises, one starts to wonder: who, in fact, is this man eulogized by the poets? Where is he hiding? What is the reality behind the screen of ornate description? His presence—often, it is true, in some ways an authoritative presence, arbitrating claims, confirming grants and other administrative arrangements—usually seems only faintly perceptible, a hint of shadow behind the horizon. We remain largely ignorant of the personal histories, the small but crucial details that alone can give a sense of a real, developing person, affecting the rule of Chola kings.[42] The great kings mentioned in the thousands of medieval inscriptions are far less palpable, seemingly less real figures, than the much less powerful warrior-heroes sung by the ancient Caṅkam bards. The Caṅkam heroes often achieve, in the compositions of their poets, a winning individuality conveyed by unique, dramatic details; we would be hard pressed to find anything so convincingly individualized in the Chola eulogies.

In short, the medieval South Indian king eludes us as a person.[43] The shadowy quality that attends his presence is also apparent in plastic representations. Thus in a rare Chola portrait from the eleventh century—a fresco from the great Bṛhadīśvara temple at Tanjore—we behold Rājarāja I, the builder of this shrine, in the tantalizing guise in which he must have appeared to his contemporaries.[44] (See Figure 2.) The king's body is largely hidden here by the impressive figure of his court poet, Karuvūrttevar, with his Brahminical thread, white beard, and haunting eyes. Indeed, Rājarāja's eyes are also *his* most striking feature: it is almost as if the rest of his body might dissolve at any moment, leaving behind only the simple golden ornaments that adorned him—a concrete memory of glory—and the last vision, clearly turned partly inward, still reflected in the eyes.[45] Or, perhaps, Rāja-

[42] Kulke has argued convincingly that the personal history of Kulottuṅga I (1070-1118) underlies the expanded legend of Hiraṇyavarman at Cidambaram: Kulke (1970), pp. 155-213. This would constitute a highly unusual instance of a legendary "biography" based upon the actual record of a royal career.

[43] On the more general problem of "personality" in Indian culture, see Shulman (1978).

[44] The Bṛhadīśvara frescoes as a group constitute one off the most striking expositions available of Chola cultural thematics. See below, III.2 and VIII; Nagaswamy (1980), pp. 111-21, especially plate 7.

[45] The powerful eyes of the Chola frescoes—the same feature is prominent in the Tripurāntaka painting from this shrine—recall the staring eyes of the all-seeing Buddha at the shrine of Svayambhūnāth in the Kathmandu Valley.

Figure 2. Rājarāja Chola and Karuvūrttevar

rāja's vision is fixed upon the god, as in the verse of this same court poet, Karuvūrttevar, who claims:

nĕṟṟiyiṟ kaṇ ĕṉ kaṇṇiṉ niṉṟ' akalā

The eye in his (Śiva's) forehead
never departs from *my* eye.[46]

[46] *Karuvūrttevar tiruvicaippā*, 2, in Somasundaram Pillai (1958), p. 48.

Poet and patron, Brahmin and king complete one another in this vignette, just as together they delimit the heart of the South Indian political structure. The painter has caught this unity with its inherent dynamism. For this portrait has nothing of stasis: it suggests to us, rather, flesh on the point of transformation, while the eyes alone retain a trace of hesitation upon the threshold. All the sadness and subtle beauty of Chola kingship at its height still flow out from this picture.

Whence comes this sense of an elusive king always close to disappearing? How are we to understand the political system built around him as a center? In recent years Indian kingship has benefited from much scholarly attention, both in its historical and its ideological aspects.[47] We have clearly come some way from those earlier models—largely derived from stereotypical images of Western polities—which envisaged Indian states as great imperial structures equipped with centralized bureaucracies and exercising a large measure of control over a highly structured periphery. These images turn out to be an historians' fancy, chimeras far more removed from reality than any of the myths which we will cite. In their place, several alternate approaches have begun to emerge. Thus Louis Dumont, in a seminal essay on the ideological structure of classical Indian kingship, has stressed the apparent divorce of "spiritual" from "temporal" authority, the former vested in the Brahmins, the latter in a "secularized" kingship.[48] As we shall see, this is a rather problematical formulation which does, however, point to the fundamental issue of the king's legitimation. More recently, a new model of the medieval South Indian state has been proposed in a major study by Burton Stein.[49] Drawing on Southall's work on an East African society, Stein describes South Indian society as "segmentary," a term used to suggest the following formal features (among others):

a) a relatively weak center whose control diminishes consistently with distance, so that one finds a series of relatively autonomous peripheral centers;
b) a tendency for these peripheral centers to "replicate" the structure of authority evident in the major centers;[50]

[47] See Gonda (1969); Heesterman (1957); Dumont (1970), pp. 63-88; Drekmeier (1962); Ghoshal (1959); Altekar (1949); Rau (1957); Richards (1978); Derrett (1976); Coomaraswamy (1942); Lingat (1973), pp. 207-56; Thapar (1980). On South Indian kingship, see Mahalingam (1967), pp. 17-102; Dirks (1976); Price (1979a); Sheik Ali (1972); Spencer (1969) and (1970); Breckenridge (1978); Narayanan (1977); Waghorne (1980); Stein (1978).

[48] Dumont (1970), pp. 63-88.

[49] Stein (1980).

[50] This process is analyzed from a somewhat different point of view by Tambiah

c) a pyramidlike organization of the sociopolitical segments in relation to the central authority (Stein sees this as perhaps "the most distinctive feature" of Southall's segmentary model);[51]

d) a ritual or symbolic hegemony that replaces effective political control as a major integrating force in the polity;

e) a dynamic, shifting, fluctuating system of relations between the various segments, the more peripheral of which can easily switch their allegiances.[52]

Stein finds these features in the Chola state, with its basically weak center endowed with immense symbolic importance but little real coercive power; its localized foci of authority vested, for example, in the Brahmin-peasant alliances and expressed through the assemblies of the villages and the "micro regions" (*nāṭu*); its interpenetrating yet quasi-autonomous networks of power, resources, and prestige (such as sectarian movements with their educational and other institutions;[53] pilgrimage temples;[54] merchants and artisans;[55] tribal groups newly assimilated to the wider medieval polity;[56] and the overarching groupings of the right-hand and left-hand "divisions," seen by Stein as providing in themselves a framework for such assimilation of new groups[57]); finally, its rooted instability reflected in the relative independence of local leaders—an independence most clearly evident in the areas of taxation and warfare—and in the corresponding impossibility of creating an enduring, more powerful center.[58] There is no doubt that this model is far more accurate than the older "imperial" one developed by Nilakanta Sastri and his school. (The two views are so radically at odds that it is difficult to believe that they were constructed on the basis of the same epigraphical evidence!) Nevertheless, basic questions remain unanswered, including the most basic of all:

(1976), pp. 102-31 (Tambiah's term for these replicating structures is "the galactic polity").

[51] Stein (1980), p. 269.

[52] This list has been summarized and rephrased from Stein (1980), p. 265; cf. the attempt to apply the segmentary model to North Indian rajput lineages by Fox (1971), pp. 56-57. I have stressed here only certain points of direct relevance to the analysis below.

[53] See Stein (1980), pp. 351-52; for a later period, Appadurai (1978).

[54] See Spencer (1969).

[55] See the fine study by Hall (1980).

[56] This process has been studied in another context—premodern Orissa—by Kulke (1976, 1978, 1979).

[57] Stein (1980), pp. 173-215; see also Appadurai (1974).

[58] This picture is considerably altered in Vijayanagar times, although Stein still regards the Vijayanagar state as "segmentary": (1980), pp. 336-485. For a discussion of Stein's overall thesis, see Kulke (1982); Hall (1981); Champakalakshmi (1981).

Why? The structural weakness of the medieval polity is by now quite clear—but why was it there? Why did it remain so salient a feature throughout the medieval centuries? The given dynamics of the segmentary model cannot fully explain the self-limiting aspect of state formation in this society, which was also clearly driven toward expansion and structural development. These questions become more pressing when we consider the differences between South India and the East African segmentary polities that provided the basis for Stein's model: the Chola state is incomparably more complex, more loaded with inherent stresses and conflicts, than Alur society.[59] Moreover, as Stein himself has recognized, the differences are immediately apparent in the symbolic and conceptual realms.[60] Perhaps, too, it is in these areas—in the symbolic integration of society and the articulation of its conflicts—that we can most conveniently seek the reasons underlying the given facts of a distinctive South Indian development.

That, in any case, is the hypothesis adopted here. Our starting point is the evident relative weakness of the medieval South Indian political center. We shall attempt to view this fact in the light of the major theoretical issue of the king's authority and legitimation. This linkage has been most suggestively worked out for ancient India by Heesterman, who uses the king's ultimate separation from the transcendent authority rooted in Brahminical values to explain the constraints upon the development of a strong political center.[61] The following pages seek to delineate the convoluted patterns this problem takes in the specific geographical and historical conditions of medieval South India as reflected in literary texts; the classical dynamics of the medieval polity are studied through this society's symbolic articulation of kingship. In addition, I have attempted to outline certain semantic factors informing the life of this society as a whole—including, of course, the political edifices it constructed. Here Geertz's controversial approach to the traditional Balinese state has pointed the way toward an analysis that takes such factors seriously.[62]

[59] A more fruitful comparison might be made with the early medieval states in Europe. Cf. Eisenstadt (1980), pp. 624-31; Thapar (1980); for specific case studies replete with parallels to the South Indian material, see Duby (1979); Leyser (1979).

[60] Stein (1980), p. 270. For comparative materials on African kingship, see Gluckman (1965); de Heusch (1972).

[61] Heesterman (1978) and (1979).

[62] Geertz (1980). We may note in passing that South Indian kingdoms present a number of similarities to, but also many striking differences from, Geertz's depiction of the Balinese state. The former would include the "theatrical" nature of kingship, and of political action generally, as well as the drive toward replicating cosmic structures

Rather than engaging in polemical discussions of theories and other models, I have tried, insofar as possible, to let the sources speak for themselves. Before turning to the literary texts, however, we would do well to look more closely at the surface images presented by the more traditional sources for South Indian history, above all the inscriptional record. These images help to define our problem in its most concrete expression. We might begin by painting a synthetic portrait of the medieval South Indian state as seen from a vantage point at least in part external to the culture. A Western historian who wandered, like the Connecticut Yankee, into such a state might begin by searching for its center. He would, of course, be disappointed; no single center exists. Neither would he find the center's necessary counterpart, a periphery: the state has no real boundaries.[63] Instead, he would gradually become aware of a varied, shifting series of centers of different kinds and functions, connected with various interlocking networks. There would be local "kings" and supralocal ones, each with his capital or capitals and his palaces; temples linked as stations on a wandering pilgrimage route, or as members of a localized set with interrelated deities; merchant towns, quarters, and ports; Brahminical academies for Vedic learning as well as itinerant teachers, yogis, magicians, and devotees maddened by the love of god; respected peasants in control of village and regional assemblies; local adventurers and strongmen with their private armies and allies, their supporting factions locked into traditional patterns of conflict with their rivals. The great majority of the population would be tied to the land as agricultural workers, and the resources produced from their cultivation would be exchanged for the most part in local relations, with little intervention from the outside. Nevertheless, within this somewhat confusing, highly diffuse polity, our stranger would soon become aware that certain figures are endowed with enormous significance in the minds and hearts of men. Inevitably, he would find himself directed to the courts of the dynastic kings.

There, hidden behind the arras, our Western spy could observe how the South Indian king spends his day. He might overhear the Brahminical ministers and advisers assuring the king that he is fulfilling his major duty, *prajānāṃ paripālanam*, the protection of his subjects.

---

in earthly images and forms; yet the South Indian king is hardly an impassive, immobile icon (Geertz, p. 130) but rather a shadowy escapist torn by inner contradictions, a self-transforming actor charged with safeguarding the equally elusive, internally divided dharmic order.

[63] Thus the Cera king can grant lands in an area occupied by a Chola army: Ludden (1978), p. 99.

But this protection is very widely defined, to say the least, so that the king who spends long hours with his concubines, or entire weeks hunting in the forests, is still carrying out the fundamental requirement of his role.[64] Our intruder will no doubt see a good deal of these pursuits, just as he will witness the king's involvement in arbitrating disputes (in the court as well as while on tour among the villages) and in performing a rather bewildering series of ritual duties. For the king protects his subjects partly by virtue of his mere existence (as one can see from the commonly expressed horror of the "kingless" state) and partly through his ritual accomplishments. Here the king's identity as first sacrificer, *yajamāna*, is of crucial importance. Yet this very role tends to expand metaphorically to the point where it subsumes all others in the perspective of the traditional texts: the king appears as *yajamāna* not only by performing actual or symbolic sacrifices but also by punishing evildoers (wielding his staff, *daṇḍa*, the symbol of his basic claim to power), by arbitrating otherwise insoluble claims and guaranteeing the solution reached, by leading his armies into war, but above all simply by being himself. His embodiment of a sacrificial persona is more decisive for his kingdom than any action he may take or any decision he may make. In a sense, the king is most "real," most palpably present, in the context of ritual drama, as the leading protagonist in the periodic re-creation of a dramatically visible social order—for example, when he receives his investiture from the goddess during the annual Durgā festival;[65] or as patron and protector of the gods' procession around their temple in the spring;[66] or in war.[67]

The ritual roles of the king are by no means static;[68] we can trace important historical developments and transformations. Nicholas Dirks has demonstrated in Pallava inscriptions a significant shift of

64 On *paripālana*, see Lingat (1973), pp. 222-23.

65 In Vijayanagar and Nāyak times: Stein (1980), pp. 384-90; Breckenridge (1978); van den Hoek (1978).

66 Hudson (1978) and (1982).

67 Cf. Geertz, pp. 98-120 (and n. 62 above).

68 See Inden's analysis of medieval Indian kingship as reflected in the *Viṣṇudharmottarapurāṇa*. Inden (1978), pp. 58-59, distinguishes broadly between two phases of an *internal* dynamic of the Indian king—a transcendent phase connected to the ruler's ritual sovereignty (a passive form of kingship), and an immanent phase in which he rules actively as administrator and warrior (the political sovereignty bound up with coercion, *daṇḍa*). The royal role is structured around his oscillation between these two parts of a cycle, which may be seen as analogous to the cycle of *nivṛtti* and *pravṛtti* in Hindu cosmology; cf. in this connection Held's interpretation of the *Mahābhārata* (1935, pp. 127-29, 139-47). *Nivṛtti* leads to the renewal and revitalization of the king, his kingdom, and the cosmos (cf. Chapter V below).

emphasis from the classical sacrificial role of the king to his outstanding medieval persona as donor—the giving of gifts (*dāna*) comes to replace the blood sacrifice.[69] As in other areas of Indian culture,[70] the actual performance of the sacrifice gives way at some point to a symbolic equivalent, which is seemingly less violent and less loaded with evil consequences. Royal endowment thus becomes one of the hallmarks of the king's ritual character. There is, on the one hand, a continuity with the ancient Tamil heroic ethos: the Caṅkam hero's liberality was one of his defining features, a moral trait no less central to his identity, and to his claim to fame (*pukaḻ*), than courage in battle. On the other hand, the medieval dharmic ruler's compelling interest in endowment goes well beyond this inherited heroic virtue—just as the medieval polity transcends, in scope and dynamism, the limited nature of the ancient "heroic" kingship. As the Vedic king was compelled to renew, again and again, his ever tenuous consecration,[71] so the medieval South Indian monarch was driven, as if by an inner obsession, to endow. This is perhaps the first fact that strikes one who opens any volume of epigraphical records: an enormous percentage of the inscriptions is devoted to records of endowments either initiated, or simply guaranteed, by the kings. In innumerable cases the king renounces his own "share" of income from lands or other property—this, in any case, is the idiom of the inscriptions, an idiom of "renunciation" (*tyāga*) that recurs regularly in varying contexts, with respect to village lands in peacetime, urban properties, and, significantly, lands newly "won" in war. Often we may suspect that the idiom of *tyāga* masks a reality in which the king's control over his proper "share" is somewhat theoretical; at times he quite clearly renounces what he in any case lacks the power to appropriate. But this is hardly the rule of royal endowment; the compulsion is obviously there, and the chosen idiom is in itself highly significant. Watching the king perform this act of apparent self-sacrifice over and over, our snooping Western historian must ask himself ever more urgently: Why?

If we leave him to his quandary—for it is more than likely that no one in the medieval state could answer his question in full—and from

[69] Dirks (1976); on royal *dāna*, see also Inden (1978), p. 57; Price (1979); Trautmann (1981), pp. 278-85. On *īkai*, generosity, as a cardinal virtue of the ancient Tamil hero, see Kailasapathy (1968), pp. 252-54; cf. *Tirukkuṟaḷ* 221-30. Stein (1978) sees the development of Pallava kingship, including the institutionalized role of *dāna*, as paradigmatic for South Indian states. And cf. the relation of gift and sacrifice in medieval Europe: Duby (1979), pp. 16-35.

[70] Shulman (1980b), pp. 90-137, 317-52.

[71] Heesterman (1979), pp. 75-77; (1978).

the distance of our libraries, look to the inscriptional record for an answer, we shall surely be disappointed. The "facts" are there, for what they are worth; but the inner reality, the linkages, the motivations, are stated, at best, only elliptically, or by implication. Let us take an example, chosen more or less at random. In a recently discovered copper-plate inscription from the year A.D. 932, the early Chola king Parāntaka I orders the gift of three villages in the Tŏṇṭai region of Tamil Nadu as *brahmadeya*, that is, villages a major share of whose income will be devoted to the maintenance of Brahmin households there. The inscription begins with a poetic Sanskrit version of the Chola genealogy (not wholly unlike another one that will concern us in a moment); but the heart of the inscription, at least in terms of the factual transaction it describes, is the following laconic statement:

> That Parāntaka whose lotus feet are worshiped by all earthly kings without exception, bestowed with faith and devotion (*śraddhā-bhaktiyuta*), by pouring a flood of water from a golden pitcher, (the villages of) Tālaiveṭam, Mayaṅkāṟu, and Kīḻakal entirely with 3,000 *khāri* (= *kāḍis*) of paddy and nine *niṣkas* upon the Brahmins of Meliruñceṟu learned in Veda and Vedāṅgas, including the Sāma Veda with its 3,000 branches (*śākha*).[72]

This is followed by a delineation of the boundaries of the villages and by a Tamil portion giving details of the supervision and execution of the grant by the local families included in the assembly (the *nāṭṭār* of Tiruttaṇi). The exact exemptions from a variety of taxes are then specified.

Note that at no point in this inscription does the king indicate by even the slightest hint his reason for making this gift. It all seems axiomatic—as if any king in his senses, and especially one graced by *śraddhā* and *bhakti*, would naturally hasten to divest his treasury of income that could go to support learned Brahmins. Indeed, the reference to "faith" and "devotion" is as much as we get in the way of personal statement. For the rest it is a thoroughly cut-and-dried affair, self-explanatory and self-sustaining. This is, moreover, a representative example of what we can read in a great mass of inscriptions from this period (and, indeed, from earlier and subsequent periods, as well). We can imagine Parāntaka listening, with a slightly bored expression, as the *śilpin* who engraved the inscription read it back to him in all its conventional, formulaic detail.

We are only slightly better off when we turn to a more elaborate inscriptional statement, from a section dealing not with the mechanical

[72] Text in Nagaswamy (1979); cf. translation, p. III.

details of an endowment but rather with the perception that the endowing ruler had of his dynastic origins and of the classical patterns established by his predecessors. The king in question is Vīrarājendra Chola (1063-1069), who has left us in an inscription at Kanyākumārī a remarkable version of the medieval Chola genealogy.[73] Within this mythic account of Chola dynastic history, particular interest attaches to the few verses, couched in ornate Sanskrit, that relate the story of an eponymous founder of the kingdom:

In that family was born a king,
Coḷa by name,
who tore asunder with his prowess a host of kings;
who was Death to the mighty monarchs;
who ruled the entire earth as if it were his capital,
so that the forests on every side
became gardens for his games. (28)

At one time he, the resort of the wise,
resplendent as Hara,
was spending his days in the forests
inhabited by hosts of sages.
He did not lack opportunities for pleasure— (29)

when, once, while he wandered in the wilderness
unaccompanied by many soldiers,
patient
and intent upon hunting down herds of deer—
he who was gracious to his subjects[74]
was suddenly carried off to the south
in pursuit of a demon who took the form of a deer. (30)

His swift steed which followed after that deer
brought him to another wilderness
thick with many trees.
He was swiftly followed by the commanders of his
fast-moving armies,
which were always ready to set off, at a moment's notice,
for a long campaign. (31)

[73] *TAS* 3, no. 34 (edited by K. V. Subrahmanya Aiyar), pp. 87-158. This version of the Chola genealogy differs in a number of interesting ways (including the episode translated below) from other accounts, such as those of Kampaṉ (*Irāmāvatāram* 1.712-23) and Cayaṅkŏṇṭār (178-206). I am indebted to Professor Hermann Kulke for making the text of this inscription available to me at a pressing moment.

[74] The editor of the text translates *prakṛtidakṣiṇa* as "he who was by nature skillful."

There the king slew that night-roving demon
and then proceeded, with his many spies, along the Kāverī
  which carries in its tremulous stream,
  here on earth,
  that same drink of life
  won by the gods by churning the ocean of milk. (32)

He bathed there . . . (text undecipherable)
  for Brahmins;
he whose mind was controlled
saw none.
Then from Āryāvartta
he brought eminent Brahmins
and settled them there on the banks. (33)

Resolutely,
he cleared the wilderness entirely
and laid out a perfect wood
  with areca palms and many betel creepers,
while with other small groves
  he made the banks of the Kāverī
  everywhere covered with shade
    and bearing many kinds of fruit. (34)

People often bathe in the heavenly river (Gaṅgā)
and perform *tapas* on its banks:
they torture themselves
  out of a longing to reach heaven.
But a bath *here*
  or fierce *tapas*
will ensure a dwelling in a place
  far better than the world of the gods
for those who are good. (35)

The major innovation which these verses introduce into the official Chola genealogy is the adaptation of a well-known episode from the *Rāmāyaṇa*—the fateful ploy of the demon Marīca, who takes the form of a golden deer to lure Rāma deep into the forest, away from Sītā.[75] This episode initiates the central trauma of the narrative, Rāvaṇa's abduction of Sītā. The link between Chola tradition and the *Rāmāyaṇa* is made explicit in Vīrarājendra's inscription: the verses directly preceding the passage I have quoted (24-27) deal with Rāma, the para-

[75] *Rām.* 3.43-44.

digmatic ruler "who performed to perfection the supreme acts of kingship" (*mahīśacaritaṃ kārtsnyena cakre param*, 26), as one of the ancestors of the Chola dynasty. This linkage has several obvious functions. First, it brings to bear a prestigious, classical model on a wholly local dynastic claim. Second, it places the origin of the Chola rulers in the hallowed North, whence they were, in a sense, "exiled" to the untamed lands of the South. Third, it incorporates a highly meaningful pattern—with real historical roots—according to which the kingdom is said to emerge from the wilderness.[76] Moreover, in the present instance this transition from wilderness (*kānana*) to the cultivated paddy fields of the Kāverī delta is very accurately linked to Brahmin settlement. The very foundation of the historical Chola kingdom is connected in this text to the eponymous founder's "importing" of Brahmin settlers from Āryāvartta. Even if we disregard the conventional claims to northern origin (of both the dynasty and the newly imported Brahmins), we can affirm that the royal granting of lands to Brahmins—*brahmadeya*, as in the inscription cited earlier—was a major element both in the formation of the medieval South Indian state and in its perennial attempts at expansion.[77] And yet, once again, the inscription fails to provide any real explanation of this pattern. At the very moment of the state's origin, "Coḷa" acts in the quintessential pattern of the dharmic South Indian king—and we are not told why.

At this point we must, it seems, go beyond the bald statements of the text to a consideration of its central images, which we may be able to interpret with the help of other, far more explicit and self-conscious texts. We might start by pressing further the analogy drawn between "Coḷa" and Rāma. Is it not, perhaps, significant that this episode in the *Rāmāyaṇa*, with its disastrous consequences for the epic hero, elicits from Rāma one of his most sustained and moving tirades of guilty self-torment and self-reproach?[78] (By following the golden deer, he has abandoned Sītā to her fate; how will he ever be able to face his father-in-law, Janaka, again? And so on—although these feelings are mixed with other powerful emotions, such as rage, shock, anxious fear, and anger at Lakṣmaṇa for failing in *his* protective role.) Our South Indian dynastic hero has no such specific occasion to reproach himself—and yet, like Rāma, he is entangled in an ambiguous role that inevitably implicates him in evil (though not necessarily in

[76] Cf. Falk (1974); Shulman (1979a); for another instance of this theme, *Tiruviḷaiyāṭaṟpurāṇam* 1.3 (*tirunakaram kaṇṭa paṭalam*).

[77] See Stein (1980), pp. 141-72.

[78] *Rām*. 3.57-65; cf. *Irāmāvatāram* 3.8.151-61. Rama has significant impulses in this direction in any case!

guilt-ridden ways). He is, after all, explicitly compared to Death itself—a flattering trope, of course, but one that leaves no doubt as to the violent aspect of the classical kingly role. Moreover, this aggressive, destructive side of the king as warrior finds another expression in his preferred manner of recreation: "Coḷa" is "hunting down herds of deer" in the forest when the demon in disguise entices him to the south. Hunting may well be a paradigmatic royal activity in South India,[79] but it is hardly free from opprobrium. Quite the contrary—like battle, it stains the king with the evil consequences of *hiṃsā*, "harm" to living beings. The king is expected, of course, to absorb this harm as his native "portion"—it is all part of the job. The sacrifice of life on earth must go on, and it is the king's duty to manage it according to rule. But this does not mean that he wants to hold on to the consequences of his actions forever. We should bear in mind that such traces of evil (*pāpa, pāpman*) are regarded in South India not as some ethereal, immaterial moral quality but rather as something more akin to a concrete, viscous, uncomfortably possessive power.[80] Small wonder, then, that the king who accumulates too much of this *pāpa* becomes intent upon, even obsessed with, ridding himself of it through effecting some kind of transfer. And it is the Brahmin who is the natural candidate for the role of recipient.

In fact, the problem goes far deeper. The king's contamination by evil must be seen as bound up with the very essence of his activity as a ruler, or, in the language of the royal symbols, with his exercise of force—*daṇḍa*, the power of the staff, symbol of his right and duty to punish.[81] Again, we know that the king can by no means avoid wielding his staff—were he to abandon it, the world would fall apart. This is the major thrust of the speeches addressed to Yudhiṣṭhira, the conflicted hero and reluctant ruler of the *Mahābhārata*, by his brothers and their common wife Draupadī *after* the epic battle that guarantees Yudhiṣṭhira his throne. At this crucial moment (described in the opening chapters of the *Śāntiparvan*, a section of the epic that constitutes one of the major classical discussions of the problem of *daṇḍa*), Yudhiṣṭhira sits inconsolate at the thought of the irreparable loss and ruin brought about by his readiness to fight for his kingdom. Each of the heroes pleads in turn, eloquently and relentlessly, the case for *daṇḍa*—in the

[79] See, for example, the magnificent Kirāta hunting scene depicted in the Lepākṣi murals; and see below, V.2 at note 54.

[80] This force may even be personified in wholly concrete images—for example, when Brahminicide takes the form of an Untouchable hag with blood-soaked garments to pursue Indra: *Bhāgavata* 6.13.10-12; cf. below, V.2.

[81] Lingat (1973), pp. 214-15; Inden (1978), pp. 35-36.

hope that Yudhiṣṭhira will come to terms with his kingly imperatives. Perhaps the most convincing exponent of this cause is Arjuna, the central warrior hero of the epic, who offers what is in effect an elaborate *stotra*, a hymn of praise, to *daṇḍa*:

> All the limits established in the world, O king, are marked by *daṇḍa*. . . . No man will sacrifice if he is not afraid, nor will he give gifts or hold to his promise. No one can attain great glory (*śrī*) without striking at others' vitals, or without doing terrible deeds, without killing like a fisherman (*matsyaghātin*). Only a killer has fame on earth, and wealth, and offspring. Indra became Mahendra by killing Vṛtra; thus he attained lordship over all the worlds. People worship those gods who are killers—gods such as Rudra, Skanda, Śakra, Agni, Varuṇa, Yama, Kāla, Vāyu, Mṛtyu, Vaiśravaṇa, the sun, the Vasus, Maruts, Sādhyas, and Viśvedevas, O Bhārata. These are the gods people worship, influenced by their power—not Brahmā or Dhātṛ or Pūṣan. Only a few men sacrifice to those who are impartial toward all creatures, the restrained, pacified deities intent on tranquillity. I see no being which lives in the world without violence. Creatures exist at one another's expense; the stronger consume the weaker. The mongoose eats mice, just as the cat eats the mongoose; the dog devours the cat, O king, and wild beasts eat the dog. Man eats them all—see *dharma* for what it is! Everything that moves and is still is food for life. This is a law laid down by fate (*daiva*); he who knows it is not confused. Please just be who you were created to be, O king. . . .[82]

Like other partisans of *daṇḍa* Arjuna prides himself on taking what could be called a realistic view: the initial statements on the necessary moral force provided by *daṇḍa* (sacrifice, giving, faithfulness, and so on are all dependent on the ruler's power to punish) give way to a more general, somewhat cynical view of violence as the law of life. Power—that is, violent, lethal power—argues for itself; Yudhiṣṭhira is advised to "see *dharma* for what it is." This bitter exhortation is followed by the practical demand that the king accept his role, as he accepts the violence implicit in his willingness to go on living: Yudhiṣṭhira should simply be the person he was created to be. The problem, of course, is that Yudhiṣṭhira has profound doubts on this very score; he is far from convinced that life is worth living, at the

[82] *MBh* (SR) 12.15.10, 13-23. See discussion of this passage in Biardeau (1976), pp. 164-67.

going price. Nor is he alone in these doubts—Yudhiṣṭhira's struggle epitomizes an entire dimension of moral questioning in the epic, and, indeed, in traditional Hindu society generally. Moreover, not even Arjuna, the biting exponent of *daṇḍa* in this passage, can remain blind to the sorry state of a universe constructed upon his premises:

> *evaṃ paryākule loke vipathe jarjharīkṛte (sic)*
> *tais tair nyāyair mahārāja purāṇaṃ dharmam ācaret*

> O king, one must accomplish the ancient *dharma* by these various ordinances
> in a world which is topsy-turvy, off course, and falling apart. (12.15.53)

This is the sort of world with which the king, like everybody else, must make do—although all the brothers, including Yudhiṣṭhira, seem agreed that the king's responsibility is greater than others'. That, indeed, is Yudhiṣṭhira's dilemma. Note, however, that even Arjuna admits the existence of a problem here: glory (*śrī*) is within the king's grasp—however chaotic and distasteful the mundane setting may appear—but only by slaying creatures "like a fisherman." The simile is by no means accidental: the fisherman, whose victims inevitably die with their unblinking eyes staring at him in horror, symbolizes violence in its most brutal and polluting form.[83]

Daṇḍa, then, sets up a tension within each king and for every kingdom. Yudhiṣṭhira's dilemma remains the inheritance of all medieval South Indian kings. Alone, the king is burdened by the evil consequences of his violent role. But this dilemma is then played out in relation to the Brahmins, the repositories and symbols of the supreme values of the tradition—above all the freedom from taint expressed in the Brahmin claim to purity, and the link with renunciation that underlies this claim. We shall discuss this Brahminic complex of values at some length below, but already the central dynamic is apparent: the king will seek to transfer his load of evil to the Brahmins who take his gifts; they, for their part, are meant to dispose of it—a ritualized role predicated upon the Brahmin's unique, innate facility with problematic "remnants." Not that the royal bequest of *pāpa* was in itself welcome to the Brahmin recipients—the reverse is true, as one can see from the theory that developed in response, to the effect that royal gifts accompanied by gold or betel nut (as opposed to sesamum seed) were without inauspicious consequences. In theory, such gifts

[83] See below, on *matsyanyāya*—the "law of fishes"—II.5 at n. 120. And cf. Shulman (1980), pp. 214-16.

could be distinguished from outright *payments* to the Brahmin for fulfilling his priestly role within the context of the *jajmāni* service-order. In either case, however, the king's peculiar dependence is conspicuous; his ability to carry on, indeed his legitimacy in the widest sense, is inseparably tied to his ability to give gifts to the Brahmin.

We must also note how close we are to the ancient sacrificial models. In the sacrifice, the patron-protagonist, the *yajamāna*, divests himself of the evil adhering to him by transferring it to the Brahmin priests together with their payment in gifts (*dakṣiṇā*). As we have seen, the king is traditionally regarded as the *yajamāna* par excellence. This is not to say that the medieval political order reproduces the precise patterns of the Vedic *śrauta* ritual—for the latter has already gone far toward extricating itself, and its performers, from the endless cycle of violence and the need to redistribute its consequences.[84] Indeed, the dangerous interdependence of *yajamāna* and priest was a motivating concern in the priests' attempt to elaborate the idealized world of the *śrauta* rites outside the normal social order. The medieval paradigm reflects both an earlier stage in the development of the sacrifice—a stage in which this interdependence remained a constant, and a constantly problematic, factor—and the profound fissure that has opened up in the classical period between the pure, detached Brahmin and his royal patron. Ideally, the king and Brahmin should form a stable pair; in reality, they have been divided, and with this division the integrity of the sacrificial universe has been disturbed. The Brahmin is now committed to a sacrifice without remnants, without evil, and without visible connection to the king's polluted and polluting sphere of violence and power. This leaves the king in the invidious position of performing a sacrifice that can never be whole, can never reach its logical conclusion of legitimate destruction and regeneration; for it is the destructive aspect inherent in sacrifice, in creation, that the Brahmin rejects in his move beyond the everyday sphere. The Brahmin carries with him the ultimate values of the society, and its ultimate authority; the king must now rule a world that always looks outside itself, and in any case beyond *him*. He can hardly hope, in these conditions, for lasting balance, harmony, or stability; rather, he finds himself in endless motion, vainly pursuing his lost authority even as he is pursued by accumulating evil. What may once have been a fairly homogeneous, unified role—in the heroic kingship of Caṅkam times, let us say—has, by the Pallava period, become segmented into separate carriers, each with his own tensions, his own loneliness, his peculiar

[84] See Heesterman (1981), pp. 60-61.

relation to the sacrifice, and his nostalgia for a time when power and authority were more easily combined.

There was, however, another possibility for the South Indian king, an option not unrelated to the first (Brahmin legitimation) and not necessarily competing with it. The service performed by the Brahmin could also be accomplished by a god. We can see this pattern clearly in the story of Kūṟṟuvanāyaṉār, the Śaiva saint and soldier who succeeded in subduing the entire earth (presumably, that is, the Chola country in which he was born). Cekkiḻār tells the tale of this upstart *kṣatriya* in several simple, vivid verses:

> The guardian of the fertile earth (= Kūṟṟuvanāyaṉār, who had just completed his conquests) asked the Brahmins who dwell in Tillai to anoint him with the jeweled crown. But they said: "We crown none but kings from the ancient line of the Cĕmpiyar (Cholas)." Refusing thus, they went to Malaināṭu of the Cera. After the Tillai Brahmins, leaving behind a single family to safeguard their unique right to service (*ŏrumaiy urimai*), had gone to the land of the pure Ceras of great lineage, he (Kūṟṟuvanāyaṉār) grew despondent through doubt; he worshiped the anklets which dance in the *sabhā*.[85] Holding fast to the thought, "Tonight I *must* receive His lotus feet as my crown," he went to sleep—and the god indeed gave him his lotus feet in a dream. Through this act of mercy, he became the guardian of the entire world.
>
> He worshiped in each of the many temples favored by the lord who performs his dance of unending ambrosia in the golden *sabhā*—and the inhabitants of this world knew keen joy. To the gods' delight, he gave away his kingdom and reached the feet of the lord.[86]

The Śaiva hero's search for an alternative form of legitimation results from his failure to achieve the more usual kind—from the Brahmin priests at Cidambaram. The explosive nature of the Brahmin-king relation is evident here, for the Brahmins who refuse Kūṟṟuvanāyaṉār's request, on the grounds that he is not of the proper lineage, feel compelled to abandon their homes and to migrate to Kerala in the far southwest. The king clearly has the power and hence, it might seem, the right to demand Brahmin cooperation; denied it, he turns to another authority, the god established in the shrine (who is, of course,

[85] This is a reference to Naṭarāja-Śiva's dance (the *ānandatāṇḍava*) in the *ciṟṟampalam* at Citamparam.

[86] *PP* 2.7.4-7.

worshiped by these same Brahmin families). The universalistic claims of Śaiva *bhakti* are seemingly vindicated by the god's acquiescence: the king's *abhiṣeka* now takes the form of his being crowned by the deity's feet. Anointed in this manner, the king can rule his domain. Note, however, that this pious ruler seems fairly indifferent to the usual demands of kingship; he spends his time visiting temples until, at last, he renounces office altogether in favor of a death-in-worship. *Bhakti* absorbs, without resolving, the basic tensions of the renunciatory ideal.

This hagiography has its correlation in a dominant historical pattern in our period. Endowments to Brahmins exist alongside massive endowments to temples and their deities. In both cases we may discover a dynamic of exchange and transformation, as the donor converts his burden of sorrows into *śrī*—a newly attained, and always vulnerable, prosperity, wholeness, and regal splendor. Indeed, this precarious but infinitely desirable state is precisely what is claimed for the newborn Chola kingdom in the last verse quoted above from Vīrarājendra's inscription: having settled his northern Brahmins on lands carved from the wilderness, along the banks of the Kāverī which is compared to the divine ambrosia, the king finds himself in paradise—not, it should be stressed, a celestial garden of delights (such as could be attained by bathing in the Ganges), but a wholly terrestrial, visible, immediately accessible domain created through his kingly actions of violence (slaying the demon deer), demarcation (clearing the forest, laying out gardens and groves), and renunciation. Kingship becomes, it would seem, a divine drama holding the promise of supermundane rewards, enacted and realized in the uniquely human realm of life on earth.

4. Paradigm and Transformation

The patterns just outlined provide the initial framework for our study. We need now to examine each of the actors on his own terms and in his relations with the others; as we shall see, the literary texts have a great deal more to say about the major roles and their permutations. At this point we can attempt to draw out some of the implications of the discussion in the form of a provisional paradigm of the kingly role.

In order to take into account the dynamic nature of the political order, this paradigm must distinguish two phases of a cycle, both of them connected, as we might expect, with sacrificial concepts. There is first, the "normal" order of the everyday: here the king appears as arbiter of an unending process of recirculation; in the inscriptions, his voice guarantees the allocation of local resources in ways that serve his own purposes and needs as well as those of the community as a whole. We may relate this pattern to the well-known *jajmāni* system of parceling out "shares" in connection with service roles: each group in the village receives its portion, while the king as *yajamāna* (the sacrificial term underlying the title given to the system, *jajmāni*) supervises the entire process of distribution.[87] But this process is neither simple and smooth nor ever truly satisfactory for any of the parties involved. The distribution is rarely stable; it must be renewed constantly in response to the strains of competing claims. Not least among these are the king's own compulsive attempts to prop himself up, at least momentarily, above the body politic by means of an endowment that will extricate him from the entangling *pāpa* of the community and allow him the transcendent aura of renunciation (*tyāga*). Thus we find the king offering his portion—a kind of *śeṣa* or sacrificial remnant—to the Brahmins, or to the god. But this gift, while allowing the sacrificial order of *dharma* to survive another hour under the aegis of the donor king, is never enough: it ties down both the Brahmins and the temple deity in uncomfortable ways; and it can never finally free the king from his ever-accumulating burden of evil. The first problem, that of the dangerous level of dependence, drains away the transcendent power of the gift; the central symbolic figures become locked in restrictive patterns of interaction. Thus the king demonstrates his kingship by acting for the god—presenting him with the precious remnant, and redistributing the tangible and intangible signs of his grace (*prasāda*)—whereas the god, for his part, requires this human mediation, for he has allowed himself to become immobile, trapped in stone, in the interests of stimulating and receiving the gift of human love. A similar interdependence strains the relation of Brahmin and king, as we have seen. The second problem, the temporary nature of the solution, means that the process can never be completed; one is always forced to divide up the portions again, to reorder the circulating resources, to redirect the moral flow and the ranking of honors (*mariyātai*), to give still another set of gifts—even as the resource base tends to diminish before one's eyes.[88] Moreover, as the

[87] See Dumont (1972), pp. 138-50; Heesterman (1981); Reiniche (1977); cf. discussion in Stein (1980), pp. 377-78, of the *amara* tenure of Vijayanagar times. It should be stressed that the village assembly, from the Pallava period onward, can itself take on the king's symbolic role as overseer and donor (*ibid.*, p. 230). The royal *yajamāna* may be a corporate persona. And see Dirks (1983), p. 11.

[88] The need to repeat, with cumulative or innovative effect, the earlier ordering of

internal stresses build up, the pressure to endow more and more intensifies: thus we have the phenomenon of "crisis endowment," at moments of open conflict when the political actors—the king himself, his subordinates in their various factions, his rivals, his Brahmin priests—rush to the nearest (or the most magnificent, or the most popular) temple to offer their gifts.[89]

This everyday side of the cycle is characterized by normative, hierarchical claims: the king himself is deeply involved in regulating and sustaining the hierarchy in the midst of a confused web of rivalries and fluctuating conditions. The picture as a whole has what might be called a "tragic" aspect connected to its bounded condition, its inability to solve its internal tensions within the given frame, and its self-conscious partiality—the loss of ultimacy to the Brahmin boundary figure.[90] And, sooner or later, the attempt breaks down; the inner stresses are too much to bear, the local resources too limited to meet the unending demands. Help has to come from outside—in the form of resources gained through predatory conflict, in a manner that undermines, at least temporarily, the entire hierarchical structure even as it sets loose the energies checked by the normative restraints. The tensions of the everyday pattern propel the kingdom in the direction of expansion. Thus the king will lead his armies into battle, or on long raids into enemy territories; the conflict-ridden body politic reaches beyond its borders in what would seem a symbolic expression of its essential unity. But this appearance is deceptive: although the warrior-king, who sometimes remains largely impassive and helpless,[91] does unite around his person, as a symbolic focus, the disparate fragments of the temporarily dissolved village polity, these fail to achieve even in warfare a greater coherence than they usually attain at home. Nor is the dramatic quality, which we have seen to mark the king's ritual roles in peacetime, lacking during a campaign: the medieval monarch leading his troops takes on something of the character of a circus manager desperately calling upon his refractory, essentially autonomous actors to appear. In breaking out of the nor-

---

resources is strikingly evident from many temple walls, with their inscriptions piled upon inscriptions. One should also note the care with which earlier records of endowment were preserved—often recopied, engraved anew at the order of successive rulers.

89 For an instance of this phenomenon, from the time of Acyutadevarāya (1530-1542), see Stein (1960), pp. 170-71. Cf. Ludden (1978), p. 102.

90 This use of the term "tragic" will be explained below: see section 5 of this chapter, and Chapter VII.

91 As, indeed, he is sometimes portrayed in the literature: see Shulman (1979b), discussing Rāma in the *Catakaṇṭarāvaṇaṉkatai*. And cf. the "transcendent" phase of kingship in Inden's analysis (above, n. 68).

mative cycle, the king has opened himself, and the kingdom he represents, to the indeterminate and the unbounded.

This disorderly phase has a logic of its own as well as real, important consequences. Its antithetical aspect recalls the institutionalized chaos of the village festivals for the goddess, with their inversions of roles, attack upon hierarchy as such, the release of pent-up forces, their sometimes comic touches.[92] All of these features are present in medieval South Indian warfare, as we shall see. But we can also discern here an overriding rationale of plunder: as George Spencer has demonstrated,[93] raiding provided the medieval kingdom with its major source of free-floating resources. Not only property in the narrow sense—such as livestock, produce, gold, and silver—could be plundered and brought home to the political "center" or centers; South Indian armies were also quite capable of looting temples and kidnapping their deities. Certain popular gods in medieval Tamil Nadu—such as Vātāpi Gaṇapati at Tiruccĕṅkāṭṭaṅkuṭi and Tiruvārūr[94]—were acquired in this way. War thus activates anew the ancient agonistic model of the sacrifice—with the king cast, as ever, in the *yajamāna*'s role. Whether engaged in the slaughter of battle or merely robbing his rival of his god, the king finds himself sinking under a new load of *pāpa*. In a sense, he is now at the very heart of the ancient sacrifice, the central moment of destruction and the unpredictable unleashing of chaotic forces. But the ancient rite has been superseded by the Brahminical ideology of distance and control—and it is in this context, of a state largely informed by Brahminical values, that the king must function. Once again, the sacrifice is not allowed to take its course; more than ever, the king needs someone to receive his gifts. Thus, if he has conquered new territory that he hopes to incorporate into his kingdom, he will invest in lands—by endowing *brahmadeyas*. The gold he has acquired will be granted to a deity as an ostentatious symbol of the king's *bhakti*—and of his need for the god's support. The more resources have been plundered, and the greater the potential for new concentration in the hands of the victorious warrior-king, the more

[92] See Brubaker (1978).

[93] Spencer (1976 and 1983).

[94] Vātāpi Gaṇapati as worshiped at Tiruvārūr, Tiruccĕṅkāṭṭaṅkuṭi, and other Tamil shrines may have been brought to Tamil Nadu after the Pallava conquest of Vātāpi/Bādāmi (A.D. 642). Ironically, this same deity is said to have been kidnaped by brigands from Tiruvārūr and taken as far north as Kaliṅga before he "escaped" and returned home to Tiruvārūr: *Tiyākarācalīlai, kaṭavuḷ vāḻttu* 29; Taṇṭapāṇi Tecikar, p. 32. For an instance of looting temple deities during the reign of Kulottuṅga I, see Stein (1980), p. 174. And cf. "sacred thefts" in medieval Europe as described by Geary (1978).

eager he will be to exchange these resources for the intangible but always necessary *śrī*—the royal splendor, divine luster, the basic concomitant of his position—which he has darkened, or, perhaps, entirely forfeited during the campaign.

Both the tremendous dynamism and the inherent limitations of the medieval South Indian state stand out clearly in this view. Although a powerful center never emerges as such in this period, neither does the state remain at a low level of development; on the contrary, it is given to constant flux and expansive drives. In economic terms, it needs the resources that are available only from plunder; ideologically—to the extent the king absorbs the Brahmin vision, in the hope of acquiring Brahmin support—he can maintain himself only by renewed endowments dependent in part upon expansion. The kingdom cannot remain forever small, wholly tied down to local factors, but neither can it become truly "great"; the drive to incorporate new elements (hitherto excluded social groups; wilderness lands or territories conquered from a rival; foreign deities, or the power networks associated with heretical groups such as the Buddhists and Jains) is always shattered by the compulsion to replicate the original, delicately balanced ordering of the social universe. The fragile alliance of Brahmin and king both impels the kingdom to break out of its normally contained state and places obvious limits on the reconstructive potential of this break. Similarly, the mirror relation of king and temple deity—each partner reflecting the inner divisions of the other—works against any real consolidation of power in the hands of the ruler: the latter cannot ultimately transcend his own god. These dynamics reproduce themselves on all levels of the society; they apply no less to a local ruler exercising minimal control over a tiny, ill-defined territory than to his Chola overlord at the symbolic center of the wider kingdom. Moreover, the relations between these levels can never be fully regulated and defined, given the inherent limits on the power of the dynastic center: local rulers may, indeed, seek to project their own intolerable tensions on to the major kingly figure, thereby achieving a temporary release and the protection of a higher, more prestigious, and somewhat more powerful political actor,[95] but the latter is effectively prevented from utilizing in a permanent, dependable way the loyalties and resources of his supposed subordinates. Rather, he will

[95] See Hart (1980). We may note in this connection Inden's useful distinction between a major king and the less powerful *sāmanta*: the *rājarāja* acts as a *yajamāna* for his own *abhiṣeka*, whereas the *sāmanta* has his overlord acting for him as *yajamāna* (as a father does at his son's *saṃskāras*). See Inden (1978), p. 38.

radiate his power back into the diffused local sources from which it springs.[96]

We can, however, note a rise in the intensity of the conflict, and an added dimension to its structure, as we move up from lower, more localized levels to wider regional or supraregional systems of power; this rise also transforms the idiom of exchange between the patron-king and his supporting Brahmins. If within the local, village context of *jajmāni* relations the Brahmin receives payment in exchange for concrete ritual services, once the actors are lifted out of their local roles their mutual dependence deepens, while their claims upon each other, and upon themselves, are articulated anew—the king now seeks recognition as a great (even universal) ruler after the model of the classical Kṣatriya icons of Sanskrit texts, whereas the Vedic Brahmins, no longer village priests but rather rarefied, pure exemplars of detachment, offer the king their support in exchange for grants of land. This transformation in perspective and style should perhaps be seen as yet another attempt to propel the major figures out of the enmeshing web of local relations, thereby creating, as it were, an encompassing boundary of ideal relations between Brahmin and king, above the interlocking mass of normal social interests and struggles. Yet its effects upon the structure of power seem to reduplicate the pattern of the lowest levels: the conquering king can claim more power only by renouncing more power, by investing his "gains," such as they are, in the symbolic legitimation of Veda-chanting Brahmins. They, for their part, hold even more firmly than their village counterparts to their identification with the ultimate Brahmin values of renunciation and purity—thus denying the political center the very legitimacy it seeks. In other words, the king's recognition can be achieved only by his acknowledging his subservience and by his renouncing any desire to cumulate resources for his needs. Power, in medieval South India, is won by conspicuous and ever-renewed powerlessness, self-impoverishment, and ritual self-denial.

Thus the greater the ruler's claim to authority, the less raw power he may actually concentrate in his hands. One can sometimes trace the assimilation of this pattern by "peripheral" kingdoms which, in the course of expanding and becoming more "central," gradually achieve the institutionalized weakness of the South Indian royal center. The effect, in the major kingdoms, is to leave power, such as it is, in

[96] See Inden (1978), pp. 34-36, on the king as microcosm symbolically identified with the (macrocosmic) realm, and on the "immanent" *tejas* focused in the king but made accessible to the wider kingdom.

the hands of its original, quasi-autonomous regulators—the local foci of authority such as caste and kinship networks, Brahminical groups (priests, teachers, landowners, sectarian lineages), merchant associations, and village assemblies. Royal intervention in the ongoing life of such groups, while by no means a rare or insignificant occurrence, tends to reflect and, often, to conserve their configurations of power rather than to disrupt or subsume them. In general, the forces concentrated at the center have more to do with the symbolization of the conflicts rife within the society as a whole than with their resolution in a way that could allow for the accumulation of power and resources; the integrative process in this polity allows for, indeed effectively ensures, its continued fragmentation.[97]

This conclusion, highly abstract as it must seem, and still very much in need of proving, receives support from another set of factors that emerge with great clarity from the literary sources on kingship. These have to do with the inner, implicit perceptions of the world and of the human tasks and identities within it. Instability and change characterize this inner vision; boundaries blur, one role readily merges with another. As we shall see, the major symbolic types in South India—including the political actors we have mentioned: king, Brahmin, even the *bhakti* god, but with the notable exception of the bandit-hero—are composite figures incorporating multiple personae, which come into view and then dissolve in relation to other such identities. The king presents us not with one face but with a series of fleeting images projected from a mirror. It is all one can do to arrest these apparitions for a moment's scrutiny—for there is an underlying urge to self-transformation and self-transcendence; nothing remains the same for long. In conjunction with one another, the social types appear to unfold their hidden aspects in kaleidoscopic patterns; isolated, they recede before our gaze, or disappear into their own antithesis. The result is a complex system of great dynamic potential and basic structural weakness, in which the major actors collide with one another, and with their own internal forces, thereby upsetting the tenuous balance associated with the prime cultural ideals. Moreover, these ideals are themselves no less elusive, problematic, and open to transformation: *dharma*, the king's concern and support, is repeatedly said to be *sūkṣma*—delicate, subtle, difficult to define; *bhakti*, the ethic of devotion that informs the entire system, is often conceived in South

[97] Some of these formulations owe much to discussions with S. N. Eisenstadt and S. J. Tambiah. For integration as preserving fragmentation (in the very different setting of traditional Rajasthan), see Stern (1977).

India as tense, antagonistic, and ridden with conflict. In this respect—the fractured, dynamic, self-transforming nature of things—both the conceptual and the symbolic orders seem to reflect accurately enough the social reality of their times.

We must, then, beware of drawing too sharply the contours of the emerging model. This is a state of infinite thresholds: transformations await us everywhere.[98] The analytical distinction we have drawn between two phases in the royal paradigm must not be taken to imply that these phases are wholly separate in reality, even in simple temporal terms; in fact, they tend to interpenetrate consistently. Nor can we discover any real separation between "secular" and "sacred" areas of authority: the spiritual powers of the Brahmin and the martial or administrative talents of the king are not permanently distinct and opposite forces but internally divided and mutually dependent symbolic clusters. Each contains something of the other, may indeed turn into the other. The basic dynamic of relations is transformational—Brahmin to warrior to renouncer; king to clown to king. Our task now is to map the ranges, and to explore the meanings, of these metamorphoses.

5. Modes of Meaning and Experience: *viraha* and *viḷaiyāṭal*

Before abandoning the abstractions of our analytical paradigms, we might attempt to bring them down to earth by relating them to certain recurrent emotions, experiences, and themes. I have referred in passing to the "everyday" paradigm as "tragic," whereas the second, non-ordinary phase of inversions and chaotic expansion may be said to contain "comic" elements; both these terms, borrowed from Western poetics, need to be defined and explicated in relation to the South Indian context to which I wish to apply them. This, too, is part of my intention in the following chapters. For the moment it is, perhaps, sufficient to point to an important tension between two pervasive concepts, which may also serve to replace our borrowed terminology.

If the everyday is tragic, the reason lies in its being suffused by the experience of *viraha*, "separation" (Tamil *pirivu*). As Friedhelm Hardy as shown, *viraha* is for the Tamil Vaiṣṇava poets (especially Nammāḻvār) perhaps the predominant mode of experiencing the divine:

[98] On Hindu thought as concerned with the "*transformability* of certain states," see comments by Appadurai on Ferro-Luzzi (1980), p. 54.

> They opened themselves to the beauty of the temple images and rituals and to the eros of the myths and tried to communicate them in turn through their sensual poetry. But the more they took in from this sense- and emotion-filling nature of Krishna, the closer they thereby came to him and the more they thus fulfilled themselves as human beings—the more they suffered. This peculiar experience of suffering in one way could only be explained as due to Krishna's very presence in their hearts, and in another way they saw this as the reflection of human incapability to contain or encompass the transcendental.[99]

This conceptualization is not, I would argue, by any means limited to the Tamil Vaiṣṇava poets—among the Śaivas, the *Tevāram* poets present similar notions—nor, for that matter, to the realm of religious feeling. Life itself, in its ordered, normative aspect, is conceived as an arena of separation, which may be experienced on various levels—the metaphysical separation of man from his divine source; the more generalized sense of limitation and partiality inherent in mundane reality; and the emotional torment involved in separation from those whom one loves. This latter category has, in itself, several distinct levels: there is the everyday experience of loss (through absence, temporary or permanent, and above all in death); the ill-defined longings which arise so mysteriously in the course of our normal lives and which may have no conscious object;[100] and—here we find what appears to be the most profound development of the theory of separation in South India—that amazing sense of separation, loneliness, and loss that accompanies the *possession* of the object of one's love. This is the feeling described by Hardy in the passage quoted above: the very presence of the deity, his revelation before our eyes, evokes in us the unbearable sense of his absence—of our finitude, our inability to hold the god here, our frustration at the awareness of his total transcendence. But the same emotion is present in any kind of loving, even, the medieval Tamils would argue, in the moment of ecstatic union with the beloved. The closer we approach the other, the more clearly do we realize the ultimate unknowability of another person and our

[99] Hardy (1981), p. 9; this thesis is expounded in full in Hardy (1976). Compare the doctrine of separation in Bengali Vaiṣṇavism: Dimock (1971), noting similarities with the poetry of the troubadours; and cf. O'Flaherty (1980), pp. 122-24.

[100] Here we may mention, as a special subcategory, the longings described by Kālidāsa in a famous verse (*Śakuntalā* V, 2)—that is, those arising from beholding a lovely sight, or hearing sweet sounds. Kālidāsa connects these feelings to lost memories of former lives (see the story of Āputtiraṉ: below, II.3).

inability to cross, once and for all, the border which divides us. Love, in its different aspects, is as much a form of separation as of merging.

This metaphysic of paradoxical separation-in-union apparently first developed self-consciously in Tamil Nadu in the *bhakti* traditions of the early medieval period. Its roots may lie in the much earlier Caṅkam love poetry, which shows a pronounced fondness for tragic images of love: of the five main phases of the conventional lovers'-drama, correlated, respectively, to five external landscapes (*tiṇai*), four contain explicit situations of separation. Thus *mullai*, the forest region, is the setting of the beloved's patient waiting for the lover's return; *nĕytal*, the seashore, is connected with anxious waiting; *pālai*, the desert wasteland, is the landscape of separation par excellence;[101] *marutam*, the alluvial plains, the landscape proper to married union, is the scene of quarrels and infidelity—here we often encounter the wife whiling away the night in loneliness, as her husband is away with the courtesans. Even the fifth landscape, *kuṟiñci*, the mountainous setting of the joyous premarital union (*kaḷavu*) of the lovers, contains the seed of suffering—for *kaḷavu*, as its very name indicates, is at best a stolen pleasure, fleeting and laden with anxiety. The medieval poets, starting with this rich legacy, have expanded upon its hidden premises: separation now becomes not only a common, concrete reality in the lives of nearly all lovers, who are forced into a physical or, more painfully, an emotional distance from one another; rather, it is seen more and more as the outstanding characteristic of love even in—or especially in—its fulfilment in union.

Beyond this, separation serves as a many-faceted metaphor for man's normal state of being in the world, a state characterized by actual or potential loss and by ever-present fragmentation and limitation. Herein lies, it would seem, much of the affective power of Kampaṉ's *Irāmāvatāram*, large portions of which are devoted to expressing the trauma of separation that the heroes, Rāma and Sītā, must undergo. Many of Kampaṉ's most powerful passages explore what he perceived as this most basic human experience. Thus when Rāma first returns to his hut in the forest and finds it empty—for Sītā has just been kidnapped by Rāvaṇa—he is overwhelmed by confusion and bitterness: the poet compares him to "a life which has left its containing body and returned to seek it—but in vain" (3.8.158); or to a man whose life depends upon his only treasure, which he has hidden in a box buried in the earth—only to discover that thieves have made off

[101] See discussion in Shulman (1981).

with it (159). Rāma's loss calls up in him a cry of existential protest, in a moment of total antagonism and outrage at the world:

> That great one trembled—
> was he raging against *dharma*?
> or against mercy (*aruḷ*)?
> or against the gods, or the sages,
> or the prowess of the evil?
> How would it all end?
> Was he raging against the Veda itself? (3.8.161)

Note how the overwhelming reality of separation induces in the hero a general hostility to a world in which such experiences are possible, even usual. But this is only Rāma's first reaction to his loss; from this point until almost the very end of the long poem, *viraha* is his predominant mode of feeling. At times, as at the start of the *Kiṭkintākāṇṭam*, Rāma comes close to losing his reason because of the unendurable suffering that he is forced to know. Sītā, for her part, has very similar experiences: indeed, she is described at one point, in her captivity, as "a woman fasioned from sorrow (*piṇiyāḷ*)—as if the grief of separation (*pirivu*) which afflicts lovers, full of desire for one another, in the world, had taken on tangible form" (5.3.7). Kampaṉ's poem may be seen as in large part a lyrical and dramatic exposition of *viraha* in all its pain, its pervasive and unavoidable familiarity, and—we must not forget—its uniquely attractive beauty.

For *viraha*, however suffused by suffering, need by no means be seen in a wholly negative light. Quite the contrary is true of the Tamil *bhakti* poets: they extol the pangs of separation, which are also evidence of real love. Such suffering is, in their eyes, quite literally divine—a reflection of the god's need and longing for the lowly creatures who are, for their part, obsessed with their own yearnings for him. *Viraha*, as the hallmark of the everyday, is the inevitable concomitant of *saṃsāra*, the phenomenal world—and the *bhakti* poets, far from wishing to be released from this scene of suffering, ask rather to be reborn again and again so as to taste each time anew the wonder and joy of loving the absent deity.[102] The god may torture his devotee by his

[102] See, for example, *PP* 143. The Caṅkam poet Kapilar expressed a similar viewpoint, in a "secular" context, in *Kuṟuntŏkai* 288:

> He is dear to me, that man
> far away in his mountains
> where the pepper-vine grows thick
> and monkeys feed upon the tender leaves.

apparent indifference or, for that matter, by actively afflicting him with misery; but these sorrows are apprehended as signs of the living relation between the two parties, hence of the rapturous connection which only separation makes possible:

kaṣṭā te sṛṣṭiceṣṭā bahutarabhavakhedāvahā jīvabhājām
ity evaṃ pūrvam ālocitam ajita mayā naivam adyābhijāne/
no cej jīvāḥ kathaṃ vā madhurataram idaṃ tvadvapuś cidrasārdraṃ
netraiḥ śrotraiś ca pītvā paramarasasudhāmbhodhipūre rameran//

"Cruel is your creative act,
bringing innumerable sorrows
to all who are endowed with life."

So I had always thought,
Invincible One,
but now I reason:

how else could living beings
delight in drinking in,
with eyes and ears,
this form of yours,
supernally sweet
and liquid with awareness
in the flooding ocean filled
with the nectar of truth?[103]

This verse, by a brilliant sixteenth-century poet from Kerala, points to the normative, ordered aspect of the *viraha* mode: god is in his temple (embodied in the image accessible to his devotees), and all is wrong—painfully, wonderfully, passionately wrong—with the world.

For the delights of *viraha* hardly serve to alleviate the tragic character of human life. The tragedy inheres in the pain—and yet this remains an essentially life-affirming stance. This conclusion should not surprise us; a similar claim could be made for the Greek tragedians (certainly for Aeschylus) as well as for Shakespeare or Racine. The tragic vision of the world tends to entail a deep engagement in the world's life, even, it could be argued, a basic acceptance of life, for all its horrors.

And now I wonder:
is the sorrow caused by those we love
not sweeter than the sweet joys
they say are found in heaven?

[103] *Nārāyaṇīya* 1.7.

The possibility of human nobility, so basic to tragedy, is partially predicated on this assumption. These are issues we shall discuss at greater length below with reference to a Tamil version of the tale of Karṇa, which even Aristotle would have deemed tragic. Our interest here is in the tragic component of the *bhakti* world view, which seems remarkably close to Lucien Goldmann's definition of the tragic as the simultaneous presence and absence of God.[104] And one further point that requires emphasis: underlying the *bhakti* poets' view is, as mentioned earlier, the idea of delimitation: the terms of *saṃsāra* are such that revelation can be, at best, but partial and paradoxical; the transcendent god can never be contained by our reality. As we shall see, the tragic vision depends upon just such a delimitation, a closing off of semantic space. The tragic world is bounded, fragmented, and full of meaning.

Some of the medieval Tamil poets were quite aware of this, and, as I hope to show, they therefore undermined their own tragic perspective. The same boundaries that appear so precious, so in need of defense against all outer attacks—the boundaries of the conventional order, with its hierarchical claims, its pressures for a balanced and stable definition of roles, and its ever-increasing, painful sense of its own imperfections and limitations—are also subject to a constant assault from within. The delicious distress of *viraha*, so real to us, is conceivably less so to the god. Harsh as it may seem, harsh as it really is, our torments are his amusements—*līlā*, or in Tamil, *viḷaiyāṭal*. At this point another mode of experience opens up before us, much as the delimited, ordered paradigm of the everyday is forced open, by its own tensions, to a new, less controlled or controllable form of being. *Viḷaiyāṭal*, the deity's favored mode of relating to the scattered parts of himself and to his world, is by nature chaotic—unpredictable, uncontainable, undefinable in terms of everyday perceptions. It eludes meaning: creation itself, seen as the god's play, is a teleological mystery. The point, if there is one, could only lie in its pointlessness, and in the emotions that this quality engenders.[105] This is not to deny the everyday experience of suffering, *viraha* in all its tragic reality and centrality to our emotional life; on the contrary, this experience is also basic to the *viḷaiyāṭal* mode of perception, which, as we shall see, is infused with the knowledge of evil. *Viraha*, in a sense, *is* the god's *viḷaiyāṭal*. Nevertheless, there is a transformation of perspective: the

[104] Goldmann (1955), pp. 46f.

[105] Here the Śaiva Siddhāntins would take issue, offering instead a rational teleology. See Shulman (1980b), p. 281.

closed boundaries have been invaded by a new, heretical spirit. In a sense, *viḷaiyāṭal* encompasses and transcends the human vision of *viraha*, in much the same way that a clown encompasses, from the outside, the bounded reality that he wishes to illuminate. It is a question of where one stands—wholly inside, hermetically enclosed by the sensation of pain, loss, and protest; wholly outside, if that were possible, hence impassive, remote, detached; or, like the god, the clown, or the magician, on the slippery and invisible border where the outer reaches in.

And once more: these modes, like the two phases of the paradigm to which they are related, are never pure or truly isolated. They interact and interpenetrate, in ways we must now attempt to understand.

· II ·

Royal Masks

Like a golden palace aflame,
fine food mixed with poison,
like a lotus-pond full of crocodiles—

so is kingship
at once delight
and disaster.[1]

1. The Icon

We begin with what might be called the iconic portrait of kingship—the idealized picture of a prototypical, South Indian dharmic ruler. This portrait draws implicit support from the *dharmaśāstric* injunctions but goes beyond them by working out their symbolic implications.[2] The rather extreme image that emerges retains, like most other Hindu icons, a certain dynamic character suggestive of a reflexive stance: the icon tells its story and yet points beyond it; like the speaking curtain in the Vikramāditya stories,[3] the icon is a veil that is meant to be removed.

Our text, the *araciyar̲ paṭalam* from the first book of Kampan̲'s Tamil version of the *Rāmāyaṇa*, is devoted to the perfect rule of Daśaratha, Rāma's father, over a thoroughly South Indian Ayodhyā:

> The king of that splendid city
> was king of kings.
> Over all the seven worlds,
> alone,

[1] Aśvaghoṣa, *Buddhacarita* 9.41.

[2] See summary in Lingat (1973), pp. 207-56; also Nagaswamy (1978); *Manusmṛti* 7.1-226.

[3] *Vikkiramātittan̲ katai*, pp. 116-17.

he wielded his glorious straight staff—
like the very form of good *dharma*
who gave birth to that hero of jingling anklets
called Rāma,
the lord of this majestic tale. (169)

First of all, wisdom;
then mercy, *dharma*, composure,
flawless might and heroism,
generosity,
adherence to what is right—
if other kings had *half* of these,
all of them served him (Daśaratha). (170)

In the ancient world circled by the
powerful sea,
there was no hand unmoistened
by the water that accompanied his gifts.[4]
Other kings might not complete
the Vedic sacrifices proper to their station:
he accomplished them all. (171)

In giving love, he was like a mother.
He was like *tapas*
in producing results.
He resembled a son who stands before his parents
and shows them the right way.
If any sickness had appeared there,
he could have been its cure.
To anyone with eyes to see,
he appeared like subtle learning
or like knowledge itself. (172)

By giving
he crossed the sea of supplicants.
Through studying endless books,
he crossed the ocean of knowledge.
With his sword blazing,
he crossed over the sea of enemies.
He crossed the sea of pleasure joined to *śrī*
by immersing himself
to his heart's content. (173)

[4] The pouring out of water is the ritual sign of gift giving in South India.

Floods,
birds,
wild beasts,
and the harlots' hearts—
Daśaratha of undeniable glory,
with the sharp sheathed sword,
generous king of kings,
held each of these
to a single course. (174)

The Cakravāla Mountain appeared to be his ramparts,
the brilliant sea beyond the border—his moat.
Other hills were his jeweled palaces;
the earth itself resembled Ayodhyā,
great city of this king. (175)

His spear, from constant use against his enemies' valor,
had always to be whetted—and was thus worn thin.
His golden anklets, rubbed against a myriad
of bejewelled kingly crowns,
were also worn away. (176)

That moon which was the parasol of the king
waxed ever without waning,
spread its cool shade over all lives on earth
and drove away the darkness—
as if to render that moon superfluous
that was left in heaven. (177)

He who had a lion's strength,
who wore ornaments wrought from diamonds,
cherished all lives as his own;
in this world without blemish,
he became the single body
in which dwelled all life,
animate and still. (178)

The triumphant discus of the hero
whose mighty shoulders rose up like mountains
wandered the world,
ever rising,
like the burning sun—
the one

protector of all lives
wherever it came to rest. (179)

No enemies came at him like arrows;
his drumlike shoulders itched without battle.
He ruled sweetly, protecting the entire world,
as a poor man nourishes his patch of ground. (180)

Kampaṉ has given us in these verses a picture of perfection—a socio-political perfection that serves as the backdrop to crisis when Rāma, true scion of this family of paragons, follows the logic of royal duty into exile. Indeed, Kampaṉ's *Rāmāyaṇa* could easily be read as a sustained attempt to scrutinize the South Indian royal ideal in the light of a perception of reality that renders that ideal profoundly problematic; Rāma's own career brings out many aspects of this problematic reality, including the outstanding issue of the king's inevitable contamination by evil. But let us remain for the moment with the original, iconic grasp of kingship presented in these verses. What are the attributes of the perfect king? Verse 170 offers, at first glance, a jumble of fairly predictable traits, one of which is explicitly ranked first by the poet—*mati*, wisdom. The emphasis is instructive. Wisdom implies the discrimination necessary for making choices; the king can err. He needs profound learning in the tradition (verse 173) as well as the understanding which enlightens it. Already, in the first attribute of kingship, we can sense the king's position on the thin edge of an abyss.

Wisdom is followed by *aruḷ*—mercy, compassion, grace. The king shares this attribute with the gods, who are constantly asked to manifest it. But whereas wisdom is calculating and careful, *aruḷ* tends toward spontaneity and danger: *aruḷ* can redeem, but it can also carry one beyond all limits. Thus when Viṣṇu appears as a dwarf before the all-too-generous king Bali, he asks for the deceptively modest gift of the space covered by three steps—and he couches his request in terms of *aruḷ*: give, if you have *aruḷ*. Bali follows his generous instinct and is dethroned.[5] *Mati* and *aruḷ* need not conflict; the royal exemplar can no doubt contain both virtues. Nevertheless, a certain tension is clearly implicit, and it is surely significant that the first two attributes listed gravitate toward opposite poles—the first toward control and fine distinctions, the second toward uncalculated, freely flowing emotion.

Next comes *dharma* (*aṟaṉ*), which the king in effect embodies (cf. verse 169). This is not a simple demand for righteousness: much of Kampaṉ's poem is given over to showing the complexities and moral

[5] *Irāmāvatāram* 1.436; see discussion in Shulman (1980b), pp. 332-33.

ambiguities of *dharma* as revealed by Rāma's career. In fact, something of this ambiguity may be suggested by the alliteration, reinforced by the *sandhi* and metrical divisions, of the first line of this verse. The line reads: *ātim matiyum maruḷummaṟa ṉumma maivum*. The *m*, repeatedly geminate because of *sandhi*, dominates each metrical unit; it also seems, at first hearing, to dominate the meaning of the words, so that we have *maruḷ* ("confusion") rather than *aruḷ*, and *maṟaṉ* ("*adharma*"; also "valor") instead of *aṟaṉ* as attributes of the king.[6] Given the general thrust of Kampaṉ's attitude toward *dharma*,[7] it is perhaps not wholly fanciful to discover here a designated irony and ambiguity.

For all that, the king must, of course, keep to what is proper and just—*nīti*, the final term in Kampaṉ's series. *Nīti* is unambiguous but almost inhumanly demanding, as we shall see. Between *dharma* and *nīti* we find *amaivu*, composure, followed by two of the most basic attributes of the classical Tamil hero—undaunted courage (*vīram*) and unstinting liberality (*īkai*). The moral basis of the latter has already been discussed;[8] we will return to the former in our final chapter.

So much for the bare list; subsequent verses take up again several of its themes. What is noteworthy even at this stage is the totalistic attitude: other kings fail to realize these virtues completely, whereas Daśaratha, the perfect monarch, in effect transcends them, for they are said to serve him. The ideal king embodies and encompasses the royal virtues; to be true to the iconic image, he cannot fail in any respect. It is really a question of all or nothing. The total demands upon the king are demonstrated further in verse 171 with its striking hyperbole: no hand in the entire world remained without the sign of the king's generosity (the water that accompanies the gift in South India). Moreover, Daśaratha can lay claim to the outstanding symbol of wholeness and perfection in the orthodox Hindu tradition—the completed sacrifice. The major Vedic sacrifices have, no doubt on principle, an incompleteness about them; they always leave behind a remnant as the seed of the next sacrifice.[9] Daśaratha brings all *his* sacrifices to completion.

By now, two main features of the icon are beginning to emerge: the theme of an encompassing wholeness or perfection, and the sense

[6] *Aṟam* and *maṟam*, *aruḷ* and *maruḷ*, are in any case frequently opposed terms.

[7] See Shulman (1979).

[8] Above, I.3; cf. Price (1979), pp. 211-12; Hart (1980). On the royal virtue of heroism, cf. Beck (1978), pp. 173-78, and Chapter VII below.

[9] See Shulman (1980b), pp. 120-22; (1984). The persistent and troubling remnant of the sacrifice (*yajñasyodṛc*) is connected to the recurring, desperate attempts "to bring the sacrifice to an end (*sam-√āp*)."

of the implicit complexity of this wholeness. The next two verses develop contrapuntal themes even as they elaborate the initial images of this chapter. Verse 172 announces the notion of royal love (*aṉpu*), which is compared to a mother's love for her child. *Aṉpu* contrasts with the largely formal requirements mentioned so far, but there is no doubt about its place among the fundamental components of ideal kingship. The king and his people should be bound together by powerful mutual affection: the Vedic sacrificial texts describe the marriagelike bond between the king and his subjects (*viś*),[10] whereas Tamil sources stress the emotional axis of *aṉpu*. Thus when Daśaratha seeks to retire from the kingdom and to crown Rāma in his place, he repeatedly asks his ministers about Rāma's suitability for the job; they reassure him by speaking of *aṉpu*:

> Just as Rāma is filled with love of many kinds
> for all the living beings of the world,
> so, in so many ways,
> do they love him.[11]

The same verse that compares the king to a mother also imagines him as a child, the *object* of a parent's love (this may also be a hint of Kampaṉ's approaching focus on Daśaratha's own son, Rāma). Both similes speak to the personal and emotional element of South Indian kingship—an element that serves here to intensify the pressure of the ideal.[12]

Verse 173 presents a significant opposition. The poet extols again the king's preeminence in giving gifts, in learning, and in war; but while in each of these three cases the king "crosses over" the respective "sea," his strategy is rather different with regard to the "sea of pleasure" (*poka pauvam*; cf. Skt. *bhoga*). Perhaps *bhoga* has no real limit; in any case, the iconic monarch remains submerged. This aspect of kingship will be discussed in Chapter VI. But the following verse, 174, seems to check this royal tendency. Here, in perhaps the most striking

[10] Especially clear in the *daśapeya*: see Heesterman (1957), pp. 226-27. According to Heesterman, this bond is largely replaced by the "marriage" of the king to the *purohita*.

[11] *Irāmāvatāram* 2.83. This chapter, as we shall see, may be regarded as a kind of commentary on the *araciyaṟ paṭalam* under discussion.

[12] Cf. Sheik Ali (1972), pp. 23-24: "Indian society is basically different from the Western in its approach to both private and public affairs. The Western society is stern, rigid and matter of fact in its dealings of public affairs, but it is sentiment, emotion and personal attachment that counts most even in politics in India." On the maternal imagery of kingship, see below; and cf. *Irāmāvatāram* 4.432, where Rāma advises the newly crowned Sugrīva to guard his subjects so that they may think, "He is not our leader but the good mother who gave us birth and nurtured us."

expression in this short chapter, we see the king's nature externalized, as it were, in the struggles of nature. The wild forces of nature, including the epitome of sensual abandon, the harlot's heart, are held in place by the king's very existence. The king functions here as a kind of symbolic limit, a brake upon the notoriously unstable forces at large in the world. It is as if the king were charged with carving out the channels for the endless flux of vital powers in his kingdom, and with supervising the flow, lest it get out of hand; or, to employ another favored metaphor, as if governing were a form of *yoga*, a concentrated "yoking" of unruly forces (such as the raging horses of the senses)[13] to an acceptable, highly energized level of activity. This theme of controlled power, especially sensual power, echoes the very first verse of Kampaṉ's *Irāmāvatāram*, a verse that sets the tone for much of what is to follow in this poem:

> The five senses are arrows
> which engage us in error;
> arrows, too, are the eyes of women,
> whose breasts ripple under their gold.
>
> Let us sing the beauty
> of that river which adorns Kośalā,
> where these arrows never stray from their course.[14]

Like so many of Kampaṉ's verses, this first utterance of the poet has an unresolved ambiguity about it. First, the verse opens a chapter, the *āṟṟuppaṭalam*, devoted to descriptions of the flooding waters which descend from the Himālaya to rage through Daśaratha's kingdom—hardly an image of power contained and controlled! Second, the arrows that "never stray from their course"—the senses generally, and the coquettish glances of beautiful women, more specifically—presumably strike their targets unerringly. In other words, women intoxicate those men, who may or may not be their husbands, upon whom they cast their gaze. Just how proper, then, is the order exemplified in this idealized landscape? If in Daśaratha's kingdom all the dynamic and vital forces are said to flow in the single correct direction, the underlying sense is one of tense and never wholly convincing—and perhaps not wholly desirable—control.

Linked to this ambiguous control, and plagued by its tensions, is the king's accountability: by maintaining proper order he guarantees

[13] *Kaṭha Upaniṣad* 1.3.3-9; cf. *Arthaśāstra* 1.6 and Inden (1978), p. 35.

[14] *Irāmāvatāram* 1.13 (the first verse of the text proper, after the preamble, the *taṟcirappuppāyiram*).

fertility and prosperity. Thus the king is responsible, for example, for safeguarding women's chastity;[15] and the woman, as a famous verse tells us, is responsible, through her chastity, for the rains.[16] These images feed into one another: the shared notion is one of holding in check, by sheer power of the will, the violent, emotion-tinged forces upon which life ultimately depends. Indeed, in a sense these forces are the very stuff of life itself: thus Kampaṉ can compare the flooding waters rushing into gardens, fields, forests, and ponds—an image of unbounded, chaotic power—to "Life flowing into different bodies" (1.32) or to "*karma* trailing after lives" (1.29). This perception suggests a deeper aspect of the problem. To anticipate a point that will occupy us at a later stage, we may note that the real difficulty, for both king and woman, is not the technical one of establishing and maintaining control over chaotic forces but rather an internal challenge to balance such control with a countervailing attraction to unmediated and unlimited vitality.

Nature's struggle and the internal dynamic of kingship are thus seen as homologous. A necessary drive toward containment within highly ordered boundaries is pitted against the urge to make contact with life's forces in their raw, unlimited state. Having hinted at this precarious balance, the poet can return at this point to the images of wholeness. In a series of verses that play brilliantly on conventional, cliché-ridden tropes,[17] Kampaṉ compresses the world into a single unit identified first with the kingdom and then, in effect, with the king himself ("the single body in which dwelled all life, animate and still," 178). Note that this compression takes place along both a vertical and a horizontal axis. Celestial space is telescoped by celebrating two royal symbols, the parasol and the discus (*ājñācakra*): the former renders redundant its conventional poetic partner, the moon, whereas the latter overtakes the sun (177, 179). The clear superiority of the royal regalia over their heavenly counterparts is beyond doubt: the parasol "waxes ever without waning"; the discus rises without ever setting. Verse 178, which connects these two extended images, states the implicit theme of unity: all life is contained within the king, just as the heavenly bodies are located in his symbols. The world is one, its center and focus the wholly terrestrial locus of kingship.[18] Similarly,

[15] *Irāmāvatāram* 2.1.15.

[16] *Tirukkuṟal* 55. The association of sexual continence and rainfall is a prominent theme in the Ṛṣyaśṛṅga cycle: see O'Flaherty (1973), pp. 42-52.

[17] See the more detailed discussion of this passage in Shulman (1978).

[18] The *dharma* literature somewhat similarly identifies the king with time and the *yuga*-scheme: *Manusmṛti* 9.301-302; Lingat (1961); Biardeau (1976), pp. 157-71.

we move along the horizontal axis from the seven worlds mentioned in the first verse (169) to a world coextensive with the city of Ayodhyā (175), and from here to the final verse, where the universe has shrunk to the dimensions of a poor peasant's field. The king protects the world "as a poor man nourishes his patch of ground" (180). This transition has a startling freshness about it: not only has the universe collapsed into more manageable proportions, as the king is made to encompass all existence and to create thereby a unified symbolic whole; at the same time, the king of kings has been identified with the poorest of his subjects, the lonely, impoverished peasant. This equation works in both directions. The king is clearly identified with the body politic, which he effectively constitutes; on the other hand, every man is, in a sense, a king. The royal struggles and transformations transpire within each member of the kingdom. One senses in this final verse of the chapter, with its striking immediacy and imaginative empathy, the emotional power of kingship in medieval South India. The South Indian sees in his king a mirror of his own nature, his longing for wholeness and his own innate complexity and tension.

We have discovered the following elements in Kampaṉ's iconic vision of kingship: a holistic sense of the king as encompassing and containing the world; a potential for conflict and tension within this royal wholeness; a focus upon a terrestrial center (rather than, let us say, a celestial, transcendent point of reference); an inherent problematic of control vis-à-vis chaotic forces; a symbolic correspondence between the king and the least of his subjects. It should be clear from the above that the king's role, even under the most ideal circumstances, is far from simple. Even the iconic portrait is suffused by tensions. Nevertheless, the icon reveals a basically positive ideal: Daśaratha's kingdom is a vision of human happiness on earth. Given this uncompromising vision of an ideal rule, one might be excused for wondering how it is seen to bear upon experienced reality. Kampaṉ provides no easy answer to this problem—extreme idealism is, in fact, a general problem in the Rāma literature, and not only in its South Indian variants[19]—but he does present us with a fascinating inversion of his own icon at the beginning of his second book, the *Ayottiyā kāṇṭam*.

Here, as we saw in the verse about *aṉpu* quoted earlier, our iconized ruler Daśaratha is considering relinquishing his throne and retiring to the forest. He uses the occasion to give vent to what might be considered his "real" feelings about kingship; and it now transpires that this best of all kings, ruling the best of all kingdoms in the most

[19] See Shulman (1978).

perfect manner, perceives kingship in its essence as no better than poison:

How can one cast aside
the fresh ambrosia (of release)
and devour instead its opposite,
the terrible poison (of kingship)?
If one realizes that there is no certainty
in the richly caparisoned elephants,
the regal peacock feathers,
the royal parasol casting shade over all—
then how long can one swallow
these soiled remains (*ĕccil*)?
What joy (*iṉpam*) can come of that? (2.25-26)

These verses, like others from this chapter, are directly linked to the iconic images of the *araciyaṟ paṭalam*, the text with which we began this discussion. Only the values have been transformed: the same parasol which is earlier described as bringing cool shade and protection to the entire world, thereby reducing the moon to redundance, is now a saliva-stained remnant, a vessel of utter impurity to be abandoned in disgust. Kingship itself has become the poisonous antithesis to truth, certainty, and freedom. Our icon has been debunked. No wonder, then, that Rāma's assumption of the throne is described in the next verse (27) as an infliction imposed on the divine hero, or, in a later verse (70), as a duty (*kaṭaṉ*) reluctantly accepted by the prince. Rāma clearly shares Daśaratha's basic hostility toward kingship, even to the extent of sharing the metaphors expressive of this attitude: for Daśaratha, kingship is "the sorrow of a lame buffalo yoked to an overburdened cart" (2.66); when Rāma is temporarily reprieved from ruling, because of Kaikeyī's machinations, and is faced instead with fourteen years of exile in the forest, he feels his troubles vanish "as when a black bullock yoked to a cart, driven hard by his owner, is released by some merciful person" (*aruḷ uṭaiy ŏruvaṉ*, 2.294). The people of Ayodhyā may become ecstatic at the mere thought of Rāma's scheduled coronation (2.52-58, 75-88), but for the ruler-elect there is no joy in power: the king is haunted by the personal horrors of kingship, by the proximity of evil, by his never-ending responsibility for the dharmic order in a world in which "nothing is more cruel than dharma" (2.46).

What are we to make of this striking contrast between the idealized images of the *araciyaṟ paṭalam* and the poet's own subsequent attack upon them? What is the meaning of the ambivalence so much in evidence here? On the one hand, Daśaratha's sudden hatred of kingship simply expresses the latent tensions already present in the icon. Even a wholly righteous king cannot avoid the struggles we have observed—the dynamic of wisdom and compassion, the necessity of maintaining control over powerful forces ever straining to break out, the superhuman, total demand for eternal vigilance, correctness, and success. He may, like Daśaratha, accomplish all his sacrifices, distribute gifts to every outstretched hand, conquer the whole earth—but only at the cost of unflagging struggle with the world, and with himself. As we shall see in the following pages, *dharma* allows the dharmic ruler virtually no margin of error. But there seems also to be a more radical level of rejection in Kampaṉ's verses, a level related to the poet's reflexive stance and to his attempt to grapple with the wider problematic of evil. The biting metaphors he uses suggest this more extreme rejection: kingship has become the epitome of impurity, the despised (if necessary) remnant (*ĕccil*), or the poisonous draught of death. Here the poet appears to have exposed his own idealized portrait: like the images of the deities worshiped in a Hindu temple, the poetic icon simultaneously reveals and obscures its object,[20] and there comes a moment when its presence is more problematic than instructive. In the case of a sociopolitical ideal, this is the moment when intractable conflict becomes palpable. Clearly, for Kampaṉ's Daśaratha kingship is inevitably opposed to the ultimate values of truth and freedom from evil—hence his yearning for renunciation at the end of his long reign. Still, his renunciation is contingent upon his finding a successor: Rāma reluctantly steps into the iconic slot. Both father and son are well aware of the limits of the iconic vision; behind the icon lurk the terrors of evil—both the inherent evils of ruling, above all killing and punishment, and the potential evil of kingly error in judgment—and with these terrors, the sense of a wholeness not simply pregnant with potential conflict but rather shattered beyond repair.

These are the first lessons of dharmic kingship, at least as seen in Kampaṉ's South Indian perspective: those who embody it also condemn it. Those who praise it also revile it. Its emotional power is correlated to its fragility. Seeking total control, it always risks total failure. It is in some sense deeply opposed to the ultimate values of the tradition. Moreover, the two royal faces we have noticed—iconic perfection, on the one hand, and radical rejection, on the other—seem

[20] See discussion in Shulman (1980); Hardy (1976); Ramachandra Rao (1979), p. 116.

intimately linked. We shall see how easily they can issue into one another.

2. Royal Error: The Pāṇṭiyaṉ and the Fury

There is in Tamil literature no more striking illustration of the perils of royal power than the climactic chapter of the *Cilappatikāram* in which the heroine, Kaṇṇaki, confronts the Pāṇṭiyaṉ king of Maturai. Within the space of thirty-four dramatic lines, the author, Iḷaṅko, powerfully expresses the transformative potential of kingship as conceived by the classical South Indian tradition. In a sense, his portrait of the Pāṇṭiyaṉ king bridges the gap between the two levels—the icon and its reevaluation—which we discovered in Kampaṉ. Before turning to the text, let us summarize the events leading up to the dénouement in the Pāṇṭiya court.

The hero, Kovalaṉ, has come to Maturai from his native city of Pukār, the Chola seaport, together with his wife Kaṇṇaki. He is turning over a new leaf; having squandered his resources on the dancing-girl Mātavi, he wishes to start life afresh in a new town, with the only capital he has left—Kaṇṇaki's golden anklets. He takes one of these anklets to sell in the town, but here he is accused by a scheming goldsmith of the latter's own crime—the theft of the Pāṇṭiya queen's golden anklet. Incriminated by the goldsmith's false testimony before the king, who is preoccupied with appeasing his moody queen, Kovalaṉ is cut down by the royal guards at the Pāṇṭiyaṉ's order. When the news of her husband's death reaches the faithful Kaṇṇaki, she is transfigured with grief and rage; in this wild state, her hair disheveled, her remaining anklet ominously raised in her hand, she makes her way to the palace gate. The gatekeeper, shocked by this apparition—all too reminiscent of the violent goddesses Kŏṟṟavai, Aṇaṅku, and Kāḷi—announces her arrival to the king, who asks that she be ushered into his presence. Their dialogue begins with his greeting:

"You who have come before me,
  your eyes flowing with tears,
young lady! Who are you?"
Thus spoke the king, and she replied:

"Heedless king—I have something to say to you.
My city is famous Pukār,

city of that king of spotless glory (Śibi)
who allayed a dove's distress;[21]
and of another who, tormented by the tears
falling from the eyes of a cow
who rang the bell of justice at the royal gate,
crushed his own beloved son under his chariot's wheel.[22]
In that city a merchant's son
was born in a great family of fame and faultless glory:
seeking a livelihood and driven by fate (*ūḻviṉai*),
he entered your city,
O king whose feet are graced by anklets,
with the intention of selling *my* anklet.
That was Kovalaṉ, killed
by you;
I am his wife, Kaṇṇaki by name."

"Fearsome lady (*pĕṇṇaṇaṅke*),
to kill a thief is no perversion of justice—
it is kingship itself with its gleaming spear."

Replied the woman:
"King of Kŏṟkai, you who have strayed from the
good path—
within *my* golden anklet are embedded precious stones."

"Fine words well spoken!" cried the king;
"our anklet contains pearls—
bring it here!"
When it was placed before him,
Kaṇṇaki cracked open her anklet
adorned with precious stones:
a gem shot forth and struck the king on his face.

[21] Śibi saved a dove (Agni or Dharma in disguise) from a hawk (Indra) who pursued him, by offering to weigh his (Śibi's) flesh against the dove's weight in a scale. Cf. *Jātaka* 499; *Kathāsaritsāgara* 7.88. This highly popular story was claimed by the Chola genealogists as early as Caṅkam times: cf. for example *Puṟan*. 37.5-6 (and parallels listed by the editor, Cāminātaiyar). The medieval Chola kings continued to include Śibi among their ancestors: *Kaliṅkattupparaṇi* 190; *Irāmāvatāram* 1.718.

[22] When the son of Manunītikaṇṭacoḻaṉ accidentally ran over a calf with his chariot, the mother-cow rang the bell for justice at the gate of the palace; the king gave justice by driving his chariot over his son's body. See Shulman (1980b), pp. 100-101 and plate II.

The king looked at the jewel.
His parasol collapsing,
his staff sagging down,
he said:
"Am I, who listened to a goldsmith's words,
 a king?
 I am the thief.
I have failed in my trust
 of guarding the southern land with all its people.
Let my life
  fail now."

As the king uttered these words,
he fainted and fell,
and the great queen of the Pāṇṭiyaṉ,
 trembling and distraught,
 thinking, "There is nothing to say or show
  to women who have lost a husband,"
fell, too, still worshiping
his feet.[23]

So swift is the narrative pace of this short passage that the reader or listener struggles to assimilate its implications: with an unusual economy of speech and image, Iḷaṅko describes a world suddenly turned upside down. He does so with minimal intervention by the narrator; the terse dialogue of the two characters carries the burden of the action until the final revelation of the bitter truth, at which point Iḷaṅko allows himself a brief but utterly effective descriptive comment. Thus the emotional charge building up in the two main actors has to be inferred from the suggestive overtones of their speeches.[24] We are left with a study in contrast—two powerful figures each undergoing a far-reaching transformation at his own very different pace. For Kaṇṇaki, the scene in the Pāṇṭiya court is but the beginning of her revenge; she will go on to cast her breast at the city of Maturai, thereby engulfing it in flames.[25] These are stages on her path to apotheosis, a process of central interest to Iḷaṅko, as to the mythic sources on which he drew. The king, however, is at the end of his road—a sudden, tragic end wholly unforeseen before it arrives. Or so, in any case, it might appear to the unwary.

[23] *Cilappatikāram* 20 (*vaḻakkurai kātai*), 48-81.

[24] This careful and suggestive use of dramatic dialogue was later developed still further by Kampaṉ in his *Irāmāvatāram*.

[25] For this part of the story, see Shulman (1980b), pp. 192-211; van den Hoek (1978).

In fact, the king's transformation has all the terrible familiarity of a repressed traumatic memory suddenly breaking into consciousness. Let us follow the course of the contrasts that Iḷaṅko has depicted. The initial opposition is complete: on the one hand, the king, still honored and secure, still confident enough to address Kaṇṇaki with the superior tones of authority ("Young lady! Who are you?"). He has just been informed by his wife of her inauspicious dream—she has dreamed of his staff and his royal parasol falling, and of the bell of justice at the gate ringing incessantly—but he is apparently not yet overly upset by the evil omens. Kaṇṇaki, on the other hand, is a wild specter of raw emotion: her loose hair recalls the chaotic forces of the forest;[26] she is covered with the dust of the street, where she has just left the blood-soaked body of her husband; above all—this is the feature Iḷaṅko repeatedly stresses[27]—she is clutching obsessively her remaining golden anklet, symbol of the shattered wholeness of her married life.[28] It is hardly surprising that the gatekeeper is reminded of the goddess Kālī! In fact, over the last three cantos (18-20) Kaṇṇaki has slowly but remorselessly been taking on a new character. In the early parts of the poem, she is the classically demure, ever-enduring wife, often reminiscent of Sītā—for example, in the scene in which Kovalaṉ and Kaṇṇaki leave Pukār for Maturai, when after only a short walk in the early morning the delicate wife, already exhausted, asks her husband if they have not yet reached their goal.[29] Now that tragedy has overtaken her with Kovalaṉ's death, Kaṇṇaki has acquired stature. In a crescendo of fury, she heaps scorn on the gods and the inhabitants of Maturai:

> Are there no women here?
> Are there no women here, or only such as could bear
> the evil suffered by their husbands? . . .
> Are there no noble men (*cāṉṟor*)
> who could care for their own children?
> Are there no noble men? . . .
> Are there no gods in Maturai,
> where the king's sharp sword has erred? (19.51-58)

In the same tone, she sarcastically questions the wisdom of *dharma* (18.41). She has become decisive: when she sees Kovalaṉ's spirit rise

[26] See Hart (1975), pp. 112-13, commenting on *Cil.* 20, *vĕṇpā* 2: "her black hair enveloping her like an entire forest." Cf. the similar symbolic value of Draupadī's loose hair: Hiltebeitel (1980).

[27] As in line 27: *iṇaiy aric cilamp' ŏṉṟ' entiya kaiyaḷ*; also line 42; *vĕṇpā* 3.2.

[28] On the symbolism of the anklet in the *Cil.*, see Zvelebil (1973a), pp. 182-83.

[29] *Cil.* 10.36-43.

up from his body toward heaven, leaving her behind, she says at once, "I shall not seek my husband until my burning wrath is assuaged" (19.70). Clearly, she can no longer be intimidated by a weak and erring king. Kaṇṇaki, in short, is now a woman whose inner nature has been transformed, and whose potential power has been activated and revealed by crisis. No longer capable of being controlled or contained, she stands on the edge of outright divinity.

The Pāṇṭiyaṉ, for his part, undergoes a far more sudden and in some ways less dramatically engaging transformation—and one that leads in the opposite direction from Kaṇṇaki's. If Kaṇṇaki is on the verge of transcending mortality, *karma*, and the boundary between human and divine—she will soon become the goddess Pattiṉi—the king, who begins as a kind of human-divine hybrid, is now reduced to a wholly mortal man, who must pay for his mistakes by his death. At first he retains a rather touching faith in dharmic kingship: is not the execution of a thief the very stuff of kingship? (See lines 64-65: "to kill a thief is no perversion of justice—it is kingship itself with its gleaming spear"). But when Kaṇṇaki proves her charge—Iḷaṅko adds the dramatic touch of the jewel that flies up to strike the king's face—the Pāṇṭiyaṉ is instantly transformed. One moment he is as usual, the king upon his throne; the next, he has become a caricature of himself. It is as if his image had been reduced to a negative; a shadowy antiself, wholly opposite to the former bright image, emerges. The sudden reversal leaves the king utterly at one with his new attributes: he is "the one with the collapsing parasol and the sagging staff" (*tāḻnta kuṭaiyaṉ taḷarnta cĕṅ kolaṉ*). There is no transition, no time to absorb the shock; as the Pāṇṭiyaṉ himself exclaims, he is no longer a king but instead a thief, wholly identified with the very crime he had thought to punish. He has failed, and, given the peculiar requirements of his position, he has nothing more to do on earth; only by death can he atone for his error. The terrible aspect of truth is revealed in a single flash; as we are told in the first of the *vĕṇpās* that bring this canto to a close, "To those who do wrong, *dharma* is Death (*kūṟṟam*)." We become aware that the king has all along been treading a narrow line on the border of death; one slip, and he is swallowed by the abyss.

We might formulate this notion in somewhat different terms. The outstanding point is the uncompromising vision of the king. The demands upon him are total. Note that the Pāṇṭiyaṉ has, after all, erred in good faith; his mistake was to accept the (not unconvincing) testimony of the goldsmith without further inquiry. But this makes no difference whatsoever—error exists here in a wholly objectified, final form, and no extenuating circumstances can have any effect upon its perpetrator. The only link between the king and his former righteousness is his readiness for death as the only possible expiation.[30] The ruler is either a wholly righteous king or the exact antithesis, a thief (this is the Pāṇṭiyaṉ's own conclusion, which we shall see recurring in other stories). There is no attempt to mediate these extremes; the transition from one to the other can be instantaneous and total. Indeed, so extreme is this dichotomy, and so swift and inevitable the transformation from one pole to the other, that the two aspects seem intimately bound up with one another: the thief *always* hides behind the iconic mask of righteousness. The first false step destroys the mask and reveals the thief. It is in this way that the Pāṇṭiyaṉ's tragedy unites the two levels we discussed with reference to Kampaṉ: the Pāṇṭiyaṉ acts out the basic ambivalence of kingship. He moves from iconic perfection to a latent, anti-iconic reality. Moreover, it is the latter stance—the erring, all-too-human, guilt-laden monarch—that seems most powerful and most predictable. Again and again, the dharmic icon collapses into ruins.

In theory, of course, the dharmic ruler could go on forever, always holding to his narrow course, never quite toppling over into the chasm gaping at his feet. Even in this case, as we have seen, he may have reason to wish to renounce the unhappy task. But the emphasis of the texts is on the fragility of the ideal: the awesome responsibility, and the probability of failure. By this point we can begin to understand the obsessive or "neurotic" aspect of South Indian kingship—the appallingly severe standards constantly invoked for the king's conduct. The king bears a unique responsibility for the rule of *dharma* in his kingdom; any infraction of the rules—such as might be revealed by an untimely death, disease, lack of rainfall, or a variety of other disasters that can hardly have been rare in any historical Indian kingdom—is immediately laid at his door. Hence the concern for perfection with all its implications. Rāma stands out as the classic exemplar of this ideal carried to its farthest limits, for example in his banishment of Sītā in response to his citizens' slanderous gossip about her. The Sanskrit poet Bhavabhūti shows, in a pathos-laden scene, Rāma's agony over what he knows to be Sītā's totally unmerited punishment.[31] Apparently, Rāma has no real choice: he must preserve a state of utter blamelessness, leaving no room for reproach. But it is perhaps significant that, having determined to exile Sītā, our ideal ruler falls into

[30] This is the implication of the later passages in the *Cil.* (such as the *kaṭṭurai* which concludes the *maturaikkāṇṭam*) which still refer to the Pāṇṭiyaṉ's righteousness.

[31] *Uttararāmacarita* of Bhavabhūti, Act I (from verse 40 on).

a paroxysm of *self*-blame and *self*-hatred—he calls himself a horrifying monster, a poisonous tree, a criminal, even an Untouchable Caṇḍāla. In this rather startling scene, the ruler's unflinching, self-abnegating righteousness ironically brings out his darker aspect or, perhaps, what may be seen as the tragic side of dharmic kingship: the personal cost of too much *dharma* is, for the king, a kind of evil. Yet this personal tragedy is a direct reflection of the built-in ambivalence we have noted: the icon contains the elements of its own destruction; the hidden horrors are every bit as real as the mask.

3. The Maternal Monarch (1): The Would-Be Renouncer

Iḷaṅko's description of the Pāṇṭiyaṉ's sudden, guilty death exemplifies a fairly typical sequence in the South Indian tales of kingship—the iconic flux from paragon to criminal. Given the importance of this pattern, especially in psychological terms, and its associated moral background, it is hardly surprising that the classical Indian ideal of renunciation holds a peculiar fascination for the righteous king. We have seen this to be the case for Daśaratha, our aged icon; but one also thinks immediately of the epic hero Yudhiṣṭhira, whose renunciatory impulses constitute one of the major themes of the *Mahābhārata*.[32] Indeed, the *Mahābhārata* locates this theme at the heart of its myth dealing with the origins of kingship. According to this text,[33] the first kings created by Viṣṇu would have nothing to do with the job—they preferred *tapas* and renunciation. As a result, in Jan Heesterman's apt expression, "kingship in fact all but failed."[34] We can by now understand something of these kings' reluctance to rule. Indeed, even when kingship is finally established by the good king Pṛthu, who announces at his birth that he will follow the dictates of his Brahmin advisers,[35] the office retains an unsettling impetus toward renunciation. It is not for nothing that even Kauṭilya, that most earthy and power-conscious of all Brahmin theoreticians, sees the king's greatness in his control of his senses (*indriyavijaya*)—an emphasis which, as Heesterman has noted, places the king in line with the

[32] See Zaehner (1962), pp. 102-24; Biardeau (1978), pp. 94-111. Arjuna's crisis also has a clear renunciatory flavor.

[33] *MBh* 12.59.93-98. Cf. Heesterman (1978), pp. 7-9.

[34] *Ibid.*, p. 8.

[35] *MBh* 12.59, 104-15. On Pṛthu, see below, section 4.

Brahminical values of detachment and transcendence.[36] If this is the case in the *Arthaśāstra*, small wonder that renunciatory kings remain stock figures in the later literature.[37] The king is the exemplar of all virtues, including the classical Brahmin ideal of renunciation, to which in any case he may incline for his own good reasons; on the other hand, the king-turned-*sannyāsin* abandons the world to insupportable chaos.[38] Hence he must be stopped in his tracks, if necessary forced to rule at whatever personal cost: thus Yudhiṣṭhira has constantly to be dissuaded from renouncing the world by his more practical and socially conscious companions, rather like one of Kafka's unhappy clerks pressured to return to the office. However—again like Kafka—the Indian texts remain extremely sensitive to the inner conflict embedded in this reality. For reasons that will become clear, royal renunciation is a recurring problem for our authors.

To explore this problem in its South Indian guise, we turn first to the Buddhist sequel to the *Cilappatikāram*, Cīttalaiccāttaṉār's *Maṇimekalai*. The heroic king in this poem is Āputtiraṉ, clearly one of the central figures of the work and a male counterpart of sorts to the heroine, Maṇimekalai (daughter of Kovalaṉ and of his abandoned mistress, Mātavi). Āputtiraṉ has a checkered career spread out over two births. His "first" mother—the first one about whom we hear—is Cāli, a Brahmin lady from Vārāṇasī who has transgressed the bounds of chaste conduct (*kāppukkaṭai kaḻintu*, 13.5) and who has given birth to the child during a pilgrimage to Kaṉṉiyākumari. Mercilessly, she abandons him in a hidden garden beside the road. There he is discovered and nursed for seven days by a cow—until he is found and adopted by the pious Brahmin Iḷampūti. The child—given the name Āputtiraṉ, "son of a cow"—is brought up in the Brahmin's village and given a proper Brahminical education, at which he excels. His childhood is thus spent in the traditional milieu of the South Indian Brahmin *agrahāram*, with all its ritual concerns, its encompassing ethos, its delight in inherited knowledge; the initial traumas of the boy's birth and desertion are apparently forgotten.

But one day Āputtiraṉ discovers a cow decorated and garlanded for a sacrifice and terrified "as a deer caught in a net, awaiting the cruel arrow of the murderous hunters" (13.31-32). Unable to bear the cow's sorrow, the boy waits until midnight, when all the village is asleep, and escapes with the animal. But to no avail—by morning the theft

[36] *Arthaśāstra* 1.6; Heesterman (1971), p. 9.

[37] See, for example, Zimmer (1984), pp. 38-42. For an early Tamil example, see *Puṟan*. 363. And cf. the dénouement of the tale of Yayāti: Defourny (1978), p. 167.

[38] On the horrors of the kingless land (*arājaka janapada*), see *Rām*. 2.67.

is discovered, and the villagers hasten after the young Brahmin thief. Overtaking him on the road, they abuse him and beat him; this enrages the otherwise pacific cow, who turns against the villagers, disembowels several of them with its horns, and escapes into the forest. In the ensuing argument, the circumstances of Āputtiraṉ's birth are revealed by one of the Brahmin elders; the others indignantly denounce him as Untouchable and a thief.

Nevertheless, the young Āputtiraṉ has the last laugh (*amar nakai cĕytu*, 13.92) at the Brahmin ritualists' expense. He reminds them: were not two great Brahmins (Vasiṣṭha and Agastya) born when Brahmā became infatuated with a dancing-girl (*katavuṭ kaṇikai*—Tilottamā)?[39] What fault, then, could attach to his mother Cāli? If his captors cast aspersions on his mother's honor and his own pure birth, Āputtiraṉ, like the learned Brahmin he has become, responds with the sharpest of his weapons—a clever pun. Not only is his mother thus compared to the divine Tilottamā, and his own birth to that of the revered Vasiṣṭha and Agastya, but his listeners are also clearly meant to recall that Vasiṣṭha's wife, Arundhatī—the conventional paragon of wifely chastity—shares the Tamil name of Āputtiraṉ's mother, Cāli.[40] The Brahmin adulteress has thus been posthumously elevated to exemplary virtue by her witty son; the enraged Brahmin villagers drive the punning cow-thief from their homes.

By this point, poor Āputtiraṉ has already undergone more than a few transformations—Brahmin birth, adoption by a cow, Brahmin education, and a sudden reversal into Untouchability. His progress to kingship is no less miraculous and dramatic. Hounded from the village (the Brahmins fill his begging-bowl with rocks), the young saint-in-the-making takes refuge in "Southern Maturai," where he lives in the courtyard of a shrine to Sarasvatī; each day he distributes his earnings from begging among the blind, the deaf, the lame, and the sick. This virtuous habit has already earned him the title "protector" (*kāvalaṉ*, 13.115)—one of the most common kingly epithets, and an intimation of what is in store. The Brahmin lad has become obsessed with the desire to sustain other suffering creatures. To this end, the goddess herself bestows upon him an inexhaustible bowl, with which Āputtiraṉ nourishes all who are in need.

[39] Thus the commentator, Pŏ. Ve. Comacuntaraṉār (p. 289); and cf. *Nīlakeci, vetavātac carukkam*, comm. on v. 3. But the more usual story of the birth of these two sages involves Urvaśī and the seed of Mitra and Varuṇa: *Bṛhaddevatā* 5.149-52; cf. Shulman (1980b), pp. 315-16.

[40] Or Cāliṉi: see *Cil.* 1.51; *Paripāṭal* 5.44-45. On Arundhatī, see Shulman (1980b), p. 149.

Sarasvatī's unique gift leads to an unusual, Buddhist reversal of the common puranic pattern of Indra's jealous competition with mortals:[41] here the king of heaven feels threatened by Āputtiraṉ's great magnanimity and therefore spitefully sends an abundance of rain to the Pāṇṭiya land—thereby rendering Āputtiraṉ's magic bowl superfluous. The flourishing Pāṇṭiya kingdom, now sated with plenty and subject to the corruptions of idleness and debauchery, is no longer suitable for the frustrated saint with his insatiable need to alleviate *others'* hunger; feeling, we are told, like a virgin growing old (*kumari mūtta*), he wanders helplessly about, mocked or ignored everywhere, like a shipwrecked merchant who has lost all his wealth to the sea. Fortunately, however, for our increasingly desperate, spinsterish hero, famine strikes the Cāvaka land across the seas; he takes ship at once with his beloved bowl. But the saint's path to fulfilment is rarely direct: the ship is damaged by a storm and puts in for shelter at the island of Maṇipallavam; Āputtiraṉ disembarks, only to discover shortly thereafter that the ship has set sail again without him. This is too much for our hunger-hungry hero: there is, alas, no one at all to feed on Maṇipallavam; he throws his now useless bowl into the Gomukhī ("Cow's-mouth"!) Tank and then proceeds, with impeccable logic, to starve himself to death.

But not even death can deter the single-minded ascetic. Āputtiraṉ is reborn—from the same cow that nourished him in his former birth, although this creature has itself been reborn, equipped this time with golden horns and hoofs, in the hermitage of a sage in the Cāvaka land. Āputtiraṉ has too much merit to undergo the tribulations of existence in the womb, even in the prestigious womb of a cow; so the marvelous cow lays a miraculous, golden egg, out of which our hero is gloriously hatched. Most wonderful of all, he has reached his goal, the long-suffering Cāvaka land, whose childless ruler adopts the boy and grooms him for the throne. At length, Āputtiraṉ is crowned king. Since his coronation, the Cāvaka land has flourished as never before: rains fall in their season, and there is food for all. Āputtiraṉ has, quite unconsciously, achieved his earlier mission.

Let us pause briefly to review the hero's dizzying progress to this point. Āputtiraṉ has gone from the Brahmin village of his "first" childhood to the courtyard of the Sarasvatī temple in Maturai, and thence to a suicidal death on the island; reborn from his favored maternal figure, the cow, he has become the righteous ruler of the Cāvaka land. All these events are clearly seen as forming a single, continuous,

[41] See O'Flaherty (1976), pp. 78-93; below, V.2.

internally consistent chain, but the mature king whom we meet in the text has, naturally enough, forgotten them all—not only the experiences of his former birth, but even those of his childhood with the golden cow in the hermitage. It will be the task of Maṇimekalai, the insistent, ascetic heroine of the book, to lead the king back through the maze of his lost memories. This desire to recover the lost but haunting fragments of the distant past recurs as a leitmotif throughout this gentle and ingenious book; the narrative present frequently dissolves into reminiscence, nostalgia, or dream. And so it is with our king: the process of recovery is initiated by Maṇimekalai, who, newly arrived in the Cāvaka kingdom, chides Āputtiraṉ for his forgetfulness:

> Having attained great royal riches,
> you have become confused;
> you have no knowledge.
> And while you may not know about *that* (former) birth,
> how have you managed to know nothing
> even of *this* birth of yours
> from the womb of a cow? (25.23-25)

Now, of course, the king must possess the truth, and—interestingly—he seeks it from his foster mother, the queen. She reveals the tale of his birth, and with wonderful effect—for at once Āputtiraṉ begins to dream of renunciation.[42] The king is saddened and ashamed of his own dramatic history (including the story of his former birth and abandonment, which he has also come to understand, 25.77-79). It is all too much to bear, the endless trials and transformations, the restless movement from one incomplete identity to another. Although the text nowhere states this explicitly, it seems Āputtiraṉ's deepest longing is for his last-but-one human role, that of the wandering, compassionate ascetic. In any case, he is definitely ill at ease in his present circumstances; the vision of the past has undermined his thoughtless security. As if to reinforce his depression, he suddenly sees through the façade of his "normal" existence; the royal joys have become empty, and he is weary of his rounds—the warrior-kings waiting patiently for an audience with him, the praises (how sincere can they be?) of the noble men around him, the dancing and the music, and—with particular emphasis—the futile intoxications of love, the recurring tiffs and quarrels that always require him, the king, to prostrate

[42] This story, we may note, reverses the classical Sāṅkhya parable of the king's son brought up in exile among low-caste mountaineers: there the prince has to discover his properly royal nature (as the soul must discover its divinity). See Zimmer (1969), p. 308; below, VII.4 at nn. 80-81.

himself before the feet of his sulking wives, to draw pictures with *kuṅkuma* paste upon their breasts, to dress their tresses with flowers. How humiliating, and how disgusting, it all seems to him now! Would it not be much better simply to renounce this way of life (*tuṟattal naṉṟu*, 25.92)?

These are dangerous thoughts. Divining them, the astute minister, Caṉamittiraṉ, harangues his suddenly recalcitrant king:

> Long live our king!
> Listen, please, to my words:
> before *your* kingly father received you,
> for twelve years this good land,
>   perfect for habitation,
> was without rain, and its living creatures perished.
> Mothers had no mercy on their children
> but were quite capable of devouring them,
>   alone in their hunger.
> Then you appeared, garlanded lord,
> like a raincloud in the burning summer.
> Since then, the heavens have not failed;
> the prosperity of the soil is unabated;
> souls held in bodies know no hunger.
> But if you leave, all your country
> will call out to you like a child without its mother.
> This world is given over to sorrow:
> if you, not wishing to protect it,
> seek the higher state of the Other World,
> this is the end for many living beings here,
> O lord—
> you will save yourself alone!
> This is no part of the Dharma
> of that First One of all living beings (the Buddha),
> who cared nothing for his own life but cherished others'.
> It is the very opposite of wisdom—
> think, O king! (25.99-118)

We must look closely at this speech, which evokes the problematic perfection of the royal icon, albeit from a Buddhist perspective. Perhaps the most striking feature of the passage is the central, duplicated image of motherhood. Here the underlying tensions of kingship emerge in a characteristically warm simile drawn, like so many Tamil root metaphors, from the life of the family. We have already met the association of the king with a mother in Kampaṉ's idealized description;[43] here the full depth of the image is revealed, as its negative aspect is brought into play. The symbolism of the mother in Indian myth and folklore is richly ambivalent,[44] and both sides of it apparently apply to the king. The righteous king protects his subjects—at whatever personal cost—as a good mother protects her child; but the face of the dark or evil mother stares out at us in the king's renunciatory persona. A profound antagonism to the king's impulse to renounce the kingdom is articulated through the emotional image of the child crying for the mother who has abandoned him. This is an ancient motif in Tamil literature: it appears in the classical war poetry as a trenchant image expressing the desolation of the conquered land (the country of the defeated enemies cries out like a motherless child).[45] Indeed, Āputtiraṉ's entire history is suffused by this theme: his own mother heartlessly deserts him by the roadside,[46] just as he now wishes to abandon his subjects; the Brahmin villagers declare him an Outcaste precisely because of his mother's action, while he, ironically, defends her. To these circumstances we may add the symbolism of the cow, a conventional substitute for the mother in Indian stories: the dark pole of motherhood is clearly suggested by the violent actions of the sacrificial cow which, freed by the young Āputtiraṉ, murderously attacks the Brahmin villagers and then flees into the forest.[47] These images are further sustained by the stark description in the minister's speech of the evil mother at her most extreme—the famine-stricken mothers who would pitilessly devour their own children.[48]

On the other hand, the positive associations of motherhood are also symbolically expressed in Āputtiraṉ's story: we have the golden cow that nourishes him in two separate births, as well as Āputtiraṉ's own imitation of maternal qualities—not only his protection of his kingdom, but above all his delight in feeding the hungry. Maternity in its dual aspect is clearly a symbolic focus for the *Maṇimekalai*, at least in its attitude toward kingship; we may deduce that Āputtiraṉ, like the South Indian king generally, is felt to have a feminine persona that is inherently ambivalent—capable of nourishment and protection, and of the mother's comforting love for her children, and yet potentially

[43] See above, section 1.

[44] Shulman (1980b), pp. 223-94; O'Flaherty (1980), pp. 77-129.

[45] *Puṟan.* 4.18-19; 230.7; 379.14-15.

[46] Note the way the phrase used to describe this event recurs with reference to Āputtiraṉ's urge to renounce: *īṉṟa kuḻavikk' irankāḷ āki* ("having no mercy for her child": 13.9); *īṉṟāḷ kuḻavikk' irankāḷ āki*, 25.103; cf. *tāy oḻi kuḻavi pola*, 25.111.

[47] On the symbolism of the murderous cow, see Shulman (1980b), pp. 229-34.

[48] Cf. Lamentations 2:20; 4:10.

violent and cruel, like the ancient Tamil mother of ferocious instincts who drives her young son to a hero's death on the battlefield.[49] This polarity suggests a link between the king and the violent goddess (Durgā or Kālī), who both sustains and destroys her worshipers; the symbolic parallel imparts an interesting complexity to the king's relationship to this goddess, who, as we shall see, is often portrayed as the direct source of the king's power.[50] For the moment, let us note simply that it is the darker side of the mother—her murderous, unfeeling aspect—which is related by our text to the king's "higher" instincts, that is, his yearning for renunciation.

Before we attempt to summarize the lessons of Āputtiraṉ's story, let us follow his career through yet one more stage. The minister's speech has the desired effect: the king, presumably stricken by remorse at his implicit resemblance to his own hard-hearted mother, is convinced to remain on the throne. However, overpowered by a desire to see Maṇimekalai once more on the magic island of Maṇipallavam—the same island where he had previously given up his life, and to which Maṇimekalai has now, quite literally, flown—Āputtiraṉ demands that his minister grant him at least a month's leave, and at once sets sail for the island. New emotional shocks are in store for him here. First, the miraculous Buddha seat, the focal point of the pilgrims to Maṇipallavam, confirms to Āputtiraṉ the tale of his former birth. Then the guardian deity of the island reveals to him the sequel to his former death: the forlorn ascetic had, as we recall, succeeded in starving himself to death out of frustration at being unable to feed anyone else; but no sooner was he dead than his traveling companions returned to the island, discovered his lifeless body, and resolved to follow his example; their servants followed them, too, into death. Thus, concludes the deity, Āputtiraṉ had, for all his good intentions, in effect committed murder: "You took your life, and then you took the lives of those who came feeling compassion for you. Are you not a killer, you who became a king?" (*kŏlaivaṉ allaiyo kŏṟṟavaṉ āyiṉai*, 25.172-74). Compassion, it appears, can be a double-edged sword: as in the story of the Pāṇṭiyaṉ's judicial error, again a righteous king is revealed as a murderer; but this time the circumstances are, if anything, still more extreme, since it is Āputtiraṉ's empathy with suffering creatures, expressed in his relentless drive to feed them, that has in effect caused his companions' death. The hostility to renunciation enunciated in the maternal imagery of the minister's speech is, it would seem, also active

[49] *Puṟan*. 279; cf. Villi's portrait of Kuntī, below VII.7.

[50] See Chapter VI.1.

in this narrative invention; but there are further overtones to this development that need to be explored.

Let us stop for a moment to consider Āputtiraṉ's state of mind. We might expect this king, still in the throes of his crisis of renunciation, by now thoroughly convinced of the emptiness and weary strain of his former royal existence, to find support for his new understanding at the miraculous shrine. But in fact the oracles go beyond this: not only are the tales of his former incarnation confirmed; they are also fleshed out with new and horrifying details. The king cannot even pride himself on his former ascetic achievements—this well-meaning savior led others to disaster. Āputtiraṉ's identity keeps expanding in uncomfortable ways: he has by now incorporated some sense of an existence before his present royal career, but the more he delves back through the mists into his former life, the more complex and ambiguous it all seems. For our author, no life seen only on its own terms, delimited by a single birth and a single death, is truly intelligible—the chain is much greater than any single component—yet even within the larger perspective, each life remains replete with paradox and mystery. In contrast with the Buddhist *Jātakas* and the standard perception of the Buddha's former births—as a relatively straight path of ever more refined consciousness and more radical compassionate action—the Tamil Buddhist exploration of the cognitive experience of reincarnation finds the resulting awareness to be baffling, even terrifying.

For this is by no means the end of Āputtiraṉ's discoveries. Guided by the deity and in the presence of his mentor, Maṇimekalai, he proceeds to unearth the buried bones of his former body. Did he not, after all, die on this same island? As the commentators on this chapter have recognized,[51] this scene is heavily laden with pathos; indeed, who but a Tamil could bring abstract theory to earth in so dramatic and human a fashion? If there are former births, there must be former bodies, and one could, in theory, exhume oneself from the grave. The poor king—pushed, by now, to the outer limits of his endurance, staring into his own grave—is understandably stupefied. Fortunately, however, Maṇimekalai is by his side, eager, as always, to draw a moral from these events:

> "What has happened to you, great garlanded king?
> I came to your land and called you here
> to teach you of your other births. . . .
> If kings who rule the wide earth

[51] See the introduction to this chapter in the SISS edition (1951, p. 570).

take to the merciful *dharma* (of renunciation),
is anything left behind to remove others' faults?

If you ask what the thing called *dharma* is,
listen and don't forget:
it is nothing but food, dress, and dwelling
for all mortal souls."

The king spoke: "Whether in my land or other lands,
I shall always perform the good *dharma*
uttered by the lady with the lovely forehead.
You have taught me of my birth;
you have created me!
I cannot separate myself
from you."

"Grieve not," said the lady, properly adorned;
"your great land, full of sorrow at your departure,
is even now calling out for you.
Board your ship and return. . . ." (25.221-39)

With these words, Maṇimekalai flies off into the air, leaving Āputtiraṉ languishing in confusion. So much for renunciation! The unhappy king must go home. Once again he has been abandoned by a woman in the hour of his greatest need; and if Maṇimekalai is clearly too young to be regarded as his adopted mother, she seems nevertheless to have served, at least temporarily, the hero's need for some such figure of female guidance and authority. Now that the traumatic revelation has been accomplished, Maṇimekalai seems no less hard-hearted than Āputtiraṉ's former mother, Cāli: she gives the king his orders, explains concisely their rationale, and departs, despite his pleas that he cannot bear another separation. As so often in these stories, karmic patterns seem to have a cyclical, self-fulfilling quality: Āputtiraṉ, drenched with his newly recovered memories, must find his present situation all too reminiscent of earlier ones. Loneliness and desertion are apparently his most familiar experiences, and kingship, we must note, has hardly alleviated their effects; if anything, it has exacerbated them. Āputtiraṉ must return now to a role that he detests, fortified only by the lonely insights he has been granted and, perhaps, by a vision of kingship as a necessary vehicle for compassionate action.

Āputtiraṉ's experience may be atypical even of the idealized literary accounts of kingship in medieval South India: this is, after all, a Buddhist text, with an underlying Buddhist ethos. Nevertheless, it is striking that this text does not adopt the most prevalent Buddhist expression of the king's divided person, the conception of the Bodhisattva-king.[52] Royal *dharma* is given its due in Maṇimekalai's last speech to Āputtiraṉ—the ruler's duty to provide for his subjects is clearly stated, as is the bald rejection of the king's drive to renunciation—so that here, as in early Buddhism generally, the political sphere has a certain inherent legitimacy and affirmed value.[53] For all that, Āputtiraṉ remains a deeply conflicted figure, and in this way he is still remarkably close to the classic South Indian dilemmas of kingship. His career incorporates many of the traditional personae of the South Indian king—Brahmin, Untouchable, ascetic, thief, lonely Rip Van Winkle—although their links with kingship are never made explicit here, as they are in other texts that will concern us below. The closest we come to a clear linkage is perhaps the statement of the island deity: "Are you not a killer, you who have become a king?" But even this connection belongs to the one problematic area of kingship on which the *Maṇimekalai* does expand—the king's interest in renunciation. We have seen how grimly this royal urge is depicted; and Āputtiraṉ's early history only reinforces the attempt to separate the *dharma* of kings from that of monks or ascetics.[54] Any blurring of this boundary is dangerous, both for the world as a whole and for the renouncer-king himself: an overdose of compassion can kill, as the fate of Āputtiraṉ's traveling companions reveals. One man's charity is another man's murder. The king, for everyone's sake, had best stick to his throne.

Yet this provides no resolution of the conflict that Āputtiraṉ, the world-weary monarch, discovers in himself; it does not even significantly moderate its range. If the early life (or lives) of this hero has any implications for his later career—and that this is the case is a fundamental assumption of this text, with its profound interest in karmic continuities—then we might well conclude that Āputtiraṉ is by nature unfit for kingship. His outrage at the impending sacrifice of a cow is strong evidence of this conclusion: kingship is, in itself, a kind of extended sacrifice, as we shall see. And yet it is hard to avoid the feeling that Āputtiraṉ's eventual assumption of kingly duties is

[52] See Tambiah (1976), pp. 72-101. The same characterization of the king as Bodhisattva is seen in Tibet.

[53] Tambiah (1976), pp. 32-53, sees the ideal of the *cakravartin* as a necessary counterpart to the monk's *dharma*: "Kingship as the crux of order in society provides the conditions and the context for the survival of *sasana* (religion)" (p. 41). Without elaborating on this point, we may note that the affirmation of politics in Buddhist traditions tends—among other effects—to limit the range of oscillation around the political center (as opposed to the extreme transformations of the Hindu royal types).

[54] For an explicit formulation of this distinction, see *Buddhacarita* 9.48-49.

seen as the result of those same characteristics that make him balk at sacrificial violence—his compassion, the sensitivity to others' suffering, the tendency toward *self*-sacrifice, the passion for ultimate truth; in short, the main components of his renunciatory drive. In other words, if Āputtiraṉ embodies, like Daśaratha, the royal ideal, then kingly legitimacy seems bound up with the king's impulse toward renunciation. The perfect king can hardly be without this feature—it is, as we shall see, a major part of his claim to transcendent authority—yet it is denounced in the strongest images available. Only a king abandoned by his mother at birth can be made to feel the evil consequences of a ruler's renunciation of his kingdom. For Āputtiraṉ, like Yudhiṣṭhira, the only possible conclusion is a life of duty riddled with doubt and the pervasive tension of unfulfilled aspirations.

4. The Maternal Monarch (2): The Sacrifice of Vena

So far we have been dealing with essentially "good," even ideal kings, although even these well-intentioned heroes have been liable to grievous error. Their careers, especially that of the richly experienced Āputtiraṉ, reveal an innate complexity and a compounding of symbolic roles, with a consequent instability and impetus toward self-transformation; it takes all too little to change a paragon of protective virtue into a Caṇḍāla filled with disgust for his own life, or a thwarted, confused renouncer. But there is another type of king recognized by our sources as being fundamentally important in defining the parameters of the institution: the evil king who deliberately flouts the dharmic ideal. This type is familiar from many myths and stories, but its outstanding representative is Vena, the evil antihero of one of the major Hindu myths of kingship.[55] This is a myth of origins: Pṛthu, the righteous king, emerges from the wreckage of previous attempts at establishing ordered rule.[56] It is also a very old myth: Vena is known to the Veda both as the father of Pṛthu[57] and as a "first king" or as "the brahman that was first born of old (or in the east, *purastāt*)."[58] These early references to Vena are hardly pejorative; rather, they seem to focus on the king's role as embodying the cosmic center and thereby

[55] On the Vena myth, including its analogues in other Indo-European traditions, notably the Roman, see O'Flaherty (1976), pp. 320-69; Dumézil (1943).

[56] See *MBh* 12.59.99-103; Heesterman (1978); above, II.3 at notes 33-34.

[57] *RV* 10.148.5; 10.94.14; 8.9.10; see O'Flaherty (1976), p. 322.

[58] *AV* 4.1 (Whitney's translation); see discussion by Heesterman (1957), pp. 150-51.

encompassing, as the central *brahman*-power, the entirety of creation.[59] This role is never wholly lost in the much later puranic versions of the story, in which Vena's character has been blackened beyond recognition; the centrality of the king—even an evil king—is now bound up with the notion of sacrifice. As we shall see, the sacrificial idiom also embraces another use of the maternal imagery of kingship that we discovered in the Tamil tale of Āputtiraṉ.

The myth of Vena and Pṛthu has recently been discussed in detail by Wendy O'Flaherty, who has illuminated its symbolic ties with motherhood: Vena is closely allied to the darker aspect of the mother, or, at a still deeper level, to the mother's "bad" (poisonous or milk-withholding) breast (as opposed to the "good" breast flowing with milk).[60] There are also important connections to the symbolism of the Hindu androgyne, with the associated themes of sexual and sacrificial violence.[61] Some of these associations will be discussed below, but our main concern is with the implicit attitudes toward kingship embedded in this story. O'Flaherty offers a wide-ranging synopsis of the mythic variants; we will limit ourselves here to a close reading of a single South Indian version, that of the *Bhāgavatapurāṇa* (4.13-15).[62]

The story begins with Vena's father, King Aṅga (the version of *MBh* 12.59 refers to him as Anaṅga, "Bodiless"—a common title of Kāma, Desire), who has one of the most common problems of kings in these stories: he has no son to carry on his line. In fact, the king's childlessness has even more immediate implications here: it is revealed during a sacrifice, at which the gods fail to appear to take their portions; when the king breaks his vow of silence to ask his priests what has gone wrong, they inform him that it is all because he has no son. (This unhappy situation is itself, however, the result of some evil in a former birth, *prāktanam agham*.) The sacrifice is swiftly converted into a rite to gain offspring, and, indeed, a person (*puruṣa*) appears from the sacrificial fire with a concoction of rice in a golden bowl; the king feeds this miraculous potion to his wife Sunīthā, and in due course she gives birth to Vena.

Sunīthā, however, is the daughter of Death himself, and, unfortunately, the child takes after his maternal grandfather. He is a hunter, so cruel by nature that whenever he appears, people take to their heels

[59] *Ibid.* On the king's "Brahminical" identity, see below, III.4 and V; cf. Malamoud (1976-1977), p. 179.

[60] O'Flaherty (1976), pp. 321-69.

[61] See Shulman (1980b), pp. 176-211, 297-98.

[62] For other versions, see *MBh* 12.59; *Brahmāṇḍa* 2.36.127-227; *Padma* 2.27-41; *Skanda* 7.1.336-37; *Vāmana, saromāhātmya* 26.1-62, 27.1-34.

with the cry, "Here comes Vena!" Even as a child, he enjoys slaughtering his own playmates, "as if they were sacrificial beasts." His father, observing his nature, attempts to restrain him, but to no avail. This household tragedy prompts one of the narrator's not infrequent gnomic interventions: the one good thing about a wicked son is that he predisposes his father toward renunciation! And this is precisely what happens to Aṅga: depressed, insomniac, he steals out of his own palace one night and disappears, abandoning his wife (pointedly referred to by the text simply as "Vena's mother"—but one wonders how reluctant Aṅga really is to escape the bed of Death's daughter). In the morning the notables of the kingdom search fruitlessly for their vanished monarch ("like wrong-headed yogis who search outside themselves for the hidden *puruṣa*," 13.48). When they return empty-handed, the sages anoint the evil Vena as king in the conspicuous presence of his mother.

At first, things are not as bad as might have been expected: for example, thieves (*dasyavaḥ*) go into hiding at once, "like rats terrified of a snake." Soon, however, power goes to the head of the evil king, and he breaks all bounds: he drives about in his chariot, causing the heavens and the earth to quake; worse still, he forbids the Brahmins to sacrifice or to receive gifts. Now, of course, the sages—ever mindful of their own responsibility for Vena's coronation—feel they must intervene, for the world is caught between two possible calamities: thieves and bandits, who would run rampant in the absence of a king; and the power-mad king himself, a kind of archbandit bursting with evil desires. Given these alternatives, the kingdom's situation is that of an ant trapped in the middle of a firebrand burning on both ends (*dāruṇy ubhayato dīpte*, 14.8).[63] Swallowing their pride and restraining their anger, the Brahmins approach the king in a conciliatory manner, eager to instruct him in *dharma*.

But Vena will have none of this: he rejects the Brahmins as fools (*bāliśāḥ*). Their love for the great god Viṣṇu, whom they have just extravagantly praised in Vena's presence, is like that of a wife for her lover (*jāra*). The king is greater than any god; indeed the gods—Viṣṇu, Brahmā, Śiva, Indra, Vāyu, Yama, Sūrya, Parjanya, Kubera, Soma, Earth, Agni, Varuṇa, "and others" (14.26-27)—make up the king's body. Therefore it is only proper that the Brahmins worship and sacrifice to Vena alone, the foremost embodiment of divinity. So much for Vena's interest in *dharma*; the irony lies in the partial truth of Vena's

[63] This seems to be a translation of a Tamil expression, *irutalaik kŏḷḷi ĕṟumpu*—further evidence, if more is needed, of the Tamil provenance of the *Bhāgavata*.

boasts. For the king is, indeed, said to incorporate Viṣṇu's divinity (*nāviṣṇuḥ pṛthivīpatiḥ*);[64] he is a portion (*aṃśa*) of Viṣṇu manifest on earth; and both the sacrificial texts and the *dharma* literature are fond of identifying the king with a series of eight divinities, all of whom appear in Vena's list of his divine body parts, and who are furthermore correlated with the points of the compass.[65] This is the theme of the king's identification with the world, the "holistic" pattern of Kampaṉ's *araciyaṟ paṭalam*;[66] the king unites within himself the dispersed powers of creation. Vena's mistake is to take these notions literally and to deduce operational conclusions on this basis. His boasts reveal his perfect logic and his faulty consciousness: the king who vaunts his divinity is in danger of losing it. Put somewhat differently, *self*-sacrifice is the keynote of dharmic kingship, as we have seen from our earlier examples (Rāma, the Pāṇṭiyaṉ, Āputtiraṉ); and if Vena seeks to deny this recommended attitude, the Brahmin sages will have their own way of helping him to execute his duties. In fact, the irony goes considerably deeper here, for in other versions of this story Vena proudly claims to be, like the Vedic Puruṣa or Prajāpati, "sacrificer, victim, and divine recipient of the sacrifice all in one."[67] This claim looks suspiciously like that of the renouncer, who has "placed his sacrificial fires within himself":[68] inebriated by the sense of royal omnipotence, Vena has unwittingly drifted into the paradigm of the single (Brahmin) sacrificer who rejects the world of reciprocal relations and agonistic rivalries, such as those which characterize the conventional Brahmin-Kṣatriya pair. Vena's motivation is clearly far from Brahminical (it has nothing of the quest for wholeness and purity), but the result is the same—the Brahmin priests are declared redundant. They in turn respond with an equal and opposite overreaction: taking Vena at his word, as an incarnation of the cosmic Puruṣa (*yajñapuruṣa*), they proceed to slay him with shouted *mantras*—a spontaneous sacrifice sprung, we may assume, as an unwelcome surprise on the arrogant Vena.[69] The Brahmins then retire to their *āśramas*, leaving the world

[64] See Raghavan (1956).

[65] *Manusmṛti* 5.96; 7.4, 7; *BĀU* 1.4.11 offers a different list for the gods' *kṣatra*-power. Cf. Heesterman (1979), p. 74. Vena's list seems to conflate the earlier ones.

[66] See above, section 1.

[67] Heesterman (1978), p. 3; see *Harivaṃśa* 5.

[68] *Manusmṛti* 6.25, 38; cf. Heesterman (1964).

[69] The Brahmins' literal-mindedness, which runs parallel to Vena's and applies to his statement, may also extend to the metaphor he uses for their *bhakti*—the adulterous love of a married woman. Later (Bengali) Kṛṣṇaism develops this theme deliberately: love of god is like that of a married woman for her paramour. We may assume the usage here is intended to be satirical.

kingless. Only the grief-stricken Sunīthā, the dead king's mother—again surprisingly present in a dynamic role—thinks to safeguard the king's corpse by magic arts (*vidyāyogena*).

And she is surely right to have done so, for, in the absence of any king, all hell breaks loose. The nightmarish visions of the *dharma* texts, which never fail to warn against the dangers of a kingless state, come true. The sages are the first to notice: seated on the bank of a river and engaged in telling sacred stories, they suddenly become aware of a great cloud of dust swirling through all the quarters of space. They know exactly what this means: the dust has been raised by the busy feet of bandits and thieves, who are now rushing about preying upon the helpless and also attacking one another. This is precisely what the Brahmins had feared when they hesitated to take action against Vena; the kingless country is wholly delivered over to thieves and has become devoid of truth (*cauraprāyam . . . hīnasattvam*). Indeed, the situation is even worse than predicted, for the Brahmins are now caught in a new predicament. In their zeal for righteousness, they have clearly exceeded their mandate, just as the Brahmin warrior Paraśurāma goes beyond all reasonable limits in his relentless campaigns against the Kṣatriyas;[70] and the result is the necessity of further Brahmin intervention, potentially compromising for the Brahmin values of purity and detachment. In fact, for the *Bhāgavata*'s authors, the true Brahmin cannot escape involvement in the world: when the perfectly composed, ever-tranquil Brahmins—those possessed of the controlled equanimity so highly praised by the classical sources—pay no heed to the cries of the suffering, Brahminical power flows out of them "like milk from a broken pail."[71] We may note here the polemical *bhakti* stance against the *Bhagavadgītā*'s goal of detachment: clearly, the Brahmin must act when the situation demands it—as it usually does—regardless of the consequences to his personal karmic account. In the present instance, failure to act is no less serious a threat to Brahminical wholeness than abstention from action.[72]

Thus the Brahmins, suddenly recalling that the line of Aṅga has produced many fine kings after all, hasten back to the palace, where Sunīthā has so thoughtfully preserved Vena's corpse. They set to work at once churning (*mamanthur*) the dead king's thigh, out of which arises a dwarf, black as a crow, with red eyes and copper-colored hair. The sages order him to take a seat (*niṣīda*)—hence, we are told, his

[70] See below, III.3.

[71] *brāhmaṇaḥ samadṛk śānto dīnānāṃ samupekṣakaḥ/ sravate brahma tasyāpi bhinnabhāṇḍāt payo yathā* (4.14.41).

[72] See further discussion of this point in Chapter III.

name, Niṣāda; he is the ancestor of the wild tribes who dwell in the hills and jungles. In his birth the Niṣāda obligingly takes upon himself all the impurities of his father, Vena (*aharaj jāyamāno venakalmaṣam ulbaṇam*, 14.46). This leaves the corpse essentially pure, at least in karmic terms; hence the sages can now churn out of its arms the marvellous twins, Pṛthu and Arcis. Pṛthu, identified at birth as a portion (*kalā*) of Viṣṇu, will become the ideal Hindu king, always ready to be guided by his Brahmin advisers; his sister, a manifestation (*saṃbhūti*) of Lakṣmī, will become his wife.

Before looking at Pṛthu's career, let us pause for a moment to consider the symbolism of Vena's disastrous reign. The maternal imagery in this myth has been discussed by O'Flaherty: Pṛthu, who will soon encounter a far more positive maternal figure in the Earth-cow, is produced from the anomalous "masculine" mother Vena. The maternal persona of the king is once again a dark and malevolent one, although in this case its links with renunciation seem almost accidental; the king who declares himself to be Brahmā or Prajāpati, sole sacrificer and recipient of the sacrifice, arrives at this position on the basis of wholly impure intentions. Indeed, Vena might be seen as delineating the very bottom line of kingship, the evil, egoistic, predatory potential of the king, while the true renouncer-kings, such as Āputtiraṉ, illuminate the upper limit. It is noteworthy that both the lower and the upper limits have clear associations with Brahmin elements (for Vena, the total sacrifice; for Āputtiraṉ, sincere renunciation); we will return to this point. Note, too, how maternal imagery of a negative cast can "frame" the entire range of royal possibilities, with most kings presumably falling somewhere in the middle, where the more positive role of the mother (nourishment, protection) is relevant to kingly duties. Pṛthu, as we shall see, embodies this middle road of kingship. This interpretation of the symbolism is reinforced by the remarkable role granted to Sunīthā, Vena's own mother, who seems almost to haunt the myth as a shadow to her son. Other versions of the myth bear out the assumption that Sunīthā is the vital link between the evil king and the legacy of his grandfather, Death.[73] Sunīthā is present, in lieu of any other family representative, at Vena's coronation; and she magically preserves her son's corpse, out of which the future king must be born. This part of the myth is serious and evocative: it is as if the authors wished to underline and exemplify in story the common comparison of the king—especially the warrior-king—to Death.[74] But this turns out to be more than a hackneyed simile; even the righteous

[73] See discussion by O'Flaherty (1976), pp. 323-24, 328-29, 363-65.

[74] See, for example, *Puṟan*. 19.3, 16; 42.22-24. This simile is common in the Sanskrit epics and in *kāvya*, as it is in medieval Tamil literature.

king emerges ultimately from the womb of Death's daughter. Looking back through his genealogy, the king finds his origin in the destructive side of *dharma*, imparted to him through the instrumentality of the mother.[75] We may recall the passage from the *Cilappatikāram* dealing with the Pāṇṭiyaṉ's fate: the king who errs finds that *dharma* has become Death.[76] The Vena myth teaches us a more extreme lesson: even the king who embodies *dharma* is bound up with death, which is an integral part of *dharma*. Yama, lord of the dead, goes by the title Dharmarāja; the same name is frequently applied to Yudhiṣṭhira, the righteous king of the epic, who is all too conscious of its sinister implications.[77]

The Vena myth thus clearly points to the close connection between kingship and death, or between kingship and evil in a more general sense; yet also crucial to this myth is the attempt to separate out the complexities of kingship and, specifically, to divest the king of evil. The royal corpse divides its moral burden between the outcaste Niṣādas, on the one hand, and the dharmic Pṛthu and Arcis, on the other. We shall see in a moment that this distribution is not entirely successful; even the virtuous Pṛthu has a residue of evil. Nevertheless, our myth clearly aims at an idealized vision of kingship, a vision based on the principle of *separation* from evil, which will, however, continue to exist in some excluded form (the jungle-dwelling Niṣādas). From Pṛthu's point of view (as well as that of his Brahmin godfathers), the main goal is to externalize the king's darker aspect by transferring it to someone else. Once the Niṣādas have borne away the royal onus, we are left with a purified, perfected king.[78] We should note the close parallel with another myth of "churning," the *amṛtamanthana*: there, too, the ocean churned by the gods and demons first produces the terrifying Hālāhala poison, which Śiva—the excluded, outcaste deity—must swallow; only after the poison is neutralized can the ocean's bounty—ultimately the *amṛta*, elixir of immortality—appear, just as Pṛthu's birth follows the exile of the impure Niṣāda.[79] We will return to this parallelism below.

Pṛthu's story is a happier one than his father's; we shall be concerned

[75] Our text describes Death—Vena's maternal grandfather—as born from a portion of *adharma* (*adharmāṃśodbhavaṃ mṛtyum*, 4.13.39). In terms of royal origins and identity, the point lies in the king's association with what might be called the *adharmic* side of *dharma*. For a discussion of *dharma*'s self-destruction, see Shulman (1979).

[76] Above, section 2.

[77] See Biardeau (1978), pp. 94-111.

[78] In other versions, the theme of purifying Vena is more elaborately developed: the righteous son is said to save his father. See *Skanda* 7.1.336.95-253; *Brahmāṇḍa* 2.36.127-227; O'Flaherty (1976), pp. 324-25.

[79] *MBh* 1.15-17; *Rām.* 1.45; see discussion by Long (1976).

here only with its central episode, the milking of the earth. This episode portrays Pṛthu's response to the crisis he has inherited from his father: his subjects are dying of hunger, for the earth has ceased producing crops, and Pṛthu is called upon to act. We subsequently learn the reason for this famine: when all men had become thieves (at the death of Vena; *coribhūte 'tha loke*, 17.7), the earth had swallowed, for the sake of future sacrifices (*yajñārthe*), all the plants created by Brahmā. The stress upon sacrifice is clearly significant here; Pṛthu, too, thinks in sacrificial terms when he accuses the earth, as one of the deities invited to the sacrifice, of refusing to do its part by producing rice in exchange for the offerings it consumes (17.22). This is instructive: the king acts as the arbiter and guarantor of a ceaseless process of exchange and redistribution,[80] a process described in sacrificial metaphors; he must, then, be prepared to blast open any blockage in the system. The remarkable point is that the king's supervision of this circulatory process is perceived as sacrificial and essentially violent. Thus Pṛthu seizes his bow[81] and pursues the terrified Earth, which has adopted the form of a cow; after a fascinating, pathos-laden dialogue between the two—the aggressive king, who is compared both to his great-grandfather, Death (Kṛtānta), and to Tripurāri-Śiva (17.13, 17, 28), and his vulnerable, feminine victim bloated with seeds—the earth instructs Pṛthu to level her surface[82] and to milk her of "milklike desires" (*kṣīramayān kāmān*, 18.9). Pṛthu, using Manu ("Man") as a calf, "milks" the earth of plants; he is followed by the various other classes of beings (sages, gods, demons, *gandharvas* and *apsarases*, *pitṛs*, *siddhas*, *vidyādharas*, magicians, *yakṣas*, *rākṣasas*, *bhūtas* and *piśācas*, Nāgas, animals of forest and village, birds, trees, and mountains), each of which milks the inexhaustible mother of a needed form of sustenance or power.

The paradigmatic relation here is clearly that of the first "milkman," the king, to the earth. Once again we are faced with rich maternal imagery: the earth itself appears as a mother who first withholds and then delivers her bounty;[83] and the king who feeds his famished subjects in this way is, like Āputtiraṉ and Kampaṉ's Daśaratha, a symbolic

[80] See Appadurai and Breckenridge (1976); above, Chapter I.

[81] In *MBh* 7, Appendix 1 no. 8, p. 1116, Pṛthu takes the bow of Śiva (and cf. 12.29.128-36). This is instructive in view of what follows.

[82] Hence, by popular etymology (from √*prath*, to level), his name—and the earth's title, *pṛthivī*.

[83] This pattern (which is related to the complex symbolism of milk) is itself widespread in South Indian myth and legend: see the story of Kuntī and Karṇa, below, VII.7 at notes 148-49.

"mother" of his kingdom. But the contrast between Pṛthu and Āputtiraṉ is also illuminating: while the latter seems determined to reenact his own unhappy birth story (albeit from an earlier existence) by abandoning his subjects, Pṛthu, the son of an equally dark mother, reverses the force of the maternal symbolism entirely. Pṛthu, although endowed with the violent characteristics of the martial king, is wholly benevolent toward his subjects. In fact, Pṛthu's maternal character is much less clear than his father's; the text seems intent on taking him through a wider series of symbolic family roles. Although he uses Manu—mankind—as the calf to milk the earth, in a sense Pṛthu is himself portrayed as the calf or child drawing forth the mother's milk. He is further said to be the earth's father, on the basis of a rather heavy-handed pun: when the milking (from the root $\sqrt{}$*duh*, to milk) was at last accomplished, Pṛthu, highly pleased, regarded the earth affectionately as his daughter (*duhitṛtve cakāremāṃ premṇā duhitṛvatsalaḥ*, 18.28). We should also recall that the king is conventionally married to the earth;[84] and although one hesitates to pursue these metaphors too literally, we may nevertheless suspect that incest comes as naturally to the king as to one of his exemplary models, the creator Brahmā[85]—for Pṛthu weds not only the earth (at once his "daughter" and his "mother") but also his twin sister, Arcis.

Let us try to draw together the different strands of the Pṛthu-Vena myth that have engaged our attention. This is a myth of sacrifice, indeed of two opposed sacrificial paradigms, both of which are germane to the historical realities of kingship in medieval South India. The first paradigm, that of Vena, suggests the dangers and impurities inherent in the institution; the second is seen as normative, and as an institutional response to these same dangers. Vena embodies the sacrifice in all its aspects—sacrificer, recipient, and victim; Pṛthu performs the sacrifice within his more limited role of patron and warrior-king, but also as the successor to Rudra in the ancient agonistic model of the rite.[86] The myth contains an implicit progression from a monolithic to a dualistic conception of the king's sacrificial task; and we must ask why the first possibility is so bitterly rejected.

It is not simply a question of Vena's wickedness or arrogance, although both these traits are important. The heart of the matter is Vena's attempt to go it alone, without Brahmins, gods, or any other outside forces: Vena caricatures the king's normal claim to constitute

[84] See Chapter VI.1.

[85] See discussion by Bailey (1981).

[86] See Heesterman (1964); Shulman (1980b), pp. 90-93, 110-16; Kramrisch (1981), pp. 3-10.

the "body" of his kingdom as the single force that encompasses and unites the divided elements. Taken literally, this claim means that the king must produce the kingdom out of his own self—more specifically, through his role as microcosmic victim in the ongoing sacrifice of life on earth. Creation depends upon sacrifice in this as in other areas of Indian thought: thus only in death can Vena give birth to both the Niṣāda—the outer limit of his kingdom—and the properly righteous (if incestuous) royal couple. Many other examples of this pattern exist, for example in the origin myths of several South Indian castes. To cite but one instance:

> A Kammāḷaṉ (artisan) had two sons, the first by a Balija woman and the second by his Kammāḷaṉ wife. He was unjustly slain by the king of Kāñci. His two sons then avenged his death by killing the king and dividing his body: the Kammāḷaṉ took the head to make his weighing-pan, while the Balija woman's son used the skin to make a pedlar's carpet and the sinews as threads for stringing bangles.[87]

This story repeats the theme of the king's death in atonement for error, as in the *Cilappatikāram*; but its major aim is to explain the origins of several conventional caste attributes from the corpse of the sacrificed king. The king constitutes his kingdom in a literal, hence necessarily violent fashion. In sacrificial terms, this is a paradigm of self-contained wholeness and dangerous independence—like that of the demons who are said in the *Brāhmaṇa* texts to have sacrificed into their own mouths.[88] The same pattern recurs later in the Pṛthu-Vena myth in the motif of the earth, which has swallowed all the seeds of Brahmā's plants. And, as in the case of the overly self-sufficient demons, this unilateral step has to be reversed—by the king who is committed to the contrasting, bilateral model of sacrifice. For the attempt to realize in the kingly role a literal, all-embracing wholeness has two closely related consequences: first, it leaves no room in the system, which, turned in upon itself, begins to build up pressure against its boundaries, to overheat, as it were, with no possibilities for help from outside to intervene; second, given the extent of the king's implication in the world—he is not, after all, a renouncer free to roam the forests at will—his identification with the kingdom requires him to absorb all his subjects' violence, including the ineluctable

[87] Thurston (1909), 3:117-18; cf. Appadurai (1974), p. 238.
[88] *Śat. Brāh.* 11.1.8.1.

sacrificial onus that accompanies the maintenance of ordered life.[89] In Vena's monolithic model, the king serves as a kind of magnet for negative *karma*; he attains the fruits of the never-ending sacrifice only at the cost of sustaining the burden of sacrificial evil. Small wonder that Vena appears as a dark, malevolent figure. His claims to total identity with his kingdom, indeed with the entire world—*l'état c'est moi* would have been Vena's motto—recall the ancient *Brāhmaṇa* portrayal of Death as the creator, Prajāpati.[90] There is, indeed, a conception of wholeness here, but it is a wholeness bursting with innate tension and sacrificial violence. In this sense Vena, too, can make the traditional kingly assertion of being possessed by Viṣṇu: he imitates Viṣṇu's role as the all-encompassing center, the wholeness that is about to give birth from within to the divine violence and terror of the avatars.[91]

Pṛthu, by way of contrast, opens up the doors that his father had sealed. He remains, it is true, closely linked to the sacrifice: even this ideal king has a violent bent to his nature, as we learn also from the explicit comparison of Pṛthu to Śiva. Indeed, this comparison is used to underline an action—Pṛthu's pursuit of the Earth-cow—that implicitly suggests one of the basic myths of Rudra-Śiva, the Vedic tale of Rudra's pursuit of the incestuous Prajāpati (who has the form of a stag).[92] Pṛthu's milking the earth thus seems to express the terrifying (*raudra*) side of the king's nature; Pṛthu stands in relation to the earth as the sacrificial butcher Rudra to his victim. This relation is fundamental to Indian kingship. Nevertheless, Pṛthu, too, is more closely tied to Viṣṇu, who is said to possess (*ā-√viś*) the king at his birth. These contrasting associations with Rudra and Viṣṇu belong to every South Indian king; here we may agree with Biardeau's analysis of the avatar, with its combination of "rudraïque" and "viṣṇuïque," Kṣatriya and Brahmin elements, as paradigmatic for Indian kingship.[93] Yet the king seems to have a much more intimate and natural connection with Viṣṇu, just as the Brahmin, as we shall see, is more basically linked

[89] In theory, the proper king seeks to avoid acquiring his subjects' demerit by the proper fulfillment of his duties. *Manusmṛti* 8.308 states the negative case clearly: the king who fails to protect his subjects but still receives his sixth share of produce as taxes takes upon himself all their impurities. But the theory as a whole has the look of a stopgap; the king's conscientious "protection" is a flimsy defense against the relentless accumulation of evil that kingship, like life itself, entails. Even a far better king than Vena needs the Brahmins to deal with this problem.

[90] For example, in *Bṛhadāraṇyaka Upaniṣad* 1.2; *Śat. Brāh.* 10.6.5.1-8.

[91] On the violent associations of the avatars, see Biardeau (1976), pp. 175-203.

[92] *Aitareya Brāhmaṇa* 3.33.

[93] Biardeau (1976), especially pp. 175-85.

to Rudra (here I am at odds with Biardeau); the mythic identities are merged or exchanged in the course of the transformations that the king and the Brahmin effect in their relations. In the present myth, Pṛthu's association with Rudra seems to reflect his adoption of the agonistic, bilateral model of royal sacrifice. It is not by chance that Pṛthu's first act as king is to shower gifts on the Brahmins and other groups (17.1-2). Pṛthu has restored the king's classical role as *yajamāna*, the sacrificial patron dependent upon the Brahmin priests—whom he amply rewards—for the proper accomplishment of the rite. Within this paradigm, evil passes from the patron (the king who bears responsibility for the moral balance of his kingdom, including the inevitable violence and inherent conflict) to the priests, who "digest" it[94] or transfer it further into the outer zone of transcendence. The result is, in effect, an open-ended system with power flowing regularly among men and gods, subjects and king, Brahmins and patron, while the necessary residue of evil travels outward via the Brahmin gatekeepers. Whereas Vena had broken the circulatory cycle, closed the boundaries, and accumulated a lethal surplus of poisonous evil, Pṛthu accepts his need for Brahmin advice and sacrificial services, thereby orienting the kingdom as a whole toward transcendence and liberating its internal dynamism.

Lest this solution appear to be airtight—as it has to those who see in the hierarchical superiority of the Brahmins India's ideological answer to the problems of power and political morality—we hasten to note its delicate nature. True, Pṛthu acknowledges Brahmin preeminence in wisdom and confirms the dualistic paradigm of sacrifice; but this same paradigm of Brahmin-Kṣatriya cooperation and interdependence is, as we shall see, profoundly problematic for the Brahmin. Nor can the king escape for long his own inheritance of totalistic claims, as symbolized by his identification with Viṣṇu. Pṛthu shows us less of an exemplary solution to the problems of kingship than a momentary and precarious balance riddled with contradiction. One sees this clearly enough in his subsequent adventures: Pṛthu's very virtue propels him into inevitable conflict with a jealous Indra, who stoops to stealing Pṛthu's sacrificial horse and is nearly killed in return by Pṛthu's son.[95] Pṛthu must be convinced to abstain from completing his hundredth and final sacrifice—lest Indra be dethroned and heresy

[94] See discussion by Parry (1980); and see Heesterman (1964) on the Brahmin role in the sacrifice.

[95] *Bhāgavata* 4.19. On the rivalry between Indra and other kings, see below, V.2.

become rampant on earth.[96] Eventually, at the end of his reign, Pṛthu, too, retires to the forest to perform *yoga* and meditate on Viṣṇu. The king who resorts to renunciation at the end of a long career is, of course, much less of a problem for the tradition than one who, like Āputtiraṉ, yearns too early for this release. For all that, the renouncer-king's relief speaks for itself: kingship, however properly ordered, entails the unchanging process of contamination by evil.

To sum up the main lessons of the Pṛthu-Vena myth for our purposes, we may extrapolate the following abstract notions from our text:

First, kingship is pervaded by sacrificial concepts. The kingdom is rooted in sacrifice, created by a form of sacrifice, maintained by sacrifice.[97] This means, at least in India, that the king is faced with unavoidable evil, the consequence of the sacrificial violence. Indeed, this evil seems to preexist, perhaps even to condition the appearance of the powers of royal splendor and prosperity (*śrī*).[98] In the myth of the churning of the ocean, poison precedes the discovery of the *amṛta*; Pṛthu has to be churned out of the corpse of the evil Vena. The ancient Brahminical sacrifice was based on the exchange between two parties of *śrī*, the sacrificer's goal, and *pāpman*, the sacrificial evil.[99] The same challenge awaits the king: before he can attain *śrī*, he must deal with the *pāpman*—either through exclusion (the Niṣāda exiled to the jungles), absorption (Vena), or some form of transfer (Pṛthu). The myth clearly recommends the first and the last alternatives and condemns the second.

Second, the kingly claim to wholeness, symbolized by the association with Viṣṇu, puts the king in tension with the Brahmins and saturates him with evil. These are the results of Vena's attempt to realize in his person the entirety of worldly power, thus obviating the need for gods or Brahmins. The king who remains very much a part of the world cannot adopt the paradigm of the single sacrificer without amassing an unbearable burden of evil. Maternal imagery of a negative cast expresses this attitude toward the king as embodying the sacrifice alone, just as it is used to condemn the king who turns too early to true renunciation. Schematically stated, kingship is framed by upper and lower limits related, as we shall see, to the bifurcated role of the

[96] This is another myth of the origin of heresy: Indra disguises himself to steal Pṛthu's horse; the masks he discards become the Pāṣaṇḍa heretics.

[97] Cf. the somewhat similar conclusion of Hocart (1969), pp. 113-16; and see also Yamaguchi (1972), and the contrasting view of Waghorne (1980).

[98] On *śrī* generally see Hiltebeitel (1976), pp. 143-91; below, VI.1.

[99] Heesterman (1964).

Brahmin—renunciation, on the one hand, and total responsibility for the sacrifice on the other. But whereas the Brahmin can hold these opposed roles in suspension—their very combination in a single figure gives the Brahmin his flexibility and his symbolic power—the king who drifts toward either end of the permitted range finds himself, and his world, in trouble. Despite his real demand for wholeness, and despite his need for the legitimation that only renunciation can ultimately grant, the king must cling to the center, where he is forced into relation with the Brahmins and other parties to the kingdom. This leaves him weak, constrained, and always tempted to exceed his proper limits.

Finally, the dualistic model recommended by the example of Pṛthu is itself more than a little problematic. It puts a strain on the Brahmins, who accept the king's gifts and the sacrificial residues that go with them; it also leaves them with more authority than they can use, while the king now *lacks* the authority to act independently. One has, in short, a system of delicate balance in which a heavy surplus of evil flows outward via the Brahmin priests, under the watchful eyes of a weakened arbiter, the king; in which royal splendor, *śrī*, can only be extracted from the sacrifice, hence from an unending circulatory process that creates the Brahmin-king interdependence; and in which control over this process is always threatening to break down as both the major figures, saddled with impossible ambivalence toward each other and toward themselves, cling reluctantly to the thin lifeline of their common (and somewhat theoretical) distaste for disorder.

5. Caricatures and Cripples: The Icon in the World

We began this chapter by exploring the iconic image of the dharmic king in medieval South India; and we have seen the icon unfold into highly complex and ambiguous symbolic forms, some of which seem to question the prescriptive power of the dharmic ideal itself. Yet so far we have barely scratched the surface of royal symbolism in South India; in subsequent chapters we shall strive to penetrate further behind the iconic mask toward the symbolic center of kingship in this culture—a center by no means as clearly defined for us as the iconic images, yet no less significant a presence for all that. But we have by no means finished with the icon; and, as a form of interim stocktaking, we may review certain of its features in relation to the stories discussed above.

First, we have seen how the iconic image dissolves into its own antithesis. The tensions it contains are exemplified in individual careers: they impel Āputtiraṉ toward renunciation, and Vena toward a sacrificial death. Icon and antithesis are experienced by the Pāṇṭiyaṉ king-turned-thief as a progression in time—indeed, an astonishingly dramatic and rapid progression, which seems dependent upon an a priori perception of the interrelation of these two poles (ruler and thief). The Pāṇṭiyaṉ's transformation results from royal error, which constitutes but one delimited aspect of this perception. There are, as we have seen, much more extreme expressions of the king's potential for flouting the dharmic ideal: the Vena myth is an outstanding example of what might be called the "anti-iconic" persona of the king. But perhaps the most striking examples come from another genre entirely. As we shall have occasion to note several times in later chapters, certain comic modes seem to offer particularly trenchant insights into the problems implicit in other, less self-conscious sources. Comedy has a way of giving voice to the unutterable; its caricatures, inversions, and wild exaggerations are no accidental outgrowths of a deliberately uncultivated garden. Rather, they point to the very heart of the culture.

Thus if we turn, for example, to the medieval literature of Sanskrit farce, we find anti-iconic kings such as Anayasindhu ("Ocean of Bad Policy") in Jagadīśvara's *Hāsyārṇava*.[100] Anayasindhu's kingdom has gone awry: as he learns from the spies he sends out to investigate, men embrace only their own wives, rather than others'; the Untouchable sews sandals, while the Brahmin is honored in his assembly; people have absolutely nothing of which to be ashamed. *Horribile dictu!* The whole kingdom is topsy-turvy (*evaṃ maṇḍalavaiparītyam adhikaṃ jātaṃ mahābhūpateḥ*, v. 11). The king decides it is all his fault: for many days and nights his mind has been absorbed, and his aged body worn out, by adulterous amours, and he has therefore neglected his duty of touring the realm. But it is not too late: he sets out at once on a tour of inspection, and he is quite prepared to use force (*daṇḍa*) to set things "right." The play recounts the scenes in the court he establishes in Bandhurā's brothel, where we meet the king's *purohita* Viśvabhaṇḍa ("Everyone's Fool"), who has come to teach the courtesans the arts of love; the physician Vyādhisindhu ("Ocean of Disease"), who boasts that not even the long-lived Mārkaṇḍeya could survive his treatments; the barber-surgeon Raktakallola ("Billow of Blood"), who drags a

[100] I have used the Chowkhamba edition, Varanasi, 1963. On the *Hāsyārṇavaprahasana*, see Lévi (1963), pp. 253-55.

blood-soaked victim into the court and demands compensation for the latter's timidity and unfortunate aversion to pain; the police chief Sādhuhiṃsaka ("Scourge of the Good"), who cheerfully announces his delight at the fact that the city is entirely in the hands of armed thieves; and the valiant general Raṇajambuka ("Jackal of Battle"), who describes his masterly execution of a leech—after donning his armor and covering himself with his shield.[101] We need not pursue these parodies further at this point—the relation of kingship to comedy is explored at length in Chapters IV and V—but let us at least note the symmetrical inversions of the icon: Anayasindhu is no less aware than Daśaratha, Āputtiraṉ, or Vena of the king's total responsibility for his kingdom, and of the need for royal force (*daṇḍa*) to keep everything in the desired order—in this case, the kind of order that absolute disorder can represent. In other words, the icon and the caricature inhere in one another. We may wish to distinguish now between the anti-iconic figures (such as Vena, or the bandit-kings discussed below) and the iconic inversions (Anayasindhu and other comic types—but not, as we shall see, the mainstream images of royal clowns).

Clearly, the dharmic icon veils a world of subtle and highly significant transformations. Admittedly, the icon has a peculiar power over the imagination, so much so that one is often tempted to take it at face value—a pandit's ploy sometimes followed even by Indologists and historians. It required the insight and complexity of a poet such as Kampaṉ to place the icon within the contours of an anti-iconic reality. We would do well to follow in Kampaṉ's path in this respect. Indeed, we might regard the dharmic icon as an instance of the "social obfuscation of reality" that Cohen and Ben Ari have seen as existing alongside the commonplace "social construction of reality."[102] For Cohen and Ben Ari, this obfuscation is linked to a deeper reality, and in particular to the existence of fundamental conflicts or irreconcilable contradictions within a society. If social reality is constructed on the premise that it is congruent—that there is no ultimate cognitive disjunction, and that its truths can never conflict—then when such conflict does arise (as in the revelation of incommensurable values underlying opposing options), it elicits attempts to deny or to mask it. The dharmic icon, with its implicit suggestion that an ideal kingship is possible without compromising the ultimate values of the tradition (on the part of the king or the kingdom he represents), seems well suited for analysis along these lines. In particular, the king's impulse

[101] *Hāsyārṇavaprahasana*, pp. 9-47.

[102] Cohen and Ben Ari (1979).

to renounce his kingship—an impulse that affects all the more positive royal figures, and that springs from an identification with the ultimate Brahminical values—is not really capable of being assimilated by the icon of the perfect ruler.

Yet perhaps the most striking analytic feature in the materials we have examined in this chapter is the extent to which they themselves reveal the transparent nature of the iconic "obfuscation." The congruence of social reality seems rather different here, where disorder can be a form of order, and the partial, limited nature of any statement, system, or concept tends to be explicitly recognized by its authors. Perhaps the Western drive toward congruence, harmony, and the resolution of contradiction takes a different form in South India—no doubt a less harmonious and homogeneous form. There seems to be room for many incongruities in this kind of cultural congruence. Thus it is that beside the dharmic icon we have to place the innumerable stories that stand this icon on its head, examine it critically, and declare it wanting. We may mention in this connection the amazing number of stories about kings who are afflicted by some physical flaw or disablement. Leprosy or some other skin disease is perhaps the most common of these legendary ailments (for example, Karikāla Chola at Tanjore,[103] King Camatkāra at Tiruvārūr,[104] Kulaśekhara the Cera at Tirupperūr,[105] the epic hero Sāmba,[106] King Maha of Anantāmātya's *Bhojarājīyamu*,[107] Hiraṇyavarman of Cidambaram,[108] and even the familiar Vena[109]), but we may also think of Kūṉpāṇṭiyaṉ's hunched back,[110] Mucukunda's monkey-face,[111] Koccĕṅkaṇ's red eyes,[112] and a whole series of lame or crippled kings (including the heroes of the late medieval "cripple-dramas," the *nŏṇṭināṭakam*).[113] In the epic alone

[103] *Bṛhadīśvaramāhātmya* 11, cited in Somasundaram Pillai (1958), p. 43.

[104] *Skandapurāṇa* 6.10.1-24; *Tiruvārūrppurāṇam* 18.1-60.

[105] *Perūrppurāṇam* 29.1-24.

[106] See von Stietencron (1966).

[107] *Bhojarājīyamu* 1.90.

[108] The prevalence of this motif may help to explain the ease with which Hiraṇyavarman's original ailment—a lion's body—was transformed, with the help of a textual error, to leprosy. See Kulke (1970), pp. 188-89. (The later tradition often refers to Hiranyavarman's leprosy.)

[109] *Skandapurāṇa* 7.1.336.95-253; cf. O'Flaherty (1976), p. 325; for yet another leprous king, see Artola (1965), pp. 47-48.

[110] *Tiruviḷaiyāṭaṟpurāṇam* 62.

[111] Below, V.4; a similar story is told of Piratattarājaṉ in *Aruṇācalapurāṇam* 11.1-13.

[112] *Tiruvāṉaikkāppurāṇam* 19; *PP* 4210-11.

[113] On *nŏṇṭināṭakam*, see VII.6 below. One thinks of Yudhiṣṭhira's toe, blasted by Gāndhārī: *MBh* 11.15; cf. Gehrts (1975), pp. 271-72; Hiltebeitel (1977a). Similarly, Brahma Nayuḍu, the hero of the Telugu folk-epic *Palnāṭi virula katha*, suffers a broken

we have the blind Dhṛtarāṣṭra and the impotent Pāṇḍu.[114] These epic figures and the legendary South Indian kings of the *sthalapurāṇas* form an impressive group of maimed or otherwise impaired monarchs; indeed, so prevalent is this type that one might almost regard it as normative. Whatever else it may mean—each story must, of course, be examined in its own terms—the pattern as a whole suggests a conception of the king, even the iconic exemplar, as innately flawed, weighed down with an inescapable onus, and always in need of healing by some outside power such as a temple deity, Brahmin, or magician. Like the image of *dharma* itself as an originally four-legged creature that loses one of its legs in each successive *yuga*,[115] the dharmic ruler of the Kaliyuga, our present degenerate moment of time, is profoundly unbalanced, crippled, pathetically lacking the wholeness he is meant to symbolize.[116]

He is also tragically weak. We have noted the king's identification with his kingdom, and his consequent enmeshment within the social fabric of the whole, with all its problems and attendant evils. What must also be stressed at this point is the vulnerability that this structural position entails. The king is "flawed" not only by contamination with *adharma*, or with evil in a variety of forms;[117] he is also impaired by his congenital impotence. At best *primus inter pares*, he can never achieve the legitimacy that could impart autonomy, security, and lasting power; indeed, the more power he accumulates in temporary triumphs, the less legitimate he becomes, and the more in need of Brahminical support. Vena's ill-fated attempt at autonomy is witness to this conceptual scheme. In part, the king's very centrality is to blame for his predicament; the depth of his involvement ties his hands. Whatever his personal difficulties—and they are usually severe—at no point is the king safely beyond the sorrows of his subjects. In effect, he is one with them, but far more constrained than any other member of the kingdom by the accumulated burden of their ills and their demands.

Kampaṉ, as we have seen, links the centrality of kingship with the king's control over unruly cosmic forces. In spatial terms, the king is marked out as the center—heaven and earth are compressed into his

---

toe: Roghair (1982), p. 273. On "lameness" in the family of the sun, see Shulman (1978b), pp. 121-23.

[114] And the "eunuch" Arjuna: below, V.6.

[115] *Manusmṛti* 1.81-82.

[116] The major exception to this composite portrait is Rāma—admittedly born in an earlier age—whose major flaw seems to be his perfection.

[117] See the discussion in V.1-4.

throne room—even as he embodies the principle of separation and movement between the cosmic realms: as archetypal sacrificer, the king maintains the cosmic processes in their proper courses. Pṛthu levels the earth, the site of the sacrifice, the main arena of the cosmic dramas played out between heaven and the nether world (and in which man is the main actor).[118] Each king seated upon his throne is an incarnation of Indra and an embodied memory of the *skambha*, the cosmic pillar that holds the heavens high above the earth.[119] Although these boundaries can become blurred, as we shall see, in principle the king is put into a position of maximum vulnerability. The texts never tire of demonstrating this point: pitted against the cosmos in this fashion, solely responsible for the perfection of the center and the precise separation of spheres, the king is inevitably subject to recurring crises. His position is brittle, fragile, ludicrously dangerous; at any moment the whole madly whirling machine, with its powerful, antithetical currents racing through intersecting channels, may collapse and crush him. One is reminded of a Buddhist tale about the great emperor Kaniṣka: this king is said to have been reborn as a fish with a thousand heads; because of his evil actions during his reign, a wheel of knives continually cut off these heads. "Thus in each of his successive rebirths he was constantly decapitated, the wheel continued to turn, and his heads filled the vast ocean."[120] As so often in Indian stories, the punishment is but an intensification of the situation that leads to the initial crime: Kaniṣka's fate as a fish merely makes more explicit the premises of his kingship. The murderous wheel (*cakra*) of the *cakravartin*, the "roller of the wheel," continues to revolve after his death—and to bring home his need to die over and over for his deeds. It is not at all surprising that the *cakravartin* turns up as a fish: the "law of the fish" (*matsyanyāya*, the Hindu equivalent of our "dog eat dog") is the standard Indian metaphor for anarchy. Often this metaphor is cited to exemplify the horrors of a society without a king; but even a universal emperor (and a renowned patron of the Buddhist *dharma* at that) is not, it would appear, so far removed from this same "law."

Thus we may note a correlation between the realistic weakness of the Indian king and his symbolic centrality. He is the pivot of the whole system, but he lacks true power; normally, he is utterly dependent upon others. Heinrich Zimmer once pointed out another

[118] See Biardeau and Malamoud (1976).

[119] On the *skambha*, see Ogibenin (1973) and Shulman (1979a); for the link with the throne, see Auboyer (1949).

[120] Rosenfield (1967), p. 39.

characteristic symbolic expression of this correlation in the Indian game of *caturaṅga*, the forerunner of chess: like the kings familiar to us from the texts, the king of the Indian chessboard is endowed with enormous symbolic significance but virtually no scope for real action. He needs a good deal of luck (of the dice) as well as the help and protection of his ally; in the end, he is perhaps most closely akin to the pawn.[121]

In short, the dharmic icon issues into the dilemmas of kingship. The Indian obfuscation of reality is paper-thin: again and again the texts show us the king's struggles rather than his successes, his relations not merely with *dharma* but with what might be called the adharmic side of that *dharma*. Crippled, impotent, burdened with sacrificial residues, identified with the community and uniquely responsible for its evils, the king must weigh his options. Several of these have become apparent in the stories we have studied: 1) he can go on as before, hoping always for the best, but in perpetual danger of slipping fatally (the Pāṇṭiyaṉ); 2) he can seek to arrogate greater power than he deserves—and than he is likely to retain (Vena); 3) he can attempt to share the burden, or, more exactly, to pass it on to someone else, preferably the Brahmin (Pṛthu's ideal solution)—but this is problematic for the Brahmin; 4) he can renounce the kingdom (as Āputtiraṉ longs to do)—but this is unacceptable for the kingdom; 5) finally—a solution we have not yet discussed, but one that will occupy us at length below—he can watch, and take part in, the momentary dissolution of the entire edifice and, even more strikingly, of his own carefully constructed, iconic self.

[121] Zimmer (1937). To some extent, this is, of course, still apparent in today's chess. Cf. the related case of *cenne* (mancala): Claus (1980). The South Indian king's weakness and vulnerability are also cogently expressed in the allegorical medical drama *Jīvānanda* of Ānandarāyamakhī (Tanjore, 17th century): here the king Jīva is, as in Sāṃkhya, wholly inactive, dependent upon his minister Vijñānaśarman. See the summary by Zimmer (1948), pp. 64-68.

· III ·

Brahmin Gatekeepers

> But from this delightful heresy
> we need not be delivered.
> We fall into it again
> each time we fall in love.[1]

1. The Burden of *Saṃskāra*

The iconic persona of the king, with all its dynamic tensions, its tendency to unfold into self-mockery and antithesis, has no true counterpart in the symbolic depiction of the king's closest associate, the Brahmin. It is a commonplace in the *dharma* literature that king and Brahmin are indissolubly linked—"married," according to the outstanding metaphoric usage of the texts.[2] Together, these two figures appear to delimit the field of politics; they comprise the minimal basis for "statehood" in classical theory, and this theory clearly recognizes their mutual dependence: there are no Kṣatriyas without Brahmins, and vice versa.[3] Their properly ordered relationship should, as many have claimed, serve as the major paradigm and guarantee of the proper workings of Hindu society as a whole.

And yet it does not, except in the thinnest and most idealized of social visions; and Hindu theorists were the first to recognize this painful fact, however they may have striven, against all odds, to reverse it. Far from sustaining one another and thereby society at large, the king and Brahmin more usually collide, thereby undermin-

[1] Mandelstam (1916), n. 63.

[2] Coomaraswamy (1942); Heesterman (1957), pp. 193-95, 226-27; Trautmann (1981), pp. 347-48.

[3] A number of early myths explore this proposition: thus Aurva's tale recounts a Kṣatriya attempt to do away with Brahmins; Paraśurāma reveals the reverse. See discussion below, section 3.

ing any enduring stability in the political realm, or in their own roles. Indeed, it is in the very nature of these roles, or perhaps of the political order that defines them, to impel their actors into such unending confrontations. If this is a marriage, then it would seem to fit the ancient Tamil conception of the married state (the stage of love proper to the *marutam* agricultural tract) as rife with conflict, quarrels (*ūṭal*), and persistent betrayal.

In short, South Indian Hindu polity is built not upon a reasonable, "rationalized" balance between king and Brahmin but upon the shifting ground of Brahmin and royal dilemmas. This chapter explores the Brahmin's side of this problematic relation. The Brahmin's roles are essential to the syntax of South Indian kingship: wherever the king turns, he encounters another Brahmin mirror reflecting back his image. This mirroring process has its own internal dynamism, and the images vary from caricature to idealistic criticism to faithful reproduction and imitation. The Brahmin acts out his own versions of the royal dramas, even as he seeks to transcend them. In the following pages we shall observe something of his potential range of transformation.

Let us return to the opening sentence of this chapter: in what sense does the Brahmin lack an "iconic" definition? After all, an idealized image of the best or "most real" Brahmin does exist in the classical Sanskrit texts: this best of Brahmins is, no doubt, closely tied to the renunciatory ideals of *sannyāsa* and *mokṣa*, which he in effect symbolizes by his emotional detachment, his purity, and his complete control over such human drives as sexuality and anger.[4] He is, in a word, *śānta*—literally, "extinguished," hence free from passion, at peace. Yet the *śānta* Brahmin is not a true icon, capable of dissolving into its own implicit realities—as in the case of the king—but rather one quite realistic half of a wholly divided symbolic image. The king's anti-iconic stances are something of a surprise, to be discovered each time anew, as if by drawing back a veil; the Brahmin's internal conflict is a basic feature of his identity, a feature recognized, albeit somewhat

[4] This sentence already puts me into conflict with Dumont, who distinguishes the Brahminical value of *purity* from the renunciatory complex of values: (1972), *passim* (see especially pp. 114-18). My understanding of the Brahmin role is closer to that of Heesterman's (see his articles of 1964 and 1967). See also Parry's illuminating study of the Benares funeral priests (1980). Velcheru Narayana Rao (private communication) distinguishes between two types of Brahmins in medieval Andhra—the active ritual-priest working within the jajmāni framework of interdependence, and the detached reciter of sacred texts. This empirical distinction appears to reflect the Brahmin's classic *inner* division, which will be traced below.

reluctantly, by the texts. It is this internal dialectic which imparts so poignant, and so obsessive, a character to the never-ending attempt in our sources to find, enshrine, and immobilize the "true" Brahmin.[5]

This Brahmin dialectic emerges with great clarity from the Brahmin's outstanding role as guardian and ritual enactor of the processes of *saṃskāra*. This richly evocative word connotes, among other things, the giving of form, the realization of an innate potential for achieving form, a process of definition and perfection.[6] The same root gives us *saṃskṛta*, the native term for Sanskrit—language in its paradigmatic, most perfect form. Sanskrit is the Brahmin's inheritance and trust; it epitomizes with its classical, theoretically unchanging structure the Brahminical drive toward refining, imposing limits, defining the margins of *all* structured experience.[7] This drive affects Hindu society as a whole in various spheres (most obviously, in cult and ritual, but also in politics, in the arts, in intellectual life). The Brahmin projects *saṃskāra* onto whatever he touches. He can never leave things alone, always refuses to let nature take its (usually degenerative) course; rather, he insists on fashioning himself, and his society, in the images sanctified by tradition. He enables, or more often compels, proper forms to emerge out of their disorderly, raw reality. He can effect this partly by virtue of his knowledge—the technical mastery, with or without understanding, with which he has been charged—and partly by virtue of his own symbolic identification with the ideals of perfection, demarcation, and self-containment: at the highest point in his society, he is, or ought to be, the most chastely fashioned of all vessels, a living landmark of purity, excellence, and limpid definition.

Yet *saṃskāra* has other sides to it: the processes of separation, categorization, and the imposition of pure limits are not without their price. Indeed, this price is a high one, both for the Brahmin worker of *saṃskāra* and for the society informed by his values. To begin with, *saṃskāra* requires a problematic detachment from the given world: the boundaries the Brahmin is eager to impose constitute a rarefied microcosm within which reality, and its Brahmin purveyors, are theoretically encapsulated. "Theoretically" because, seen from the outside, the relation of microcosm to macrocosm, of samskaric metonym to the chaotic, unstructured, everyday world, is largely fictive (like the

[5] See discussion by Heesterman (1964).

[6] See Ramanujan's afterword to his translation of Anantha Murthy's novel (1976).

[7] That Sanskrit did, of course, continue to undergo profound changes, even after it ceased to be an everyday spoken language, was not always recognized by the tradition. For a fascinating example, see Sandahl-Forgue (1977).

relation of Veda to *dharma*).[8] The Brahmin constructs his perfect forms, his controlled, rigidly ordered sphere, in an internalized atmosphere of frustrating isolation. Given the basic drive toward *saṃskāra*, the frustration can only exhaust itself in ever more obsessive attempts to maintain the fiction, to wring perfection out of a recalcitrant world, or—most dangerous of all—to realize the elusive link between microcosm and macrocosm in the most literal, concrete way. *Saṃskāra* is a war against the world, a war the Brahmin is doomed to lose; individual battles give rise to tragic figures such as Paraśurāma, to be studied below. But even in its own terms, seen from within, the samskaric microcosm is riddled with difficulty. Its very detachment works against it: as the Brahminical tradition itself recognizes, even perfect boundaries become brittle, while the worlds they contain can slowly die. Like other South Indians, the Brahmin knows a hidden ideal of "melting," becoming soft, fluid, subtle, and thus flowing past or through normal boundaries and defined forms.[9] We could state this differently by relating it to the normal tensions of symbolism: *saṃskāra*, in structuring the boundaries of experience through the momentary encapsulation of an orderly, metonymic realm, simultaneously fractures and veils the subtle wholeness that transcends the symbol. The metonym both embodies and divides the whole; like other symbols, it always points beyond itself. The Brahmin stands on its edges, looking past it, but also through it, toward an absolute, unshattered, nonsymbolic dimension of oneness. Committed to preserving samskaric form—despite the cleavage that it, too, must bring to the world—he becomes divided in himself; part of him will always pursue the process of *saṃskāra* to the end, while another part rebels against its limitations and seeks to transcend it. Having detached himself from crude, polluting reality, the Brahmin finds himself now doubly engaged—with the "real" world, which continues, inevitably, to attack and invade his isolated microcosm, and with the latter's own enduring tensions and partiality.

There is irony here: beginning as a kind of nostalgia for lost wholeness, *saṃskāra* becomes a continuous struggle between the Brahmin and the world, and ends by dividing him from within. But the irony is still more bitter. For the tradition tells us, as we shall see, that the very act of withdrawing from the world—the Brahmin's desperate *nivṛtti*—is precisely what fuels the creative, sacrificial process of *pravṛtti*. The former ultimately gives birth to the latter. Just as Rudra-

[8] See Heesterman (1978a).

[9] Egnor (1978), pp. 19-22.

Śiva in the Vedic myth tries to interrupt the Creator's incestuous, world-engendering lust[10]—and thereby causes that lust actually to erupt into a real, externalized world—so the Brahmin's *saṃskāra*, in pitting itself against refractory reality, is seen ultimately to generate *more* life, more power, even, perhaps, more impure violence. *Saṃskára*, in short, remains a kind of sacrifice, however refined and remote from other, less controlled rites.

As such, it proceeds in different patterns. Most often, one senses an attempt to arrest the degenerative flow of time and chaotic experience: samskaric ritual may freeze time and form into a pristine, deathless permanence—or, at least, it may create the illusion of having done so. Another, contrasting path is to open up the structured realm of existing forms (*sát*) to homeopathic doses of disorder (*ásat*): this, in effect, is what happens in the Brahminical sacrifice, where the boundaries are deliberately breached by their guardians under the laboratory conditions of the highly controlled and structured ritual. Both cases, we may note, have a violent aspect. Moreover, the processes of *saṃskāra* leave the Brahmin to deal not with a whole, undivided world but with fragments or, to use the more common metaphor, remnants of such a world—he is himself, in fact, just such a remnant, embedded in a remnantlike domain set off from the larger, impure sphere he has rejected, which is itself yet another residue. In this sense, the Brahmin is surprisingly like his polar opposite, the Untouchable—as many traditions, stories, and rituals tell us.[11] The Brahmin serves the world, purifies it, deals with the remains of sacrificial violence and with the impurity bound up with handling disorderly, menacing power; the resulting closeness to the Untouchable is particularly evident whenever the Brahmin fulfils his classic priestly roles, either as servant to a ruler or as temple priest.[12] The Brahmin's advantage lies

[10] *Ait. Brāh.* 3.33-34; see Kramrisch (1981), pp. 3-26.

[11] See, for example, Whitehead, pp. 117-19; Beck (1978a), p. 58; Hart (1975), p. 123; Tripathi (1978), pp. 224-25; V. Das, p. 50. Dumont (1972), pp. 92-98, has spoken here of a structural opposition which makes the two categories inseparable; but the relation appears to be based less on opposition than on hidden affinity. And see Marriott, pp. 128-29, addressing the phenomenon in terms of related strategies of "asymmetrical exchange."

[12] The latter is contemptuously referred to by the texts as *devalaka*, "hireling of a god." *MBh* 12.77.8 equates the Brahmin priest who performs worship for others, for a fee, with the Caṇḍāla outcaste. The degraded category of Brahmin temple priests (*ādiśaivas, civācāriyar*) in South Indian temples today bears witness to this viewpoint; see the analysis by Appadurai (1983), and also Trautmann (1981), pp. 280-82, on the Brahmin's relation to his gifts. V. Narayana Rao attests to the fact that the sight of a Brahmin priest is considered inauspicious in Andhra villages.

only in the dimension of transcendence with which he is also linked—transcendence of the sacrifice, of the symbol, of all that is limited and fractured, and, in the end, of *saṃskāra* itself.

Situated on the boundary of the symbol, looking beyond it, the Brahmin marks the cultural center. It is not enough to call him simply "liminal,"[13] though he is surely that as well; his normal, divided role is not truly anomalous, nor is his position at the boundary interstitial, removing him from other defined domains. Rather, he has the ambiguity of a center that is open to both sides—to the limited order, and to its disorderly transcendence—and which, indeed, combines both sides in a dynamic, fluctuating, self-transforming bond.[14] The Brahmin's *saṃskāra*, with its inherent tensions, creates and nourishes the South Indian cultural core.

2. The Subversive Ideal: The Tripura Demons and the Buddha

The inner workings of the Brahmin's double identity, in its complex relation to the social order as a whole, become clear through parallels and contrasts with analogous types. I wish to present an extreme example and to suggest, for the sake of the argument, a somewhat far-reaching analogy, whose contrastive features can be analyzed as well. The example, a medieval South Indian version of the classical *tripura-saṃhāra* myth, touches upon one of the major roles conventionally attributed to Brahminism: the definition and preservation of Hindu "orthodox" ideology.[15] I hope to show how even on this rather theoretical plane of consciously articulated ideals, Brahmin thinking has a dynamic, open-ended, unresolved quality. But it is not only a question of abstract theorizing, by any means: the issue of "orthodoxy," or of the self-definition of the Hindu community, has a vital historical reality behind it in South India, where the medieval Hindu cultural synthesis emerged in the course of a long struggle with various "heretical" groups, both within the Hindu community (for example, iconoclastic Siddhas discussed below) and outside it (Buddhists and

[13] V. Das (1977), pp. 130-31.

[14] This formulation, which will be expanded in the following pages, has been influenced by Ohnuki-Tierney's analysis of anomaly (1981, pp. 119-29) and by Egnor's discussion of the "middle" (1978, pp. 106-13). See also Shulman (1980c), pp. 126-27.

[15] See Staal (1959) on this term, always problematic for Hinduism. I have retained the word "orthodox" in referring to the ideological structure of the Brahmin tradition in its confrontations with dissenting groups.

Jains). The eventual Hindu triumph over the major heretical groups in this region is usually seen in connection with the rise and crystallization of the *bhakti* movements there—and the problematic nature of the *bhakti* ideal is another focus of the Tripura myth.

This myth, borrowed from classical Sanskrit sources,[16] underwent a long process of development in South Indian Tamil and Sanskrit texts, and in the ritual traditions of South Indian shrines.[17] Śiva's destruction of the demons' Triple City is seen as one of the eight heroic feats accomplished by that god in the Tamil land—in this case, at the famous shrine of Tiruvatikai (South Arcot District).[18] This is not the place to chart the evolution of the Tripura myth in South India; suffice it to say that the Tamil myths follow the lead of the classical Sanskrit *purāṇas* in combining the destruction of the Triple City with the story of Viṣṇu's avatar as the Buddha.[19] According to the Sanskrit *purāṇas*, Viṣṇu corrupts the Tripura demons—who are usually said to be imbued with power derived from asceticism, or from sacrifices, or in later texts from *bhakti*—by means of heretical doctrines described as Buddhist (the texts in fact generally offer a synoptic blend of heresies culled secondhand from Buddhist, Jain, Materialist, and other sources); once they have been corrupted, the demons can easily be killed by the gods; but the heresy first taught by Viṣṇu in heaven frequently survives the slaughter of his demon-converts in order to spill over on to the earth—and thus the presence in India of living, all-too-human heretics is explained.[20] As O'Flaherty has shown, there is nothing syncretistic about these myths of the Buddha avatar, much modern scholarly interpretation to the contrary notwithstanding. Rather, Viṣṇu's propagation of Buddhism is simply part of the long and varied series of deceitful acts perpetrated by the gods (often, indeed, by the tricksterlike Viṣṇu, the master of *māyā*) on their demon or human enemies. Yet by the time the myth appears in a full-fledged Southern version—such as that of the Sanskrit *Śivarahasyakhaṇḍa*, summarized below[21]—Viṣṇu's role has become pro-

[16] See *MBh* 8.24; *Śivapurāṇa* 2.5.1-12; *Liṅgapurāṇa* 1.71-72; *Matsyapurāṇa* 125-40, 187-88.

[17] Reiniche (1979), pp. 104-11, discusses the adaptation of this myth to a Tirunĕlveli temple festival. The antiheretical thrust of the myth may have made it a favorite of the Cholas: see discussion below, VIII, of its depiction in the famous mural at the Bṛhadīśvara temple, Tanjore.

[18] On the eight *vīraṭṭāṇam*, see Shulman (1980b), pp. 81-82.

[19] On the history of the myth in its classical Sanskrit versions, see O'Flaherty (1976), pp. 180-89.

[20] *Śivapurāṇa* 2.5.1-12.

[21] *Śivarahasyakhaṇḍa* (published as *Śrīskāndamahāpurāṇa*) 7.70.10-102, 7.71.1-109,

foundly problematic, and it is no longer a simple matter to corrupt the ideals of one's enemies:

> The lords of the demons, Vidyunmālin, Tarakākṣa, and Kamalākṣa, won from Brahmā three castles, of iron, silver, and gold, on earth, in heaven, and in the middle region between them. They also asked for eternal life, but Brahmā was unable to grant this, being mortal himself like all the gods except Śiva. They were, however, granted their wish that they could be destroyed only by a single arrow after a thousand years, when the three cities came together. Maya, the architect who had built the cities, advised these demons to worship Śiva so as not to come to harm. They followed this advice, and each received a *liṅga* from the god.
>
> The gods were distressed by these demons, who flew everywhere in their cities. They wished to kill the demons, but Viṣṇu said, "They are devoted to Śiva, and their wives are chaste; no one can kill them." The gods replied, "They are really without *bhakti*. They merely perform worship of Śiva because of Maya's advice, and Śiva has no love for such a service." Viṣṇu recalled the boon they had won from Brahmā; nevertheless, the gods proceeded to make a sacrifice from which spirits (Bhūtas) emerged, and the gods sent them to kill the demons. When the Bhūtas saw that the demons were covered with sacred ash and *rudrākṣa*, they fled to a garden where they feasted on fruits, like a pack of monkeys. The demons hit them with clods of earth and sticks and, by the order of Śiva, the Bhūtas died. In revenge for being attacked, the demons plundered the worlds of the gods, and the gods took refuge in a cave on Mount Meru.
>
> Then the gods went to Kailāsa to see Śiva, but the doorkeepers said it was not the proper time and refused to let them in. The gods raised their voices and cried, "Śiva! Maheśāna!" Angered at this racket, the doorkeepers beat the gods with sticks, and the gods fled. "How are we to address Śiva?" they asked Viṣṇu, at a safe distance. "We were beaten because we cried so loudly," he said; "the doorkeepers could not bear the noise." "True, true," they said, rebuking one another and calling, "Hush! Hush!" After

7.72.1-34. It is difficult to suggest a date for this text; Zvelebil has argued that it is, perhaps, a late spinoff of the Tamil *Kantapurāṇam* of Kacciyappacivācāriyar (see his forthcoming study of Murukaṉ). My own conclusion is different (1980b), p. 360 n. 17, but the issue remains undecided.

some deliberation, they decided to send Viṣṇu to corrupt the demons with his *māyā*.

Viṣṇu became Buddha and Nārada became his disciple, and they deluded the demons with a *māyāśāstra* and sweet words and destroyed the chastity of their wives by gifts of ornaments and jewels. "Who is this man?" the demons asked Nārada. "He comes from the end of the world, and whoever becomes his disciple achieves all desires," the sage replied. Viṣṇu created for them clothes, ornaments, money, and women, and soon all were clamoring to be his disciples. "I am Buddha. You must worship me. There is no use in worshiping Śiva," said Viṣṇu, so all of them abandoned Śiva. Moreover, their wives were deluded and constantly felt love for men other than their husbands. Only three demons—Paramayogin, Śīlapara, and Viraktayogin—remained steadfast in their devotion to Śiva.

Then, leaving a Buddha from part of himself, Viṣṇu left with Nārada. They wished to climb Kailāsa to see Śiva, but evildoers are unable even to approach that mountain, and Viṣṇu and Nārada could not climb it. Viṣṇu at once realized that this was because he had led creatures away from the worship of Śiva. He meditated on Śiva, and the latter appeared to him and said, "Alas, you two are fools; you led astray my devotees for the sake of the gods' affair. Now go to Lake Mānasa and complete that affair."

Viṣṇu plunged into the lake and performed *tapas* surrounded by the gods. The gods performed the Pāśupata vow, and Śiva was pleased and agreed to do battle against the demons. He looked at Devī and smiled, and from his eyes fire darted forth to burn the three cities. In the wake of the fire, Śiva sent from the bow which was Mount Meru and the bowstring which was the serpent Vāsuki an arrow composed of the bodies of the gods, with Viṣṇu as its tip. The demons died, with the exception of the three steadfast devotees, who hid in the sea and meditated on Śiva. "Look what would have happened to us if we had been deluded by that Buddhist teacher," they said; and Śiva made them his doorkeepers on Kailāsa. The gods concluded: one must have no truck with heretics (*pāṣaṇḍasaraṇiṃ gatāḥ*), even if they are very fond of *dharma* (*api dharmaratā bhṛśam*).

The myth begins by stating a practical difficulty which is, in itself, wholly conventional in puranic depictions of the world: the gods' enemies, the demons, are powerful and must somehow be defeated, against all odds. It is important to note that the gods—who are, by definition, that party whose victory man desires—have no apparent moral superiority over their rivals. Indeed, the reverse is often true, as in our present example. And this is precisely where our South Indian text expands upon the difficulty that is latent in earlier, classical versions, by imparting a powerful moral dimension to its reading of the story. Here the demons' strength derives from their adherence to those very values that the tradition itself regards as supreme, whereas the gods—the good guys—fail signally in respect to these same ideals. In itself, this is nothing new; the novelty lies in the great seriousness with which the South Indian authors view this situation, and in the implications it selects from the story's ending.

Our text subsumes its supreme values under the single rubric of devotion to Śiva; other Tamil versions of the myth are somewhat more specific (the demons worship the *liṅga*, wear Śaiva emblems, are proficient in the Āgamas, enforce a strict regime of worship and *tapas*).[22] Above all it is stressed that *bhakti* must be based upon an inner reality of feeling rather than upon utilitarian self-interest. Intention counts more than bare action;[23] our text has a clear aversion to anything that smacks of automatic, magical effects, so much so that at some points it reads almost as a parody of mechanistic conceptions of the outer trappings of devotion. Thus the gods who call out the names of Śiva—an act said in many *bhakti* texts to bring instant salvation—achieve at first no more than a beating at the hands of Śiva's gatekeepers. Their fate is thus little better than that of the Bhūtas-turned-monkeys, who at least had the sense not to attack the Śaiva demon-*bhaktas*. The sincerity of the latter is impugned by the gods, and this jaundiced viewpoint appears, in the end, to be borne out—for the demons, all but three, lose their faith, whereas the gods manage to win Śiva over by performing a vow. Given the whole history of this conflict, Śiva's attitude toward his importunate divine adherents is presumably closer to weary resignation and repugnance than to enthusiastic acceptance.

Still, it is the original identification of the demons with the devotional ideal that raises fundamental questions. We need not be surprised that a major ideal belongs with the demons and must be taken away from them by trickery and violence; this is a recurrent pattern in Hindu myth. Recall the deception, by Trivikrama-Viṣṇu, of the exemplary

[22] *Kāñcippurāṇam* 30.2-42; *Tiruvatikai talamāṉmiyamum tevāra patikaṅkaḷum* of Ka. Rā. Civacitamparam Mutaliyār, 6-7 (pp. 17-27).

[23] Ironically, this attitude may itself be a Buddhist legacy to South Indian Hinduism.

demon-king Bali; or the demons' appropriation of the Veda[24] and the *amṛta*,[25] and the consequent necessity for the gods' intervention (again, in both cases, with the help of Viṣṇu). In fact, this pattern goes even deeper, as we shall see in a moment. In the present instance, the alignment of moral forces has two important consequences. First, the demons' challenge to order, or to the proper workings of *dharma*, has a partly idealistic twist, despite the fact that their grasp of the ideal is somewhat hollow. The inhabitants of the three cities are *bhaktas*, albeit perfunctory *bhaktas*; as a group, they have as much access to the rewards of devotion as anyone else—yet they must *not* be saved. This may be seen as one of the central problems posed by the text; certainly, it is the problem that occupies the gods from the beginning. The demons' violation of the dharmic order is supported by a higher logic; as Reiniche has remarked, discussing the classical versions of this myth in connection with a village festival that partially enacts it: "How can this religion affirm the necessity of acting in conformity with the socio-cosmic rules of *dharma* and at the same time permit these rules to be transcended by devotion alone?"[26] The association of the demons with faith and its rewards places the gods in the position of defenders of dharmic norms; the old agonistic pattern of rivalry between these groups has been taken over to express the opposition between order itself and a universalistic ideal.

Second, this challenge is clearly met—by betraying the ideal. Viṣṇu corrupts the gods' enemies and is forced to expiate this "crime." It is true that the text tries to distinguish sharply between the roles of Viṣṇu and Śiva; the former performs the evil deed, while the latter remains aloof. In this, as in other stories, Viṣṇu serves as Śiva's scapegoat: he saves Śiva from embarrassment by leading the devoted demons astray, thus rendering them vulnerable, both morally and in terms of cold *Realpolitik*, to the attack that must come if cosmic order is to be restored. Śiva, safely remote and not implicated in the evil acts of his disciples, can even call Viṣṇu a fool for having served the gods' interests. But what was Viṣṇu's choice? Should he have withdrawn from the cosmic scene in order to pursue the absolute ideals of unwavering devotion and untainted purity of heart and deed? How serious is this rebuke of Śiva's? Note that he immediately orders Viṣṇu to complete the process he has begun. If the price of corrupting the

[24] *MBh* 12.335.21-65 (Madhu and Kaiṭabha steal the Vedas); *Bhāgavatapurāṇa* 8.24.7-57 (the demon Hayagrīva does the same).

[25] At the time of the churning of the ocean: *MBh* 1.15-17. In the *Brāhmaṇa* texts, the demons are constantly attempting to steal the sacrifice.

[26] Reiniche (1979), p. 106.

demons must be paid, it is certainly not Viṣṇu alone who pays it. Rather, we witness the triumph of the principle of universal yet relativistic order over the troublesome ideal. This would seem to be the purport of the rather puzzling moral pronounced at the end by the gods: heretics, even righteous, dharmic heretics—those, that is to say, who have put into practice the supposedly all-embracing vision of *bhakti*—cannot be allowed to get away with their quasi-utopian design.

Not that the ideal is simply defeated or pushed aside. After all, an ideal solution remains possible for the three devoted demons who resist the temptations of apostasy: they survive as the gatekeepers of Śiva's home on Kailāsa. For our purposes, this is one of the most intriguing elements of the myth, for it establishes a similarity between these demon paragons and the Brahmins. Both the Brahmins and the pious demons are gatekeeper figures holding fast to an absolute ideal attacked by a social order whose limits they demarcate. Both are paradoxical, boundary figures; both have a vision of wholeness and freedom. If we push the analogy to its logical conclusion, we might say: like the pious demon, the Brahmin, in his commitment to transcendent ideals, represents an implicit threat to the social order he delimits. Of course, the similarity can easily be blurred by "bracketing out" the question of *bhakti*'s moral power, or by stressing the historical role of the *bhakti* movements in sustaining, rather than undermining, social order (and, in fact, the same could be said of Brahminism's historical contribution).[27] But this is precisely what our text refuses to allow; it prefers to confront the problem head-on, to work out the implications of proclaiming an openly subversive ideal. It thus quite naturally underlines the fact that a major value of the tradition is in the hands of a gatekeeper figure, an outsider of sorts. And in this respect, our story is in line with a structural component of the South Indian world view—an assertion, proceeding from the very foundations of this culture's symbolic ordering of the universe, that truth exceeds the cultural limits and forms and is thus vested with those who stand at, or just beyond, the boundary, in various groups, in varying degrees of proximity to this border: groups such as Brahmins, *sannyāsins*, sages (on the one hand), and demons, Untouchables, prostitutes, and bandits (on the other).

The similarities are there: the tradition does not shrink from expressing them, playing with them, seeing how far they can be taken. Thus prominent demons become the natural recipients of a divine

[27] See Shulman (1978).

revelation, whereas bandits become both kings and gods.[28] Transformations within, and between, the categories are legion. Yet the texts also point the way to vital distinctions. The symbolic analogies are qualified by cognitive differentiations. In the present case, Brahmins and pious demons can still be distinguished in crucial ways: for one thing, the demons' ideal is *exclusively* linked with their devotion, whereas the Brahminical ideals have a wider range. More important still is the difference in attitudes toward the equivocal bounds and limits. The demon devotees have inherited only the revolutionary side of the *saṃskāra* dialectic, without the Brahminical obsession with demarcation—the heart of *saṃskāra* as a process. The drive to salvation through *bhakti* becomes, in the hands of the demons, an uncompromising assault upon the world, where limitation is the key to order. The Brahmins, for their part, are no less committed to this limited order than to its transcendence. A threefold process is at work in the orthodox view: first, truth is vouchsafed to the outside, the other, the transcendent (hence the rapprochement between the Brahmin and the asuric claim to wholeness); second, the outside is somehow brought in, made central, assimilated to the inner life of the limited order (through ritual, through *saṃskāra*, by a symbolic opening to the outer forces); third, self-limitation becomes the hallmark of the orthodox community, which prefers the tension of living within borders and always looking beyond them to the resolution of this tension in uncompromising revolt against order. Demons and heretics can reject compromise and seek the immediate, unlimited realization of their ideals; the Brahmin, pulled in the same direction, struggles to stay in place, and to keep the world on its same, self-limiting, self-defeating course.

The profundity of this tension, and its unresolved character, will become evident when we study the stories of Paraśurāma and Aśvatthāman, two supposedly anomalous Brahmins, both of them unable to keep these conflicting drives in suspended opposition. Note that the demons of the Tripura myth are *not* anomalous, for all their piety—not only is demonic *adharma* accorded its own proper place within the Hindu order;[29] it is also wholly appropriate that the pious demons be worshipers of the richly ambiguous deity Śiva, and that as such they continue to disturb that order from within. Again like the Brahmin, the demons' association with the outer limits does not

[28] See Chapter VII, below.

[29] Reiniche (1979), p. 107, argues that this is one of the basic lessons of the Tripura myth.

make them truly liminal. They are a category in their own right, however contradictory their role may seem: they are there to be excluded, a necessary challenge to be overruled.

Very similar is the function of Viṣṇu, the divine corrupter, in this version of the Tripura myth. Here Viṣṇu—a false heretic—recalls the original Nāstika of the preclassical sacrificial ritual, who "denies" (his opponent's sacrifice) so that the agonistic contests can go on.[30] For much the same reason—in order that the cosmic order, based as it is on conflict and violence, can continue to exist—Viṣṇu teaches heresy to the pious demons. The struggles of the gods and demons must never reach a final resolution if the world is to survive, for it is created and maintained through a dialectical alternation, a positive movement of *pravṛtti* and a negative, backward pull of *nivṛtti*; the gods and demons gravitate to opposite poles of this process, and neither side can opt out, not even in the name of basic values of the tradition. If these values tend to be articulated in the "negative" idiom of *nivṛtti*—that is, a "demonic" universalism, or a universal detachment and salvation, as seems to be professed by the pious Tripura demons—then the tradition must somehow compromise itself and its goals. The *nāstika* preacher comes from within, in order to save the dharmic order by defeating enemies who are also initially within its range, inasmuch as they uphold the traditional ideals of freedom. One is thus left with an "ordered" center that is, in principle, wholly ambiguous: it affirms a subversive ideal profoundly unsettling in its implications even as it consciously attempts to limit the immediate effects of this ideal, and thereby betrays it. A dynamic tension remains active within the very core of South Indian Hindu culture. It is noteworthy that in the Tripura myth it is this tension which is, in effect, the underlying source of heresy, seen as a divine invention aimed at restoring a cosmic order threatened by a universal salvation. This formulation of the myth is, in fact, a direct outgrowth of historical forms of dissent in medieval South India.

This is not the place to discuss at length the phenomenon of dissent in South Indian Hinduism. Let us simply note, in passing, that groups such as the iconoclastic Tamil Siddhas (*cittar*), the radical anti-Brahmin rebels such as the famous, pseudonymous "Kapilar"[31] or the Telugu poet Vemana, and the mystical visionaries who were later to shape the interface of *bhakti* Hinduism and Tamil Islam,[32] tended to identify

[30] Heesterman (1968-1969); see below, IV.2 at nn. 47-49.

[31] Author of a famous anti-Brahmin *akaval*. For the history of the Tamil Siddhas, see Zvelebil (1973); Kailasapathy (1969), pp. 183-212; Buck (1974 and 1976).

[32] See Shulman (1984a).

themselves almost exclusively with the idealistic, antinomian side of the Brahmin's own inheritance. They speak of inner illumination, the conquest of desire and of egoism, and the transcendence of form (texts, temples, rituals); they attack that part of the samskaric process which is committed to creating, or recreating, the symbolic boundaries of a proper order endowed with all its consequent tensions. But in attacking the Brahmin on this score, the dissidents inevitably distort his vision into a false stillness. The Brahmin's investment in *saṃskāra* exists only in symbiosis with his "disorderly" potential for transcendence: thus the temple, for example, is a *tīrtha*, at once a metonymic expression of divinity captured in space and a point of transition (literally a "ford" or "crossing place") toward a still uncaptured wholeness.[33] The entire society built around the Brahminical vision is caught up in ceaseless motion and transformation; what the heretic or rebel rejects is not its goals or transcendent ideals but only the maddeningly pliant ambiguity which it brings to those ideals, and with which it structures their relation to the partial, fragmented reality of the everyday social order.

Fragmentation and a frustrating partiality: these are the enduring features of mundane reality as seen by what we might call Brahminical realism. It is a reality simultaneously affirmed and rejected by the Janus-headed Brahmin gatekeeper in his perpetual oscillation between poles. The double movement of *saṃskāra*—the sacrificial imposition of limited forms, and their transcendence—allows the community that adheres to it to outmaneuver the rebels obsessed with only one side of this process. The Brahmin encompasses his rivals not so much by virtue of his association with the encompassing power of the pure whole, the *brahman* that he symbolizes, as through his identification with the two extremes of social vision, the radical realism of the sacrifice (with its attendant pollution and limitation) and the no less radical idealism of release. For their part, his iconoclastic rivals will be forced toward their own ironic compromises and accommodation if they are to survive as a group: thus the revolutionary Vīraśaivas become, in effect, another caste (or group of castes); Tirumūlar, the Tamil Siddhas' most authoritative figure, even achieves the formal status of a Śaiva saint with the incorporation of his *Tirumantiram* in the orthodox Śaiva canon. Having a history effectively denies the iconoclast the residual consistency of the mythic heretic: only the Tripura survivors retain a simple, pristine idealism at Śiva's gate.

To sum up: the Brahmin's relation to his society is a paradoxical

[33] See above, I.1.

one—more complex, and also more flexible, than that of the majority of his rivals; but also marked by unresolved, indeed unresolvable, ambivalence. A living incarnation of the supreme values of renunciation, the Brahmin also remains, as the Upaniṣad tells us,[34] the "womb" of kingship—and of the world. Even in his problematic effort at detachment, he carries the world within him; the creative sacrifice is all too likely to erupt from within his isolated sphere. Indeed, he may even seek such an eventuality, which can at least reconnect him to the everyday order and overcome the fiction of his symbols: thus the microcosm inflicts its violent power on the macrocosm. The remainder of this chapter will be devoted to two prominent Brahmin figures who exemplify, each in his own way, this peculiar relationship.

3. The Brahmin Warrior (1): Paraśurāma, Matricide and Regicide

Nowhere is the explosive potential of the Brahmin's inner conflicts more evident than in the puranic versions of the Paraśurāma story. This myth has a long, complex history dating back to the epic,[35] to which it may, in fact, have been intended to serve as something of a symbolic reference or "key."[36] In the myth's earliest versions, there is no mention of Paraśurāma's divine identity: he is simply the startling, unruly product of a horrifyingly mixed union—for this Brahmin boy's grandmother was the Kṣatriya princess Satyavatī, his mother the Kṣatriya Reṇukā.[37] Brahmin and kingly blood flows in almost even quantities in his veins, and he acts accordingly, in a tragic life guided throughout by conflicting impulses. (We shall ask ourselves to what extent the dread "mixing" of genetic strains is the true source of his troubles.) By the time of the major puranic versions, of course, our hero has become an avatar of Viṣṇu; in this guise he appears in the two South Indian texts we shall consider here—the Vaiṣṇava Sanskrit version of the *Bhāgavatapurāṇa*, and a later Tamil rendering from a local shrine.

A disingenuous note of warning before we begin: although the

[34] BĀU 1.4.11.

[35] Studied exhaustively by Gail (1977).

[36] See n. 60 below.

[37] The story is sometimes told in conjunction with the tale of Viśvāmitra, the uncle of Jamadagni (thus Paraśurāma's great-uncle). In many ways, Viśvāmitra, the Kṣatriya striving for Brahminhood, is an inversion of Paraśurāma, the kinglike Brahmin. (This conjunction of the stories occurs in the *Bhāgavata* text discussed below.)

standard interpretations of this tale are "cautionary" ones, as we shall see—that is, Paraśurāma is seen as exemplifying the extreme dangers of anomaly, of deviation from Brahminical ideals—we would do well to remember that "real" Paraśurāmas were not at all uncommon in medieval South India, if we are to judge from the claims made by many dynasties and historical heroes. Indeed, Brahmin warriors seem to have been, in many cases, more the rule than the exception: we may recall the Brahmin generals (*brahmādhirāja*) of the Chola armies.[38] This pattern endured well into Vijayanagar times.[39] The Kadambas, the Gaṅgas, and the Pallavas all developed traditions of Brahminical origins (the latter via the Brahmin warrior Aśvatthāman).[40] Apparently, the image of the Brahmin king or fighter held a fascination for medieval South Indian society. How are we to understand this supposedly "anomalous" situation? Does the widespread popularity of the Paraśurāma myth attest, at least in part, to its affinity with existing historical claims?[41]

Bhāgavatapurāṇa 9.15-16

The *Bhāgavata* has rearranged several important elements of the myth that it inherited from the epic and other puranic accounts. Nevertheless, it offers a remarkably complete version of the four major events of the myth, which may be summarized as follows:

1. *The slaying of Kārtavīrya.* The Haihaya king Arjuna (= Kārtavīryārjuna) received from Dattātreya, who is a portion of Nārāyaṇa(!), a thousand arms and virtually unlimited powers, which—like most of the threatening puranic kings—he abused. He came to the *āśrama* of Jamadagni, Rāma's father, and, after being received there as a guest, coveted the sage's magical cow; he sent his men to seize the cow together with its calf and to take them to his city, Māhiṣmatī. When Rāma heard about this crime, he was enraged, like a serpent crushed

[38] Mahalingam (1967), p. 263.

[39] Thus Kopaṇṇa, the Brahmin minister and commander of Kampana Uḍaiyār II of the Sāṅgama dynasty, was instrumental in the Vijayanagar penetration of the Tamil countryside. See Appadurai (1978), pp. 57-58.

[40] Stein (1978), p. 126; Chakravartinayanar (1975), p. xi; Pillai (1975). Perhaps the locus classicus for the description of Brahmin warriors is *MBh* 1.179-81, where the Pāṇḍavas, disguised as Brahmins, fight the assembled Kṣatriyas for Draupadī. Kalkin, too, will be a Brahmin fighter: see Biardeau (1976), p. 184. One may be reminded of a similar "mixed" type, the Sufi *ghāzis* of the Deccan: Eaton (1978), pp. 19-44.

[41] One strand of the story—the matricide and its consequences—has become the most widespread village myth in South India. See Brubaker (1978); Gail (1977), pp. 112-15. The village variants cannot be considered here.

by someone's foot; taking his terrible axe (*paraśu*), his armor, bow, and arrows, he ran off to Māhiṣmatī in pursuit of the king. When Arjuna beheld this amazing sight—a sage dressed in his deer's skin, radiant as the sun with his long, matted hair, and carrying bow, arrows, and an axe—he sent his army against him; but Rāma, endowed with the power of mind and fire (*mano'nilaujas*), cut them all to pieces, so that the earth turned into a blood-soaked bog. Arjuna himself entered the fray, throwing mountains and trees at his enemy; but Rāma cut off his thousand arms and his head with his sharp axe.

Rāma then returned—with the unfortunate cow—to inform his father and his brothers of his successful act of vengeance. One wonders if he was surprised or disappointed by his father's disapproving response: "O Rāma, Rāma, great-armed one—you have committed an evil deed (*pāpa*) by slaying, for nothing, a king who comprises all the deities. We are Brahmins, my son, revered for our patience (*kṣamā*). . . . The Lord, Hari, is pleased with those who are patient. The slaying of an anointed king is more serious than the killing of a Brahmin. Expiate your evil in a pilgrimage." Thus chastised by his father, Rāma—ever the obedient son—spent a year visiting holy places.

2. *The matricide.* Reṇukā, Rāma's mother, went down to the Ganges, and there she beheld the Gandharva king Citraratha sporting with the celestial nymphs. Feeling a bit attracted herself to Citraratha (*kiṃcic citrarathaspṛhā*, 16.3), she forgot that the time for offering was near. By the time she hastened back, it was too late: her husband had divined all that had happened, and he ordered his sons to slay their wicked mother. Only Rāma obeyed this command: he killed his mother and his disobedient brothers, who refused to carry out Jamadagni's gruesome demand; but he did so knowing his father's powers of *samādhi* and *tapas*, and with the intention of using them to reverse the effects of his action. And, indeed, when his father, highly pleased with Rāma's blind obedience, offered him a boon, Rāma chose to have the dead revived without any memory of their traumatic deaths at his hands. Reṇukā and Rāma's brothers arose as if from sleep.

3. *Jamadagni's death and the battle with Kārtavīrya's sons.* Arjuna's sons knew no peace after their father's death. One day when Rāma had gone into the forest together with his brothers, the vengeful sons invaded the *āśrama* and killed Jamadagni while he was seated in the hut where the sacrificial fire was kept, his mind sunk in meditation on the Lord. Reṇukā, striking herself in agony, called out to her son Rāma. He hurried back to find his father slain, and he became confused by grief, anger, and distress (*tadduḥkharoṣāmarṣārtiśokavegavimohitaḥ*, 16.15). Leaving his father's body with his brothers, he took his axe

and, determined to put an end to *all* Kṣatriyas, ran to Māhiṣmatī, where he created a great mountain with the severed heads of Arjuna's sons. He also created a terrible river flowing with blood; and, after destroying the Kṣatriyas twenty-one times over, he made lakes of blood at Samantapañcaka.

4. *The gift of the earth.* Returning home, Rāma joined his father's head to his body and performed a great sacrifice to the Lord, at which he gave the entire earth to the Brahmin priests (the East to the *hotṛ*, the South to the *brahman*, the West to the *adhvaryu*, the North to the *udgātṛ*, the intermediate points to the others, the center to Kaśyapa, Āryāvarta to the *upadraṣṭṛ*, and other areas to the *sadasyas*). He then performed the *avabhṛtha* bath in the Sarasvatī River and was freed from his remaining evil (*kilbiṣa*). Jamadagni thus received his body back and rose up to heaven as one of the Seven Sages.[42] But lotus-eyed Rāma retired: in the coming Manvantara he will reveal Vedic speech (*vartayiṣyati bṛhat*), but in the meantime he resides on Mount Mahendra, having laid down his arms (*nyastadaṇḍaḥ*) while his thoughts have become tranquil (*praśāntadhīḥ*); Siddhas, Gandharvas, and Cāraṇas sing his tale.

What is the meaning of this gory tale of the avenging Brahmin? How do the various parts relate to one another? The text announces one possible "moral" in introducing its version: "Rāma, who is called a portion (*aṃśa*) of Vāsudeva, the destroyer of the Haihayas, thrice seven times cleared the earth of Kṣatriyas; he destroyed the evil *kṣatra*, the non-Brahminical burden on the earth, covered as it was with *rajas* and *tamas*, although their (the Kṣatriyas') fault was but a small one (*phalguny api kṛte 'ṃhasi*, 15.15)." The kings are associated with the non-Brahminical *guṇas* of *rajas* and *tamas*—as well they might be—but their actual fault, it would seem, hardly merited their extermination. Rāma is therefore guilty, at the least, of a violent overreaction. This element of excess has, in general, been related by those scholars who have addressed this myth to Paraśurāma's anomalous behavior: he is a most unbrahminical Brahmin, an exception so horrifyingly extreme that he cannot but illuminate and reinforce the rule. Thus Robert Goldman has connected the myth to a wider corpus of so-called "Bhārgava" materials known to the epics and marked by a highly problematic predilection for violent themes; in Goldman's view, the assimilation of these stories by the Sanskrit epic tradition is the first recorded instance of "Sanskritization."[43] Madeleine Biardeau, who has devoted

[42] This revival of Jamadagni is an innovation in the *Bhāgavata*.

[43] Goldman (1976).

a series of important studies to this myth in its different versions, sees Paraśurāma as a typical embodiment of the avatar, who is always, in her view, a paradoxical combination of opposites (creative and destructive, Brahmin and Kṣatriya, "viṣṇuïque" and "rudraïque").[44] But this working out of the avatar themes is, according to Biardeau, only one side of the myth; the other, no less powerful component is a cautionary one illustrating the necessity for the true Brahmin to abjure violence of any kind. Thus Jamadagni's passive acceptance of his death reveals his transformation from the earlier angry, Kṣatriyalike sage who can order his wife's execution to a true exemplar of Brahmin values.[45] Biardeau's interpretation has been attacked on textual grounds by Gail[46] and van Buitenen;[47] the latter also put forward a convincing reconstruction of the textual "prehistory" of the story, based on its links with the tale of Aurva in the first book of the *Mahābhārata*.

Since the Aurva story is so closely bound up with the Paraśurāma myth, it may be briefly summarized here:

> There was a king called Kṛtavīrya, who gave rich gifts to the Brahmin Bhṛgus. When he died, his impoverished relations demanded that the Bhṛgus return some of this wealth; but some of these Brahmins buried their treasure in the earth, and others gave it away to other Brahmins. One day one of the kings uncovered some of this wealth by chance, while digging in the earth in the home of one of the Bhṛgus. At this the kings ranged over the whole earth, slaughtering the Bhṛgus everywhere down to embryos in the womb.
>
> One of the Bhṛgu wives hid her unborn child for a hundred years in her thigh, so that her husband's line might not be wiped out. When the Kṣatriyas found her at last, the child burst from her thigh (*ūru*) in a blinding light that robbed the kings of their vision. They begged the young Bhārgava to pardon them, and he gave them back their sight.
>
> But this Bhārgava—known as Aurva, since he was born from his mother's thigh—was still filled with burning anger, and he strove to bring about the destruction of the entire world. At length his ancestors appeared from the world of the fathers and pleaded with him to restrain his wrath: they had not died helplessly, so

[44] See above, II.4 at n. 93.

[45] Biardeau (1967-1968; 1968; 1970); (1976), pp. 185-90.

[46] Gail (1977), pp. 210-11.

[47] van Buitenen (1978), pp. 146-50.

> they informed him, at the hands of the Kṣatriyas, but had in fact engineered their own massacre through weariness with their long lives on earth. Aurva remained angry: whatever the Bhṛgus' motivation may have been, he could not make peace with a world in which kings and rulers had not endeavored to save his ancestors. Yet, pressed by the fathers, he at length cast his anger into the ocean, where it burns the waters in the form of a great horse's head.[48]

The Brahmin-Kṣatriya struggle of the Paraśurāma cycle—symbolized by the violence directed by a Bhārgava descendant against the line of a "Kṛtavīrya"—occurs here in all essential details,[49] along with a thematic pattern strikingly reminiscent of the Paraśurāma myth: Aurva's impatience with an imperfect world, a world in which fathers are unjustly slain by overpowerful rulers, recalls Paraśurāma's adolescent reaction against *all* the world's kings. In both cases, it is clearly crucial that the protagonist is a (young) Brahmin, who uses innate violent powers in the service of a dangerously totalistic (possibly even idealistic) goal. In both cases, it is the continuity of life in the world that is at stake. Always, it seems, the Brahmin's reaction is extreme: the chain of circumstances produces an escalating conflict, the height of which is the Brahmin hero's threat to undermine or to destroy entirely the social order. In the story of Aurva, the Kṣatriyas embark on genocide out of a partly legitimate grievance—the always problematic transfer of royal wealth to Brahmin recipients, that is, the classical pattern of royal self-impoverishment—but neither this consideration nor the appropriate Brahminical argument of the Bhṛgus' spirits (that they had contrived their own murders out of disgust with the world) can alleviate the avenger's anger. Aurva, like Paraśurāma, brings the world to the edge of a holocaust out of an understandable sense of righteous rage.

If we look back at the *Bhāgavata* version summarized above, it is clear that Biardeau is right in regarding the anomalous, violent Brahmin as a focal problem for the myth. One feels this at once in the text's lingering, quasi-iconic description of the wild Brahmin, with his matted ascetic's hair and his terrible weapons, as he enters the city of his foes.[50] Something here obviously intrigued the authors of our

[48] *MBh* 1.169-71.

[49] See van Buitenen (1978), pp. 146-50, for a detailed analysis. We may add another link with the Paraśurāma cycle: the Aurva myth is related in the *citrarathaparvan*, called after the Gandharva king who, we recall, plays a catalytic role in the matricide.

[50] See the summary above. Such loving descriptions of Paraśurāma are common in

text. One sees the same issue in Jamadagni's shocked, pathetic comment to his son, who apparently needs to be instructed in tones usually reserved for a still unenlightened child: "*We* are Brahmins, my son. . . ." Rāma's actions undoubtedly belie the ideal Brahminical identity (and reveal his Kṣatriya inheritance); the myth relates a serious lapse, or rather a series of lapses, from the well-established Brahmin values of nonviolence and detachment. And yet is there not still something quite naturally Brahminical about this warrior, who simply exploits his gift of Brahminical power in a wholly unrestrained manner? Paraśurāma, we are even told, has "the power of mind and fire." The power is clearly there for him to use; the question is only how its violent realization is assessed.

We may note in this connection the chromatic texture of the story—its preference for intense reds and yellows (the blood-soaked earth; the blood river at Māhiṣmatī; the blood-filled lakes at Samantapañcaka; the blazing splendor of the angry Rāma as he enters the battle; the fire of the sacrifice at which he expiates his crimes), and the alternation of these strong colors with the more tranquil tones of other scenes (the peaceful green of the hermitage, the Ganges where Reṇukā sees Citraratha, Rāma's final refuge on Mount Mahendra). It is as if the violent events of the story kept erupting through the deceptively quiet surface of its setting. Here the parallel between Rāma's battles and the Reṇukā episode is particularly striking: the violence that, rightly or wrongly, takes place outside the hermitage suddenly wells up from within, with horrifying if not totally irreversible consequences. Rāma's destruction of the Kṣatriyas and his matricide thus seem to run along parallel lines, in a way that may help to explain their linkage in the myth and that may also give us some insight into the authors' perspective on this story.

In our text, as in its prototype in *MBh* 3.115-16 (indeed in the Sanskrit tradition generally), the Reṇukā matricide remains largely undeveloped—so much so that it is difficult to gauge the authors' attitude toward it. There is, nevertheless, a tell-tale addition in our text's narration of the story: not only is Paraśurāma's awareness of his father's power—to curse him? to revive the dead?—explicitly stated, but the episode also concludes with an afterthought that repeats this same notion. "Knowing the powers of his father's *tapas*, Rāma slew his loved ones" (*pitur vidvāṃs tapovīryaṃ rāmaś cakre suhṛdvadham*,

Sanskrit literature; see, for example, "Bhāsa" 's *Karṇabhāra*, verse 9: "the best of sages, the destroyer of the *kṣatra*, his head piled high with matted locks gleaming red like a flash of lightning, and in his hand the axe glowing with an ever more intense light. . . ."

16.8). It is not certain whether Rāma is simply terrified of his father's capability of harming him, or is banking on a reversal of the effects of his obedience, or both. The implication would seem to be, in any case, that at the very least, a certain ambivalence attaches to the matricide. As to Rāma's other violent deeds, there can be no doubt about the ambivalence they arouse. In the *Bhāgavata* this theme is evident from Rāma's need for expiation, through a sacrifice at which he gives away the entire earth. Even this event is problematic, for the sacrificer's gift of the entire earth is expressly prohibited in the *dharma* literature, although it is also attested in other stories.[51] But the true extent of the opposition to Rāma's bloodthirsty revenge becomes clear in other versions, in which the *pitṛs*, sated by the endless blood-oblations which Rāma has been force-feeding them, beg him to desist from his revenge—just as the *pitṛs* demand from Aurva that he cast off his deadly anger.[52]

All this might seem to support Biardeau's "cautionary" interpretation of the story: the violent Brahmin is condemned, ultimately transformed (Jamadagni rids himself of anger and is slain without resisting; Rāma retires, his mind at peace, to his mountain refuge). Yet even if we limit ourselves to these two instances, the thrust of the story remains unclear: we know that Rāma has the unsettling habit of reappearing in his old, violent guise, not in the least pacified (*praśānta*)[53]—as if the apparent resolution of the *Bhāgavata* version were not really to be taken seriously. As for Jamadagni's death, the alleged proof of his ultimate acceptance of the traditional Brahminical ideal, is there not a heavy measure of irony here: the nonviolent sage mirroring in his passive demise the overviolent folly of his royal murderer? Think, for example, of Vasiṣṭha's very properly Brahminical resistance to the violent attacks of the Kṣatriya Viśvāmitra.[54] Moreover, his father's death merely serves to pour fuel onto Paraśurāma's fires. There is something wrong in the story, a nagging, unresolved difficulty that is capable of upsetting any theoretically harmonious conclusion, just as the violent events the myth relates keep breaking through the apparent calm of its setting.

Indeed, were this not the case, the myth might well have died a

[51] See Bailey (1981), pp. 113-14; Biardeau (1970), pp. 293-94.

[52] *MBh* 3.117; cf. *Skandapurāṇa* 6.66-68.

[53] *MBh* 5.174-87 (the *ambopākhyāna* describing Bhīṣma's battle with Paraśurāma, who is once again forced to lay down his arms by an intervention of the *pitṛs*); *Rām.* 1.74-76 (Paraśurāma's contest with Rāmacandra). See discussion of the latter story by Marglin (1977), pp. 253-55.

[54] *Rām.* 1.52-56.

deserved death long before the Brahmin authors of the *Bhāgavata* set about their task. I would like to suggest that our obviously anomalous Brahmin warrior is also seen in some sense—admittedly an abstract, projected, nonimitative sense very much at home in Indian myth—as normative. Paraśurāma carries to a mythic extreme an enduring Brahmin conflict: on the one hand, restraint, purity, nonviolence, detachment; on the other, inherent power, and the recurring temptation to use it in the violent pursuit of an uncompromising vision. Indeed, the myth implies that the Brahmin can never be wholly free of violence, although it fails to specify its precise nature. Is it the ineluctable violence of the sacrifice, which accrues to the Brahmin priests? Or (a common puranic view)[55] the violence which Brahminical ideals—absolute purity, complete detachment—inflict upon the fabric of ongoing life in the world?[56] We have already noted how the Aurva and Paraśurāma myths seem to converge upon this "anti-idealistic" position. But perhaps it would be closer to the ambiguous truth of the myth to attempt a more inclusive formulation of the problem. Thus we may see in Paraśurāma's career both the paradigmatic Brahminical commitment to an ideal vision of the world and the Brahmin's essential association with the sacrificial antithesis to that ideal: Paraśurāma, intent upon ridding the world of royal evil once and for all, in effect performs a sacrifice more terrible than all others. Seen in this light, both the matricide and the destruction of the Kṣatriyas—the former resulting from a blind obedience to paternal authority exercised (or rather abused) in the service of a superhumanly severe ideal of female chastity, the latter based upon an equally absolutistic standard for the world—reflect innate, problematic components of the Brahmin identity. Neither the ideal nor its compromises can be finally relinquished; the volatile combination of conflicting drives produces the discharge of violent action on the part of the mythic figure who can no longer contain them.

There is a tragic aspect to this story, an aspect rooted in a basically realistic appraisal of the Brahmin's unresolved inner conflict, and of the always frustrating relation between the Brahminical ideal and the "real" world of limitation and sacrifice. In village versions of the myth, Paraśurāma has the makings of a true tragic hero who chooses wrongly, out of the right motives, and must face the terrible conse-

[55] Cf. Shulman (1980), pp. 234-36.

[56] Biardeau has applied this notion to Aśvatthāman, the closest analogue in the epic to Paraśurāma: (1976), pp. 210-12.

quences of his action.[57] The *Bhāgavata*, a product of a Brahmin Vaiṣṇava milieu concerned with establishing its claims to Vedic legitimacy and high Brahmin status,[58] seeks a closure for the myth in which the conflict is at least partly pasted over and contained—hence its typical puranic "happy ending" (with Jamadagni revived and Paraśurāma himself at least temporarily rendered calm). For the same reason, the attack upon Paraśurāma's extremism is oddly muted here; it is only through suggestion and implication that the text expresses its hostile attitude to the matricide and the revenge upon the kings. In other words, we find an extreme inner conflict articulated only in highly ambiguous terms, while the lack of any true resolution is obscured by the purity and peacefulness of the tale's conclusion. For all that, the latent tragedy cannot really be suppressed. In the North Indian tradition of the *rās līlā*, Paraśurāma sometimes appears as a clown—no doubt because of his incongruous fusion of opposing traits[59]—but more generally, in both puranic and village sources, he is a rather grim figure, an unsettling reminder of the disastrous potential of the Brahmin's anger.

By now we may also begin to understand why the Paraśurāma myth seems to serve as a kind of symbolic "key" to the *Mahābhārata*, which refers back to the myth at the very onset of the Sūta's narration as well as at later points in the story.[60] The pools of blood at Samantapañcaka are both the geographical and the thematic precedents (during the juncture between the Tretā and Dvāpara *yugas*) of the bloodbath that takes place at this same site, Kurukṣetra, during the *Mahābhārata* war. Paraśurāma's oscillation between a peaceful, ideal-Brahminical persona and a violent, Kṣatriyalike identity adumbrates the conflict repeatedly evident in the epic between the violent, sacrificial side of *dharma* (especially the royal *dharma*) and the universalistic drive of renunciation; and Paraśurāma is no more capable of resolving this conflict than is Yudhiṣṭhira. The difference lies in Paraśurāma's Brahmin identity; the conflict is built into his inheritance in a way that it is not for Yudhiṣṭhira. And if the king can be forced, at least at times, to come to terms with his role—to rule, however reluctantly, and to

[57] Compare the tragic heroes discussed in Chapter VII below. I discuss the village versions of this myth in a forthcoming paper.

[58] Van Buitenen (1971).

[59] Personal communication from Krishna Prakash Gupta. On incongruity and clowning, see Chapter IV.

[60] *MBh* 1.1.11, and especially 1.2.1-12. The Sūta's audience is clearly meant to perceive a continuity between the Paraśurāma story and the events of the Epic. It is also striking that Duryodhana's death must take place at Samantapañcaka (see 9.52.1ff, 9.54.5-7).

accept the burden of evil this entails—the Brahmin warrior seems never to be at rest.[61] Again and again he clears the earth of kings, and then bequeaths the awkward prize, in toto, to the priests. Each time it is all or nothing—or rather, if we take the story as a whole, both all and nothing, in a paradoxical, unending struggle with the demands of reality and the ideal.

This view has important implications for the construction of the social order in historical Hindu states. The myths express in their hyperbolic imagery the restless quality of a center structured around these unbalanced, dynamic figures; they also point to essential distinctions in their roles. For all the complexities of his ever-fluid identity and the transformational character of his position, the king is ultimately *less* divided than the Brahmin, whose inner being must remain open to two opposite extremes. Ex officio, the king becomes tainted by impurity (the accumulating evils of war, hunting, punishment, and the unhappy concomitants of passing judgment), but he can, at least, dispose of his burden with the help of the Brahmin. But the latter can never wholly emerge from the confusing combination that defines him: perhaps the only truly anomalous Brahmin is one who rejects anomaly and identifies himself with only one side of his inheritance. A move of this sort can lead, as we have seen, to heresy and exclusion; similarly, the Brahmin who gives way entirely to the violent aspect of his identity becomes a horrifying figure, far more so than any king. We shall see something of this pattern in the epic story of Aśvatthāman. But the opposite move is equally weighty with consequences. The next version of the Paraśurāma myth to be studied requires a divine intervention to restore to the young Brahmin his native and vital imbalance.

Kāñcippurāṇam 45-46

This Tamil version of the story, by the eighteenth-century Veḷāḷa poet Civañāṉayokikaḷ, is separated from that of the *Bhāgavata* in time (perhaps by some nine hundred years) and in social context: its setting is one of Śaiva devotionalism in the temple town of Kāñcipuram. The sectarian transformations it works in this myth of Viṣṇu's avatar are immediately obvious, as is another reflection of the religious history of Kāñci—the attempt to legitimate a "folk" shrine (of the goddess Reṇukā) within the Brahmin temple complex focused on the god Śiva. Despite these evident factors, the problems posed by our militant

[61] This becomes literally true of Aśvatthāman, as we shall see.

Brahmin hero are no less powerful and alive than in the earlier version of the Sanskrit *purāṇa*; only their imaginative expression has been altered and expanded. The *Kāñcippurāṇam* tells the tale of Paraśurāma in two cantos, in which the natural chronological order of the mythic events is reversed: canto 45 describes Paraśurāma's struggle with Kārtavīrya and the Kṣatriyas, whereas canto 46 deals with the prior events of the matricide and Jamadagni's death. The reversal may be related to the relative importance of the two subshrines described here, Paracirāmeccaram and Ireṇukeccaram; but in retelling the two cantos, I have rearranged their order in order to facilitate the comparison with the *Bhāgavata*'s version. We begin, then, with canto 46:

> Reṇukā, the daughter of King Varma, was the ultimate in earthly beauty. She married Jamadagni and lived a flawless, chaste domestic life with him. One day she was seen by Kārtavīrya—by the power of *karma*—when she went to fetch water. He was immediately seized by desire, but she had her eyes fastened on the ground and thus failed to notice him. He then hovered in the sky above the lake, and Reṇukā, at last, caught sight of him. Then Kāma revealed his power to a slight extent: but the good lady at once forced her mind back to the way of truth, filled her pot with water, and headed home.
>
> But her husband in his wisdom had divined the reason for her delay—the action of that cruel idiot, Kārtavīrya. Angry as the mare's-head fire,[62] he turned to his son: "O glorious Rāma—that poisonous Kārtavīrya has approached your mother lustfully, desiring her beauty which is as great as the sea. With his youth, his kingly power, and his incurable foolishness, he will now come to take her, thinking nothing of us. Go and quickly cut off her head!"
>
> Rāma obeyed the word of his *guru* and went out, taking his mother. Sorrow it is to be born a woman; even greater sorrow, to be young; even greater, to be endowed with beauty; even greater, to be the refuge of those who seek boons!
>
> Rāma cut off his mother's head with his sharp sword and returned to bow at the sage's feet. Said Jamadagni in his grief: "Today I have seen that you are indeed the son of a Kṣatriya princess, and that you love me. You have accomplished my command. Matricide, however, is not a good thing (*tāykŏlai naṉmaiy aṉṟu*); the world will condemn it. So now follow this order: go there and join her head to her body; worship her golden feet,

[62] Cf. the end of the Aurva myth, above at n. 48.

praise her, and say, 'Mother, go wherever you may wish.' Remove her thus from that place, and return."

Jamadagni thought to himself: "Anger makes for bad *karma*. Anger destroys good characteristics, *tapas*, and vows; anger ruins knowledge. There is no enemy worse than anger." So he abandoned his anger and was dwelling in peace and quiet when that evil king (Kārtavīrya), having heard all that had happened, cut off his head and went away.

Restored to life by her son, Reṇukā was stricken by grief at the loss of her good husband. She went to Kāñci, where her son had worshiped, and set up a *śivaliṅga* there. Śiva and Pārvatī appeared to her. Said Reṇukā: "I have been disgraced; now you must protect me. They say a husband is sweeter than anyone else, and that he is master of his wife's body. Śiva is husband, father, and mother to all living beings. My husband instructed me in these things day after day. You are like him; numberless are those who have been saved by worshiping you. Now that I have fallen from high estate to innumerable sorrows, let me flourish as a deity worshiped by the people; let me give them their delights (*pokam* = Skt. *bhoga*)." In this way Reṇukā became a divinity (*tĕyvatam*), equipped with serpent-ornaments, shield, and sword, surrounded by Potarācaṉ and other attendants in Kāñcipuram; she grants low-caste people their desires in the Kaliyuga.

The startling sequel to these events is related in the longer, playful canto 45:

Viṣṇu was born through Bhṛgu's curse as the son of Jamadagni and Reṇukā; obeying his father's command as *dharma*, and because of her own fault, he killed the mother who had given him birth and nurtured him. Thus he suffered an unhappy fault; but, by the sage's grace, he revived her. Jamadagni joyfully abandoned anger and entered *samādhi*, in which state he was slain by the enraged Kārtavīrya.

Now Rāma was furious; he wished to destroy the entire race of kings. He went to Kāñci and worshiped Śiva, his senses controlled, absorbed in *tapas*. The god felt pity for him and came down to earth as an Untouchable Pulaiyaṉ, a slaughterer of cows—wearing leather sandals, a tattered garment, and with a body darker than darkness itself—together with Umā, Gaṇapati, and Murukaṉ, and with the four Vedas as sharp-clawed dogs.

He approached the young Brahmin at noon, as he was beginning his rites on the riverbank. Rāma, who was concentrating his mind on worship, suddenly became drunk on the smell of toddy. When he saw the approaching Untouchable, he waved at him with the flowers he had brought for worship, hoping to scare him off; but the Pulaiyaṉ came ever nearer to that pure sage. Now Rāma addressed him angrily: "What impudence is this, you low-down Pulaiyaṉ, eater of cow-flesh, you who are far from dharmic truth? Do you think there is no one here to use force against you?"

Śiva set the dogs on him, and Murukaṉ and Gaṇeśa seized his hands; Pārvatī intervened, saying, "O poor Brahmin beggar—you are in trouble now." And Rāma was enraged: "Why did you touch me? This is not *dharma*; it is evil for you!" Said Śiva: "Can you say if the evil is yours or mine? Who are you anyway? You look as if you are related to me."

"What are you saying?" cried Rāma; "I am the good son of Jamadagni; you are a Pulaiyaṉ. Are you not ashamed to pretend that you are related to *me*?" "If you are indeed the son of the incomparable Jamadagni," replied the Untouchable, "then we are *extremely* closely related—no doubt about that. Your mother Reṇukā is very much beloved by my flawless wife—therefore I love you too!"

By this point Rāma was beside himself with fury. "There is no punishment for you, who have spoken thus to a Brahmin, except to have your tongue cut out." Said Śiva: "Evil one, you who willingly committed the horrible crime of killing your mother—cut out my tongue if you are able, cut off my head. Listen, shameless one: who would not embrace a relative? Even if his relatives are as sour as the tamarind, a sophisticated person will not abandon them." And again he set his dogs upon Rāma, who took up his staff and threw it at the lord; Gaṇeśa cut it in two. The god who danced with Kālī was angry now: "You son of a Pulaiyaṉ's maidservant, you threw your staff at my son; you have no mercy (*aruḷ*), you were not even afraid of matricide. I shall kill you at once." As he approached the sage, Rāma took to his heels in fear, but the moon-crested god pursued him and touched him with his hand. At this touch, Rāma's hairs bristled in great joy, though he was confused and anxious because of the pollution he had incurred. "Alas," he cried, "I have been seized by a Pulaiyaṉ, with whom one should not even speak! I and my *tapas* are ruined."

Śiva addressed him: "You claim to belong to a family of flawless Brahmins—but you are the lowest of Brahmins (*pārppaṉakkaṭai*-

yaṉ), lower than me; my work entails destruction, but you slew your thin-waisted mother. You are lower than the low; you are my servant. Rejoice, for I shall support you." So spoke the god, and Rāma, angry as a serpent, struck the lord with his lotuslike hands. The god slapped him on his face, bound his hands and legs, and kicked him far away under a thickly leafed tree.

Rāma opened his eyes and lamented his lot: "I was born in the family of the best of Vedic Brahmins; I studied the Veda, Vedāṅgas, and logic, and all kinds of weapons. Now, through evil *karma* from a former birth, I must suffer. I beheaded my mother, and I bear the disgrace (*paḻi*); my father died at the hands of that foolish king. On top of all this, I have been touched and humiliated by that Pulaiyaṉ. How is it that I am still alive? They say that those who praise Śiva feel no sorrow; but, strange to say, though I cling to his feet, I see no end to my disgrace. I have erred greatly; let me now praise Śiva again and remove my fault."

Hearing his praises sung by the sage, the lord was pleased and revealed his true form together with Pārvatī and their sons. Rāma sank into a sea of joy and confusion. He asked Śiva for the power to destroy the race of him who had killed his innocent father, so that he might offer his blood to his father. Śiva glanced at his axe, which created a portion of itself; this weapon Śiva bestowed on Rāma along with the name "Paraśurāma." The god disappeared after promising that he would grant boons to those who worshiped him there on Mondays. Rāma, filled with anger, slaughtered the anointed kings, performed his obligation to his fathers with rivers of blood, and experienced true bliss (*iṉpam*).

It should be apparent at once that we have moved into a cultural context quite different from that of the Sanskrit *purāṇa*: there is an immediacy and freshness about the description, despite the high literary style—as if the author had deliberately set about filling in the human details of the bare narrative skeleton; the rich dialogue brings the mythic characters down to earth and reveals their psychological complexity; one senses the personal involvement of the author in the story, his readiness to take a stand, to articulate values; the tale is bathed in the intense noonday light of South India, which reveals a wholly real world exposed to a great range of emotional experience and, perhaps above all, to the comic, reflexive stance of its observers. The concrete presence of the shrine, and the less tangible but no less real presence of its deity, loom over the mythic events. In addition to these changes in focus, there are a number of striking differences between this version and that of the *Bhāgavatapurāṇa*, which we shall attempt to isolate and to understand. Adalbert Gail has noted the probable dependence of our text upon the *Brahmāṇḍapurāṇa*, where Paraśurāma is similarly tested by Śiva in humble disguise (as a Kirāta hunter—the whole episode thus directly recalling Arjuna's contest with the Kirāta-Śiva);[63] this link reinforces a well-known historical connection between the Kāñci tradition and the *Brahmāṇḍa* text.[64] Nevertheless, Civañāṉayoki has gone far beyond anything in the relevant chapters of the *Brahmāṇḍapurāṇa*; Paraśurāma's encounter with Śiva at Kāñci has developed a new, dynamic character quite different from that described in the Sanskrit prototype. Neither the sectarian coloring of this version, nor the transparent attempt to legitimate the worship of a local goddess within the Brahminical shrine, should divert our attention from the author's creative effort to address the basic issues of the ancient myth.

Let us begin with the matricide episode. Note that Reṇukā's troubles are related here not to her usual tempter, the Gandharva prince Citraratha, but to Kārtavīrya, Jamadagni's conventional enemy. This tidies up the story and provides a new background for the matricide: the old motif of rivalry over the sage's wishing-cow has been scrapped, so that conflict now centers quite explicitly on the woman, whose perfect chastity must guarantee the safety of the male inhabitants of the *āśrama*. This is a typical South Indian scheme that has invaded the myth.[65] Given this transformation of the story, it is interesting to see how the text relates to Reṇukā's responsibility: in a striking illustration of the South Indian feminine ideal, Reṇukā fails, at first, even to notice Kārtavīrya—her eyes are exactly where they should be, on the ground. When she does finally see him hovering in the air, she has a momentary lapse (as in the *Bhāgavatapurāṇa*, where she is *kimcic citrarathaspṛhā*): as our author states with careful delicacy, "Kāma revealed his power to a slight extent" (*kāmaṉuñ ciṟitu taṉ matukai kāṭṭiṉāṉ*). But Reṇukā recovers at once, wills her mind back to order, and pays no further heed to the king. Has she erred significantly? Not even her husband seems to think so, in this version of the story. Jamadagni makes no mention of his wife's fleeting desire, although we may sense, in his panic, a

[63] *Brahmāṇḍapurāṇa* 2.3.22-23; Gail (1977), pp. 212-14. Cf. Śiva's disguise as the Kirāta who tests Arjuna: *MBh* 3.40.1-62.

[64] Thus the final section of this *purāṇa*, the *lalitopākhyāna*, is devoted to the goddess Lalitā, who is identified with Kāmākṣī at Kāñcipuram. See Shulman (1980b), pp. 169-76.

[65] On the woman as the focus of inherent conflict in South India, see Hudson (1978), pp. 113-17.

certain lack of faith—as if he were not quite sure that she could pass the test again, if confronted with Kārtavīrya, in the flesh, inside the *āśrama*. But this is nowhere stated, not even when Jamadagni commands his son to kill Reṇukā; the only reason he cites is his horror at Kārtavīrya's approaching violation of the heritage.

We learn nothing of Rāma's feelings as he proceeds to decapitate his mother—as so often, the mythic silences are even more suggestive than the explicit statements—but the narrator does allow himself a lyrical verse on the sorrows of womanhood, especially young and beautiful womanhood. This verse is suggestive of his stand toward the matricide generally, a much more explicit stand than that we saw in the *Bhāgavata*: our author is clearly horrified by Reṇukā's fate (indeed, even Śiva is made to refer to it with horror in canto 45). And, in fact, Jamadagni also regrets the deed as soon as it is accomplished. As he tells his son with disarming bluntness: matricide is not a good thing. Not that he is particularly disturbed for the sake of his late wife—rather, he claims to be worried about public opinion. Underlying this feeble statement of regret there is, however, another more powerful concern. The sage sends his son to revive Reṇukā and to ask her to remove herself from the vicinity; presumably he knows, as would any Tamil villager, that the spirits of those who die prematurely or in unjust circumstances return to plague the survivors.[66] This is surely the basis for Jamadagni's boon in this version. Note how far we have come from the Sanskrit text, in which it is Rāma, the matricide, who initiates his mother's resurrection. We are now dealing with a typical case of transition from the ordinary human condition to a state of dangerous divinity—a transition almost always dependent upon violence and usually upon some form of sacrifice.[67] A village goddess has been born.

But the text has more to say of this episode. First, Jamadagni has learned something of the evil effects of anger, and he vows to renounce this emotion—much as in the version of the *Reṇukāmāhātmya* studied by Biardeau, where the matricide is a key moment in Jamadagni's "conversion" to true Brahminhood.[68] Yet the lesson in this case seems radically different from that drawn by Biardeau, who, as we have noted, regards Jamadagni's transformation as an affirmation of the Brahmin ideal. Even more than in the *Bhāgavata* version, the Tamil text is replete with irony, as is evident in the terse description of

[66] Whitehead (1921), pp. 20-21.

[67] See below, VII.4, on the theme of the "tragic apotheosis."

[68] Biardeau (1968).

Jamadagni's death: no sooner has he abandoned his impulsive anger once and for all than he loses his head in a much more literal sense. For Civañāṉayoki, at least, this hardly seems a recommendation for Brahminical detachment.

Furthermore, Reṇukā—revived already as a *widow*, a unique development of the myth and one that links her immediately to the Tamil village goddesses—goes on to consolidate her newly won divinity. The irony deepens mercilessly: they say, remarks Reṇukā, that a husband is sweeter than anyone else; no doubt she is thinking of her own sweet-tempered spouse. She is still burning with humiliation, and it is this fact—her fall from high estate to undeserved sorrow, a career that endows her with an excess of violent emotional energy—that serves as the basis of her demand from Śiva that she be worshiped as an effective, boon-granting goddess during the Kaliyuga. We are given a description of the village goddess as she stands, with sword and shield, beside her usual attendant Poturāja,[69] explicitly sanctioned by the myth. But the granting of blessings to the devotees hardly hides the essentially tragic stance of this new deity, who remains subject to periodic violent attacks—usually visited on these same devotees—as well as to the inherent bitterness and loneliness of her situation: her divinity expresses but cannot assuage her personal tragedy. Let us take note of the stark contrast with the *Bhāgavata*'s serene conclusion.

As we might expect, this perspective on the matricide finds a parallel expression in the description of Paraśurāma's subsequent history. What is the lesson of Śiva's Untouchable appearance before the young Brahmin obsessed with purity? We seem to find the very opposite of Biardeau's ideal resolution: not only is the eventual universal regicide allowed to pass without comment (except for the candid remark that Paraśurāma seems to have enjoyed it), but as preparation for the holocaust the Brahmin avenger is made to see another side to his identity—the angry, violent, impure side that makes a mockery of all his pretensions to purity and high status. This is not to say that the slaughter of the kings is ultimately condoned, any more than is the matricide (several South Indian temples claim to have witnessed Paraśurāma's subsequent expiation for the evils of matricide and regicide).[70] But the emphasis of the text is on the necessity for Paraśurāma to come to terms with his own darker persona; his awareness must somehow encompass the Brahmin's well-known relation to the Untouch-

[69] Cf. Hiltebeitel (1978), pp. 775, 785-86; Whitehead (1921), pp. 24, 40.

[70] For instance, at Tirukkovalūr and Tiruvañcaikkaḷam (Cranganore).

able.[71] Śiva, who can call upon the ancient link between Rudra and the *brahman*-priest of the sacrifice,[72] is the perfect teacher for this lesson, for Śiva is both the guardian of proper order (Vratapā, Vāstoṣpati) and the wildly antinomian destroyer of that order.[73] The Brahmin has inherited both of these classic roles; the first commits him to notions of hierarchy and his own purity, the second imparts to him a revolutionary character based on a higher ideal, a vision of absolute wholeness and freedom. Once again, as in the *Bhāgavata* version, there is an ambiguity about Paraśurāma's relation to this inheritance: is his violent potential that of the subversive ideal itself, as expressed in the blind obedience of the matricide and the urge to realize a world free of kings? Or is it the reflection of the Brahminical power that is linked to sacrifice and *dharma*? One thing is clear: Paraśurāma's claim to conventional ritual purity—the noonday bath in the river, the purity of his *pūjā*, his isolation from polluting contact with lower castes—is exposed as hollow by the god, who transcends such claims even as elsewhere he seeks to sustain them. Paraśurāma becomes, in the words of the text, a "Brahmin-Untouchable" (*pārppaṉakkaṭaiyaṉ*), lower than the lowest of social categories. The moral crime of matricide is used here to rationalize an affinity affirmed by countless texts. This relationship between the Brahmin and the Untouchable may even be said to be the symbolic heart of the Tamil version.

The Tamil text thus goes beyond merely impugning the conduct of a single, anomalous Brahmin warrior. It boldly lays bare the double nature of the Brahmin, attacks his claim to purity and ideal conduct, and hints at the antithetical side of Brahminism, its Śivalike "outsider" quality, and also at the difficulty that the Brahmin normally has in accepting this part of his identity. (Paraśurāma has literally to be forced to acknowledge it.) We see the closeness of the Brahmin and the Untouchable, the potential for transformation from one category to the other. Here Brahminism is no longer a detached ideal—that has become more pretense than reality—but rather an internally divided set of conflicting drives and powers. Paraśurāma's violent actions thus appear to reflect a normal part of his identity, once his relation with Rudra-Śiva has been established; the god himself informs him of this relation and emphatically reaffirms it when the Brahmin indignantly denies it. The point is not, of course, to reduce the Brahmin's role to its violent component, or to identify him wholly with the Untouchable; rather, it is his unending oscillation between poles, his creative

[71] See section 1 above.

[72] Cf. *Śatapatha Brāhmaṇa* 1.7.3.28, 1.7.4.19. In effect, the *brahman*-priest may be said to act out Rudra's role in the sacrifice.

[73] See Kramrisch (1981), pp. 3-26.

and energizing imbalance, which the myth seeks to explore. Like Rudra-Śiva, the Brahmin is both outside and in, Untouchable remnant and symbolic center, ideal and its antithesis, guardian and destroyer. A revolutionary anti-Brahminism is part and parcel of his identity; he is closely tied to both ends of the social scale. He holds within him the upper and lower boundaries of the society: the supremacy based on purity and the ultimate values of renunciation, nonviolence, and detachment (themselves the real basis for the claim to purity), as well as the Untouchable's entanglement in the world with its impurities. In any case, both upper and lower limits are themselves refracted or divided further, for the two boundaries can interpenetrate and coincide: the *sannyāsin* and the Outcaste are in some ways strikingly alike.[74]

Thus the Brahmin's associations with destruction and death have a rationale expressed through ambiguous mythic statements: Paraśurāma is both a Brahmin sacrificer gone wild and a closet idealist at war with an unjust world; both possibilities implicate him in the impurity of violence, although it is the second, quasi-idealist side that seems to have intrigued the puranic authors more. A similar ambiguity, tilted perhaps in the other direction, pervades the epic's tale of Aśvatthāman—another Brahmin warrior, in this case explicitly identified from the beginning as an incarnation of Rudra.

4. The Brahmin Warrior (2): Aśvatthāman, Butcher and Renouncer

Although Aśvatthāman has never been an overly popular character—he is quite clearly a major villain, in a text in which it is far from easy for *any* character to be wholly villainous—he nevertheless represents one of the outstanding Brahmin types in the epic. It would be tempting, if only the text would allow it, to try to exorcise him as a wholly negative example, to see in his story another tale of warning about Brahminism gone wild—and thus to exclude him from our models in much the same way that the Hindu gods, and their human followers, sought to deny the wild Rudra-Śiva his place in the sacrifice.[75] But this is precisely the point: Aśvatthāman is an incarnation of Rudra,[76] and the shocking but palpably pressing fact is that he represents for

[74] As we shall see in the next section; also below, VI.1 (the affinity of the prostitute and the *sannyāsin*).

[75] This is to a large extent the thrust of Karve's interpretation: (1974), pp. 111-21.

[76] More precisely, he is born from a mixture of Mahādeva (Śiva), Antaka (the Destroyer), Krodha (Anger), and Kāma (desire): *MBh* 1.61.66. See discussion by Dumézil (1968), p. 213.

the epic poets not merely some form of dreadful aberration but rather an available Brahmin truth. He can be denied, as Śiva is denied, only at the cost of a near-total destruction.

Aśvatthāman combines a tragic fate with unconscious parody of the Brahmin's bifurcated role; as with Paraśurāma, his actions can be interpreted as reflecting both a strangely powerful form of Brahminical idealism and a grimly realistic strand of the Brahmin's inheritance. There are, nonetheless, important differences between Paraśurāma and the epic hero: unlike Paraśurāma, Aśvatthāman's lineage is pure; he is a Brahmin through and through, but a Brahmin born to fight—as the son of Droṇa, the Brahmin teacher of both the Pāṇḍavas and the Kauravas, the epic's heroes and anti-heroes. There is no question in Aśvatthāman's case of a residue of Kṣatriya blood working itself out in outrageous acts. If Paraśurāma reveals the avatar model with all its ambivalence and conflict,[77] as well as the peculiarly Brahminical dilemmas we have discussed, Aśvatthāman remains closer throughout to a native Brahmin identity—or at least to certain aspects of it. His Brahminical characteristics, including the status of reputed sage (*muni*) and adviser, are stressed repeatedly in the course of the epic narrative. In addition, as we shall see, Aśvatthāman embodies the deeply Brahminical passion of refusing to make peace with a shattered world.

Still more significant, perhaps, is the explicit stress placed by the epic poets on the necessity for Aśvatthāman's unpalatable deeds. The grisly Brahmin's brutal raid on the Pāṇḍava camp brings to completion the horrific but divinely appointed and ineluctable sacrifice of war. As the incarnation of Rudra, Aśvatthāman is the necessary instrument for the realization of that god's destructive designs, which are themselves a basic part of the divine fate (*daiva*) at work in the epic universe. This is our point of departure: the first fact to be grasped is that Aśvatthāman's actions, however terrible, have a certain positive power behind them in the epic's own perspective, and that Aśvatthāman himself can by no means be simply condemned or despised.

To explore the problems suggested by Aśvatthāman, we must turn to the *Sauptikaparvan*, the short, hard-hitting tenth book of the *Mahābhārata*, which narrates the events at the conclusion of the epic war. Throughout the earlier books of the *Mahābhārata*, Aśvatthāman plays a relatively minor role; like his father, he sides with Duryodhana and his Kaurava brothers against the Pāṇḍava heroes. But if he seems somewhat neglected until the battle nears its end, the *Sauptikaparvan* is almost entirely his. Let us briefly recapitulate its description of events

[77] As Biardeau would have it: see above at n. 44.

in the original Sanskrit version, before turning to Villiputtūrār's medieval Tamil account.

The catastrophic war is virtually over; the slaughter has been immense. Duryodhana has been mortally wounded—unfairly, of course, as in all the major confrontations between the Pāṇḍavas and their enemies[78]—by Bhīma and is lying paralyzed, slowly dying, beside the pool where he had hidden. Here (as recounted in the final chapters of the *Śalyaparvan*, immediately preceding the *Sauptika*) he is visited by Aśvatthāman and two other survivors of the war, Kṛpa (another Brahmin warrior) and Kṛtavarman. The meeting of Duryodhana and Aśvatthāman is marked by powerful contrasts played out against the ghastly backdrop of limitless destruction: on the one hand, there is the dying king who seems, on the whole, at peace with life and with fate—he has accomplished his duty and achieved a death befitting a noble Kṣatriya; on the other hand, we have the king's Brahmin friend and supporter working himself into a fury at the unfairness of it all, and above all at the unrighteous means that the Pāṇḍavas have used against Duryodhana and most of the other Kaurava stalwarts. Aśvatthāman is simply not prepared to accept the outcome staring him in the face, and he asks Duryodhana to make him, Aśvatthāman, the last Kaurava general (*senāpati*) in the interests of revenge: he swears by all his accumulated merits, gifts, and *tapas* that he will slay all the Pāṇḍava supporters that he can find. Duryodhana acquiesces and anoints him on the spot.

This is the point at which the *Saputikaparvan* opens: Aśvatthāman and his two followers, bloodstained and exhausted, are wandering through the night in a dense, eery, demon-infested forest near the Pāṇḍavas' encampment. Aśvatthāman, consumed by grief at Duryodhana's fate, is nursing his anger and resentment; these highly charged emotions, festering in the dark wilderness setting pierced by the cries of the savage animals of the night, slowly drive him to the brink of madness. A strange vision pushes him over the brink: he sees a huge and terrifying owl swoop down on a multitude of crows sleeping peacefully on the branches of a banyan tree. This slaughter of the crows serves Aśvatthāman as an inspiration: he has no chance of surviving an open combat with the Pāṇḍavas, but he could accomplish his vengeful goal by catching them unawares, in their sleep. And he feels wholly justified in resorting to this cruel ruse: have not the Pāṇḍavas perpetrated deceitful and blameworthy crimes at every step of the conflict (10.1.49)?

[78] See Hiltebeitel (1976), pp. 244-86.

It is important to note the care with which Aśvatthāman's emotional state is portrayed; it is this state which allows him to take his fateful decision. If he is mad—and he is clearly regarded as such by his two companions when he informs them of his plan—there is still logic to his madness: the grief and rage that overwhelm him have a profoundly realistic basis in the cruel and conspicuously unrighteous deaths of his friends, his king, and, closest to him, his own father Droṇa. Let us listen for a moment to Aśvatthāman's angry lament:

> How terrible is the sorrow of that person who must always recall, in this world, his father's death: it burns my heart relentlessly, night and day. I saw my father killed by evil men—you saw it all, too—and that, above all, cuts into my inner parts. How could someone like me live on in the world for even a moment after hearing from the Pāñcālas that Droṇa was slain? I cannot bear the thought of living unless I kill Dhṛṣṭadyumna in battle: he killed my father, so I must kill him and all those Pāñcālas who follow him. Those groans that I heard coming from the king as he lay with his thighs broken—who is so cruel that his heart would not burn at that sound? Who is so lacking in compassion that he would not weep after hearing those words of the wounded king? Those with whom I sided have been defeated, and I am still alive—that heightens my sorrow, as a raging flood fills further the sea. How can I sleep tonight or feel at ease, with my mind filled, as it is, with this single concern? (10.4.23-29)

This is no rationalization, no searching for excuses to justify the urges of an already latent violent temperament, but an obviously genuine outpouring of overpowering emotion from a person who has been grievously hurt, and who is now obsessed with finding release from his inner pain. One can hardly help but sympathize with a person crazed by so much sorrow, and there is every reason to believe that the epic poets wished to arouse such an empathetic understanding, even if, on another level, they failed to condone Aśvatthāman's actions. As we shall see, there is also a matter of principle involved. Given the intensity of the Brahmin's reaction to the mounting series of tragic losses, we can also understand why Kṛpa and Kṛtavarman are unable to sway him from his chosen course. The three heroes argue, in a gloomy parody of a learned debate, replete with proof texts and logical claims and counterclaims. Their discussions—reported with a vicious verisimilitude characteristic of comedy in its cruel or mocking aspect[79]—touch upon one of the core problems of

[79] See below, V.8 at n. 188.

the epic, the complex relations between fate (*daiva*) and human effort and responsibility.[80] Kṛpa, praising *yoga* and human effort (*utthāna, puruṣakāra*), seems to echo the *Gītā* (10.2.22-24); and although his speeches are not wholly consistent, his basic intention is to dissuade Aśvatthāman from committing a deed that will be "like smearing blood on a white background" (10.5.15). But it is all to no avail; Aśvatthāman has by now been entirely possessed by the divine fate driving onward to disaster. He refuses his friends' advice (to get a good night's sleep, come back to himself, and then fight a fair battle in the morning) and rushes off toward his enemies' camp, with Kṛpa and Kṛtavarman following rather reluctantly behind.

Before he can enter the camp, he must pass a trial that emphasizes his identity with Rudra: a huge spirit (*bhūta*) emitting flames from thousands of eyes bars his way at the gate. Unable to defeat this apparition, Aśvatthāman worships Śiva—the real source of this test[81]—and offers himself in self-sacrifice (*ātmayajña*) upon a golden altar that has miraculously appeared. The sacrifice (another classical Brahmin value attached to this seemingly un-Brahminical avenger) has the desired effect: an immediate epiphany, in which Śiva himself reveals that the Pāñcālas' time has run out, gives Aśvatthāman a glittering sword, and enters into his body, making it glow with an unearthly brilliance.

What follows is the heart and climax of the *Sauptikaparvan*, the unforgettable eighth chapter, a masterpiece of lurid description expressed with an unusual economy of form. It would be hopeless to try to paraphrase this passage, with its wealth of detail and vivid suggestion. Suffice it to say that Aśvatthāman, drunk on anger, grief, and the divine power within him, rampages through the camp of his enemies, most of whom he brutally slaughters in their sleep. The first death sets the pattern: Aśvatthāman wakes Dhṛṣṭadyumna (the slayer of his father, Droṇa) with a violent kick, seizes him by the hair and pummels him into the earth; when Dhṛṣṭadyumna, still half asleep and unable to resist, pleads with his tormentor to slay him quickly, with his sword, so that he may reach the heaven of heroes killed in battle, Aśvatthāman heartlessly refuses; instead, he pounds him to death with his feet (10.8.12-21). And so it goes, in a horrendous orgy of screams, panic, and gore; the five Pāṇḍava heroes, who have gone to sleep outside the camp at Kṛṣṇa's prescient instigation, survive the slaughter, but their sons, grandsons, and allies are all killed. The few who manage to flee Aśvatthāman's avenging sword are cut down by

[80] See the statement of the question by J. D. Smith (1980), pp. 67-68. The epic's dualism in this respect is a persistent theme in Biardeau's ongoing research and interpretation.

[81] See discussion by Kramrisch (1981), pp. 85-88.

Kṛpa and Kṛtavarman at the gates. The graphic descriptions of the holocaust are suffused throughout by sacrificial metaphors and similes; Aśvatthāman is compared to the Destroyer let loose by time (*kālasṛṣṭa ivāntakaḥ*, 10.8.72). The whole frightful nocturnal scene has all the compelling horror of a nightmare coming true—and indeed the heroes see before them, in the moment of their death, the smiling, red-eyed, red-faced, red-garmented lady with a noose in her hand (Kālī, Kālarātri, Śikhaṇḍinī) of whom they had dreamt each night, in terror, since the war began (10.8.64-67).

At last it is over: dawn finds Aśvatthāman drenched in human blood, the hilt of his sword clenched so firmly in his hand that it has become one with his body (10.8.136). And he is happy; he has carried out his promise to Duryodhana and discharged his debt (*ṛṇa*) to his father. With his two companions he hastens to inform the dying king of his revenge, and with this comforting news Duryodhana expires. Aśvatthāman, grieving for the king but also, it would appear, afraid that the Pāṇḍavas will pursue him, takes to his chariot.

He has one last role to play on the epic stage. First the Pāṇḍava heroes must discover the extent of their loss; early reports of the carnage inspire Yudhiṣṭhira's succinct cry of mourning, more terrible in a way than all his subsequent agonies of remorse:

> *jīyamānā jayanty anye jayamānā vayaṃ jitāḥ* (10.10.10)
>
> The others, though vanquished, have won;
> we, in our victory, have been defeated.

But it is Draupadī's bitter lament at the site of the carnage that is most telling; and it is Draupadī who, in keeping with her character as a fierce and high-minded Kṣatriya wife and mother, thinks first of vengeance. As in previous emergencies and disasters, she turns to Bhīma, the only one of her five husbands upon whom she can always rely; she demands that he bring her the jewel that Aśvatthāman has carried on his forehead since birth.[82] Bhīma rushes off, to be followed almost at once by Yudhiṣṭhira and Arjuna, who have been warned by Kṛṣṇa of Aśvatthāman's dangerous power—specifically, his possession of the dread *brahmaśiras* weapon. They find him, covered with dust, his hair disheveled, but otherwise in a classic Brahminical pose: seated on the bank of the Ganges near the venerable sage Vyāsa, wearing a garment of *kuśa* grass, his body smeared with ghee. In fact, Aśvatthāman seems at this moment like a specter from the past: we may

[82] The congenital forehead-ornament links Aśvatthāman with the serpent (said to carry a precious stone on his hood) and with Rudra-Śiva, with his third eye.

be reminded of the wild Vrātya with his vision of Rudra, or of the long-haired, poison-drinking sage of the Vedic hymn.[83] And it is, it would appear, still as a representative of Rudra that Aśvatthāman enters into his final confrontation: he casts his weapon "for the destruction of the Pāṇḍavas" (*apāṇḍavāya*), while Arjuna, at Kṛṣṇa's behest, shoots to neutralize this threat. The resulting stand-off nearly destroys the world; Arjuna accedes to the request of Vyāsa and Nārada to withdraw his weapon, but Aśvatthāman cannot do so—he has none of Arjuna's superb control, nothing of his truthfulness or chastity, and he is unable to recall the missile he released in wrath. It will end only by destroying all the embryos carried in the wombs of the Pāṇḍava wives, including the future king Parikṣit, who will be stillborn and then revived by Kṛṣṇa.

For this, Aśvatthāman is cursed by Kṛṣṇa: for three thousand years he will wander the earth, alone, reeking of pus and blood, without friends or companions, in forests and uninhabited countries, burdened by all forms of disease. Aśvatthāman divests himself of his forehead-jewel and accepts his punishment. "I shall survive," he says to Vyāsa, "*together with you* among men." He is, no doubt, wandering among us still.[84]

The violent Brahmin's jewel, it is interesting to note, becomes the righteous king's crown. The heroes rush back to Draupadī with the jewel, and Bhīma hands it to her—a sign, he says, that the slayer of her children has been defeated, his glory destroyed; all he has left is his body. Because of his Brahmin birth, however, he has been set free. This satisfies Draupadī: "The son of the *guru* is like the *guru* in my eyes," she states as she gives the jewel to Yudhiṣṭhira. The latter, venerating it as a gift (or remnant, *ucchiṣṭa*) of his *guru*, places it on his head in what has been appropriately described as a "postwar crowning ritual."[85] Perhaps the violent, indeed murderous aspect of kingship inheres in this symbol. As for Aśvatthāman, his loss of the jewel no doubt expresses, as Biardeau has seen, a double deprivation: "It is as much his brahmanic power as his (doubtful) talent as a warrior that he thus abandons."[86] This is Aśvatthāman's final act of self-sacrifice, but unlike Karṇa, who also relinquishes a congenital safeguard and

[83] *RV* 10.136.1-7. See Kramrisch (1981), pp. 88-91, on the Vrātya hymns.

[84] Aśvatthāman is said to be present wherever the *Mahābhārata* is recited. His wanderings make him available as a possible dynastic ancestor for various local kings—the Pallavas, for example.

[85] Hiltebeitel (1981a), p. 194.

[86] Biardeau (1976), p. 213.

treasure—the divine armor that he bestows upon Indra[87]—Aśvatthāman evinces no nobility in this gesture; his only concern is to save his life. His tragedy lies in his lack of any truly tragic, heroic stature.

The symbolic force of this last exchange is even more apparent in another South Indian version of the concluding scene recorded, like so many other fascinating elaborations of *Mahābhārata* themes, in the first *skandha* of the *Bhāgavatapurāṇa*. Here the confrontation between Aśvatthāman and Arjuna has a different resolution: Arjuna succeeds, alone, in withdrawing both his and Aśvatthāman's terrible weapons, and then binds Aśvatthāman with a rope, "like a sacrificial victim." Thus bound, the hapless Brahmin (here referred to repeatedly by the pejorative term *brahmabandhu*) is dragged before Draupadī. But it is Kṛṣṇa who, at first, insists that Aśvatthāman be killed, for he is in the inglorious class of those who slay innocents, children, sleepers, and other unfortunate victims. Still, Arjuna is reluctant to slay his *guru*'s son, and Draupadī, in a flash of eloquence and compassion, supports him: "Let the Brahmin go. He is Droṇa alive in his offspring. . . . Let not his mother, Kṛpī, weep, as I weep, for the death of a child." This plea more or less carries the day; it is, as the narrator states, clearly just and righteous (*dharmyam . . . nyāyyam*). Only Bhīma remains eager for Aśvatthāman's blood. Now Kṛṣṇa restates the matter with his conventional ambiguity: a *brahmabandhu* should not be killed, but an *ātatāyin*—an attacker[88]—should. It is up to Arjuna to divine the god's mysterious intent: he takes his sword and cuts off the jewel in Aśvatthāman's head along with his hair. Aśvatthāman, freed from his bonds but deprived of his jewel and his Brahminical splendor (*tejas*), is then driven from the camp—for, we are told, the shaving of the head, the loss of property, and exile are all equivalent to the execution of a *brahmabandhu* (and Aśvatthāman suffers all three).[89]

As in its version of the Paraśurāma myth discussed earlier, the *Bhāgavatapurāṇa* cannot let the violent Brahmin survive in this form: Aśvatthāman is humiliated, punished by a symbolic execution, even subjected to an ironic inversion of his self-image, for this incarnation of Rudra, the sacrificial butcher of Vedic myth, is here reduced to the condition of a bound and helpless sacrificial victim (*paśu*). His title in this text, the scorned *brahmabandhu*, is sometimes applied to the debased Brahmin clowns who will interest us in Chapter IV (just as

[87] See below, VII.7.

[88] The *ātatāyin* is an important and intriguing category sometimes said to include arsonists, poisoners, thieves, adulterers, and other perpetrators of violence. In early texts the term is sometimes used pointedly to refer to a Brahmin warrior.

[89] *Bhāgavatapurāṇa* 1.7.13-58.

Paraśurāma appears as a clown in North Indian dramatic tradition); but there is nothing very funny about this savage shadow of the ideal (detached, controlled, nonviolent) Brahmin. Indeed, Aśvatthāman's story points to the essential seriousness of the Brahmin's inner conflicts as seen from the vantage point of a basically realistic appraisal of the world: in this light, the world is transparently saturated with evil, impurity, and pain, and must be *rejected* by anyone affirming a radical ideal. There is no question of reconstruction, of a moderate, sustained attempt at mending. The evil is far too overwhelming, as an emotional experience, for such a stand; Aśvatthāman's agitation, which springs from causes inevitably conducive to such a state, demonstrates this emotional truth. Having seen his father and his king cut down in unfair combat, he can no longer contain the Brahminical power within him from seeking violent retribution; at the same time, he is acting out the divine horror at creation which the myths attribute to the antinomian outsider, Śiva. The perspective here is a somber one, allowing no true resolution; moreover, this vision is, as it were, sealed off in a tragic closure that allows one to feel little else than the terrible sense of total loss, unfairness, an undeserved and unending victimization. Aśvatthāman may be anomalous as a Brahmin; he may be too cowardly and self-seeking to be a tragic hero such as Karṇa; but the tragic consciousness he personifies is an integral aspect of experience for anyone who takes the world of "facts," of human deprivation and limitation and the emotions they arouse, as ultimately real.

This essentially "realistic" attitude—which involves, above all, a cry of protest against an imperfect world—helps to distinguish the case of a "mad" Brahmin such as Aśvatthāman from that of the mad, or inverted, or exiled king; as we shall see, the king's exile, which might seem analogous to Aśvatthāman's punishment, is an essential component of his role; but it tends to be part of the largely comic, and transformative, aspect of the king. The latter's comic inversions help to impair the validity of *any* purely external, and truly self-limiting, reality.[90] Not surprisingly, Brahmin "realism" also constitutes only part of the Brahmin's symbolic role; and even in the epic, Aśvatthāman's "tragic" stance is subject to an implied critique. Here irony serves the epic poets as the vehicle for veiled commentary: the more one considers Aśvatthāman's career, the more ironic it appears. There are several levels to this use of irony. Look, for example, at Aśvatthāman's punishment according to the *Mahābhārata*: the peripatetic exile that puts him in a class with Cain and with the wandering

[90] See Chapter V.

Ahasuerus of medieval European folklore. On the one hand, this punishment is clearly one of the most severe in the epic, far worse, it would seem, than a mere death in battle (though not, perhaps, much worse than surviving the war to rule a decimated world, as Yudhiṣṭhira must do). On the other hand, even this punishment appears to mimic, like the rest of Aśvatthāman's life, a classic Brahminical role—that of the lonely, homeless, forest-roaming *sannyāsin*. Aśvatthāman is something of a willy-nilly renouncer, just as earlier he is, in a sense, a driven, unnatural sacrificer. In both cases authentic elements of his Brahmin identity are distorted, unbalanced, pushed to an extreme where they are almost unrecognizable. And yet what we find here is not merely a cynical travesty of Brahmin roles but rather an imaginative extension of these roles to their symbolic limits in such a way that the hidden closeness of these extremes becomes apparent. This is the deeper level of irony that Aśvatthāman's tale brings to light. The blood-stained sacrificer blends with the Renouncer; the uncompromising idealist becomes a butcher. Whereas Paraśurāma's story focuses upon the fundamental, creative imbalance and oscillation of the Brahmin, torn between two poles, Aśvatthāman reveals that the two poles, in their most extreme forms, at least partly coincide.

One way in which this subtle insight is worked into the epic tale is through the poets' use of myth to illuminate the events of the epic narrative. Hiltebeitel has convincingly shown that the conclusion of the *Sauptikaparvan*—with an important version of the myth of Śiva's exclusion from the gods' sacrifice (Chapter 18)—is a deliberate evocation, in myth, of themes central to the entire *parvan*.[91] Without repeating Hiltebeitel's arguments, we may note the overall replication of meaning in myth and epic tale: the excluded Śiva of the myth proceeds from an emotional stance similar to Aśvatthāman's to destroy—and thereby to complete—his opponents' sacrifice. In an important sense, the sacrifice is carried out by someone who resents its taking place in the first place. Śiva's grudge against the world is evident in many stories: it underlies his attack upon the incestuous Prajāpati (an ancient multiform of the Dakṣa myth in which Śiva is barred from the sacrifice),[92] and it can be heard in the anguished cry of the infant Rudra at his birth.[93] Yet the ambivalent Śiva is also the guardian of sacrificial order, as we have seen, and in his myths, as in the story of Aśvatthāman, the effect of his *raudra* protest is always the same: the

[91] Hiltebeitel (1976), pp. 312-35.

[92] *Śat. Brāh*: 1.7.4.1-8; see discussion by Kramrisch (1981), pp. 3-26.

[93] *Kauṣītaki Brāh.* 6.1-14; *Varāhapurāṇa* 33.4.

performance of the sacrifice, with all its violent horrors. Indeed, the very attempt to deny these horrors is what brings about the disastrous violence of a total sacrifice, a sacrifice without remnant or rebirth.[94] This is precisely what Aśvatthāman accomplishes: he succeeds where the sacrificer is meant to fail—in reaching the "end of the sacrifice," an absolute, final destruction. He is driven to this achievement by his limitless rage, his protest against injustice, against fate and failure; and, ironically, this protest only serves to complete the workings of divine fate (*daiva*), with its inevitable, frustrating dimension of unjust evil. Extreme idealism becomes a form of violence inflicted upon a world it cannot hope to change: Aśvatthāman has something of the uncompromising fanaticism of modern ideologues, convinced with murderous sincerity of the absolute correctness of their vision. The resulting catastrophe—the horrific completion of the sacrifice of battle—is thus unavoidable, tragic, and yet, in the epic's own terms, inconclusive.

For a completed sacrifice without remnant belongs to a world without limits, a world wholly unlike the one that fascinated and perplexed the epic poets. "Normal" sacrifices have as their proper end the ambiguous, "impure" remnant that will be the seed of the next sacrifice; and the extraordinary battle-sacrifice of the epic must therefore be redeemed by the miraculous intervention of Kṛṣṇa, who produces a remnant, after all, from Aśvatthāman's overly successful sacrifice in the stillborn Parikṣit, the future king. For his part, Aśvatthāman must be punished; his excess must not serve as a model for other Brahmins in their sacrifices, their otherworldly protests,[95] or their wars. Despite the inexorability of the divine power working through him, Aśvatthāman cannot represent an acceptable idealistic choice. In the moving vision of the epic poets, the Brahmin must face the implications of his ideals for the social order constructed around them—an order in which the longing for wholeness leads to disaster, and the greatest destruction of all is brought about by the outsider who rejects the realities of limitation and loss.

Villiputtūrār Pāratam 10.1-46

Aśvatthāman's extreme reactions involve him in patent evil; but his integral relation to the basic Brahmin identity should stand out clearly

[94] Cf. Biardeau (1976), pp. 210-12.

[95] Biardeau, *ibid.*, has interpreted Aśvatthāman as embodying the violence that otherworldly, absolutist Brahmin idealism wreaks upon the world. For another view, see Dumézil (1968), pp. 213-22.

from the above discussion. It is this relation which is crucial to our concerns in this chapter; and it is thus fascinating to observe the stress placed on Aśvatthāman's Brahminical features by the medieval Tamil poet Villiputtūrār in his rendering of the epic. If in the Sanskrit original Aśvatthāman intensifies the Brahmin's inner division to the point of an ambiguous, and partly ironic, explosion, in the Tamil version his image is largely rehabilitated, and the tragic tone of his tale made somewhat simpler and more direct. The Tamil poet makes no attempt to whitewash the murderous Brahmin, but his sympathetic portrayal is taken to a new limit; moreover, Aśvatthāman's dismissal from the scene marks the virtual end of Villiputtūrār's narrative, as if there were no more to be said once this oddly heroic figure had accomplished his deeds. Let us see how Villiputtūrār treats the terrible *Sauptika* sacrifice and Aśvatthāman's subsequent fate.

First, the basis for Aśvatthāman's action is slightly altered. Aśvatthāman finds the dying Duryodhana lying, barely conscious, beside the pool where he has been felled; the Brahmin lifts the king's body and holds him in his arms as he weeps for him in a grief greater than that which he felt for his father's death, and so touching that even the gods in heaven melt in sympathy (9.200). Embracing the king, the Brahmin sage (*muṉi*—note the pointed use of this epithet here) finds this the proper moment to bring home several pressing truths (*vāymaikaḷ*, 9.201):

You paid no heed
  to the proper way for kings—
  the words which must be said
    so that justice does not perish
    and so that mercy reigns;
  the nobility of not envying others,
  dharma, and the wielding of the staff
    to win the respect of all on earth.

You failed to heed the forceful words
spoken by my white-haired father (Droṇa),
  by the son of the heavenly river (Bhīṣma),
  by Vidura of the broken bow
  and other elders,

you who have the form
  of a good family's mark of honor.[96] (9.202)

[96] *tilaka mā mūrttiye*, literally "the form of the forehead-mark."

Aśvatthāman has been converted into an embodiment of Brahminical sagacity and solicitude for righteous order, a considerable transformation of his role in the Sanskrit original, but a transformation consistent with other moments in the Tamil version of his career (for example, when he eloquently urges Duryodhana to make peace, in the interests of humanity and the prosperity of the kingdom, right before Karṇa's fatal battle with Arjuna).[97] But does the dying Duryodhana need to hear another lecture on the proper duties of the perfect king? Even Aśvatthāman seems to perceive the inappropriateness of his remarks, as he suddenly reverts to his more usual military manner:

> "Like mountain peaks struck by lightning,
> the heads of frenzied Bhīma and the rest
> will be sundered from their bodies,
> and all their armies will be torn to pieces
> by my fight:
> before the dawn, I shall return,
> and the sevenfold world will be *yours*—
>
> so he (Aśvatthāman) promised,
> and the serpent-bannered (Duryodhana) gave him leave;
> gave, too, to that sage's son,
> graciously and easily,
> the jewel upon his crown
> in the hope he would return. (9.203)

Note the relatively cool tone that characterizes Aśvatthāman's promise: there is as yet no sign of any frenzy, of the volatile mixture of anger and outraged sorrow that pervades the Brahmin's mind in the Sanskrit text. Here Aśvatthāman makes a calculated move: he is still capable of conceiving a Kaurava victory, in the last moment of the war; and, as we subsequently learn (10.5), he is also concerned with keeping Duryodhana alive for even a few hours more—hence the reference to his return before dawn. Aśvatthāman wants his king to hang on in expectation of a final, auspicious reversal of fortune. The royal *cintāmaṇi* that Duryodhana bestows on his last commander clearly recalls the crest-jewel with which Aśvatthāman was born; in this case the transfer marks the attainment of Kṣatriya status, in a more formal sense, by the Brahmin warrior intent upon his final mission. Yet Aśvatthāman is still endowed with the "proper nature of the Brahmins (*pūcurar pĕrun takai parittāmā*, 9.204)" as he leaves, together with Kṛpa and Kṛtavarman, for the Pāṇḍavas' camp.

[97] *Villiputtūrār Pāratam* 8.2.179-81.

This time there is no council in the forest; Aśvatthāman observes the symbolic attack of the owl on the sleeping crows (10.1) and at once perceives his duty (*kaṭaṉ*). But the terrible *bhūta*—here said to have been sent by the order of Kṛṣṇa (*mātavaṉ vitiyāl*, 3)!—bars the way into the camp; the three heroes struggle against him in vain. "If need be, we must die at this *bhūta*'s hands," thinks Aśvatthāman—but then another idea strikes him.

"Whether the deed we planned is accomplished
or not,
worshiping Śiva is meritorious (*puṇṇiyam*),"
he thought;
he bathed in a cool pool of water that was there;
then, fixing in his mind
the husband of that woman who is the very form of music,[98]
he offered flowers of many kinds
and, reciting the five syllables,[99]
as the Āgama requires,
he worshiped at his feet. (6)

The lord who has ashes and the bull
rejoiced in this worship according to Vedic rite
and stood before him, in his mercy,
  a feast for eyes and heart.
The son of the powerful sage
stopped trembling
and said: "Give me a weapon
  to crush my foes."
Before he had finished speaking,
the lord offered him this weapon. (7)

This divine weapon frightens off the *bhūta*, and Aśvatthāman can now enter the camp of his sleeping enemies, after stationing Kṛpa and Kṛtavarman at the gate. He feels the joy of battle, like Murukaṉ (*kaṭappamālaiyāṉ*, 9)—hardly a Brahminical image, but surely a positive one nonetheless—as he makes his way straight to Dhṛṣṭadyumna's bed and beheads him without further ado (and also without the gratuitous cruelty that accompanies this killing in the Sanskrit text). By now the alarm has been sounded, and a fierce battle breaks out in the middle of the camp (*pāḷaiyatt' iṭaiye*); Aśvatthāman, his mind now

[98] Śiva as joined to Umā.
[99] The *pañcākṣara, namaḥ śivāya* ("homage to Śiva").

overwhelmed with anger (*mel vĕkuḷum cittamoṭu*), piles the severed heads of his Pāñcāla victims into a mountain (11). He rushes through the encampment searching for survivors, and thus reaches the spot where the Upapāṇḍavas, the heroes' sons, are resting:

> Unaware
> that their fathers, who had seized the entire earth,
> had gone away,
> or that their uncle (Dhṛṣṭadyumna) had perished
> at the hands of the sage's son,
> the beloved sons of the great woman born from the fire[100]
> were sleeping:
>
> the garlanded sage with his terrible sword
> appeared to them
> like a dream. (12)
>
> "These are the ones
> who have conquered
> and taken for themselves
> the whole earth!"
>
> So he thought,
> he who was like a jewel upon the crown
> worn by severe ascetics—
> for *they* were like a flame
> lit from another flame.
> He reeled in anger;
> as if drunk on toddy,
> in a frenzy,
> in a split second,
> before they could grab their weapons,
> he cut off their heads with his sword. (13)

Aśvatthāman has replaced Kālarātri of the Sanskrit *Sauptika* as the nightmarish vision come true: *he* is now the dream of death that the sleep-filled heroes see materializing before them. And although he is now intoxicated with the slaughter, he is still a sage (*muṉi*, 12) who can be compared to the ascetics' crowning ornament (*tiṇ ṭavar tamakkuc cikāmaṇiy aṉaiyāṉ*, 13); moreover, he makes, in essence, an honest mistake in taking the Upapāṇḍavas for their fathers (his prime target)—for these sons are the very image of their fathers, "like a flame lit from another flame." All in all, despite the horrendous result,

[100] Draupadī, born in the sacrificial fire.

Aśvatthāman's rampage has lost some of its ghastly character; and when it is over—after a desperate, doomed intervention by none other than the Chola king, who must also be cut down (14-15)!—the murderous hero can still be described, not wholly sarcastically, by a positive epithet:

The kings of the eighteen lands,
the fierce armies they had mustered
  replete with elephants, chariots, horses, and foot-soldiers—

all these he slew at midnight
in a fight ten times more terrible
than any fought by day:

for he, Aśvatthāman,
endowed with rare, proper learning,
was the son of the god with the garlanded matted locks. (16)

After crushing, in violent anger—
  just as he had planned—
all who were in the camp,
he (Aśvatthāman),
full of frenzy like a wild bull,
joined his fellows at the gate.
Holding the five heads of those splendid young men—
  to the horror of the gods—
he reached the Kuru king
  before Vĕḷḷi[101] rose in the sky. (17)

This is the moment Villiputtūrār chooses to underline this "learned Brahmin's" identity with Rudra-Śiva, here described as Aśvatthāman's "father"; but the identity is even more powerfully affirmed by the striking adaptation of a mythic image: Aśvatthāman holds in his hands the Upapāṇḍavas' severed heads, just as the Brahminicide Śiva is left holding Brahmā's skull.[102] Aśvatthāman, it seems, always calls up the haunting images of the distant past. And it is in this cruelly evocative guise that he now returns to the dying Duryodhana for a final, tragic interview (translated here in full):

[101] Vĕḷḷi = Śukra, the planet Venus.

[102] *Śivapurāṇa* 3.8-9; see O'Flaherty (1973), pp. 123-27. Aśvatthāman's links with Śiva are obviously sustained through the repeated comparison with Murukaṉ/Skanda (verses 9, 16).

"I have come, my lord.
The *bhūta* sent by Mādhava[103]
turned his back and fled.
I slew all in the camp,
scattering their great crowns;
and I have taken the lives of the five heroes. (18)

Those kings,
the lion-bannered (Bhīma) and the rest,
have perished—here are their heads!"

With these words, the sage's son
placed the boys' heads before him. (19)

Looking at those heads,
the king subject to avid desire
felt some comfort—
but then he said,

"In truth,
the faces of these children
are very like the bright faces
of their loving fathers." (20)

To these words of the king,
the wise sage learned in the Veda
said nothing;
he just stood still.

Said Duryodhana to that hero:
"Evil performed by Brahmins
is a terrible fault;
how could you have done it? (21)

"From the first day of the Bhārata war,
you fought with your arrows,
defeating many kings;
what heroism was there today
in beheading those children?
What were you thinking?
What have you done? (22)

[103] Kṛṣṇa, here unambiguously the source of Aśvatthāman's trial (see n. 81 above).

"Is there anything left
in our two families,
   which are but *one* family—
for us or for them?
You have snapped off the Kuru's last shoot,
you who are the flawless son of an excellent family. (23)

"From the day we played in the water of the river,[104]
how I have hated the son of the wind![105]
Truly, my own deeds burn me now
as I enter Death's gate—
what words[106] have I left to say? (24)

I have lost
   all my relatives
      with their fine words,
      their armies of elephants with thick, long trunks,
   and all my companions.
I stand alone:
who is there, upon the earth,
who could be compared to me?" (25)

So he said, in several sentences,
and then gave leave to depart
to that son (of Droṇa) who had killed
others' sons.

"Go," he said,
and that your evil acts performed in battle
may leave you,
live on,
   performing *tapas*." (26)

Duryodhana clearly derives no real comfort from Aśvatthāman's revenge, for he still has the perspicuity to identify the Upapāṇḍavas correctly and to point, in sorrow, to Aśvatthāman's error. The conversation, couched in an abruptly shortened verse form (four lines with four metrical feet each), hovers on the brink of silence: Duryodhana, fully aware by now of his responsibility for the disastrous

[104] Duryodhana tried to drown Bhīma during their youthful period of rivalry: *MBh* 1.119.

[105] Bhīma.

[106] *kūṟṟiṉ vāyp pukunteṟk' ĕṉṉa kūṟṟ' ayā*, punning on *kūṟṟu*, "Death," and *kūṟṟu*, "utterance."

war, asks rhetorically in verse 24 if there is anything left for him to say; he enlightens Aśvatthāman in a remarkably terse, sadly gentle and indirect statement about his victims' true identity (20); whereas Aśvatthāman, for his part, is dumbfounded by this revelation, so that he hears the rest of Duryodhana's rebuke in total silence. In fact, Aśvatthāman's words in verses 18-19 are his last directly reported speech in the epic text: he seems, from the moment he is made to realize his mistake (his tragic *anagnorisis*),[107] to assume the silent posture proper to the ascetic sage (*muṉi*) he now truly becomes. The entire scene is played out with a tragic simplicity of painful awareness succinctly expressed in words, and at the same time with a certain softness; Duryodhana's death acquires a nobility reflected in his joyous reception in heaven (31-32), while Aśvatthāman is sent off to the forest not as a cursed and reluctant parody of a *sannyāsin* but as a chastened Brahmin who can, and who must, purify himself from his evil past.

This conclusion is reinforced by a last meeting with Vyāsa, a meeting that replaces the entire climactic battle of the *astras* in the Sanskrit original:

> The learned son of the sage
>   with the bound bow in his hand
> and his uncle (Kṛpa)
> and Kṛta(varman)
> were bewildered by the true words
>   of the Kuru king, who had the prowess of the sword.
> They went to Vyāsa—
>   he who was as if the three rare fires of the sacrifice
>   had been born together, in a single form—
> bowed, and told him
>   of the strength of the five (Pāṇḍavas),
>   of what they, themselves, had done,
>   and of the death of the king
>   whose crown was not revered. (33)
>
> He (Vyāsa) appointed the forest,
>   proper for *tapas*,
> for Kṛpa and for Droṇa's son, Aśvatthāman,
> and said to them: "Stay in that place."
> Then he allowed Kṛta(varman) to depart.

[107] See VII.7.

And they, as he had said,
meditated on Lord Śiva
and performed *tapas* in the wilderness
surrounded by mountains,
to the amazement of the gods. (34)

Vyāsa confirms Duryodhana's parting advice: Aśvatthāman is converted into an honest Renouncer devoted—as he has been throughout his life, including the crucial moment of difficulty before his murderous nocturnal raid—to the god he represents. And that is all there is to it. There is no confrontation with Arjuna, no imminent universal conflagration to be warded off, no violence to the Pāṇḍava embryos in the womb, *and no curse*. The stained Brahmin warrior simply leaves for the forest. What appeared, in the Sanskrit *Sauptika*, to be a bitterly ironic ending to a darkly convoluted career has become, in the Tamil poem, a rather clear-cut, nonviolent resolution of a tragic cast, but not without some promise of redemption.

Villiputtūrār does not, however, attempt to reduce the powerful ambiguity of the epic tale. When the Pāṇḍavas learn of the slaughter, and of Aśvatthāman's responsibility, Bhīma and Arjuna still cry out for revenge; but this time Kṛṣṇa restrains them with a number of oddly related arguments. First the god explains Aśvatthāman's motivation: he had sworn an oath to Duryodhana to make the earth subservient to him and to kill the Pāṇḍavas (before dawn). Then there is the state of his mind: he was filled with a twisted anger (*tiruku ciṉattŏṭum*), and he had worshiped Śiva out of love (*pĕṭpu*). In short, he was like Murukaṉ (again the comparison with Śiva's warrior-son, as in verse 9)—who can recount his prowess (42)? Moreover, if he were to use his *apāṇḍaviyam* weapon, who could save the Pāṇḍavas then? (Here Aśvatthāman's secret weapon remains a threat, which the god advises his protégés not to put to the test.) Finally, Kṛṣṇa has, after all, kept the promise he made before the war began: to safeguard the lives of the five heroes. And it has not been easy, as he says to Draupadī: "Why grieve over the lives of your sons? Look how many devices (*tantiram*) I had to use—over a crore—just to keep your *husbands* alive!" (44). Anyway, who can overcome fate (*vitiyiṉaiy ĕvare vĕlpavar*, 43)? No doubt the heroes had failed to imagine that the god would save *only* their lives, in a literal fulfilment of his word—that they would emerge from the war bereft of their children and their friends, as the now unchallenged rulers of an empty kingdom. But such an outcome is hardly inappropriate when it comes from the hands of this shifty, elusive deity who is referred to, in these final verses, as *cūḻcci vallāṉ*—

"he who is skilled in contrivance" (43). And the murderer, as we have seen, is simply let off the hook: his exit to the forest, as a *real* ascetic, marks the end of the story. No wonder that, according to Villiputtūrār's final verse (46), the Pāṇḍava heroes are left "thinking about *dharma*'s way" (*aṟaṉĕṟiye karuti*) as they protect the world; for as everyone knows, *dharma*'s infuriating subtleties, its essential inscrutability, can keep any sensitive king pondering for the whole of his life.

Let us return briefly, in conclusion, to the point made at the outset of this chapter. If any properly ideal (*śānta*) Brahmins have ever existed, they seem not to have made their way with any prominence into the vast corpus of Hindu myth and legend. Rather, the Brahmin ideals of detachment, purity, and control exist in relation to a reality of violent engagement in a violent world. These two sides of the Brahmin coexist in a dynamic tension within him; all that is required to see this division is to intensify it in such a way that the bonded energy bursts forth—usually in a hypertrophy of one aspect, but a hypertrophy that reflects the interpenetration of the two poles (as with Aśvatthāman). A violent potential is part of the Brahmin's symbolic identity: it is not, after all, so surprising that Paraśurāma would accept only Brahmin pupils who wished to study the art of war,[108] just as Brahmin generals had their natural place in the Chola armies. On the other hand, even these Brahmin warriors retained their claim on Brahminical ideals. The South Indian Brahmin is an unstable amalgam given to internal oscillation between conflicting pulls in a process activated by his relations with other figures, above all his royal patron. Note that this perspective does not confirm the "non-dualistic" scheme that has been eloquently argued by Marriott and Inden.[109] The union of incompatible drives within the Brahmin remains a profound problem on all levels: personal, social-structural, philosophical, symbolic.[110] The problem cannot be wished away, any more than it can be solved by reaffirming the Brahmin's theoretical supremacy in the caste hierarchy—a supremacy that is itself only an extreme restatement of the tension.

In short, it seems we may have to abandon the Dumontian ideal, connected though it is to a very real part of Hindu theory, of the supremely pure and pacific Brahmin, and instead make do with a far more complex, fractured figure. It is this dynamic figure who con-

[108] *MBh* 12.2; "Bhāsa," *Karṇabhāra*, after verse 9.

[109] Marriott (1976); Inden (1976).

[110] Thus Parry (1980) finds the Brahmin funeral priests of Benares to be caught up in an ongoing "moral crisis" incapable of resolution.

fronts the South Indian king in the "marriagelike" bond that forms the nucleus of the Hindu state. The complex and unresolved nature of both these actors becomes apparent under the strains imposed by their union, as hidden fragments of their identities are unlocked, heightened in power, and released into the external world. These fragments may at times be mirror images—and here we find an extension of an ancient pattern revealed by Heesterman in the sacrificial and legal texts, a pattern of regular alternation of Brahmin and Kṣatriya roles: king and Brahmin tend to exchange their identities.[111] The Brahminical "breakthrough" toward a transcendent orientation based on the absolute values of renunciation was aimed at arresting this endless alternation and at separating out the two roles. But the stories we have been discussing show the persistence of the older pattern even within the context of the transcendent orientation: in fact, the absolute values have become part of the old cyclical exchange, so that we now find renouncer-kings pitted against Brahmin warriors in unending self-transformations. Unless we take account of this transformative drive, and of its effect both upon the major symbolic roles and upon the reality in which they are embedded, we shall fail to grasp the dynamic and open-ended character of the medieval South Indian sociopolitical system as a whole.

The Brahmin is the gatekeeper of this system, his place the threshold of a gateway that opens in two directions: to the world, and away from it. But this gateway is placed at the cultural center, a monument of saṃskāric form. On one side lies the perfect, deathless world of the sacrifice without remnant, without evil, without end—a sacrifice that can take place only outside the mundane order. Ultimate authority and ultimate values arise only there. On the other side lies crude, uncontained impurity, a vital mixture of dyings and rebirths, and the unmediated emotions of terror, joy, and love. The congealed ideal and the wholly real, a dry harmony and a lively dissonance, are divided by this door. Yet, strange to say, these two realms, reached through opposite movements, soon flow together; to go through the gateway in either direction is ultimately to return, through a baffling circularity, to the same, literally "liminal" spot. This *limen* is the point of departure and of return, a boundary made center; or, in the words of a Bengali Caryāpada: "the courtyard is within the room."[112] Always the same open gateway awaits its Brahmin guard.

[111] Heesterman (1978), pp. 16-17.

[112] Kukkurīpāda II, in Mojumdar (1973), p. 32. The statements in this summary are not made in a "deconstructionist" mode: it is one thing to equate center and periphery, inner and outer, with the loss of all distinctions; quite another to regard the experience

His is not, however, an easy stance, and very often the Brahmin grows weary of the gate, yearns to tear it down from without, or to melt down its hidden counterpart within himself—and thus to do away with gates, thresholds, the whole divisive apparatus of perception and prescribed modes. But this yearning in itself belongs to the threshold and essentially contributes to its preservation at the society's self-transforming core. The urge to transition and transformation gives the gateway its symbolic power and its centrality in this culture; whereas for the Brahmin, to cross over the threshold once and for all, in a unilateral, irreversible movement, would be to lose the dynamic orientation of his life. It is this orientation that the Brahmin bequeaths to the kingdom, to which he remains equivocally tied. The state, like its Brahmin gatekeepers, is caught up in ceaseless movement; its goal, like theirs, is the same gateway from which it departs.

---

or perception of marginality as crucial in the processes of forming a cultural center (as in India).

· IV ·

A Kingdom of Clowns: Brahmins, Jesters, and Magicians

> Besides, I am a Brahmin: for me everything becomes reversed, like a reflection in a mirror; left seems to be right, and right becomes left.[1]

1. Introduction: Kingship and the Comic Mode

Were the antinomies discussed in the previous chapter the only major parameters of the Brahmin experience, that experience might well have seemed unbearable. In fact, for all its tensions, it is very far from that. The Brahmin's relation to the ultimate values of his society—the relation that underlies his prestige and his authority—has its own complexities and surprises. At certain points, irreconcilable conflict opens up to a new dimension; a radical perspective transforms the struggle of uncompromising idealism with the tragically limiting and polluting engagement in the real world. In part, this perspective proceeds from a redefinition of what is real: this slips the ground out from under the opposing "idealistic" and "realistic" drives. A different kind of transcendent orientation emerges; its essence is comic; it forms an integral part of the Brahmin role. Briefly, there is an historic link between the Brahmin and the clown, a link that also deeply affects the symbolic ordering of the South Indian social universe, including the structures of kingship. This link, and the more general relation between South Indian kingship and comedy, will be studied in this and the following chapters.

A book on South Indian kingship is not the place to develop a theory of comedy. Nevertheless, we can hardly avoid addressing the

[1] *Mṛcchakaṭika* I (after v. 16).

outstanding comic themes that recur in the stories relating to the political order and its transformations. These stories will take us beyond the period and the geographical area of our primary concern. We cannot understand the role of the Brahmin court jester, for example, without reference to the Vidūṣaka of classical Sanskrit drama, or to his last surviving representative in the Kūṭiyāṭṭam tradition of Kerala. Nor can we analyze the comic roles of the king himself without exploring the phenomenon of clowning in the village and in folk traditions of South India, for these village clowns enable us to perceive something of the nature of Indian comedy generally, its distinctive features and effects. Many of these features turn up, with surprising force and regularity, in the cluster of symbols and concepts that comprise the royal role. For, as suggested earlier, kingship in South India is expressed through different modes, with related metaphysical and structural characteristics; specifically, a "tragic" mode of *viraha* and a "comic" one of *viḷaiyāṭal* have been outlined above.[2] It is the second of these, with its inversions, its mirror effects, its transformative powers, its ludic approach to the realities of the inner and outer worlds, that concerns us in this chapter.

Our analysis will necessarily remain incomplete. Nothing like the whole spectrum of Indian comedy could be considered here. To mention but one lacuna: no full study of Indian comedy could ignore the tropical garden of Indian (and especially Brahminical) comic forms to be found in Malayalam and Sanskrit literature from Kerala. I have left this area untouched. Still, material for this chapter has expanded alarmingly, as if infected by the comic spirit itself; while my attempts to hold it within reasonable bounds were no more successful than Manu's experiments with the fish. Comedy, it appears, has laws of its own. We will seek initially to understand its workings within several South Indian contexts by surveying the major comic carriers—first of whom is the Brahmin clown.

Is there a psychology of Brahmin clowning? What underlies this affinity? The link is an ancient one, and not only in the classical tradition of Sanskrit drama. Let us look, for example, at a poem from the late-Caṅkam collection of *Kalittŏkai*—a text that offers, in many of its poems, fascinating mixtures, parodies, or expansions of the classical Tamil types and conventions. In the following poem (*Kalittŏkai* 65), the heroine's confidante is supposedly telling the hero-lover about a rendezvous that failed:

[2] See above, I.5.

A Kingdom of Clowns

You with your fine clothes—listen
to the joke all the village is enjoying:

I was waiting for you,
all dressed up, with my jewels,
in the dark dead of night—
no sign of life anywhere—
when that old crippled Brahmin
whom you're always telling me to respect—
  with his bald head, woolen cloth,
  his body wasted from leprosy;
  the one who never leaves the village street—
looked at me, bowed low, and said,

"Who are you to stand here
at this untimely hour?"
He was like an old buffalo seeing straw.
"Don't go away," he said, opening his bag;
"have some betel, lady."

I said nothing, standing there.
He retreated swiftly:
"Little lady," he said,
"you're trapped—
I'm a different sort of demon
than you.
Be kind to me.
If you trouble me,
I'll take all the offerings you get from this village."
He chattered on like that,
and I saw the old Brahmin was scared,
so I grabbed some sand and threw it at him.
At that, he began to scream!

It was as if a trap laid by hunters
for a fierce-eyed tiger
had caught instead
a useless jackal—

a pitiful sight for a lover.
All the village is abuzz:
that old Brahmin's whole life
is a farce.

The scene described in the poem parodies the standard *akam* theme of the clandestine, nocturnal meeting of the lovers: the rendezvous is spoiled by the fumbling efforts of the ridiculous Brahmin cripple to play the role of heroic lover to the heroine's companion. We should note the realistic portrayal of this comic attempt at a seduction; there is clearly no question here of the lyrical, refined sentiment of the classical Tamil love poetry, but rather a bluntly accurate depiction of a grotesque but very human encounter on the village street. This "everyday realism" is a recurrent comic feature that we will discover again in connection with the Vidūṣaka and other clowns; here, as in European comedy, it can be related to the appearance of "low" (non-heroic, nonexemplary) characters.[3] Indeed, the foolish Brahmin of this poem recalls in a number of ways the classical Brahmin clown of the drama: like the Vidūṣaka, he is deformed, easily frightened or intimidated, and, it would seem, quick to think of food (his attempt to pick up the young woman consists solely of an offer of betel). Moreover, the context of his comic actions is the proper erotic love of the true hero (here the listener addressed in the poem)—much as the Vidūṣaka's role depends upon his master's noble love. Let us note, too, that the Brahmin of the Tamil verse is wholly unconscious of his comic effect; from his viewpoint, the episode must surely seem rather painful, as his sudden claim to be a demon hungry for offerings might well suggest. This element—the self-awareness, or lack of it, of the clown—is, as we shall see, a crucial indicator in any typological classification of comic types.

The grotesque Brahmin of *Kalittŏkai* 65 is remarkably close to the clowns of South Indian folk theater; but the connecting links must include the comic figures of Sanskrit drama in its various genres, especially the *nāṭaka*, the somewhat less prestigious *prakaraṇa*,[4] and the *prahasana* or farce.

2. The *Vidūṣaka*: Losing the Illusion

Of the many comic characters known to the Sanskritic tradition, surely the most outstanding, and by far the most familiar, is the clown of the drama. A considerable literature treats of this stock figure of fun.[5]

[3] Thus Auerbach, in his famous study (1957), traces the growth of realism in European literature from Roman comic genres (among other sources: see his analysis of Petronius, pp. 20-28). And cf. Aristotle's statement on the "low" character of comic figures: *Poetics* 1449a.

[4] For example, the *Mṛcchakaṭika*, parts of which are discussed below; and see Dimock et al. (1974), p. 88.

[5] The major modern study, concentrating on the problem of origins, is Kuiper (1979), where most of the available literature is cited; but see also Bhat (1959); Parikh (1953); Schuyler (1899); Jefferds (1981); Wells (1963), pp. 14-15; Welsford (1935), pp. 62-65.

The Vidūṣaka is *not* a court jester or court fool:[6] his comic powers are rarely self-consciously directed at his companion, the *nāyaka*—the play's hero, often a king. The Vidūṣaka is funny despite himself, often against his will; at times he protests against being forced into a comic role.[7] Yet by his words, his physical appearance, his attire, and his actions,[8] he provides a humorous counterpoint to the main action of the play.

The dramaturgical textbooks offer definitions of the Vidūṣaka's character and lists of his main attributes, which may or may not correspond to the empirical usages of the dramas. They do, however, provide a convenient point of departure. Thus the *Nāṭyaśāstra* describes the Vidūṣaka as "a dwarf, with projecting (or jagged) teeth, a hunchback, double-tongued, with a disfigured face, bald, yellow-eyed."[9] The emphasis is clearly on a grotesque appearance characterized by deformity and ugliness.[10] This effect was, in theory, heightened by the Vidūṣaka's makeup and attire, including, perhaps, a comic three-cornered hat and a loosely tied, messy *dhoti*.[11] The element of physical deformity links the Vidūṣaka with the comic cripples of the medieval Tamil folk-drama;[12] the distorted body—a failure of form, an insult to the "proper" ordering of nature's categories—suggests a much more profound psychological or cognitive function. Already we may sense a comic antithesis: like many other clowns, the Vidūṣaka is a categorical challenge, a blow against *saṃskāra* in its widest sense of creating, maintaining, and refining conventional limits and forms.

Why is this funny? Why do we laugh at the first appearance of the hunchbacked, dwarfish, limping Vidūṣaka? Questions such as these, which will haunt our discussion, will hardly be resolved in its course.[13]

[6] As stressed by Coulson in his introduction to *Śakuntalā* (pp. 32-33).

[7] *Karpūramañjarī* I (Kapiñjala protests against his humiliation in a verbal contest with the serving girl).

[8] The first three items are mentioned in *Nāṭyaśāstra* 13.138. See discussion by Kuiper (1979), pp. 214-17.

[9] *vāmano danturaḥ kubjo dvijihvjo vikṛtānanaḥ/ khalatiḥ piṅgalākṣaś ca sa vidheyo vidūṣakaḥ: Nāṭyaśāstra* 35.57.

[10] Yet, as Kuiper remarks (pp. 216-17), the *Nāṭyaśāstra* distinguishes the Vidūṣaka from its main categories of deformed or crippled characters. He is commonly referred to in the plays as monkeylike (e.g. *Nāgānanda* III, after v. 11).

[11] See Bhat (1959), pp. 54-59 (on the *triśikha*, perhaps depicted in a Gupta panel).

[12] The *nŏṇṭināṭakam*: see below, VII.6. Cf. the "lumpish," unfinished character of the European clown: Handelman (1981), p. 328.

[13] See the summary and suggested typology at the end of Chapter V. Attempts at universal interpretations of comedy, such as the essays of Meredith and Bergson and Freud's ingenious study, are clearly germane to this discussion; but my approach has been guided by the effort to set the Indian data in their cultural context, and to explore their symbolic and "metaphysical" properties.

But if we are to approach an answer that will fit the Indian materials, we must look beyond the external characteristics of the clown—suggestive as they are—toward an analysis of his overall impact on the drama. Scholarly consensus would probably support Huizinga's characterization of the Vidūṣaka: "The *vidūṣaka* is a counter-stroke of the spirit of the play itself; the loftiness of the sentiments comes out the more strikingly by the contrast of his vulgarity."[14] This view would also suit the tradition of Sanskrit poetics, which insists on the essential subordination of the comic mode—*hāsya*—to the dominant emotion of the play (usually *śṛṅgāra*, love).[15] Thus the Vidūṣaka's role is seen as enhancing, by contrast, counterpoint, or simple human relief, the general *rasa* or "taste" of the drama. Jefferds has argued in this vein in an insightful study:

> A totally homogeneous field remains "unfelt" until interrupted by variation. . . . The status quo—even the passionate love-longing of the Nāyaka in Sanskrit theater—may fade, by our habituation to it, from too-persistent foreground to forgotten background. To take a metaphor from *kāma-śāstra*, the Vidūṣaka is like the little bites which paradoxically enhance the prolonged love act. . . . The Vidūṣaka, by the sheer contrastive force of his "style," does not diffuse but rather refines and shapes our response to the total tone, tempering, as an alloy tempers, the intensity.[16]

We shall seek to qualify this interpretation, but Jefferds is surely correct in underlining the Vidūṣaka's contrastive function. The point can be stated even more strongly: whatever the total force of his role in the drama—integrative in a broad fashion, as is generally believed, or, as will be argued below, largely "disintegrative" in a distinctly Indian style—the Vidūṣaka acts as a kind of negative pole to *rasa* as such, a bungling, incongruous lump of refractory, unrefined feeling and perception.[17] This is the aspect of the Vidūṣaka which we must first investigate through the dramatic texts.

Perhaps its clearest expression is in the Vidūṣaka's relentless hunger—an "oral fixation"[18] that specifically offsets the *nāyaka*'s far more

[14] J. Huizinga, *De vidūṣaka in het indisch toonel* (1897), p. 41, cited (and translated) by Kuiper (1979), p. 206.

[15] Thus the *Nāṭyaśāstra* sees *hāsya-rasa* as *śṛṅgārānukṛti* (6.45). Later poeticians elaborate upon this perspective. Cf. Jefferds (1981), p. 69, n. 9.

[16] *Ibid.*, p. 62.

[17] Biardeau (1981) notes that the Vidūṣaka's deformities are similar to those that disqualify one from being a *yajamāna*, that is, from participating in the outstanding samskaric expression of ritual identity.

[18] Jefferds (1981), p. 70 (n. 23).

complex state of desire, longing, and romantic love. In the Vidūṣaka's bag of verbal tricks, the most worn and predictable is his attempt to channel any conversation (but especially a high-flown, lyrical speech by the hero) into purely gastronomic lines: his similes, more often than not, are taken from the world of kitchen and table, and he is certain to interpret any statement or query as referring to matters of food. He sees the world with the eyes of Tantalus, except that his focus is more narrow, for the Vidūṣaka's true craving is for cakes and sweetmeats, *modakas*. Thus the rising moon quite naturally appears to him as a *modaka* broken in two.[19] The greatest disaster that can befall a Vidūṣaka is a case of indigestion, as we learn from Bhāsa's Vasantaka, who moans that his poor stomach is revolving like the eyes of the cuckoo.[20] Generally, however, the Vidūṣaka has a Rabelaisian capacity for eating: in one late Sanskrit drama, the aptly named Mahodara ("Great Stomach") enters holding up his belly with his hands.[21] For most Vidūṣakas, no problem is too thorny to be solved by a feast. It is as if this figure had taken the multivocal Sanskrit root *bhuj*—"to eat, partake of, enjoy, make love"—and reduced it to its single most primitive meaning. In this respect, the contrast with the *nāyaka* is complete, for the latter hopes to "enjoy" his beloved in many ways—physically, of course, but also emotionally, in a wide spectrum of feeling and experience. The Vidūṣaka consistently deflates these aspirations; the only way he could "enjoy" a woman would be, quite literally, to eat her up. He often appears to cultivate a bemused tolerance of his companion the king's ardent love-sickness; and although he may, at times, be coopted into furthering the *nāyaka*'s cause, in his own awkward fashion, his heart is never really in this enterprise. Indeed, he regularly mocks it.

It should, then, come as no surprise that the Vidūṣaka is almost never allowed to play a role in a comic, erotic subplot such as we know from the Roman comedies and their European descendants.[22] He may, it is true, be married—to a usually nameless "Brāhmaṇī" whose task, we may imagine, would be to keep her husband fed. More in character, it would seem, is the misogyny preached in eloquent language by Maitreya, the Vidūṣaka of Śūdraka's *Little Clay*

[19] *Vikramorvaśīya* III, after verse 6.

[20] *Svapnavāsavadatta* IV, *praveśaka*.

[21] *Adbhutadarpana* of Mahādeva, V (cited by Bhat [1959], p. 52).

[22] Including, of course, Shakespearean drama. See the classic treatment of this subject by Levin (1971) and, for the Roman comedy, Duckworth (1971), pp. 184-90. Cf. Jefferds (1981), p. 70, n. 23: "There is no question of the Vidūṣaka seriously interacting erotically with a woman."

Cart. This nonerotic (and at times antierotic) character of the Sanskrit clown is one of the features that distinguish him from South Indian folk clowns, as we shall see. This statement holds good for the Vidūṣakas of all the early plays; but there is some development of the role, over time, perhaps even under the influence of the living folk theaters. Thus later dramatists such as Śrīharṣa and Rājaśekhara contrive scenes—burlesque skits might be a better description—in which the hapless Vidūṣaka is put into embarrassing, erotically suggestive situations. In Act III of *Nāgānanda*, for example, the Vidūṣaka, covered from head to toe in red garments borrowed from a woman with the aim of hiding himself in this way from the bees following his powerful scent, is mistaken by the drunken Viṭa (the dissipated "rake") for his beloved Navamālikā; the appearance of the latter saves the clown from the Viṭa's embraces but inspires a further humiliating trial of his Brahminical pretensions.[23] More elaborate still are the comic interludes of Rājaśekhara's *Viddhaśālabhañjikā*, one of the most colorful of the medieval dramas: here the queen plays a practical joke on the Vidūṣaka, Cārāyaṇa, by arranging a second marriage for him: with a lady named Ambaramālā ("Garland in the Sky"), the daughter of Śaśaśṛṅga ("Horns of the Hare"—a Vedāntic metaphor for the impossible) and Mṛgatṛṣṇikā ("Mirage"). The bride is played by a servant lad who even forgets to use feminine gender in referring to himself in the Vidūṣaka's presence—and is corrected, in a pedantic flourish, by the intended bridegroom himself. Cārāyaṇa is so flattered by the proceedings that he is completely taken in, dresses up for the occasion, and gets halfway through the wedding ceremony before realizing his mistake. He takes his revenge on the queen and her maidservants by a daring plot of his own.[24] These latter-day Vidūṣakas have clearly moved some way from the classical models of Kālidāsa and Śūdraka—another indication of this development is their increasingly obscene, insulting speech—and both the cases just cited are built around a transvestite motif reminiscent of the androgynous clowns of other Indian comic genres.[25] Nevertheless, it should be noted that even here the "later" Vidūṣakas are by no means erotic figures with romantic interests of their own to set against the heroes' noble love: they are,

[23] Asked to prove his Brahminhood by reciting Vedic *mantras* but unable, of course, to remember even one, the clown claims that the Vedic sounds have been concealed by the stench of wine emanating from the Viṭa.

[24] *Viddhaśālabhañjikā*, Acts II and III. On the Vidūṣaka and the mirage, see below.

[25] See below at notes 135-136; Chapter V.6 (the Virāṭa episodes); and cf. the Javanese clown Semar: Scott-Kemball (1970), plate 19; also Bouissac, p. 174 (the androgynous circus clown).

at best, the butt of others' sexual innuendoes, fantasies, or pranks, and thus still an essentially neutral, and neutralizing, sexual type.

From the above we may deduce that the Vidūṣaka is, in general, far closer to a foil than to a parodic shadow of his heroic companion.[26] The distinction is important: the foil serves to heighten, by contrast, the serious nobility of the hero; the parody, expressive of a deeper similarity between the clown and his mocked companion, ultimately assimilates the latter to the comic perspective of ridicule and wry debunking.[27] Though the two functions can sometimes coexist within the same comic character, classical Sanskrit drama structures the relations of the Vidūṣaka and the *nāyaka* along the lines of the former pattern: the relation depends for its forcefulness upon an essential incongruity, the high-flown sentiments of the hero wedded to the absurdly human, earthy, and corporeal attitudes of his clown. At the same time it may be suggested that the two constitute a fundamental unity: "Just as no *pravṛtti* can be conceived without its negative counterpart of *nivṛtti*, so the *nāyaka* can only be understood in relation to his counterpart, the *vidūṣaka*."[28] Together these two figures articulate the composite image of the hero (usually a royal hero at that), in which two sides are always active in dynamic tension and internal flux—an active, exemplary side wholly engaged, unself-consciously, in the present's tasks, hopes, and feelings; and a reflexive, commentating, self-mocking side. Without the Vidūṣaka, the *nāyaka* is only half himself. To pursue this dialectic, we must analyze the *internal* incongruities that give the Vidūṣaka his true power within the imaginative reality of the drama.

Here it is not so much a question of contrast with the hero as of an oddly disharmonious blend of attributes peculiar to the Vidūṣaka himself. One can see this in several interrelated areas: his Brahmin identity coupled with his debased, anti-Brahminical characteristics (such as his Prakrit speech—for the Vidūṣaka rarely breaks into Sanskrit); his ignorance and foolishness, together with a marked propensity for wit and for uttering plain truths; a crucial association with language in general, although he is effectively debarred from fine utterance; and, most complex of this set, an ontological ambiguity that places the clown on a fine line between realities (or illusions).

Let us begin with the question of his intelligence and learning. Though often despised by others for his foolishness, the Vidūṣaka is

[26] This point is also made by Jefferds (1981), p. 68.

[27] Levin (1971), pp. 109-47; cf. Nevo (1980), pp. 31-32.

[28] Kuiper (1979), p. 210. *Pravṛtti* is the positive movement of creative engagement in life, *nivṛtti* a retreat or withdrawal (or the reabsorption of the created in the divine).

by no means a simpleton; he seems, rather, to have been too lazy to acquire the Sanskritic education to which he is entitled by his Brahmin birth. He exemplifies the notion that *half* an education (which, according to the *Kāmasūtra*, is precisely what the Vidūṣaka can claim) is worse than none.[29] The plays abound in references to his precarious grasp of knowledge: he offers to keep the heroine from slipping away, "like what I remember from my studies";[30] when he fails to decipher a written message, it is because "these letters were not in my textbook";[31] he cannot recite a single Vedic *mantra*[32] or even remember the number of Vedas;[33] he thinks the *Rāmāyaṇa* is a text on dramaturgy.[34] His pretensions to erudition derive from the fact that his father-in-law's father-in-law used to carry around books in someone else's house.[35] Small wonder that he serves as a butt for others' jokes, while his bungling inefficiency and mental torpor sometimes entangle the hero in new embarrassments (necessary, of course, for the development of the plot)—as when the clown loses Urvaśī's love letter in the second act of *Vikramorvaśīya*. And yet he has a ready wit and, often, a keenly observant eye. Unlike Falstaff, who must be reminded by Prince Hal, "What, is it a time to jest and dally now?"[36] Maitreya, perhaps the most perspicacious of the classical Vidūṣakas, is quite aware of his limits: "I am not such a fool that I don't know the proper time and place for a joke!"[37] In this vein another Vidūṣaka, Cārāyaṇa, boasts that the learned (*paṇḍidā* = *paṇḍitāḥ*) are distracted, like monkeys, by recondite or imaginary constructions and thus are left with useless "leaves" hanging on the branches of a tree, while the fools go straight for the fruit fallen at its root.[38] This metaphor has the added advantage of turning the tables on the "straight" characters, who often compare the Vidūṣaka to a monkey; here it is the pandits who are simian, whereas the fool takes pride in going to the root of the matter. A deserved pride, at that—for the Vidūṣaka, like so many clowns and ceremonial fools throughout the world, has the freedom both to see and to state simple, sometimes shocking truths. Thus when Maitreya is loath to go out at night to offer, on behalf of his friend, to the

[29] *Kāmasūtra* 1.4.46 (*ekadeśavidya*).
[30] *Nāgānanda* I, after verse 17.
[31] *Avimāraka* II, *praveśaka*.
[32] *Nāgānanda* III, after verse 3.
[33] *Priyadarśikā* II, after verse 1.
[34] *Avimāraka* II, *praveśaka*.
[35] *Karpūramañjarī* I, after verse 18.
[36] *Henry IV*, Part I, V.iii.
[37] *Mṛcchakaṭika* III, after verse 23.
[38] *Viddhaśālabhañjikā* II, after verse 14.

goddesses at the crossroads—he is, of course, a coward, another common trait of the Vidūṣaka—he rationalizes his refusal with a blunt statement of fact: "The gods never respond even if you worship them—so why bother?"[39] The problem of the gods' unpredictable, often invisible response to human worship kept generations of Mīmāṃsikas busy theorizing;[40] the Vidūṣaka's quasi-heretical stance emerges from the obvious.

Were this all there were to it, the Vidūṣaka could take his place in the series of comic characters famous for their incongruous blend of wit and folly—a long series stretching from Aristophanes through Gargantua and Shakespeare's beloved fools.[41] In fact, the Vidūṣaka does not belong in this series, as Jefferds and others have clearly seen. His "wisdom," such as it is, has little critical force behind it; and his relation to higher truth is of a different order than, say, the Fool's in *Lear*. We are not yet at the point of a true reversal of identities, or of Folly's triumph. On the other hand, the Vidūṣaka does have a bearing upon what may be seen as the ontological issues of the drama. He may be less penetrating, in his psychological and social observations, than the Shakespearian clowns, but he is at least as deeply involved as they are in defining and examining the nature and the true limits of the heroes' experience (especially his romantic passion). Indeed, the Vidūṣaka's role in this respect is central, recurrent, and often explicit. Look, for example, at the following short passage from *Śakuntalā*, Act VI. Love-sick, remorseful King Duṣyanta has been staring at a portrait he has drawn of his lost love, Śakuntalā; the clown and a passing Apsaras, Sānumatī, have been observing the king's deepening immersion in the picture, to the point where he seems no longer to recognize its true nature. The clown's bantering comes to a sudden halt when he hears the king threatening to incarcerate a bee which, as part of the painting, is troubling Śakuntalā's painted image:

VIDŪṢAKA: Surely that bee ought to be afraid of your fierce punishment.
(*Smiling, to himself*). He's crazy—I hope it's not catching.
(*Aloud*). Sir, you know it's just a picture.
KING: What do you mean, "just a picture?"

[39] *Mṛcchakaṭika* I, after verse 15.

[40] See the fine discussion of the *apūrva* concept by Halbfass (1980).

[41] There is an enormous literature on wise fools (largely anticipated by Erasmus): see, among other works, those of Welsford (1935; the classic survey); Willeford (1969); Swain (1932); Goldsmith (1955; on Shakespearean fools); and Huizinga (1952), pp. 72-76, interpreting Erasmus.

SĀNUMATĪ: Now I understand—he experienced the picture as real.
KING: (*Dejected*). Friend, look what you have done:

> I was enjoying the delight of seeing her, in person, before my eyes,
> with my heart full of her presence,
> when you reminded me and turned my love
> back into a picture. (*He wipes away a tear*).[42]

The clown brings the hero crashing back into a prosaic and unhappy world. As his very name might warrant,[43] the Vidūṣaka "spoils" the king's illusion; romantic union is converted back into everyday loss and separation. But this is only an epitome of the Vidūṣaka's more general effect upon romantic visions and noble sentiment—as we might expect from his over-identification with the primitive appetite, the oral, and the concrete. He specializes, we might say, in collapsing the hero's intangible constructions of emotion and fantasy. To cite but one more striking example: in a marvellously extended passage in Rājaśekhara's Prakrit drama, *Karpūramañjarī*, the *nāyaka* and the Vidūṣaka share their dreams. The *nāyaka* has, naturally, dreamt of his beloved: he caught hold of her sari, which she then left in his hand—and disappeared along with the dream. The Vidūṣaka proudly announces that he, too, has had a dream, in which—as we learn while the king slowly prys the precious details out of him—he underwent a series of astonishing transformations: he dreamt that he fell asleep beside the Ganges, was swept away by the current, became absorbed by a rain cloud, was rained into the ocean where he became a pearl within an oyster, was then fished out and made into part of a necklace that adorned the breasts of the queen of Kanauj, and was suffering the terrible pain of being squashed between those full breasts and the chest of her husband during their love making, when—at last—he awoke. The king, upon hearing this dream, clearly perceives the clown's intent: "You knew that my dream of meeting my beloved was unreal, and you sought to drive it from my mind with the report of your counterdream!"[44] Note the Vidūṣaka's wry use of an erotic image—his helpless discomfort during the royal love-making—to

[42] *Śakuntalā* VI, verse 20.

[43] There is considerable controversey over the etymology and meaning of the name: see Kuiper (1979), pp. 192 (n. 320), 193, 204 (especially n. 355), 208-10; Bhat (1959), pp. 85-89, citing the Sanskrit theorists.

[44] *Karpūramañjarī* III, verses 3-8. See below at n. 139; and cf. Bottom's suggestive dream in *A Midsummer Night's Dream* IV.1; discussion by Willeford (1969), pp. 137-40.

comment upon, and in effect to puncture, the lyrical eroticism of the king's overwrought emotional state.

The motif of the clown's dream has a certain poignancy about it, for it evokes—especially in this instance, which is supposedly a dream within a dream—the classic character of the clown, any clown, as a magician who tinkers with reality from his position on the boundary between inner (visionary, imaginary) and outer, conventionally ordered experience. But in the case just cited, as in the great majority of the Vidūṣaka's at times unsettling statements, the effect is anything but magical. The Vidūṣaka is no more a conjurer than a critic. If he is indeed a creature of the boundary, as of counterpoint and unlikely conjunction, his movement tends toward a single direction: from enchantment to the commonplace, from poetic fancy to common sense. Duṣyanta wishes to curse the ring that slipped from Śakuntalā's finger (with the result, he believes, that he failed to recognize her); "very well," says the Vidūṣaka, "I shall curse this stick for being crooked."[45] The clown's comments take the *nāyaka*, and with him the audience, back down to earth. This descent to the concrete or to the grotesquely commonsensical is always comic in character, as if the energy invested in elaborating the fanciful forms and modes of sustained poetic feeling were suddenly released in the uncontrollable ripples and convulsions of laughter.[46] The Vidūṣaka governs the transition, poised as he is in relation to the hero to deflate, dissolve, undo the work of *saṃskāra* and the classical iconography of emotion. He may seek to achieve this effect deliberately, as in the case of the dream just recounted; more often he works at debunking by means of the unconscious force of his traditional habits and attitudes. To some extent, this faculty derives from what may be a universal feature of clowning—the reflexive gift of the commentator, who is capable of framing experience or, even more significantly, of switching frames almost at will. But in part we may have here a specific inheritance that the Vidūṣaka received from his origins in late Vedic myth and ritual. Let us recall Maitreya's pseudo-heretical remark quoted earlier (on the uselessness of *pūjā* offered to the gods): here the Vidūṣaka is almost a comic Nāstika, not in the classical sense of the word as a bona fide heretic but rather in the older sense of the Vedic "nay-sayer," the willy-nilly skeptic who is ritually pitted against his opposite, positively affirming ritual player.[47] The clown's "negation" is specifically tied to the *nāyaka*'s

[45] *Śakuntalā* VI (Bengal Recension).

[46] This quasi-Freudian view finds some support in recent physiological research: see Handelman (1981), p. 365 n. 12.

[47] Heesterman (1968-1969); see above, III.2 at n. 30.

positive "illusion," and the two form a unity, as we have seen. Here we must mention Kuiper's theory that the Vidūṣaka in the drama effectively substitutes for Varuṇa, the primeval *asura* whose negative role in relation to Indra was an essential feature of Vedic rituals still dimly reflected in the structure of the drama.[48] The Vidūṣaka stands in relation to the *nāyaka* as the complex, inauspicious Varuṇa stood in relation to Indra, specifically in the Vedic verbal contest (*vívāc*) that expressed the cosmogonic strife of the two cosmic powers—the forces of the *asuras* against those of the *devas*, the pole of *nivṛtti* as opposed to that of *pravṛtti*, withdrawal and wholeness pitted against creation, division, and sacrifice.[49]

From this vantage point it is highly significant that, according to the *Nāṭyaśāstra*, the protecting deity of the *nāyaka* is Indra, whereas the Vidūṣaka's protecting deity is the syllable *Om*—that is, language as creative symbol and embodiment of the Absolute (*śabdabrahman*).[50] Kuiper has argued that here, too, the Oṃkāra is a substitute for the dread Varuṇa, "who was too inauspicious to act (or, to be named) as the protector of a dramatic character."[51] Yet even if this view is correct with respect to the evolution of the dramatic tradition, the association with primeval speech is clearly crucial to the Vidūṣaka's classical role. His *nivṛtti*-negations of the *nāyaka*'s romantic pretensions are dependent upon his peculiar use of language, albeit the debased Prakrit speech of the Mahābrāhmaṇa or, as he is sometimes called, the Brahmabandhu (that is, a "low" Brahmin excluded from ritual, especially sacrificial, performance).[52] The clown's identification with *Om*, the *praṇava*-mantra, is not coincidental: it hints, rather, at two sides of the Vidūṣaka's function as ontological referee and commentator. Our unbalanced, incongruous clown is caught up in a partial paradox never fully articulated in the plays themselves or in the critical literature about them. On the one hand, he stands in a somewhat tenuous relation to a truth that transcends the particular dramatic situation in which he acts. He offers immediacy and tangibility in place of the *nāyaka*'s lugubrious enchantment; his humorous statements hint at a context wider than

[48] Kuiper (1979). Kuiper's rich and, on the whole, convincing argument cannot be summarized here.

[49] *Ibid.*, pp. 208-209.

[50] *Nāṭyaśāstra* 1.97. Similarly, Sarasvatī protects the heroine, and Śiva the rest of the actors. See discussion by Biardeau (1981).

[51] Kuiper (1979), p. 176.

[52] Not that the Vidūṣaka is actually excluded in this way (in fact, he takes part in Brahmin rituals); the point is in the application of the epithet. And see Biardeau (1981): the Vidūṣaka's deformities are those that debar someone from being a *yajamāna*.

the hero's own, top-heavy perspective; to a certain, rather limited extent, his comic deflation of *saṃskāra* "opens up" the drama to outer, nondramatic reality. Our laughter is the key to his success. As the Hebrew poet Bialik has said of the wordless languages of music, weeping, and laughter: "They begin where words end, and their proper function is not to close but to open. They well up from the abyss, they are its tide."[53] The Vidūṣaka's link with Oṃkāra symbolizes this idea. Words, on the other hand, mask the abyss: and this, too, is part of the Vidūṣaka's habitual task. Even in the earliest dramas, he is already, in some sense, a translator (a role which, as we shall see, becomes central in the South Indian comic traditions): representing, we might say, the very idea of language, and given to stating uncomfortable truths in bluntly comical ways, the Vidūṣaka filters his insight through the crude vessel of his own absurdity. He can be garrulous, even unnervingly eloquent—for example, in Maitreya's verbose depiction of the palatial brothel in Ujjayinī[54]—but this linguistic power is somehow cloying, ineffectual, debased. His truths, bound up, as they must be, with the *nāyaka*'s illusions, are translations, pointing imperfectly at an invisible original. They have both the freedom and the loss of the only partly formed.

Perhaps the hidden original is itself far from perfect; the Omkāra, as *śabdabrahman*, can be seen as "the inferior *brahman*, in relation to the supreme *brahman* that transcends sound."[55] The Vidūṣaka is thus a "brâhmane gaffeur" who contrasts with the superior Brahmin as much as with the *nāyaka*. It would, perhaps, be equally helpful to adopt a metonymic view of these relations: just as the *praṇava*, as *śabdabrahman*, simultaneously embodies and symbolizes the transcendent wholeness of the absolute, so the Vidūṣaka's use of language veils as much as it reveals, very much like the royal icons discussed in Chapter II. In either case, a contrast emerges between the Vidūṣaka, voluble but limited in his hold upon truth, and the silent *muni*, the sage who denies the legitimacy of language in his serious demand for perfection and ultimate freedom. If silence transports the sage into the unlimited, the clown's rude Prakrit speech clearly binds him to the mundane; he is on this side of transcendence, however incisive his perceptions. We might note, however, that this contrast between sage and clown cannot be simply defined in hierarchical terms: the *muni* is no less vulnerable in his pretensions than the *nāyaka* to the clown's

[53] Bialik (1979), p. 112.
[54] *Mṛcchakaṭika* IV (after verse 27).
[55] Biardeau (1981), p. 299.

mockery; debased, debunking comedy can easily outwit the grimly serious sage, or even turn him into a clown himself.[56]

The comic spirit may triumph; but the Vidūṣaka's limitations should by now be clear. He may be capable of suggesting another "frame" for the hero's noble sentiments, but he is himself locked into his rather helpless role. In the end, his perspicuity does him little good. Even his potential for galvanizing others, or for thickening the plot by his unintentional clumsiness or folly, is severely limited. Like so many comic figures, his wit can flourish only by virtue of his practical impotence. Comedy contains him, defuses the impact of his own deflating words. At his most perspicacious, the clown is most absurd. His linguistic gift endows him with a certain power to transform perception—without transforming reality; in a sense, he is trapped by his own wit, enmeshed in the verbal webs he weaves around himself, just as the Creator is said to weave the world out of and around himself, like the spider.[57] The arachnid metaphor works both ways—the god is both the source and the victim of the creative process of weaving a world, *māyā*, in all its beauty and its entangling danger—and we might well expect the clown to follow this example. Indeed, the Indian folk clowns do have an important relation to the notion of *māyā* as a magical, transformative power to construct, and to dissolve realities.

But the Vidūṣaka, as we have seen, is no magician. He may "spoil" others' illusions, but he is victimized by his own: thus Cārāyaṇa leaps at the chance of marrying a transparent mirage.[58] The Vidūṣaka even falls prey to the most hackneyed of all Vedāntic trials of perception: he is frightened by the sight of a rope that he mistakenly perceives as a snake.[59] This joke hits home. The Vidūṣaka is hardly a wry, detached observer in control of his own mind, and capable of tampering with others'; he is the object of others' sport rather than a playful figure in his own right, just as he is closer to foil than to parody, more truly foolish than truly wise. His witticisms emerge, almost by serendipity, from the earthy obsessions of his temperament. If he applies his own brand of *Entzauberung* upon the hero within the play and upon the audience outside it, this effect is only semiconscious. Moreover, the Vidūṣaka's assessment of the world is ultimately no more convincing

[56] For a fine example, see the *Bhagavadajjuka* (the sage Śāṇḍilya as clown). One thinks also of Rāvaṇa's unconscious parody of a sage when he comes, disguised, to Sītā in the forest: Kampaṉ 3.826–830.

[57] Cf. *Bṛhadāraṇyaka Upaniṣad* 2.1.20.

[58] Above, n. 24.

[59] *Svapnavāṣavadatta* V, after verse 2. This is something of a cliché in Sanskrit drama; cf. *Subhadrādhanañjaya* I. On the snake and the rope, see O'Flaherty (1984).

than the *nāyaka*'s, as we can see from the usual happy endings in the drama, when the lovers' passion finds fulfilment. In a sense, the Vidūṣaka is subject to the most profound illusion of all, that which passes for ordinary "reality." For it is no less deceptive to live with the merely tangible, with gross objects and the compulsions of hunger, fear, and *Realpolitik* as the final bedrock of reality, than it is to cultivate lyrical or romantic visions. We may laugh at the Vidūṣaka both for his mockery of the *nāyaka*'s experience and for his failure to recognize its truth.

Laugh "at" rather than "with"; the Vidūṣaka in the classical dramas does not consciously control our response. His clowning operates within a carefully constrained field and has a fairly predictable range, at least in those plays which set the norms for the classical tradition. As Jefferds has noted, he is not a critic.[60] Moreover, the outstanding aspect of so many other (including other Indian) clowns—their transformative powers, their ability to play with the play, to move into the unpredicted and the uncontained—is largely frozen in the Vidūṣaka's case. He never quite reaches the centrality of the Shakespearean clowns, who so often illuminate the entire development of the drama. Think, for example, of the *Midsummer Night's Dream*, where the amorous heroes, in both their "seriously" sober and their enchanted, befuddled states, often seem ironically to parody the antics of the clowns. And unlike Puck, the Vidūṣaka almost never gets the last word. By the same token, it is not easy to ascribe to him the "lightning-rod effect" of "sanctioning the release . . . of our anarchic impulses and feelings, under controls which prevent them from threatening the adult, civilized norms of the main plot, even as they are prevented from threatening these norms in the spectator himself and in society at large."[61] The Vidūṣaka but rarely reaches down to the level of anarchy, protest, or revolt.

These comparisons may seem unfair: the Vidūṣaka is clearly not meant to be central in the manner of Shakespeare's clowns. Their point is merely to suggest the beginnings of a typology, as we move from the Vidūṣaka to other, South Indian comic figures. For our purposes, two points should be stressed again: first, though he is no magician, the Vidūṣaka does open up the issues of proper perception and the stratified nature of reality, both by his pointed comments, in contrast with the *nāyaka*'s statements and feelings, and by the challenge that his incongruous blend of attributes constitutes to our normal

[60] Jefferds (1981), p. 67.

[61] Levin (1971), p. 146.

categorical distinctions. He may help to blend the overall "flavor" of the drama, but at the same time he corrodes its ontological assurance. Second, if he is not "central," he is nevertheless crucially important as a comic complement to the *nāyaka*'s "straight" character. King and clown comprise a unified but internally diffuse, and disharmonious, set.

Excursus: On Triads and Twins

The Vidūṣaka completes the *nāyaka*; together the two are one. But their mutual dependence is unequal: the *nāyaka* can probably get by without a Vidūṣaka,[62] but the latter does not stand alone. Is it because of the clown's fundamental loneliness that, throughout the world, he tends to appear together with one or more companions? As commentator or reflexive mirror, the clown is, of course, paired to the ridiculed norm. But there are shadows carved from shadows, and mirrors within mirrors. The echo, which Bergson saw as basic to laughter as such,[63] can reverberate repeatedly in the direction of its source.

We may detect here a general feature of comedy, its capacity for self-regeneration through division, distortion, and a creative reflection of, and upon, existing forms. Whereas tragedy seals itself within its given limits—thus leaving conflicts and contradictions locked in opposition, without hope of resolution—comedy is infinite regress, an "implosion" in the mind focused inward upon itself.[64] A "benign doubling and redoubling"[65] reveals the comic process in action. The resulting profusion of forms is expressed through the comic groups of two, three, or more, which map out in their interrelations the unstable parameters of the comic vision. These relations appear to be subject to a rule of polarization: within a comic set, the various figures sort themselves into graded levels leading from the "raw," chaotic forms of slapstick and simple farce through ironic observation to more complex and integrated forms. The rule applies to India no less than to the comic configurations intimated by the author of the *Tractatus*

[62] There are, of course, dramas without a Vidūṣaka. We may think, for example, of Bhavabhūti's Rāma plays; and note that Rāma functions generally as a kind of royal anticlown (with Hanuman as his Vidūṣaka?).

[63] Bergson (1956), p. 64.

[64] See Babcock (1978), pp. 16-17; on tragedy, see Chapter VII below.

[65] Nevo (1980), p. 16.

Coislinianus, which must serve us as surrogate for the lost Aristotelian theory of comedy.[66]

These levels of comic representation are germane to our study, although a full typology of Indian comedy would, of course, disclose many more distinct roles. Nor do the Indian materials reproduce exactly the three major types distinguished by the *Tractatus*: the rather crudely buffoonish Bōmolochos; the elusive, ironic commentator, Eirōn; and the pretentious and vainglorious impostor, Alazōn.[67] As we might expect, these types are often collapsed into the latent potential of a single comic figure, only to emerge as clear-cut facets of his identity in relation to another character. Each comic scene, each series of actors, has its own calculus of comic permutations. Let us look briefly at one classical example, from the first act of the *Little Clay Cart*, where three "clowns" are suddenly thrown together to their mutual discomfiture and our delight.

Two of them, in fact, have been together from the start—the evil and pompous Śakāra, brother-in-law to the king; and his slick, sycophantic companion, the Viṭa or Libertine. They have been pursuing the elegant courtesan Vasantasenā, for whom Śakāra lusts ("love" is hardly his emotion); she, disgusted by his attentions, has found shelter in the house of the play's hero, Cārudatta. It is night: the pursuers have lost their prey; in their confusion they attack Cārudatta's maidservant, who is accompanying the Vidūṣaka, Maitreya. After a few moments of wild slapstick, with blows raining down freely on all sides, the Vidūṣaka raises his walking-stick and cries:

> VIDŪṢAKA: Enough of this! Even a dog gets violent in his own house—so why not a Brahmin like me? This stick is as crooked as my luck: I'll use it to pound that lousy head of yours until it pops like dry bamboo!
>
> VIṬA: Forgive us, O great Brahmin![68]
>
> VIDŪṢAKA (*looking at the Viṭa*): You're not the one who offended. (*Looking at Śakāra*): *He* is. So it's you, Saṃsthānaka, brother-in-law to the king, you evil man. It may be true that Cārudatta has become poor, but is he not still an ornament to the city of

[66] See the edition by Cooper (1922); discussion in Nevo (1980), pp. 12-14.

[67] See Bhat's rather unhappy attempt to apply these types to the Vidūṣaka and other characters of the Sanskrit drama: (1959), pp. 170-71.

[68] *Mahābrāhmaṇa*. One should note that this epithet is also used to refer to an allegedly degraded class of Brahmin funeral priests. Its application to the Vidūṣaka may therefore be somewhat ironic.

Ujjayinī? What gives you the right to enter his house and beat up his servants? . . .[69]

VIṬA (*uncomfortably*): Forgive us, great Brahmin. It was not out of arrogance that we did this, but simply a mistake:

We were looking for a lustful lady . . .

VIDŪṢAKA: Who, this one?

VIṬA: God forbid!

Someone young, her own mistress,
whom we lost—and thus committed
this inelegant confusion.

There is nothing left of us but apologies. Please accept them. (*He throws off his sword and falls at the Brahmin's feet.*)

VIDŪṢAKA: Get up, my good man, get up. I reproached you out of ignorance; now that I understand, I am sorry.

VIṬA: You are the one who deserves an apology. I will get up, on one condition.

VIDŪṢAKA: Speak.

VIṬA: That you won't tell Cārudatta about this incident.

VIDŪṢAKA: I will not tell him.

VIṬA:

Your grace, O Brahmin, graces now my humbled head;
we came at you with swords, and your disarming goodness
overcame us.

ŚAKĀRA (*jealously*): Why are you cringing before this worthless Brahmin?

VIṬA: I'm afraid.

ŚAKĀRA: Afraid of what?

VIṬA: Of Cārudatta's virtues.

ŚAKĀRA: What virtues are there in a man in whose house there is nothing to eat?

VIṬA: Don't say that—

His poverty is the result of his caring for people like me;
and never did he lord it over anyone.
He has dried up, like a lake in summer,
after giving everyone his fill.

ŚAKĀRA (*angrily*): Who is that son-of-a-bitch anyway?

The famous Pāṇḍava Śvetaketu?
Rādhā's son Rāvaṇa, sired by Indra?

[69] The Vidūṣaka sings a verse at this point.

Aśvatthāman, the son Kuntī bore to Rāma?
Or is he Jaṭāyu, born to Dharma?[70]

VIṬA: You idiot! He is the excellent Cārudatta:

Wishing-tree to all in need,
weighed down with the fruit which are his virtues;
a father to all good men,
a mirror to the learned,
touchstone of proper conduct,
an ocean bounded by fine character,
excellent host, never disdainful,
a veritable treasure-house of manliness,
his whole being noble and resourceful—
only such a paragon is truly alive;
the rest of us just go on breathing.

Let's go.

ŚAKĀRA: Without Vasantasenā?
VIṬA: Vasantasenā is lost.
ŚAKĀRA: What do you mean, lost?
VIṬA: Lost—
like the sight of a blind man,
like a sick man's former health,
an idiot's understanding,
an idle man's hopes of success,
or like true knowledge in an absent-minded rogue.
As soon as she met you, she disappeared,
as pleasure does in the presence of a foe.

ŚAKĀRA: I won't go without Vasantasenā.
VIṬA: Haven't you heard:

An elephant can be held by a chain,
a horse by the reins;
but you need a heart to hold a woman—

and since you don't have one, you could just as well be gone.

ŚAKĀRA: You go if you want to—I'm not going anywhere.
VIṬA: So be it. Off I go. (*Exit.*)[71]

Only with difficulty could these three comic figures be assigned to the categories of the *Tractatus Coislinianus*; the comic division of labor

[70] All the Śakāra's genealogical statements are, of course, hopelessly muddled, a ridiculous amalgam of gross ignorance and pretentious name-dropping.

[71] *Mṛcchakaṭika* I, following verse 42.

is nevertheless patent. Note how the Vidūṣaka has risen in the world—from Bōmolochos-Buffoon (as he appears when juxtaposed with the noble Cārudatta) to the most respectable and serious of the three characters in this scene. The Viṭa's verbose attentions drive the Vidūṣaka almost into silence, although he continues, in effect, to represent the idealized presence of his friend, Cārudatta. In this way Maitreya helps to reveal the foolishness of the Viṭa, his mirror image (as the Vidūṣaka himself is mirror to Cārudatta): the Viṭa, too, is a Brahmin, and an educated one at that, but his learning merely enhances his effect as a shifty, self-dramatizing, absurdly effete fool. Van Buitenen aptly calls him "precious";[72] his witticisms tend to be phrased in an idiom both grandiose and slick, and they merely glance off his unworthy patron, the oaflike Śakāra. That the Viṭa allows himself to serve such a master is evidence enough of his slippery, rationalizing temperament. Irony would suit him—as, indeed, it often does in the comic genre of *bhāṇa*, where the Viṭa figures as the narrator and sole observer of the action;[73] here, however, the pressure from below has pushed him further toward the Alazōn type—for in Maitreya's company he is ashamed of, and seeks to disguise, his sycophantic dependence on Śakāra. And yet whatever the Viṭa says or does discloses his instability and hyperbolic folly, his clumsiness of mind if not of word; observe how he overreacts, throwing off his sword and falling at Maitreya's feet, in the orgy of apologies to which the two Brahmin clowns treat one another (to Śakāra's obvious distaste).

The "pressure from below" derives from the presence of Śakāra, whose ludicrous grossness and wicked nature become more and more dangerous as the drama unfolds. That aspect of comedy that is linked with cruelty, or with evil generally,[74] finds expression in this character. And, in true Indian fashion, the two ends of the scale converge, for Śakāra is both a crude Bōmolochos, amusing by virtue of his unrestrained and exaggerated appetites, and a conceited impostor given to grotesque shows of "learning" (as in the verse he utters in this passage) which only serve to expose his ignorance. In the *Little Clay Cart*, Śakāra's impudent buffoonery at times "ennobles" the Vidūṣaka even as it thrusts the Viṭa into an ambiguous middle range of comic attitudes. The three clowns act upon one another, and upon the drama as a whole, in a rich interweaving of comic roles that become distinct only through these relations.

[72] In the introduction to his translation of the play (1971), p. 38.

[73] On the *bhāṇa*, see the fine study by Janaki (1973) as well as a forthcoming book by Lee Siegel; a typical example of the genre is the *Ubhayābhisārikā*.

[74] See V.8 below; Duckworth (1971), pp. 309-11 (the derisive aspect of laughter).

Such triads are not at all rare. The set of Vidūṣaka, Viṭa, and Ceṭī (maidservant) appears in the third act of *Nāgānanda*, as mentioned earlier; and we shall see a triangle similarly laden with sexual tensions in the Andhra puppet theater. Sanskrit farce also offers a number of intriguing examples (as in Mahendravarman's *Mattavilāsa*). But, in general, the more prevalent pattern seems to be that of doubling, a pattern that, inevitably, turns out to have two main forms of its own. There is, on the one hand, the type we have already seen exemplified by the Vidūṣaka and the *nāyaka*: a clown coupled with a frankly noncomical, perhaps idealized figure whose words and deeds fuel the fires of the clown's wit or mimicry. This type is extended in interesting ways in the stories of a king and his court jester, to which we turn in a moment. On the other hand, the exemplary figure may himself be converted into a clown without losing his identification with propriety and order. We then have two, polarized clowns, like the White Clown and the Auguste of the European circus; the former holds absurdly to his claim on the normative world of rules and proper categories, while the latter revels in antinomian, exuberantly childlike, or more often childish, pranks.[75] The circus pair, White Clown and Auguste, offer great scope for comic invention; since both are clowns, they illustrate both a mockery of the norm and a mockery of the norm's mocker. Each of the two performs a necessary exegesis of the other. This polarization operates with regularity: we may think of the deadly serious sage and his rebellious and skeptical disciple in the *Bhagavadajjuka*.[76] But, as we shall see in the next chapter, perhaps the most striking development of this pattern occurs in the South Indian myths about kingship.

3. The Clown on the Kerala Stage

Surrounded by his rival clowns, the Vidūṣaka of the classical dramas may achieve a certain elevation that carries with it an implicit critique of these others. But a true transformation of the Vidūṣaka into an explicit and forceful critic can be seen in the Kerala dramatic tradition of Kūṭiyāṭṭam, which bases its performances on the texts of Sanskrit

[75] See Fellini (1976), pp. 124-26, 129-30. Fellini remarks that this "game" (the White Clown vs. the Auguste) "is so true that if you have a white clown with you, you are bound to play the Auguste, and vice versa" (p. 130). And cf. the conventional two Zanni of the *commedia dell'arte*: Nicoll (1963), p. 265.

[76] This couple turns into a triad, then widens still further, after the entrance of the courtesan (around whose sudden death the plot of this farce revolves).

plays.[77] These texts are performed in the Kūṭiyāṭṭam tradition in greatly elaborated forms, with many striking features apparently unique to this area, for the relation of Kūṭiyāṭṭam to ancient Sanskrit drama, as to the *Nāṭyaśāstra* schools of Sanskrit poetics, is not yet wholly clear. With respect to the role of the Vidūṣaka, the Kūṭiyāṭṭam tradition itself recognizes that major innovations have been made, innovations that are generally attributed to the poet Tolan, said to have been the jester and companion of King Kulaśekharavarman (11th century?), himself the author of Sanskrit dramas still performed in Kūṭiyāṭṭam.[78]

The Vidūṣaka in Kūṭiyāṭṭam shares with his classical predecessor a partly grotesque appearance: he has a red turban with a golden rim and black stripes; huge rolled or rounded earrings; a thick, racoonlike black stripe across his eyes; a long, black, twirled mustache; and red or brown polka dots scattered over the white paste covering his face and chest (in a manner somewhat reminiscent of the costume of European circus clowns).[79] He wears a dhoti and, of course, his Brahminical thread. In one play he enters in a largely disabled state—his hands and legs have been broken by a fall from a horse—so that he reminds us of the crippled clowns of the South Indian folk genres.[80] But the visual effect he produces is undoubtedly secondary to his verbal impact; the Kūṭiyāṭṭam Vidūṣaka is one of the most articulate of Indian clowns. He treats the audience to a feast of satirical and ironic comment, self-conscious parody, and spontaneous wit. Of all the South Indian comic figures, he is closest to Menippean jest. These verbal functions are clearly responsible for his centrality in this theatrical tradition; as K. Kunjunni Raja has said, "the Vidusaka is the most prominent and the most popular figure in Kootiyattam and Koothu.

[77] It is imprecise to refer to Kūṭiyāṭṭam as a "surviving" form of classical Sanskrit drama; it appears rather to represent a local development of the ancient tradition, in which genuinely classical elements have mingled with specifically local and popular ones. The following pages owe much to the performances and seminars given by the troupe of Vasudevan Namboodiripad (of the Kerala Kalamandalam) at the University of Wisconsin in September 1982, and to discussions with Vasudevan Namboodiripad and Clifford Jones. The responsibility for the conclusions presented here is, of course, solely mine.

[78] There is much controversy over Kulaśekhara's date; see Unni (1977), pp. 21-48. Tolan is the subject of a monograph by P. V. Krishna Warrier: *Tolamahākavi* (Kozhikode: P. K. Brothers, 1953), in Malayalam—unfortunately unavailable to me.

[79] From observations at a performance in Madison, September 15, 1983. Cf. the photograph in Bhat (1959), opposite p. 48; and Unni (1977), p. 179.

[80] *Tapatīsaṃvaraṇa*: see Tarlekar (1975), p. 275; and see below, VII.6, on the Tamil *nŏṇṭināṭakam*.

In course of time he came to overshadow all the other characters in a play."[81]

This central role, which constitutes an enormous expansion of the Vidūṣaka's part in the classical dramas, has three major analytical components. First, the Kūṭiyāṭṭam Vidūṣaka has become a wholly legitimate and necessary "translator"—he translates the Sanskrit and Prakrit verses spoken by other characters (when he is on stage) into Malayalam intelligible to the audience. In the process of doing so, he also elaborates and comments upon the translated text. The classical Vidūṣaka's close association with language generally, and his implicit role of translator of truth into "corrupt" human speech (as discussed above), have been realized in specific and concrete ways in Kūṭiyāṭṭam. The Vidūṣaka's use of Malayalam—one of the innovations attributed to Tolan, and a practice criticized in some of the dramaturgical treatises from Kerala—endows him with an obvious and immediate power over the dramatic representation. At the same time, it neatly splits off his intradramatic function as one of the play's characters from his identity as translator and commentator: the latter aspect has been isolated and lifted out of its context, so that the Vidūṣaka now offers a double image, partly inside and partly outside the play. From this position on both sides of the boundary, it is a short step to the role of a more general mediator of dramatic reality; and thus it is surely no accident that in an important subgenre of Kūṭiyāṭṭam called Cākyār-kūttu, when there is but a single actor/narrator engaged in presenting a story before an audience, that actor is always dressed as a Vidūṣaka. In some sense, the clown appears as the true persona of the storyteller as such.

Second, we have the Kūṭiyāṭṭam Vidūṣaka's role as critic, especially as seen in the expository monologue with which he introduces himself to the audience. Like other characters in Kūṭiyāṭṭam, the Vidūṣaka has a *nirvahaṇa*—a rich presentation of the character's background (often a kind of "flashback" to the narrative antecedents of the major dramatic figures) on the occasion of his first appearance on stage. The *nirvahaṇa* can be very lengthy; in the case of the Vidūṣaka it may extend for four or five entire nights, during which he entertains the audience with a humorous, largely satirical exposition—part of which is prescribed for him by tradition, while the rest is extemporized in a process of interaction with the audience. Here the Vidūṣaka may choose to comment upon local issues or events or to address, directly or obliquely, individuals sitting before him. His role as live com-

[81] Kunjunni Raja (1974), p. 2.

mentator is clearly in evidence in this capacity. It is nevertheless contained by the traditional structure of discourse ascribed to the clown, a discourse focused during the *nirvahaṇa* on the four goals of human life (*puruṣārthas*)—*vinoda* (entertainment, enjoyment, pleasant distraction); *vañcana* (deception); *aśana* (feasting); and *rājasevā* (serving a king).[82] The wholesale parody of the classical series of *kāma, artha, dharma*, and *mokṣa*—desire, personal profit, duty or righteous behavior, and final release—combines various disciplines and attitudes: *vinoda* and *vañcana* have an erotic cast (an exposition of *Kāmaśāstra*); *aśana* is a direct outgrowth of the classical Vidūṣaka's insatiable appetite; *rājasevā* expands upon the ambiguous and problematic association of Brahmins with kings.[83] At this point there seems to be a transition toward a more serious "*parabasis*," with the Vidūṣaka lamenting the state of kingship in his time and decrying those rulers who have lapsed from the dharmic ideal; he also points to the ineluctable power of *karma*. Simultaneously, his satire becomes harsher and more generalized as he describes the corruption and pervasive folly of an entire village, a South Indian Chelm called Anadhītimaṅgalam: here the power of the deity in the local temple is being ruined by the self-seeking designs of the temple servants; the village fools devote their common energies to deceiving and robbing the local prostitutes; in short, a whole society is subject to delusion and decay.[84] Note that the Vidūṣaka's depiction of this village is in no way a sanctioning of folly, or a carnivalesque suggestion of an acceptable Feast of Fools; rather, the Vidūṣaka here is a contemporary critic engaged in a formalized but essentially comic exposure of a world identifiably linked (despite the distorting, exaggerated perspective) with everyday realities.

Finally, the contrastive, "spoiling" effect of the Vidūṣaka in the classical dramas takes a new turn in Kūṭiyāṭṭam. In translating, and responding to, his companion's lovelorn lyrics, the clown now toys with satirical *inversion* in ways that go far beyond the classical precedents. Many of these remarks, including the parodic *pratiślokas* ("counterverses") that the clown utters in Malayalam, are recorded in the dramatic handbooks that the Cākyār community has preserved for the Kūṭiyāṭṭam plays. For example: Arjuna sings the praises of Subhadrā's eyes, which seem to him to be begging for his love, promising the gift of her affection, and hinting at their future union; upon

[82] *Ibid.*; Unni (1977), p. 181; Tarlekar (1975), p. 272.

[83] Tarlekar (1975), p. 272.

[84] This structure of the Vidūṣaka's *nirvahaṇa* is also ascribed to Tolan.

hearing this verse, the Vidūṣaka says in Malayalam (supposedly expounding the text):

> Dear friend, I am extremely happy; for those charming corners of the eyes of the servant-maid contain the request: will you give me a little pan and betel-nut; the hint that "I live in the servant's room," etc.[85]

The Vidūṣaka's interpretation is colored by his traditional interest in food, before all else; but in offering this rendering of Arjuna's verse, the clown both destroys its entire force and denigrates the object of the hero's passion—for Subhadrā is reduced to the status of a maid-servant. This tendency has become habitual with the Kūṭiyāṭṭam Vidūṣaka, who seems to have developed the misogyny of earlier clowns, such as Maitreya, to an extreme. Here, for example, are the Vidūṣaka's comments on the verse in which Arjuna introduces Subhadrā:

ARJUNA: *Asti* (*There is . . .*)
VIDŪṢAKA: Who my dear friend? Lord Kṛṣṇa?
ARJUNA: *Subhadrā nāma* (*someone named Subhadrā*)
VIDŪṢAKA: Oh my friend! I know well. Alas! You are attracted by that aging Subhadrā.
ARJUNA: *Prastutatāruṇyā* (*still young*)
VIDŪṢAKA: What a young girl? Oh! You are in love with that lame, squint-eyed, teeth-protruding ugly servant-maid?
ARJUNA: *Atyantasundarī* (*extraordinarily beautiful*)
VIDŪṢAKA: What! Very beautiful and young damsel. Let me think about it. Oh. I know. You are a prince of the lunar race and the friend of Kṛṣṇa. Yet you fall in love with a servant-maid. Alas!
ARJUNA: *Bhaginī Vāsubhadrasya* (*the sister of Vāsubhadra*)
VIDŪṢAKA: The sister of Vāsubhadra? (*Laughing*). How pitiable for a learned man like you to love a woman married to somebody. By this time she must have three or four children!
ARJUNA: *Kanyakā* (*an unmarried girl*).

At this point the Vidūṣaka has no choice but to admit his mistake; Subhadrā is, after all—to the clown's despair—an appropriate bride.[86]

The transition from the *nāyaka*'s Sanskrit to the Vidūṣaka's Malayalam is here accompanied by a steep fall in the level of discourse; the

[85] Unni (1977), p. 188, citing Krishna Warrier.

[86] *Ibid.*, p. 185, citing Keralavarma Ammāman Tampurān, *Kūttum Kūṭiyāṭṭavum* (Trichur, 1114 M.E.), in Malayalam (unfortunately unavailable to me). I have quoted verbatim Unni's translation of the Vidūṣaka's Malayalam.

passage illustrates the popular view of Sanskrit as elevated speech, language at its most chaste and perfected. The linguistic contrast runs parallel to an emotional one: Arjuna's chaste vision of his beloved is parodied at every step by the scornful, crudely pretentious clown. Here it is not the *nāyaka* who is being mocked but rather the Vidūṣaka who appears ridiculous by virtue of his stubborn, somewhat pathetic persistence in misunderstanding and devaluing his friend's intent.

Parody can easily become travesty. Arjuna praises his beloved with a variation on a hackneyed theme: she is a paragon of feminine virtues, all of which have been lavished upon her by Brahmā, the creator—to such an extent that if he ever wishes to fashion another woman, he will have to beg them back from her (*sraṣṭum vāñchati cet karotu punar apy atraiva bhikṣāṭanam*). The Vidūṣaka translates this as follows:

> All the feminine qualities such as stink of the mouth, the foul smell emanating from the body, wrath, harsh words, terrible looks, etc., have been exhausted by Brahman in the creation of Cakki, so that in order to create another he has to beg them from her.[87]

By now nothing is left of the *nāyaka*'s positive sentiments but the bare syntactical frame in which he expressed them. Even this has been turned inside out: the romantic thesis has evolved into a clownish antithesis, hyperbolic praise has become abuse. It is amazing that the two verses, *śloka* and *pratiśloka*, lofty adulation and coarse, ironic denigration, can coexist within the same context, in close juxtaposition, and with the same referent. To achieve anything like the same effect, we would have to interweave, as consistent, immediate echoes of one another, the statements of Falstaff's "anti-kingdom" of riotous delight with those of Henry's strait-laced court. Kūṭiyāṭṭam standardizes this kind of alternation in idiom and image. Both sides of the coin are clearly demarcated and made conspicuous: if clown and prince are still two parts of a symbolic whole, their internal differentiation could hardly be more complete.

Imaginative bifurcation of this kind—a toying with the properties of inversion and parodic echoes—might seem to belong, by right, to dramatic and literary genres, in their supposed isolation from a more real world of events and unmediated experience (if such a thing exists). Perhaps a tradition like that of Kūṭiyāṭṭam, with its patient expansion of each detail, each complex facet of the classical art, can afford to indulge in comic mirror effects and radical self-commentary imbued

87 *Ibid.*, p. 193, citing Krishna Warrier (p. 81).

with satire. Even the Kūṭiyāṭṭam Vidūṣaka is safe from counterattack, safe even from being taken seriously. Yet this isolation within artistic frames no longer seems axiomatic;[88] the Vidūṣaka has his counterpart in the sphere of political symbolism. The three major roles of the Kūṭiyāṭṭam clown—his control over language and his association with its limits; his critical capacity; and his penchant for satire, irony, and stark inversion of whatever is given—all recur in the popular traditions, from elsewhere in South India, about the most famous court jester in the region's history.

4. Tĕnāli Rāma: The Obliquity of the Real

In turning to the folktales about the South Indian court jester, we cross a double boundary: from classical or semi-classical genres to the perspective of a folk culture; and from carefully delimited comic roles to a coherent vision of radical comic transformation.[89] The jester's stories are marked by a boldness and an intensity never attained by the Vidūṣaka, in either Sanskrit classical drama or in Kūṭiyāṭṭam, although the jester has inherited many of the Vidūṣaka's traits. In crossing over from drama to the symbolism of the royal court, an inhibition is released: the clown is now gifted with pure intentionality and a comic inventiveness entirely legitimate within his assumed context. He is entirely self-conscious; his raison d'être lies in his wit. Unlike the Vidūṣaka, even at his most foolish the jester can never really be a fool.

There is only one such jester in the Tamil and Telugu traditions, the folk-hero Tĕnāli Rāma (Tamil Tĕṉālirāmaṉ) or Tĕnāli Rāmaliṅgam, who is associated by a host of popular stories with the famous Vijayanagar king Kṛṣṇadevarāya (1509-1529). Tĕnāli Rāma's historicity is entirely in doubt: there is no evidence, aside from the folk stories, that Kṛṣṇadevarāya ever had a "real" jester; nor is there any reason to believe that Tĕnāli Rāma has anything to do with the well-known poet Tĕnāli Rāmakṛṣṇuḍu, the author of Telugu *kāvyas* such as the *Ghaṭikācalamāhātmya* and the *Pāṇḍuraṅgamāhātmya* and a contemporary of this king. The village of Tĕnāli in Guntur District could certainly have been the ancestral village of more than one prominent Rāma. Nor can we date the stories themselves: they exist today in a variety of oral and written forms, the latter ranging from bazaar chap-

[88] See, for example, Victor Turner's work on "social dramas": Turner (1974) and (1982).

[89] This section has profited greatly from discussions with Velcheru Narayana Rao and Don Handelman, to both of whom I am deeply indebted.

books, in Tamil and Telugu, to modern literary reworkings of varying quality and closeness to the folk sources. There is no way of knowing if these stories go back as far as Vijayanagar times, or farther: as will soon become clear, they incorporate themes and motifs that have an almost universal distribution and that may, therefore, have been current in South India from much earlier times. But we have as yet no evidence of the existence of actual court jesters in the medieval Tamil kingdoms. This does not mean that there were no such figures: already in the *Cilappatikāram* we find suggestive but enigmatic references to comic players (*nakaiveḻampar*) attendant upon the king in his military expedition,[90] and it is possible that other roles mentioned in this text—such as that of the hermaphrodites (*peṭi*) exhibited with defeated kings[91]—had comic overtones. Given the profusion of comic elements formalized in the Chola court literature, it seems likely that similar functions were maintained in the medieval Tamil courts.

What can be said with assurance is that Tĕnāli Rāma serves with equal prominence in premodern Tamil and Telugu folk literature as the major exemplar of the court jester; that as such he is immensely popular, a heroic figure in more ways than one; and that he is clearly related to Indian counterparts such as Birbal, the jester (sometimes said to be from Andhra) associated with the Mughal emperor Akbar, and the beloved Gopāl Bhāṛ of Bengal.[92] It is also entirely possible that this symbolic type emerges in its full scope only with a more powerfully structured political system such as that of the Vijayanagar kings, and in particular in connection with some royal figure who comes to be perceived as prototypical or symbolically dominant.[93]

Only a few of the Tĕnali Rāma stories will be examined here. The corpus itself is quite large and merits a full study, which might seek to define the peculiarly South Indian transformations of those narrative patterns the stories share with other literatures.[94] Tĕnāli Rāma is close,

[90] *Cil.* 26.130-31; also at court: 5.53 (with Aṭiyārkkunallār's comment).

[91] *Cil.* 27.179-91; cf. *Maṇimekalai* 3.116-25.

[92] On the latter, see Dimock (1963), pp. 183-88. Cf. Kuiper (1979), pp. 205 and 226.

[93] A parallel case is that of Hārūn al-Rashīd and Buhlūl.

[94] I have used the following collections: *Tĕṉṉālrāman katai*; Kāḷahastirājeśvara Rao (1967); Campantam (1963); Robinson (1885), pp. 342-56; Panchapakesa Ayyar (1947); Narrainsawmy (1839), pp. 27-53; *Rama the Jester*, "Muttamiḻmaṇi" (1951). This list is obviously not exhaustive. A nineteenth-century collection by Natesa Sastri was not available to me. In addition, I have benefited from V. Narayana Rao's recounting of oral versions of the stories. Since none of the written versions I have used can claim great authenticity, I have in general followed the Tamil chapbook (the first source listed above) but have added significant details from other sources; my summaries are, therefore, sometimes hybrid versions.

on the one hand, to such local figures as the Tanjore Rogue[95]—a foolish trickster and scoundrel—and, on the other, to comic heroes such as Till Eulenspiegel, Hershele Ostropover, Nasreddin Hoca, and the African tricksters. His affinities with the European court fools are also apparent.[96] But if his iconography and morphology are remarkably similar to those of these other, well-known counterparts, his syntax is entirely his own. He is rooted in the milieu of the late medieval South Indian court as perceived by the local village. His contribution to the symbolic ordering of that milieu lies in the imaginative working out of a reflexive perspective that profoundly alters the normative attributes of the king.

At first glance Tĕnāli Rāma might appear to be, like certain of the European court fools, a specialist in ironic reversal and satire. In fact, reversal serves him merely as a tool to achieve a much more powerful statement; the linguistic playfulness and contrapuntal habit of the dramatic clowns, including the critical Vidūṣaka of Kūṭiyāṭṭam, are now the means to a wholesale symbolic violation of the norm. This is not, of course, to say that these means are accidentally chosen or insignificant; we could apply to the jester what has been said of human endeavor generally—that while laughter is in the realm of ends, the means, on the contrary, are always serious.[97] This would seem to hold true even where laughter is the instrument of a profoundly serious cognitive end, as we may observe from the usual story of Tĕnāli Rāma's "conversion" to his professional role:

> One day a passing *sannyāsin* came to Tĕnāli, where he noticed the fine character and excellent bodily form of the young Brahmin lad, Rāma. The holy man taught Rāma a *mantra* which, if recited 30 million times in a single night in the Kālī temple outside the village, would cause the fierce goddess to appear. At night, Rāma went to the Kālī shrine and recited the *mantra*. (Some say: his mother was so vexed at the impudent, hyperactive boy that she sent him in despair to Kālī, as the only "mother" who could handle him.) The goddess appeared in her terrifying form, with a thousand heads, and with two pots in her hands—one with the elixir of wisdom (*vidyā*), the other with that of wealth (*dhana*). She asked Rāma to choose whichever one he desired. The im-

[95] Natesa Sastri (1908), pp. 492-505.

[96] Such as Triboulet, Claus Narr, Brusquet; see Welsford's classic study (1935). On the African jester, see Gluckman (1965), pp. 102-103.

[97] Steiner (1981), paraphrasing Bakhtin. See the similar view of Peacock (1978), p. 221.

pudent lad snatched both pots from the goddess and drank them to the bottom. Kālī was enraged, but Rāma, quite unafraid, began to laugh. "How dare you laugh at me!" cried the ferocious Kālī, until Rāma explained: "I suddenly thought how much trouble it is for us, with only one head and two hands, whenever we have a runny nose—and how much worse it must be for you with your thousand heads!" The goddess cursed him: "You will become a ridiculous jester (*vikaṭakavi*) from this time forth." But Rāma was pleased: "You have given me a great boon; whichever way you look at my title, it reads exactly the same."[98]

Kālī, marveling at the boy's wit, felt compassion, and promised him that he would be praised for his jests at the royal court. Then the goddess disappeared, and Rāma left for the capital to pursue his new career.[99]

Like most of the clowns surveyed so far, Tĕnāli Rāma is a Brahmin; the Brahminical association with comedy and reversal is still, obviously, seen as integral by the folk milieu. But the story adds to the "liminal" resonances of the Brahmin identity of its hero two explicit links to the "outside"—the wandering *sannyāsin*, who makes the entire sequence of events possible; and the site of the revelation in the shrine to the wild goddess, beyond the village bounds. The jester's special faculties emerge from an outer zone of unstructured potentiality. But these faculties in themselves have a recurring structure beautifully symbolized in the goddess's double-edged curse, which the jester transforms by his cleverness into a boon. The palindrome epithet points to Tĕnāli Rāma's peculiar path to truth. Reversal is of his very essence, a perceptual stance which, as the story indicates, imparts a certain creative or transformative power to its possessor; it can turn curse into blessing, death into life. The jester is a walking palindrome: his double vision, which flows naturally out of the contrary move-

[98] *Vikaṭakavi* is a palindrome in the Indian syllabic scripts (Tel. వికటకవి).

[99] *Tĕṉṉālrāman katai* (TRK) 1, pp. 48-49; Robinson (1885), pp. 342-43; Kāḷahastirājeśvara Rao (1967), pp. 5-7. The Telugu retelling lacks any mention of the palindrome as boon. Panchapakesa Ayyar adds a fine touch: the *sannyāsin* arrives in the village after a long drought, and his arrival is immediately followed by rains, which the villagers credit to his power. Tĕnāli Rāma meets him and congratulates him on the "jolly old palmyra tree"—a reference to a famous illustration of false causality, the *kākatālīyanyāya* (the palmyra fruit falls to the ground *by chance* at the moment that a crow alights on the tree's branch, so that it appears the bird is responsible for the fruit's fall). The *sannyāsin*, perfectly aware that he is being wrongly credited with the miracle, is impressed with the Brahmin boy's wit and directs him to Kālī (pp. 4-8).

ments within his nature, inevitably precipitates reversals in any seemingly stable entity or concept which he approaches.

The reversal that begins Tĕnāli Rāma's career has its own logic: true to his origins beyond the pale, the jester is always only one step away from the abyss. A major part of his appeal lies in his insouciance in the face of terror. Indeed, the clown's mockery of all that is most fearsome—his sometimes magical, sometimes witty and sophisticated triumph over mortal terror, such as that represented by the gruesome Kālī—is a seemingly universal aspect of his role.[100] The danger is, nevertheless, entirely real, an essential component of the jester's experience, while his triumph over it is no simple victory but more of a continuous, dialectical battle between fear and wit. In Tĕnāli Rāma's case, this battle is *not* the backdrop to heroism—his "heroics" lie elsewhere—but he does play out his antics in the shadow of an always imminent, ultimate punishment. Time and again he escapes a death prescribed for him by his capricious, easily offended king. On one occasion he deceives his two executioners by asking to be allowed a final, purifying bath; they are to strike him with their swords when he gives a signal upon emerging from the temple tank. The two executioners position themselves on either side of their victim; he cries, "Now!" and dives into the water—and the executioners strike out and decapitate one another.[101] Another time he is taken out to be trampled to death by the royal elephant; the king's agents bury their victim up to his head in the ground and go to look for the elephant; a hunchback happens by, and Tĕnāli Rāma at once convinces him that he has just undergone a magical cure for a hunched back. He emerges erect from his hole; the hunchback, impressed by the miracle, willingly assumes the victim's place.[102] The jester survives, by his wit, the disasters his wit has brought upon him. This type of brinkmanship is his "occupational hazard";[103] it evokes the drama of his message and highlights the potential impact of his power; without it, he would be in danger of lapsing into inconsequentiality.

Tĕnāli Rāma's career is all that the goddess had promised—and more. He is, in the eyes of the folk traditions, as essential to the life of the court as the king himself. Though there are various versions of his entry into the royal presence, they usually involve a crafty

[100] Torrance (1978), pp. 16-27, 274-77; Willeford (1969), pp. 102-103; Sachs (1978), p. 26. This attribute may be connected to the clown's gift of "magical reparation"—Ulanov and Ulanov (1980), p. 11.

[101] TRK 3 (p. 50); Robinson (1885), p. 344.

[102] TRK 2 (pp. 49-50); Campantam (1963), pp. 40-45; Robinson (1885), p. 343.

[103] Willeford (1969), p. 163.

humiliation by Tĕnāli Rāma of the king's Brahmin *purohita*, who becomes in the stories Tĕnāli Rāma's mortal enemy. This rivalry is expressive of a basic theme running through the entire corpus—the jester's comic iconoclasm, which is directed against all forms of privilege, pretense, and convention. Brahmins, and Brahminical ritual, are first on the list of his targets (and again we must remember that the antithetical jester is himself a Brahmin). This theme dominates what is perhaps the most famous of all the Tĕnāli Rāma stories:

> As the king's mother lay dying, she expressed a final wish: she wished to taste once more the sweetness of the mango fruit. Unfortunately, mangoes were out of season; and although the king sent his messengers to bring a mango from some distant land, they arrived too late—the king's mother was already dead. The king now feared that his mother's ghost would wander forever, haunted by the unappeased craving with which she had died, and he sought the counsel of his Brahmins in dealing with this problem. The Brahmins came up with a simple solution: if the king were to give a golden mango to each of one hundred Brahmins, his mother's soul would rest in peace. So Kṛṣṇadevarāya invited the Brahmins to a feast at which they would receive their gift.
>
> On their way to the royal banquet, the Brahmins saw Tĕnāli Rāma standing at the door of his house and beckoning to them; in his hands he held iron rods, their tips red-hot from a fire. "Do you not know," he asked them, "that any Brahmin who will allow himself to be branded twice or thrice by these irons will receive *two* or *three* golden mangoes?" Many of the Brahmins happily volunteered to undergo this penance. But when they claimed their additional golden mangoes from the king, Kṛṣṇadevarāya was shocked and angry; he summoned Tĕnāli Rāma to the court to explain his actions. The jester boldly informed the king: "Your Highness, *my* mother died suffering the torments of rheumatism, and the doctors advised me before her death to place hot irons on her painful joints; but before I could do so, she died. So I followed your example: just as you sought to allay the distress of your mother's ghost by your gift to the Brahmins, I sought, through these same Brahmins, to achieve a similar aim."[104]

[104] TRK 7 (pp. 53-54); Kāḷahastirājeśvara Rao, pp. 34-35; oral account by V. Narayana Rao.

This story hardly calls for comment; its effective satire of a ritual that confers great privilege on a greedy priestly caste helps to explain the folk perception of the jester as a comic hero engaged on behalf of the unprivileged common man.[105] Yet the satire has the further effect of casting common-sensical doubt upon the truth of ritual as such—a doubt which, in fact, ranges far beyond the sphere of cultic practice, and which involves the jester in what we might call "cognitive heroics." His words and actions are aimed, in perhaps a majority of the stories, at producing a transformation in consciousness. Note that this aim has a kind of ritual quality of its own: the jester's legitimate role is to undermine *any* nonliteral, impalpable, invisible, or wonder-working act or intention. And since the Brahmins have no monopoly on this kind of thinking, they can easily find themselves the reluctant allies or dependents of the jester:

> Irāyar [King Kṛṣṇadevarāya] slept one morning till an hour and a half after sunrise. As it was his day for being shaved, the barber came, and having gently operated while he lay in bed, without disturbing his sleep, went away. After awaking and rising, the king looked into the upright mirror, and saw how nicely he had been shaven. Greatly delighted, he called for the barber, and asked, "What is there that you wish?" He said, "Swamy, I would like to be made a Brahman." Irāyar assembled the Brahmans, and promised them exemption from taxes if in six months they should receive the barber into their order. Exceedingly distressed, they subjected him to various ablutions and ceremonies. When the six months were over, Irāyar determined to go to their village, and see the barber sit and eat in their ranks. They went weeping to Tennālu-Rāman. He said, "You have no need to fear; I will do a trick to get you off." He tied a rope round the neck of a black dog, dragged it along after him, made a sacrificial pit on the bank of a tank near the village, and employed four Brahmans to perform the needful rites. He then dipped the dog he had brought, and it barked repeatedly. Then he drew it round the pit he had dug, bathed it once more, and made it again circumambulate. Irāyar coming while he was acting thus, demanded, "Why do you treat the dog in this way?" Tennālu-Rāman said, "I am going to make this black dog white." Irāyar replied, "Madcap, how can a black dog become white; it is impossible." Tennālu-Rāman said, "When a barber can be made a Brahman, is turning a black dog white a wonder?" So soon as he heard that, the king

[105] Yet this hero is "heroic" in a sense very different from that adopted by Torrance (1978), *passim*.

reflected, "Right! I spoke without deliberation." He did not go to the neighborhood of the Brahmans, but returned to his palace, and summoning the barber, pacified him in another way, and sent him home. Hearing the news, all the Brahmans were delighted.[106]

The Brahmins panic as the king is about to beat them at their own game of ritual nonsense; only the jester, who is never tainted by these rules, can save them—once again, by an apt parody of the ritual itself, with its magical "ablutions and ceremonies." The story plays with the common association of barbers and Brahmins—the two ends of the social scale[107]—and ends by reaffirming their distinctiveness, despite the suggestive parallel between the barber's ambition and the Brahmins' stereotypical greed (in this case, for a remission in taxes). In other versions, the king adopts the more likely course of threatening to seize the land that the Brahmins hold free from taxation if they fail to "convert" the barber to their caste.[108] In any case, the king has acted, as he comes to see, "without deliberation," and his repentance is a highly significant element in the story: it is the jester's mock ritual that brings the king back into line, as it were, with an obvious reality and a necessary truth, and which in effect makes the erring monarch responsible for his deeds.

These two, rather simple stories—of the golden mangoes and the black dog—are closely akin, although they pit the jester against different "foes" (first the Brahmin court priests, then the king himself). Their interest lies in the semi-ritualized demonstration of ritual limits and, to a lesser extent, in the conspicuous power of the creative wit working through carefully selected imagery, and upon emotion (the king's guilt at his mother's death; the Brahmins' panic; the barber's confused ambition). The deeper ranges of Tĕnāli Rāma's semiotic commentary upon the kingdom are explored in other stories, many of which turn, as we might expect, on linguistic concerns. Thus a series of stories about the great Telugu poets associated with Kṛṣṇadevarāya's courts—famous figures such as Pĕddana, Timmana, and Bhaṭṭumūrti—displays the jester's own poetic talent, and the peculiar uses to which he puts it. One such story is that of Tĕnāli Rāma's "exposure" of the poet Dhūrjaṭi:

One day in court, Kṛṣṇadevarāya proposed a riddle: What was the source of the incomparable sweetness (*mādhurī*) of the wise

[106] Robinson (1885), pp. 353-54; cf. TRK 16 (pp. 63-64), *Rama the Jester*, pp. 11-14.
[107] See above, III.1 at n. 11.
[108] TRK, p. 64.

poet Dhūrjaṭi's verse? Some said it was fate (*adṛṣṭa*), some ascribed it to his purity, or to the grace of the goddess Śāradā. Tĕnāli Rāma determined to find a better answer. He followed Dhūrjaṭi at night when the poet made his way to a courtesan's house, and waited for him there till morning. The next day Tĕnāli Rāma was able to proclaim in the court:

> *hā tĕlisĕn bhuvanaikamohanoddhatasukumāravāravanitā-*
> *janatāghanatāpahārisantatamadhurādharoditasudhārasadhārala*
> *groluṭaṃ jumī!*
>
> "Aha! I have discovered (the secret)—(the sweetness comes from) sipping the streams of nectar issuing from the sweet lips which remove great distress, the lips of delicate but aggressive women who delude the whole world."[109]

Mādhurya, the "sweet" quality attributed to Dhūrjaṭi's verses, is one of the analytical features of poetry discussed by the handbooks of poetics;[110] Tĕnāli Rāma, in a Rabelaisian mode, reduces this abstract virtue to a corporeal, wholly sensual context. And the court applauds his travesty: Tĕnāli Rāma has found the "true" answer to the king's question—as if the entire apparatus of critical appreciation and analysis were suddenly revealed to be irrelevant, hollow, ridiculously wanting. The jester has performed his classic debunking role, and the court joyfully crashes down with him to a level of pure sensation expressed in a one-to-one correspondence of literal words and bodily deeds. Poetry itself has been demoted to the status of a parasitic outgrowth of a courtesan's kisses, although this reversal is itself expressed in a verse carefully crafted to mimic the "high" poets' Sanskritic diction. The jester turns language against language to effect a switch in sensibilities; the ensuing collapse threatens not merely the high style of court poetry but also the very self-image of the court as the repository of proper, ornate, erudite, saṃskāric form. This is the standard outcome of the jester's pranks: whether he is at odds with poets, with pretentious pundits,[111] with an arrogant gymnast,[112] or with the royal paragon himself, Tĕnāli Rāma is certain to claim the final word.

The game can be played with great seriousness. Indeed, the basic contrast is not, I would argue, between a "serious" assemblage of conventional figures—sitting ducks for the jester's barbs—and the

[109] Kāḷahastirājesvara Rao, pp. 25-26.

[110] E.g. *Kāvyaprakāśa* 8.72; cf. Raghavan (1978), pp. 261, 268.

[111] Kāḷahastirājeśvara Rao, pp. 21-23; TRK 11 (pp. 57-58); Campantam (1963), pp. 151-59.

[112] TRK 14 (pp. 61-62); Robinson (1885), pp. 351-52.

latter's comic rebellion. The situation is somewhat different from that projected by Bakhtin for medieval Europe, where somber "agelasts," as he calls them, might seek to sabotage the life-giving "parodic-travestying" comic genres, thereby exposing themselves to unceasing parodic attacks.[113] Rather, we have in this folk vision of the Vijayanagar court an opposition between two kinds of seriousness: a pretense-riddled, self-limiting, linguistically confined type (with strong affinities with the tragic), and a comic seriousness no less laden with philosophical significance, and perhaps even more clearly linked to transcendence. This playful seriousness, or self-conscious playfulness, is powerfully reflexive; its favorite toy is human speech, which it isolates, dissects, and exposes; it is itself a major constitutive feature of South Indian kingship. Let us see now how the jester works upon language and linguistic convention, and upon the imagination that has been given shape by these conventions.

First a story that points the way to these concerns:

> The king had a lovely terrace built and invited a painter to cover its walls with pictures. When the painter was finished, he invited the king and his courtiers to admire his work. Tĕnāli Rāma, staring at a figure drawn in profile, asked innocently, "Where are the other parts of this one's body?" The king laughed and replied, "Do you not know that you must *imagine* them because of the painter's use of perspective?" "Now I understand," said Tĕnāli Rāma.
>
> When some months had passed, the jester came to the king and said: "I have been practicing the art of painting for months; I would like you to see my skill." "Fine," said the king; "you can wipe away the faded paintings in my palace and cover the walls with *your* work." Tĕnāli Rāma erased the older paintings and produced his own: he drew a fingernail here, a lone finger somewhere else, two hands in another spot. When the walls were filled with these disjointed elements, he called the king to see his work. "What is this?" cried Kṛṣṇadevarāya at the sight of his palace murals. "Have you forgotten about the imagination (*pāvaṉai*) necessary to appreciate art?" asked Tĕnāli Rāma.[114]

There is a close parallel to this story in the Eulenspiegel corpus: the prankster received a commission to paint the murals of a princely

[113] Bakhtin (1981), pp. 56-60. Bakhtin (1968), pp. 205-206, offers a specific list of such targets: "feudal kings . . . aged masters of the Sorbonne . . . hypocritical monks, morose slanderers, gloomy agelasts. . . ."

[114] TRK 18 (pp. 65-66); Campantam, pp. 35-37; Kāḷahastirājeśvara Rao, pp. 62-65.

mansion; when his patron arrived, with his courtiers, to inspect the new paintings, they saw only an empty wall; Till Eulenspiegel then announced that his art was invisible to bastards—and thus no one would admit that he saw no painting.[115] But the thrust of the South Indian folktale is rather different. There is, to begin with, a parody of the artist's conventions, a parody that extends ultimately to the entire artistic enterprise: the jester fails to accept the painter's illusory reproduction of the outer world. But more telling still is the shockingly surrealist world that Tĕnali Rāma himself creates: the mural of dismembered limbs could serve as a fitting symbol of the jester's compulsion to deconstruct, to sever whatever is normally connected, to impeach the whole. And does not the palace mural accurately reflect the jester's chaotic inner world, where outer relations are initially reversed only as a step toward their ultimate dissolution? As usual in these stories, a striking visual image perfectly articulates the cognitive stance of the clown, or of his creators. This concrete visualization of an internal process is integral to the story, which is, at least in part, *about* imagination and illusion (*pāvaṉai*—the key term in the Tamil version). To the jester, symbolization of any kind is suspect, and imagination, once conventionalized, becomes an object of play and mockery. But this attitude must itself be represented in visible form; the imaginative freedom of the jester, with the suggestion of an unlimited flexibility and infinite creative potential, is wholly rooted in the immediate, the tangible, the concrete. Were Tĕnāli Rāma sent to comment on an exhibit of abstract painting in the Museum of Modern Art, he would probably produce a mockingly naturalistic drawing "true" to life.

Note the mechanism of literal-mindedness which the jester uses for his purposes. He has, after all, simply applied in earnest literalness the rules of representation taught him by the king. This mechanism, which always leads to absurdities, is central to many of the stories. A courtesan (*veśyā*) invites him over (*mīda*) to her house: Tĕnāli Rāma walks over (*mīda*) her roof.[116] The king is so angered by one of his jester's impudent tricks that he orders him never to show his head in court again; Tĕnāli Rāma covers his head with a huge pot and comes back into the king's presence.[117] This penchant for the literal is extended to other areas of experience, such as storytelling: Tĕnāli Rāma was once invited to recount the story of the *Rāmāyaṇa* to a courtesan (note

[115] Welsford (1935), p. 45.

[116] V. Narayana Rao.

[117] TRK 4 (p. 51); *Rama the Jester*, p. 20. Cf. the similar story about Marcolf, Solomon's jester-nemesis in European folklore: Welsford (1935), p. 37.

the impropriety of the Brahmin's reciting to a *veśyā*!); he began by saying, "Once Rāma went to the forest," and then fell silent. "Well?" prompted the courtesan. "Wait," said Tĕnāli Rāma; "he is still walking there."[118] The jester as narrator dissolves the convention of narrative time, even as a painter he collapses the conventions of representing space. There can now be no distinction or disjunction between "real" time—always the present—and story time, and as a result there is virtually no room left for the story: Tĕnāli Rāma's version of the *Rāmāyaṇa* goes by the name *yathārtharāmāyaṇa*, "the *Rāmāyaṇa* as it really is," and his method is utterly simple; "Hanuman burnt Laṅkā—just like this," he says, as he sets fire to the *veśyā*'s home.[119]

It is the jester's fascination with the *yathārtha* order of experience—with things as they "really" were, or are—that motivates his expressive acts and words; and it is the consistent perspective that he brings to bear upon this problem which gives Tĕnāli Rāma an unusual measure of coherence compared with other, far more unstable figures in the spectrum of South Indian comedy. The mirror that he holds up to reality is, from a normative point of view, highly distorting; but from the jester's viewpoint, it is "reality" itself which is hopelessly askew—the "real" is a monstrous and crooked parody of itself. The *yathārtha* world, where things are as they normally are—or, rather, as they are normally said to be—takes on a blatantly arbitrary character. This is true, above all, of the linguistic domain; and here the jester concentrates his attacks on the most obvious weak spot of all, the alleged link (which we take for granted) between language and the world. This link turns out to be much too weak to sustain the burden of meaningfulness that we impose upon it.

The point is made through the jester's simple-minded adherence to the literal, an attitude that actually presupposes a considerable sophistication, and that is clearly but the other side of the jester's obvious skill with language, his gift for witty repartee. The effect of this literalness can be analyzed on several levels. There is, no doubt, a certain rebellious force in evidence—like that of a stubborn child who eludes his parents' authority by literalizing their demands. When Tĕnāli Rāma covers his head with a pot, he is literally fulfilling, but in truth defying, the king's command. Then there is the powerful presence of irony, a dependable byproduct of preferring the literal to the figurative.[120] The jester's role at court provides a dimension of insti-

[118] V. Narayana Rao.

[119] V. Narayana Rao.

[120] For several striking modern examples—from the First World War—see Fussell (1975), pp. 165-66.

tutionalized irony, which the king desperately needs. But irony, like love, is both infinitely variable and highly specific in its manifestations, and Tĕnāli Rāma's variety follows a definite design: instead of saying one thing and meaning another, he reduces others' intentions to the verbal shells that seem to contain them. Here the distinctions made by the Indian philosophers of language may help us: the jester invariably chooses the level of literal meaning (*vācya*) over that of secondary, "transferred," or metaphoric usage (*lakṣaṇā*). But language without *lakṣaṇā* is really no language at all, as the Indian schools clearly saw; some, such as the Yogācāra Buddhists and one branch of the Mīmāṃsā, regarded *lakṣaṇā* as a primary feature of *all* utterance couched in sentences.[121] Tĕnāli Rāma would have agreed. He acts out, with implicit criticism, what the linguistic philosophers knew: that there is in all language, in A. K. Ramanujan's phrase, an "obliquity of a sort."[122] To remain only on the level of *vācya*, excluding *lakṣaṇā* by design, both distorts the speech act and exposes its limits, its inevitable saturation with metaphor and transferred meaning. Watching or listening to the jester, one sees at once that words do not mean what they are thought to mean; that their relation to the "outer" world, or to our mental images of it, is at best a tenuous one easily undermined by any self-conscious attempt to discover it. Language, as Bakhtin has beautifully put it, is "maliciously inadequate to reality."[123]

An interesting parallel now emerges between the jester's distorting literalness and the character of poetic utterance, which is seen by Indian poeticians as a *misapplication* of literal modes of thought. "The expressions of poetry are in the broadest sense characterized . . . by a negative correlation with the universal positive goal of discourse: the truth."[124] But where poetic theory sanctions this "twist" or "crookedness" (*vakrokti*) as the necessary hallmark of poetry, the jester exposes a similar rooted crookedness in ordinary speech. Moreover, the jester moves in an opposite direction from the poeticians, as Velcheru Narayana Rao has remarked; the two strategies are symmetrical but reversed. The poeticians' basic concern is with hidden, suggested meanings (*vyaṅgya, dhvani*) embedded within the poet's words; they go beneath the everyday level of language in search of something in its depths. Tĕnāli Rāma, on the other hand, moves away from suggested or implicit meanings as well as from the everyday level of *lakṣaṇā*; his

121 Kunjunni Raja (1969), p. 248.

122 "Indian Poetics: An Overview," in Dimock et al. (1974), p. 116.

123 Bakhtin (1981), p. 309.

124 Gerow (1971), p. 17; cf. pp. 16-22, 48-50. The classical statement of this view is Kuntaka's *Vakroktijīvita*.

direction is upward, toward the surface of language, in an excess of literalness (an *ativācyatā*).[125] The result is a radical difference in perspective: if the poeticians disclose the open-endedness within language, with its suggestive potential, and thereby affirm its value and its truth, the jester reveals an open-ended, unbridgeable gap between language and reality. Any linguistic ordering of experience, of thought or feeling, now appears to be suspended over an abyss.

The jester's literalizing is thus a tool in his ludic surgery of speech, a means of exposing the overwhelming obliquity of language and of thought. The jester dissects the word and displays its disconnected parts; like the surrealistic painting in the palace, language presents a disjointed, incoherent guise. Its semiotic capacity is by now in doubt; truth can only exist outside it.[126] This doubt has an immediate existential effect. Just as Cervantes may be said to reveal, in Don Quixote, a hero "alienated in analogy,"[127] Tĕnāli Rāma discloses an entire world alienated in metaphor, a world of transferred meaning and substitute experience, inhabited *only* by ludicrous Quixotes and pretentious fools. Only, that is, with the exception of the jester, whose binding and loosening of linguistic ties still points the way to a deeper truth; and of fellow spirits such as the angry poet Cuntaramūrtti—also a clown of sorts, as we shall see—who could sing of his god:

> I placed before him
> my head
> and my tongue;
> I even offered him
> my heart.
>
> I didn't try to cheat him.
>
> But whenever I talk of being
> the servant of his feet,
> I'm just a man of metaphors
> to him,
>
> our supreme lord of Pāccilāccirāmam,
> that madman
> who ties his loincloth
> with a hooded serpent:

[125] V. Narayana Rao, in discussion, December 1982.

[126] Cf. Bakhtin (1981), p. 309 (with reference to Rabelais): "Truth is restored by reducing the lie to an absurdity, but truth itself does not seek words; she is afraid to entangle herself in the word, to soil herself in verbal pathos."

[127] Foucault (1970), p. 49.

if *he* doesn't want us,
can't we find some other god?[128]

Even more, perhaps, than the jester, the *bhakti*-poet is impatient with metaphor-laden speech; his truth—the "mad" god Śiva—is by nature antithetical to order, and to ordered thought. Hence the poet has little hesitation in sacrificing to him his head, tongue, and heart (the *trikaraṇa*); his complaint is that this sacrifice is not repaid or even noticed by the elusive trickster-god, who remains as "crooked" in his own way as any conventional act of speech.

Note that the jester's "analysis" of language, and of the linguistically ordered concepts of time and space, proceeds in two stages: he demonstrates the simplest and most profound of all the Indian clown's truths—that the literal, the *yathārtha*, or whatever is usually perceived as real, is wholly ludicrous and false; but this very demonstration also shows that the nonliteral is equally absurd. There is a cumulative magic about these vanishing displays, even if the magician himself is a ridiculous joker playing the fool. His distinctiveness should by now be clear: Tĕnāli Rāma goes far beyond the classical Vidūṣaka, who never attempts this type of commentary since he is himself half a victim of the defects of speech, and only partly conscious of his comic role. Tĕnāli Rāma is entirely aware; he embodies reflexivity at its limit, through the active observation, exploitation, and display of the linguistic prison of consciousness. The Menippean features of the Kūṭiyāṭṭam clown—the linguistic playfulness, the critical concern, and the use of ironic, satirical inversions—are all present in the jester's stories, but they, too, are exceeded by the range and purposefulness of his antics. In particular, the use of ironic reversal has been transformed: whereas the Kūṭiyāṭṭam Vidūṣaka remains entirely bound up, in his debunking comments, with the positive assertions of the *nāyaka*, Tĕnāli Rāma uses reversal to transcend the limits of speech; his ironic literalizing detaches meaning from language even as it reverses the direction of a given statement. The palindrome that defines him points to the dynamism which he brings to perception: it is more "true" (the jester may suggest) to see things in a double direction, or in internal oscillation, than in merely one linear movement; but this double vision is meant to propel us toward a still greater freedom of perception, to a stance within an unstructured and always unfinished creative domain. In this Tĕnāli Rāma, for all his predictable iconoclasm, is less a representative of disorder *per se* than an ironic advocate of movement and transformation within the royal world that subsumes him. In

[128] Cuntaramūrtti *Tevāram* 134 (*patikam* 14.1).

terms of Handelman's analysis of ritual clowns, he is not an "enemy of the boundary" but is rather "of the boundary" itself, and thus an exemplar of the principles of flux, ambiguity, paradoxical openness to either side, and internal change or dissolution.[129]

What is crucial for our purposes is the way this figure is integrated into the general symbolism of kingship. The jester belongs in the central hub of the kingdom, which can never dispense with his ironic truth. Stated schematically, the point is the boundarylike characteristics of the South Indian royal center: as we have seen in Chapter III, it is this center which is conceived as ambiguous, open-ended, inclusive of ordered limits as well as of their transcendence, and given to dynamic movement and transformation. The jester enacts these features in an institutionalized corrosion of any stability in the royal realm. In another culture, a literalizing mania such as Tĕnāli Rāma's might demand exclusion: thus Feodosiy Kosoy in sixteenth-century Russia was branded a heretic, having reduced a sacred symbol to its most literal content.

> Kosoy says that those calling themselves orthodox worshipped wood instead of God. . . . Only they do not understand, only they do not want to understand, although they could understand by themselves, for if someone beats to death the son of another man could that man love the stick with which his son was killed? In the same way God hates the cross because his son was killed on it.[130]

This is heresy in orthodox eyes: but, as the Tripura myth has shown us,[131] "heresy" is no less central to an "orthodox" Hinduism than is the jester to the proper image of a South Indian court. The folk perception of a mighty king *requires* the presence of his irrepressible jester. Whatever the king constructs—together with his ministers, his wives, his Brahmin priests and advisers, his poets—the jester can be counted on to undermine or to unravel. The two constitute the two contrary vectors of a single process of life and movement. Their association is fundamental; we shall see in the next chapter how the two roles collapse in a single royal figure.

Two final stories may be cited here to illustrate the specific character of this interdependence of king and jester. Both deal with the deeply evocative theme of the jester's death. The idea of the dying clown

[129] Handelman (1981), pp. 340-42.

[130] Cited by Lotman and Piatigorsky (1978), p. 237.

[131] See above, III.2.

recurs, with obsessive poignancy, in much of the world's comic literature; there is clearly a profound reluctance to allow the comic hero—so often a symbol of vitality itself, of the eternal movement and regenerative powers of life—to die.[132] And in some stories, such as the following, the clown seems to triumph dramatically over death.

> One day the king noticed that his jester was depressed. "Why are you grieving?" he asked. Replied Tĕnāli Rāma: "The astrologers have predicted that I have but a month or two left to live; and I have made no provision for my family after my death." "Have no care," said the king; "I can provide for your family ten times better than you can." "But," said Tĕnāli Rāma, "everyone says never to trust the rich in matters such as this." The king reassured him and pledged that he would always care for the jester's family.
>
> After some time, Tĕnāli Rāma let it be known that he was dying. Meanwhile he hid away his gold and jewels; then one day, after publishing the news of his death, he hid himself in the family money chest. No sooner was the king informed of the jester's demise than he sent his servants to appropriate Tĕnāli Rāma's treasure chest. With great effort they dragged the heavy box into the court and struggled with the lock; but when the lid was finally opened, to everyone's astonishment Tĕnāli Rāma himself climbed out. "What, you are not dead?" cried the embarrassed king. "With someone like you as my family's guardian, how can I afford to die?" the jester replied.[133]

Although Tĕnāli Rāma is never truly threatened by death in this tale, his rising out of the sealed casket conveys something of the emotive image of the clown who mocks the grave. Indeed, the jester seems to toy with death, and to manipulate its psychological power, even as elsewhere he toys with time and with language. As usual, this play has the clear aim of testing a word, or the reality behind it: the jester's trick puts the king's trustworthiness to the test and thus exposes its utter hollowness; the king stands revealed not simply as a liar—al-

[132] On the clown's relation to death, see Ulanov and Ulanov (1980), p. 5 (it is "as if his whitened face, huge mouth, deeply fixed, encircled eyes prefigured the face of death"); Fellini (1976), pp. 127-28; Oreglia (1968), pp. 98-100 (on the death of a famous Pulcinella); Willeford (1969), pp. 88-93, 131 (the fool as ambiguous scapegoat-victim and master of death); Bakhtin (1981), pp. 193-204 (the clown who dies laughing—a cheerful death); Hastrup and Ovesen (1976), p. 22. In Lorca's *Asi que pasen cinco años*, Act III, the clown carries a death's head. One thinks, too, of Quixote's sad demise.

[133] TRK 19 (pp. 66-67); Campantam (1963), pp. 193-96; Robinson (1885), p. 355.

though his lie is, in this case, much more serious than that which the jester discovers in *all* language—but also as the greedy thief or bandit that he is. In this story, there is no doubt about the jester's alliance with the truth.

One can easily imagine, on this evidence, how much the king is felt to be in need of the jester's corrective power. The interdependence of the two figures is asymmetrical, as with the *nāyaka* and his Vidūṣaka, but the balance has now shifted: if the *nāyaka* can survive without a clown, the same cannot be said for Kṛṣṇadevarāya and his jester. The latter, it is true, can flourish only in the context of the court; his wit as well as his life depend upon the royal presence. Yet he always has the upper hand with his royal patron, who, at least in the popular perception, relies upon the jester to maintain his precarious relation to reality and to truth. We can see this clearly in other stories that deal with the jester's death—a real death, this time, which leaves the king helpless and forlorn.[134] One such story, of somewhat dubious authenticity, appears in a modern, perhaps "novelistic" reworking of one of Tĕnāli Rāma's most famous feats:

> Tĕnāli Rāma, weary of the anger constantly directed at him by the king and by the king's Brahmin minister, decided to teach them both a lesson. He first went to the minister and told him in confidence: "A man and his wife have come from the northern country to stay with me. The woman has no equal in beauty on this earth, and the husband never lets her out of his sight." The minister pleaded with Tĕnāli Rāma to arrange a meeting for him with the mysterious lady, and, after much persuasion, Tĕnāli Rāma agreed to help. He instructed the minister, because of the delicate nature of the affair, to come dressed as a woman, at night, to his house.
>
> The jester then repeated the secret story to the king, and, once again, allowed himself to be persuaded to arrange a rendezvous—under the same conditions. That night he arranged a bed in one of the inner chambers of his house and awaited the arrival of his "guests." The minister was the first to arrive; Tĕnāli Rāma escorted him into the dark chamber. Soon the king appeared, also in woman's garb; the jester admitted him to the room and then locked the door from the outside. The minister and the king flew into each other's ardent arms, only to discover, to their chagrin, that the other was a man. They cursed Tĕnāli Rāma and ordered him to open the door; but the jester refused to do so until he was

[134] Thus Campantam (1963), pp. 197-200.

promised impunity. Having no choice, the king gave his word; but as he was leaving, he said in exasperation, "Go hang yourself!" He then tore off his female attire and marched back to the palace.

But Tĕnāli Rāma sat up, contemplating matters, through the night. He realized that, after a whole lifetime spent in jesting, he could not expect any one to credit his story or take anything he said seriously. As dawn arrived, he prepared a noose hung from the ceiling and took his own life.

When the king heard the news, he was troubled. The jester was given a magnificent funeral attended by the king, his ministers, and the priests. Which was as it should be—for "it would have been no laughing matter if he started to come back to earth to play some more practical jokes on those who had offended him."[135]

This story suggests several interpretative possibilities, none of which can be shown to agree with the authors' intent; it would help if other versions could be found to corroborate the unusual ending. The main body of the story, dealing with the transvestite assignation, is perhaps the most spectacular traditional example of the jester's humiliation of his king. The basic images may have been borrowed from the Virāṭa escapades of the epic—Bhīma's transvestite encounter with Kīcaka, and Arjuna's disguise as the dancing-master Bṛhannaḍā[136]—but here they serve to illuminate the jester's transformative capacity, which works, quite naturally, upon sexual identity and upon the royal self-image. The king's humiliation at the hands of his jester hardly diminishes the ruler's need for this outrageous trickster-hero, and the grief expressed at the latter's funeral is surely genuine, even if the narrator hints at another explanation: the fear of reprisal from the victim of a tragic death. This theme—the "tragic apotheosis" of the dead, self-sacrificing hero[137]—could, indeed, be applied to the jester, whose tragic side can be seen in the enforced limitations of his role: he is condemned to be funny, trapped, as it were, in a zone of comic commentary; the transformations he works are in part a function of his virtual impotence as a member of the ordered, "real" world. This, in fact, is the "moral" drawn by the narrator: since no one will ever take the jester seriously, he might as well die. If the moral is correct—as well it might be: the tragic side of clowning will come up again in our discussion of the royal clowns in the next chapter—then this story

[135] TRK 6 (pp. 52-53); *Rama the Jester*, pp. 25-30.

[136] See below, V.6.

[137] Discussed at length below, VII.4.

marks a violent change in tone and attitude from the other Tĕnāli Rāma tales; there the jester is normally content with the degree of seriousness accorded his remarks, whereas in the present case he longs to escape back into a world of everyday seriousness and normative discourse—the same *yathārtha* world he has so often ridiculed. But it would seem more likely that his suicide is meant in another spirit, as a continuation of that mockery and a further derision of language, and of death itself. There is, after all, a logic of sorts in his relation to the king's facetious command: the logic of "spoken in earnest, taken in jest; spoken in jest, taken in earnest." The familiar principle of ironic reversal is still at work. Note, too, that the jester remains in control: he has been given impunity, and thus is free to choose his death rather than submit to it as punishment. And the death itself now becomes the ultimate commentary on kingship: once again the king is shown as one whose words lead—by the simplest, most literal route—to misapprehension and even disaster. Kṛṣṇadevarāya, it seems, will never make himself understood. Even if Tĕnāli Rāma's suicide is not a "cheerful death" such as those celebrated by Rabelais—such as Anacreon's, by choking on a grape pip, or that of Zeuxis, the painter, who died laughing at the features of an old hag he had just painted[138]—it still contains an element of his conventional triumph over the king. Without his jester, the ruler is stuck, preyed upon by a literal reality and by his own inner falseness, a parodic counterfeit of the proper royal image that he can no longer aspire to, or even properly perceive.

The Tĕnāli Rāma stories we have analyzed provide an insight into the symbolic structure of South Indian kingship within the folk culture. They reveal an integral, comic component of kingship, which other sources—including "high" literary genres of myth, epic, and lyric—elaborate. Certain of the mechanisms proper to this comic aspect should by now be clear; others remain to be studied in still living representatives of the South Indian folk-comic traditions. In lieu of further summary, and as a bridge to the scatological side of those traditions, let us conclude this section with another Tĕnāli Rāma story, one that illustrates, yet again, the jester's inevitable victory over his royal rival, and that provides another remarkable variation on the "magical" theme of the clown's dream:

> The king decided that he must, for once, pay Tĕnāli Rāma back for his persistent impudence; so, one day, when all the courtiers were assembled before him, he called the jester near and an-

[138] Rabelais (1979), IV.17.

> nounced that he had had, that night, an unusual dream: "We were walking," said the king, "just the two of us, in some unfamiliar, deserted place. Suddenly we found ourselves on a narrow footpath between two deep pits: one of them was full of honey, and the one on the other side was filled with stagnant gutter-water, urine, and faeces. We hesitated for awhile, but finally decided that we must somehow traverse this path. Though we were walking with extreme care, somehow or other I slipped and fell into the pit of honey. But *you* fell into the pit of urine and excrement."
>
> At this, the courtiers clapped their hands in delight—what an appropriate fate for Tĕnāli Rāma! The king silenced them and continued, "Well, I swallowed as much honey as I could and then worked my way back onto the path. I couldn't bear to see what state you were in: you were breathing hard, struggling somehow to reach the shore. But halfway up you lost your grip and fell back into the pit, head first. At that moment I suddenly awoke."
>
> Tĕnāli Rāma stood still as a rock, while all the others giggled.
>
> The next day he came to the court, as usual, in the morning. "Yesterday you told me your dream," he said to the king, "and last night I saw its continuation in *my* dream. You were out of the honey pit, while I, after a great effort, finally got back up on the path. But we could hardly go home in that state: so I licked off all the honey on your body with my tongue, and you then cleaned *me* in the same way."[139]

Two false dreams, which seem to parody nightmares reported in the *Brāhmaṇa* literature (Bhṛgu's nocturnal ramblings through a landscape of liquid terror).[140] But unlike the Vidūṣaka, the jester here has no need to deflate the spurious vision: he is far more a master of the imagination than the hapless king, who foolishly chooses this medium for another contest with his court fool. And, as usual, the jester's imagination works to precise symbolic effect: is it by chance that Tĕnāli Rāma triumphs by means of a honeyed tongue?

5. Folk Clowns: Fertility and Disharmonious Form

Tĕnāli Rāma is a folk creation cast into the world of the royal court. The link he suggests between comedy and royal symbolism is basic to the perception of kingship in the popular culture; and we shall see

[139] Campantam (1963), pp. 190-92.
[140] *Śat. Brāh.* 11.6.1.1-13.

in the next chapter how this link is sustained, deepened immeasurably, and also partly obscured by a profusion of narrative and lyrical description in classical works. Before studying these sources, however, we must briefly survey the series of folk clowns still alive in various South Indian theatrical traditions. These clowns embody many of the specific comic features discussed with reference to the Vidūṣaka and the jester, but they add to these features a further dimension important for our understanding of the royal comedies. In the clowns of the South Indian dramatic genres, we find a full range of self-conscious, carefully articulated comic forms combined with a creative or transformative power explicitly recognized and put to ritual use.

Look at the following description of a Tamil village clown (*komāḷi*): he wears a conical cap ending in a crooked point—and this cap may be covered in golden or yellow paper to resemble a crown; he has the Vaiṣṇava *nāmam* on his forehead; he wears a full mustache and white beard, which may be plaited with hemp; his teeth are crooked and unevenly spaced; he creates this effect with two rows of cowry shells strung together on a cord over his mouth, and thus always appears to be grinning grotesquely; from his neck hangs a long bag, into which he puts whatever comes his way—an odd assortment of unrelated items, which he may someday need; he has the paunch of a glutton (*tīṉikkāraṉ*), a fact emphasized by the disorderly fashion in which he ties his dhoti; small bells jingle on his legs; his gait is awkward, distorted, uneven. He acts, in general, like a madman—guffawing without reason, jumping, dancing, singing his songs; these tend to describe beatings he receives, for example from a gardener who finds him stealing flowers or grain from his garden.[141] In some cases (see Figure 3) the clown's pointed cap is adorned with a crude representation of a face, with pointed nose and wildly staring eyes;[142] these features seem to have much in common with folk depictions of demonic figures from myth and local epic. The village clowns are associated with ritual occasions such as Māriyammaṉ festivals or the *rātā-kalyāṇam* festival (when comic actors dressed up as Hanuman, the monkey-hero of the *Rāmāyaṇa*, are present alongside the clowns).[143] In southern Tamil Nadu, a buffoon directs the *karakam* dancers on festival days; he comments on the performance, taunts the dancers, and makes obscene remarks.[144]

[141] Jagannātaṉ, with texts of two songs.

[142] I am grateful to Brenda E. F. Beck for these photographs of a village clown (Coimbatore District).

[143] Jagannātaṉ, p. 143.

[144] Personal communication from Erica Claus.

Figure 3. Tamil Village Clowns

This ritual connection is of decisive importance in evaluating the clown's role; unfortunately, the available data are an insufficient basis for interpretation. There may be, as Tapper has suggested for the clowns of the leather-puppet traditions,[145] an element of focusing upon these figures any inauspicious forces (as in the evil eye, *dṛṣṭi*), thereby deflecting these forces from others. But it is still more likely that the clowns are also meant to arouse or stimulate these same forces by their unique, misshapen form and their patent reversal of normative behavior; in their challenge to the ordered domain of social life, the

[145] Tapper (1979).

Figure 3. Tamil Village Clowns

clowns bring into play the vital, creative powers usually excluded or subdued. Even in the absence of more contextual details, the iconography of these comic figures suggests several specific themes: there is, again, an association with kingship (through the mock crown and, perhaps, the Vaiṣṇava sign);[146] as in the case of the Vidūṣaka, we find an emphasis on oral appetite and a ludicrous corporeality, a feature that also recalls, as Vāsudeva Jagannātaṉ notes, the clownish god Gaṇeśa, with his ungainly paunch (indeed, the village clown is sometimes referred to as *vikaṭa vināyakar*, a "ridiculous Vināyaka/Ga-

[146] On the king's relation to Viṣṇu, see above, II.4 at n. 93.

ṇeśa");[147] and the bag of assorted knickknacks hanging from his neck suggests the clown's role as *bricoleur*, eclectic manipulator or transformer of whatever materials come to hand. This latter trait is partly a function of the clown's imaginative power: to a masterful clown, nothing is "only" itself, for all things (or feelings or perceptions) are but the starting point of unending transformations and a temporary point of reference in an unlimited series of creative relations with other, equally unstable things. This "magical" potential of the clown is far better articulated in the village and folk-dramatic contexts than with the Vidūṣaka or even the jester: the debunking habit is by now much reduced, and the clowns are less given to comic attacks upon others' "illusions" than to the creation and dissolution of their own.

Finally, the village clown's association with slapstick—his pathetic descriptions of the beatings he receives—is integrally related to the dynamism he imparts. This attribute is less simple than it might seem; it is also a regular feature of the clowns in the leather-puppet shows. Slapstick here expresses an immediate liberation of suppressed force—a characteristic concomitant of clowning—and also hints at various complex, perhaps antithetical attitudes. It is partly the result of the clown's comic violation of the norm (usually by thieving, a broad and ambiguous category in itself)[148]—and thus constitutes a deserved punishment and a reassertion of order. But it also reveals the clown's irrepressible resistance to punishment, the vitality of an eternal victim who can never truly be overcome, disciplined, or confined. The beatings merely underscore his basic immunity and capacity to survive, even as they contribute to the violent reordering and revitalization that the clown engenders.

The clown's iconographic disharmony is even more pronounced in the South Indian leather puppets, which have preserved some of the region's most colorful comic forms. Thus the Killekyāṭa—among the Karnataka leather puppets, the central comic figure, who has, in fact, lent his name to the entire caste of performers—is a mixture of contrasting attributes: he has a dark black body, with a crooked nose, disheveled top-knot, the hairs standing on end; a straggly beard, pot belly, protruding hips, misshapen and unbalanced limbs (one rather muscular arm, the second lean and too short). He wears a striking, large necklace, which seems at odds with his dark and ungainly body. His facial aspect expresses an unresolved tension; his eyes are large and bulging, his lips red and overly full, his general expression some-

[147] Jagannātaṉ, p. 144. And are not the village clowns, like Gaṇeśa, removers of obstacles—to true perception? (Don Handelman, personal communication.)

[148] See below, VII.6 on the bandit as clown.

thing between frightful and funny. An ithyphallic variety also exists. The general grotesqueness of this figure, and in particular his dark coloring, seem designed to contrast deliberately with his Brahminlike tuft—as seems to be the case with the clown figure of the Tamil leather-puppet tradition. The Killekyāṭa's wife, the lovely Baṅgārakka, is equally striking in appearance: heavy-set, her hair standing straight on end, her mouth parted in an almost demonic, tooth-filled grin; her two pendulous breasts ending in black, torpedolike nipples; a thick neck and double chin suggesting a repulsive sensuality, and an overall impression of coarseness rendered ridiculous by her many ornaments, such as the enormous gold ring that adorns her large and crooked nose. Unlike her husband, she is relatively light in color, as may also be implied by her name ("the golden lady"—an endearing title conveying something like "little darling"). She is also known ironically as Sundari or Nakali Sundari, "the Beautiful."[149]

This blatant incongruity of form is accompanied by an even more suggestive incongruity of manner. Here the comic roles seem predicated largely upon outrage and violation. Thus in the Andhra puppet theater, the play (usually derived from the two major epics) is "framed" by a comic introduction following immediately upon the invocations to the gods (Gaṇeśa, Sarasvati, and the ancestor/*guru* of the players);[150] in this introductory skit, as in later comic interludes that punctuate the play, obscene dialogue predominates in the relations of the major comic triad—Baṅgārakka; her aged husband, Juṭṭupoligāḍu; and her nephew, son-in-law, and lover, Ketigāḍu.[151] The sexual tensions within the triad are voiced in provocative and explicit terms: Juṭṭupoligāḍu's virility is mocked, and that of Ketigāḍu extolled; a violent fight inevitably erupts between the two males, at times with suggestions of homosexual rape.[152] These comic scenes are "easily the

[149] Nanjundayya and Iyer (1931-1935) find her "hideous" (3:516). My description is based on the figures in the Folklore Museum, Mysore University, and on those used by Hombaiah and his troupe in performance at Ambalajīrahaḷḷi (Nāgamaṇḍala taluk of Mandya District, Karnataka) on September 3, 1980. I am indebted to Professor J. S. Paramashivaiah for introducing me to this performance. See also Seltmann (1971), p. 479; *Asian Puppets, Wall of the World* (1976), p. 34.

[150] Seltmann (1979).

[151] The names vary: Juṭṭupoligāḍu is also Juṭṭuprutigāḍu, Juṭṭupolugāḍu (< *juṭṭu*, the Brahmin top-knot) and Allatappayya. Other characters include the Vidūṣakalike Gandoligāḍu.

[152] GoldbergBelle (1982). Note the similar pattern in Chhattisgarhi versions of the Loriki-Candainī epic: Candainī's husband is impotent (or cursed to be an ascetic), whereas Loriki, with whom she elopes, is highly virile. The triad replicates the Andhra puppets' inner alignment; the elopement is the favorite scene in Chhattisgarhi performances (Joyce Burkhalter Flueckiger, private communication).

most popular portions of the show."[153] They are not, however, directly linked to the main plot; by now the dissociation of the clown from the major dramatic action—a split that we first observed in the role of the Kūṭiyāṭṭam Vidūṣaka—is complete, and the comic figures have established their total autonomy. They are, at the same time, central to the performance as a whole; they introduce it, at times comment upon the action,[154] and (at least in the Karnakata tradition) mediate between the dramatic reality on the screen and the everyday life of the village by referring, in a stream of puns, witticisms, and ironic observations, to current issues.[155]

As with the Tamil village clown, the comic mode of the leather-puppet clowns is slapstick and crude farce; the violent explosion into blows is standard, and again expresses the shock of reversal, for it is the younger, more manly Ketigāḍu who is beating away at an elder to whom he normally would owe respect. This violation of the norm suits the general tone in these scenes of a riotous obscenity—the two male characters often have grotesquely elongated phalluses—and a wild scatological delight. The same violent rule of slapstick (somewhat akin in spirit to the English Punch and Judy shows)[156] is maintained in the Tamil leather-puppet theater, but here the sexually charged triad of Andhra is replaced by an all-male set of buffoons: Uccikkkuṭumpaṉ, Uḷuvattalaiyāṉ, and the younger Mŏḷumŏḷu. They come to blows among themselves on various pretexts, including the predictable obsession with food (including cigarettes and sweets), its high cost, and their heroic capacity for consumption (*cāppāṭṭup parākkiramam*).[157] These clowns, too, summarize and introduce the main story, offer previews of the coming night's performance, apologize for any errors committed by the players, and quiet down the audience in preparation for the coming action; their routines may also include an elaborate parody of magicians and their spooky use of *mantras* (*oṃ, namaḥ śivāya,*

[153] GoldbergBelle (1982), p. 14.

[154] Tapper (1979) cites an example in which Ketigāḍu and Gandoligāḍu wager on the outcome of a battle between the Kauravas and Ghaṭotkaca.

[155] Seltmann (1971), pp. 479-82; Nanjundayya and Iyer (1931-1935), 3:516, 533-34; Devasahayam (1973), p. 12. Tapper (1979), however, denies this; in any case, the puppet clowns' comments are apparently less topical than those of the Kūṭiyāṭṭam Vidūṣaka, or of the Javanese puppet clowns.

[156] Speaight (1970).

[157] Irāmacāmi (1978), pp. 118-40. (I am grateful to Stuart Blackburn for making this unpublished dissertation available to me.) The Tamil leather-puppeteers, like those of Andhra and Karnataka, are of Maharastrian origin. Once again, the clowns' names are expressive: Uccikkuṭumpaṉ appears to reflect *uccikkuṭumi*, the Brahmin's tuft; Mŏḷumŏḷu is "Chubby."

hrīm)—an unusual, sophisticated transformation of the Vidūṣaka's debunking drive.[158]

What is the secret of these figures' power over their audience? What meaning is to be ascribed to their impropriety, obscenity, and deliberate offensiveness to the norm? Again their ritual effectiveness must be taken into account: the puppet shows are sometimes performed to bring rain in times of drought,[159] just as the "carnivalesque" *Virāṭaparvan* of the epic is recited for this same purpose. Apparently, the inversion of everyday standards coupled with the release of contained energy is felt to be capable of reversing a cosmic state—or of revitalizing the liquid flow in the universe which has, for whatever reason, become arrested and blocked. The breach self-consciously opened up in the normative social order has its counterpart in the unseen realms of gods and demons; and the rebellious emancipation from the illusory objectivity of social limits allows a corresponding chaotic energy to make itself felt in the world at large. The clown brings renewed movement to whatever he touches, and to whatever he suggests to the mind. Thus, as with the court jester, reversal and shocking violation are not simply ends in themselves for the leather-puppet clowns but rather stages in a much wider process of energizing and release. First the antithetical undercurrent is given expression, in word and form; *then* a fertile, creative, open-ended freedom is made accessible to the mind and to a world which it can now imaginatively reconstitute, change, re-form.

The particular character of these clowns seems to be derived from the combination of their flagrant reversals and the "magical," transformative powers that accrue to them as a direct result of abrogating prescribed order. It is the latter component—their fertilizing, life-giving aspect—which may strike us as singular; none of the clowns discussed earlier could claim this power to the same degree. We have reached the end of a spectrum stretching from the Vidūṣaka (in the classical drama and its development in South India) through the Telugu court jester to the leather-puppet clowns; from dramatic foil through cognitive trickster to autonomous comic master and magician; from only partly conscious butt through ironic commentator to fully self-conscious, complex manipulator of realities; from a bumbling, orally fixated, distorting reflection of the *nāyaka* through the playful and

[158] *Ibid.*, pp. 127-28. Here the Tamil clown may remind us of the "debased" magicians or sorcerers from whom some have derived the Russian *skoromokhi*: Belkin (1975), pp. 30-31.

[159] As was the case—with successful results, of course—in the Killekyāṭa performance I witnessed at Ambalajīrahaḷḷi.

coherent court fool to the powerfully transformative, overtly obscene, internally disharmonious puppet clown. The spectrum as a whole offers varying types and degrees of reflexivity upon the given order and its representatives, as we have seen. This point can now be refined with respect to the leather-puppet clowns, where the iconic disequilibrium is most intense. For the centrality that these full-fledged comic characters have acquired is clearly connected to their reflexive role as boundary figures illuminating the dramatic world; and it is their internal organization—or rather dynamic and fluid disorganization—that allows them to function in this way. These clowns are intentionally incoherent, a confusing jumble of antitheses: sexually ambiguous (like the androgynous Semar in Java—and Arjuna-Bṛhannaḍā), simultaneously virile and impotent (Juṭṭupoligāḍu, with his long phallus mocked by his wife; or the hunchback lovers of various traditions[160]); at once old and young, Brahminical and anti-Brahminical, abusive masters of elegant speech, and so on. They are subject to constant movement within themselves, an oscillation between opposing attributes and attitudes; they are thus never wholly formed, always in the process of becoming, and transcending, themselves. This internal movement induces oscillation and transformation in anything that comes within their range, particularly in the cognitive domain; they thus tend, as Don Handelman has shown, "to make clear-cut and routinely accepted precepts into ambiguous, confused, and problematic ones."[161] Jumbling categories within their own unfinished character, they bring doubt and movement to categorization in general, and thus identify themselves with the problematic reality of boundaries in their formation, their tenuousness, their hidden artificiality. The ritual clown is "an ambulatory manifestation of 'boundariness' "[162] endowed with primary features of the boundary such as paradoxicality, fluidity, inconsistency, self-transformation, and a powerful sense of being "in process." He is stable only in movement, or in instability; and it is this dynamic, dissonant identity that enables him to dissolve other entities, to take apart the given world as part of its process of movement toward a not wholly determined future. The clown identifies himself with this process rather

[160] E.g. *Pañcatantra* 5.10 (pp. 285-89); *Jātaka* 536 (Draupadī's hunchback-lover). Cf. Natesa Sastri (1908), pp. 277-79; related figures include the dwarf-lover (*Kalittŏkai* 94, where he unites with a hunchback woman) and the old Brahmin lecher (above, section 1). We have already had occasion to note the famous royal hunchback Kūṉpāṇṭiyaṉ.

[161] Handelman (1981), p. 342. The leather-puppet clowns would seem to have, in Handelman's terms, elements of both "anti-structure" and "in-process."

[162] *Ibid.*, p. 341.

than with any rigid moment of its unfolding—including the recurring moment of his antithetical revolt, when an existing stability is first broken through.

If this view is to be accepted, we shall have to modify the still commonly held belief that the clown provides a "safety valve" for his culture; that the reversals he engineers serve ultimately to reinforce the inverted norms and to integrate protest against them, or to compensate in some way for the deprivation they entail. We may recall that an interpretation along these lines is still generally applied to the Vidūṣaka.[163] And in itself, symbolic inversion does seem to fulfil this purpose. As Turner has said (in reference to the Javanese theater), "all social classification of living humans means existential deprivation for those classified, and the resulting loss and frustration are compensated for by symbols of reversal, such as *ludruk* transvestism and clowning."[164] Similarly, James Peacock has shown how Javanese symbols of reversal ultimately "call forth enchantment with the form and veneration for the cosmic categories it embodies."[165] We shall return to this question when we discuss the festive inversions of the king's normal role. But the above analysis has allowed us to distinguish two rather different aspects of the puppet clowns' effective function (though both aspects inhere in the same complex figures): an antinomian mode of reversal, "antistructure," and attack (like the Auguste of the circus), and a transformative, energizing, reflexive mode. The latter dissolves boundaries even as it illuminates their artificial and ambiguous existence; the former consciously transgresses them or inverts their contents, and in this way helps ultimately to sustain them (in Peacock's terms: to maintain the essential enchantment with form). The iconography of the clown (the confusing interplay of attributes) best expresses his transformative and dynamic side; his verbal and dramatic actions tend to express his revolt. There may, indeed, be a form of integration in this combination of modes, but, as with the notion of cultural "congruence" discussed earlier,[166] it is clearly an extraordinarily complex, ambiguous, and disharmonious integration predicated on the always open-ended and unfinished character of that which is being integrated. To paraphrase Turner's observation: if all socially accepted classification or ordering of reality entails existential deprivation for those partaking of that order—for reality always exceeds the categorical limits, so that vital remnants remain outside—

[163] See section 2 above (notes 14-16).

[164] Turner (1978), p. 285.

[165] Peacock (1978), p. 222. Cf. Sachs (1978) on Aristophanes, pp. 23-25.

[166] See II.5 after n. 102.

the resulting cognitive loss and frustration are expressed, explored, and at times transcended through complex symbols of inversion, in the first instance (with the inherent suggestion of an ultimate reversion and reaffirmation), and of transformation toward an indeterminate future, in the second.

It may be the peculiar feature of medieval South Indian culture to have made this recognition of the essential partiality of all cultural categories and forms a central aspect of its relation to reality.

The transformative side of the clown gives him his prominent role as reflexive "framer" or mediator of the drama (including ritual drama in the festivals). This framing technique is found throughout the South Indian folk-dramatic genres. In the Kannada *yakṣagāna* dance dramas, the *koḍaṅgi* clowns appear at the beginning of a performance and during dramatic interludes; the *koḍaṅgi* is usually a child or young student, who begins his apprenticeship in the troupe by performing this role. A more mature clown, the *hāsyagāra*, also appears in the *yakṣagāna* as a frequent commentator (through improvised dialogue) on the actions of the other characters: we may note here the internal differentiation in clown roles combined elsewhere (for example, the Kūṭiyāṭṭam Vidūṣaka). The basic reflexivity of the clown may explain why it is a clown who plays the role of a main character whenever that character is in disguise (such as the transvestite Bhīma in the *Kīcakavadhe*): there is a wonderful sophistication in this use of the character who normally illuminates the threshold into the magical world of the drama, in a context when an *internal* identity boundary is crossed.[167] Of course, disguise in itself is native to the clown, who often lacks a stable identity of his own but is "at home" in an endless progression of temporary masks and magical self-transformations.

A similar role on the boundary of the dramatic illusion is given to the clown (*kaṭṭiyaṅkāraṉ, tŏppaikkūttāṭi*) in the Tamil street dramas (*tĕrukkūttu*): here the clown introduces all the other characters, comments upon the action, and concludes the performance.[168] In the little-known, unstudied *Bhāgavatamela*, a *koṇaṅki* clown begins the play with his dance during the invocation; he is followed first by Gaṇapati (as in the leather-puppet traditions), then by the *kaṭṭiyakkāraṉ* or *sūtradhāra*, another comic character serving as stage master for the drama.[169] The same title, *kaṭṭiyakkāraṉ*, is applied, to the introductory clown of the more literary *kuṟavañci*—a genre that emerged, toward the end of the

[167] Ashton and Christie (1977), pp. 7, 42-43.

[168] Durga (1979), pp. 47-48; personal communication from M. Shanmugam Pillai.

[169] Durga (1979), p. 41. Cf. the Vidūṣaka's roles in the *trigata, with* the *sūtradhāra*: *Nāṭyaśāstra* 5.136-40; Kuiper (1979), pp. 177-93.

medieval period, out of the substratum of popular tradition (still replete with fragmentary memories of the classical past).[170] In concluding this chapter, let us briefly examine the *kuṟavañci*'s clown.

The *kuṟavañci* itself has a set pattern: it describes the love of the heroine for a local hero (usually the god, but also possibly a local lord or king), whom she beholds during his procession (*pavaṉi*); the lovesick girl is visited by a Kuṟatti fortuneteller (hence the name of the genre), who predicts her eventual union with her beloved; the Kuṟatti is then herself reunited with her gypsylike husband (often a bird catcher). Lyrical descriptions of the local landscape are interspersed with these dramatic events. The clown's place is, as we by now expect, at the beginning: immediately after the initial invocations to the deities, he announces the hero's setting forth on his procession. In some works of this class, the clown also introduces each major stage of the plot.[171] His appearance offers several familiar features: he holds a staff in one hand, has the triple thread drawn over his breast, is smeared with white ash; on his forehead he bears the Vaiṣṇava *nāmam* or a vermilion *tilaka*; he wears a turban, ochre trousers, and a belt; he sports a fierce, twisted mustache.[172] His arrival on stage is heralded by descriptive verses such as the following (from the most famous of all *kuṟavañci* poems, Tirikūṭarācappakkavirāyar's *Tirukkuṟṟālak kuṟavañci*).

Into the springtime streets
  blown by the south wind, Kāma's chariot,
the rich lord of Kuṟṟālam
is about to come on his procession,
  riding the bull married to the Earth.[173]
Here to announce his coming (*ĕccarikkai kūṟa*)[174]—
  with twisted thread hanging in a straight line upon his breast
  and a staff in his long hand—
comes the *kaṭṭiyakkāraṉ*,
  like the approach of a dark cloud.

[170] On *kuṟavañci* see Muttuccaṇmukaṉ and Mohaṉ (1977); Zvelebil (1974), pp. 224-26; for classical antecedents, see Shulman (1980b), pp. 288-89. Representative examples of the genre are the anonymous *Tañcaivĕḷḷaippiḷḷaiyār kuṟavañci, Kumpecar kuṟavañci* of Pāpanāca Mutaliyār, and the outstanding *Tirukkuṟṟālak kuṟavañci* of Tirikūṭarācappakkavirāyar.

[171] Muttuccaṇmukaṉ and Mohaṉ (1977), p. 65 (e.g. in *Carapentirapūpāla kuṟavañci*).

[172] *Ibid.* Cf. *Kumpecar kuṟavañci* 12.

[173] Viṣṇu is identified as the bull, Śiva's mount; his wife is the Earth.

[174] *ĕccarikkai*: "exclamatory word enjoining care, silence, uttered in advance on the approach of a king, or any exalted personage" (*Tamil Lexicon*, s. v.).

He has come,
the *kaṭṭiyakkāraṉ*,
from the gates
of the bearer of the straight staff
which protects the kings of men on earth,
godly kings, and all others,
he who made great Meru into his bow,
giver of boons,
Kuṟṟālam's lord.[175]

Perhaps the most striking note in these verses is the implied association of the clown with the god in his regal aspect (the divine king in his local shrine). The two "arrivals"—that of the clown-servant preceding that of his divine master—seem to merge in the telling; and the *kaṭṭiyakkāraṉ*'s simple staff (*pirampu*) is assimilated by verbal suggestion to the royal scepter (*cĕṅkol āṉa pirampu*). This playful overlapping of identities—the clown slipping into the king/deity—points toward the royal clowns of the next chapter. The *kaṭṭiyakkāraṉ* is the god's gatekeeper and, as the triple thread suggests (and as we might expect from his place on the threshold), a Brahmin—though again an odd Brahmin—with his martial mustache, his royal associations, and above all his dark color (like that of a dark raincloud). The Brahminical traits of the leather-puppet clowns (their persistent Brahminical top-knots still reflected in their titles: Uccikkuṭumpaṉ, Juṭṭupoligāḍu) have been deepened here into another full-fledged Brahmin clown, albeit a somewhat debased Brahmin like the Vidūṣaka; these Brahminical features may explain why the *kaṭṭiyakkāraṉ* of the Tamil Christian *kuṟavañci*, *Pĕtlakem* (= Bethlehem) *kuṟavañci*, is the teacher and holy man, John the Baptist (Yovāṉ Snāṉikaṉ).[176]

The Brahmin clown of the *kuṟavañci* brings us back to the question with which this chapter began, that of the psychology of Brahmin clowning. And while we may still not be able to provide a full answer to explain the historical affinity between Brahmin and clown, certain keys to the relation have emerged from the various analytical features of Indian comedy we have discussed. Among these may be stressed the clown's inherent complexity, his unresolved oscillation, his association with the borders (linguistic and symbolic); the deeply rooted reflexivity that he brings to his varying contexts; the "disintegrative" integration that he masterminds through his efforts at reversal and decomposition of given forms, and the revitalizing, regenerative ca-

[175] *Tirukkuṟṟālak kuṟavañci*, p. 8.
[176] Muttuccaṇmukaṉ and Mohaṉ (1977), p. 66.

pacity that flows into this same process; the comic articulation of hidden truth (utterable only by the clowns) and the drive toward a transcendence based on the principles of indeterminacy, movement, and dynamic transformation; the central role given to ambiguity, ambivalence, and anomaly as enacted by the clown in the symbolic heartland of kingdom and culture; and, finally, the clown's relation to ontology, his contrary motion of disillusionment (as in the case of the Vidūṣaka) on the one hand, and of magically purveying "illusory" visions (as with the folk clowns), on the other. This last attribute requires elaboration, as it contributes to the metaphysical foundations of this culture. From his apparent safety within the entrenched zone of the boundary, the clown—like the magician, or like the *brāhmaṇa* priest of the sacrificial ritual, whose job was to think through the entire sacrifice in total silence—argues for the reality of the inner worlds of vision, intuitive perception, hallucination, nightmare, or dream. In a word, he exemplifies the world's status as *māyā*, at once tangible and real, and immaterial; entirely permeable by the imagination; always baffling, enticing, enslaving, and in the process of becoming something new and still more elusive. His attitude toward these phenomena varies from comic detachment (ironic, perhaps dispassionate) to passionate and playful engagement in further creation, though always through an initial act of violation or dissolution; while in the middle range we find the clown's common-sensical and yet ridiculous acceptance of immediate, sensuous reality. The essence of *māyā* is contradiction—the incongruous wonder of the absolute transformed into sensible form; the innate, mysterious, dynamic contradiction of the clown. And this the clown shares with the Brahmin, with the latter's characteristic ambivalence toward a baffling and violent reality as well as his stance upon the border facing the ultimate on either side—transcendent wholeness through "outer" release, or the creative metonymy of samskaric form.

The Brahmin's internal oscillation, like the clown's, engenders the ambiguous movement of *māyā*. Rejected or reaffirmed, the world is never still; the violence of the sacrifice, transformed, becomes a violent ideal. Truth lies somewhere on the border, neither here nor there; but the border *is* the center, in all its ambiguity and unrest. Brahmin and comic hero merely enact the anomalous norm: in its own eyes, in its own wisdom, the medieval South Indian state is a kingdom of clowns.

· V ·

Royal Comedies and Errors

A little Madness in the Spring
Is wholesome even for the King,
But God be with the Clown—
Who ponders this tremendous Scene—
This whole Experiment of Green—
As if it were his own.[1]

1. Introduction: The Importance of Being Exiled

The intimate association of kings and comic figures (such as the Vidūṣaka or the court jester) is not, of course, limited to India. Western traditions reveal a similar symbolic symbiosis of these types: Rabelais repeats the ancient belief that kings and clowns have the same horoscope.[2] A host of stories explores this relation, which is also present, in culturally distinct patterns, in Biblical and Islamic traditions.[3] And, as in India, the European sources describe two levels or aspects of this connection: the "formal" or "surface" association of the king with his court jester or fool, who may, like Tĕnāli Rāma, provide a necessary corrective to the king's human inadequacies and deviations from truth; and, on a deeper level of perception, an implied closeness of identities or even an exchange of personae, such as we find in *Lear*. The king's clownlike attributes were played out, as Bakhtin tells us, in the medieval folk carnival:

[1] Dickinson (1955), no. 1333 (3:921).

[2] Rabelais (1979), 3.37; cf. Bakhtin (1968), p. 198.

[3] See the materials gathered by Welsford (1935). Muslim tradition offers the example of Hārūn al-Rashīd and Buhlūl (among others). The Biblical figure of David has pronounced "clownish" features: recall his feigned madness in captivity, and his dancing before the Ark.

> In such a system the king is the clown. He is elected by all the people and is mocked by all the people. He is abused and beaten when the time of his reign is over, just as the carnival dummy of winter or of the dying year is mocked, beaten, torn to pieces, burned, or drowned. . . . The clown was first disguised as a king, but once his reign had come to an end his costume was changed, "travestied," to turn him once more into a clown. The abuse and thrashing are equivalent to a change of costume, to a metamorphosis. Abuse reveals the other, true face of the abused, it tears off his disguise and mask. It is the king's uncrowning.[4]

This type of festive "uncrowning" is also, as we shall see, an important part of the Indian king's symbolic career.

These similarities should not, however, mislead us. Fundamental differences divide the comedies of kingship in South India and late medieval Europe, in ways directly resulting from the varying nature of sociopolitical order in these cultures. This chapter will pursue the king's comic side in relation to the conceptual model of medieval South Indian society that has been emerging from our discussion. Royal clowning brings the "dis-integrating" dynamic of this culture into its symbolic center: the same figure who is held responsible for the society's proper order may be seen to undermine this order, to unravel the fabric even as it is being woven, to open up his kingdom to indeterminate forces of transformation and flux. He does this by undergoing far-reaching changes himself, in a series of recurrent patterns, as the exemplary protagonist in the ongoing dramas of cultural self-definition. The comic transformations of the South Indian king form part of an always unfinished process of the kingdom's "becoming."

The Western king, by way of contrast, seems driven toward a more stable form of "being." His development may require that he taste, at some point, the tempting sensations of comic rebelliousness and the ludicrous anti-self—witness Hal's "training" at the hands of Falstaff—but his movement inexorably tends toward exorcism of the comic demons, or the mature sealing off of the royal self from disorderly and irreverent excess. Falstaff will thus be exiled by Hal upon his accession.[5] As Willeford writes:

> Thus the hero's demonstration of kingly qualities is part of a gradual differentiation that also causes his folly to gain a voice

[4] Bakhtin (1968), p. 197.
[5] See Nevo (1980), p. 16.

separate from his own, to consolidate, to become a human partner with whom one can have a dialogue. The king at the center and the court jester beside him are a picture of the result of this process, the king being free to allow the jester because the king is (symbolically) detached from his own folly and that of the world.[6]

If the festive "uncrownings" of the folk traditions seem to represent an exception to this general rule of the king's increasing separation from the clown (as seen in the "high" culture of the courts), they must at the same time be recognized for the rather limited types they are: carnival inversions, as we shall see, are one of the major integrative mechanisms in the Indian royal comedies; their scope is relatively predictable and confined, and they inevitably imply a reversion to the king's normally ordered state. On the other hand, a Western king who, like Lear, becomes trapped in a foolish persona is quintessentially tragic; the nobility he attains in this state is created from the conditions of his tragic "recognition," *anagnorisis*, of his own folly; and if, as with Lear, this recognition drives him mad, his madness conveys, above all, an awesome horror. The terrible vision of the crazed king-turned-fool is redeemed only by the tragic consciousness it evokes. The Fool, of course, lucidly states Lear's folly and, appropriately, offers him his coxcomb;[7] but by the time the king fully understands the bitter truth, the Fool himself is no longer strictly necessary and can thus disappear from the drama—since both his insightful wisdom and his comic foolishness have been subsumed within his royal master.

A tragic *anagnorisis* of this kind is denied the Indian king, whose clowning remains unconscious, in contrast to the Brahmin and folk clowns (with the exception of the Vidūṣaka) studied above. By the same token, however, the dimension of horror is largely lacking: neither the king nor his subjects need be appalled by a folly that demands no tempering, no exorcism, since it will always remain as a recurrent and necessary component of the royal identity. Even madness is only a temporary, and not overly frightening, experience belonging to the probable unfolding of *any* royal career.[8] And it is the king who must himself act out this experiential mode. The process of differentiation is arrested before it can congeal into stable, homogeneous halves: although in some cases the king is set against a wholly externalized comic self—*nāyaka* vs. Vidūṣaka, emperor against jester—the two parts nevertheless always comprise a unity; still more signif-

[6] Willeford (1969), p. 166. See also Hastrup and Ovesen (1976), p. 20.

[7] I.iv.

[8] See below, VI.3, on the conventional royal madness of romantic love.

icantly, the major stories of kingship display the processes of unending transformation: king to clown to king; "serious" ruler to even more serious comic exile; tragic exemplar to self-mocking shadow. The Indian king needs his foolishness to be king at all, for it provides him with his most creative and dynamic attributes in a world of transformations, where the greatest disaster is to become stuck in a single, nontransitional form.

Thus Henry V may exile Falstaff, thereby stabilizing his rule and his own regal identity; but the South Indian king must himself suffer exile. His kingship is a double pulsation, systole and diastole, or, as Inden has suggested,[9] immanence and transcendence, a *pravṛtti* and a *nivṛtti*. Without the exilic phase, both king and kingdom will be lost in the tragic rigidity of a false but impenetrable reality; but given the painful possibilities of exile, they become endowed with the capacity for regeneration and creative play. Beyond this, perception is altered, and hidden layers of existence unveiled; exile itself becomes a cogent metaphor for the essential nature of human experience in the world.

The various patterns of the king's *nivṛtti*—often, but not always, comic in character—will be traced below, in relation to specific stories, symbolic characters, or textual genres. Three features common to all these patterns may, however, be noted briefly in advance.

First, the king's comic withdrawal or exile, which reflects both his own self-transforming identity and the transformative powers that he brings to bear upon the kingdom, also expresses the limitations of the king's actual power. The comic king shares the clown's basic impotence. Even, or especially, in terms of *Realpolitik*, the king's power (to cumulate resources, to give commands, to act decisively in his kingdom's interests) is rooted in a kind of conspicuous powerlessness. The comic transformations of exile mark the moment of royal weakness, self-denial, or even more radical loss of self, out of which the king's claims to authority are articulated.

Second, the exemplary comedies of kingship illuminate both the ludic undercurrent flowing through the foundations of the South Indian state and the ontological underpinnings of this structure. The entire edifice is knowingly erected on the thin surface dividing, and at the same time connecting, inner and outer worlds. In such a state, in which concretely external realities are declared, in principle, to be deceptive, subject to internal flux, and in any case no less tangible or "real" than the visionary experiences of the mind, the king himself is the first to become permeated by his inner shadows; his plunge into

[9] Inden (1978), pp. 58-60.

alienation, antithesis, or extravagant fantasy is not an isolated phenomenon pertaining only to his individual nature and career but a powerful demonstration of the interconnectedness of being—of the bonds that unite inner with outer, individual with communal experience. Like Don Quixote in Américo Castro's historical exegesis,[10] the Indian king shows the impact of the inner life of the imagination and of feeling upon a malleable and changing external world; the history of his kingdom is, in its own perspective,[11] a "living out" (in Castro's terms: *desvivir*), in ordinary, everyday reality, of the open-ended processes of self-definition and self-demolition through the interweaving of the imagined, the sensed, and the perceived.[12] Note that the king's exilic identity, expressed in shadow and disguise, is in no way less authentic than his normally "ordered" self; in fact it is the latter, as we have seen, that is constituted by a series of royal masks, while in exile the king is brought into contact with an area of experience perhaps ultimately *more* "real" than any prescribed role. *Nivṛtti*, comic or otherwise, has a transcendent aspect crucially important for the king.

Finally, the royal *nivṛtti* has an innate link to the king's perception of evil. These royal comedies are but rarely light-hearted, nor are they "therapeutic" in the sense that Shakespearean or Aristophanic comedies are sometimes said to be.[13] Their darker side is linked to the tragic themes of disposession, impotence, and loss; and they share something of the deadly comic seriousness of the jester, with his epistemological concerns.[14] Indeed, the South Indian king is never simply comic (as the Brahmin clown may be); his comedy develops out of an ambiguous tragi-comic stance that can turn wholly tragic if the transformational process ever halts. The king enacts in his exile both the magical transcendence and the personal tragedy characteristic of the clown.

2. Indra: The King as Buffoon

We begin with Indra, king of the gods. Is it by chance that this divine monarch, the mythic model for human kings, consistently appears in

[10] Castro (1977), pp. 77-139.

[11] See the fine "ethno-historical" essay by Dirks (1982) on the historical self-understanding of the South Indian little kingdom.

[12] On *desvivir*: Castro (1977), p. 119.

[13] Nevo (1980), pp. 16, 34, 223-25.

[14] See above, IV.4.

a ludicrous light in the epic and puranic literature? Among Indra's many traits—his vaunted prowess on the battlefield, at table, and in the harem; his sacrificial prerogatives; his ambiguous connection with Śrī and, through her, with notions of prosperity, royal splendor, and proper order—perhaps none is so striking as his recurring tendency to become embroiled in embarrassing situations. The Ahalyā episode, no doubt one of the best known and most explicitly humiliating for the god—he slinks away from Ahalyā's house in the form of a cat, his body disfigured by the marks of a thousand vaginas through the curse of Ahalyā's jealous husband Gautama[15]—is only one of a long series of similar scrapes. Why have the authors of our texts reduced the divine king to this sorry state? There can be no doubt as to the seriousness of his condition; the purāṇas depict Indra as a startlingly pathetic creature, constantly threatened by the emergence of some new rival (who may be demonic or, more often, merely human) and forced to resort to the most devious and cowardly tricks simply in order to retain, or in many cases to regain, his throne. What can this mean?

Some scholars have seen here the effects of an historical process within the myths: as new gods, such as Śiva and Viṣṇu, became preeminent, the older heroes were transformed into much poorer figures. Even if this hypothesis has some merit, we must observe that Indra's ludicrous aspect has quite a venerable antiquity in our sources. The *Brāhmana* literature often portrays Indra in a highly questionable light, for instance as adopting the form of a monkey in order to disrupt a sacrifice,[16] or disguised as a woman in the house of Vṛṣaṇaśva.[17] These stories seem even to have offended some sober scholars; Oertel, for example, regarded the transvestite motif as "admirably fitted to a folk tale . . . but . . . ill adapted for exploitation in hymns of the ritual."[18] One can only wonder if the *Brāhmaṇa* authors had so solemn a view of the ritual. Moreover, we may assume that for them, as for

[15] Kampaṉ, *Irāmāvatāram* 1.546-47; cf. *Rām.* 1.18-19. The cat motif is also present in *Kathāsaritsāgara* 17.114. Zvelebil (1973), p. 213, follows A. K. Ramanujan in regarding the cat and the thousand vaginas as folklore motifs; and cf. Neogi (1916), pp. 90-94 (Indra cursed to become a cat in the house of a hunter).

[16] *JB* 1.363; *ŚB* 1.6.9-18; cf. Oertel (1905). Cf. the later myth of Indra's paternity of the monkey Vālin, and the associated sex-reversal (Indra is seduced by a male monkey who has become female): *Tiruvāṉmiyūr stalapurāṇavacaṉam* 2 (p. 8). And see the Mucukunda myth discussed below, section 4.

[17] See Oertel (1905); *RV* 1.51.13. Other ancient transformations of Indra's include a ram, a quail (see Sāyaṇa on *RV* 10.119), an ant (*Tai. Ār.* 1.5.1-2), horsehair, and a peacock (*Rām.* 7.18.4-5).

[18] Oertel (1905), p. 177.

their puranic successors, Indra's peculiar transformations carried some meaning. However eroded his status within the classical pantheon, this forlorn and antiheroic god continues to claim his royal title; and historical rulers felt no hesitation about describing themselves as an "Indra among kings." Both the continuity in the mythic role and the attention accorded Indra's adventures in the epic and puranic sources suggest that the process depicted in these stories—the divine king threatened, exiled, humiliated, and reinstated—is felt to be significant in its own right.

We shall try to bring this issue into better focus by looking at two versions of one of the basic myths about Indra: a classical account from the epic, and a medieval South Indian text.

Mahābhārata 5.9-18

The ancient myth of Indra's Brahminicide[19] is narrated at length in the early chapters of the *Udyogaparvan*, in a context heavy with troublesome implications for Yudhiṣṭhira, the dharmic king. The story is told by Śalya, whom Yudhiṣṭhira, in his "first attempt at perfidy,"[20] recruits as a kind of half-hearted double agent in his role as Karṇa's charioteer; both Śalya and Yudhiṣṭhira must be aware of the relevance of Indra's unhappy errors and misadventures for the Pāṇḍava hero aspiring to the throne.

The myth opens with a set piece, one of the classic problem situations of Hindu mythology: Indra discovers to his dismay that he is threatened by the ascetic power, the piety, and the ambition of a rival, in this case the demon Tvaṣṭṛ's son Triśiras-Viśvarūpa.[21] Viśvarūpa has been created by his father out of hatred for Indra (*indradrohāt*), and he seeks Indra's position (*aindraṃ samprārthayat sthānam*); he is gentle, self-controlled, intent on *dharma* and *tapas*—and for all that, a monster with three heads, one of which recites the Veda while the second drinks wine and the third stares into space as if about to drink up the cardinal points. Seeing Viśvarūpa's ascetic power, Indra becomes depressed but, inevitably, eventually decides upon his usual tactic of

[19] Originally hinted at in the Veda; see O'Flaherty's translation and commentary to *RV* 1.32: (1981), pp. 139-40, 148-51; Holtzmann (1878); Dumézil (1969); Kramrisch (1962), pp. 135-36; van Buitenen (1978), pp. 159-66; Hiltebeitel (1977).

[20] Van Buitenen (1978), p. 166. See also Hiltebeitel (1976), pp. 241-43, 280-81.

[21] There are hints in the Vedic material that Tvaṣṭṛ is also Indra's father. If this notion is still relevant for our myth, Triśiras would thus be Indra's half-brother. See O'Flaherty (1976), p. 102. The *Udyoga* account uses both names, Triśiras and Viśvarūpa, for the demon.

sending out the celestial dancing-girls. The latter make a supreme effort (*yatnaṃ paraṃ kṛtvā*) to divert Triśiras from his *tapas*; and, for once, they fail, so that Indra must, reluctantly, take action himself. He is determined to strike before his enemy grows any stronger; and, in a burst of aggressive energy, Indra succeeds in dispatching him with his *vajra* weapon. It all happens so fast that one might wonder why the god hesitated in the first place.

However, Indra had, of course, good reason to shrink from slaughter: Triśiras, though definitely dead, emits such burning splendor (*tejas*) that he appears to be alive. Scorched by this fire, Indra turns to a woodcutter (who conveniently happens by) and commands him to cut off Triśiras's three heads. The woodcutter is most reluctant: for one thing, his axe will not cut through the huge corpse; for another, he is loath to commit a rather dubious deed (*karma*) that is condemned by the good (*sadbhir vigarhitam*). Even when Indra identifies himself as king of the gods and repeats his command, the woodcutter hesitates: "How can you not shun such a cruel deed? Why are you not afraid of Brahminicide?" "That is easy," answers Indra in what seems almost a deliberate parody of the ritualists' attitude; "I will purify myself later by some dharmic rite." He also promises the woodcutter a share of the sacrifice (the symbolically crucial head of the victim).[22]

So the woodcutter proceeds to decapitate Triśiras[23] and then goes home, as does Indra, without telling anyone what has happened. Perhaps he hopes to get away with what is clearly seen as a crime, the murder of a Brahmin (albeit a demonic Brahmin). And, naturally, he fails: for after a year has passed, the *bhūtas* of Paśupati-Śiva proclaim so that all can hear that Indra is a *brahmahan*, the slayer of a Brahmin. Now action of some sort is again required. Indra, true to his earlier statement to the woodcutter, performs a vow (*vrata*), after which he succeeds in divesting himself of the evil by spreading it among four carriers—the seas, the earth, trees, and women.[24]

So far, it would seem, nothing too extraordinary has happened; the pattern of Indra's encounter with Triśiras-Viśvarūpa is par for the course. Perhaps for this very reason we should take a moment to

[22] On the head of the sacrifice, see Heesterman (1967); on the woodcutter, and the related figure of Trita Āptya, see O'Flaherty (1976), pp. 153-60.

[23] From the demon's three heads issue forth three kinds of birds: heathcocks, partridges, and sparrows.

[24] This passage is missing from the BORI "critical" text; it appears in SR and is clearly important to later versions, including that of the *Tiruviḷai*. to be discussed below. Hence I have restored it in my summary. On the general problem of Indra's transfers of evil, see O'Flaherty (1976), pp. 146-61.

notice the traditional elements in Indra's role: his initial panic at the emergence of someone better (that is, more dharmic, more ascetic, better controlled, *and* more powerful) than himself; his immediate attempt to meet the threat by devious means; his obvious reluctance to do battle, even though he is clearly armed with the most effective of weapons; and, above all, his puerile attempt to avoid the consequences of his actions, as in the empty rationalizations he offers the woodcutter (whom, incidentally, Indra desperately needs as his henchman) and in his doomed efforts to hush up the whole case. If, in the end, Indra succeeds in regaining a state of purity and renewed power, he does so only by passing the evil on to various other vehicles in the world—not, it would seem, the most heroic of solutions, even if one is prepared to see this as a feature rooted in the ancient agonistic structure of the sacrifice.[25] All in all, the god appears in a most unseemly light—so much so that one cannot but suspect that the myth is meant to be appreciated in this way, as an amusing, perhaps tragicomic farce whose main protagonist consistently moves between the heroic and the ridiculous, more of a clownish, cloddish antihero than a positive exemplar of royal virtues. This initial portrait gains in clarity and forcefulness in the following episodes.

For the sorry cycle begins again: Tvaṣṭṛ, enraged at the death of Viśvarūpa, creates from the sacrificial fire another son, the terrible Vṛtra. Vṛtra's challenge to Indra lies first of all in his apparently uncontrollable growth: he swells up, propping up the sky (*divaṃ stabdhvā*);[26] he swallows the worlds, including the five elements, tastes, smells, and other sensory perceptions—and finally Indra himself. The god is rescued from Vṛtra's jaws only when the gods quick-wittedly invent the Yawn, so that Indra, making himself small, can slip through the yawning mouth of his adversary. Clearly, the demon is too powerful for the god; Indra gives up any thought of battle and, together with the other gods, takes refuge with Viṣṇu. The latter advises the gods to use one of the classic ploys against an enemy, familiar from the *Arthaśāstra: sāman*, the conciliatory stance aimed at beguiling the foe.

This plan succeeds all too well. Vṛtra is delighted when the gods and sages suggest, in gnomic *triṣṭubh* verses, a pact between him and Indra; his conditions for acceptance are that he never be slain by Indra

[25] According to Heesterman (1964), the "pre-classical" model of Vedic sacrifice required the two parties to the rite to exchange, in endless cycles, the burden of evil generated by the sacrificial slaying.

[26] Note that this is Indra's classic role in the Vedic cosmogonic myths! See Kuiper (1975).

or the other gods with anything dry or wet, with rock or wood, weapon or nonweapon,[27] by day or night. So it is agreed, and Indra manages to hold fast to the letter of this agreement even as he violates its spirit; he eventually kills Vṛtra (with Viṣṇu's help) at twilight, with foam from the ocean's waves.

At this point we might have expected the myth to conclude on a joyful note, with our divine hero reinstated by virtue of his cleverness. That such is not the case points to the nature of our authors' concerns; Indra's victory, far from concluding the story, opens the way for further significant developments, some of which are focused on moral issues. Indra has kept his word to Vṛtra, but the word is not the truth—as we have learned from the court jester Tĕnāli Rāma, whose ironic literal-mindedness Indra mimics.[28] In effect, the god has violated the pact (just as the jester violates language by taking it at its most literal level); to win by a technicality, by reading the small print, so to speak, is perceived here as obviously wrong; hence Indra is now overcome with falsehood (*anṛta*) in addition to suffering, yet again, the effects of Brahminicide. The rest of the universe can rejoice in its liberation from Vṛtra's suffocating growth, but for the divine protagonist of the tale it has all become rather too much: he goes out of his mind (*naṣṭasañjño vicetanaḥ*) and flees to the end of the worlds (*antam . . . lokānām*), where he hides himself, writhing like a serpent, in the waters.

The king, demented, terrified, loaded down with evil, has gone into hiding; the world pays the price. No rain falls, rivers and lakes dry up, the earth becomes treeless, ravaged. This state cannot be allowed to last: enter Nahuṣa, the human king to whom the gods turn in desperation with the request that he take Indra's place. Nahuṣa, although he is endowed with *śrī (śrīmān)*, protests that he is too weak for the job. The gods reassure him: they will give him their own *tapas*; indeed, he will have the faculty of acquiring the *tejas* of whatever beings come within the range of his sight. So Nahuṣa is anointed king of heaven, and immediately a transformation begins; he who delighted in *dharma* now becomes intent upon *kāma (dharmātmā satataṃ bhūtvā kāmātmā samapadyata)*. At first content to play with the celestial maidens while being entertained by enchanting stories and concerts, Nahuṣa all too soon shows signs of overbearing pride—a trait that seems to come with this position. The primary symbol of the change is his

[27] Following SR; the BORI text reads "with thunderbolt or weapon."

[28] See above, IV.4.

sudden desire to possess Śacī, Indra's grass-widowed consort. From this point on, Nahuṣa moves steadily toward his doom.

We need not recount at length the details of Nahuṣa's wooing of Śacī, including her flight to Bṛhaspati, *guru* of the gods. Bṛhaspati faithfully protects her, not only from Nahuṣa but also from the gods, who, utilitarian as always, are quite prepared to hand her over to Nahuṣa in the interests of maintaining peace in heaven. Upon Bṛhaspati's advice, Śacī asks and is granted leave by Nahuṣa to seek her husband. We now have three separate "quests" (I borrow the term from Alf Hiltebeitel)[29] for Indra: first the gods, apparently led by Agni, find the still terrified (*bhayodvigna*) Indra and, at Viṣṇu's instance, perform an *aśvamedha* to purify him;[30] again Indra manages to rid himself of evil by distributing his Brahminicide among the trees, rivers, mountains, earth, and women. But unlike the first such redistribution, this one does not suffice to restore Indra's confidence. He takes one glance at the current state of affairs in heaven, with Nahuṣa still swelling (like Indra's erstwhile opponent Vṛtra) from the *tejas* of other creatures, and disappears once again—leaving Śacī calling pathetically after him. The second quest is hers, accompanied by Upaśruti ("Whisper," "Rumor," "Divination").[31] They discover the divine monarch cowering inside the stalk of a lotus growing in a pond on a far-away island. No sooner does Śacī find her long-lost husband than, still touchingly loyal, she sings his praises, reminding him of his former victories and at the same time bringing him up to date on Nahuṣa's plans. Time is drawing short, she tells him; soon the respite granted her by Nahuṣa will be over.

Indra's first words to the wife who has traveled across the world to find him are little short of surly: "Why have you come here, and how did you find me out?" He then adds with his usual fighting spirit: "This is no time for courage" (*vikramasya na kālo 'yam*). And once again he proposes a devious plan: Śacī must tell Nahuṣa that she will welcome his advances if he comes to her in a palanquin carried by the (seven?) sages. The point, of course, is to turn Nahuṣa's pride to use against him; he in fact quickly agrees to Śacī's suggestion and yokes the sages to their task.

29 Hiltebeitel (1977).

30 In the version of *MBh* 12.329, this *aśvamedha* is performed *after* Nahuṣa's fall from heaven, as a preliminary to Indra's return (verses 39-41).

31 "Whisper" is van Buitenen's translation; "Rumor" is Dumézil's, following E. W. Hopkins; "Divination" is used by the Roy-Ganguli translation. See Hiltebeitel (1977), p. 335 n. 22.

Thus the third quest seems almost redundant:[32] Bṛhaspati dispatches Agni, at first dressed as a woman, to search for Indra; eventually Agni, somewhat against his will, enters the waters[33] and discovers Indra hiding, with a tiny body, inside a lotus fiber. Bṛhaspati hastens to the hideout and calls on Indra to rise up; Indra—inflated, it would seem, by his priest's hymns of praise—resumes his old form and disingenuously asks, "What is left to be done? Are not Viśvarūpa and Vṛtra dead?" Bṛhaspati reminds him of Nahuṣa, the human king who is tormenting the gods and sages. Indra now wants to hear the whole story of Nahuṣa's rise to power, from the beginning, and Bṛhaspati patiently obliges. By this time Kubera, Yama, Soma, and Varuṇa have arrived, and Indra pleads with them to help him against Nahuṣa; they claim to be afraid of him, and Indra is forced to bribe them by the offer of their respective "shares" of kingship or the sacrifice (Kubera wins lordship over the Yakṣas and their wealth, Yama the kingship of the dead, Varuṇa that of the waters, and finally Agni is allowed to share Indra's sacrificial portion). This settled, the five guards now assure themselves that they can conquer Nahuṣa—a somewhat smug assumption which any audience that had followed Indra's adventures to this point would have reason to doubt. Indeed, the whole scene could have been lifted from a picaresque novella—the shrunken king, only recently emerged from his lotus stalk, dispensing regal gifts of sovereignty on his cowardly cohorts; the greedy deities, drunk on bargaining and dreams of glory, readying themselves for their march against the awesome human monarch who has become a living magnet for others' *tejas* and power. Fortunately for all involved, one imagines, the gods' resolve is never put to the test. For while Indra is still racking his brains for some means to kill Nahuṣa, Agastya arrives with the happy news that the danger has passed: while being carried by the sages, Nahuṣa had foolishly allowed himself to become involved in a debate,[34] in the course of which he had denied the authority of certain Vedic *mantras*; he had then committed the terrible mistake of kicking Agastya in the head. At once he had lost his *tejas* and his *śrī* and,

[32] The version of *MBh* 12.329 in fact knows only two "quests": Upaśruti leads Śacī to Indra; Śacī returns to the same hiding place *after* Nahuṣa's fall.

[33] Water is here conceived of as the womb of fire; as Bṛhaspati tells Agni, in a context replete with incestuous overtones: "Everything loves its source (womb, mother—*yoni*)."

[34] The term used is *vivadamāna* (. . . *munibhiḥ saha*). Given the sacrificial setting of the myth as a whole, one wonders if this *vivāda* is not analogous to the *brahmodya*. Nahuṣa continues in this mode of discourse in *MBh* 3.175-78 (his riddling-contest with Yudhiṣṭhira).

cursed by Agastya to become a serpent, had fallen from heaven to earth.

So the way is now clear for Indra's restoration. The various cosmic disasters, with all their consequences, have somehow passed—little thanks to Indra himself; but the god may now reassume his throne, give out handsome rewards, become reunited with Śacī, and protect his subjects again according to *dharma*.

The cycle is complete; the text can return to the epic's concerns (and Yudhiṣṭhira can be left to agonize over the implications of Indra's normative career for a merely human king). But Yudhiṣṭhira's questions are largely ours as well: what does this richly imagined tale have to say about Indian kingship? How are we to understand Indra's actions, his fall from power, his subjection to evil? We must limit our commentary to these issues, merely noting in passing the obvious continuity between the epic version and the Vedic cosmogonic myth of Indra's war against the serpent-demon Vṛtra.[35] More directly present, perhaps, are echoes of the Brahminical sacrificial ritual, which the myth's antecedents in the *Brāhmaṇa* literature make clear.[36] Indra's contamination by evil (*anṛta, pāpman*) recalls the similar state of the sacrificer, who seeks to transfer this burden to his rival contender (as Indra transfers it to various carriers); both the year-long trial of the evil-laden god and the period of hiding in diminished form in the lotus pond must be linked to the gestationlike *dīkṣā* of the sacrificial cult.[37] Indra becomes, in effect, the embryo carried in darkness, surrounded by impurity, awaiting a violent birth. Although the transposition of these themes into the mythic narrative is not quite smooth enough—the sequence of sacrificial stages is unclear, as is the role of the *aśvamedha* which fails to redeem the hidden king—the ritual background is an essential part of the myth and one to which we must return.[38] The Nahuṣa episode also alludes to important astrological and seasonal concerns, as Alf Hiltebeitel has shown:[39] in particular, we may posit a relation between the king's *dīkṣā*-like period of hiding and exile and the period of regeneration and renewal associated with the monsoon.

For our purposes, however, the central point is the comic coloring of Indra's exilic experiences. This comic tone is *not* a stylistic overlay

[35] See Kuiper (1975); Brown (1942); extended interpretation in Kramrisch (1962).

[36] *Śat. Brāh.* 1.6.3.1-17; *TS* 2.4.12.1; cf. van Buitenen (1978), pp. 159-61; Hiltebeitel (1977), pp. 331-34.

[37] See discussion by Kaelber (1978).

[38] See section 6 below.

[39] Hiltebeitel (1977), pp. 339-50.

or an accidental accretion in the epic text but rather a matter of principle. Indra's *dīkṣā*, his burden of falsehood and Brahminicide, his flight from the throne, his immortal terror—all are part of a comic persona entirely proper to this king. Although other characters in the myth are also funny (especially the other gods), it is Indra who repeatedly elicits laughter: by his cowardly, awkward actions; his transparent self-deceptions; his farcical dialogues with his *guru* Bṛhaspati and with Śacī. Not that he intends to be comical or grotesque; in fact, he seems oblivious of this effect. The exiled king is a pathetic, driven, unconscious clown. A comic figure of this sort has a tragic aura about him, reinforced in Indra's case by the oppressive onus of evil that adheres to him, and that he is continually trying to parcel out among any suitable receptacles: just as the human king in his "ordered" mode supervises the ceaseless redistribution of the kingdom's resources, the divine king in his exilic phase attempts to redistribute his own suffocating surplus of evil.[40] But the very process of accumulating this burden has a cruelly comic aspect patently evident in Indra's struggles with Viśvarūpa (alive *and* dead) and in his ironically literal interpretation (and actual betrayal) of the pact with Vṛtra. In this respect Indra recalls the antinomian "Auguste" of the circus, who delights in disorder and rebellion and takes the consequences of his tricks; but Indra is also his own White Clown, the Auguste's counterpart who is always on the side of propriety and order.[41] As the White Clown, Indra reigns in heaven, *before* his fall—but always preyed upon by his neurotic obsession with any potential rival or threat (demonic or human), always scheming to survive through deceit, disguise, or flight. Such a king parodies his own role even at his most stable and orderly. But the deeper parody emerges during his inevitable and necessary descent into the boundarylike sphere of exile—note even the geographical marginality of Indra's hiding place in the pond on a distant island—where he is transformed into a shadowy antiself, demented, terrorized, staggering under a burden of evil, and given to the ludicrous urges of the Auguste. In this phase his earlier identity is largely masked, while a surprising closeness emerges between the fallen king and his erstwhile enemies. Indeed, the myth's authors seem to revel in a deliberate blurring of identity boundaries: thus Vṛtra acquires Indra's traditional feat of propping up the heavens (the *skambha* motif);[42] whereas Indra is described as a serpent writhing in the waters—an

[40] See above, I.4 and II.4.

[41] See above IV.2 at n. 75.

[42] See n. 26.

image all too reminiscent of his ophidian foes (both Vṛtra and Nahuṣa have strong affinities with the serpent).[43] Moreover, Indra's rival/ replacement—Nahuṣa in our version—always holds up a mirror for Indra himself: the lustful, arrogant Nahuṣa may well claim to have become Indra, and his fall imitates Indra's flight at an earlier point in the cycle.

Charades of this sort are a regular feature of the king's comic withdrawal from the throne. "Disguised" as a shadowy caricature of his former self, the exiled king finds mirrored fragments of himself littered around the ominous landscape of his trials. It is no wonder that he is afraid, or that his fear persists beyond his restoration; the eery images of his lost self will haunt his memory as a living presence until they assume external form again, in his next exilic phase.

Indra's clownish characteristics are extensively developed in later, puranic versions of the Vṛtra-Viśvarūpa Brahminicides: the pusillanimous hero sinks to a new low by ambushing his unarmed enemy (Vṛtra, now transformed into a demon-yogi) and then protesting, in the outraged tones of mock innocence, when the evil of Brahminicide afflicts him: "I have killed many demons in my time, and never suffered untoward results."[44] The exiled Indra is also described as an Untouchable, an important element to which we will return. Occasionally, however, the comic concomitants of this role are blurred, as in the Tamil version of this myth by Parañcotimuṉivar, that will occupy us next.

Indra at Maturai: Tiruviḷaiyāṭaṟpurāṇam, Canto 1

The *Tiruviḷaiyāṭaṟpurāṇam* (seventeenth century?), one of the most famous of all Tamil *sthalapurāṇas*, is to a large extent a book *about* kingship and its relation to the worship of the god and goddess in their local shrine.[45] The author's conception of kingship was probably formed, at least in part, by the political atmosphere of Nāyak rule in Maturai; this context may underly the somewhat sober tone that Pa-

[43] Nahuṣa's ophidian identity is explicitly established at the conclusion of the myth, but it may well be implicit in the central motif of his poison-glance (*dṛṣṭiviṣa*). Hiltebeitel (1977), pp. 332, 334, has noted the symbolism of eyes in this myth. Nahuṣa also has a serpentlike forehead ornament (500 burning lights—*MBh* 12.329.30). His name is mentioned among those of the snakes (*MBh* 1.31.9). The name has no agreed etymology; Tuvia Gelblum once suggested to me that it could be related to the Semitic words for snake (e.g. Hebrew *naḥaš*).

[44] *Skandapurāṇa* 6.8-9. Cf. *ibid.*, 1.1.15; *Bhāgavatapurāṇa* 6.7.1-40.

[45] See Shulman (1980b), pp. 202-203, and the forthcoming work by William Harman on this text.

rañcoti applies to the exuberant classical myth.[46] The comic symbolism of Chola kingship seems to have come under a restraint in subsequent centuries, or to have been revised upward in the direction of the local god, whose pranks and amusements form the ostensible subject matter of this purāṇa. It is instructive, nonetheless, to find a variant of Indra's major myth as the first story related by this text—its introduction to the history of Pāṇṭiya kingship that it seeks to record.

The myth opens with a lush description of Indra's heavenly estate (perhaps projected out of perceptions of the Maturai royal court). The king of the gods is ensconced upon the cushions that pad his royal throne, his attention mesmerized by the dancing-girls performing before him. Indeed, he is wholly overcome by passion as he watches their dance and listens to their honeyed songs; and it is at this moment, with Indra "drowning in a sea of drunken joy" (3), that his priest and *guru*, Bṛhaspati, arrives. The timing could not be worse: Indra fails even to notice the presence of his mentor; offended, Bṛhaspati hastens away, taking with him some measure of Indra's regal splendor. Indra senses this loss at once, and realizes its cause: "I have erred in not honoring my excellent old *guru*" (5). Sorrowfully, he sets off in search of Bṛhaspati.

Note the total transformation of the background to Indra's exile: the entire Viśvarūpa-Vṛtra cycle develops here from his intoxication with his dancing-girls. In the *Udyoga* version, Indra becomes unconscious or demented (*naṣṭasañjño vicetanaḥ*) in the wake of his victory over Vṛtra; in the Tamil text, he *starts off* in this condition (as Parañcoti states baldly in verse 4: "Alas, he was lost in the maidens' mad charm; did he have any wits at all?" *tamakk' ŏru matiy uṇṭ' āmo*). As in the Ahalyā myth, Indra's problems stem from a sexual infatuation, which causes him to upset the delicate balance between king and *guru*-priest.[47] The result is disastrous: unable to find Bṛhaspati anywhere, Indra turns for help to Brahmā, who advises him to make Viśvarūpa his priest. Brahmā is, in fact, plotting against Indra, but the latter suspects nothing (*malarmakaṉ cūḻcci teṟāṉ*); he makes the demon his *purohita* and orders him to perform a sacrifice. Viśvarūpa, true to the ambivalent nature of various mythic *purohitas*,[48] calls on the gods to accept the offerings but in his heart devotes them to the demons. This split between consciousness and external action adumbrates a major element in the resolution of the myth, but at this point it costs Viś-

[46] This context requires further study and analysis. On Nāyak rule in Maturai, see Sathyanatha Aiyar (1924).

[47] See Chapter VI below, on the king's erotic ties to his dancing-girls.

[48] O'Flaherty (1976), pp. 104-27.

varūpa his life: Indra, divining what is going on, cuts off Viśvarūpa's three heads, allowing birds to fly forth from each of them; he then feeds the demon's flesh and blood to other demons (*alakai*) in apparent accomplishment of the ancient Tamil precept of the battlefield sacrifice.[49]

By now we have returned to the classic problems of the earlier versions of this myth: Viśvarūpa is dead, but Indra is seized by the sin of Brahminicide (*pirama pāvam*). He distributes the evil among the usual carriers (trees, earth, women, water). Characteristically, however, the Tamil text is not content with this first redistribution; each of the carriers is granted a way to rid itself of the unwelcome gift (evil flows out of the water as foam, out of the earth as brackishness, out of women as menses, and out of trees as sap). Each of these carriers of the god's evil thus gains the possibility of achieving purity, albeit temporary and always subject to renewal; in addition, each is rewarded for bearing the evil in the first place—women are given the ability to enjoy love-making (with their husbands!) during pregnancy; the earth will bear no scars when pits are dug in it; water will always spring up afresh when drawn; and trees will continue to grow even after being cut. As we might expect, these rewards for temporary contamination by evil are all connected, in one way or another, to notions of regeneration, fertility, and growth: the same conceptual conjunction that we have suggested with respect to the king's impure exile and subsequent restoration or rebirth.

And Indra, too, is now pure once more (though still without a priest), "like a polished gem"; but Tvaṣṭṛ seeks revenge for the death of his son. He creates Vṛtra and commands him to slay Indra. A battle ensues, "like a contest between *dharma* and evil"; and at first evil has the best of it. Vṛtra attacks Indra with an iron bar, and Indra swoons; when he regains consciousness, he recognizes his relative weakness and repairs to Brahmā's world. Brahmā takes him to Viṣṇu, who informs him that his, Indra's, *vajra* is simply too old to kill anyone; the god needs a new weapon, which he can obtain from Dadhīci—for, long ago, when the gods and demons had churned the ocean, they had deposited their weapons with this sage; and he had swallowed them after a long time, when no one came to claim them. These weapons had fused within him and become his backbone: it was this that Indra needed for his new *vajra*.

So Indra and the gods rush over to Dadhīci, who, of course, is perfectly prepared for the sacrifice demanded of him: as an enlightened sage, and the very form of mercy (*karuṇaiy* or *vaṭivam*), he cares

[49] See section 7 below.

nothing for his body. As he says to Indra: "Is it (the body) not the same as a serpent's skin or the nest of a bird? Shall I say 'I' am the body inhabited by the five (senses) which perform like dancers?" (33). There is a gentle irony in Dadhīci's rhetorical questions; Parañcoti has used this episode to underscore his original theme. Dadhīci's simile takes us back to Indra's intoxication with the heavenly dancing-girls, the opening error in this cycle; the self-sacrifice of the sage presents a clear contrast to Indra's witless, self-seeking career. And Indra remains trapped, at this stage, in the dynamics of conflict and its evils: Dadhīci effortlessly splits open his skull by the force of his mental concentration and ascends to heaven, leaving his priceless spine for the gods;[50] Viśvakarman (*kammiyappulavaṉ*) fashions the weapon, and Indra can return to the fray.

It is a long fight, fraught with the clichés of medieval Tamil war poetry. In stark contrast to the epic version, Parañcoti depicts the battle as an open, essentially fairly fought contest, although Vṛtra is described throughout as a deceitful thief (*kaḷvaṉ, paṭiṟaṉ, vañcakaṉ*—see verses 41, 45, 46, 48). Each of the main warriors is backed by his usual army, and thus we can enjoy the standard scenes of decapitated corpses dancing on the battlefield, demons grinning as they eat their way through mountains of corpses, and so on. These surrealistic vignettes are themselves endowed with a partly comic coloring, as we shall see. In the end, Vṛtra flees to the ocean to hide. Now Indra cannot find his enemy; Brahmā directs him to the sage Agastya, who dwells on Mount Pŏtiyil near the southern tip of the Indian subcontinent. Agastya cheerfully obliges the god by drinking up the waters of the sea.

The insertion of this episode, which is well known from earlier texts,[51] seems to be a unique feature of the *Tiruviḷai.* version of the Vṛtra myth. It serves several purposes: it prefigures Agastya's role in the Nahuṣa episode, as inherited from the *Udyoga* text; it ties the myth even more closely to the localized Tamil milieu (since Agastya is the Tamil sage par excellence, at home in the Tamil land; he is also the supposed narrator of the *Tiruviḷai.* in its entirety); and it allows a much-needed respite from the battle scenes, in pure *kāvya* fashion, for the poet gives us three delightful verses describing the picturesque state of the ocean devoid of water (a forest of coral is revealed, as if the mare's fire had come to light; fish and serpents writhe on the dry

[50] This is, in fact, a Vedic survival: cf. *RV* 1.84.13-15. Cf. Shulman (1980b), pp. 112-15, 230-32.

[51] *MBh* 3.102.16-23, 3.103.1-3. Agastya, identified with the star Canopus, contributes to the astral symbolism of the Nahuṣa myth discussed above: see Hiltebeitel (1977), pp. 342-43, 347.

sea bed; ships are stranded, broken; kites swoop down on their exposed prey). And here is Vṛtra—"As if evil done by the king of heaven had taken form and was performing *tapas*" (57)—meditating on a mountain that has now emerged into view.[52] These verses fill in the contours of a diptych, a study in similarity and contrast: on one side Vṛtra, a deceitful yogi (*kaitava no<u>n</u>pu no<u>r</u>kuṅ kaḷva<u>n</u>*, 58), exposed on the ocean bed by Agastya's swallowing of the waters; on the other side, the falsely heroic Indra, soon to be hiding under water (and elsewhere himself swallowed by his demonic foe). The inherited theme of suggestive masquerade is still alive. The act of slaughter confirms it: when Indra overcomes his rival, "as if testing the new *vajra*" (58), Brahminicide (*piramac cāyai*) seizes him again, this time in concrete and alarming ways. The evil has acquired a tangible, demonlike presence; it leaps at Indra, strikes his chest, rolls about, laughs, gnashes its teeth; worst of all, it will not leave him! The god, thoroughly frightened, hurries away toward the northeast, where he falls into a tank of water and hides himself in his famous lotus stalk.

We now have a short version of the Nahuṣa episode, with a few changes from the *Udyoga* account. Nahuṣa has just finished an *aśvamedha*, and the gods quickly recruit him for their king. He undergoes no transition: he is king of heaven, and he demands Śacī at once. Śacī acts the chaste Hindu wife: she indignantly asks Bṛhaspati, "Is it *dharma* for someone to take me as his wife while my life-companion (Indra) is still alive?" (62). Bṛhaspati—is he still sulking because of Indra's original insult?—offers no comfort beyond a single statement: "If he comes in a bejeweled palanquin borne by the Seven Sages, then *he* is Indra; he, indeed, will be your lover." In the *guru*'s eyes, apparently, the office is what counts; Indra has become reduced to a wholly depersonalized state, while anyone who acts like Indra may properly claim his perquisites. Śacī readily agrees to these conditions and sends for Nahuṣa, who, overcome by lust and not expecting trouble (*pu<u>n</u>kaṇ noy viḷaivum pārā<u>n</u>*, 64), urges the sages to their task with the Sanskrit imperative *sarpa* ("move!"). Agastya, straining under the front pole of the palanquin, finds this the perfect opportunity for a pun: "Become a serpent (*carppam āku*, 65)," he curses Nahuṣa, who at once assumes this form and departs.[53] Parañcoti comments in the homilist's disap-

[52] The *Hālāsyamāhātmya*, a probable source for Parañcoti's version, adds a few details: Vṛtra is seated in *padmāsana*, immovable as a rock (*pāṣāṇa iva niścalaḥ*), his senses controlled, his mind concentrated on the Absolute (*parabrahman*): 4.91-92.

[53] This popular explanation of Nahuṣa's serpent-transformation is also known to *Skandapurāṇa* 1.1.15.83-86, a version very close to that of the *Tiruviḷai.*; and cf. *Bhāgavatapurāṇa* 6.7.1-40.

proving tones: "An ignoramus has no greater enemy than good fortune" (65).

It is time for Indra to return: Bṛhaspati himself, urged on by the gods, calls on Indra to emerge from his hiding place (as in the epic version); but, in contrast to the epic's account, Indra is still stained with Brahminicide when he comes out of the lotus stalk. Bṛhaspati suggests a solution, as only he can, for only a *guru* can redeem a fault (*kuṟṟam*) done to a *guru* (68). Indra must go on a hunting expedition on earth; his evil will depart only there. Thus the king of heaven sets off on a hunt—a traditional royal recreation[54]—which takes him to innumerable terrestrial shrines and, at last, to the Kadamba forest that will become the shrine of Maturai. There, his disgrace detaches itself from him (*tŏṭutta paḻi veṟ āki viṭuttu*, 71). Indra worships the *liṅga* he finds there, bathes in the tank—which he names the Golden Lotus Tank—clears the forest, levels the ground, and covers the god with his royal parasol to protect him from the burning sun. A radiant *vimāna* descends from heaven to become the nucleus of the new temple. Indra arranges the major elements of worship and sings to the god: may he, Indra, be one of Śiva's devotees. Śiva appears and promises that Indra will worship him each Cittirai and attain the result of a full year's worship; but he must return to heaven to enjoy pure (*cutta*) pleasures while his *karma* wears away; Śiva will grant him *mokṣa (vīṭu)*, so that he will forget his desire to be born in the still higher stations of Brahmā and Viṣṇu.

Parañcoti concludes his chapter with a picture of Indra, purified and restored to his home: the heavenly maidens wave chowries, the gods adorn his feet with their heads; Indra's body sinks into a flood of sexual passion as he bathes in Indrāṇī's full breasts; but his heart (*uḷḷam*) is submerged in the flooding mercy of Cuntaranāyakaṉ (Śiva). Thus "the lord of heaven followed the ancient way (*tŏṉ muṟai*, 97)."

This ending raises an important question. Has any real, lasting transformation been achieved, for once, in the divine protagonist? The Indra of verse 97 seems a somewhat different figure from the drunken monarch of the opening verses. Of course, he is still immersed in an intoxicating, intense eroticism—this is no doubt very much a part of the "ancient way" he follows—but the text suggests a crucial split between mind and body; the "new" Indra acts like the old one, but

[54] This royal hunt forms a central motif of the version by Pĕrumparṟappuliyūr Nampi (*Tiruvālavāyuṭaiyār tiruviḷaiyāṭaṟpurāṇam* 1.1-36). Here Indra slays only Vṛtra and divides the sin into four parts; eventually he goes hunting, since the dancing of his heavenly maidens fails to take his mind off his burden of evil (a reversal of Parañcoti's account, where he is overly excited by the dancers). This version knows nothing of the episodes involving Bṛhaspati, Viśvarūpa, Agastya, and Nahuṣa.

his consciousness is given over to devotion. This is precisely the kind of transformation that some *bhakti* movements sought to achieve in their historical contexts in South India.[55] But it also resonates with earlier moments in the myth: Viśvarūpa's false intent as he acts out the sacrifice, and Dadhīci's straightforward preference for "mind" (or soul) over body. Indra ends up somewhere between these two; if Viśvarūpa has a flawed consciousness coupled with theoretically correct actions, whereas Dadhīci transposes himself into consciousness alone and dispenses with bodily deeds, Indra attempts to hold on to the awareness of Śiva's truths while maintaining his grip on life, with all its pleasures. The suggestive closeness to Viśvarūpa's inner division goes only this far. In a sense, the split career described in the epic text—White Clown to Auguste, parodic ruler to self-mocking exile—has been replaced by the splitting of mind and physical action within the king's new mode of being; but now the "mad" side of the king will be expressed through his ecstatic, devotional consciousness, while the "orderly" aspect of the reinstated ruler—the White Clown secure upon his throne—has been demoted to a necessary but clearly inferior state (its declared object being merely the erosion of Indra's *karma*). One can see here the tendency of Tamil myths to break out of the conventional mythic cycles that they inherited and to seek solutions, on a different level, for some of the problems posed by the stories. At the same time, Indra remains something of a clown; although he never achieves the level of a royal "fool of god" such as Ceramāṉ Pĕrumāḷ,[56] he has moved in that direction; and even here he is still subject to parody, for his new-found *bhakti* is held up to scrutiny in later chapters of this purāṇa, where Indra continues to serve as an easy target for various human heroes (the Pāṇṭiya kings).[57]

And yet, as already stated, this Tamil version of the myth has done much to diminish its overtly comic tones. Paradoxically, the *Tiruviḷaiyāṭaṟpurāṇam*, this most playful of texts, seems to start off on a relatively serious note. But this statement needs clarification. Indra is, it is true, somewhat rehabilitated in this retelling; he has become more heroic, in the conventional sense, whereas his opponents have been

[55] Shulman (1978).

[56] Below, section 5.

[57] Thus Ukkirapāṇṭiyaṉ insolently seats himself on Indra's throne and knocks off Indra's crown (*Tiruviḷai.* 14). The painting of this scene reproduced in the Maturai edition of the *Tiruviḷai.*, opposite p. 266, shows Indra as a much-diminished monarch, as opposed to an elegant and casually vigorous Ukkirapāṇṭiyaṉ; without his crown, Indra appears as a rather plump, awkward, and aging official, hardly a heroic figure. (The painting is taken from the complete *Tiruviḷai.* series on the temple wall.)

portrayed as deceitful and explicitly evil—so that his killing them has a clear rationale, whatever the personal consequences to the divine king. The basic ambiguity of the epic version has been reduced. Yet the latent comedy bubbles up of its own accord—in the initial depiction of the royal figure literally demented by lust; in the persistent elements of masquerade and diffusion of identity; in the comic overtones of the battle scene (to be discussed below); in the playful narration of the Nahuṣa episode; and in the mild sarcasm of the conclusion, given the future fallings-off from grace of the apparently enlightened (and yet still essentially inebriated) divine king. Parañcoti has failed to contain the irrepressible force of this story's images of kingship; for our purposes, Indra is still quite enough of a fool. But there is still another consideration, one basic to our understanding both of this text and of the wider issues it evokes. The seemingly "serious" tone can be misleading, for, as we have seen in connection with the court jester's commentaries upon life and language,[58] there are at least two kinds of seriousness, one connected to notions of order and decorum, the other linked to a comic transcendence of order. The second type of seriousness often finds its metaphors in play, laughter, and various types of comic roles; it strains toward spontaneity and freedom; being reflexive by nature, it illuminates the gap between reality and all attempts to order or to limit it, between roles of any kind (social, mythic, dramatic) and the emotional realities of the individual actors who embody them. And this brand of comic seriousness, so like the jester's iconoclastic wisdom, is connected to this text's own definition of this story as a *tiruviḷaiyāṭal*, a divine amusement or game (Sanskrit *līlā*). The ultimate perspective here is that of the supreme god, who watches the antics of the mythic characters from the safety of absolute distance, and who nevertheless intervenes—irrationally, for the sheer joy of it, or for the hell of it, as a game—to translate Indra's sufferings into a less painful idiom. Seem from Śiva's vantage point, the ups and downs, or ins and outs, of the king of heaven are no less amusing than Śiva's own adventurous transformations and masquerades.

3. Triśaṅku: Upside Down and Autistic

Indra's divine difficulties find many parallels in tales told about human kings. One of the most powerful of this type is the story of Triśaṅku, which first appears in the Sanskrit *Rāmāyaṇa*. We will be concerned

[58] Above, IV.4 at n. 113.

here with Kampaṉ's concise Tamil version of this story; but we must begin with the narrative outline as given by Vālmīki.

Triśaṅku's trials are only one episode in the longer set dealing with the king Viśvāmitra's thorny road to Brahminhood; like other parts of this cycle, this episode shows Viśvāmitra in a rather poor light as he vainly struggles against his native, royal instincts. The impetus to Viśvāmitra's quest is his humiliation by the Brahmin Vasiṣṭha; convinced of the superior power of the Brahmin, Viśvāmitra takes up ascetic practices with the clear ulterior motive of becoming stronger than his rival. He remains arrogant, egotistical, and subject to violent rages—a prime example of the type Richard Brubaker has aptly named the "pathetic ascetic"[59]—until the moment of his final transformation.

Triśaṅku, the king of Ayodhyā, arrives at Viśvāmitra's forest *āśrama* after suffering a violent change himself. He wishes to perform a sacrifice that will allow him to enter heaven with his human body; but his *purohita*, Vasiṣṭha, has refused to officiate at such a ceremony. Triśaṅku, somewhat ashamed at this rejection, has then tried to enlist Vasiṣṭha's sons in the enterprise; they also have refused and, angered at his stubborn arrogance, have called him a fool (*bāliśa*) and cursed him to become an Untouchable Caṇḍāla. It is in this state—his skin darkened, wearing dark garments, his hair in disarray, covered with garlands from the cremation ground and iron ornaments, and abandoned by all his former subjects—that he meets Viśvāmitra. Triśaṅku pours out his heart to the royal sage (*rajarṣi*—the level that Viśvāmitra has so far attained by his austerities): he, Triśaṅku, has always been a good king, has never uttered a lie (*anṛta*) even under pressure, has safeguarded his subjects, sacrificed and satisfied his *gurus*; but he has not achieved the desired fruit of his sacrifices. He concludes that cruel fate (*daiva*) is supreme, human effort meaningless; perhaps only Viśvāmitra could overcome fate and help him.

And this is precisely what Viśvāmitra rushes to do. Although he is filled with pity for the king, he is also clearly pleased at the opportunity to prove his newly attained ascetic powers—and to overshadow his rival, Vasiṣṭha. He promises that he, Viśvāmitra, will perform the sacrifice by which Triśaṅku will reach heaven with his present, Untouchable body. Viśvāmitra's disciples are sent to invite all the sages to this ceremony, and many respond to the invitation; only one called Mahodaya and the sons of Vasiṣṭha refuse. The latter send a scornful message: how can the gods and sages partake of offerings from a sacrifice commissioned by a Caṇḍāla, and at which a Kṣatriya is the

[59] Brubaker (1977), p. 61.

officiating priest?! Viśvāmitra is, predictably, infuriated by this reply and curses Vasiṣṭha's sons to be burnt to ashes and, after seven hundred reincarnations, to become Untouchable Muṣṭikas, eaters of dog's flesh; Mahodaya is cursed to become a cruel Niṣāda hunter. So much for those who bring up questions of purity and propriety when this power-hungry "sage" is about to conduct a spectacular rite!

Viśvāmitra embarks upon the sacrifice, with the sages assisting him in priestly roles; they are afraid to cross him, lest he curse them, too, in anger. Everything proceeds according to the rules, but the sons of Vasiṣṭha are proved right: no gods come down to partake of the offerings. Now Viśvāmitra is even angrier: raising the sacrificial ladle, he cries, "Behold the power of my *tapas*!" Triśaṅku ascends into the sky, while all the sages gaze in wonder. But Indra sees the approach of this human missile and is ready for him: "Go back, Triśaṅku, you do not deserve to dwell here; you fool, cursed by your *guru*—fall head downwards to earth." Triśaṅku falls, screaming for help. Viśvāmitra, in a paroxysm of anger, calls out, "Stay!" Thus Triśaṅku is caught, upside down, in the sky, while Viśvāmitra—realizing that he cannot win for his *protégé* entrance into the real heaven of Indra but still intent on fulfilling his promise—creates for Triśaṅku a complete, topsy-turvy world in the southern skies, with its own seven sages and groups of stars. As he is about to create another Indra and a complete set of deities, the gods, demons, and sages intervene and beg Viśvāmitra to desist; he agrees, on the condition that the world he has created in anger will endure as long as the other worlds. Thus Triśaṅku still hangs upside down in heaven;[60] he has, in a sense, achieved his aim. Viśvāmitra can move on to his next trial, and the sages can go home (*Rāmāyaṇa* 1.57-60).

Before we examine Kampaṉ's retelling of this story, let us note the similarity between Triśaṅku and the exiled Indra. As in some versions of the Vṛtra myth,[61] the king turned away from his throne has become an Untouchable;[62] but unlike Indra, who ultimately regains his higher status, Triśaṅku is left to languish in the limbo of Viśvāmitra's angry

[60] Triśaṅku is a constellation in the southern skies—perhaps Orion, as H. H. Wilson suggested long ago (p. 297 n. 8). There are important parallels between the Triśaṅku story and other myths (Greek and Semitic) about Orion: for example, the *Midrash Shemḥazai Va'azael* (Jellinek, 4:127-28), depicts Shemḥazai hanging, like Triśaṅku, head downwards between earth and heaven.

[61] See n. 44 above.

[62] The theme of the king-turned-Untouchable is also explored and expanded by the *Yogavāsiṣṭha*: see the discussion by O'Flaherty (1984).

creation.[63] The Triśaṅku story thus offers a different—but in certain ways no less paradigmatic—pattern of kingly fortune. For what Triśaṅku seeks is, in a way, no more than *any* king's desire: the object of the sacrifice, for the sacrificial patron, includes an ascent to heaven (and, in the normal course of events, a subsequent return to earth). But in order to follow this path, the *yajamāna* must normally divest himself of his body, which he leaves in the care of the Brahmin officiants pending his safe return from the skies.[64] Triśaṅku wishes to bypass this rather risky stage in the ceremony; by implication, he also seeks to avoid the total reliance on the priest's good faith that the classical sacrifice requires. When Vasiṣṭha indignantly refuses to cooperate, and Triśaṅku persists nonetheless, the stage is set for a striking demonstration of the fate in store for a king who disregards his *purohita*'s advice.

But this is more than a simple cautionary tale: just as there is something of Paraśurāma in every Brahmin, so there is something of Triśaṅku in every king. It is in the nature of the monarch to seek to realize his independence, to conquer heaven, with or without the help of his priests; he might even be said to err by abandoning this goal. Thus Triśaṅku becomes a hero of sorts; a late Upaniṣad begins with a *śānti-mantra* described as "Triśaṅku's Vedic utterance": "I am the destroyer of the tree (of *saṃsāra*); my fame (*kīrti*) is as the mountain's peak; I am *amṛta*, pure as the sun; I am splendid wealth, wise, immortal, indestructible."[65] Triśaṅku is here the Vedāntic hero who has fought his way to *mokṣa*—or, perhaps, the sacrificer who chooses the path of no return, the final conquest of heaven.[66] This is one side of his coin: the king who exemplifies the yearning for transcendence, and who shows the way to its attainment; such a king, as we have seen, can present an unusually cogent claim to legitimacy.[67] The other side of the coin is the insupportable result of just such a royal quest, with its implications of a single, unilateral direction of movement: Triśaṅku becomes permanently trapped in his exile, unable to break out of the perilous state of *nivṛtti*; the king remains an Untouchable, frozen in place somewhere between heaven and earth, upside down, a lonely,

[63] Folk versions sometimes poke fun at this *viśvāmitrasṛṣṭi*: the sage does not quite manage to create properly, and his creatures are thus malformed or askew.

[64] See Malamoud (1976). Brian Smith (1979) discusses two main types of sacrifice—that mentioned above, and a one-way sacrifice in which the sacrificer ascends to heaven and fails to return. Both types are represented in the *Brāhmaṇa* literature.

[65] *Brahmānubhava Upaniṣad, śāntimantra*, in Swami Sivananda (1973), p. 173.

[66] See n. 64 above.

[67] Above, II.3.

pathetic creature inhabiting his own uselessly self-contained world. He experiences perhaps the worst of all possible fates in a transformational world—the fate of becoming stuck in an isolated, nontransitional form.

Let us now see how Kampaṉ has developed the story. Kampaṉ devotes only eleven verses to Triśaṅku; he tells the tale in utter simplicity, letting the events speak for themselves. There can be little doubt, however, that he saw the story as comic. The characters themselves are frequently described as laughing, although their laughter carries with it the bitter flavor of derision, even of self-mockery, as we can see in the verse that introduces the episode. Viśvāmitra is engaged in *tapas* with the aim of acquiring Brahminical splendor; as usual, the existence of such a single-minded ascetic alarms Indra, who sends his dancing-girl Tilottamā to seduce him.[68] And Tilottamā succeeds admirably:

> As soon as the king beheld her body, he was pierced by the arrows of Aṉaṅkaveḷ (Kāma); he lost his good sense, sank into the sea of desire. But after passing some indescribable days with her, he recalled the good truths of the books known to the wise. "This is poison," he laughed in rage. (1.660)

Viśvāmitra is disgusted with himself, and angry at both Indra and the celestial courtesan; his eyes red, his heart black, he curses Tilottamā to become a mortal woman. As so often, the sage projects his own failing onto the victim of his curse; the *apsaras* seems headed for an earthly career as an insatiable human temptress—the kind of woman that Viśvāmitra, like many of the sages in these stories, usually finds irresistible. For now, however, Viśvāmitra heads south to begin his austerities anew. Here he encounters Triśaṅku:

> While the king (Viśvāmitra) was performing *tapas* in the southern quarter, the powerful King Triśaṅku of Ayodhyā approached his family *guru* and said: "Help me reach heaven with my body *today*." Said Vasiṣṭha: "I know not how." (662)
>
> "Sir, if you are unable, I will search the long earth for someone else, someone after my own heart; then I will perform the sacrifice." So spoke (the king), but the priest replied: "Fierce lord of great anger, you have wronged your ancient preceptor (*tecikaṉ*). So you seek someone better for you—become an Outcaste!" (663) At this curse spoken in wrath by Brahmā's son (Vasiṣṭha), that

[68] Kampaṉ places this seduction *before* the Triśaṅku story; in Vālmīki, Menakā seduces Viśvāmitra only after the Triśaṅku and Śunaḥśepa episodes (1.63).

king of kings lost the splendor that he had shared with the sun. His face—that lotus which blossoms at dawn—lost all luster. He took on a form ridiculed by all. (664) Necklaces, crown, adornments—all turned to iron ("black gold"). His garments, triple thread, garlands looked now like animals' skins. His body, black, stained with dirt, lost all loveliness. Thus he entered his town—and all mocked him, calling, "Cī, Cī!" Shocked, he took to the forest. (665)

After spending a few days in the midst of the forest, he approached the grove where King Kauśika (Viśvāmitra) was performing *tapas*. When he drew near, the ascetic said, "Who are you, Outcaste? Why have you come here to me?" The king bowed and related all that had happened. (666)

"Is that so?" he said, and laughed: "*I* will hold a sacrifice and project you, with your body, into heaven!" He called other ascetics together, but when the sons of Vasiṣṭha arrived they said, "We have never heard of a king holding a sacrifice for an Outcaste (*pulaiyaṉ*); (667) we could never agree to *that*." Enraged, Viśvāmitra cried: "Depart as hunters (*kirātar*) of base action." No sooner had he said this than they became hunters (*ĕyiṉar*), wandering through the forests.

Viśvāmitra then completed his sacrifice and called the gods down (for their portions). (668) But they laughed in scorn: "A king completes a sacrifice for an Outcaste and then calls us to come in haste. How very fine!" Said (Viśvāmitra) to the king with elephants of fine trappings: "*I* promised you, by virtue of my *tapas*. Go to heaven!" And indeed he rose up, with his *vimāna*, into the skies. (669) As he approached heaven, the immortals were angered: "What is this, an Outcaste coming *here*? Go back down to earth." Having no support, he fell, crying, "Help, O sage!" Viśvāmitra raised his arms, laughed like thunder, and called: "Stop, you, stop." (670)

"The gods do not respect me; they have scorned me. I will create their world anew, and the entire heavens." Thus he thought, and began to plan a sun, planets, *nakṣatras*, moon, all with their steady light, along an axis south to north—and all that moves and is still besides. (671) The king with the fragrant (*kalpa*-) tree (Indra), the four-faced god (Brahmā), black-necked Rudra, and all the other gods came to him together and said: "Please be patient, O sage; it is right to protect one who has sought refuge with you. Let him become a constellation, (672) while *you*

> become a *rajarṣi*; five *nakṣatras* will move south to illuminate your skill." Thus said the gods, as they departed. . . . (673)

There are superficial differences between this version and Vālmīki's: Viśvāmitra has already been seduced by the *apsaras*, and is thus all the more ready to show off his renewed ascetic powers; Vasiṣṭha himself curses Triśaṅku without the help of his sons; the latter actually arrive at Viśvāmitra's sacrificial ground; we are not explicitly told that Triśaṅku falls from heaven upside down. More significant is the alteration in tone: Vālmīki's four chapters have been compressed into a few comic verses; Kampaṉ carefully exploits the image of the Untouchable king bounced helplessly between heaven and earth. The result is a delightful intermezzo, of increasing dramatic intensity, a duet played for us by the two comic kings. Viśvāmitra builds his own ruin on Triśaṅku's mistaken goal; Triśaṅku foolishly entrusts himself to the self-serving care of the megalomaniac king-turned-sage. The context of the tale—Viśvāmitra's disaster-laden project of self-transformation—imparts satirical force to Triśaṅku's career, so that we have, in effect, two royal clowns egging each other on by their respective folly. Viśvāmitra, obsessed with Brahminhood, is driven toward typical royal errors (lust, egoism, rage) by his inner nature: he succumbs at once to Tilottamā; becomes trapped in the hopeless project of forcing Triśaṅku's entry into heaven; and, in the next episode, foolishly curses his four surviving sons to become Outcastes when they refuse to obey his command (to take Śunaḥśepa's place as sacrificial victim). Triśaṅku lives out his kingly fate, suspended between the worlds, caught forever in a celestial no man's land. He pays the price of looking for help to a compulsive, ego-ridden king pathetically trying to put *tapas* to tangible use. Which of the two kings is more of a buffoon—or more tragic?

4. Mucukunda: The Mad Chola King

Triśaṅku is only one of a series of human kings who rise to heaven and then fall back to earth; and he is not the only one who ends up suspended in midair. His son, Hariścandra, suffers a remarkably similar fate. We have seen how Nahuṣa, the mortal king who replaces Indra during the latter's exile from his throne, undergoes a dramatic fall from heaven (because of his lust for Śacī and his disrespect for the Seven Sages, especially Agastya);[69] in this, Nahuṣa is essentially im-

[69] See section 2 above.

itating the flawed prototype whose title he has usurped, for Indra, too, must fall to earth. But it is perhaps Nahuṣa's son, Yayāti, who is the most famous exemplar of the "falling king" motif.[70] So pervasive is this motif that its symbolic importance can hardly be doubted; we shall look at one last example, from another South Indian statement about kingship.

The Tamil tradition gives considerable prominence to a king called Mucukunda, who is known to the *Mahābhārata*[71] and to several Sanskrit purāṇas[72] (where he appears as a Rip Van Winkle figure associated with Kṛṣṇa), but who figures in Tamil sources as a legendary Chola ruler.[73] Mucukunda is said to have brought down from heaven the famous image of Tyāgarāja-Śiva at Tiruvārūr; the same story informs us that Indra, because he gave away this image, had to take the form of an Untouchable to worship at the Tiruvārūr shrine—another striking example of the theme of the Untouchable king.[74] The Tamil purāṇas also connect Mucukunda to another myth about Indra's "fall":

> A Brahmin of Kaliṅga had a daughter named Sukumārī, who on reaching the age of twelve expressed the wish to overcome rebirth by worshiping Śiva. Her father gave her *dīkṣā*; she would rise early in the morning and spend each day in worship. One day a Gandharva saw her when she went to pick flowers after her bath; he followed her, full of desire, and she cursed him to become a monkey. He turned into a langur (*mucu*) wandering in the woods.
>
> One day the langur was jumping about on a *bilva* tree beneath which Śiva was playing with Pārvatī; his jumping caused leaves and blossoms to cover the body of the god. Pārvatī was angered and cursed him to retain his langur's face even after his curse was expiated; but Śiva blessed him for showering him with *bilva* leaves. He told him he would be reborn as a universal monarch; thus the langur became Mucukunda, the monkey-faced son of the Chola king.
>
> The demon Akitavuṭṭiraṉ conquered Indra, who went into hiding on the slopes of the Himālaya. There he saw the daughter

[70] *MBh* 1.70-88; *Padmapurāna* 2.64-83, discussed by O'Flaherty (1976), pp. 237-43; Defourny (1978).

[71] *MBh* 12.75.3-20.

[72] *Viṣṇupurāṇa* 5.23-24; *Harivaṃśa* 2.58.43-67.

[73] Aṭiyārkkunallār on *Cil.* 6.14-17; *Kaliṅkattupparaṇi* 189; Kampaṉ, *Irāmāvatāram* 1.717.

[74] *Kantapurāṇam* 6.23.49-123; *Tiruvārūrppurāṇam* 8.12-236. Cf. Shulman (1978a).

of Bhṛgu and tried to take her by force. Bhṛgu cursed him to become a Rākṣasa because of this Rākṣasa-like action.

Now the gods were driven from heaven, and they sought Mucukunda's help. He killed the demon and, at the request of the gods, ruled the three worlds, which he protected from the Rākṣasas. One day one of the celestial dancing-girls, performing in court, pointed out Mucukunda's face—and all the girls broke into laughter. Mucukunda was deeply ashamed. He left the heavenly kingdom and returned to earth to worship his family deity, the sun. Sūrya told him that only Śiva could change his face to that of a man. The king wandered from shrine to shrine until he reached Tirimūrttimalai, where he threatened to commit suicide unless Śiva appeared to him. The god sent him to bathe in the Kāñci River at Tirupperūr; there he received a human face. Mucukunda still had no desire to return to his kingdom; not even his ministers and his family could persuade him to do so. Instead, he wandered like a madman among the shrines of Śiva.

The gods were now without a king, so Nārada went looking for the Rākṣasa-Indra. When Indra caught sight of him, he was delighted and ran forward to seize and devour him; Nārada hastily sprinkled him with water and recited a Śiva-*mantra*. At this, the Rākṣasa hastily withdrew his paw. Nārada led him to the Toṇi River at Tirimūrttimalai; the Rākṣasa balked at entering the water, so Nārada took hold of him and shoved him in. Indra emerged in his old form but in a state of total amnesia. Nārada patiently explained the events of recent history to him, and Indra returned to rule heaven as Mucukunda's friend.[75]

As in the Nahuṣa myth, we find again the hidden Indra, sadly transformed, and his mortal replacement, who must ultimately return to earth. The two figures are both contrasted and implicitly compared; indeed, this text goes far beyond any discussed so far in working out the affinities between Indra and the human king called to his throne. Although their development diverges in the course of the story, the figures share certain basic features—for example, the tendency toward rape, which in both cases leads to a transforming curse. Indra, as so often, is victimized by his rampant lust; the result is a demonic transformation that exaggerates this very fault. Mucukunda, however, goes from rape to reform; his experiences as a langur and as king are merely stages in his progression from Gandharva to saint. He thus falls from

[75] *Tirimūrttimalaipurāṇavacaṉam* 12-13 (pp. 91-108); cf. *Perūrppurāṇam* 13-14. See also discussion of this myth in O'Flaherty (1976), pp. 152-53.

his celestial throne not because of an infatuation with the dancing-girls—such as we might expect from Indra—but because of his embarrassment and shame at their ridicule; lust may lurk in his nature, a residue from his Gandharva days, but he seems also to have acquired a certain distaste for erotic pleasures, a potential for renunciation. Even in his fully simian period, he shows a tendency for unconscious devotion to Śiva; this streak becomes dominant during his pilgrimage to the shrines and eventually precludes any possible return to heaven. Mucukunda becomes a mad *bhakta* wandering from shrine to shrine. In this respect, he contrasts sharply with the Rākṣasa-Indra, who seems quite indifferent to *bhakti* in any form, and who actively resists his redemptive bath in the sacred river at the shrine. Underlying this contrast, however, there is still another connection: the madness of devotion in Mucukunda's case replaces the madness that affects Indra in the Vṛtra cycle; moreover, this seemingly more acceptable form of insanity remains as a permanent attribute of the exiled king. Mucukunda never recovers from his intoxication with the god. Indra, on the other hand, is eventually saved from himself (and thus the gods, too, are delivered from the menace of Rākṣasas—such as their erstwhile king); he can now return to his throne, to await his next fall. As far as Indra is concerned, only one thing has changed: he now rules as Mucukunda's friend; the final superiority of the human king and devotee over his celestial counterpart has been established.

Despite the differences in their development, which are crucial to the moral perspective of the myth, the two kings remain strikingly alike, to the point of mirroring one another at given moments in their cycles; in this, they may recall Solomon and the demon Ashmedai (Ṣakhr in Muslim traditions), who assumes Solomon's likeness in order to exile him from his throne.[76] We might mention again that Indra has his own monkey-avatar;[77] and the Mucukunda myth suggests yet another ancient theme, that of Indra's ambiguous rivalry with the monkey Vṛṣākapi.[78] Both the Vṛṣākapi hymn of the Veda and the Tamil Mucukunda story build upon the comic associations of the monkey.[79] These associations may have attached themselves to Mucukunda, who is never said to have a monkey's face in early Sanskrit sources, through a Tamil folk etymology (*mucu* = langur); but

[76] See Shulman (1984a).

[77] See n. 16 above.

[78] *RV* 10.86. See commentary by O'Flaherty (1981), pp. 257-64.

[79] The clown in the north Karnataka puppet theater is known as Hanumannāyaka (not specifically identified with Hanuman of the *Rām.*, who, as suggested earlier, might be seen as Rāma's Vidūṣaka).

the result is to emphasize the latent comic aspect of kingship. Both royal figures in this myth are, in any case, grotesque and ridiculous. Indra as a demonic Rākṣasa is more amusing than frightening; he is clumsy, coarse, and ignorant; indeed, he remains confused even after his bath in the Toṇi River, until Nārada can bring him up to date on current events. The monkey-faced king of heaven is a hilarious spectacle for his own dancing-girls. For both divine and human kings, comedy is an integral aspect of their royal career.

Let us restate some of the themes that have emerged from the stories cited in this chapter. These stories suggest that the royal role involves a process of radical transformation and restoration, a process that brings the king into contact with various areas of darkness—Untouchability, a generalized impurity and/or moral evil, exile and hiding, a demonic antiself or an extreme loss of self—and that structures this contact around comic forms and themes. This process applies both to the paradigmatic kingship of the gods and to exemplary human kings: just as Indra acts out an aspect inherent in human rulers, so the "falling kings" of heaven show us an essential part of Indra's career. This "fall" may be explained by reference to some specific fault (as is sometimes said to be the case for the tragic heroes of Western drama)—for example, Yayāti's boastful pride, or Nahuṣa's lust for Śacī. But there is clearly much more to this motif. In a sense, every king has fallen to earth from heaven, for the Hindu king establishes his tenuous legitimacy by sacrifice, that is, by ascending to heaven and returning thence to earth. This route represents a particularly trenchant claim to transcendent authority on the part of the sacrificing ruler; it is also a graphic representation of his always anomalous position, with its attendant weaknesses and dangers. The king is a lonely figure, nowhere truly at home; he is both man and more than man, a repository of divinity, separated from his fellows; his throne is a vulnerable, unsteady vehicle oscillating between heaven and earth.[80]

The "yo-yo motif" (Triśaṅku bounced back and forth between the worlds) accurately reflects this anomaly as well as its hazards: at once human and partly divine, the king is a tragi-comic hybrid given to restless movement; ultimately he may be frozen, upside down, in a world of his own. Or he may come crashing down from heaven, especially if he seeks to realize his theoretical superiority in tangible ways—by going to heaven bodily, or by marrying Śacī, or by conquering the gods, or by demanding to receive sacrificial offerings in

[80] See above, II.5 at n. 119.

his own right.[81] As in Indian poetic theory, it is the suggestion that counts, never the literal attempt at realization: the king's divinity, such as it is, *must* be left vague and implicit, just as his renunciatory side must be submerged until the end of his life. The very suggestiveness of this role points to the ontology of South Indian kingship: from his unique symbolic position between spheres, the king serves as master functionary and overseer of the magical apparatus of transformation, which brings inner worlds into external light. But unlike the self-conscious Brahmin clowns and magicians, the king cannot claim to manipulate this process; rather, he takes part in it from within and, if things go wrong, he becomes its victim. If he demands too much of his position, if he seeks to pin down the suggested or the imagined to something literally true, to undo the symbolic quality of this world of symbolic transformations, to build for himself a structure of power concentrated in tangible, external objects and in "realistic" facts, then, in the perspective of the South Indian storytellers, he is likely to find himself trapped in an all-too-real world of empty objects, inverted directions, and cruelly powerful tricks of the mind. His only real safety lies in giving himself over to the unending cycles, in relinquishing his claims to power, in accepting the temporary falls and loss of self and the essential fluidity of his role. But this fragile and fluid sense of his identity leaves the king, at least in certain recurring moments, a clown.

5. Ceramāṉ Pĕrumāḷ and Cuntaramūrtti: The Fools of God

One way to narrow the range of this oscillation and to attain both a greater stability and a more secure legitimacy for the royal role is to relegate the king entirely to his "mad" aspect. (To move in the other direction—toward stabilizing and securing the wholly "proper" or "ordered" aspect of the king—was apparently felt in South India to be inappropriate or, indeed, impossible, as the discussion in Chapter II would suggest.) In this pattern, the mad king never returns from exile, as we saw to be the case of the peripatetic *bhakta*, Mucukunda. But by the same token, such a total exile, which expresses the crazed inner state of the king, could just as easily take place at home. The king who is overwhelmed by the ecstasies and torments of devotion, his mind and spirit abandoned to the god who directly sanctions and sustains his rule, can exemplify the process of a renunciatory "fall"

[81] As does Vena: above, II.4.

from the throne while still fulfilling his royal role. Seated on his throne, in his palace, he exiles himself in his heart, and at the same time plunges into the comic circumstances of this phase of his kingship.

An outstanding example of this type is the story of the famous Śaiva devotee and Kerala king, Ceramāṉ Pĕrumāḷ, although the comic coloring of his "biography" is somewhat dulled by the severe, pedantic style of Cekkiḻār, who has recorded the tale (*PP* 2.7.2, verses 3748-3922; 2.13, 4229-81). The inherent complexities of a career as both ruler and devotee are, however, conspicuous in Cekkiḻār's account. Indeed, we learn that this king had, from the beginning, grave doubts about accepting the job. While still a prince, he had given himself over entirely to worship: he would rise at dawn, bathe in water, then submerge his body in sacred white ash; then he would work in the god's garden until it was time to bring the deity his fresh garland. He had nothing to do with the business of ruling (*aracar tŏḻil puriyār*, 3754), for he felt that there was no power (*uṟuti*) in worldly ways or in kingship (*araciyalpu*, 3755). But one day the old king retires to the forest, and the Brahmin ministers decide that our hero is next in line for the throne. At first, afraid that kingship will interfere with his devotion, he hesitates; in any case, he must first inquire of the god. Śiva reassures him: not only will he continue, after his accession, to feel the keen desire of worshiping the god—that desire which is itself the most desirable of states—but he will also attain the unusual ability to understand the utterances of all beings (hence this king's epithet, *kaḻaṟiṟṟ' aṟivār*, "he who knows speech"). In addition, he will have all the usual attributes of kingship—victorious strength, unstinting generosity, armies, vehicles, and so on. So Ceramāṉ Pĕrumāḷ is convinced; he announces to the Brahmins that, despite the inevitable loss to his single-minded devotion, the god's command is that he accept the throne. The Brahmins happily crown him king, thus "bringing the two worlds (heaven and earth) under one crown"—a hackneyed cliché which, as we shall see, turns out to be literally correct.

And at the very moment of his coronation, the royal madness begins to show itself in dramatic ways. As the new king is being carried by the royal elephant in procession around his capital of Kŏṭuṅkoḷūr (modern Cranganore), he catches sight of a washerman (*vaṇṇāṉ*) carrying sacks of salt-soap (*uvar*) on his shoulder; the washerman's body has become white by contact with the salty substance dissolved in rainwater. "This man has the form of Śiva's servants," cries the new king as he leaps from his elephant and prostrates himself, with vehement longing and desire, at the low-caste washerman's feet. The washerman, needless to say, is startled and upset. "Who does your

Honor think I am?" he stutters; "I am only a lowly washerman" (*yār ĕṉr' aṭiyeṉaik kŏṇṭat' aṭiyen aṭivaṇṇāṉ*, 3766). "And I," replies the king, "am a lowly Ceraṉ, your servant—for you have reminded me of the brilliance of sacred ash."

This vignette already expresses the essence of Ceramāṉ's extraordinary character. Extraordinary—and yet also exemplary: the South Indian king is, indeed, the humblest of all the god's servants.[82] He will demonstrate this humility in a series of ritualistic self-abasements, which are integral to his role; his glory lies in casting off his royal glory, even as whatever power he posesses springs from the vivid demonstration of his essential powerlessness. Like other clowns we have studied, he has a transformative potential rich in emotional content, but the secret of this skill is the royal clown's impotence in the "real" world of nonsymbolic acts. The effective stature of the king is achieved through the extremes of his self-abnegation and self-parody.

Thus the incident at his investiture is soon followed by an even more striking symbolic statement. A low-caste poet and singer, the *pāṇar* Pattiraṉār, arrives from Maturai with a palm-leaf letter of introduction from the god Śiva himself, asking the Cera king to enrich his devotee. The king breaks out into violent trembling at this sign of the god's mercy in thinking him, the king, worthy of his command; he grasps the palm-leaf letter, smooths it out, worships it, weeps copiously over it; then, leaping from his throne—Ceramāṉ obviously has a penchant for such sudden leaps—he orders all his storerooms emptied out. When this is accomplished, the king bestows everything he has—horses, elephants, jewels, and, in the end, *the kingdom itself*—on the astonished bard. The latter disappoints his royal benefactor by rejecting the gift of his throne; he will take only what he needs to survive (which turns out to be whatever he can load onto the royal elephant). Still weeping—is it because he must resume his weary office?—Ceramāṉ Pĕrumāḷ follows Pattiraṉār to the city limits to see him off to Maturai again (3773-85).

Note that the king's attempt to give away his kingdom—to the lowly *Pāṇar*!—is not condemned; the devotional ethic that motivates this move apparently overrides the usual considerations which, in the classical literature, prohibit such a gift.[83] Nevertheless, like Āputtiraṉ, the frustrated renouncer-ruler is sent back to work; but unlike the Buddhist king, Ceramāṉ Pĕrumāḷ devises new ways to subvert his royal duties. If he cannot, at first, abandon the kingdom entirely, he can at least spend his time in the restless pleasures of pilgrimage. This

82 See Appadurai (1981), pp. 50-51.

83 See above, III.3 at n. 51.

part of the story is connected to the major focus of Ceramāṉ's hagiography, that is, his intimate tie to the poet-saint Cuntaramūrttināyaṉār (Cuntarar). These two devotees form a pair: yet another symbolic union of king and Brahmin (for Cuntarar is an Ādiśaiva, from the caste of Brahmin temple servants, although he was brought up as a prince). In this case, however, the "marriage" of Brahmin and king takes on a new character, for both figures are endowed, simultaneously, with obvious clownlike qualities; moreover, they meet in a way that, appropriately, involves the clownish god they both worship, so that the three form, for a moment, another comic triad. As always, the interrelationships of this triad reflect the rule of comic polarization discussed above.[84]

The meeting results from an instance of divine forgetfulness, a momentary lapse that is not, in fact, uncharacteristic of Śiva, who is quite capable of surrendering to passing passionate urges. Ceramāṉ Pĕrumāḷ was used to hearing, at the end of his daily *pūjā*, the jingling sound of Śiva's anklet as the god danced in the temple at distant Cidambaram. But one morning this divine reward is denied him:

> One day he performed the service of his worship
> to the god in whose matted hair
> the celestial Ganges is hidden,
> but he did not hear the anklet's chiming
> during the dance of the bearer of *kŏṉṟai*, soaked in honey,
> at the end of his weighty service—
> and his mind was disturbed. (3788)

> Hastily, he concluded his worship
> and, sobbing, he said:
> "How has your servant erred?
> What happiness will I ever know again
> in this body given to desire?"
> Then he unsheathed his flashing sword
> and set its point against his breast.
> Swiftly the lord rang out his anklet's chiming,
> loud and clear. (3789)

> Upon hearing the anklet's sound,
> he removed the sword and,
> cupping his flowerlike hands above his head,
> fell to the ground, worshiped, rose,
> and spoke long words of praise:
> "O you who were hard to seek

[84] IV.2 (Excursus).

for Viṣṇu, Brahmā, and the rare Veda—
why did your mercy fail just now?" (3790)

So he said, and the god, without appearing before him,
answered in a hidden voice:
"The Harsh Devotee came and worshiped
our dance in the temple hall
and praised us, with feeling focused upon union,
by singing songs rich in meaning.
We stood and listened—
that is why we were late." (3791)

The god, entranced by the poetry of Cuntarar, his "harsh devotee" (*vaṉ ṟŏṇṭaṉ*), has forgotten himself again—with nearly fatal consequences for his other, despairing devotee far away on the west coast of South India. Śiva's sheepish explanation inspires the king to seek out the wondrous singer who could cause such a delay in the deity's normal schedule. Ceramāṉ leaves his capital and proceeds, via the Kāverī and Cidambaram, to Tiruvārūr, the poet's town. There Cuntarar, returning from another of his innumerable pilgrimages, finds him waiting:

He bowed to the king
who was bowing before him;
they rose, and each
embraced the other,
with love and with desire;

like swimmers
plunged in the midst of an ocean of joy
and unable to climb out,
their very bones dissolved,
their spirits became one
just as their bodies were
as one. (3812)

From this moment, the two become inseparable companions whose innermost feelings have fused (*kalantav uṇarvāl*, 3814) in their shared passion for the god. They eat together (in deliberate contravention of the rules of commensality—3819-22); they spend weeks together on the road, in pilgrimage to the shrines of Śiva. To the world they perhaps appear as two crazed devotees in love with a crazy god. The bond with Cuntarar has released any lingering royal inhibitions in Ceramāṉ; like Mucukunda, he now lets madness engulf him as he sings and worships his way through South India. The darker aspects of the king's exile, which we saw in the myths of Indra and Triśaṅku, are missing in this case, washed away by the transcendent truth and value of devotion:

> When are we beside ourselves? When the spirit breaks its fetters and tries to escape from its prison and aspires to liberty. That is madness, but it is also other-worldliness and the highest wisdom. True happiness is in selflessness, in the furore of lovers, whom Plato calls happiest of all. The more absolute love is, the greater and more rapturous is the frenzy. Heavenly bliss itself is the greatest insanity.[85]

Note Huizinga's choice of words: ecstasy is, literally, a standing outside, "beside ourselves"—another habitual feature of the clown, who always stands, in a sense, beside himself in the reflexive and open-ended zone of the boundary.[86] The Cera king is, as usual, reflexive only by default; lost in this normative form of madness, he cannot but show up the vacuity of any kingship that might *lack* such ecstasy. But an additional reflexive element emerges from the king's association with Cuntarar, who for his part has all the makings of a whole-hearted divine clown, a "fool for Śiva's sake."[87] Cuntarar's checkered career is riddled with comic episodes; he specializes in a kind of ironic chutzpah, an outrageous attitude rooted in his claim to intense intimacy with the god. Cuntarar is *tampirāṉ toḻaṉ*, "companion of the lord"; he presumes upon this familiarity to blackmail Śiva, to extort gold and other rewards from him, even to make him act as a weary matchmaker in the poet's romance with Caṅkiliyār (who becomes Cuntarar's second wife); later, the god is forced to trudge back and forth an entire night between the errant saint and his *first* wife, Paravaiyār, on a tedious mission of reconciliation.[88] Cuntarar's "foolishness" in these and other instances is matched by that of his god, with his fondness for pranks and practical jokes: thus Śiva takes the form of an old Brahmin to disturb Cuntarar's sleep one night by lying down repeatedly with his dusty feet on the devotee's head;[89] on another

[85] Huizinga (1952), p. 75.

[86] Above, IV.5; on the clown's "empty" selfhood, see Ulanov and Ulanov (1980), pp. 22-24.

[87] On the closely comparable type of the Byzantine "fool for Christ's sake," see Syrkin (1982).

[88] *PP* 3467-3534. (I have discussed these stories at length in the introduction to a forthcoming translation of the Cuntarar *Tevāram*.)

[89] *PP* 228-34.

occasion the god sends his ghosts, dressed as bandits, to rob Cuntarar of his possessions.[90] Often we can observe the two clowns, poet and deity, in comic interaction: thus Cuntarar wins from Śiva the gift of 12,000 gold pieces, which he throws, at the god's behest, into the Maṇimuttā River at Tirumutukuṉṟam—with the promise that he can reclaim then later, in Tiruvārūr (far to the south); but when Cuntarar enters the great Kamalālaya Tank at Tiruvārūr and asks for the gold, the god procrastinates, pretends not to hear; finally, the poet sings a verse that Śiva simply cannot ignore, and the gold appears in the water of the tank. But Cuntarar knows the habits of his playful divine "friend," and he has wisely brought along a touchstone, just in case. He tests the gold and, of course, finds it below standard; another round of joyous praises is then necessary before the god surrenders, stops playing, and brings the gold back up to scratch.[91]

The same playfulness characterizes the friendship of Cuntarar and Ceramāṉ: when they are together, they are oblivious of the world's demands; their days are devoted to the pursuit of their internal worlds of feeling and fancy, in a manner marked by both the curious detachment from the everyday world and the passionate engagement of players in a game.[92] It is not surprising that we find them occupied with spectator sports and other amusements (*vinotaṅkaḷ*, 3901)—ball games, water sports, elephant fights, wrestling matches, and, of course, gourmet feasts—during one of Cuntarar's visits to the Cera capital (the king, after all, has his royal tasks to perform at home).[93] This kind of entertainment is a royal prerogative, which Ceramāṉ is only too happy to share with his friend. But, like clowns everywhere, these two are not simply equated or locked into a single level of being; their interaction has its own dynamics, including the "tragic" element of sudden separation and loss—as when Cuntarar, overcome by homesickness and yearning for the god of Tiruvārūr, suddenly breaks off his playing and heads home, leaving his royal playmate languishing in his office (*PP* 3903-3906). A moment such as this reflects Cuntarar's tragic side; he is, in the end, the "harsh devotee" who bears within him a hidden grudge against the god he worships. This angry vein in Cuntarar's character affects the spirit of his clowning. Thus when the two devotees are seen together, it is the king who frequently seems the more extreme, more playful or "mad," so that in this case the familiar pattern of king-clown relations is reversed: normally the se-

[90] *PP* 3911-18.

[91] *PP* 3281-92.

[92] See Huizinga (1971), pp. 28-32.

[93] *PP* 3901-3902.

rious royal hero faces a comic Brahmin (the Vidūṣaka in the drama, the court jester in the folktale); or the *nāyaka*, in his romantic madness, is the "straight" White Clown to the Vidūṣaka's Auguste. On the divine level, this model may suggest the relation of the central, "royal" Viṣṇu to the Brahminical boundary figure, Śiva. But in the story of Ceramāṉ and Cuntarar, the king is clown to the Brahmin—or, perhaps, Auguste to Cuntarar's White Clown. When the deity they both worship is also present before them, the comic set becomes complete with a Bōmolochos-Buffoon.

We can see this pattern of relations in the final episode in the lives of both Cuntarar and Ceramāṉ, the episode that concludes Cekkiḻār's monumental purāṇa by bringing us back up to Śiva's heaven, where it all began. Cuntarar has come back to the Cera capital to visit his friend (on the way there he performs one of his most famous miracles—restoring life to a Brahmin boy who had been swallowed by a crocodile some years before). After some days spent in worshiping at various shrines, Cuntarar approaches the major Cera shrine of Tiruvañcaikkaḷam (at Cranganore). The long road that he has followed, separated from Śiva, is approaching its end (4256). He sings his *patikam* to the god at this shrine; the implicit theme (*uṭkuṟippu*, 4258) of the poem is a request that the bonds binding him to life on earth be cut. (Cekkiḻār seems here to be glossing the poet's statement in the eighth verse of this *patikam*: "I hate the householder's life; I have renounced it completely.")[94] And, from his place on Kailāsa, Śiva hears this prayer and understands. He orders the gods: "Go and bring our Ūraṉ (Cuntarar), whose mind is one with me, on a celestial white elephant." Brahmā, Viṣṇu, and the other gods bow and take leave; with a pure, resplendently white elephant, they come down to earth in the Cera capital, where Cuntarar sees them upon leaving the shrine. "This is the merciful command of the god whose matted hair is overflowing with water and flowers," the gods inform him; unable to do anything else, Cuntarar bows and mounts the elephant. We may note in passing that the reversal of Brahmin and royal roles continues, for it is the Brahmin poet who is given the white elephant, a conventional royal symbol, to ride. On this celestial mount, as flowers rain down from the skies, Cuntarar takes off for Kailāsa—though not without a passing thought for his erstwhile companion, the Cera king (4262).

The latter intuits what has happened, no doubt by virtue of his longstanding relation with the saint:

[94] Cuntarar *Tevāram* 39 (4.8).

As soon as the lord of the Ceras
  knew what the Lord's companion had done,
he leaped on the horse he had standing nearby
  and rode to Tiruvañcaikkaḷam.
Seeing the true devotee
  joyfully flying through the heavens
  on his valiant white elephant,
he (the king) could no longer stay on the ground:
he sent his horse galloping
  along the route already taken
  by his mind. (4263)

This is the king's final great leap, the last of a spectacular series: he mutters the Śiva-*mantra* in his horse's ear, and the horse at once climbs into the heavens, circumambulates the mysterious white elephant carrying Cuntarar, and then leads the way to Kailāsa. The impetuous Ceramāṉ has obviously had enough of separation; unable to relinquish his beloved friend, he leads the charge against heaven's ramparts in a mock-heroic end to a most unmilitary royal career. Meanwhile, back on earth, the king's soldiers follow this startling ascension with their eyes, until their lord is no longer visible; then, "with mature love," they fall upon their swords in order to escort him into heaven with their subtle bodies (4265-66).

A poet to the last, Cuntarar spends the dramatic ride through the skies composing one last *patikam*, to the lord of Kailāsa (Tirunŏṭittāṉ malai); and, as the white elephant glides over the ocean visible beneath him, the poet teaches this poem to Varuṇa, the lord of the ocean, who will bring this final composition to the Tiruvañcaikkaḷam shrine.[95]

But at Kailāsa, the Cera king is stopped at the gates, whereas Cuntarar simply rides through on his elephant. Reaching Śiva's presence, he is overcome with desire, "like a calf which has been sent on a long journey and which once again sees its mother" (4270). The god addresses him: "So, Ūraṉ, you have come—for the good of the world (*ulak' uyya*)." And the harsh devotee (*vaṉ ṟŏṇṭar*)—even at this moment, the old epithet comes first to the narrator's mind—opens himself to a flood of happiness, "as if supreme joy had acquired form and was standing there," as he answers the god: "You bore with my mistakes and possessed me for yourself; you removed my entanglement—yet how could I have merited the great mercy (*pĕrun karuṇai*) of your

[95] Traditionally, this is *patikam* 100, which closes the Cuntarar *Tevāram*. In its final verse, Cuntarar addresses the "king of the ocean" and asks him to deliver the poem to Añcaiyappar, the god at Tiruvañcaikkaḷam (*āḻi kaṭal araiyā añcaiyapparkk' aṟivippate*).

endless path?" Still, in the midst of these encomia and ecstasies, Cuntarar manages to remember his party-crashing friend left, forlorn, at the gate. "Ceralaṉ is outside," he says to the god. When Śiva orders the king brought in and sees him bowing profusely, at a considerable distance, the god cannot resist a smile: "Just tell me," he asks, "how you got here without an invitation! (*iṅku nām aḻaiyāmai nīy ĕytiyat' ĕṉ*, 4273)."

Not even Śiva, it seems, can set limits for his devotees. Ceramāṉ Pĕrumāḷ answers without embarrassment: "Your servant came praising the anklets of Ārūrar and serving that elephant with its trappings; I have been allowed to enter after being carried along by the overflowing ocean whose limpid waves are your mercies." This florid image is perfectly fitting: in many shrines on earth, Cuntarar has praised the local river for sweeping along a load of jewels, coral, aloe wood, peacock feathers, and other assorted rarities, an unconscious offering to the god; the king now transposes his friend's image in describing his own arrival as a passive gift borne by the waves of emotion set in motion by Śiva himself. Ceramāṉ has a last request—that he be permitted to sing his composition (*tiruvulāppuṟam*) in the court. Śiva listens receptively to his praises, then orders the two friends to become leaders of his hosts (4276).

Thus the circle is closed. The Brahmin poet's painful, ludic pilgrimage on earth transports him, finally, back to heaven (whence he had originally been exiled by Śiva's curse); his clowning is at an end. The clownish king has stormed into heaven with his friend, and will remain there; in the Cera capital, the worthy Brahmins will once again have to go searching for a ruler. Note that Ceramāṉ has succeeded precisely where Triśaṅku fails, in reaching heaven with his body—through a spontaneous, impudent act of devotional excess. His *bhakti* makes this possible, and atones for any flaws; Ceramāṉ is totally devoid of Triśaṅku's egoistic concerns. In the end, kingship proves to be no obstacle to this devotee, who spends much of his rule in ecstatic states, in pilgrimage and song, until the moment he disappears before everyone's eyes. Indeed, in an important sense he has not really been there all along: for as Cekkiḻār tells us—and as this king himself intimates repeatedly in *his* poems[96]—he has long ago melted into the love of god. Ever the exemplar of cultural ideals, this king lives out the fervently admired processes of softening, flowing, dissolving one's heart and mind in the liquid sensation of ultimate truth. In Ceramāṉ Pĕrumāḷ's own words:

[96] The *Pŏṉvaṇṇattantāti, Tiruvārūr mummaṇikkovai*, and *Tirukkayilaiñāṉavulā*.

I have set my mind
  to concentrate on him,
my tongue
  to speak of him,
my head
  to bow before him,
my hands
  to worship.
I have set my love
  to make me bound
and my body
  to blossom:

all this I have prescribed
for the sake of the lord
  whose ornament is burnt
white ash.[97]

Such are the royal ordinances which the *bhakta*-king prescribes (*vitittaṉave*—the final word of this verse). They apply only to his own inner life; his interest in his subjects appears to be minimal, his royal power is invested in the pursuit of powerlessness, in humility, in a kenosis of all that is merely human, regal, or mundane. In the world's eyes, he may be mad, a crazed devotee who spends his mornings waiting anxiously for the sound of the god's distant anklet; yet madness of this sort is highly regarded in this culture, for it mimics the alluring madness of the god. And in this extreme and idealized case, the South Indian kingdom is again a state without a center—in a much more literal sense than we have implied before—for the royal figure at its center is himself no longer solidly present at all; his innermost being has collapsed in love. The symbolic focus of this South Indian kingdom is a black hole, out of space and time, a point opened up to infinity, generating from within universes of feeling and passionate play, encased in comedy, and made accessible to the imagination through the hollow form of the mad king and devotee upon his throne.

6. The Androgynous Clown: Bṛhannaḍā at Virāṭa's Court

The stories we have been examining are part of a much larger set, which includes other distinct comic, or tragi-comic, types: for ex-

[97] *Pŏṉvaṇṇattantāti* 92. On the "liquid" devotional ideal, see Egnor, pp. 20-21.

ample, the gambler-king, driven from his throne by his vice (Yudhiṣṭhira, Nala);[98] or a noble tragic buffoon such as Rāvaṇa, in Kampaṉ's masterful portrayal.[99] (The latter case is a finely articulated mediating category between the essentially comic and the largely tragic components of the royal role; and it is not by chance that this mediation is enacted by a heroic demon who merits a sympathetic depiction.)[100] One major subset—the king's "romantic" madness and its consequences—will be briefly examined in the following chapter. But instead of extending the present chapter further in a solemn effort to describe *all* the major types represented in the literature, I wish to concentrate in what follows on two major categories of comic transformation, each of which is basic, in its own way, to the royal norms. The first is a category of festive or carnival *inversions*, deeply linked to the ritual context of Indian kingship; the second involves the king's temporary immersion in the chaotic experiences of war.

The outstanding example of the king's "carnivalesque"[101] inversions emerges, inevitably, out of a context of royal exile. Indeed, it serves as the dramatic climax to this exile, and, in effect, as a symbolic statement of its very essence. This is the story of the Pāṇḍavas' thirteenth and final year of exile from their kingdom, a year that they spend disguised, in hiding, at the court of the Matsya king Virāṭa. Their adventures during this year are described in the fourth book of the *Mahābhārata*, the *Virāṭaparvan*—undoubtedly one of the most popular parts of the entire epic.[102] In Tamil Nadu, Villipūttūrār's Tamil version of the *Virāṭaparvan* is recited in times of drought, as a ritual attempt to bring down rain; this ritual function, clearly related to the "inversions" the book describes, points to the conceptual background of this section in the epic. As has become increasingly clear from recent studies,[103] the *Virāṭaparvan* is no mere accretion interpolated into the "original" *Mahābhārata*—as an earlier generation of scholars believed[104]—but a critically important statement of major epic themes

[98] "Gambling" is clearly felt to constitute a royal imperative, as at the *rājasūya*: see Heesterman (1957), pp. 140-57; Beck (1982), pp. 199-205.

[99] For example, in the subtly ironic scene in the Aśoka garden, when Rāvaṇa pleads with Sītā (5.406-80).

[100] On the tragic and heroic demon, see below VII.7.

[101] The term is van Buitenen's, from his introduction to the *Virāṭaparvan* (1978), pp. 3-10.

[102] See the introduction by Raghu Vira to the BORI text of the *Virāṭa*, p. xvii.

[103] Biardeau (1978), pp. 187-200; Hiltebeitel (1980a); Dumézil (1968), pp. 93-94; van Buitenen (1978), pp. 3-10.

[104] This was the view of E. Hopkins, among others: see van Buitenen (1978), pp. 18-21.

and concerns. Not least among these is the epic's understanding of kingship with all its problems, its varied aspects, its ritual and symbolic exigencies. In this respect, as in others, we may agree with Hiltebeitel's view of the *Virāṭaparvan* as embodying "the 'deepest' level of their [the epic poets'] play with symbols."[105]

Our concern is with the nature and meaning of the Virāṭa images of kingship as seen, above all, in the central heroic figure among the Pāṇḍavas: Arjuna, the son of the divine king Indra, and the subject of the most extreme of the heroes' transformations. Biardeau has described Arjuna as the epic's major exemplar of kingship;[106] and although this interpretation is open to question—the other brothers (especially Yudhiṣṭhira!) have their own claims on kingly identity, and their masks and transformations are also intriguing and obviously significant—it is true that Arjuna focuses our attention on the painful comedies of the exiled king. To a large extent, the comic tone of the *Virāṭaparvan* is a function of Arjuna's clowning, which is bound up with his disguise as Bṛhannaḍā—the eunuch (*ṣaṇḍha, klība*) dressed as a woman, who is sent to the harem to instruct Virāṭa's daughter how to dance. Bṛhannaḍā presents us with as stark an image of the Indian king as can be found: the royal figure is here reduced to impotence, transvestism, the assumption of a female persona, and a ludicrously nonheroic occupation. There is no reason to believe that this transformation is accidental or in any way peripheral to the Indian king's normative self-image. Rather, it expresses a necessary and enduring component of that image, one that is, as will be shown, fundamentally comic. Although van Buitenen's "carnivalesque" interpretation of the *Virāṭaparvan* as a whole has been criticized,[107] one would be hard put not to notice the comic character of the episodes devoted to Arjuna-Bṛhannaḍā's escapades.

Before turning to these episodes (first in the Sanskrit original, then in Villiputtūrār), let us recall the narrative background and the disguises adopted by Arjuna's brothers and by Draupadī. The *Virāṭaparvan* opens with the Pāṇḍava heroes on the verge of their thirteenth year away from their kingdom; according to the terms of the dice game that had sent them into this exile, they must get through this year unrecognized by friend or foe. They elect to spend the year at Virāṭa's court in the following disguises: Yudhiṣṭhira, the king to be, becomes the Brahmin dice player Kaṅka; the brawny Bhīma becomes

[105] Hiltebeitel (1980a), p. 148.
[106] Biardeau (1976) and (1978), pp. 87-204.
[107] De Jong (1980).

Ballava, cook and wrestler; Arjuna appears as Bṛhannaḍā; the twins, Nakula and Sahadeva, assume the guises of a horse trainer and cattle expert, respectively; Draupadī, the common wife of the heroes, presents herself as a *sairandhrī*, servant girl and hairdresser. These disguises have elicited much recent comment; each of them is clearly expressive of a range of designated symbolic meanings. For our purposes, we may stress the "ludic" character of Yudhiṣṭhira's disguise, as well as its Brahmin overlay: in effect, Yudhiṣṭhira stands on the threshold of a more explicit comic role, for in India the dice master shares the playfulness and the generative power of the Creator, whose work may be represented in the game of dice.[108] Nevertheless, Yudhiṣṭhira's comic side remains undeveloped, in contrast with Arjuna's startling role.

We must also note the dark background to these masquerades. The heroes' assumption of new, dramatically engaging identities is not a simple form of play but a response to the experience of exile, danger, and loss; and the prolonged "festival" at Virāṭa's court, however rich in playful inversions and ludicrous situations, has a somewhat Nietzschean tone. Much of the *Virāṭaparvan* takes place in darkness, either the literal darkness of night or the metaphorical and more pervasive darkness of disguise. The heroes wander through this book in a daze, hugging the shadows of the palace in which they are never at home, never safe, always intent upon keeping up the masquerade; they struggle for self-control in humiliating circumstances that leave them burning with suppressed violence—until they can contain it no longer, and an explosion occurs. Their inner state is an unhappy one, no doubt familiar to many participants in the world's carnivals, of loneliness, anomie, and oppressive helplessness. Indeed, the ritual context of this festive drama seems to require just such a state of intense self-alienation, which may be the most basic element of the carnival experience. One senses this dark undercurrent of pain and struggle in the *Virāṭaparvan*'s first extended story, the episode of Bhīma's slaying of the lascivious Kīcaka (undoubtedly one of the *Mahābhārata*'s finest narrative passages). Kīcaka lusts for the beautiful *sairandhrī*-Draupadī, who, in despair, turns to the loyal Bhīma; the latter adopts yet another disguise, that of a woman, in a midnight "tryst" with Draupadī's tormentor, whom he kills; Bhīma must then effect a hair-breadth's rescue of Draupadī from a forced suttee with the body of her would-

[108] See n. 98 above; Hiltebeitel (1976), pp. 86-101. Yudhiṣṭhira as "Brahmin" gambling companion thus has something of the Brahmin magician-clown. On the disguises in Virāṭa generally, see Gehrts (1975), pp. 215-28, and the sources cited in n. 103 above.

be lover. Although we cannot analyze this episode in detail here, we may at least notice how deeply it, too, is imbued with the carnival spirit of this book: Bhīma, like Arjuna throughout the *Virāṭaparvan*, takes on a transvestite disguise; Draupadī, humiliated by Kīcaka in the court, excoriates her "impotent" (*klība*) husbands in a powerful harangue reminiscent of the ritual revilings in South Indian goddess festivals, or of the Billingsgate speech of the European carnival;[109] and the final episode—the rescue of the reluctant suttee victim—crowns the cruel, comic melodrama with another grimly humorous slaughter, a timely reminder that these charades can be deadly serious after all.

But we must concentrate on the key figure of Arjuna, who dominates the stage from chapter 33 on (the entire second half of the book). Indeed, Arjuna's disguise is a matter of heightened interest from the very beginning: as Dumézil has noted, "It is Arjuna, the false eunuch, who most richly inspired the poets."[110] From the moment of his arrival at Virāṭa's court, Arjuna presents an incongruous, even grotesque appearance, which the epic's authors exploit to good effect:

> Then another man appeared, endowed with wondrous form,
> a great man[111] covered with the ornaments of women,
> with earrings like buttresses or palace walls
> and gilded conch shells, resplendent and long.
>
> Shaking his long, thick hair which fell disheveled about him,
> that great-armed hero with a wild elephant's stride
> made the earth tremble under his step
> as he came toward Virāṭa in the midst of his court. (4.10.1-2)

King Virāṭa, beholding this apparition, is understandably perplexed: Arjuna-Bṛhannaḍā's features simply do not harmonize (he is "a handsome man . . . with a braid and wearing earrings," 10.5). He concludes, quite correctly, that what he is seeing is an archer who is "wrongly attired" (*paridhāya cānyathā*, 10.6). For "her" part, Bṛhannaḍā sticks to her transparently inappropriate disguise, with the added remark—very much in the spirit of the *Virāṭaparvan*'s own brand of comedy—"And as to why I have this form—even to talk about that increases my pain!" (*idaṃ tu rūpaṃ mama yena kiṃ nu tat prakīrtayitvā bhṛśaśokavardhanam*, 10.9). And off he goes, sad and yet comical, hav-

[109] See Bakhtin (1968), pp. 15-17, 27-28, 187-95; Gaignebet and Florentin (1974); for South Indian festivals to the goddess, see Brubaker (1978). Ritual abuse remains an important feature at festivals such as the Bharaṇi celebration of Bhagavatī at Kŏṭuṅkoḷūr (Cranganore).

[110] Dumézil (1968), p. 93.

[111] *bṛhatpumān*: cf. Biardeau (1978), p. 189.

ing somehow passed a mysterious royal inspection of his identity as a eunuch, to teach the young princess Uttarā how to dance.

Arjuna-Bṛhannaḍā puts in a short, unhappy appearance during the Kīcaka episode (he, too, has to suffer Draupadī's reproaches) but he comes into his own only later, when the Kauravas stage their cattle raid in Virāṭa's kingdom. The king is away with Arjuna's brothers, still disguised, of course, at a second front opened by the Kauravas' ally Trigarta; the defense of the kingdom therefore rests with Virāṭa's son Uttara. This sets the scene for the comic vignette in which Bṛhannaḍā will cast off "her" disguise, clearly a climactic point in the Virāṭa story.[112] Let us follow Arjuna's transformations carefully, as they are portrayed in the Sanskrit text.

When the alarm is raised—the Kauravas are making off with Virāṭa's cattle—our heroes are (where else?) in the harem; the vain Prince Uttara is being entertained by the women. Upon hearing the news, he boasts that he will rout the entire Kaurava army and bring back the cattle; if he had been on the spot, he says, the disaster could never have happened in the first place, but now the Kauravas would see him in action "as if Pārtha-Arjuna himself were tormenting them!" This finely chosen simile—Uttara, of course, has no inkling that Arjuna is anywhere near—has a disquieting effect upon Draupadī, who overhears the prince's boasts; at her prompting, Princess Uttarā pleads with Bṛhannaḍā to serve as her brother's chariot driver (Sūta). Draupadī, with her keen eye, has apparently sized up Uttara correctly; but at first Bṛhannaḍā offers only disingenuous protests. "What power do I have to drive a chariot? If you are interested in a song, a dance, a musical recital of one kind or another, then I will be happy to help you." But he allows himself to be persuaded, although his games (*narma*, 33.17) are not over: he dons the armor they give him upside down, and all the girls burst out laughing. In this light-hearted spirit, this unlikely Quixote (pointedly referred to by one of his more ominous titles, Bībhatsu, "the Terrifier"—33.26) drives off with Uttara in the direction of the Kauravas, after promising to bring back bright garments from the battlefield for the girls' dolls (*pāñcālikārtham*).[113]

From this point on we have a comic diptych: on one side, our two heroes in a clowns' duet, on the other, the Kaurava antiheroes un-

[112] Dumézil has, once again, noted the crucial importance of this episode: "Euripides or Aristophanes would not have done better." (1968), p. 93.

[113] On this rather loaded term, see Hiltebeitel (1980a), pp. 166, 171; Biardeau (1978), pp. 197-99. Whatever the suggestive overtones of the word, we should note its mirroring capacity—the doll (*pāñcālikā*) calls up the image of Pāñcālī/Draupadī, herself reduced in Virāṭa to a restricted and impure image of her normal role.

wittingly indulging in their own amusing antics. Once again we see the "doubling and redoubling" so characteristic of comic forms,[114] as well as another striking instance of the playful exchange of identities: Uttara and Bṛhannaḍā offer, in their interaction, distorted images of one another as they slowly slip into a total reversal of their roles. This scene reveals Arjuna in the greatest depth of his self-parody as hero and king, at the moment of his transformation back to his "native" self, as if he were required to touch bottom before bouncing back to a more heroic vision of himself in the world. Uttara prompts this transformation by his own ludicrous transition from vainglorious heroics to abject cowardice: no sooner does he catch a glimpse of the Kaurava army—advancing, in the unsettling manner of Birnam wood, "like a forest creeping through the sky" (36.5)—than he panics and wishes to go home. How can he fight, he asks his supposedly effeminate driver: he is a mere child, all alone, never tried in battle; his hairs are standing on end out of terror. But Bṛhannaḍā, surprisingly, refuses to turn back. In what must surely be a self-conscious parody of the opening chapter of the *Bhagavadgītā* (where it is Arjuna who suddenly balks at the battle), he asks Uttara why he will not fight.[115] This is followed by a grim promise: Bṛhannaḍā will drive the prince into the midst of the Kauravas, hungry as vultures for flesh, even if they are hidden inside the earth. Besides, says the charioteer, the women would laugh at the prince if he came home empty handed.

Uttara is unimpressed: "Let them laugh at me!" And in a flash he leaps from the chariot, leaving behind "his pride and his bow." But Arjuna is after him, his long braid flapping over his red skirts as he flounders over the battlefield in the wake of the cowardly Uttara. It is an utterly ridiculous sight, and the Kauravas, watching from the distance, guffaw—until it slowly dawns on them that something here is wrong. All the incongruity of Arjuna's disguise suddenly takes on meaning: the skirts and the braids hardly seem to fit those stout arms and thick neck, that heavy gait which shakes the earth. The same doubt that had assailed Virāṭa on Bṛhannaḍā's first appearance in the court now begins to work on them: this person has "something of a man and something of a woman" (*kiṃcid asya yathā puṃsaḥ kiṃcid asya yathā striyaḥ*, 36.30); could it possibly be Arjuna? They are not yet sure, but they have reason to feel afraid. Meanwhile, the duet approaches its conclusion: Bṛhannaḍā catches the fleeing Uttara by his

[114] See above, IV.2 at nn. 64-65.

[115] See Dumézil, (1968), p. 93, and van Buitenen (1978), pp. 15-16, on the link with the *Gītā*'s opening scene.

long hair.[116] Desperately, and wholly inappropriately, the prince chooses this moment to offer his bellicose driver a bribe: he will give him one hundred golden coins, eight gems, a chariot, ten rutting elephants, if only he will let him go home. Arjuna laughs and drags the whining, moaning Uttara back to the chariot.

By now the disguise is dispensable: Arjuna announces that *he* will fight and Uttara will drive the chariot. There is a further farcical moment when Arjuna takes the prince to the *śamī* tree where the Pāṇḍavas had hidden their weapons upon their entry to the Matsya territory: Uttara refuses to climb up to retrieve the hero's bow, for he has heard that a corpse is tied to this tree. And he is right: the Pāṇḍavas had indeed placed a corpse there to frighten off curious passersby. Uttara fears pollution—is this a parody of the classical motif of the king who carries a corpse?—or else he is grasping at straws; in any case, Arjuna blandly lies to reassure him.[117] Equipped with his great bow, Arjuna can now reveal his true identity and prepare the still cowering Uttara for his role in the coming battle.

As the two clowns emerge from their fluid, comic roles and assume a more properly heroic stance, their enemies become more muddled, perhaps partly in compensation. Another one of the Kauravas' interminable debates breaks out: Droṇa, the Brahmin teacher, points out a number of evil omens and urges caution. This moves Duryodhana to a satirical attack upon all teachers and pandits: they are good, he remarks, at showing up others' weaknesses, at telling stories at their ease in courts and palaces, at analyzing human behavior, and, of course, at finding fault with the food they are served—but never consult them in a real emergency! (4.42.26). The discussion rambles on: Karṇa glories in the approaching fight with Arjuna (now identified with certainty), but Kṛpa turns on him with an analogy: if someone ties himself up and hangs a heavy rock around his neck in order to swim across the ocean, what manliness (*pauruṣa*) would there be in that? Manliness, of course, is a symbolic issue at this juncture, given Arjuna's recent experiences. But for the Kauravas, it is in any case too late: Arjuna charges into their army and sends one after another of the major heroes fleeing.

The poets enjoy a final ironic scene: King Virāṭa, returning home, is worried when he discovers that his son has gone to war with Bṛhannaḍā. "With a eunuch as his charioteer, I fear for his survival!" He is

[116] We might note that the *Virāṭaparvan* appears almost obsessively fascinated by hair (Bṛhannaḍā's long locks; Draupadī's unbound hair, etc.): see 4.15.36; 4.15.7; 4.21.47; Hiltebeitel (1981), *passim*.

[117] Biardeau (1973-1974), p. 99, offers a different interpretation.

disabused of his perception when all the heroes discard their disguises. The book's conclusion—from the blood-stained dicing match to the princess Uttarā's marriage to Abhimanyu, Arjuna's son—cannot detain us now.

In analyzing the inversions of the *Virāṭaparvan*, above all Arjuna's symbolic role, we must explore both the specific associations aroused by the central images and the ritual context from which they emerge. Arjuna's appearance as a eunuch, although "explained" in the epic itself as the result of a curse he received in heaven (from the dancing-girl Urvaśī, whose advances he had rejected),[118] is an important statement about the Indian king; as we have already noted on several occasions, "impotence" is a basic attribute of the king. Bṛhannaḍā embodies this truth in its simplest, most literal form; and although in this case the king's impotence is limited to his state of exile, in general this feature carries over, on a more abstract level, to the king's "ordered" phase. Indeed, Arjuna's far-reaching inversion in Virāṭa's kingdom may be seen as actualizing an always latent dimension of the king's reality; in this sense it goes beyond the mere reversal of his normal attributes by revealing a hidden, dynamic side to his role. This sense of liberated dynamism may also be related to Arjuna's position at Virāṭa's court as the dancing master in the harem, for the dance suggests, here as elsewhere, the power of movement as opposed to stasis and limitation.[119] Arjuna-Bṛhannaḍā thus brings, through his own transformation and inner flux, a measure of revitalized movement to his surroundings; the clown, who is stable only in transformation, corrodes the seemingly secure façade of the social order in which he acts. We may begin to sense here the reasons for the energizing impact that this book as a whole is felt to produce on the world: the inversions and transformations that the disguised heroes act out in the Matsya kingdom have the effect of opening up a dimension normally less accessible to experience, and this effect, *within* the narrative, may also extend *beyond* it to the point of releasing rain in times of drought.[120]

All of this is closely bound up with clowning and other comic features. As Bṛhannaḍā, Arjuna takes on the classic role of the androgynous clown—seemingly a universal clown type, and one that we have already met in connection with the Vidūṣaka and the court jester.[121] We may recall the androgynous clown Semar of the Javanese

[118] *MBh* 3.App. I.6 (lines 124-35).

[119] Similarly with Naṭarāja-Śiva's cosmic dance, a study in the stability of instability. (I am grateful to Don Handelman for this observation.)

[120] See above, IV.5 at n. 159.

[121] IV.2 at n. 25 and IV.4 at notes 135-36.

shadow-theater, a close analogue to the popular Bṛhannaḍā of the Andhra shadow-puppeteers.[122] Hiltebeitel, in a recent study, has delineated Bṛhannaḍā's associations with Ardhanārīśvara-Śiva, the god in his androgynous form.[123] This comparison is instructive: although in general, as we have seen, the ancient Indian king's affiliation seems to lie most closely with Viṣṇu (while it is the Brahmin who is linked to Rudra-Śiva),[124] in the present case the *inverted* king is related to Śiva by virtue of their common sexual ambiguity. Even in Śiva's case, it should be noted, androgyny is frequently the occasion for comic remarks, sometimes wholly playful in tone, but at other times linked to the cruel sense of frustration that even the god must feel in this sexually unsatisfying form.[125] The clown's natural affinity with the androgyne, or the transvestite, derives from his habit of dissolving boundaries and categories—including those of sexual identity—and of producing incongruous combinations. As we should by now expect, this kind of play, with all the concomitant effects of blatant impropriety, inversion, and reflexive commentary upon the supposedly "serious" norm, finds its most intense symbolic expression in the portrayal of the king.

In fact, Bṛhannaḍā is by no means the only androgynous Indian king. The epic also knows, for example, the tale of Bhaṅgāśvana, who was changed by Indra into a woman and later elected to remain in that state (because, as Bhaṅgāśvana claims to have discovered empirically, a woman's sexual pleasure is greater than a man's).[126] But the most significant precedent is provided by Arjuna's own divine father and prototype, our familiar royal buffoon Indra. Already in Vedic texts, as has been noted earlier, Indra is said to disguise himself as a woman.[127] This transvestite guise is surely one of the best suited to this god in his never-ending oscillation between his "properly" regal and ludicrously antithetical selves; and thus it is not, after all, surprising that Indra should share this essential feature with Arjuna, his representative in the epic. One late South Indian text—the *Pañcavaradakṣetramāhātmya*, which recounts the myths of Uttaramerūr—

[122] For Semar see Scott-Kemball (1970), plate 19. Jon GoldbergBelle informs me that Bṛhannaḍā is among the most beloved of the Andhra shadow puppets.

[123] Hiltebeitel (1980a).

[124] Above, II.4 and III.3.

[125] See Shulman (1980b), p. 270.

[126] *MBh* 13.12.2-49; cf. Shulman (1980b), pp. 303-304.

[127] See n. 17 above. On androgyny and kingship more generally, see Miller (1971); and see above, II.3-4 on the "maternal" monarch.

connects the Virāṭa stories (extended in various ways) to a local tradition about Indra:

> During their exile from their kingdom, the Pāṇḍavas worshiped Viṣṇu-Varada (in Uttaramerūr); after spending a year in disguise in the Matsya kingdom, and subsequently regaining their throne in battle with the aid of Varada (as Kṛṣṇa), they continued to come each year to worship the god in this shrine—as did Virāṭa and other kings.
>
> One night Indra, thinking himself preeminent among the creatures of the fourteen worlds, disguised himself as a pregnant woman and approached his mother. "Help me," he pleaded; "I am pregnant; my husband was angry at me, beat me, and drove me from the house. I have no mother, brother, father, or other relatives. You are all I have." Indra's mother was filled with compassion and took the woman in. But when she discovered that "she" was really a man, Indra's mother was not amused. "I will *not* be made a fool of (*parihāsāspadā nāham*)," she said in anger; and while she did not kill him—since he *was* her son—she cursed him to become a leper. Indra went home, ashamed; by dawn his body had become white with leprosy.
>
> For three days he hid in the house, with his body covered with garments. His wife, Paulomī, found him weeping on the floor. "Just look at me!" he cried, removing his covering and embracing his wife; "how can I enter the assembly, or see the gods?" In despair, he decided to take his own life. Suddenly a voice from Viṣṇu's heaven directed him to the shrine at Uttaramerūr, where he was eventually freed from his affliction.[128]

As usual, Indra's inflated pride precedes his fall to a pitiable state; only Varada's intervention can save his life and restore him to his position. Here the transvestite guise, adopted as a joke, is the occasion rather than the symbol of his exile; the god's lame attempt at comedy evokes only grim displeasure in his severely "proper" mother, who will brook no offense to her matronly dignity. (Many other myths, we may note in passing, describe the strained relations between Indra and his mother.)[129] Again we see the common image of the paradigmatic, leprous king.[130] It is also highly significant that this text links Indra's

[128] *Pañcavaradakṣetramāhātmya* 4-5, in Gros and Nagaswamy (1970), pp. 14-23 of the text.

[129] Shulman (1980b), pp. 53-54; also 248-50 (Indra's attack upon the Maruts in the womb of Aditi).

[130] See above, II.5 at notes 103-109.

transvestite prank and consequent punishment with the Pāṇḍavas' stay in Virāṭa's kingdom; later chapters of the *māhātmya* recount the arrival in Uttaramerūr of Virāṭa himself, together with his son Uttara, who lends his name to the village (as well as to the local god, the goddess, and the sacred tank).[131]

To return to the Virāṭa "carnival": the integral nature of Arjuna's transvestite transformation, and its comic overtones, should now be apparent; what remains to be shown is its integrating function. Here we must characterize the nature of this carnival more precisely. As we have seen, it is hardly a joyous affair, despite its comic inversions, its moments of dark farce, its melodramatic rescues, its ludic delight in masquerades, secret names, and new identities.[132] The comedies of Virāṭa are played out against a shadowy background of exile, personal loss, and severe personal trial. In ritual terms, this year of hiding, like Indra's period of fearful concealment in the lotus pond,[133] is a kind of *dīkṣā*—a moment of ritualized separation, "regression" to an infantile (or, indeed, embryonic) state, and, at the end, an initiatory rebirth (in this case, a rebirth as warriors moving toward the climactic battle-sacrifice).[134] In the words of the epic text itself, the heroes spend their year in disguise "like creatures dwelling in the womb" (*garbhavāsa iva prajāḥ*, 4.2.11).[135] This womblike *dīkṣā* has other features in harmony with the sacrificial rituals: thus Biardeau convincingly relates Bṛhannaḍā's "impotence" to the notion of ideal chastity (*brahmacarya*) associated with the detached, yogic king; but the *dīkṣita*, too, must be chaste.[136] We might even go a step farther and see Arjuna's period in the seraglio as a kind of Gandhian trial of innocence and self-restraint—it is, in fact, never made wholly clear whether Arjuna is truly reduced to the state of a eunuch or is merely masquerading as one,[137] and after it is all over Arjuna seems to imply, in an interesting speech, that it has not been easy for him in the midst of so many women (above all

[131] *Pañcavaradakṣetramāhātmya* 6-8; see discussion by Gros and Nagaswamy (1970), pp. 10-11.

[132] The emphasis on secret nomenclature is nicely stated by M. V. Subramanian (1967), p. 143: "In buccaneering vein they also settle on a set of code names for all the five brothers."

[133] Above, section 2 (see at notes 36-38).

[134] For Virāṭa and *dīkṣā*, see Biardeau (1978), pp. 187-88 (n. 3); Gehrts (1975), pp. 215-28; Hiltebeitel (1980a), p. 149.

[135] See comments by Hiltebeitel (1980a), p. 149; Gehrts (1975), p. 217.

[136] Biardeau (1978), pp. 189-93.

[137] As Hiltebeitel remarks (1980a, p. 154): "The epic descriptions leave it amusingly imprecise and ambiguous whether Arjuna is physiologically a eunuch, a hermaphrodite, or simply a transvestite."

his lovely pupil, Uttarā).[138] The false eunuch's self-control would put Arjuna-Bṛhannaḍā in the same class as the medieval South Indian kings, whose impassivity in various seductive situations is a conventional theme in panegyrics.[139] In other circumstances, of course, Arjuna is anything but impassive—his erotic adventures are typical of the king in his passionate aspect (another facet of his potential for madness and extreme transformation)—but sexual license is clearly *not* a part of the Virāṭa carnival experience.

In general, it would seem, this is a carnival of sadness. It produces a regeneration or revitalization by way of painful inversions; its comic elements have a measure of cruelty; even the imaginative playfulness it incorporates is permeated by built-in frustration and conscious restriction. The major participants undergo experiences of intense alienation, self-mockery, and bitter struggle with the demands of their disguise:

> L'homme ivre d'une ombre qui passe
> Porte toujours le châtiment
> D'avoir voulu changer de place.[140]

But the Indian king simply cannot follow the ironic advice of Baudelaire's owls; he is condemned to know all the sorrows of the shadow, to subject himself to ceaseless movement and the turbulence of dissonant emotions; his place in the world is a perennial "changing of place"—and all this without ever becoming fully aware of his own fate. The reflexivity inherent in his transformations is, from his standpoint, unconscious (though, seen from the outside, it is no less powerful because of that); he is entirely absorbed in the experiences of these relentless cycles, far more a tragi-comic victim than a ludic master of his transformations. Bṛhannaḍā shares little with the Brahmin magician-clowns. The king brings movement to the world at the cost of being "moved," in oppressive and even dangerous ways, himself.

Hence the essential limitations of these carnival inversions. Despite the important energizing effect of the king's period of disguise, the entire episode tends ultimately to sustain or to reinforce the given contours and dynamics of the everyday order. The carnival is not truly

[138] *MBh* 4.67.1-7.

[139] See below, VI.2.

[140] He who is drunk on a passing shadow
forever pays the price
of having sought to change his place.
Baudelaire, "Les Hiboux" (*Spleen et Idéal*).

open-ended, in the sense that nothing really new is created; instead, it merely reveals a latent aspect of the king (or of social reality in a wider perspective). The range of its forms is restricted and fairly predictable; it seeks far-reaching inversions as its favored mode, with the suggestion of their eventual reversion to the origin. This kind of festive playing, in both India and Europe, thus seems to function basically as an integrating mechanism that safeguards, and periodically revitalizes, the fundamental "enchantment with form."[141] Inversion, even of a very dramatic or seemingly chaotic type, can go only so far; its cognitive contribution is in hinting at a more stratified ontology than we normally conceive. Thus in the *Virāṭaparvan*, as in South Indian festivals for the village goddess, a hidden dimension of vital reality is opened up in a sudden moment of crisis and antithetical movement—only to be covered up again. By the end of the book, the disguises have been discarded; the heroes can now resume their conventional royal masks.

Villiputtūrār's Virāṭa

This forced limitation of the carnival experience may help to explain why Villiputtūrār does little to develop the suggestions embedded in the Sanskrit text. To be more precise: while clinging fairly closely to the original (with a few notable exceptions), the Tamil poet indulges his playfulness above all in the linguistic domain; his *Virāṭaparvan* is thus a feast of paronomasia, double entendre, sly verbal twists, and pleasant ironies. One imagines him at work composing with the wry, contained smile of a Tĕnāli Rāma on his lips.

We shall follow him through only a few of these verbal pranks. First, however, we should take note of one area in which Villiputtūrār clearly exceeds the inherited guidelines of his source: in his playing with the comic properties of androgyny and transvestite disguise. Thus in the Kīcaka episode, Bhīma takes on a complete feminine costume for his midnight rendezvous with Kīcaka (3.63); the latter is entirely fooled, falls at the ankleted feet of his "beloved," and utters three slavish, erotic verses in "her" praise. As usual in this part of Villiputtūrār's *Mahābhārata*, these verses are heavily laden with irony, for Kīcaka speaks with an unintentional ambiguity built into the hackneyed metaphors he chooses; these metaphors, as both the disguised Bhīma and Villi's Tamil audience clearly perceive, are about to become

[141] Above, IV.5 at notes 164-65.

literally, violently true. Thus Kīcaka pleads with the dark figure whom he takes to be Draupadī:

> I have not yet seen you open
> your mouth—so like a parrot's,
> or like a *kiñcukam* flower—
> to favor me with just one statement:
> "Don't be afraid."
> When will you relieve
> my failing spirit
> with a gracious glance
> from the corners of your eyes,
> dark as poison? (69)

The "poisonous" image, wholly conventional for the beloved's eyes in Tamil poetry, could hardly be more appropriate; the "relief" (*ĕṭup-patu*) that Kīcaka seeks is, more literally, a "taking (away)"—he is on the point of being "relieved" of his very existence. But he has, as yet, no intimation of this imminent disaster:

> You are the only deity
> I worship;
> you are everything to me.
> I never look any more
> at the inferior faces
> of other women;
> for I am far gone
> in the sickness of desire. (70)

Just how far gone he really is he now learns from the disguised Bhīma, who smiles at him "like a god who destroys vile birth, but who rejects the service of a worshiper whose heart is impure" (*malaṅ kŏṇĕñcuṭai pūcakar pūcai kŏḷḷāta puṉ pava nācakak kaṭavuḷ po'ṉakaittu*, 71). The poet aptly reverses Kīcaka's hyperbolic metaphor of worship, as he brings Bhīma's perspective to the fore; perhaps the commentator is right to recall here Śiva's smile during his devastating attack upon the Triple City of the demons.[142] Bhīma proceeds to crush Kīcaka in a lethal embrace described in terms ironically evocative of the embrace of love (76).

Among the Pāṇḍavas heroes, Bhīma is the most brawny, the most impetuous, and the most inclined to the use of raw force in any circumstances; hence the startling, ludicrous effect of his feminine disguise. Villiputtūrār finds an opportunity to project an opposite

[142] Commentary to v. 71; for the Tripura myth, see above, III.2.

inversion—from demure, delicate woman to Amazonian warrior—in his description of the Kauravas' invasion of Virāṭa's kingdom. In the Tamil version, the enemies arrive at the northern gate of the Matsya capital after setting fire to the crops in the fields and capturing all of Virāṭa's cattle—as the frightened shepherds hasten to inform Prince Uttara, in his father's absence. They reproach him for doing nothing: "why are you staying in your home, like a fledgling eagle in its nest (4.27)?" (The enemy king is, after all, Duryodhana, with the serpent—the traditional enemy of the eagle—on his banner: *mācuṇakkŏṭiyoṉ*, 26.) But before Uttara can say a word, his mother, the queen, looks at the row (*nirai*) of her serving-girls and commands them:

> Until the king returns,
> take weapons in your bright hands
> and go together
> to stand guard on the city walls. (28)

Perhaps the queen knows her son too well to expect any real help from him; she prefers to transform her ladies-in-waiting into soldiers. (Even here the poet cannot resist a pun—for the rows, *nirai*, of women about to be armed are verbally assimilated to the cattle, *nirai*, which have just been stolen by the enemy.) But now Uttara rises to the occasion with a boast which, like Kīcaka's, is pregnant with unconscious irony:

> Quickly,
> Uttara bowed to his mother,
> as she finished speaking,
> and laughed aloud—
>
> "Grey-haired lady,
> how excellent
> is this sacred speech
> of yours!
> *I*, adorned with
> finely ground sandal,
> necklaces and garlands,
> have arms massive as mountains:
> have I nurtured them only
> so that *women*
> would go to war?
>
> In the blink of an eye,
> *I* shall defeat
> the kidnappers of our cattle

with their entire army,
roaring like the sea:
I shall see
how one turns his back
and runs. . . ." (29-30)

Uttara's laughter is the prelude to his own comic disaster; it will not be the Kauravas who turn their backs on the battle (note the ambiguity of the phrase he chooses, *mutuku kaṇṭ' iṭuveṉ*—literally, "I shall see the [turning of] the back"). Still more to the point, only a "woman" will, in fact, save him; the prince would have done better to go on preening his massive arms, with his sandal paste and garlands, than to try his luck on the battlefield. From this moment on, a harsh, derisive laughter—often ironic, always cruelly appropriate—echoes continually in the background of the poem.

At this early stage, Uttara is aware of only one problem: he has no charioteer of "like mind" (*ĕṉ niṉaivŏṭ ŏppat or cārati*, 30) to drive him into battle. Draupadī hears this complaint and points to the powerful (*taram pĕṟu*) hermaphrodite (*peṭi*) Bṛhannaḍā, who (she says) used to drive Arjuna's chariot (31). In itself, of course, this suggestion is wholly ridiculous: the *peṭi*, in general, is a symbol of all that is useless and comically unfit, especially in a context that demands masculine prowess. Thus *Tirukkuṟaḷ* 727, for example, compares the erudition of a man afraid to speak up in the assembly to a sword in the hands of a *peṭi*;[143] the commentator Parimelaḻakar defines the *peṭi* as a woman who has some masculine characteristics but a predominantly feminine nature (*pĕṇ iyalpu mikku āṇ iyalpum uṭaiyavaḷ*). Nevertheless, the false *peṭi* Bṛhannaḍā is about to reach for her sword; and again it is the queen who has the wit to act swiftly and realistically, in the prince's better interest, by embracing Bṛhannaḍā and recommending her to Uttara: "Son, if you agree (to take her as your charioteer), you will conquer the kings in battle and come back all the sooner (32)." The queen's praise has a tinge of wonder or amazement (*viyantu*); has she sensed that Bṛhannaḍā is more than she appears to be? For his part, Uttara says nothing at all; Bṛhannaḍā finds horses and weapons, and soon the two depart from the city as crowds of women cry out their blessings (33). This traditionally heroic exit might seem to indicate a welcome reversion to more traditional sexual identities: the women, relieved of their Amazonian duties, can now cheer on their glorious, pugnacious prince; the entire scene could be classed with the conventional *puṟam* genre of *karantai*, in which the heroes set out to recover

[143] See also *Tirukkuṟaḷ* 614; *Nālaṭiyār* 251.

cattle that has been stolen.[144] The real transformation, of course, still lies ahead; here it is interesting to note that the *karantai* conventions include a moment of ludic dancing and even, perhaps, of "childlike" joy in battle on the part of the warrior-hero.[145]

Not that playfulness of this sort can be expected of Uttara: the hero of the Tamil epic's *karantai* episode turns out to be a coward who makes a mockery of the conventions. As he catches sight of the Kaurava host, his hands begin to tremble, his legs tremble, his mind wanders, his mouth becomes dry, his breath comes in spurts, he begins to stutter—indeed, his whole body starts to shake, so that the bright crown trembles on his head (36). Bṛhannaḍā tries to calm him:

"Don't be afraid!
Don't be afraid!
Just set your mind
  to achieve two things—
the slaughter of your enemies
and your own death in battle.
If you return unwounded
after coming to the battlefield,
great hero,
what won't the creeperlike women say,
    with their deceitful hearts?" (37)

The prince, predictably, finds this advice anything but soothing; he is already beyond caring about "deceitful" women, even as the deceit connected with his companion's womanliness is becoming apparent. Bṛhannaḍā embarks upon a crash course in military matters—"Look," she says, "these are horses, those are elephants, there are horse-drawn chariots, and foot-soldiers"—but Uttara, who knows nothing of all these things (*niṉṟavai yāvaiyum iyā vĕṉat tĕriyā*, 39), decides that safety (*uṟuti*) lies only in going home. Leaping from the chariot, he takes to his heels (*aṭit talam piṭar aṭittiṭa*, 41). Now, in the space of two verses, Bṛhannaḍā undergoes her change of form: first, in verse 40, "she" promises (with a feminine verb, *uraittaṉaḷ*) the frightened prince to do his fighting for him—to rout the Kauravas and recover the lost cattle

[144] See *Puṟappŏruḷ vĕṇpāmālai* 22-35 (*karantai* is differentiated in this work from the cattle raid, *vĕṭci*; the more ancient tradition combined these categories).

[145] *Ibid.* 28-30 (*āḷ ĕri piḷḷai, piḷḷaittĕḷivu, piḷḷaiyāṭṭu*). The connotations of *piḷḷai* are not solely those of childhood here, but the commentators do speak of the child's innocent disregard of danger as an element in the hero's makeup. Held (1935, p. 271) refers to a passage in the *MBh* in which the heroes go into battle "playing and dancing" (*krīḍann iva nṛtyan*)—a theme akin to those discussed in section 7, below.

"within the blink of an eye" (recall Uttara's boast to his mother in verse 30); then, in verse 41, "he" (with a masculine verb, *piṇittāṉ*) chases after the fleeing Uttara, brings him back, and literally ties him to the chariot.[146] As in the Sanskrit original, this moment of pursuit marks Arjuna's transition back to his "normal" self, though Villiputtūrār does nothing to highlight the ludicrous degradation that precedes this change; Arjuna can now recover his hidden weapons from the tree and, in a delightfully ambiguous and delicate conversation, let Uttara in on the secret of his true identity (43-45). The period of enforced disguise is almost over, and in a few moments "Vijaya will appear"; the childish prince (*ciṟuvaṉ*, 46) understands perfectly (*aṟintu*), falls at Bṛhannaḍā's feet, and, freed from his bonds, assumes the role of driver. The *peṭi* now attacks, "so that the enemies would celebrate his femininity as if it were masculine strength (*taṉ pĕṇmaiyaiy āṇmaiyāyp piṟar kŏṇṭāṭa*, 48)." In the heat of battle, deafened by the terrifying noise, Uttara has a momentary relapse and faints in fear, but Arjuna revives him (63-64); soon the Kauravas identify their foe, revealed in his native glory as Nara—as when the sun emerges from a fog that has temporarily hidden it from sight (60). Even the monkey Hanuman, dancing for joy, resumes his proper place on Arjuna's banner (58, 61). The Kaurava army is devastated, and now Arjuna mocks Duryodhana with pointed, scornful taunts that seem perfectly to suit the tone of the Tamil *Virāṭaparvan*:

> If you turn your back
> and run from the battle
> with your bow still in your hand,
> what won't women,
> their heavy breasts bound with a strap,
> say to you as you ride your elephant
> in procession through your city's streets? (70)

The all-too-familiar refrain must spring naturally to the mind of a hero who has had to hide for a year among women; to suffer the ignominy of a woman's reproaches now seems to Arjuna the worst fate for a warrior. Or almost the worst—for, as the erstwhile androgyne knows from bitter experience, there is the still greater shame of

[146] The scene recalls, both visually and verbally, an earlier moment in the Virāṭa story, when King Virāṭa battles against Trigarta; the latter manages to bind (*piṇi*, 4.15) the king to his chariot. In the Tamil text, as in the Sanskrit original, Uttara and his father Virāṭa are clearly cut from the same cloth: both are slightly ridiculous, vainglorious figures, unable to act the hero. (In the Sanskrit version, Trigarta drags Virāṭa off as the latter is "screaming like a woman"—43.8-9.)

actually being a woman, or seeming to be one. This is the insult that Arjuna hurls at Duryodhana at the climax of his harangue:

> Suppliants,
> youths,
> poets singing praises,
> messengers,
> the aged,
> Vedic Brahmins,
> women,
> cowards on the battlefield,
> and one's elders[147]—
>
> to kill any of these
> is an evil act. (74)

Hence, Duryodhana is to understand, Arjuna refrains from killing him; and, given the context of the Virāṭa masquerade, there is little doubt that the penultimate category in the list—the cowards among whom Duryodhana is meant to be classed—is deliberately, suggestively paired with the preceding category of defenseless women.

This sardonic style spreads contagiously. No sooner does Arjuna fall silent than we hear it again in the bitter recriminations that the defeated Kaurava heroes fling at one another (thus Aśvatthāman against Karṇa, 82-83). The cruel Virāṭa comedies continue to unfold. Villiputtūrār is far from finished with his games, but for our present purposes we have probably seen enough. We may sum up the Tamil poet's contribution to the Virāṭa "festival" by remarking again on the essentially linguistic character of his playfulness here. As often with Villiputtūrār, the narrative description is oddly turned in upon itself, so that the very language embodies or enacts, in its own terms and within its limits, the general features of the Virāṭa exile: the comic toying with conventional properties and boundaries, the pervasive disguises and inversions, the ironic displays of restraint, and, at times, the brief, chaotic explosions of hidden energy. A revel of paronomasia discloses, and at the same time contains and circumscribes, the dark carnival at Virāṭa's court. In one important respect, however, Villiputtūrār draws near to an innovative form of comedy that is truly chaotic and far more open-ended than the Virāṭa inversions, by transposing the poetic conventions of the *karantai* cattle war into a humorous and partially parodic vein. Bṛhannaḍā's farcical battle with

[147] *Pĕrun kuravar*: according to the commentary, these are the king, one's teacher, mother, father, and elder brother.

the Kaurava raiders anticipates the tragic, sacrificial slaughter at the main epic battleground of Kurukṣetra; but its comic aspect may be related to the ghastly comedy of warfare depicted in an earlier, Chola masterpiece, to which we now turn.

7. Heroic Clowns: The Circus-Comedies of War

It may, perhaps, be thought unfeeling to speak of war as a comedy—until we recall that comedy arises out of incongruity and contradiction, which must surely be outstanding features of most men's experience of war. Nowhere, in fact, is the gap between theory and reality, between conception and perception, more evident. Is the mindless slaughter of battle ever truly susceptible to being ordered in the categories we bring to bear on it (to say nothing of the ideological ones that any "official" viewpoint might seek to impose)? This question, of course, is asked from a Western perspective, with its inherent drive toward rationality or, at any rate, the illusion of rational order; our minds balk at the impossibility of penetrating or absorbing the chaotic moments of random destruction that constitute the truth of any war. Unprepared for the absolute loss that even a single death entails, we dream of commensurate compensations; but the lingering belief that war is somehow still part of a nation's meaningful struggles, an innately purposeful tool in the pursuit of its needs or ideals, makes any real experience of battle deeply ironic—as Paul Fussell has demonstrated with respect to the First World War. Fussell's exploration of the war's impact upon the minds of its participants (and of *their* impact upon *it*) is built upon this fundamental, pervasive, overwhelming sense of irony. No doubt this ironic perception befits the immense, senseless sacrifices of that particular war; but, as Fussell's work reveals, in this respect the Great War is truly paradigmatic: the savage comedy of ironic killing and being killed haunts all modern wars.[148]

Perhaps, then, we can allow ourselves to see how Cayaṅkōṇṭār, the brilliant court poet of Kulottuṅga I, could produce a battle poem that is, in some ways, a comic tour de force. But it is not irony that informs this comic point of view, for nowhere do we hear that a medieval South Indian war was "meaningful," in the perverse modern usage. Irony of the type Fussell describes springs from the relation of reality to hope; its recessive emotion is disappointment, its antecedents innocence or idealism. The Chola vision of warfare, on the other hand,

[148] Fussell (1975), especially pp. 29-35.

is profoundly uninnocent. Here the comedy of battle emerges not from the disparity between a horrible truth and a romantic or idealistic overlay but from a remarkably lucid sense of the absurd and the chaotic as constituent features of "reality." War intensifies this aspect of the real and clears away the everyday veils that disguise it; battle thus serves as an extreme symbolic activity in which the unwieldly and disharmonious fragments of the kingdom combine in a moment of institutionalized breakdown and release. At the same time, it facilitates transformation: Chola warfare is a circus without cages, with a ringmaster drafted from among the clowns.

Certain structural features of war in medieval South Indian polity and society have been hinted at in the introduction;[149] the highly ritualized "raiding" that seems to underly much Chola warfare serves to open the kingdom to much-needed renewal of several kinds. Both the attainment of new resources and the problematic patterns of their assimilation are basic parts of the entire process. It is above all the enduring royal compulsion to endow that helps to explain why the great Chola campaigns—seemingly so impressive in scope—never ended with a serious attempt to reconstitute the political center; instead, the original, delicate balancing of royal weakness and Brahminical authority was always replicated with the help of conquered territories and other resources.[150] Yet there is another dimension to this process, of primary concern to us here: the symbolic role of war for the Chola kingdom. The symbolic domain confirms and extends the understanding of Chola warfare as essentially episodic, uncontrolled, and totally opposed to any "reconstructive" drive. In its ritual side, it is linked to the *dīkṣā* experience of inversion—as in the Virāṭa "festival"—but it also transcends that experience in the direction of an immersion in chaotic forces, from without and from within. Like Bṛhannaḍā, the Chola heroes dance their way into battle; like "her," they exemplify a comic quality or vision; but in their case the imaginative transformation of reality is taken to far greater lengths. War becomes a moment when the visionary powers of the mind assert their total autonomy as well as their superiority over conventional, ordered forms. To these traits of comedy and imaginative play we may add a third, that of reflexivity: although the ancient Tamil heroic ethic, familiar from the *puṟam* poems of the classical anthologies, survived into Chola times, in the works of the Chola court poets it has become reflexive to a large degree; the comic coloring of the battle

[149] Above, I.4 at notes 90-93.
[150] See I.4, *passim*.

poem now provides a kind of commentary upon the simpler perspective of earlier times. These three features, as we by now expect, are closely related: comedy, a ludic ontology, and reflexivity comprise a powerful solvent applied to the life of the South Indian state. Such, in any case, is the picture that emerges from a careful reading of Cayaṅkŏṇṭār's *Kaliṅkattupparaṇi*.

Cayaṅkŏṇṭār's work does not stand alone: the *paraṇi* is a recognized genre celebrating a hero who has slain seven hundred (or, according to others, a thousand) elephants.[151] By common consent, however, Cayaṅkŏṇṭār is the finest master of this genre, and his poem ranks among the most famous of the Tamil classics. It describes a "real" battle—the expedition led by Kulottuṅga's general, Karuṇākara Tŏṇṭaimāṉ, against Kaliṅga in about A.D. 1110. The Kaliṅga war is conveyed to us through the conventions of the *paraṇi* genre, which include standard features such as the introductory invocations, an "opening of the gates" (see below), and descriptions of the *pālai* wasteland inhabited by the goddess Kālī and her bloodthirsty demons; in our poem the latter complain to Kālī of their hunger, and she promises them a gruesome feast on the battlefield; the actual war is portrayed in lurid terms by the demons, who then satiate themselves on the corpses and praise the Chola king for having arranged this banquet. Much of the poem thus embodies a "demon's-eye view" of the world. Kālī's role is related to this goddess's association with the *bharaṇi* asterism which gives the genre its name;[152] the ritual background seems to be that of a *bharaṇi* festival, such as the one still celebrated for the goddess Kālī at Cranganore, where ritual obscenity and abuse (including explicit pornographic songs describing the goddess's love-making with her consort) are prominent features. The heroic exploits of the warriors thus are closely related to a "festival" context of a fairly familiar type, replete with premeditated reversals of roles, attacks upon conventional limits, and an exceeding of these bounds; above all, a stark intermingling of comedy and anxiety in an atmosphere of ambiguous, perhaps frustrating eroticism. This context is reflected in the overall tone of the poem, a tone of surrealistic, indeed phantasmagoric experience, of nightmarish revels in the cremation ground, or on the battlefield; of surrender to the overpowering sensation of the grotesque.

Nevertheless, the Tamil poem is in no way akin to the European

[151] On *paraṇi*, see Zvelebil (1974), pp. 207-212 (and the sources he cites on p. 207 n. 46); Nagaswamy (1982), pp. 22-24; and the illuminating comments by Cāminātaiyar in his introduction to *Takkayākapparaṇi* (1960), pp. x-xi.

[152] Cāminātaiyar (1960), pp. x-xi.

Romantic grotesque; it is totally devoid of melancholy and of a *romantic* morbidity; nor are its terrors meant to titillate, as in the nineteenth-century Gothic novel.[153] The graveyard imagery of Cayaṅkŏṇṭār evokes neither false sadness nor a sweetly luxuriant gloom. Rather, the work's macabre aspect tends to be funny—not in a bitter, satirical fashion, but with the lively humor of a vivid imagination playing with powerful forms from beyond the normal pale. Tamil commentators and critics have often noted the fact that the *Kaliṅkattupparaṇi* has a number of obviously comic verses (usually classed as representing *nakaiccuvai*, the comic *rasa*);[154] several of these will be discussed presently. But what has not, it seems, been generally recognized is that these explicitly comic passages are part of a more general comic tone that pervades much of the book. This tone, often very subtle in quality, flows from the poet's basic stance: he dwells on the grisly and the grotesque as immediate, sensual expressions of the chaotic process he wishes to capture in words. His text is not a farce; not a satire; not a parodic or carnivalesque extravaganza; not a comic semiotic commentary on the serious life of the court—it is wholly remote from these genres. Moreover, several of its chapters are quite "straight" or serious, in the conventional meaning of the word (for example, the cantos dealing with the royal genealogy and with Kulottuṅga's birth and childhood). Yet far more than many other Tamil poems of comparable length (it has 599 verses),[155] the *Kaliṅkattupparaṇi* is a beautifully integrated work of sustained visionary power, and one of the important strands binding together its various sections is the common note of a grisly humorous excess.

In both spatial and temporal terms, the poem is located in the boundary zone of the wilderness. The *pālai* setting proper to the goddess (originally Kŏṟṟavai, here Kālī) also incorporates—no doubt as its very essence—the burning-ground in which Kālī's temple is situated (canto 3), and which is naturally linked to the battlefield; but the desert that the poet makes us feel in intense and immediate ways is as much an internal as an external one. The poem as a whole unrolls in a kind of "wilderness time," a time when one is separated from the security of the proper social self; major sections of the poem thus transpire at night, or at the juncture of night and dawn—when dreaming and waking consciousness blend together—or in the darkest hour of all,

[153] Here I take issue with Professor Zvelebil (1974), p. 207. On the European grotesque, see Bakhtin (1968), pp. 34-52.

[154] Aṟavāṇaṉ (1976), pp. 94-97; cf. the introduction to the SISS edition, pp. 49-50.

[155] The tradition has it that the Chola king bestowed a golden coconut on the poet after each verse was recited.

the black light of noon in the sun-baked desert.[156] This complex wilderness setting, in its outer and inner aspects, becomes fully articulated only in cantos 3-6, which introduce us to the *pālai* region and its demonic inhabitants; but this important introduction actually *follows* the lush, erotic "opening of the gates" (*kaṭai tiṟappu*), that at first glance appears to contrast starkly with all the rest of the poem.

And yet this contrast masks a deeper affinity. The fifty-four verses of the "opening" are couched in the form of an appeal to anonymous women (presumably of the Chola court or capital, but including also women brought as tribute or as captives from Kerala, the Tulu region, and the Deccan, 40-41, 43) to open the bolted doors of their houses. One line of interpretation pictures the following scene for these verses: the wives of the Chola heroes, angry because their husbands have failed to return at the appointed time from their campaign, have locked themselves into their homes in a sulk; the heroes, *returning* from Kaliṅga, sing these poetic pleas to appease them.[157] This approach helps to explain the predominant theme in this canto of the lovers' quarrel (*ūṭal*); there is, as we shall see, a strong suggestion in many of the verses that the Chola women are both famished for masculine love and reluctant to receive it. However, this entire interpretation has been questioned by several scholars (such as Irākavaiyaṅkār and Cuppu Rĕṭṭiyār),[158] who prefer to see the canto as a series of songs addressed to the women (probably by other women) in order to wake them, perhaps to begin the celebration of the king's victorious return (or of the *bharaṇi* festival!)—a mode of poetic address known, for example, from the *Tiruppāvai* and *Tiruvĕmpāvai*. This latter view has much to recommend it. But the fact remains, even on this view, that in thematic terms the "opening of the gates" constitutes a remarkable beginning for a war poem; whether the verses are projected into the mouths of the husbands, other women, or of an assumed persona (such as an anonymous poet), their contents remain the same: passionately erotic, suffused with fantasy, richly emotional in tone, and often wavering on the boundary between sleep and wakefulness, night and day. Even more striking is the essential symbolic theme of "opening": no matter who the speaker may be, the refrain of each verse is a call to "open the gates"; and given the whole texture of this section, there can be no doubting the suggestion of an erotic opening that must adumbrate

[156] Cf. Shulman (1981).

[157] Thus the commentaries to both editions cited in the bibliography; cf. Zvelebil (1974), p. 208. This seems to have been the most prevalent interpretation prior to Mu. Irākavaiyaṅkār's study (1925).

[158] See Rĕṭṭiyār (1972), pp. 25-55; Aṟavāṇaṉ (1976), pp. 43-49.

the chaotic opening up of the world in battle. The ancient analogical link between love and war recurs here in a specific context, with a wealth of affective and symbolic reinforcements.

Let us look at several of these verses, first noting their density of expression: the boldness of the description usually serves here merely to suggest further reaches of the imagination, so that the verses themselves seem to imitate as well as to initiate the processes of "opening." In fact, imagination—first concretized, then lost, in dreams—is a recurrent subject in the poems:

> In the dream when all was possible,[159]
> you failed to unite
> with munificent Naratuṅkaṉ;
> so now you are sulking,
> women angry in your love:
>
> open your great doors! (24)

The women have dreamt of the king (Naratuṅkaṉ is another title for Kulottuṅga), but even in their dreams their love has taken the form of a lovers' quarrel—the leitmotif of this canto—and thus even their fantasy issues into frustration. The king, as munificent donor, would surely have given these women what they wanted most—himself—if only they could have imagined accepting the gift. In other verses, however, the frustration is the more expectable one of waking up to "reality":

> "Mine, all mine
> is the mercy
> of Vaḷavatuṅkaṉ!"[160]
>
> So you fancied in your dream,
> and all night you were happy.
>
> Now you fondle your wide breasts,
>   seeking the scars left by his nails—
> open, please, your doors! (26)

There are, presumably, no scars this time; but, as happens several times in this canto, what was first imagined or dreamt turns up later in another verse dealing with a wholly concrete or tangible experience:

[159] *kūṭiya iṉ kaṉav' ataṉile*, literally, "in the sweet dream when (he) was united (with you)"—but *kūṭiya* also implies possibility.

[160] = Kulottuṅga, the king (as also Cayataraṉ, in verse 35 below).

Like a poor man
who has found a treasure
and keeps counting it,

you go to a solitary spot,
slip off your clothes,
and stare in joy

at the marks
left by your husband's
nails
   upon your breasts—

please open up! (47)

Inevitably, given this preoccupation with the transitions from one state to another, a certain confusion can set in (indeed, the poet obviously cultivates it):

It could really happen—

you could make love
to Cayataraṉ,
awake,

but you wouldn't know it:
you would assume
it was just that same old
dream, again.

Only the smile
on your companions' faces
would make you understand—

   please open your doors! (35)

Closely allied to this mode of playing with the relations between dreaming and waking consciousness is the motif of the women's false sleep:

"They must really be asleep"—
   that is what the young husbands thought,
and they had a remedy, too:
but as their hands
crept slowly up your thighs,
lovely ladies feigning sleep,
you would not open your eyes—

   open, please open your doors! (28)

This motif is connected to that of the quarrel or love-sulk (*ūṭal*); the husbands have, apparently, failed to keep their word (not to abandon their beloved? to return from battle without delay?). Whatever the reason, the woman responds by a symbolic closing that is clearly as painful to her as to her lover:

Tormented
by your husbands' lies;

tormented, too,
by desire,

you feign sleep
until dawn,

innocent women—

open your golden doors! (36)

Frustrated desire pervades the canto and hints, no doubt, of the nightmares still to come; the poem as a whole has been aptly described as a lurid compounding of "devils and corpses and sex-hungry women and weeping widows."[161] From this perspective, the "opening of the gates" makes a natural contribution to the whole ghastly series. But all is not frustration here: other verses of this canto reveal the double-edged nature of the love quarrel, with its latent aphrodisiac effect:

"Let go of my dress;
do you hear me, let go!"

Those are the words you murmur,
soft and angry,
as if to say,
"Tear off my dress *now*!"—

gracious ladies
open, please, your doors! (25)

Other verses can thus describe the sensual delights of union—sometimes with violent, martial metaphors that look ahead to the battle scenes soon to come.

Like spears cast in battle,
your eyes
pierce men's breasts
and open wounds

[161] Jesudasan and Jesudasan (1961), p. 188.

which you salve
with the warm compress
  of your black nipples
as you bind them
  with your soft embrace—

open, now, your doors! (56)[162]

The women lose themselves in passion following a quarrel—a form of self-forgetfulness that again resonates with the altered consciousness of the dream state; having "lost" awareness in this way, they must then set out to "seek themselves" (*uṅkaḷait teṭuvīr*, 70). Confusion—now the confusing passion of union (*mayakkam*)—continues to haunt the women's minds: after their love-making, out of this *mayakkam*, they try to clothe their nakedness in the white light of the moon (34). Yet always the underlying theme of anger, frustration, and the confusion born of these emotions threatens to surface again:

Lying
in your husband's arms,
you are tormented by his lies

until you cry, "Let me go!"

His arms slip away
from yours
and you are left
disturbed (*mayaṅkiṭuvīr*)—

open your doors
  of jewel and gold! (44)

This verse is a triumph of liquid sound suggesting slippery, liquid, motion: *taḻuvuṅ kŏḻunar piḻai naliyat taḻuvel ĕṉṉat taḻuviya kai/vaḻuva uṭane mayaṅkiṭuvīr*. . . . Its sentiment, too, is liquid—a flowing out of ecstasy into anger and agitation; a movement hesitating between opening and closing; finally, a submersion in inner confusion.

Such a movement is characteristic of this canto as a whole. Although Tamil critics have sometimes seen the "opening of the gates" as an attempt by the poet to balance, with the *rasa* of erotic passion (*śṛṅgāra*), the horrors of the subsequent cantos,[163] its true function seems to be the exact opposite: to contribute from the beginning to the wild and moving *imbalance* that propels this work. This is a poem of explosive

[162] For other images of battle, see verses 55, 62, and 66.

[163] Aṟavāṇaṉ (1976), p. 48.

fantasy that seeks to open up a dimension of experience normally contained or denied. The luxuriant setting of the Chola capital turns out to be suffused, in mysterious ways, by the wilderness: the hallucinatory eroticism of this canto merely transfers to this realm the antistructural forces and feelings elsewhere associated with war. Śaivism, of course, has from ancient times connected the erotic and the horrible;[164] but here this connection takes on the specific character of a common, partly comic "opening" to an unpredictable reality. Love, like war and sacrifice, unleashes a potential for newness, for the unknown; it, too, progresses through unsettling dreamscapes and waking visions; its exaggerated images and violent emotions may be externalized in grotesque forms; according to classical Tamil conceptions,[165] it tends to oscillate between fulfilment and denial. "Confusion" here is of the essence; it is the ordered, the rational, the safely delimited, that is suspect. In short, the effusion of erotic fantasy in this introductory canto sets in motion the internal processes that will culminate, appropriately, in the bizarre imagery of the battlefield.

The calls to open the gates fall silent with a final verse (74) describing the intertwining of red *kaḻunīr* blossoms and young lovers' lives in the women's dark hair. At once we are plunged into the violent heat of the wilderness, where Kālī is at home (75-96). Wild hyperbole conveys the intensity of the desert's heat: the Sun, seeking for his lost wife Chāyā ("Shadow"), thrusts his rays into every crevice in the cruel, dry earth (79). The shadow of the circling kite flees the burning heat (80). The deer, its mouth so dry that it would drink water even from out of a fire, licks the saliva from the mouth of the sharp-toothed wild dog—and is seized by a fit of hiccups (83). The only water in that wasteland is the sweat secreted by the rainclouds and the moon in their haste to escape its terrible heat (86). Trees are charred black like the breath of demons left languishing there by the fierce goddess (88). Serpents emerging from the tree hollows are like the withered tongues of thirsty demons (89). Winds swirling through this landscape cover its scattered gems (red rubies) with ash from the burning-ground (91)—a suggestion of the affinity between the wilderness and the cremation ground (both referred to as *kāṭu*) to be explored in the subsequent cantos. This section ends with a playful thought: the monkeys who fought as Rāma's army bridged the ocean (to Laṅkā) by throwing mountains into it, because in their confusion (*mayaṅkiṉave*) they failed to realize that a single grain of sand from the *pālai* wilderness would

[164] O'Flaherty (1973), pp. 236-38.

[165] See I.1.

have caused the ocean to dry up (96). Again, the keynote of this poem is sounded: we are in a state of continuing, indeed increasingly powerful *mayakkam*; the fantastic imagery is meant to deepen this bewilderment, to pry us loose from a conventional world in which the dimension of horror is muted or repressed.

And yet this dimension is perceived by the poet as inherent in everyday experience. He introduces us to the gruesome goddess (*aṇaṅku*) who inhabits this wasteland with the statement that the world itself is really her "ancient shrine" (*paḻaṅ koyil*, 97). The horrifying presence of Kālī cannot be relegated to the liminal zone of the wilderness; in truth, she and her demons are always with us, even when we indulge in self-deluding phantasies of security. This is an important element in Cayaṅkōṇṭār's vision: as in many other comic works, the use of grotesque, exaggerated images expresses an underlying realism and an interest in the constituent aspects of everyday, "normative" experience.[166] Nevertheless, the wilderness component of reality must be articulated in all its specific qualities and forms—and thus we are now treated to an elaborate description of Kālī's *pālai* shrine, situated in the burning ground (*cuṭukāṭu*), lit by the burning pyres, where the vultures and the jackals struggle over the corpses (120). This temple is a mockery of all the prescriptions of purity and auspiciousness: it is built upon a foundation of widows' ornaments (their husbands have been slain in battle by the Chola king, 98); its walls were fashioned from a mortar of blood and fat taken from slaughtered heroes, whose heads have become its building blocks; its gateways and towers are made from bones (99, 104). Moreover, this lovely shrine is the perfect setting for a sacrifice to its presiding deity:

> Fierce heroes of untiring strength
> call out to her:
>   "Give us a boon—
>   and in exchange
>   we shall cut off our limbs
>   and offer them to you!"
> Their clamor resounds
>   like the roaring of the sea. (109)
>
> They tend the fire of a sacrifice
>   beyond words,
> feeding it the rib bones
>   they take from their bodies,

[166] See above, IV.1.

while their oozing blood
  is the ghee poured into the blaze. (110)

Suddenly
they cut their heads
at the base of the neck
and place the severed heads
  in Aṇaṅku's hands—

heads still praising Kŏṟṟavai
while the truncated bodies
stand before her in worship. (111)

The last verse uses one of Cayaṅkŏṇṭār's favored devices, the simple but unsettling repetition of a central word: here "heads" (*ciram*) occurs three times, each time presenting a more lurid image—the heads that are first cut, with a single stroke; then delivered into the hands of the goddess; then, in the triumph over death which the heroes sought, allowed to go on with their happy praises. The whole, characteristically Śākta sacrifice is carried out in an absurd, almost whimsical manner: the bodies of the self-sacrificing heroes can now play (*viḷaiyāṭum uṭale*, 113), since they have accomplished their obvious duty, while famished demons follow the cavorting corpses in anticipation of their eventual collapse—for they are afraid to touch them during their dance of joy. The *yoginī* serving-girls, who must witness these rites every day, nonchalantly carry swords in one hand and severed heads in the other as they chatter among themselves (116). Grinning heads adorn the branches of the bamboo trees, and the wild-eyed demons (*cuḻal kaṇ cūrppey*) who notice them are so upset that they are unable to sleep (117)—an interesting inversion of the dream states celebrated in the opening canto and discussed above. In short, the shrine to the goddess is the site of satire gone routine; and yet this kind of macabre satire, which tends to recur throughout the *Kaliṅkattupparaṇi*, is perhaps the mildest of the poem's comic styles and forms.

At this point we are introduced to one contingent of circuslike players: the violent yet seductive goddess herself, described in fourteen voluptuous verses (121-134); then her troupes of ghouls and demons, who fearfully cling to her side, "since death is near" (145). Comic touches abound in the rich depiction of the demons: their hair hangs down like serpents crawling over their bodies; weeds grow in their nostrils; owls nest in their ears, where bats also fly about (141); their teeth are strings of hoes and ploughshares (142). The most prominent of these clownish devils are various disfigured types, such as the demon who was crippled when he slipped on the brains of dead kings splattered over a battlefield (146), or the ones blinded when they were splashed with the hot broth of blood and intestines which they were cooking (148). These types—especially the former—may recall to us the Vidūṣaka, with his physical deformities; the crippled hero of the comic folk-dramas; and even, perhaps, the series of lame or crippled kings.[167]

By now the nature of the *pālai* setting is fairly clear. We are within the depths of the boundary, face to face with the eery creatures of the imagination in its darkest mode of playing with the world; death is present in a wealth of gruesome, sensual forms displayed in conjunction with a demonic disorder; there is no longer any gap or division between fearsome vision and external expression. Thus the "inner" (*akam*) sensation of the demons, scorched by hunger like the burning desert itself, has turned their exterior black as well (*puṟam tīntavum*, 144): the boundary between inner and outer has disappeared. We should note here that the Tamil poetic tradition has also recognized the degree to which *akam* and *puṟam* (the "inner" world of love, the "outer" world of heroism or war) interpenetrate in the *pālai* wilderness; of all the five conventional regions (*tiṇai*) of love, *pālai* is the most likely to attract and incorporate *puṟam* elements.[168] This mingling of characteristics is well suited to the boundary zone, where, as we have seen, various processes of confusion (*mayakkam*) are at work—including the breaching of categories otherwise kept separate, as well as the passionate and confusing unions of love and of battle.[169] But this "mixed" quality of the wilderness is only part of a much wider concept of "mixing": the *pālai* region is referred to by the grammarians as *naṭuvunilaittiṇai*, the "middle" or "common" landscape, that is, that aspect of experience (symbolized by the wilderness) which infuses or inheres in all others.[170] *Pālai* is the region associated with the most intense forms of separation (*pirital*); thus its designation as central or common implies the possibility of experiencing the wasteland of separation, with all its attendant emotions, during other phases of love, even when the beloved is fully present. This notion is largely tragic in force; and, indeed, *pālai* poetry, in both Caṅkam and medieval times, tends to the tragic mode.[171] But the present case is rather dif-

[167] See IV.2 and VII.6.

[168] See the fine discussion by Richman (1982), pp. 30-52.

[169] On *mayakkam*, "mingling," see Egnor, pp. 111-13.

[170] *Tŏl. Pŏruḷ.* 1.11 (p. 12). Cf. Periakaruppan (1976), pp. 168-73.

[171] See above, I.5, on tragedy and separation; Shulman (1981).

ferent: it was Cayaṅkŏṇṭār's genius to have perceived and to have revealed the latent comedy of the wilderness—or, one might say, the central character of the grotesque. The wilderness that lurks within ordered life begins, even for Cayaṅkŏṇṭār, with separation—of the self from its moorings, the hero from his home—but its true power lies in unpredictable confusion and combination, in the creative transposition of inner into outer, in the chaotic potential actualized by the unconscious clown.

As in the case of the folk clowns,[172] a magical and comic toying with "reality" now becomes possible: an aged demon (*mutu pey*) entertains the goddess with a thousand magic tricks (*intiracālam* = Skt. *indrajāla*). He conjures up all the delightful scenes of the battlefield—rivers of blood, dead horses, dismembered elephants, dancing limbs severed from their bodies—and the famished audience of demons takes these visions to be real (*ivai mĕy ĕṉā*, 169). They try to scoop up mouthfuls of the imaginary blood; they bite into empty air as they fall upon the apparitions of enticing corpses; seeing their disappointment, the *yoginīs* laugh so hard that they break their ribs (173). At last the demons beg that the magical display be terminated, before they all perish. Kālī, however, is intrigued by the old demon's skill, and asks where he has acquired it. He names his *guru*: Uruttira yokiṉi, who lives in the Himālaya (177-78); and this now gives him (or rather the poet speaking through him) the opportunity to relate something which the old demon overheard during his period of study in the north—the *irāca pārampariyam*, the genealogy of the Chola kings as recited by Nārada to the Chola hero Karikālaṉ. An entire canto is given over to this dynastic history, clearly meant to serve as a prelude to Kulottuṅga's coming exploits and to the Kaliṅga campaign that forms the proper subject of the poem.

We need not follow the entire course of this campaign as portrayed by Cayaṅkŏṇṭār, with his own magical skill: in the history of Tamil poetry, there is no greater master of the linguistic mimicry of battle sounds, nor, for that matter, of the cruelly vivid tropes of war.[173] We hear and see the battle as it is described to the goddess by a demon witness who has come from Kaliṅga (his "account" is preceded by a lyrical canto dedicated to the birth and youth of Kulottuṅga, up to the point of his embarking on the Kaliṅga war). As the armies clash, with all the gory effects that a Tamil audience anticipates from a

[172] Above, IV.5.

[173] For discussion of the sound-symbolism, meter, etc., see Zvelebil (1974), pp. 210-12. Tamil literature does, however, offer many other examples of this predilection for gory battle scenes.

"proper" war scene, Kālī's demons lick their lips: they are still hungry and confused, but they know by now that a feast is imminent. One demon—an astrologer—has even had (of course) a happy dream, in which all the horrors of the battlefield are foreseen; and unlike the deceptive, frustrating dreams of the Chola women in the opening canto, this dream is immediately, starkly, tangibly rendered true. A violent explosion of energy overwhelms the Kaliṅga land; for a moment—an extended, ghastly, chaotic moment—all is wilderness and destruction. But it is crucial for us to note that even now, during and after the battle, the poet insists upon his biting comedies. Thus the survivors of the Kaliṅga army resort to various disguises in order to escape: some, plunging into thickets, find their hair and garments plucked off by the thorns; they remove their remaining hairs and come out, claiming to be naked Jains (467). Others tie their bowstrings across their breasts and pretend to be Brahmin pilgrims, with their triple threads, on their way to bathe in the Ganges (468); some drape themeselves in blood-soaked banners, shave their heads, and claim to be Buddhist monks (*cākkiyar*, 469); some take the jewels from their dead elephants as cymbals and maintain they are musicians (*pāṇar*) from the Telugu country (470).[174] These desperate masquerades mark the completion of the Chola victory: there are no other men left in Kaliṅga except for those depicted in wall paintings (471). The battlefield is now the scene of heart-rending visions conveyed to us, again, through satirical images or ironic contrasts. Jackals cluster around the dying warriors, waiting for their lives to depart, just as suppliants gather at the side of misers who give nothing until the hour of their death (479). Bees that have hovered around the temples of elephants in rut desert these elephants when they have fallen in battle, and move on to the flowers showered down by the gods—just as prostitutes (*pŏruṭ pĕṇṭir*) abandon a fallen client for a more promising source (480). This verse is the first of a series referring to women and thus harking back, with bitter irony, to the seductive images of the "opening of the gates": the great war banners have collapsed beside the fallen elephants that bore them, and now float on rivers of blood, like chaste women who are burnt on a bed of fire (*kaṉal amaḷi*) with the bodies of their dead husbands (481). Relentlessly, the poet holds to the analogy of love and war, but this time there is a note of blatant incongruity, with resulting black comedy: as the wives search the battlefield for

[174] As John Marr has pointed out in connection with this verse, there seems already to exist, at this early date, an association of Andhra and the Telugu language with music.

their husbands' bodies, one finds her slain husband biting his lips in the grimace of death; she is angry with him (*pulavi kūrntu*—the lovers' quarrel!) for the scar inflicted on his perfect lips, and in this state she abandons her own life (483). Another wife clasps her husband's body, lest it fall to the goddess Earth; jealous of the heavenly women who come to take her husband's spirit, she takes her life in order to accompany him (484). Another, less fortunate woman wanders the battlefield trying to reclaim her husband's scattered limbs (485).

But the most explicit and far-reaching of all the Kaliṅga war comedies occur only in the final canto, *kūḻ aṭutal*—the description of the demons' gluttonous revel on the battlefield, once the fighting is over. This is the "demons' sabbath" which Kālī's ghouls have been awaiting, and the gruesome feast that they prepare is in the best tradition of Tamil war poetry,[175] a culinary triumph that must surely outdo the witches' stew in *Macbeth*. The demons set up their kitchen in the shade of the circling vultures and the elephants' carcasses, and they proceed to cook a rich broth of blood, brains, flesh, fingernails, horses' teeth, and similar delicacies. When it is ready, the demon connoisseurs, mindful of past feasts, declare this one the tastiest ever (552). The demons file past to receive their portions, according to their proper rank: first comes the Brahmin ghoul, with gaping mouth, calling piteously in Sanskrit—*bhavati bhikṣāṃ dehi*, "Lady, give me alms" (566). Then there are the Jain demons who eat only one meal a day and must be given strained soup, lest any hairs be found in their serving (567); and the refined Buddhist demons, who feast only on cooked brains (568). Alas, a demon-thief has hidden the blind demon's soup bowl, and the hungry victim of this theft is left to grope helplessly about him, whining for food (570). The dumb demon gesticulates his hunger and his satisfaction at the portion he receives (571); a pregnant demoness licks her lips in pleasure (572); idiot demons turn their bowls upside down and are distressed to find they have lost their food (573). But first things first: guests must be honored with a serving before the local demons can begin (576). The meal proceeds (with vivid onomatopoeic effects in the verses); the demons' only regret is that Brahmā, the four-headed creator who naturally boasts four mouths, endowed each of *them* with only one (581). Betel chewing follows the banquet, and the demons finally give themselves over to games, songs, and dancing. They are satiated, happy, and at peace—the chaotic "opening" of the battle is attaining its inevitable closure, as order is temporarily restored—and the poem can now end with a series of

[175] Cf. *Cil.* 235-46.

"demonic" blessings bestowed upon the Chola king: may everyone rejoice, as he protects the world from age to age (596); may *dharma* exist everywhere and always, and divine mercy flourish; may the sages' austerities bear fruit; may the Vedic path spread, while Kali, the ruinous spirit of the Kali Age, vanquished by Apayaṉ (Kulottuṅga), goes into hiding; may fame (*pukaḻ*) spread through the world, which is now secure; may the clouds give rain (599).

This final note—the prayer for rain—may recall the magical reversals associated with the Virāṭa comedies; once again a largely comic "opening" of the mind has its desired effect upon the world outside. But the demons' concluding benediction also hints at other possibilities. On the one hand, the *Kaliṅkattupparaṇi*, with its clownish demons and hallucinatory landscapes, seems almost to sketch in the proper mise en scène for South Indian kingship as a whole: this institution, for all its associations with order and control,[176] is symbolically situated at the intersection of order and necessary disorder, and it is the latter dimension—the wilderness of comic chaos—that illuminates the king's career from within. Cayaṅkŏṇṭār's "serious" cantos relating the king's genealogy and early exploits thus fit naturally into the lurid context created by the poem in its entirety. On the other hand, this setting is by no means limited to the king and his specific, royal concerns; rather, as so often, the king embodies a truth felt to inhere in others' lives as well. The demons who cry out their blessings to the ruler are, it would seem, no different from the Chola heroes who have entered their domain; no different, in the end, from the audience that listens to their song. They actualize a mode of experience which, perhaps, one shrinks from recognizing: like the clumsy, distorted, farcical demons of the battlefield, most living beings feed on corpses; the awkward, the surreal, the grotesque pervade our lives; the wilderness, with its terrors, its separations, its chaotic potential, its comedies of the border, inheres in every ordered thing. The wild destruction of the *pralaya*, the world conflagration, lies not ahead of us but within our given world; the magic "openings" (*tiṟappu*) and the creative "minglings" (*mayakkam*) of death, of sacrifice, and of love are always with us; we cross this boundary each minute—and still we are afraid. The *Kaliṅkattupparaṇi* addresses such fears with comedy, which transcends and transforms everday terrors, as the king who is both warlord and circus master tempers the tragic aspects of his role with clowning. But for his kingdom, this poem suggests, the *pralaya* is always *now*—a presence permanently embodied in the very structure of the South Indian state.

or life?

[176] See Chapter II above.

8. Summary: The Harlequin on the Throne

This chapter has explored certain aspects of the disorderly side of South Indian kingship, the side symbolically articulated in the various images of the king's exile or fall. I have argued that these images tend to have a basic comic coloring wholly appropriate to the drive toward decomposition or dis-integration: the king brings to his kingdom something of the unsettling, playful shatter-effect of the clown. This is not to say that king and clown can be identified in a simple manner. We must distinguish carefully between levels of symbolic representation, as well as between the different types within each level. Thus it is important to recall that formal, iconic images of the king, such as those discussed in Chapter II, present an exemplary figure literally glowing with an unearthly brilliance (*tejas*) that is often correlated to his essential virtue and relentless adherence to the cultural order. Such luminous images turn up regularly in panegyric and in theoretical statements on *rājadharma*. The striking fact, already noted several times, is that this level readily dissolves into its antithesis. Royal *tejas*, one soon discovers, was felt to conceal from others' eyes a reality always known to be complex and problematic:

> A man may be of low caste,
> he may be a fool,
> he may be a bastard,
> but when he has money,
> he is king.[177]

So much for the divine splendor of the dharmic paragon and defender of right! In the hands of the *bhakti* poets, such cynicism often blends with pathos:

> Kings
>   who rule the earth all alone
>   for long years
>
> will one day hobble
> on legs bitten by black dogs
>
> and beg from a broken pot
> here
>   in this very life
> with the whole world watching:

[177] *Sumatiśatakamu* 108, translated by V. Narayana Rao.

don't tarry then

think of the lord's feet
and live.[178]

Pathetic images of this sort serve the poet's polemical stance against kingship and the life of the court (as opposed to the life of totalistic devotion);[179] they nevertheless accurately reflect the "felt" reality of Indian kingship as inclusive of a dark, problematic phase of exile or downward transformation.

The various stories and poems we have examined suggest that transformations in this direction occur as normative components of the symbolism of South Indian kingship. The very regularity with which the "exilic" themes recur in the literature points to their overall necessity in the conceptual scheme of kingship, although Brahminical theory failed to isolate or to identify such themes as explicit and necessary elements in the composite royal role. Rather, they have remained as powerful affective components of the king's career as described in myth, in the epics, in legend, and in various poetic genres. As we have seen (following Heesterman's analysis of the Vedic rituals of kingship),[180] there is a historical legacy involved in these stories: the Pāṇḍavas' years in the forest, like Rāma's exile, preserve something of the ancient vision of the king who, in order to claim his authority, sets out for the wilderness in the guise of a "Brahminical" *dīkṣita*.[181] Certain important associations aroused by the descriptions of the "fallen" kings have been discussed in the light of this legacy from the *Brāhmaṇa* texts—for example, the notion of a revitalizing contact with impurity (as in the Virāṭa "carnival," with its *dīkṣā*-like features),[182] or the more generalized effect of "evil" (*pāpa*) in imparting dynamism and life to the kingdom organized around its problematic presence (as in the exemplary tale of Pṛthu).[183] In more abstract terms, we can see (with the help of the ancient ritual texts as well as of our Chola war poem, the *Kaliṅkattupparaṇi*) that the fertilizing presence of the wilderness must be incorporated within the ordered realm of the king-

[178] Nammāḻvār, *Tiruvāymŏḻi* 1.1.4, translated by Ramanujan (1981), p. 59.

[179] This poetic attitude has been discussed at length by V. Narayana Rao in the introduction to his forthcoming translation, with Hank Heifetz, of *Kāḷahastīśvaraśatakamu*.

[180] Heesterman (1978); above, III.4 at n. 111.

[181] Heesterman (1978), pp. 14-15.

[182] Above, section 6.

[183] Above, II.4; and see the important discussion of this issue by Waghorne (1980).

dom, at whatever cost to stability and safety.[184] But these concepts with their rich history of associations and narrative exemplification were assimilated in the specific patterns of the medieval South Indian state, which brought its own compulsions and historical aims to this inheritance. Here the ancient alternation of kingly and Brahmin identities, or the king's magnetic pull toward the wilderness, take on a new, specific character within the sphere of political symbolism. The fundamental problem that remains has to do with the implications of the king's disorderly phase for the symbolic ordering of the society as a whole, on a level at which basic, recurrent images are not necessarily brought into relation with consciously held notions of what constitutes the norm. It is on this level that the comic overtones of the king's career, as seen in the medieval (especially Chola) sources, are most suggestive and instructive.

Before addressing these wider implications, we must try to define more precisely the similarities and the differences between South Indian kings and clowns, in the light of major comic elements that we have noticed in the course of the discussion. The shared features may be simply stated. First, and most strikingly, both sets of figures are comic. They may not be uniformly or consistently funny—indeed, the king is decidedly *not* of such a type—but neither are they uniformly "serious," in the sense of the word that relates to order and decorum. Both figues do, however, partake of the second kind of seriousness we have seen—the playful, transformative seriousness of laughter and comic observation. In several of the stories we have analyzed, the royal hero seems to plunge deeper into comedy as the tale progresses; more precisely, he is forced to develop dramatically, at least for some time, a comic side that is always latent in his role.

Second, there is a marked convergence in the physical attributes of the clowns and the kings, when the latter attain their transformed—often Untouchable—stage. Triśaṅku becomes dark, deformed, an object of ridicule; Indra turns into a clumsy ogre, or becomes possessed by a hysterical demon; Arjuna is reduced to a transvestite or "androgynous" disguise; many legendary kings are said to have been temporarily crippled or lame. Let us recall the lumpish, deformed character of the puppet clowns, or of the Vidūṣaka. Both groups are grotesque, somewhat unsettled—they tend to be in constant motion—and unsettling, even a little frightening. Both are in some sense strange

[184] Falk (1974); Shulman (1979a); Heesterman (1978), p. 10, on the relation of *grāma* to *araṇya*. In Heesterman's formulation: the king belongs to the *grāma*, the settled zone, but his authority comes from *araṇya*—the wilderness.

or "other," hence dark and even demonic. Both are occasionally related to other alien, wilderness types such as Kālī's comic ghouls (in the *Kaliṅkattupparaṇi*) or the forest tribes or Untouchables (the Niṣāda born from Vena; the Untouchables among whom the lost king or prince builds a new life).[185]

Third, the kings share, in different ways, the clowns' essential quality of marginality. One sees this clearly even in geographical (or rather cosmographical) descriptions: the kings fall from their place in the properly ordered universe to various hidden or paradoxical situations, such as an island in the midst of the sea, the forested slopes of the Himālaya, a lotus pond in the northeastern corner of the earth (in the classical versions of the Vṛtra myth), or—most striking of all—a topsy-turvy world hanging halfway between heaven and earth. In this stage the king disappears into a boundary zone, whence he has to be rescued and reclaimed. The cycle of his transformation thus tends to involve an initial vision of "normal" order, replete with tensions and latent conflict; a stage in which these conflicts burst forth, driving the king from his throne into a shadowy world of reversals, confusion, impurity, and geographical remoteness; and a final period of restoration, in which proper boundaries are again established (the human and celestial worlds become clearly distinct again, each with its own king; in the *bhakti* texts, a new center—the terrestrial shrine—may be recognized and defined). Such, for example, is the pattern of the Indra and Mucukunda myths; in the Triśaṅku story, the inner tensions of kingship propel the hapless ruler into a final state of limbo (neither heaven nor earth), whence there is no return. This latter pattern of "neither-nor" liminality needs to be sharply distinguished from the cyclical pattern of exile and restoration. Yet in both cases we may detect two crucial components of the royal career: its "ordered" side, and its dissolved, transformed aspect. Both sides are normative, and they are interdependent, issuing into one another; whether one looks at the endless cycle of alternating stages or at the linear progression of the doomed human kings such as Triśaṅku, one sees the image of a king who is internally divided, trapped in the anomalies and ambiguities of his situation, condemned to live through these tensions in self-transforming patterns that link the brilliant exemplar with his shadow, security with loneliness and loss.

This dynamic, composite image of the king corresponds in part to

[185] As in the story of Lavaṇa in the *Yogavāsiṣṭha*: see O'Flaherty (1984). As O'Flaherty notes, the king's sojourn among the Untouchables is seen as a kind of renunciation; Untouchables, like demons, share the "outsider" quality of the renouncer or the sage. And see below, VII.4 at notes 80-81.

the clown's relentless internal oscillation. The disparity between the king's basic aspects produces an effect similar to that of the clown's essential incoherence, his intentional jumbling of attributes and actions. The cyclical pattern of exile and return simply reveals in a temporal sequence the enduring disharmony of the king's inherent features: he is both pure (or purified, white or golden) and repeatedly subject to contamination (encumbered with evil, black, Untouchable); he is endowed with royal splendor (*tejas* and *śrī*), yet often deformed (a hunchback, dwarf, or cripple); self-controlled and detached, a master *yogin*, yet given to unbridled eroticism and frequently victimized by egoism and arrogant excess; a vigorous, manly hero who is also sexually ambiguous (a eunuch or an androgyne); properly devoted to his Brahmin *guru*, yet at times openly rebellious and anti-Brahminical; partly divine and also all too human, or worse—a hideous demon. The myths tend to concentrate each cluster of attributes in a separate stage, so that we witness the "orderly" hero transformed into a grotesque clown. At the same time, they highlight the comic potential of this transformation no less than that of the synchronic, paradoxical images (for example, the comic antikings, such as Nahuṣa; or the iconic inversions of the Sanskrit farce).[186] The diachronic model gives us an intense, clownlike stage, ultimately reversed; the synchronic model is clownlike through and through.

So much for the similarities; but there are also crucial differences between king and clown that have been repeatedly evident in the stories and in our discussion. The first has to do with the self-consciousness of the dramatic clowns. The king is reflexive only by default; he is never as acutely aware of himself as is the clown; his marginality is somehow unexpected, hence all the more painful. The clown knows he is a clown and uses this knowledge to achieve a premeditated effect (although in seeking to produce this effect, the clown may be no less tragically "driven" than is the king, in *his* cycles). This distinction is a basic one, and has implications for our appreciation of the two figures: as A. K. Ramanujan has remarked, in general we laugh *at* the king, but we laugh *with* the clown.[187] (The Vidūṣaka, as noted earlier, blurs this boundary—of all the Brahmin clowns, he is the closest to the king's situation.) We could thus trace in the outlines of a typology that would embrace both sets of figures discussed above, arranged on either side of this fundamental divide in conscious awareness. On one side, the royal clowns in all their diversity—the whirligig

[186] Above, II.5.

[187] A. K. Ramanujan, private communication, August 1980.

clowns such as Indra, in his dizzying cycles of transformation (and his flawed human replacements, Nahuṣa, Yayāti, Mucukunda); the autistic anomaly Triśaṅku, a human yo-yo trapped in his own marginal, inverted space; gamblers and other ludic masters, such as Yudhiṣṭhira and Nala; the mad devotees such as Ceramāṉ Pĕrumāḷ, with his Brahmin White Clown (Cuntaramūrtti); tragic buffoons (Rāvaṇa, not discussed in this chapter); insanely romantic clowns (to be discussed in the next); truly foolish or idiotic kings (the heroes of the Sanskrit farce); the lugubrious clowns-in-exile, such as Bhīma and the androgynous Bṛhannaḍā in the Virāṭa "festival" (the series of integrating inversions); and the "heroic" clowns of the wartime circus, with its chaotic qualities of immersion and renewal. All of these clowns, like Quixote, fail to recognize their own comic qualities (except in occasional, usually very superficial ways). On the other side of the divide, we find the king's comic aspect externalized in explicit types such as the Vidūṣaka and the ironic jester. Together, the two groups form a continuum of comic figures, all of whom are endowed with basic clownish features that we have stressed—a rooted instability; virtual impotence in the "real" world of deeds; a dubious relation to that "reality," which corrodes its cohesiveness; a heavy burden of affect, which liberates for them, and for others, the powerful emotions of passionate experience and all the anxiety of the border; at the same time, a certain disengagement or comic retreat to the edges of life; a fondness for the anomalous, which is nevertheless seen as central to the norm; above all, a dynamism linked to transformative indeterminacy, which affects both their own internal organization and the everyday order to which they are exposed. These features—the list is not intended to be exhaustive—are by no means limited to Indian comedy; they merely represent an attempt to characterize a limited series of comic types that have a bearing, in this culture, on the articulation of the political order.

If we wished to rank these types into broadly differentiated strata, we might see the king in his comic transformations as belonging to a "lower" level of comedy in its cruel or derisive aspect[188]—for here the comic hero is largely a butt or victim, unconscious of his ridiculous role; he may recall the Śakāra of the *Little Clay Cart*,[189] or the abused

[188] An aspect stressed by theorists of comedy from Aristotle (*Poetics* 1449a) through Bergson (1956) ("A comic character is generally comic in proportion to his ignorance of himself. The comic person is unconscious"—p. 71). This notion is wholly inappropriate for the sophisticated Brahmin jester as well as for the self-conscious folk clowns discussed above.

[189] Above, IV.2, Excursus; and cf. Duckworth (1971), pp. 305-28.

clowns of slapstick or farce. The more sophisticated Brahmin clown types take us to a second level, of conscious reflexivity and the creative reordering of a shattered world; here we seem to move from the cruelty of mockery to the joys of cognitive play with incongruities and conflict.[190] There are still higher levels: the truly magical playfulness of the folk clowns, which the royal comedies never attain; and, perhaps at the pinnacle of comic consciousness, a compassionate clowning sometimes associated with the god. We shall observe something of this last type in connection with the tragic hero Karṇa, for Indian comedies of this kind are closely bound up with tragedy, and thus wholly remote from the "painless" forms of the comic that writers from Aristotle to Kierkegaard have described.[191]

Indeed, pain is a decisive component of much Indian comedy. But its power lies hidden within kingship to such a degree that it serves to differentiate in another respect the king from the clown: the latter can often elude this link with suffering or with evil, whereas the king cannot. A residue of tragic *determinacy* always adheres to the king, who could no more be wholly comic than he could become completely serious (in the European mold). His inner division is, in effect, tripartite: an iconic ideal (the "white" king, Pṛthu) combines with the veiled anti-iconic persona (the "black" king Vena, or the king as bandit); but this tragic Harlequinesque conjunction unfolds further into the king's unconscious comic aspect, when he is truly Harlequin—an unstable, oscillating, self-transforming clown. The comic aspect illuminates and transcends the tragically bifurcated image, but the royal amalgam remains, nonetheless, a tragi-comic blend. It is this ambiguous mixture which is symbolically located at the culture's center, and which helps to express its essential *indeterminacy* and the ambiguous unraveling of its own limits. The king holds both forces within him—tragic construction of a limited order, and its comic transcendence and decomposition—but even his comic experiences are

[190] Duckworth (1971), pp. 310-12. This is a second major theme in analytic comic theory.

[191] Aristotle (*Poetics* 1449a), with which Kierkegaard (1960) heartily concurs: "It is handsome and correct of Aristotle that he wishes to separate from the sphere of the ridiculous that which tends to arouse compassion, to which also belongs the wretched and the pitiful" (p. 459 n.). Similarly, Kierkegaard rejects any connection between comedy and despair: "A comic apprehension on the basis of despair is also illegitimate, for despair is despair because it does not know the way out, does not know the contradiction cancelled, and *ought therefore* to apprehend the contradiction tragically, which is precisely the way to its healing" (p. 464—my emphasis). A more complete contrast to certain South Indian notions of comedy—especially a "divine" comedy—is hard to imagine. See below, VII.7.

infused with darkness and with pain. We could apply to him Fellini's statement about the clown's emotional roots in disaster: "Nothing is sadder than laughter; nothing more beautiful, more magnificent, more uplifting and enriching than the terror of deep despair."[192] Among the South Indian kings we have studied, only the devotional fools such as Ceramāṉ Pĕrumāḷ can, perhaps, escape this characterization.

Not so the Brahmin clowns, whose comic powers are consciously developed and far more autonomous than the king's. Brahmin comedy ultimately subsumes the tragi-comic flux of kingship, and in this way makes a unique and necessary contribution to the workings of the state. For the Brahmin, as we have seen, is "wedded" to the king in a problematic but indissoluble bond. He brings to this marriage his own inner divisions, which correspond to the king's tripartite soul: the "serious" Brahmin is also tragically divided into sacrificer and Renouncer, two conflicting (yet also intertwining) personae; the oscillation between these two poles situates the Brahmin at the cultural boundary, in a position that naturally opens into the comic commentary of the clown. Here, staring back at the hopeless entanglements of the world, the Brahmin can play at weaving and unweaving the baffling skein of creation, at the center of which lies the always baffled king. The interaction of these two figures propels the state on its wavering course; often the strains produced by this union have the effect of liberating the comic aspect of either, or both, of these actors. In "marrying" the king—who in effect props apart the two "serious" Brahmin roles of sacrificer and *sannyāsin*—the Brahmin becomes his own caricature, the debunking, debased Vidūṣaka. Having become incorporated in the world, tied down in relation to its ruler, the Brahmin clown resorts to impugning the status of reality in its everyday manifestations—which include, above all, the romantic phantasies of meaningfulness. The king, on the other hand, faced with this complex Brahmin partner to whom he must, in theory, defer, is set in motion between *his* roles—reaching for heaven, and grasping the earth; self-abnegation, and the bandit's greed; the drive toward transcendence, and an immersion in life's impurities. He seeks vainly to stabilize the unwieldy and wildly moving kingdom that his own Brahmin *guru* teaches him to disdain or, at the very least, to perceive as ambiguous and deeply flawed. Moreover, in seeking stability from within his own fragmented inner state, the king effectively shatters the very world he would protect; whereas the Brahmin clown encompasses and "integrates" this same world by his persistent fragmentation, his

[192] Fellini (1976), p. 54.

creative disturbance and reconstruction of its refractory, changing parts.[193]

It is this combination of two inherently complex and dynamic figures that gives the state its fundamental character. Brahmin and king may strive to achieve a balance in their association, but they are both far too "unbalanced" for such a movement to become stable and dependable; one side or the other soon overloads the scales and thus brings to the surface the other's latent conflicts. Often, as we have seen, they seem to become one another—to slip into the all-too-familiar ambiguities of the partner's roles. The king plays at renunciation, the Brahmin at killing, and always with the knowledge that these identities do, indeed, interpenetrate; that each has contributed something to the other's native inheritance. But the two, although very alike, are not equal; the *dharma* theorists are, in fact, right in stressing the Brahmin's superiority. For his transformations are the more far-reaching, the more encompassing and extreme; he brings the boundary into the kingdom's center and informs the state with its ever unresolved ambiguity. He may begin, at the border, with a serious, divided role, unable finally to leave the world, or to enter it; but as he approaches the center and its key figure, the king, he transforms it through comic dissolution—first becoming a comic clown himself (thus transcending the "straight" Brahmin personae, with their tragic conflicts), then allying himself with the king in an institutionalized corrosion of the realm (Vidūṣaka with *nāyaka*, court jester with the ruler). Joined with him, the king embodies a tragi-comic inconstancy; the center has opened up to unending transformation and the comic transcendence of its own given limits. The magical transformer—the ironic or playful Brahmin from outside—is married to the major symbol of order, the tragi-comic king, who is himself transformed without rest, driven through his cycles of masks and changes, from iconic paragon to helpless buffoon.

And with him the kingdom, too, is driven through the contrary movements of building and destroying, *pravṛtti* and *nivṛtti*. Its structures are weak, and infinitely flexible; it enshrines ambiguity as an epistemological principle, and self-transcendence as an ontological "fact"; it fashions stability out of instability, and integrates by way of ceaseless disintegration and decomposition. It is always unfinished, in the process of becoming, and unraveling itself; dissonance and disharmony are its enduring features, which it recognizes and sustains. It coheres in motion and transformation; its major symbols affirm this

[193] I am grateful to Don Handelman for this perception.

state, even as they enact its processes in their stories. The royal clown at its center realizes in his own person this metaphysic of movement and shattered wholeness. In contrast with his European counterpart, who has merely loaned his crown and sceptre to the fool, the South Indian king is required to dress *himself* in motley—for, like Crazy Jane, he must discover that "nothing can be sole or whole/that has not been rent."

· VI ·

All the King's Women

No sin will ever rub off on her. Born to prostitutes, she was an exception to all rules. She was ever-auspicious, daily wedded, the one without widowhood. How can sin defile a running river? It's good for a drink when a man's thirsty, it's good for a wash when a man's filthy, and it's good for bathing the god's images with; it says Yes to everything, never a No. Like her.[1]

1. Of Courtesans and Queens

Crazy Jane, in fact, has her own place in the medieval South Indian royal court. The South Indian king is surrounded by a plethora of women, who arrange themselves around him in various complex patterns and interrelations. There are, to begin with, his human wives—at least two of them (but often many more), of whom one is usually from his own caste and one, at least, from a lower caste.[2] The king expresses through his marriage alliances his identification with the entire range of the social order; similarly, the god—whom the king mirrors in many ways—tends to have both a properly "divine" wife and a lowly human bride.[3] Then the king is clearly said to be the husband of the Earth, whom he "enjoys" (*bhuj*) in loving union, and who will be "widowed" at his death;[4] and yet this is, in itself, a somewhat ambiguous relation, for the Earth is recognized as a pro-

[1] Anantha Murthy (1976), p. 43 (translated A. K. Ramanujan).

[2] Dumont (1959); Shulman (1980b), pp. 267–94.

[3] For example, Murukaṉ is married to the prim and properly celestial Devasenā, and to the earthy Vaḷḷi; Veṅkaṭeśvara has his usual consort, Lakṣmī-Śrī, and a local Tamil bride, Padmāvatī. The two wives are frequently at odds with one another; a whole literature (the *ecal* folk genre) describes their quarrels.

[4] See the excellent study by Minoru Hara (1973).

miscuous wife (*sarvagamyā*) who has been "married" to endless kings, and who can look forward to many more "husbands" of this sort.[5] No less ambiguous is the king's intimate relation with the goddess, either in her form as Śrī, "royal splendor"—a notoriously fickle figure[6]—or as the warrior maiden Durgā or Durgā-Lakṣmī (the latter a popular icon on Chola temples). Often the goddess is seen as a major support of the king and a source of his vital powers: thus the Nāyak kings of Maturai received their scepter (*cĕṅkol*) from the hands of Mīnākṣī.[7] Moreover, at Maturai, as elsewhere in South India, the major local dynasty was said to have been literally born from the local goddess;[8] in dealing with this deity, the king was thus confronting his own direct ancestress. The king is "married" to Śrī (Tamil Tirumakaḷ), incarnate in his first queen (*mahiṣī*), as well as to Victory (Vijayā), the goddess triumphant in battle; in the latter case, the analogy of love and war seems still to hold.[9] In addition to these liaisons, we should remember that the king has a "feminine" side all his own: like the goddess, he is a "mother" to his kingdom (with all the complex associations of maternity in South India);[10] and, like Arjuna-Bṛhannaḍā, he has an underlying identification with androgyny, or a latent feminine persona. The metaphor of "marriage" is also, of course, applied to the king's association with his Brahmin *purohita*, as we have seen. Finally, and of central importance for our exploration of royal symbolism, there is the king's conventional relationship with his courtesans (*veśyā*), who are a stable, essential element of the court. This, too, is a complex, ambiguous connection that the king shares with the god, who has his own dancing-girls (courtesans and concubine-wives) in his shrines.[11]

In short, so overwhelmed is the monarch by female attention and

[5] *Ibid.*, p. 114; cf. Hiltebeitel (1980).

[6] Hiltebeitel (1976), pp. 143-91 (especially p. 163); cf. *MBh* 12.217, 221; Sternbach (1953), p. 85 (aphorisms 433 and 436). A Pallava inscription depicts Śrī seated on a swing during a battle—in doubt as to which side would win! (See the Kūram plates of Parameśvaravarman I, SII 1, no. 151; Stein [1978], p. 137.)

[7] Nagaswamy (1978), p. 126; cf. van den Hoek (1978); Östör (1980), pp. 26-27; Marglin (1980), pp. 159-60, 320-22. A similar relation seems to have obtained in late medieval Mysore.

[8] *Tiruviḷai*. 4-5. See also Breckenridge (1978), on the Cetupatis.

[9] The Chola queens are identified explicitly with Śrī/Tirumakaḷ in the *ulā* poems discussed below.

[10] See above, II.3-4.

[11] The so-called *devadāsīs*, by now a vanishing group (although their descendants can still be found scattered throughout South India). See the studies by Marglin (1980) and Kersenboom (1984). On the *veśyā* generally, see the materials collected by Moti Chandra.

demands that it is a wonder he finds time for anything else in his life—if indeed he does! As we shall see, certain Tamil poems seem to confirm our doubts. All in all, we are presented with a remarkable picture of a richly diversified feminine presence around the king, a picture that might have something to do with the relative facelessness of the ruler himself, who seems almost to be swallowed up by his women. Nevertheless, we should not hasten to conclude that the king is given over to an officially sanctioned (or, indeed, required) frenzied eroticism. As always in South India, things are not that simple. The king does, it is true, indulge in erotic pastimes, as we have learned from Kampaṉ's idealized depiction of a highly "Tamilized" Daśaratha:

> He crossed the sea of pleasure joined to *śrī*
> by immersing himself
> to his heart's content.[12]

Yet there are many indications in the literature that the king's erotic experience was both frustrating in various ways—on principle!—and subject to important limitations. Let us look, for example, at the following cautionary tale from Tirupperūr:

> King Tirilokacoḻaṉ ruled the Chola land as a devout Śaiva, and all his people, too, were devoted to Śiva and the Śaiva way. Once on Śivarātri he went to worship the god at Tiruviṭaimarutūr, and there he saw a group of Brahmin Kāpālikas who had come from Nepal. He marveled at their appearance but failed to look into their hearts. An old Brahmin from this group addressed the king: "Your Highness, our home is in Nepal, but we have come here after hearing of your fame and the richness of your country. This is our knowledge: the true source of joy in the world is sexual union with beautiful women. Some say that the world is created by a god, but they are fools; has anyone ever seen such a god? There *is* no immortal deity; only the body is lasting and real. The world is created and increases through sexual union, which is the finest thing there is; and *it* is enhanced by drinking wine. So discard all this talk of salvation, O great king!"
>
> Hearing this speech, the king became confused; he mistook lies for the truth. He therefore abandoned the Vedic way and gave himself completely to wanton excesses; thus, drunk and obsessed with women, he ruled the world. And since a king's subjects always imitate their ruler, the inhabitants of the Chola land also broke all bounds. Seeing this disastrous state of affairs, Brahmā

[12] Above, II.1 (*Irāmāvatāram* 1.173).

sent the sage Nārada to enlighten the king. Nārada hastened to his court and, while chanting the *pañcākṣara*, sprinkled water on the king's face: at once Tirilokacoḻaṉ's delusion passed, and he bowed at the sage's feet and asked how he could free himself from the evil *karma* he had now acquired. The sage directed him to the god's shrine at Perūr, where his evil deeds would be healed. The Kāpālikas, hearing that the king had been brought back to the proper path, fled the land.[13]

This late medieval tale offers us another example of the king gone "mad"—not, this time, through devotional excesses (as with Ceramāṉ Pĕrumāḷ and Mucukunda) but by heretical teaching stemming from the Himālayan wilds. (We should note in passing that this text hints at historical links between South India and the Tantric traditions of the Northeast—a phenomenon that certainly deserves detailed study.) The Nepali Kāpālikas should, by rights, be Śaivas themselves, of an extreme cast, but the doctrine they teach the Chola king is "pure" heresy; by the time of this text, the very name "Kāpālika" must have become synonymous, for pious South Indian Śaivas, with an obscene materialism and hedonism. And it is this—the hedonistic abandon—that the myth wishes to deny the Chola king, who must be cured of his heresy by the sage sent down from heaven. Note that the "Kāpālika" teaching in this tale is admirably suited to a theory that would connect sexual license on the part of the king with the fertility of his kingdom (or, indeed, of the entire world); a connection of precisely this sort is sometimes cited in explanation of the presence of the *veśyā*-courtesans in the Indian court or temple.[14] In other words, the king's eroticism, specifically as directed at the *veśyās*, would symbolize and also effectively stimulate the forces of auspiciousness and fertility in his kingdom. Although there is clearly some truth to this view, it is certainly significant that in the present case the king's erotic drive is severely *curbed*. In effect, the Chola king has to be rescued from his own eroticism, from sensual intoxications that have led him astray. This sober attitude is also relevant to the king's association with his dancing-girls.

If we look more closely at the symbolism of the *veśyā* (and of her analogue in the temple), a fascinating complexity emerges. Much more

[13] *Perūrppurāṇam* 30.1–33.

[14] Cf. Gonda (1975). Similar explanations are frequently offered for the *maithuna* figures on Indian temples. Inden (1978), p. 44, notes that the king places earth from the doorway of a courtesan on his loins during his consecration; this act is interpreted as suggesting a concentrated sexual potency.

work needs to be done on the roles played by these women and the precise interrelations of *veśyā, devadāsī*, and king; but certain recurring themes can be tentatively isolated now. The *veśyā*, like her mythic prototype, the *apsaras*, is, indeed, associated with fertility—more specifically, with rain.[15] In this respect, she is naturally brought into relation with the king, who is ultimately responsible for the continued fertility of his realm. But the *veśyā*'s stimulation of fertile powers through her erotic action works only for the world at large, never (properly) for herself—a pregnant *veśyā* is almost a contradiction in terms. The *veśyā* is clearly not meant to produce children; when she does, she is endangering her career, indeed her very essence. Here her role is sharply distinguished from that of a wife (whose fertility may be felt to come at the expense of any true eroticism).[16] The wife and the *veśyā* have split between them the roles of fertility and eroticism; but we are then left with the paradox that a symbol of barren eroticism (the courtesan) is needed to bring about the longed-for state of non-erotic fertility (in the home). This stark division no doubt oversimplifies the matter, but already we can sense that the circle of courtesans surrounding the king bring their own ambiguities to the royal court.

The ambiguities deepen when we consider the symbolic import of the *veśyās*' sexual role. On the one hand, their seductive allure undoubtedly matches the king's own inherent charm: he is himself a handsome "lord of desire" (*māninīmanmatha*, a Kāma to women) who conquers women much as he conquers his enemies in battle (here we must forget for a moment the images we have studied of leprous, crippled, or otherwise deformed kings). We shall have more to say of this theme in a moment. The *veśyās* are a particularly appropriate vehicle for expressing this royal capacity, since they bring to "love," indeed to life itself, an undying auspiciousness—being unmarried, they can never be widowed, and are therefore *always* auspicious (*nityamaṅgalī*), "daily wedded" (and, at least in theory, always beautiful?—*nityakalyāṇī*).[17] Here again they are set apart from the class of "ordinary" wives. But what is the nature of their erotic link with the king? Even to speak of "love," in quotation marks, is perhaps to go too far. In general, it is quite improper for the king to feel love for his *veśyās*—real love, as we shall see, weakens him unendurably; and, as

[15] Marglin (1980), pp. 259-75; O'Flaherty (1973), pp. 43-50.

[16] Note also that a South Indian wife should, preferably, bear male children; a *veśyā*, if she *must* have a child, should have a girl—to carry on her profession (V. Narayana Rao).

[17] As in the passage quoted as the epigraph to this chapter. Cf. Marglin (1980), pp. 255-57, 272; Kersenboom (1984), pp. 340-42.

Purūravas learns to his cost in Kālidāsa's drama, it is no simple matter to make a courtesan a queen.[18] Of course, Urvaśī, like the *veśyā*-heroine of Śūdraka's *Little Clay Cart*, does offer love to the hero;[19] but in this she is breaking ranks with her profession, for the *veśyā* is always cautioned not to fall in love.[20] She is, indeed, trained to harden herself against feeling, and above all against real attachment (*āsakti*) to a man; and, as many passages tell us, this triumph over attachment makes the *veśyā* rather like the dispassionate *yogin* or *sannyāsin*.[21] Like the renouncer, the *veśyā* should exemplify the virtues of absolute indifference. Here we may have touched upon a partial explanation for the paradoxical association of *veśyās* and *devadāsīs* with notions of chastity and even of virginity.[22] A distinction in levels must be made: on one level, the *veśyā*'s "chastity" reflects her separation from the category of common prostitutes; she is somewhat closer to a concubine, perhaps, in that her erotic relationships tend to be fairly stable and enduring; whereas the *devadāsī*, for her part, is clearly *not* engaged in a "trade."[23] But on another level, the relative openness of the *veśyā*'s eroticism and its freedom from emotional involvement make it pos-

[18] On Urvaśī, the *apsaras*, as prototypical of the hetaera, see Ruben (1956), pp. 65-78. It should be remarked in this context that the courtesan is often *compared* to the king (as Sternbach states, [1953, p. 143], this is by far the most common simile for courtesans in Sanskrit literature)—since both indulge in "sin," are indifferent to others' sufferings, blend truth and falsehood, cruelty and mercy; both, moreover, seek their own advantage before all else. And cf. *Manusmṛti* 4.85: ten courtesans are equal to one king.

[19] This may well be a universal theme—the prostitute with a heart of gold. And see Ruben (1956), p. 70.

[20] See, for example, *Ubhayābhisārikā*, pp. 16-17. In Dhūrjaṭi's *Śrīkāḷahastīśvaramāhātmyamu* (4.28), an experienced prostitute instructs her daughters in the professional ethic: "You must make love with the clients (*viṭulan*, Skt. *viṭa*) without truly uniting with them, as oil sits upon the tongue, or a drop of water clings to a lotus-leaf. . . ." (*jiḍḍu nāluka jalamu rājīvadalamu . . . viṭulā/galaciyunu galayakundanga valayu lalana*). Note the Upaniṣadic metaphor—the drop of water on a leaf—which serves elsewhere to indicate the soul's detachment from the world. The implied association of the prostitute with a kind of renunciation or detachment is significant, as we shall see.

[21] See Marglin (1980), p. 30; *Bhagavadajjuka*, p. 74; Sternbach (1953), pp. 50, 71-72; n. 1 above.

[22] Marglin (1980), pp. 275-80. Similarly for the *apsaras*, as Anantha Murthy remarks in another context: "It is said Kannada is like an apsara. In the myth, the apsara remains a virgin despite her many love-affairs. So is Kannada. It has taken on Sanskrit, Persian and English (words), but it remains Kannada." Anjaneyulu (1980). Cf. the epic heroine Mādhavī, repeatedly rendered virginal: *MBh* 5.104-121; Dumézil (1971), pp. 316-30. And see the Aruṇācalam myth below, section 4.

[23] Marglin (1980), pp. 249-50. In Orissa, the *devadāsīs*' sexual liaisons were regulated by a royal officer.

sible to apply to her the "yogic" symbolism of the prostitute, who seems almost a textbook example of the *Gītā*'s goal of detached worldly action.

Not that this is a positive image: in a culture that values, above all, intense emotional experience, the impassive prostitute is hardly a figure to be highly praised. Thus Kampaṉ, for example, refers several times to prostitutes in a rather hostile manner, always because of their "triumph" over love; in one verse he links prostitution with the renouncer's goal of *mokṣa* as two essentially equivalent images for the barren *pālai* wilderness:

> This land was without moisture—
> like the minds of those who seek *mukti*
> by destroying the two kinds of action[24]
> and overcoming the strong fortresses
> of the three inner enemies;[25]
> or like the minds of prostitutes
> fixed on their price in gold. (354 = 1.7.15)

The prostitute resembles the renouncer in this fundamental attribute: both are removed from the redemptive, life-giving truth of the god's presence, which we experience through powerful emotion; hence, for Kampaṉ, both figures suggest the void. Elsewhere, he relates the prostitute to a mirror, again because of the sense of a lifeless, relationless state of being:

> They[26] saw women playing catch,
> the shiny balls, like crystal mirrors,
> turning black from the reflection
> of their eyes, painted with kohl,
> and red from the touch of their rosy hands—
>
> like the heart of a harlot
> with her cobra-hood mound of Venus
> who gives her body and takes pleasure
> equally with her lovers
> and then takes her price. (571 = 1.10.16)

In the case of the prostitute, impassivity and detachment become (for Kampaṉ) synonymous with heartlessness. The other pole—that of helpless, extreme passion—is implicitly present in the background of

[24] Good deeds and evil deeds, both categories generative of *karma*.

[25] Lust, anger, and ignorance.

[26] Rāma, Lakṣmaṇa, and Viśvāmitra.

this verse, which marks a moment in Rāma's entry into the city of Mithilā, where he will find and win his beloved Sītā. Rāma and Sītā will lose themselves in passion, in a paradigmatic enactment of the relation between god and his devotees, and in pointed contrast to the absence of relation between the prostitute (or the courtesan) and her "lover."[27] (These verses are also interesting in the light of later Tamil tradition, which makes Kampaṉ, like the Kālidāsa of medieval literary legend, a devotee of the dancing-girls.)[28]

We may, then, begin to see further into the *veśyā*'s contribution to royal symbolism—to see beyond the simple function of encircling the king with auspiciousness and calling forth the forces of vitality and heightened fertility. Although this function is basic to the *veśyā*'s role, so are her intriguing inner divisions: she simultaneously elicits sexuality and, like the renouncer, distances herself from love, from fertility, and from the ongoing life of the world.[29] No wonder that these women, their hearts made impenetrable to true passion, are sometimes assimilated to virgins.[30] One suspects that to a large extent they are meant to excite the king's passions without fulfilling them—a tantalizing, continuous exercise in seduction undertaken, no doubt, for the sake of enhancing the kingdom's prosperity, and with little regard for the frustrating effect upon the king. As a microcosm of his realm, the king feels the awakening of vital forces within him and, perhaps, struggles to contain them while maintaining their powerful flow. But (here the rich complexity of the symbolism is most suggestive) even if the king indulges his sexual attraction to the courtesans, he is *still* engaged in an essentially barren, loveless activity, perhaps even a kind of *yoga*-through-*bhoga* reminiscent of the Tantric style.[31] Despite the explicit eroticism—or, rather, because of the necessary indifference that permeates it—the *veśyā* connection is generally unromantic, unfulfilling, empty of joy.

For the South Indian monarch is not cut out for dispassion, despite his very real urges in that direction.[32] He is, rather, defined by feeling,

[27] For more extensive discussion of this verse, see Shulman (1980).

[28] See *Tamiḻnāvalarcaritai* 13 (81-108).

[29] It is the wife, never a courtesan, who is sometimes called *saṃsāram*—the world in its unending flow.

[30] Is there a link here with the Draupadī of the South Indian folk traditions? As a woman married to five husbands, Draupadī can be taunted by her enemies (in the Kuru *sabhā*) with being little better than a prostitute (*bandhakī*, 2.61.35; Villiputtūrār, 2.2.232); yet the folk tradition knows her as the chaste (virginal?) Turopataiyammaṉ.

[31] One thinks of Śaṅkara, archetypal *sannyāsin*, masquerading as King Amaru to experience the science of *kāma*: Siegel (1983), pp. 4-5.

[32] In this respect he is quite different from the image of the ideal, yogic king drawn

by the imaginative identification with a whole range of emotional experience; and, as we have seen, his relation to the transcendent presence of the god is also characterized by intense and varied emotional states. The only detachment that comes easily to him is that which accompanies his clownish, comic aspect—but the king is also endowed with the clown's rich burden of anxiety and affect. He is closer to a parody of a *yogin* than to a sincere, controlled renouncer. At best, he could be described as a *bhaktiyogin* preyed upon by passion; he falls in love all too easily, and usually in the tragic mode; though he is driven toward renunciation of one kind or another, he must also renounce it;[33] frustration permeates even his indulgence and sexual satiety. Hence his inner link with the ambiguous *veśyā*, who enfolds him in a feminine version of his own intricate ambiguities. And who also does something else—by her maddening combination of auspiciousness, arousal, and an emotional deep freeze, the *veśyā* helps to propel the king further in his mutations. Denying love, she also denies harmony or ease; the king, whose symbolic identity is worked out partly in relation to his courtesans, is thus forced to go on with his parade of futile masks. Several of the stories discussed above show how the king's transformation regularly proceeds by way of his contact with a woman or women: such, for example, was the experience of Mucukunda, whose dancing-girls giggled at his monkey's-face—a trauma so terrible for the king that he was forced to renounce kingship altogether in order to search for some more durable, more real meaning connected with a god. In this case as in others, the courtesan may be said to reveal the facelessness behind the royal mask.

Put more abstractly, we could say that if the king's essential illusion is that of an elusive equilibrium and stability, then, clearly, he must be symbolically "married" not only to a wife and queen—who will sustain the illusion—but, above all, to a group of courtesans who will undermine or impair it. The dependable linkage between two such fragmented characters expresses the essential, underlying ambiguity and complexity of the king's truth; the symbolic universe within which the king is situated uses the *veśyā* to comment cogently upon the nature of kingship itself.

Tamil literary tradition records many stories about *veśyās* in the Chola court; indeed, the courtesan phenomenon is a very ancient one in Tamil Nadu, richly attested in Caṅkam poetry.[34] From inscriptions

by Biardeau in her work on the *MBh*. On the king's drive toward renunciation, see above, II.3-4.

[33] Above, II.3.

[34] See Hart (1974) on the courtesan in ancient Tamil Nadu.

we also learn of the presence of dancing-girls in the major Chola shrines.[35] But in studying the symbolism of the medieval king and his women, we shall begin with a different, in some ways opposite type—that embodied in a prominent literary genre of Chola court poetry, the *ulā* or "processional," which is closely related in its themes and images to the problems raised by the presence of the courtesans at the royal court.

2. *Ulā*: Narcissus in Procession

The *ulā* poems seize upon a striking symbolic moment in the life of the king (or the god): his emergence from his palace (or shrine) in order to parade through the streets, before the eyes of his subjects. Of the latter, however, it is only the women who are of interest in this genre; and they are described in accordance with a conventional division into seven age groups: *petai*, age 5 to 7; *pĕtumpai*, 8-11; *mańkai*, 12-13; *maṭantai*, 14-19; *arivai*, 20-25; *tĕrivai*, 26-31; and *periḷampĕṇ*, 32-40.[36] Women from each of these groups catch a glimpse of the hero and, in a manner appropriate to their age and maturity, exhibit signs of love and desire for him. When it is the god who is parading—as in the earliest Tamil *ulā*, the *Tirukkayilaiñāṉavulā*, ascribed to our familiar "fool for Śiva's sake," Ceramāṉ Pĕrumāḷ—the women's intoxication with the divine hero suggests the passionate feelings of the devotees; but in the case of the royal procession through the capital, we are dealing with another important statement about the component images of kingship. The king's procession before his female subjects is a dramatic and necessary feature of his "rule," as is their frenzied response. The genre as a whole reflects the symbolic quality of South Indian kingship: the king is there in order to be perceived, and to perceive himself, in highly formalized and emotionally powerful ways.

Commentators from Nacciṉārkkiṉiyar on (fourteenth century) have claimed that the women described in the *ulā* belong to the category of "common women" (*pŏtu makaḷir*) or prostitutes.[37] There is an obvious reluctance to imagine chaste, married women in the passionate

[35] For example, at the Bṛhadīśvara in Tanjore: SII 2, part 3, no. 66.

[36] See Balasubramanian (1980), p. 261 (citing *Ilakkaṇa vilakkappāṭṭiyal* 99-103); Zvelebil (1974), pp. 197-99. The list of ages varies somewhat: see the introduction by Ki. Vā. Jagannātaṉ to his edition of the *Cankararācentiracoḻaṉ ulā*, pp. 3-4. The traditional meter of the *ulā* is *kalivĕṇpā*.

[37] Nacciṉārkkiṉiyar on *Tŏl. puṟat.* 30 (85); cf. Jagannātaṉ, introduction, pp. 2 and 4; Balasubramanian (1980), p. 262.

poses depicted here. In truth, however, this seems to be an unnecessary restriction in the scope of the poems, as one can see from analogous "processionals" (also referred to as *ulā* or *ulāppuṟam*) outside the confines of the *ulā* genre proper: such *ulā* processions abound in the literature as a recurrent pattern evoked whenever the hero wanders into the streets. Thus Rāma enjoys an *ulā* before his marriage to Sītā as well as on later occasions (for example, when he is summoned to his father's court).[38] The pattern is well represented in Sanskrit literature (Śiva's "parade" before his marriage, *Kumārasambhava* 7)[39] and in Telugu.[40] In all these passages, the love sickness that the hero arouses in the women is clearly generalized. Nevertheless, as we shall see, the *ulā* does preserve something of the sense of thwarted desire which we have associated with the *veśyā*, while it focuses the theme of detachment and impassivity upon the king.

The outstanding master of the Tamil *ulā* is the Chola court poet Ŏṭṭakkūttar, who composed an *ulā* for each of three Chola kings: Vikrama (1118-1135), Kulottuṅga II (1135-1150), and Rājarāja II (1146-1173). Together, these works are famous as the *mūvarulā*.[41] There is another equally beautiful *ulā*, of anonymous authorship, on the Chola prince Śaṅkara Rājendra (apparently the younger brother of Kulottuṅga III).[42] We shall refer particularly to the latter poem as well as to Ŏṭṭakkūttar's ornate compositions and to Kampaṉ's *ulās*. This is not the place for a full study of this genre; the following remarks are aimed at clarifying the *ulā*'s portrait of the South Indian king.

Given the symbolic import of the genre—its self-conscious contribution to the essential visibility of the king and patron—it is not surprising that the royal *ulās* begin with genealogy. This staple of all the panegyric genres serves here to introduce the hero of the poem, the latest in an imposing series of valiant rulers descended from the god Viṣṇu via Brahmā on his lotus, at the moment of his awakening from sleep. He has spent the night with his queen, on "Anaṅga's couch of married love" (*kaṭi aṉaṅkap pāyalvāy*)[43]—a night of desire and erotic play, and thus clearly marked off from the experiences awaiting him by day, in his procession before the women in the streets. Dark-

[38] *Irāmāvatāram* 2.52-58 (discussed below).

[39] And cf. *Raghuvaṃśa* 7.1-16; Raghavan (1973), p. 38; *Kuvalayamālā* of Udyotanasūri, cited by Moti Chandra (1973), pp. 194-96. The Bhikṣāṭana myth, in which Śiva parades naked through the forest in front of the sages' wives, is another variation on this theme.

[40] For example, *Basavapurāṇamu* 2.90ff. (pp. 64-65).

[41] I have used the SISS edition. See Zvelebil (1974), pp. 198-99.

[42] See Jagannātaṉ's introduction, pp. 5-7.

[43] *Cankararācentiracoḻaṉ ulā* (hereafter: CRCU), 43; cf. *Vikkiramacoḻaṉ ulā*, 71-80.

ness suddenly turns white: the royal couple has slept "like a raincloud and the lightning, upon the sea of milk";[44] the king is dark, like the dark god Viṣṇu with whom he is identified, and who is also conventionally compared to the monsoon cloud, whereas the queen is the slender flash of lightning appropriately conjoined to him. But as he rises, the king is now radiant as the sun emerging from behind a dark mountain; he bathes in water brought in golden pots from the Kāviri (Pŏṉṉi—the Golden River), bestows gold upon the Brahmins, and dresses himself in brilliant white garments (*ŏṇ tavaḷat tūcum*).[45] This dazzling spectacle of white and gold—further heightened by the ornaments the king puts on, and the white ash with which he covers his forehead[46]—must now behold itself, before it can be displayed before others' eyes: the royal hero, fully dressed and adorned, stares at his own image in a standing mirror.[47] This moment, at the very start of the royal day, beautifully expresses the reflexive aspect embedded within the South Indian kingly role.

This is also a moment of transcendence: the king bows at the feet of the Supreme Being, the god Śiva.[48] Now it is time for him to begin his work: he leaves the palace, mounts his elephant—lovingly and extravagantly described—and heads for the women's street. The onerous royal duty is to progress slowly through this quarter with all proper regal splendor—chowries waving, parasol and banner raised on high—while the women thronging the streets swoon, collectively and individually, at this unbearably alluring vision. Their woeful infatuation is first described in general terms that incorporate (here as well as later in the poem) a sophisticated play with conventional tropes: the ladies lose their "heart-lotuses" to the king, who thus becomes, in all his limbs, a veritable "forest of lotuses" (*paṅkayakkāṭu*[49]—for are not the hero's hands, feet, eyes, face, and mouth habitually compared to the lotus?). "Like wax melting in fire," the women dissolve in the heat of the gentle south wind (*tĕṉṟal*), the tormentor of lovers;[50] their moonlike faces are bathed in tears; they grow pale, lose their wits, their garlands, their very lives;[51] in an astonishing acceleration of a

[44] CRCU, 43.

[45] *Ibid.*, 52-53.

[46] *Ibid.*, 54-61. Note that the king is a Śaiva.

[47] *Ibid.*, 62.

[48] *Ibid.*, 63-64. Note that this meditation takes place immediately after the king has stared at his own image in the mirror.

[49] *Ibid.*, 127.

[50] *Ibid.*, 132.

[51] *Ibid.*, 128; 133.

sequence that normally takes days of languishing in love, their bodies suddenly grow lean and emaciated, to the point where their bracelets fall from their arms.[52] These descriptions follow patterns established by centuries of romantic verse, with the women cast in the role of the conventional, love-sick heroine; what is new, perhaps, is the self-conscious isolation and extension of the inherited tropes. In the midst of the emotional upheaval caused by the king's appearance in the streets, the hackneyed metaphors of desire seem suddenly to strike out on their own, to study themselves in the poet's mirror even as the king has been made to inspect his own astounding image. This reflexive character is a regular feature of the ornamental, courtly *ulā*.

We can observe this feature and something of its effect in a greatly telescoped *ulā* by Kampaṉ: the passage describing Rāma's ride through the streets of Ayodhyā on his way to his father's palace. The entire passage requires only seven verses, and the essential development of the *ulā* themes is fully apparent in the first three:

> One by one,
> the heavy drums roared,
> like clustering thunderclouds;
> conch-bracelets clanked
> as they slipped from women's wrists;
> the gods clamored in joy,
> for their troubles were at an end;[53]
> bees buzzed in the fragrant garland
> which he bore upon his head
>
> as he (Rāma) rode by on the chariot. (2.52)
>
> Drum beats echoed through the air,
> with the rising music of song;
>
> Anaṅga's arrows flew in all directions—
> you could hear the twanging of his bow!
>
> A flood of knowledge
> burst the mighty dam
> of chaste restraint;
> like herds of deer,
> women thronged the streets,
> separated
> from all shame. (2.53)

[52] *Ibid.*, 130-31.

[53] For Rāma is now intended to assume the throne.

In the doorways,
    set with tall pillars,
and on the terraces,
lotuses flowered between earrings
    and disheveled hair—

flowered, too, from the latticed windows
  where swords,
        blood-soaked spears,
        bees
        and *kĕṇṭai* fish
stared in their confusion. (2.54)

Note the dynamic movement of the verses: the first, a rising chorus of various happy noises, already initiates the women's passion—one glimpse of Rāma, and they grow thin before our eyes; we can hear their bracelets crash to the ground. The process of desire unfolds rapidly, inexorably: in the second verse the dam of chastity (*niṟai*) is broken, and the flood carries away the last remnants of modesty or shame. By the third verse, we find ourselves in a wholly surrealistic scene, with lotuses blooming between earrings while weapons, bees, and fish "stare out" through the windows. What has happened is simple enough: verse 54 is a wild implosion of metaphors now liberated from their habitual moorings. The lotuses, of course, are the faces of the women, in their doorways and windows; the swords, spears, bees, and *kĕṇṭai* are traditional images for women's eyes (which are deadly as these lethal weapons, long as spears, agitated like bees, and shaped like the fish).[54] These metaphors are said to be "confused" (*mayaṅka*)—superseded, no doubt, by the eyes to which they are compared, but also thrown together here in a genuinely confusing sequence of seemingly autonomous images torn from their usual context. The result is a strange verse that is also strangely powerful—and close, it would appear, to the emotional state that is being described. We can hardly blame Kampaṉ's *kāvya* style for this experiment in surrealism; rather, it develops naturally out of the experiential mode of the *ulā*. It is also noteworthy that the description is entirely focused on the spectators, while Rāma himself is barely mentioned; he simply proceeds in his chariot through the havoc erupting around him. On the one side, there is a breach, a deluge, a violent bursting forth of inner forces; on the other—nothing, a blank face, a silent stone.

In a few *ulās* (including some of the most famous, which are atypical

[54] On the imagery of eyes and vision, see Shulman (1980).

in this respect), this total division into feeling and unfeeling sides is somewhat modified, and the king is allowed a limited response. Let us examine first an example from the *Caṅkararācentiracoḻaṉ ulā*, which once again offers an unusual play with conventional tropes. The Chola prince has arrived in the vicinity of the *arivai* (a mature woman aged between 20 and 25) who, like the other women, is intoxicated with desire for him. At this point a woman singer (*viṟali*) approaches, and a delightful dialogue develops between her and the *arivai*.

VIṞALI: "Is your waist not a serpent
with its jewel that dispels the dark?"
ARIVAI: "O Viṟali, if this were so,
would it let its jewels slip away
when I bow to our king
in this street covered with jewels?" (277-78)

The *viṟali* simultaneously praises and teases the *arivai* by applying a standard image to her waist (slender as a serpent); the *arivai* rejects the comparison with a logical argument—since her jeweled *mekalai* waistband slips off her waist when she bows to the king (in her lovelorn, emaciated state), there can be no serpent there; a snake would hold on to the jewel in his forehead, but *she* cannot hold on to anything in her helpless longing. The banter continues:

VIṞALI: "Are those full breasts
the hill of Agastya,
who played at swallowing the roaring sea?"[55]
ARIVAI: "If that were so, would the sandal upon them
burn and peel away
when the south wind blows?" (279-80)

The sandal paste upon the *arivai*'s breasts is parched dry by the heat of her desire, fanned by the southwind; again, the hyperbolic metaphor is rejected.

VIṞALI: "Your arms are golden bamboo
covered with golden hairs;
and does not your neck have the beauty
of the *valampuri* conch?"
ARIVAI: "Why, then, would not their pearls remain firm
even as I long for the heroic arms
which guard the earth?" (281-82)

[55] For Agastya's swallowing the ocean, see above, V.2, after n. 50. Agastya resides on Mount Pŏtiyil, which abounds in sandal-trees.

By Tamil convention, pearls are formed in the bamboo and the *valampuri* conch; but, unlike those pearls, the lady's pearl necklace falls and is lost through her love-sickness and confusion.

VIṞALI: "Are your long eyes—wider than the seven seas—
not lotuses floating in water?"
ARIVAI: "If they *were* lotuses,
would they not fold
even during nights when I am not united
with the one, unique leader
of the army which never flees a battle?" (283-84)

The clichés cannot be made to stick. In each case the *viṟali* offers a flattering, wholly familiar comparison, which the *arivai* demotes to a lower order of reality—her arms are *not* bamboo but rather all-too-human limbs that long for the touch of her beloved; her sleepless eyes are *not* a new species of lotus, unable to close at night, and the water in which they are "floating" is real, from human tears. The poet's stock in trade is held up to the light, mocked, and discarded; the well-worn metaphors are deliberately confronted with the hard, living reality of desire, which is no longer captured by their expressive capacity. This passage takes the *ulā*'s linguistic and poetic self-consciousness to a new extreme.

And the *arivai*'s determined passion seems almost to bear fruit: she draws near to the prince, "like an ocean of honey mingling with the ocean of milk" (293); their eyes meet, and he, too, is captivated:

Through this glance
they melted;
both drank in a flood
of radiant beauty
and grew languorous

until he gave his *ātti* garland
to the black-braided woman,
that her unending torment
from the sugarcane
might be contained:

then she abandoned
her stark delusion
and flowered,
inwardly and outwardly,
in a flowing
stream of joy. . . . (299-301)

This is the extent of their contact—it is all basically a matter of the eyes. Indeed, so deeply affecting is this mutual stare that his image becomes fixed in her eyes, while *hers* enters his eyes and colors them red (303). Such is the union allowed them: an eye for an eye; and the blinding exchange of images is sealed by another symbolic transfer, that of the garland that at once satisfies and overjoys the woman. The *kāvya* poet's penchant for paronomasia and ellipsis is still with us in this section: the "torment from the sugarcane" (*aṭum ālai*) is the lovesickness caused by the arrows of Kāma's sugarcane bow, now happily suppressed, though we could also read *aṭu mālai*—the torments of *evening*, conventionally the moment of the lovers' worst trials. Similarly, the "stark delusion" (*kūr māl*) that the *arivai* abandons could also be "cruel Māl/Viṣṇu"—the deity with whom the prince is repeatedly identified in this poem. In any case, the royal benefactor can now proceed with his *ulā*, leaving the lady behind. Has any real meeting taken place? As he moves away, his heart turns backwards—toward the love that might have been—while *her* heart goes forward with him (304).

His next encounter, with the *tĕrivai* woman (aged 26-31), has a somewhat similar character, but this time the theme of the unrealized union is structured around a dream.[56] Among the seven classes of women, it is the *tĕrivai* who, in this case, most closely replicates the hero's own experience: we watch her as she wakes (just as earlier we witnessed the prince's awakening); and her overwrought emotional state may suggest something of what goes on behind *his* stolid royal mask. For her, the moment of waking is one of grievous disappointment—she is agitated, "like a young goose which has lost its food, like a wave in a pool of water" (315)—for she has dreamt of passionate union with the Chola prince, and now, still half asleep, she searches in vain for the traces of their love. Alas, her jewels are still perfectly arranged in place; her breasts are not dabbed with sandal paste rubbed off his chest; her bracelets—always a key indicator of any change of state—are in perfect condition, not having been crushed during the "battles of coitus" (*kalavippūcal*, 319). Now—again like the Chola king—she rushes to the mirror to inspect her image; her lips, unfortunately, are as red as ever, not rendered pale by the pressure of a thousand kisses. The appallingly proper reflection staring back at her in the mirror is the final blow to her hopes; she succumbs to despair, with all its usual concomitants of weeping, sighing, falling, melting. Her companions suggest a recreational visit to a pool—but suddenly

[56] Compare the verses cited from *Kaliṅkattupparaṇi*, above, V.7 at notes 159-60.

the regal procession is upon them. The *tĕrivai* rushes to see her beloved, and even has the courage to address him:

"My lord (*nāyakā*)—
if you were to give me
  infinite treasures,
I would not accept them;
if you offer me the wishing-stone (*cintāmaṇi*)
  or the wishing-tree (*curar taru* = *kalpavṛkṣa*)
  or the wishing-cow (*teṉu* = *kāmadhenu*),
I will not have them;
even Mount Meru, inscribed with your tiger emblem
(after you removed the marks
  of the Cera bow and the Pāṇṭiya fish)
is not for me:

I beg of you
the sleep you snatched from me—

let me sleep again
  to dream of you. (330-33)

The dream-union is clearly the most she can hope for, if her love-sickness will ever allow her to fall asleep again. For his part, the prince is not indifferent to this poignant request; indeed, he feels "ten times more desire than she" (*māṉiṟ patiṉ maṭaṅku veṭkai paṇittāṉ*, 335). And he does bestow gifts on the *tĕrivai*—a garland, ornaments, even lands, whole villages, and heaps of gold (*aṉanta canapatamum ūrum tamaṉiya oṅkalum*, 336)—before he moves on.

This motif of the gifts to the lovelorn ladies—an unusual and irregular feature in this genre—is also taken up by Ŏṭṭakkūttar at several points in his *ulās*. Thus in the *Irācarācacoḻaṉ ulā*, the king exchanges garlands with the *arivai* woman in what might appear to be an imitation of the wedding ceremony (611-16). But this symbolic act fails to satisfy the woman, who gives voice to an extended, piteous "complaint": "Could not your club, which protects the entire universe as of old, break Kāma's sugarcane bow? . . . Could you not blow your conch just once, at daybreak, to save my life?" (617-18, 625-26). The king now notices the sorrowful condition of this love-sick admirer and offers her a greater gift—a promise that she, like his wives, will never be separated from him (*nāḷum piriyāmai nalkiṉāṉ*, 632). What is the substance of this promise? Has he really married the girl? The poet gives no explicit answer to these questions, but there is a clue in the immediate sequel to this episode, where the symbolism of marriage is again clearly suggested. The king moves on, leaving behind him his supposedly "inseparable" new beloved; and now the *tĕrivai* woman appears, in haste, "as if it were the day of Viṣṇu's former marriage" (641-42). She is, quite literally, dressed "to kill"—and the king, seeing her astonishing beauty, is terrified (*vĕruvarā*, 652). This time it is the hero who is rendered helpless by passion: he is ensnared (*tuvakkuṇṭu*, 658) by her swordlike eyes, the bows that are her eyebrows, her bamboo-shoulders—all of the conventional metaphors working their conventional magic—and he wants never to relinquish her flowerlike hands. Obviously, there is only one recourse; he lavishes gifts upon this beauty—saris worth the entire earth, garlands, jewels, a wishing-tree, gold, a pearl fishery, fabulous mountains—and she, overcome by joy, accepts them and heads home.

The commentators are surely right in viewing these gifts as similar to those offered by a prospective bridegroom to his bride (in particular, the gifts of clothes and jewels).[57] But will this wedding ever take place? The *tĕrivai* summons to her house the *pŏrunar* and *pāṇar* bards, who now enact for her the songs and dances of Kṛṣṇa's youth among the cowherds. They play the flute, as Kṛṣṇa did; dance his dance upon the serpent's hood and the "dance of the pots"[58]—recalling all the while the identification of the Chola king with this god ("Kṛṣṇa's arms and legs are the arms and legs of the Chola lord," 685-86). At length the *tĕrivai* bestows golden rewards upon the bards and sends them away; she, too, then disappears from the poem, and perhaps from the life of the king as well. Ŏṭṭakkūttar has, it is true, deviated from the more usual format of the *ulā* by describing a passionate response on the part of the hero to the advances of his adoring spectators; but it would seem, nevertheless, that this passion remains essentially blocked, limited to the symbolic exchanges during the procession. The king is allowed a mock wedding (or two, or three) as a part of the whole engaging spectacle. He may feel love for the women who crowd the streets to see him, even give them presents; but the only kind of "marriage" he can offer them is analogous to the paradoxical love of the god and his devotees—a union permeated by absence, separation, and longing, that is, with a powerful tragic component, and characterized by the unending attempts to reconstitute the god's presence by imaginative experiment, in dreams, or in the reenactment of his myths. Thus the *tĕrivai* and her bards sing of Kṛṣṇa, here the

[57] See the commentary of Ti. Caṅkuppulavar in the SISS edition, p. 110.

[58] *kuṭakkūttu*; cf. *Cil.* 17, which seems to underlie much of this passage.

mythic model for the king;[59] the latter is present in their minds as an ideal image of the lover who is nevertheless physically remote, unattainable, at best the substance of a dream.

Viraha, separation, is thus the mode of the *ulā*—*viraha* celebrated in a display of passion directed toward a largely inaccessible object.[60] Indeed, the *ulā* may be said to be constructed out of three central elements: the king's need for conspicuous, self-conscious display; the mad passion of the women, who succumb to the power of *viraha*, of love-in-separation; and the king's essential impassivity in the face of their seductive appeals. The first two elements have been discussed above; let us look briefly at a passage that pointedly stresses the third. Again we turn to Kampaṉ, this time to an earlier *ulā* of Rāma's, prior to his wedding to Sītā in Mithilā.[61] Rāma is parading through the streets, to the accompaniment of the usual chorus of groans and cries of love; the streets are littered with the debris of unrequited passion—ornaments, sandal paste, bangles, belts, pearls, and garlands, which have slipped from the women's bodies—so that our hero has some difficulty in picking his way forward (1.1157). He is cool, detached, though obviously not wholly immune to desire, since he is, after all, about to be married to his beloved Sītā. This knowledge, together with the envy it arouses, is percolating through the consciousness of the other women, some of whom now explode with explicit complaints about his heartlessness:

As their bodies poured sweat
  and their spirits grew faint,
the women sobbed
  in their suffering,

but the pure lord
paid them no heed
  in his mind,
  or with his bright eyes.

One of them wondered:
  "Is his heart
    entirely
    devoid of love?" (1.1171)

[59] With the *gopīs* cast in the role of the Chola women (even as in the later Bengali tradition they become the unchaste *parakiyā* lovers). Cf. the courtesan Kānhopatrā who stands as a *gopī*-worshiper of Kṛṣṇa-Gopāl in Paṇḍharpūr: Vaudeville (1974), p. 149.

[60] The commentators speak of a "one-sided passion" (*orutalaik kāmam*) as proper to the *ulā*: see Jagannātaṉ, introduction to CRCU, p. 12.

[61] This canto is appropriately titled *ulāviyaṟ patalam*.

Said another:
"How can he just go by
 not caring in the least
 about these women
  lost
  in love's confusion?
 Has he never heard
  of compassion?
 Is he some kind of saint?
 Or just a common murderer?" (1.1174)

Indifference can kill; a bitter irony infuses the women's perception of this simultaneously ravishing and oblivious paragon:

One golden lady cried:
"This man's ancestors
 gave their very lives
  to save their suppliants,
 but *he* won't give us back
 even our *own* dear lives!
 How did he come by such cruelty?" (1.1178)

Rāma, it now appears, is failing in one of the basic duties of kingship, the readiness to sacrifice himself in the interests of his subjects (as his ancestor Śibi, for example, offered his life to save a dove from a hawk).[62] He may be lacking in passion—indeed, this is the conclusion intimated in the following verse, where one of the women suggests that he won Sītā (by breaking Śiva's bow) not out of any real desire for her but simply in order to show off his skill (1179)—but if he had any sense of responsibility, he could not let these women die in an agony of longing for him! In fact, Rāma's "failure" is compounded: not only will he not give of himself, in a self-sacrificing mode, to those who need him, but he also appears at this moment to be wholly removed from that recklessness in loving and in desire which, as we have already hinted, is an essential attribute of the South Indian king.

But this recklessness—which we shall examine more closely in a moment—must clearly coexist in uncertain tension with its opposite, the maddening detachment apparently required and symbolically expressed by the *ulā*. Here the courtesan's "yogic" dispassion in a context suffused by erotic energies has been transferred to the king, who normally surrounds himself with courtesans partly to satisfy this aspect of his role. Like the courtesan, the king in his procession is "cool,"

[62] See above, II.2 at n. 21.

his responses limited and largely unfulfilling for the women in the streets; but this "cool" center is now set in the middle of a wildly moving frame of love-sick spectators, an encircling boundary of flames. Of course, the king, too, is in motion—it is his procession that has activated the magnetic field of attraction focused upon his person, and that has illuminated this field with the reflexive spotlight radiating from the poem. But his motion here is largely lacking in *emotion*—in sharp contrast to the passionate stances of the devotional clown (such as Ceramāṉ Pĕrumāḷ), who creates the sense of a "black hole" at the kingdom's symbolic center.[63] The latter role may by now appear to us more in character for the king; but the former—that of the impassive protagonist in the *ulā* spectacle of separation, *viraha*—nevertheless ties in well with the royal component of control and the maintenance of strictly defined order.[64] Here a boundary is tested and allowed to stand firm. Hence the "tragic" overtones (which we have earlier linked to *viraha* generally): the *ulā* may be given to irony, but it is hardly comic; its carefully orchestrated display leaves no room for a real meeting of king and subject, or king and kingdom; rather, the two—the body politic and its central symbolic representative—are essentially identified within the divisions of their ideally ordered condition. The procession articulates the inner boundaries as well as the emotional tensions that they create and contain. The powerful reflexivity of the *ulā* is that of Narcissus with a mirror: the king embarked on his procession, embodying the tragic *viraha* that is implicit in the ordered life of his kingdom, himself identified with that kingdom and its given limits, cannot truly love anyone—except his own problematic, often absent self.

3. The Pathos of Regal Romance

Yet, as we know, the king can, indeed must, fall in love. In the courtly literature, at least, he does so regularly, thereby submitting to the stereotypical torments and romantic fantasies that the Vidūṣaka regularly derides. So common is this theme of the king in love that it surely needs little exemplification here; we shall limit the following discussion to several prominent features directly relevant to the more general construction of the king's symbolic role.

As in other instances we have studied,[65] the king's love is a form

[63] See above, V.5.

[64] See II.1 at n. 13 for the king's "yogic" control over his kingdom.

[65] See above, V.7.

of symbolic "opening," a state of excess, a reaching out and beyond the "normal" order of things, a breaking through or breaking down. We might, then, expect it to be endowed with a certain comic coloring, like other transformative or disorderly states in their symbolic expressions. This expectation is not wholly unwarranted, as we shall see; but the general tenor of the king's experience of love is anything but comic, when seen from his own perspective. The "break" that occurs tends to work against the pining lover, to reduce him to an abject, "broken" condition. Look, for example, at the following description of King Nala as he longs for Damayantī (whom he has not as yet even seen!):

> His awareness trickled away;
> with his mind cracked
>   and leaking,
> he could barely
> hold on to life.
>
> Thus the king lay,
> exhausted,
> despondent,
>   like an elephant fallen into a pit
>   or like a bud
>   engulfed in flames.[66]

This verse from Pukaḻentippulavar's Tamil reworking of the Nala story paints a classical portrait of the South Indian king in the nervous prostration of desire. We should resist the temptation to smile at the king's woebegone condition; the mood here is one of strenuous suffering meant to be regarded seriously by the audience, in its empathy for the romantic hero. The latter experiences desire with the same intensity he brings to other emotions and events, and its effect upon him is enervating, paralyzing, and unrelenting; he loses his courage and his vigor (*dhairya*), his self-mastery, his mask of detachment and poise. (We may note in passing that the infatuated woman seems often to undergo an opposite development in these descriptions—her passion makes her headstrong, even brazen, so that she transgresses the bonds of her conventional modesty and shame.)[67] In this state, the helpless king becomes victimized by his emotions; he is humbled, slavish, a

[66] *Naḷavĕṇpā* 63: *keṭṭa cĕvi vaḻiye keḷāt' uṇarv' oṭa/ oṭṭai manattoṭ' uyir tāṅki—mīṭṭum/ kuḻiyiṟ paṭu kari poṟ komāṉ kiṭantāṉ/ taḻaliṟ paṭu taḷir poṟ cāyntu.*

[67] As in the *ulā* quoted above, when the *tĕrivai* boldly addresses the king (CRCU 330-333). I am indebted to V. Narayana Rao for this observation.

miserable supplicant, like Purūravas, who repeatedly begs for forgiveness from his queen as well as from his beloved Urvaśī.[68] These torments may, of course, have their positive side—we have already had occasion to point to the delicious distress of *viraha*[69]—but they are no less painful for all that, as the endless verses that describe the various kings' "sickness of desire" (*kāmanoy, kātalnoy*) eloquently attest.

There is also a question here of "madness," of a type quite different from that discussed earlier with reference to the royal clowns. This time it is not the madness of devotion, or of the trauma that can afflict the cowardly and battle-weary king, encumbered with evil;[70] this is not the madness of *nivṛtti*, in its various categories, but rather of intense *pravṛtti*—of passionate engagement in the world, with the tragic emotions resulting from this engagement. At times the hero's longing propels him into a clinical form of madness, when the experience of separation suddenly appears permanent and thus too much for him to bear; we may think of Purūravas' famous "mad" soliloquy in Act IV of the *Vikramorvaśīya*,[71] or of Rāma's crazed laments after Rāvaṇa's abduction of Sītā.[72] More often, however, we witness milder forms of temporary insanity; for example, when Rāma (our same impassive hero of the *ulā* discussed above) begins to hallucinate during the night after his first glimpse of Sītā in Mithilā:

> I know she (Sītā) has no mercy;
> but in the heat of my mind's desire
> and to assuage this fearsome sickness,
> I devoured her
> with my eyes:
>
> now the entire
>   confused world,
> all that moves and is still,
> seems to have taken on
>   *her* golden form![73]

Rāma, harried and sleepless, is talking to himself in his loneliness and mental turmoil; he projects his own inner confusion onto the world

[68] See *Vikramorvaśīya*, end of Act II; and cf. Ruben (1956), pp. 70-74.

[69] Above, I.5.

[70] Above, V.2.

[71] Where the hero even forgets himself to the point of speaking Prakrit rather than Sanskrit.

[72] *Rām.* 3.55-60, 4.1.

[73] *Irāmāvatāram* 1.696.

at large. Since setting eyes on Sītā, he is unable to discern outer objects and forms; all he can see is her golden image replicated endlessly, obsessively, before him. Is it surprising that he soon succumbs to paranoia, nicely conventionalized in the familiar *kāvya* patterns and cliché-ridden images?

> Her colorful waistband,
> her mound of Venus,
> her two
> eyes, long as swords,
> her two
> full breasts—
>
> to these instruments of Death,
> coming to consume me,
> she has added one more:
>
> her sweet smile.
>
> Can she really need
> so many
> lethal weapons?[74]

In this state of mind, nothing can be meaningless or innocuous; everything is a sign. Thus when the moon sets, toward dawn, it is as if the white parasol of the King of Night had been broken and collapsed, or as if the ornament on the forehead of the Lady of the West had been destroyed—two starkly inauspicious images, both suggestive of the disastrous state to which Rāma's kingship (or his kingly nature and bearing) have been reduced.[75]

It is this latter theme—the effect of the king's passion upon his kingship—which is of greatest interest to us here; as the example just cited suggests, when the king is in love, the ordered functioning of his kingdom may be impaired. The royal parasol is broken: disorderly excess becomes the rule. That this state is a recurring one—for the king is all too susceptible to these affairs of the heart—only strengthens the disorderly component in the structure of the kingdom. The most extreme and vivid example of this notion occurs in Kampaṉ's portrayal of Sītā's other would-be lover, the appealing, noble Rāvaṇa, a tragic buffoon who functions in Kampaṉ's poem as a caricature of the "real"

[74] *Ibid.* 1.698.

[75] *Ibid.* 1.702. The Lady of the West is considered to be the queen of the King of Night. Cf. II.2 above for another collapsing royal parasol.

(as opposed to the ideal) South Indian king.[76] Rāvaṇa's passion for Sītā, aroused by his sister Śūrpaṇakhā's elaborate description of her, causes him to undergo the usual pitiable transformation of the male lover, long before he has ever actually seen the object of his desire. Like Rāma in similar circumstances, the infatuated Rāvaṇa becomes weak, agitated, confused; but given the total inappropriateness of his love for Sītā (who is by now, of course, married to Rāma as well as being a goddess far "above" the rude demon), this passion is described in a series of pejorative images. Thus his desire keeps on growing "like evil committed, and concealed, by an unknowing fool" (3.639). Rāvaṇa is an exemplar of raw, heroic power (*maṟam*); but at this moment, his *maṟam* deserts him:

> Anger,
> heroism,
> and fierceness of pride—
>
> all abandoned him,
> like good qualities
> that cannot abide with
> evil.
>
> As one flame blends
> with another flame,
> suffering and shame
> fused with his spirit. (3.635)
>
> Even before he carried off
> the lady lovely as a peacock,
> the King of Laṅkā with its towering walls
> made his own heart
> a prisoner.
> Like butter
>   left in the summer's hot sun,
> the heart of the demon with his sharp spear
> slowly melted
>   and began to burn. (3.638)

It is, indeed, part of Rāvaṇa's tragedy—the word is by no means inappropriate to Kampaṉ's depiction of him—that in imprisoning Sītā the demon-king also "imprisons" himself in a hopeless situation of

[76] I am grateful to George Hart for a discussion of this point. On the passage briefly discussed below, see the forthcoming translation with notes by George Hart and Hank Heifetz of Kampaṉ's *Āraṇiyakāṇṭam*.

his own making; his love for Sītā may at times appear ludicrous,[77] but it is nonetheless clearly genuine, and it works upon Rāvaṇa's emotions and upon his imagination[78] in ways that both highlight his underlying nobility of character and leave him trapped in the mournful state of the lovelorn Indian male. Already at the very beginning of his infatuation, he is affected to the point where he must "step down" from his throne:

> He descended
> from his throne
> and, as all the inhabitants
> of the seven worlds
> uttered blessings,
> as conches roared
> and the people around him
> rained down flowers,
> he entered his golden palace
> with his mind grown slack
> and ruined. (3.641)

Let us note the symbolic import of this action: although Rāvaṇa, of course, remains king in his capital, his romantic madness involves him, too—like the comic kings of the previous chapter—in a kind of symbolic exile. From this point on, his kingdom becomes subject to a tragi-comic overdose of *pravṛtti*, to the madness of uncontrolled desire and obsessive sensuality, as exemplified by the king who has left his throne room to revel in tortuous, unsatisfied passion.

Rāvaṇa knows no peace. He tries desperately to alleviate the burning sensation within him. As the absolute ruler of the world, he can command the seasons and the celestial bodies to do his bidding, and he now runs through one season after another in the vain hope that a different external setting will somehow cool his torment. When even the delicate moonlight intensifies his longing and his pain, he orders the sun to rise at midnight—to the total perplexity of everyone in the kingdom, from lovers who find it difficult to plan their quarrels properly, to the roosters and the astrologers who are confused by the untimely dawn (3.669-84). In short, Rāvaṇa's love-sickness turns the world topsy-turvy; his experiments with the cosmic order (in some ways reminiscent of the jester's toying with the properties of time

[77] As in the famous "seduction" scene in the Aśoka garden: 5.406-480.

[78] Which in 3.642 (in the midst of the passage we are examining) is said to "overheat" in much the same way that Rāma's does earlier.

and space) externalize the restless disorder and disharmony within him and thus transform his kingdom into a truly unordered, nondharmic realm.

Rāvaṇa's case of romantic "illness" is, no doubt, unusually severe, and its comic results for his kingdom are also unusually far-reaching; we must also remember that, however ridiculous or amusing these "expressionistic" effects may seem to us (indeed to any audience that listens to these verses), for Rāvaṇa the whole experience is tragically serious—as is its eventual conclusion in the war with Rāma. Rāvaṇa may present us with an image of the "real" South Indian king, as perceived by the medieval culture—an image pregnant with ludicrous features and suggestive of a basic tendency toward sensual excess and disorder—but even this "realistic" figure discovers tragedy in love. This tragic aspect of love is still more pronounced in the more idealized figures, who tend to be more strongly identified with the notions of containment and control (and who give way to comic transformation only under some duress). Think, for example, of the course of Rāma's love for Sītā: the brief period as newlyweds in Ayodhyā, which is followed by exile, a violent separation (Sītā's abduction by Rāvaṇa), the agony of the search for her, a reunion which, alas, carries its own problems (Sītā's trial by fire), and then a final, grievous banishment and loss. Even in the works of those poets who sought to ameliorate parts of this story (Kampaṉ, Bhavabhūti), the heroes' experience of *viraha* remains the norm. Moreover, this pattern is largely predominant in the Indian "romance," which treats separation as its natural subject matter. A "happy ending" may take place, as when Śakuntalā is reunited with Duṣyanta, Urvaśī with Purūravas;[79] but these reunions seem often to come almost too late, after years of suffering (in the case of Śakuntalā), when both hero and heroine are well tutored in pain. There are, of course, exceptions to this generalization, for example in medieval Sanskrit romances such as Tirumalāmbā's *Varadāmbikāpariṇaya-campū*[80] and in Nayak-period Telugu works:[81] here the course of love runs relatively smoothly, despite the obligatory periods of pining and anxious separation, and ends in an early marriage. More often, the class of romantic heroines is differentiated from that of the queens, who are, for the most part, almost faceless—not

[79] This is an important difference between Indian romance and much Muslim love poetry, which tends to be overwhelmingly tragic. As is well known, Kālidāsa transformed the earlier *tragic* conclusion of the Purūravas story.

[80] Is it significant that this work was composed by a woman (the queen of Acyutarāya)?

[81] The Telugu *yakṣagānas* composed in Maturai and Tanjore.

the subjects for lyrical poems.[82] The tragic conception of love in earlier Tamil poetry has been remarked upon in another context above.[83]

South Indian royal romance thus veers away from comedy. There is nothing here of the happy resolutions of the Shakespearean comedies, which allow the still youthful lovers, at the end of their trials, disguises, and delusions, to look ahead to a life of shared, perhaps wiser love; nor do we find anything akin to Aristophanes' celebrations of sexual delight triumphant over war and other human folly. Nor, for that matter, are the South Indian poets particularly interested in the comic absurdities consequent upon loving (affecting the lovers themselves or their immediate surroundings). Rather, the king's role as a "romantic clown" is the most pathetic of all his transformations, and the least likely to develop in a "restorative," peaceful direction. Despite its potential for inducing disorder and its innate transformative capacity, romantic "madness" remains, in the South Indian sources, closer to the tragic than are other transformative patterns we have seen. Love must "happen" to every king as an inevitable element in his career—or, more precisely, even the wholly proper, or the idealized, king will tend to oscillate between conventionalized moments of passionate longing or love sickness, on the one hand, and yogic impassivity and control, on the other. Unfortunately, however, there is little promise of lasting joy at either end of the pendulum. For the king, love—like power—is a striking expression of *pravṛtti*, of his passionate, total involvement in the world: hence its essential theme is *viraha*, its mode the tragic one of painful, and in some ways questionable affirmation.

4. Playing at Prostitution: King, Queen, and God

Must we conclude that the king's eroticism is a completely hopeless affair, a painful imperative of restless movement between controlled forbearance (the "orderly" *viraha* of the *ulā*) and uncontrolled denial (the "disorderly" *viraha* of royal romance)? Is there no middle ground, and no transcendence? The question is all the more important because of the central role that the king's various women must play in the definition of South Indian kingship. There are no bachelor kings, no rulers without their concentric rings of courtesans and admirers; the

[82] Chola queens, such as Cĕmpiyaṉ Mahādevī, who *are* famous in the tradition, have achieved this place through their devotion, not their romantic careers (see the study by Venkataraman).

[83] I.5.

king needs at least one wife in order to perform his ritual tasks, and he needs his courtesans to delimit the space in which he functions as ruler, to map out the positions of court and throne. His difficulties start when he seeks love—in marriage, or with an "outside" figure such as the drama's heroines—or, conversely, when he seeks to deny it, through an inner detachment that desiccates his own life and hence that of his kingdom. In either case, it is the pervasive experience of *viraha* that awaits him, with its frustrations and its barriers.

But let us look at one last story that evokes these issues and these symbolic figures—the king, the courtesan, and the queen—and which transforms the meaning of *viraha* (perhaps the key word of this text). This is, perhaps, a synthetic story, in the South Indian fashion of synthesis—not a resolution or mediation, but a transformative upward spiral that leaves the two opposed terms in continuing, symbiotic opposition. The text, included in Ĕllappanayiṉār's sixteenth-century *Aruṇācalapurāṇam*, offers a particularly graphic image of the South Indian king (by now the "little king" of Nāyak times) in his relation to the women around him and to another basic factor in his existence, the god of his devotion. This is the story of another royal trial, and yet another divine game; a love story of separation persisting in paradoxical union.

Once there was a king, Vallāḷamakārājaṉ, who ruled in Aruṇai (Aruṇācala), where the harlots (*kaṇikaiyar*) were as chaste as Arundhatī.[84] He was an excellent king, truthful, benevolent, always praising Śiva's feet; he cared for all lives as if they were his own; he had no desire for others' wealth, and he regarded all women other than his wives as if they were his sisters.[85] With such a fine king, it is no wonder that the kingdom flourished: the tiger and the cow drank from the same watering place, Brahmins chanted the Veda, women decorated the streets with *kolams*,[86] rain fell on schedule, and the hungry were fed. In the midst of all this prosperity, the king had only one sorrow, the usual one: he had no children. He sought the advice of his Brahmin ministers, and they suggested that he proclaim his readiness to offer charity to any and all; in this way, through the compassion of Śiva, he would be given a child. So Vallāḷaṉ ordered a banner raised high in Aruṇai, to make known his determination to grant whatever anyone might ask of him. When his ministers questioned his ability to make good on this promise, the king replied: "No

[84] Arundhatī is the paragon of womanly chastity and devotion to a husband; see Shulman (1980b), pp. 245-46, 149. Quotations below are from *Aruṇācalapurāṇam* 6.

[85] See discussion of this notion below, VII.5 at notes 92-94.

[86] See above, I.1.

one will ask for something that cannot be found on earth; if someone *would, no one* could give it."

So many people—the aged, ascetics, Brahmins, yogis, *jaṅgamas* (Vīraśaiva devotees), bards, and simple beggars—flocked to the king and received his gifts. Vallāḷaṉ gave huge sums of gold to those who wished to celebrate a marriage, or to redeem their mortgaged lands, or to Brahmins who had an *upanayana* ceremony to perform; he helped to renovate the great temple of Aruṇālaca, and its associated mutts (Tam. *maṭam*, Skt. *maṭha*); he gave to the blind, the lame, the poor. Hearing of this ongoing display of generosity, the sage Nārada came to see it for himself; the king received him with honor and spoke to him of his goal, and Nārada hastened thence to Kailāsa to inform Śiva of the king's piety, devotion, and need. The god at once decided to put Vallāḷaṉ to a test. Taking the form of a *jaṅgama* devotee, with Kubera, heavily laden with gold, as his disciple and with his demon hordes disguised as Śaiva mendicants (*āṇṭi*), Śiva came down to earth, to the city of Aruṇai.

As they entered the city, the false ascetics cried, "Are there no chaste wives here, who revere their husbands as their gods? Are there no handsome sons, no one to feed the hungry, no learned kings; no women who might invite us in amazement, and who would serve us ambrosia elegantly?[87] We don't want gold, or jewels, or pearl necklaces, or the kingdom itself—but if someone were to offer us food, we would gladly eat, with love (*aṉpu*, 31)." Thus they reached the street of the harlots, and now they accosted these women and asked them how much they wanted for a whole night of love, "to remove the struggle induced by Kāma's five arrows" (33). The prostitutes answered: "You who have the look of Śiva himself! We speak no lies; we do not know how to deceive anyone. For a whole night, we charge a thousand gold coins per girl; if you can pay that, we will place body against body and overcome Manmatha's harsh deeds (*maṉmataṉ viṉai tavirppom*, 34)." This announcement—replete with the familiar ironies of the "yogic" prostitute, who speaks in the idiom of ascetics or devotees in their battle against *karma* (*viṉai*, "deeds")—was immediately accepted by the chief *jaṅgama*, the masquerading Śiva, who poured out his treasure (Kubera's gold) into the palms of the prostitutes, winked at his followers as if to say, "Don't leave these girls (*piriyātīr*)," and then proceeded himself in the direction of the palace.

Behind him, the harlots' street began to groan in passion; before

[87] This verse echoes Kaṇṇaki's lament in the streets of Maturai: above, II.2 after n. 29.

him, the king bowed low in reverence, and asked what he had done to merit this visit. "Long live the path of royal virtue," said the *jaṅgama*; "I came here in the hope that you would remove the sorrow caused by Kāma, by giving me a young girl (*kaṉṉi*, 38)." The king was happy: "I will arrange for your marriage." "No," said the *jaṅgama* (fully aware of the traditional view of eroticism as located *outside* the home); "only a prostitute would know the secret arts of healing the sickness of my desire." "If you insist," said the king, "I shall do as you wish"; and he ordered his guards to hurry to the prostitutes' quarter and bring back a suitable woman. But the guards went from door to door, and in each house they heard the singing and dancing of the harlots who were entertaining Śiva's cohorts; they therefore reported to the king that no one was available that night. The king, greatly distressed, went into conference with his ministers: "What has gone wrong? Is this the god's doing? Or some flaw in our worship? How can I break the news to *him*, after promising to help him?" But the ministers reassured him: "There is no need to worry; we shall find a girl." They raced to the harlots' street and proclaimed: "If there is one woman who lives in this quarter who will quench the longing (*virakam* = Skt. *viraha*) of a great man who has sought out our king, she will be rewarded with bracelets, necklaces, and bells, and with a pension which will keep her fed in the finest manner for the rest of her life!"

That should have done it—but, alas, the women had to inform these ministers that they had already committed themselves for the whole of that night; they had been paid in advance; if only the man could wait till tomorrow. . . . Deeply shaken, the ministers returned to the king. The latter broke out in lamentations: once again he wondered if the god was mysteriously working against him, since such a trifling matter (*aṟpam itu*, 46) was proving to be impossible to accomplish. And what about the *jaṅgama*? Was he simply waiting patiently all this while, struggling with his terrible desire? We are not told; we hear only that the king—pointedly referred to as "that pugnacious archer" (*viṟ pŏrutum ventaṉ*, 46), now clearly out of his depth, increasingly desperate, but still determined to keep his promise in one way or another—hurried off himself to hunt for a whore.

In the street of the prostitutes, the king called out his proposal: "To that woman who will enable me to keep my word to the *jaṅgama*, I will give my position on the throne; I will give her elephants and horses, gold, a palanquin of pearls—and my sceptre, which governs the world. Moreover, I myself will serve her. If she but removes the *viraha* of that great man, I shall look upon her as my mother." And then again, the demands of *viraha*: "Sages say that sexual pleasure is the highest joy available in the world. If one of you would only appease that *jaṅgama*'s *viraha*, I would offer you my very life if you asked it. Please come now!" Here, once more, we see the South Indian king at his best—intent on being faithful to his pledge, but unable to command the means to make good on it; fearful (as the commentator states)[88] of the imminent injury to his reputation (*pukaḻ*), his hero's fame; prepared to renounce his throne, and to crown a prostitute in his place, if only one would come forward to help him out of his difficulties; reduced to the unhappy state of an importunate beggar standing alone, crying for succor, in the darkness of night in his city's red-light district. The highest has become most humble once again. But the prostitutes who have heard his plea still treat him exactly like the king he is, by asking him to render judgment on their choice: "Your highness, we have only followed *your* regulations. We have already received payment to give pleasure to these devotees; what, O Master, should we do? (50)."

There could be no doubt as to the proper answer; the king could say nothing further. Ashamed (*vĕṭki*), he returned home. The arbiter of *dharma* had made the only possible dharmic decision, but he was left with another of *dharma*'s excruciating, baffling knots: unable to pry the prostitutes away from their customers, he was also unable to deny—or to fulfil—the *jaṅgama*'s demand. As he was sitting, dejected, two of his wives noticed his gloomy mood and asked him its cause. He explained to them: "An old man came here full of desire for a woman, and I agreed to help him; but there is not a single prostitute available in this town!" Hearing this, his youngest wife, Callamātevi, proposed a solution: "I don't know what you were thinking when you pledged your word to that devotee suffering from *viraha*, but if you have any thoughts of asking me to please that man, I would agree to do so." At this the king brightened, sat up and looked at his wife: "Go," he ordered—by now back in command—"to that devotee's room and do away with the distress he is suffering because of Kāma."

So the queen quickly bathed, adorned herself, and entered the room where the *jaṅgama* was staying; she took her *vīṇā* with her, and began to play sweet songs. But when she approached the *jaṅgama*, she was surprised to find him fast asleep (for she had no way of knowing that in reality he was immersed in yogic meditation). But was not her mission to make him happy? She sprinkled fragrant water on him, to wake him up; but he still would not open his eyes. Would it be right,

[88] In his prose summary of the canto, p. 368.

she asked herself, for the king's command to be in vain? Bracing herself, she fell upon him quietly (*cāntamay*, 56) and embraced him—and at that moment the god became a child in her arms, and began to cry. The baby's wailing reached the ears of the king, who—now convinced that this was, indeed, one of Śiva's amusements being played out before him, or rather through his own actions—rushed into the room, took the baby in his arms, sniffed at him and fondled him, until the child, inevitably, disappeared. Now the king was inconsolable at this loss, and he cried out to the god: "Lord, we do not know your ways. Were you testing us? You appeared as our son, and now you are gone—what is your command to us?" As Śiva appeared together with the goddess, riding his bull, the king bowed low and uttered praises; uttered, too, a request: "Please give me, in your mercy, a son to bear the burden of proper rule (*nīti*), which I still bear alone." And the god replied: "King, hear our word. *We* have become your son; and *we* shall perform your final rites." Then the god vanished—and the king lived on, ruling the world in bondage (*pantamāy*).

Thus the story ends, for once without a happy resolution of the initial problem (the king's lack of an heir). The tale has many close parallels in the rich body of *bhakti* legends (which sometimes transform the image of the prostitute into a devoted lover of the god)[89] and, in particular, in the Vīraśaiva traditions of the "paramour *jaṅgamas*" (*miṇḍa jaṅgamalu*).[90] In the latter stories, as in the Aruṇācala text, sexuality appears to have its place among the many acceptable ways of worshiping the god (or even, at times, to have pride of place, to be recommended or required by the god himself). But let us look more closely at the development of the story summarized above. This is a myth of kingship, a story focused upon the role of women in relation to the court, and to the *bhakti* god. As usual, the perfection of the social order achieved and guaranteed through the rule of a perfect king is nevertheless flawed, insufficient—for the king has no son, and thus his kingship has no future. The land may be flourishing, there is no dearth of rain, no hunger in this kingdom; but the king's individual fertility is blocked. The perfectly ordered world has an inherent sterility that always comes to light in some crucial respect. Again we may note the disorderly or "boundary" component of fertility: the king's wives are barren, despite the ideal order of the state; the myth seeks to change this situation by opening a breach in this order, in

89 For example, the reluctant prostitutes of Maturai converted to avid devotees: *Kāḷahastīśvaramāhātmyamu* 4.18-65.

90 *Basavapurāṇamu* 2.380. (p. 77).

this case through the classic "fertilizing" effect of prostitution. The god, slyly arranging the conditions for his "test," heads straight for the prostitutes' quarter, where he leaves his *gaṇas* absorbed in erotic play; he then shamelessly announces his own lustful obsession to the king, who is eventually forced to prostitute his own queen to satisfy the false *jaṅgama*'s demand. This transformation—the queen converted to the other category of royal women, the courtesans—marks the dramatic climax of the story, even as it reveals the common *bhakti* penchant for inversion or confusion of hitherto separate categories. No doubt the king, in ordering this transformation, is performing an act of renunciation, a powerful demonstration of dispassion (like the parading heroes of the *ulā*)—as is the queen, in her own way (like the indifferent *yoginī*-courtesan to whom she is now assimilated). This theme of royal self-sacrifice has already been taken up by the king's plea to the prostitutes, to whom he is prepared to offer his throne—whom he is even prepared to serve as a slave, and to regard as his own mother; note the power the prostitutes here hold over the king, and, again, the ironically positive associations they arouse (innocence, honor—they must keep their side of the transaction with the devotees—deference and respect for the king, and even chastity, as they are compared to Arundhatī and to the king's mother). All three figures—king, queen, and prostitutes—seem to have something of an ascetic or self-sacrificing character, despite the paradoxical circumstances in which it is tested and revealed; but it is the king, in his helplessness and despair, who seems, as usual, almost tragic, caught in another dharmic dilemma, and at the same time faintly ludicrous and inept.

And yet the sacrifice is rejected: the queen-turned-courtesan[91] does her best, but her acquired "yogic" eroticism confronts the true yogic stance of the god, who acts to dispel the erotic tension by a classic ploy in Hindu myth—by becoming a child in the woman's arms.[92] It is at this moment that the "synthetic" character of the story becomes apparent: for the "disorderly" pole of an improper eroticism (the queen delivered to the Śaiva beggar) is superseded, just as earlier the "ordered" pole of sterile propriety was shown to be insufficient. Both aspects, chaste dharmic order and the ambiguous breach of chastity

[91] This rapprochement of opposed categories has a modern parallel in a passage of a novel by R. K. Narayan, where a despairing wife cries out: "What is the difference between a prostitute and a married woman? The prostitute changes her men but a married woman doesn't, that's all: but both earn their food and shelter in the same manner" (1981), p. 120.

[92] Cf. Shulman (1980b), pp. 149-56, 288.

and restraint, are now subsumed in the playful god whose actions dramatically transcend each of them in turn. The king's oscillation between these poles has become irrelevant; what is left is the principle of ongoing motion and transformation, here firmly attached to the divine clown and magician in his habitual attack upon given structures, given forms. A spirit of comic transcendence has invaded the largely tragic domain of kingly love and marriage: it is this new spirit which, perhaps, explains the surprising conclusion to the story, when the god blandly reassures the king that *he*, Śiva, will perform his funeral rites; that he therefore need not worry any more about a son. This can hardly solve the king's problem; even if he is now assured of personal posthumous "salvation," he is still unable to provide for his kingdom (which, indeed, he continues to rule in a state of "bondage," as if nothing had changed). But what difference does it make? This seems to be the message of Śiva's prank. Sons, queens, prostitutes, the kingdom itself—in the end, they all pale into insignificance in the presence of the god, or in the consciousness of his comic play. We are again faced with the "black-hole" theory of South Indian kingship: ultimately the royal center, with all its radiance, its conflicts, its dynamic movement and passionate struggles, is swallowed up by the dark, unfathomable reaches of the god's *līlā*—out of space, out of time, yet somehow embedded in the kingdom's inner core.

Nevertheless, the Aruṇācala story is a tale of love, hence, in the best South Indian style, of separation, *viraha*: the word itself recurs relentlessly in the text, as our summary indicates. The story must, no doubt, rank as one of Śiva's "amusements," but its essence is hardly comic for all that; like other explorations of the king's relations with his women, it leaves a pronounced tragic impression in the end. Here it is the god who is repeatedly identified with *viraha*, understood not in the sense we have stressed repeatedly—that of the tragic longing engendered by separation—but in the simpler sense of a tormenting physical desire. Clearly, however, the former sense must lurk behind the latter; for it is the god, trying his devotees, seeking and probing for their love, with whom this story is concerned. The *viraha* he feels is real: he *needs* their love, and can never be sure of its limits, just as they long for *his*, and doubt its reality or its closeness. In true *viraha* style, the moment of realization and attainment is also the moment of separation and loss: the god disappears from the king's arms when his true identity has been established. Indeed, it is only through such disappearing acts, such dramatic absences, that the devotees come to know with certainty of the divine presence; the loss is implicit in the gain. One knows Śiva has been here only when he is gone. If this is, as we are taught, a game, then it is no less sad than it is beguiling; both god and devotee are left with their remorseless longing in the end.

Let us briefly sum up the lessons of this chapter. The king lives a life of eroticism marked by a certain prescribed recklessness, and by excess; he is himself seductive, energized, and open to the emotional labyrinth of love; he symbolizes and focuses the fertile and auspicious forces necessary for the kingdom's growth. But he also symbolizes, again through love and eroticism, the waning and decomposition of these growth-inducing powers—their containment in the tragic, ordered sphere of *viraha*, or their inverted manifestation through a "yogic" impassivity and detachment, which may be tested (with the detached and alluring courtesans) under the laboratory conditions of the court. The king is surrounded by ambiguous rings of women who define the varied frustrations of his love—cold and barren courtesans; passionate but remote admirers; faceless queens. Insofar as the king's drive toward love implicates him ever more deeply in the world, it tends to the tragic; as a romantic clown, he is usually victimized by passion, totally incapable of its creative reordering or reconstruction; the experience of separation haunts him as he swings from controlled longing to unruly despair. Transcendence lies only in the deeper *nivṛtti* of devotion, which allows both for sensual expressivity—the god himself searches for a prostitute—and for renunciation (the queen prostituted for the god), and which also points beyond these tensions even as it conserves and expresses their inherent pain.

· VII ·

Bandits and Other Tragic Heroes

PRINCE: I see a good amendment of life in thee—from praying to purse-taking.
FALSTAFF: Why, Hal, 'tis my vocation, Hal. 'Tis no sin for a man to labour in his vocation.[1]

1. Tragedy and Power

We have spoken in previous chapters of the king's "powerlessness" and its significance for the symbolic construction of his role; we have seen that this feature, far from being an accidental accretion in the myths of kingship, or a simple reflection of given structural determinants, is rather a matter of principle, a source of royal authority linked to the "disintegrative" side of the king's office—to the *nivṛtti* experiences of exile, clowning, and ascetic denial. To state the matter crudely: the wider the claims to authority made by the king, the more "impotent" he will have to be. But it is time now to speak of the king's power as well—since he is by no means all impotence and abnegation; indeed, he can adopt the latter aspect only via the exercise of a certain degree of power, which will establish his initial claim to kingly identity. The questions we must ask have to do with basic South Indian perceptions of power: its meaning within the Brahminical system that informs the state; its symbolic expressions; its relation to the problem of legitimacy and the formation of the political center; the patterns of its absorption and diffusion by the king. In pursuing these questions, we shall seek to isolate the defining features that make someone a king in South India, and that distinguish him from other powerful and symbolically central figures. At the same time, our discussion is closing its circle: we began with the royal masks, with

[1] *Henry IV, Part I*, I.ii.

the king in his "engaged," iconic aspect; we have followed him through his exile, his *nivṛtti*, the dissolution of his iconic guise; and we now restore him to his throne by recalling the *pravṛtti*—the world of power and sacrifice—out of which his kingly status was originally carved.

summary

Royal *pravṛtti*, then, is our concern in this final chapter; and, as our discussion of royal romance would suggest, this theme has a decidedly tragic aspect. Moreover, we shall see that this *pravṛtti*, again as in the case of the romantic clown, is both permeated by the experience of *viraha*—separation in varying patterns and degrees—and liable to spill over into extreme forms of disorderly excess. Both aspects inhere in what might be called the king's "heroic" past, which lives on in the tales of heroes who are both akin to, and differentiated from, kings. We shall study the heroic side of kingship in the light of these contrasting types. But let us first return briefly to the royal icons with which we began: there we found the king presiding over a world of orderly distinctions and separations, a world of *viraha* suffused by latent tensions. How does this vision relate to the king's actual *pravṛtti* mode of handling power? The iconic universe is ruled by images of an illusory balance and stasis predicated on the clear separation of major symbolic figures, such as king and Brahmin, devotee and god; these figures interact from within the bounds of their ideally defined roles (and, at least in the case of human-divine interaction, in an emotional atmosphere of unresolved yearning to transcend these bounds). But this ideal of orderly stasis can now be seen to be largely opposed to the basic thrust of South Indian social symbolism, which seeks transformation and movement as its inner law. Stasis implies the rule of illusion and false perception, a world preyed upon by rigid barriers and limits, by the artifice of fact and stubborn form. This world must break itself down in order merely to survive, or to stand in any viable relation to truth and value; and such a breakdown or decomposition ("liquefaction," *urukkam*, would perhaps be the Tamil metaphor) is in fact institutionalized by the same Brahminical world view that has contributed to the formation of the static image of order. Brahmin clowning is one powerful manifestation of this process, in its association with kingship and the state: think of the king's closest companion, the Vidūṣaka with his oral obsession, which allows him to "digest" and thereby decompose the ruler's fantasies and illusions.[2] Not all the expressions of this impulse are comic; Brahminical ritual

not just the king, but everything

[2] I am indebted to Don Handelman for this observation. See above, IV.2, and, for another "digestive" metaphor, II.4 at n. 94.

also incorporates the disintegrative undercurrents of *saṃskāra*.[3] In sacrifice, too, we see the tearing apart of reality in the interests of its eventual recomposition,[4] the entire process taking place on the thin border between the formed and the unformed—a dangerous, only partly controlled exercise in brinkmanship on the part of the priests and, at times, their royal patrons.

But there are sacrifices and sacrifices, and at an early moment in the history of Indian culture the Brahmin succeeded not only in eliminating the violent uncertainties of the ancient sacrifice but even in removing it entirely from the normal sphere of mundane relations to an "outer" zone of ideal safety and harmony;[5] and with this reformed and perfectly contained sacrifice he took his society's ultimate authority to an ideal, critical point beyond the pale. From that time on, the Brahmin could only look backward toward the political center, which he legitimized by his partial absence. This left the center in the grip of the more ancient model of sacrifice, a tragic one in which *real* violence continued to occur, and to entail *real* consequences (first of all for the symbolic magnet for sacrificial residues, the *yajamāna*/king)—but without the promise of a symbolic regeneration after the completed destruction, as in the earliest sacrificial scheme. Without the Brahmin, the royal sacrifice can only be a futile affair lacking transcendent sanction, unable to follow its natural course to the end.[6] And yet the Brahmin's backward glance became in itself a fundamental element in the construction of the Hindu state, and a major factor in its inherent dynamism. For the Brahmin's exit to the boundary still left him deeply involved in his society, as many have remarked;[7] it is his values that permeate the political center in a paradoxical movement of support and critical erosion. Officially, these values contribute to the stasis—the iconic image of harmony and balance. But in a deeper sense, the relegation of truth to the boundary could not but undermine the center, which must look outside itself for ultimate value as well as for release from the tragic limitations of a static partial order. The

[3] See above, III.1.

[4] See Heesterman (1964) and (1967).

[5] Heesterman (1964 and 1978).

[6] See above, I.3 at n. 84.

[7] Thapar (1978), pp. 63-104. Eisenstadt (1983) speaks of the paradox that "this rather extreme ideal of renunciation, of going out of the mundane world, does at the same time contain a very strong interweaving with the mundane world and with the lay life, and that just because of this the carriers of this ideal—in contrast to the monkhood or sectarians of the monotheistic civilizations—have had a much weaker leverage for the reconstruction of the mundane world, for the reconstruction of the major institutional spheres in a totally new direction." And cf. Dumont (1970), pp. 33-60.

result is the institutionalized processes of diffusion and self-transcendence which largely define the Indian political center. One begins, as it were, with an ideal of stasis, or with a precariously balanced order, but this state is inevitably transformed by creative disintegration, by the incorporation of the boundary with its ambiguities and its playful transmutational power: tragic *viraha* opens itself up to comic *viḷaiyāṭal.* In symbolic terms, the king is made into a clown. Without such a movement or such an opening, no South Indian structure of power can in the long run, successfully claim legitimacy or centrality.

This is our point of departure: the various levels and signs of this active "decomposition will be more carefully distinguished below. But what about those structures of power which do not, in fact, become wholly legitimate or central? Such structures certainly exist. One thinks at once of various peripheral mini-states sometimes organized around what might be called a "heroic" kingship (such as the Maṟavar dynasties of Ramnad District and elsewhere, or the Veṭṭuva chiefdoms in Kŏṅku).[8] Nicholas Dirks has recently explored the process by which one such group, the Ūttumalai Maṟavar of western Tirunĕlveli, accomplished—at least in their own perspective—the transition from early, "nonkingly" power to the legitimacy of a self-styled royal center.[9] How is this process seen from within the "central" sphere of traditional South Indian royal symbolism? Where do the untamed, heroic claimants of power fit into the wider scheme of the social universe? In the case of the Ūttumalai Maṟavar, as of others we shall examine, the early stage of "raw" power is associated both with banditry and with the wilderness. This association is of fundamental importance to the symbolism of the South Indian state: the bandit stands as a basic symbol of unchecked power in its natural, seemingly marginal location. Nevertheless, as we shall see, the South Indian bandit also stands remarkably close to the king.

Indeed, the bandit is marginal less because of any geographical considerations than by virtue of his relation to central values and symbols. Centricity here is a semantic, not a spatial category. In essence, the center defines itself through the processes of taming, questioning, relinquishing, or splitting off raw power. Unlike the bandit, the king cannot leave power alone: to be king, to stay king, he must be seen either to control power through ascetic denial—this is the yogic image of Kampaṉ's royal icon, discussed above in Chapter II—

[8] See Stein's remarks on the "peripheral" *nāṭu* (1980), pp. 134-40. On Kŏṅku see Arokiaswami (1956); Beck (1982), pp. 27-29. On Maṟavar kingship, see Breckenridge (1978); Price (1979); Dirks (1982).

[9] Dirks (1982).

or, better still, to surrender it again and again in symbolic moments of a prescribed kenosis. Failing this, he will be tainted in the eyes of his Brahmin guarantors with the obscenity that always appears to them to accompany unchecked power. The bandit, on the other hand, has no such compulsion—until the moment he wishes to be king. In his natural, unreconstructed state, he enjoys a pleroma of violent power that he need not hesitate to use. He is also endowed with a striking homogeneity, in stark contrast with the king. His world is the ancient sacrificial universe, which allows destruction its place—before the splitting off of Brahmin and kingship in the interests of maintaining the Brahmin's ideal, uncontaminating sacrifice. But the price the bandit pays is, not surprisingly, his own destruction: the violent sacrifice consumes him, although it also transforms him at the same time in the direction of divinity. This transformation always has a tragic coloring; the bandit appears to confirm, usually with his death, the reality and stability of the world that destroys him. Faced with what he perceives as a real boundary—that between life and death—he heroically crashes against it and dies. His royal counterpart, confronting such a boundary, transforms himself, empties himself, changes masks, and eludes its power.

Thus the bandit has a link with tragedy and sacrificial death, a link that partly marks him off from the king. His world is, moreover, suffused with continuity and with meaning: we consistently find the bandit-hero, like the martial heroes of folk epics such as the Telugu *Palnāṭi virula katha*, choosing a meaningful death, of his own making, as a final act of self-assertion and deliberate acceptance of his fate. He pursues the sacrifice to its bitter end, never doubting its final validity and reality; and he is rewarded by being transfigured: the classical aim of the completed sacrifice. But his death has no impact on the center, where entropy and involution, not a simple progression from hero to god, are the rule. Indeed, the bandit is, in a sense, twice removed from the center, which has already lost much of its authority to the Brahmin gatekeepers; the bandit is now beyond the pale of this fragmented center, however much it may continue to fascinate him with its illusions of legitimacy and splendor.

This chapter will discuss two major types, the bandit-hero and the hero as tragic exemplar, and an intermediary figure (the bandit-turned-clown). Our concern is with the relations these figures have with the king, and with the nature of the transition that allows the latter to differentiate himself from the former, thereby contributing to the construction of a recognized royal center.

2. Guardians and Thieves

Let us begin with a story that describes a *rapprochement* of bandit and king. According to the local tradition of the Vaiṣṇava shrine in Śrīvaikuṇṭam, a thief called Kāladūṣaka, leader of a band of robbers, used to live in the wilderness near the shrine. Kāladūṣaka would spend half his ill-gotten gains on prostitutes and gambling, but the other half he reserved for the god, Vaikuṇṭhanātha. Eventually the local king closed in on the thief, who sought refuge in Vaikuṇṭhanātha's shrine. The god granted him protection and then, taking the form of a robber himself, appeared to the king; admonished and instructed by the deity, the king forgave Kāladūṣaka and begged Viṣṇu to remain at Śrīvaikuṇṭam as Coranātha (Tamil Kaḷḷappirāṉ, "lord of thieves"). The king and the robber then collaborated in holding a ritual celebration: in the month of Caitra, the king and the robber decorated the town and distributed presents, especially to the Brahmins. Viṣṇu—"Lord of the Universe and Leader of Robbers"—was pleased, and he gave release to both the king and the robber. The king and Kāladūṣaka performed this festival together every year.[10]

Some versions of this story make Kāladūṣaka into a Robin-Hoodlike hero: he never oppressed the righteous but would seek out evildoers and rob them; after giving half his gains to the god and satisfying his own needs, he would distribute the rest among the poor.[11] This portrayal of the thief—which takes him out of the more common category of scandalous bandit-heroes in South India[12]—may help to justify Viṣṇu's intervention on his behalf. But the true basis for the linkage between king and robber seems to be stated by the god in his sermon to the king: "Things not given as charity will perish; kings seize them, and robbers steal them."[13] In the perspective of this story, kings and thieves can apparently be classed together; the original opposition between the two gives way to a collaboration clearly felt to be quite fitting. This relation of king to robber occurs, as we shall see, in many stories; one thinks of *Tirukkuṟal* 552, where the king who demands

[10] *Vaikuṇṭanāthamāhātmya* 5.48-52, summarized by Hardy (1978), pp. 147-48.

[11] Pāskarat Tŏṇṭaimāṉ (1971), pp. 200-201; R. K. Das (1964), pp. 30-31.

[12] Robin Hood figures do, however, exist in South Indian folklore, for example, Kochunni in Kerala and Sarjappa Nāyaka in Karnataka (my thanks to J. S. Paramashivaiah for the latter reference).

[13] Pāskarat Tŏṇṭaimāṉ (1971), p. 201. (The god says he has created Kāladūṣaka in order to teach this truth.)

money from his subjects is compared to a highwayman who stands with his spear and threatens passersby: "Your money or your life."[14]

Friedhelm Hardy, who has summarized and discussed the myth from Śrīvaikuṇṭam, interprets it in the light of local politics and society: Śrīvaikuṇṭam is situated in an area inhabited by members of the Kaḷḷar caste (whose name means "thieves"), and the chief trustee of the temple is a Kaḷḷar. The story thus describes the modus vivendi achieved by the Kaḷḷar, the Brahmins, and the local ruler, as symbolized by the festival jointly managed by the king and the head of the Kaḷḷar community. In other words, we have here "the legitimization of a particular power-structure."[15] This analysis is undoubtedly correct. For our purposes, it is important to note the symbolic roles attached to the Kaḷḷar, who, as seen above, are in a sense assimilated to the king. The Kaḷḷar, a colorful community concentrated chiefly in Maturai and Tanjore Districts of Tamil Nadu, represent the common South Indian category of institutionalized *jātis* of thieves or dacoits.[16] In South India, a bandit is not "made"—by the social and economic pressures that elsewhere create the phenomenon of "social banditry"[17]—but rather born as such, so that highway robbery becomes a traditional, socially recognized occupation of specific castes, with its own symbolic legitimation. Indeed, if someone born into a robber caste were to seek to abandon this "profession," he would, in theory at least, be guilty of straying from his *dharma*—just as demons, in the world of Hindu myth, must be discouraged from being anything but demonic.[18] Bandits, like demons, are a necessary presence in the social world.

Yet in most cases there is a certain built-in ambiguity about this role. The association with kingship, with *its* inherent ambiguities, is only one expression of this shifting evaluation, which places the bandit in varying settings of light and shadow. Thus the Kaḷḷar, despite their well-established reputation as thieves, are today for the most part settled agriculturists. As Dumont states in his comprehensive study of one branch of this community:

[14] *velŏṭu niṉṟāṉ iṭu ĕṉṟatu polum/ kolŏṭu niṉṟāṉ iravu*. And what king does *not* demand money from his people?

[15] Hardy (1978), p. 148.

[16] And not only South Indian: see Hobsbawm (1969), p. 15n.; Sontheimer (1976), pp. 85-89; Weber (1958), pp. 73-74; Winther (1972); Baines (1912), pp. 80-82.

[17] See Hobsbawm (1969), *passim*. There is a rapidly growing literature on social banditry: see, for example, Johnston (1980); Moss (1978); Rossetti (1982).

[18] Above, III.2; O'Flaherty (1976), pp. 127-36.

> In our time . . . the Kallar appears first of all as a peasant—a mediocre cultivator, perhaps, but one who is more or less tied to the soil, from which he derives at least part of his subsistance. He also has, or had, two sources of additional income: on the one hand, thievery, and, on the other, guarding against theft—the watchman's function.[19]

The thief becomes a watchman, the guardian steals from his master: the Kaḷḷar belong in this respect in the universal category of dangerous watchmen. As Hobsbawm notes, the ideal is the "formal conversion of poachers into gatekeepers. . . . In India as in Sicily the professions of village and field, or cattle-watchmen, were often interchangeable with that of bandit."[20] This role of the Kaḷḷar is bound up with the institution of *pāṭikāval*, the village police system; traditionally, the Kaḷḷar have been *kāvalkārar* in their areas.[21] In Chola times, when Veḷāḷa agriculturists were sent to settle new lands, the Kaḷḷar were sent with them as watchmen.[22] But the guardian or gatekeeper is by nature a highly ambivalent figure, whether he stands in the fields or at the threshold of a shrine. One sees this clearly in the cult of Kaṟuppaṉ (Kaṟuppaṇṇacuvāmi, Kaṟuppucāmi), who is one of the Kaḷḷar's favored deities.[23] This god stands as guardian at the entrance to the great shrine of Aḻakar-Viṣṇu (who is also known as Kaḷḷaḻakar because of *his* relation to the Kaḷḷar) at Tirumāliruñcolai near Maturai. The symbolism of the threshold is unmistakable here, for Kaṟuppaṉ has no image in this shrine; he is worshiped in the form of the massive doors to the temple, and offerings are brought to the famous Eighteen Steps beneath these doors.[24] Kaṟuppaṉ is a violent deity: his name means

[19] Dumont (1957), p. 7. For further information on the Kaḷḷar, see Thurston (1909), 3:53-91; Blackburn (1978a).

[20] Hobsbawm (1969), p. 78. Cf. Baines (1912), p. 80: "There are few countries, possibly none, in which the old counsel to set a thief to catch a thief has been more widely and conscientiously put into practise than in India." (My thanks to Diane Coccari for bringing this work to my attention.)

[21] On *pāṭikāval*, see Mahalingam (1967), pp. 246-53. Cf. the role of the Beḍar in Karnataka: Derrett (1957), pp. 7-9.

[22] Blackburn (1978a), p. 45.

[23] See Dumont (1957), pp. 368-71; (1959); Hudson (1982); Whitehead (1921), pp. 113-15, mistakenly identifying Kaṟuppaṉ with Maturaivīraṉ; Radha Krishna (1942), pp. 210-15; *Aḻakar varṇippu*, p. 6.

[24] *Census of India*, 1961, Vol. IX, Part XI-D: *Temples of Madras State*. VI. *Madurai and Ramanathapuram*, p. 107. The myth told about the Eighteen Steps—under which are said to be buried eighteen magicians from Malabar who came to steal the divinity of this shrine—is given in Whitehead (1921), pp. 113-15; Radha Krishna (1942), pp.

"the Black," and he demands blood sacrifices—indeed, one myth current among the Pramalai Kaḷḷar explains his absence from the temple of Aḻakar (that is, the absence of an image of him there?) by his dissatisfaction with the vegetarian cuisine offered in the shrine.[25] As the gatekeeper of Aḻakar (and, in other contexts, of the vegetarian god Aiyaṉār), Kaṟuppaṉ may be said to represent the higher deity; as his protector, Kaṟuppaṉ (still invisible, that is, not represented iconically) accompanies Aḻakar on his annual journey in the month of Citra, to the boundary of Maturai.[26] (During this latter festival, crowds of Kaḷḷar also accompany the god, supposedly in order to guard the great money chests which are filled with the devotees' gifts—and thus we see again the persistent paradox of the thieves made into guardians.)[27] Finally, Kaṟuppaṉ is by virtue of his violent tendencies, carnivorous tastes, dark color, and general personality no different from the demons (*pey*) against whom he must fight.[28] In much the same way, his worshipers, the Kaḷḷar, reveal a collective ambiguity in their character—part peasant, part watchman, part bandit or cattle thief. Violent power, contained or unleashed, socially conservative or boldly destructive, is a normal part of their inheritance.

Recently, a spirited defense of the Kaḷḷar has been published by Stuart Blackburn, who convincingly shows how external pressures, especially those connected to the extension of British colonial rule, may have reduced the Kaḷḷar to the "wild Collerie" image popular in British writings and, ultimately, to the status of a Criminal Tribe.[29] Blackburn emphasizes the settled role of the Kaḷḷar peasants, although he admits that in the medieval period some Kaḷḷar were "undoubtedly involved in cattle raids and possibly formed a reservoir of warriors for local military chieftains."[30] Yet this diversification would appear to be a matter of principle; the ambivalent nature of the Kaḷḷar, as indicated by their very name, is clearly mentioned in the precolonial

---

210-15. There exists a custom of swearing oaths to prove one's innocence at this site, before the doors of Kaṟuppaṉ (Whitehead [1921], p. 115)—an interesting association of truthfulness with the inherently ambivalent, somewhat menacing guardian deity.

[25] Dumont (1957), p. 369.

[26] For details, see Hudson (1982).

[27] *Ibid.; Aḻakar varṇippu*, pp. 6-7: here we learn of the initial subjugation of the Kaḷḷar by the god, after which they become his guardians. Their protection is, apparently, no longer felt to be sufficient, since today policemen also accompany the god on his journey. Kaḷḷaḻakar appears dressed as a Kaḷḷar during this festival, and the Kaḷḷars are said to have the right to pull his car: Thurston (1909), 3:84-85, citing J. Sharrock.

[28] See Dumont (1959).

[29] Blackburn (1978a).

[30] *Ibid.*, p. 44.

literature.[31] Moreover, the Kaḷḷar's own traditions indicate something of this conception. The Kaḷḷar share with the Maṟavar the story of their descent from the union of Indra and Ahalyā: according to this version of the classical myth, Indra seduced Ahalyā, the wife of the Brahmin sage Gautama, and four sons were born—Kaḷḷaṉ, Maṟavaṉ, Akampaṭiyaṉ, and Veḷāḷaṉ.[32] This story expresses the link between the Kaḷḷar and the equally martial Maṟavar and Akampaṭiyar; these three castes, sometimes referred to as *muventira kulam* ("the three families of Indra"), can claim an original royal status on the basis of their alleged descent from Indra. Again we see robber and king mutually confronted. The relatively low status of these castes can then be explained as the result of the hypogamous (*pratiloma*) union of a king (Indra) and a Brahmin woman (Ahalyā). But the story also reveals the Kaḷḷar's sense of closeness to the Veḷāḷar; a Tamil proverb even speaks of the Kaḷḷar slowly turning into the Veḷāḷar. The tradition taken as a whole thus nicely embodies the conflicting pulls of Kaḷḷar social history.

3. The Hero as Thief

Perhaps the defense of the Kaḷḷar could be undertaken from a different angle. There is every reason to suppose that the pattern of quasi-sedentary, quasi-predatory existence, or of a regular alternation between the two styles, is an ancient one in India. Heesterman has explained the engimatic rites of the Vrātyas as connected to just such a pattern, which may be preserved in the tradition that the Kuru-Pañcālas would set out during the cold season on a *digvijaya*, a "conquest of the quarters": they would seize the barley crop, forage for food, and return home before the rains in order to work their own fields.[33] If we limit ourselves to the Tamil area, we find an ancient conception of heroism as somehow linked to the raider, robber, and cattle rustler. There is, in fact, a striking fluctuation in the meanings of the basic terms. Take, for example, *maṟavaṉ*, defined in the *Dravidian Etymological Dictionary* as "inhabitant of desert tract, of hilly tract, one

[31] For example, in the Maturaivīraṉ cycle: see below, section 4. And cf. Satyanatha Aiyar (1924), pp. 273, 292, 305.

[32] The story is given by Thurston (1909), 3:62-63; 5:23; Dumont (1957), p. 5, with popular etymologies for the names of the four sons. The story is based on *Rām.* 1.47.15-32 (which, of course, knows nothing of any progeny from the illicit union); cf. the Tamil version by Kampaṉ, 1.543-550.

[33] Heesterman (1962), pp. 1-37.

belonging to the caste of warriors, person of Maṟava caste, warrior, hero, commander, military chief, cruel, wicked person."[34] We have just met the Maṟavar as a warlike caste claiming, like the Kaḷḷar, descent from Indra and Ahalyā.[35] But in the early medieval textbook of poetics, the *Puṟappŏruḷ veṇpāmālai, maṟavar* is a generalized term for the ancient class (*mūtta kuṭi*) of heroes who appeared with swords in their hands after the universal deluge, when only the mountains were visible, and the earth was submerged.[36] Note the association of the hero with a kind of primordial power. The word is sometimes used in this sense by the "Caṅkam" poets of the early centuries A.D., while *maṟam*, the related abstract noun, can mean "heroism, bravery" (usually with the added connotation of fierceness or even cruelty).[37] But the classical poets also know a distinction between the *maṟakkuṭi*, the wild, predatory communities, and the *aṟakkuṭi* or settled agriculturists. Thus in *Cilappatikāram* 12 (a canto devoted to the Veṭṭuvar or Ĕyiṉar hunters), Cāliṉi, a girl possessed by the goddess, cries out:

> In the great villages, the rich herds are flourishing;
> but the meeting places of the Ĕyiṉar with their strong bows
> are desolate.
> The inherited path of the heroes gives forth nothing new;
> like settled folk, the Ĕyiṉar are cowed,
> their spirit
> snuffed out.[38]

We also find the Maṟavar and Ĕyiṉar as the highway robbers who are the proper residents of the wilderness (*pālai*) tract, according to the textbooks of poetics. These Maṟavar are famous for their cruelty; the *pālai* region is

> a mournful way deserted even by the birds,
> where dwell the fierce-eyed Maṟavar
> with their robust bodies,
> terrible strength,
> tiger's look,

[34] DED 3900, quoting the *Tamil Lexicon*.

[35] See Thurston (1909), 5:22-48; Breckenridge (1978); Dirks (1982).

[36] *Puṟappŏruḷ vĕṇpāmālai* 2 (*karantai*).13-14; cf. the somewhat different translation by Pope (1973), p. 23.

[37] For example, *Puṟan.* 271. In later times *maṟam* becomes equivalent to *adharma*, but positive connotations linger on—hence the problem presented, for example, by Kampaṉ's antihero Rāvaṇa, who embodies *maṟam*. Kampaṉ has been accused of preferring Rāvaṇa to the dharmic hero Rama. See above, VI.3 after n. 76.

[38] *Cil.* 12.12-15.

bound bows,
curled hair,
just waiting to do evil:
they will take the life of wayfarers
even when there is nothing to steal,
just to see their bodies twist
in dying.[39]

We thus find two related notions. On the one hand, bandits and robbers are given their place within the conventional scheme of the Tamil universe; they belong in the wilderness and present a contrast to settled peasant life. On the other hand, the very concept of the hero incorporates something of the Maṟavar as marauder. One sees this in the classification of the cattle raid (in *vĕṭcittiṇai*) as the normal preliminary to war. We may thus look back to a period when cattle raiding was a standard feature of the relations between neighboring "kingdoms"—and we are speaking of the small-scale, "heroic" kingdoms of the Caṅkam period—even allowing for the somewhat artificial schematization apparent in the Caṅkam conventions.[40] The hero shades off into the cattle thief. Something of this idea survives throughout the medieval period in Tamil Nadu, as does the practice of worshiping a fallen hero by erecting a hero-stone; inscriptions on these memorial stones often point to the hero's death in the course of a cattle raid—usually while the hero was *defending* the village cattle from thieves.[41] The hero-stone, it must be stressed, is perceived as the abode of a sacred presence.

It is in this light that we may regard the Maṟavar cattle raiders and hunters of medieval times,[42] and, perhaps, the traditions linking the Kaḷḷar to highway robbery. The Kaḷḷar appear for the most part as settled peasants, but they stand outside the right-left division of Tamil society. They are not, apparently, seen as wholly rooted in their agricultural pursuits. But, whether as peasants or as raiders, they have a recognized role in society. Moreover, their seemingly antisocial

[39] *Kalittŏkai* 1.4.1-6. Cuntaramūrtti's *patikam* 49, on Tirumurukaṉpūṇṭi, offers graphic descriptions of highwaymen such as these (with whom the local deity, Śiva, has ambiguous but intimate connections). And on *pālai*, see above, V.7.

[40] For comparative evidence, see Lincoln (1976); Walcot (1979); and cf. Heesterman (1957), chapter 16.

[41] This motif also occurs in folk ballads: see Blackburn (1978), p. 135. On hero-stones, see Hart (1975), pp. 25-26; Derrett (1957), pp. 9-10; Deleury (1960; arguing, p. 198, that the famous Viṭhobā of Paṇḍharpūr is a "later development of a primitive hero-stone").

[42] See *PP* 3.3.5-7, 65.

characteristics are precisely what relates them to heroism and even to kingship. Endowed with the symbolism of the watchman-thief, they share the image of the "outsider" whose relative freedom is translated into anomalous status. Usually ranked as low, they are in some ways remarkably close to prestigious figures in the social hierarchy. Their "outsider" quality, far from implying any real form of exclusion, seems rather to connect them with central symbols of the social order.

At the same time, the traditions linked to these communities point to the tragic propensities of the outsider-hero. For the Tamil hero, as for others,[43] tragedy inheres in the relation between his dynamic power—"a kind of natural force and as such . . . never adequately judged or expressed by men's notions of moral excellence"[44]—and the bounded universe in which he is never fully at home. This power is a necessary factor in the construction of a viable society, but its violent character marks the hero as an outcast even as it links him with other disorderly figures, especially those on the other side of the boundary between man and divinity. In fact, as we shall see, the South Indian tragedies of the bandit-hero explore this transition from man to deity, even as Sophocles did in his final, heroic tragedy, *Oedipus at Colonus.* Like the aged Oedipus, like Philoctetes and Ajax, our Tamil heroes are a strangely potent mixture of outcast and superman, the cursed and the blessed.[45] A certain perversity is rooted in their way of being, and expresses the imperatives of their native power. "At bottom, the crooked spirit is an aspect of heroic character: it is the hero's need to play his match with death, never to miss a move in which he can expose himself to danger."[46] These games are often seen as deadly serious, the prelude to a grim and bloody sacrifice when the hero falls victim to his reckless drives; and in this respect he may be distinguished from the king/clown. (Perhaps we have here a partial explanation for the largely tragic themes that haunt the earliest South Indian literature on kingship, the Caṅkam poems on kings who, in general, fit into a heroic ethos with its predilection for tragedy.) The hero is engaged in a recognizable, more or less realistic world, where power, death, and suffering are all far too real to be taken lightly, or to be easily transcended; he acts within these given limitations, which confer meaning upon his fate. The "central" king of the medieval period, though he, too, must experience this tragic blend of "realistic" factors, is not limited by it in the same way; his painful *pravṛtti* is part of a

[43] Grene (1967), pp. 113-17; cf. Kailasapathy (1968); above, III.4, on Aśvatthāman.

[44] Grene (1967), p. 116.

[45] See Grene and Lattimore (1959), pp. 3-7.

[46] Hamori (1975), p. 9.

more wide-ranging process of transformation in which the given "reality" is undermined and decomposed.

Similarly for the gods, with whom the bandit-heroes are indirectly compared. If the hero who is half bandit can be deified and worshiped, it is no surprise to find a deity dressed up as a bandit. Indeed, we have already noted one instance of this possibility in the myth of Coranātha from Śrīvaikuṇṭam. South India, in fact, offers a considerable theology of thieving. But these banditlike deities are *playing*—with the world, with their devotees. We can observe this pattern in both Śaiva and Vaiṣṇava variants. Śiva, the antinomian deity *par excellence*,[47] has no hesitation about robbing his own devotee, Cuntaramūrtti, by sending his troops of demons dressed as hunters (*veṭar*) or by appearing himself as a *veṭaṉ*.[48] Śiva's specialty, however, is in turning weddings into a kind of heroic raid: in the main Tamil version of the Dakṣa myth, Śiva steals his own bride, Umā, from her father's house (just as the Caṅkam hero-lover elopes with his bride);[49] similarly, he steals the bridegroom—once again Cuntaramūrtti—at a Brahmin wedding;[50] but he is also capable of waiting for some years after the wedding, as when he makes off with the wife of his devotee, Iyaṟpakaiyār (this time with the husband's consent).[51] This conjunction of marriage and robbery is clearly a standard theme, which the *bhakti* poets use metaphorically to suggest the ravishing of the soul by the divine: God is "the thief who steals my heart" (*ĕṉṉ uḷḷaṅ kavar kaḷvaṉ*).[52] The antinomian power of *bhakti* shines through this epithet, which puts the god in the category of antisocial predators: Śiva is thus a wild bandit who preys upon the devotee, and the love which the latter feels for the god threatens to break through all of society's barriers.

The same term (*uḷḷaṅ kavar kaḷvaṉ*) is used pointedly to describe Viṣṇu as Kaḷḷappirāṉ/Coranātha,[53] thus fusing the metaphorical and the mythic usages; the Vaiṣṇava poet-saints are no less fond of referring to their god as a thief than are their Śaiva counterparts.[54] But it is, of

[47] Note that Śiva's antecedent, the Vedic Rudra, is also a robber and the lord of highwaymen (VS 16.20-21).

[48] *PP* 3911-3918 (the story is linked to *patikam* 49, on Tirumurukaṉpūṇṭi: see note 39 above). And cf. Francis (1906), p. 398; Krishnaswami (1937), p. 10.

[49] *Kantapurāṇam* 6.1-2, 5-11, 16-20; see Shulman (1980b), pp. 337-46.

[50] *PP* 147-220.

[51] *Ibid.* 404-39.

[52] Tiruñāṉacampantar, *Tevāram* 1.1-10.

[53] *uḷḷaṅ kavar kaḷvaṉ āṉa parantāmaṉ kaḷḷappirāṉākavum niṉṟ' irukkiṟār*: Pāskarat Tŏṇṭaimāṉ (1971), p. 201.

[54] For example, Kampaṉ, *Irāmāvatāram* 1.611, where Rāma is described by the lovesick Sītā as a thief who entered by way of her eyes and robbed her of her feminine modesty.

course, Kṛṣṇa—especially the young Kṛṣṇa, the butter thief and, slightly older, the cowherd who hides the *gopīs*' saris—who merits the title of robber or bandit.[55] Here again one finds a notion of divinity as transcending order and as exemplifying the wild love (*preman*) opposed to structure, sanity, and control.

One striking implication of all this is the interesting possibility that emerges for imitatio Dei. If god is a bandit, to rob is divine—especially if one robs in the name or interests of the deity. Thus Māṇikkavācakar can lavish his king's funds on various pious purposes, and the treasurer of Kṛṣṇadevarāya empties the king's treasury to build a temple at Lepākṣi.[56] More remarkable still is the story of Tirumaṅkaiyāḻvār (Skt. Parakāla) as it appears in Vaiṣṇava hagiographic literature from the *Divyasūricarita* onward.[57] Tirumaṅkaiyāḻvār is depicted in the Vaiṣṇava tradition as a highwayman who robbed travelers in order to defray the expense of feeding 1,008 Vaiṣṇavas each day; who stole the golden image of the Buddha in a famous shrine in Nākapaṭṭiṉam (in a daring raid that won him a rebuke from the Chola king); and who even waylaid and despoiled the great god Viṣṇu himself. Tirumaṅkaiyāḻvār is, of course, one of the great poets of South Indian Vaiṣṇava *bhakti*; we thus see in his case the convergence of three basic roles—bandit, poet, and devotee.

The notion of a bandit-poet recurs in the tradition: indeed, a famous story makes Vālmīki, the author of the *Rāmāyaṇa* and, according to the Sanskrit tradition, the very first poet (*ādikavi*), into a hunter-bandit. Vālmīki is said to have preyed upon hapless travelers in order to support his wife and children, until one day one of his victims (in some versions, the Seven Sages) proved to him that his family would refuse to share any part of the burden of evil he was accumulating; shocked by this revelation, Vālmīki allowed himself to be given a *mantra* (the word *marā*, the name of a tree which figures in the Rāma story); as he repeated this *mantra* incessantly, over a period of many years, the word turned into "Rāma," and an anthill (*valmīka*) grew over the immobile bandit-devotee—whence his name, Vālmīki.[58] This

[55] See Hawley (1979, 1983). A Gujarati temple myth relates how Kṛṣṇa helped his devotee steal his (Kṛṣṇa's) image from the temple in Dvārakā: Pocock (1973), pp. 106-107. The story is perfectly in harmony with Kṛṣṇa's character.

[56] *Tiruviḷai.* 58-60; Ramesan (1962), pp. 40-41.

[57] As distinct from what may be deduced about the real biography of this poet: Hardy (1979). See *Divyasūricarita* 8.1-66, 13.87-122, 14.1-103.

[58] *Adhyātmarāmāyaṇa* 2.6.64-86 (pp. 253-57); cf. Irāmacāmippulavar (1963), 2:993-95; for a delightful modern version, see Narayan (1973), pp. 126-35. A brief version, which makes Vālmīki a hunter (*veṭaṉ*) without referring to his bandit's role, appears in *Cĕy-aṅkŏṇṭār vaḷakkam*, verse 1 with commentary (p. 3). The story is absent from the *Vālmīkirāmāyaṇa*. Cf. *MBh*, SR, 13.24.6-8 (Vālmīki accused of Brahminicide).

story stresses the poet's transition from the violent life of a bandit to the saintly role of a poet-sage; it remains significant that the tradition identifies its first poet as a bandit. Poetry, it seems, like the bandit's superabundance of power, has its source in the disorderly setting of the social border.[59]

4. Maturaivīraṉ, the Hero of Maturai

With these associations in mind, we may now turn to a text that epitomizes the South Indian bandit's symbolic role. The *Maturaivīracuvāmikatai* is a Tamil folk ballad that purports to describe events in Maturai during the seventeenth century, at the time of the famous Tirumalai Nāyakkar (1623-1659). The text itself is, no doubt, later than this period; it clearly reflects a Tamil oral milieu in its language and style as well as in the viewpoint it brings to bear upon its tale. Although its hero, Maturaivīraṉ, lacks certain features we would expect from a South Indian bandit—he is not a member of a bandit caste, lives in towns rather than the wilderness, does not waylay travelers—he does exemplify many of the traits we have been discussing: the identification as a hero connected to disorder and violent force; the tendency to plunder and steal (both money or goods and, especially, women); a social role that pits him in interesting ways against the king; the symbolism of the gatekeeper-guard; the attribution of divinity with all its accompanying ambivalence and tension; a largely tragic coloring. Maturaivīraṉ belongs, moreover, in a class that includes other "disreputable" divine heroes and thieves such as Kāttavarāyaṉ, Cuṭalaimāṭaṉ (the latter more localized in his fame), and the Telugu hero Pāpaḍu.[60] Maturaivīraṉ is worshiped today in shrines throughout the Tamil area, often as an attendant or gatekeeper of the village goddess, sometimes in connection with another god.[61] His story may be succinctly summarized as follows:[62]

Tuḷacimakārājaṉ, the righteous king of Kāśī, had no children. He worshiped Viśvanātha (Śiva in Kāśī) and performed the pious acts recommended by his Brahmin advisers; Śiva was pleased and granted him a son. But no sooner was the child born than the king's astrologer

[59] A Talmudic parallel to this notion—the bandit origins of the culture hero—may be seen in the career of Resh Lakish, famous as a bandit (*lisṭim*) before he turned to study: see *Baba Metzi'a* 84a.

[60] On Pāpaḍu, see the study by Richards and Rao (1980).

[61] See Whitehead (1921), pp. 25, 38, 89, 92, 113.

[62] The edition I have used (published by Ār. Ji. Pati Company, 1972) runs to approximately 2,200 lines.

predicted that if the baby were allowed to remain in his home, the entire kingdom would perish. The grief-stricken king reluctantly ordered his son to be carried on a golden platter, honored by soldiers, musicians, and dancers, to the forest and abandoned there.

The child was deposited at the base of a tree. Soon a serpent was attracted by his cries; the serpent prophesied a great future for the child: at the age of ten he would defeat an entire army; he would rule Maturai after defeating the Kaḷḷar; he would reach a great station because of women, and would be worshiped at the feet of the goddess Mīnākṣī. Each day this serpent brought *amṛta* to sustain the baby, until one day he was found by a Cakkili woman (a member of the Untouchable caste of leatherworkers and shoemakers). She took him home to her husband, who rejoiced with her at this gift of a child by Śiva; they called a carpenter to make him a cradle, and they brought the child up according to the proper way.

Eventually, however, word spread that the king's son was growing up in the house of an Untouchable shoemaker. When the Cakkili foster parents heard that the king had learned of this, they fled with the child to another land, where Pŏmmaṇa Nāyakkaṉ the Tŏṭṭiyaṉ[63] was ruling. The father joined the ranks of the king's servant-guards.

Meanwhile, the child was growing up into a strong and fearless lad who roamed the forests hunting bears, tigers, lions, and elephants. One day his father was sent to guard the daughter of Pŏmmaṇa Nāyakkaṉ; the girl had just reached puberty and was secluded in a hut at the edge of the town during the period of her impurity. But Varuṇa sent a great storm which darkened the entire universe, and the old Cakkiliyaṉ was reluctant to go to his post. His son volunteered to take his place. There he succeeded in seducing the girl, Pŏmmiyammāḷ, after calming her fears by revealing his original, royal birth; convinced that he was not, after all, an Untouchable, Pŏmmi embraced him as her husband and her god.

Our hero, Maturaivīraṉ, remained at his post as Pŏmmi's guardian. Secretly he brought her a wedding-chain (*tāli*) and married her in the presence of the gods. He also made her a pair of fine slippers (*mitiyaṭi*) according to the craftsmanship standards of Maturai (*maturaivelai*).

After thirty days, Pŏmmi's father sent a procession to bring his daughter back to the palace. They burned her hut and took Pŏmmi

[63] The Tŏṭṭiyar are Telugu-speaking agriculturists settled in the Tamil country; their caste title is Nāyakkaṉ, and they may be descended from soldiers of the Nāyak kings of Vijayanagar. See Thurston (1909), 7:183-97; on p. 191 he notes the custom whereby a Tŏṭṭiyaṉ girl upon attaining puberty is kept in a separate hut watched by a Cakkiliyaṉ; see the summary of our text, below.

home, while the Cakkiliyar blew horns and beat drums and servant-girls waved lights to ward off the evil eye. Pŏmmaṇaṉ gave a great feast in celebration of this occasion. But that night Maturaivīraṉ longed for Pŏmmi. Taking the form of a fly, he flew past the guards and entered the palace through the eaves under the roof. Once inside, he resumed his proper form and embraced his beloved. Taking a thousand gold coins, a tent (*kūṭāram*), and the king's horse, they evaded the guards and fled together into the night.

In the morning, when Pŏmmaṇaṉ discovered that his daughter was missing, he gathered an army to pursue her. They encountered a shepherd who pointed the way, and thus they soon came upon the lovers encamped in the dry bed of the Kāverī River. Pŏmmi pleaded with Maturaivīraṉ not to kill her father, but to no avail: the hero annihilated the entire army[64] and then, refusing to regard Pŏmmaṇaṉ as his father-in-law (*māmaṉ*), slew him with his sword. He returned smiling to the tent and informed Pŏmmi of her father's death; together they burned the body and performed the proper rites.

Maturaivīraṉ and his bride then moved on to Tiruccirāppaḷḷi, where they were welcomed by the king, Vijayaraṅkacŏkkaliṅkam. The king took Maturaivīraṉ into his service as a gatekeeper at the entrance to the palace, for a salary of a thousand gold coins a month. The hero lived happily in the city; he dressed well, rode elephants or horses, seduced chaste wives, and worshiped the god Śrīraṅkanātar. But one day the king was told of the depredations of the wild Kaḷḷar in his kingdom: they would rob pilgrims to the shrine of Aḻakar;[65] they despoiled the peasants and brought agriculture and commerce to a standstill. The king sent Maturaivīraṉ with 5,000 troops to the south to subdue these unruly Kaḷḷar.

Maturaivīraṉ, the plundering hero (*kŏḷḷai kŏṇṭa vīraiyaṉ*), toured the districts south of Tiruccirāppaḷḷi, exacting tribute and service from the various local landlords and men of power (*pāḷaiyakkārar*).[66] When he arrived at the banks of the Vaikai River, in the territory of Tirumalai Nāyakkar, he was summoned to the latter's court in Maturai. He discussed with Tirumalai Nāyakkar his mission of subduing the Kaḷḷar; the ruler of Maturai kept him and his wife as honored guests in the palace. One day the Kaḷḷar descended with their boomeranglike weapons (*vaḷai taṭi*) upon the bazaar in Maturai; as they were in the midst

[64] The (Muslim) soldiers of Pŏmmaṇaṉ die with the cry *cākip calām* (p. 44).

[65] Presumably, Kaḷḷaḻakar of Tirumāliruñcolai (see above).

[66] I delete the detailed description of his reception by these "poligars," though it may be noted in passing that these pages are an excellent source for the system of collection and service in this period in Tamil Nadu.

of robbing the merchants, the alarm reached Maturaivīraṉ. He hastened to the northern gate of the city, where he fell upon the thieves as a lion attacks a herd of elephants. The Kaḷḷar perished.

Tirumalai Nāyakkar was delighted by this victory. He sent a thousand dancing-girls (*tātiyar*) to welcome back the hero, and Maturaivīraṉ fell in love with one of them, Vĕḷḷaiyammāḷ. That night he attempted to steal her away from her station in front of the shrine of Mīnākṣī. But the guards caught him at the gate: "A Kaḷḷar has come here in disguise," they cried. Maturaivīraṉ said nothing, for he was thinking: "The evil of stealing the chaste woman (*pattiṉi*) has borne fruit." He was brought before Tirumalai Nāyakkar, who failed to recognize him because of his disguise; he ordered him punished by having him taken to the forest, where his arm and leg were amputated.

The dancing-girl Vĕḷḷaiyammāḷ sought him out there and wept over him: since he had touched her, his sorrow was hers, and she would die with him. Pŏmmiyammāḷ also heard the lamentations and rushed to the forest to behold her dying husband. By now the true identity of the "thief" was known; Tirumalai Nāyakkar, stricken with remorse, prayed to the goddess Mīnākṣī to restore his hero to health. His prayer was granted: the arm and leg of Maturaivīraṉ grew back by the command of the goddess. But Maturaīviraṉ now ran to tell Tirumalai Nāyakkar of his resolve to die: life was inconstant as a bubble; he would give up his life in accordance with the fate decreed by God. With the consent of the king, his two wives, Pŏmmiyammāḷ and Vĕḷḷaiyammāḷ, entered a fire pit and were consumed. Then Maturaivīraṉ bathed in the Golden Lotus Tank and, standing at the feet of the goddess Mīnākṣī, cut his throat with a little knife. His head fell at Mīnākṣī's feet.

When, after three days, no worship had yet been offered to the dead hero, he complained to Mīnākṣī: "The people of the city are not supporting me." At her suggestion, he appeared as an Untouchable (*toṭṭi*) in a dream to Tirumalai Nāyakkar; he also prowled around the city during the night, causing havoc. In the morning, the king prostrated himself before Cŏkkar (Śiva in Maturai) and Mīnākṣī; they informed him that the trouble was due to the neglect of Maturaivīraṉ's worship. So Tirumalai Nāyakkar built a *maṇḍapa* for the hero and devoted five hundred gold coins for his daily worship. Maturaivīraṉ took possession of one of the king's servants and announced his satisfaction. Thus the worship of Maturaivīraṉ was established in Maturai. When a son was born to Tirumalai Nāyakkar, he was given the name Āṇimuttuvīraṉ in honor of the hero.

Such is the story, in its barest outline. For a Tamil audience, its power lies at least as much in those elements which our summary cannot convey—the richly colloquial language, the boldness and immediacy of the descriptions (including the unusually frank seduction scenes, which are moments of high narrative tension), the stylistic heightening of pathos and humor—as in the narrative structure. Yet even if we limit ourselves to observing that structure and its major events, we can feel the emotional impact of the bandit-hero and his tragic fate. Let us note those themes directly relevant to our concerns in this chapter.

First, we see, once again, the rooted ambivalence of the guardian. Maturaivīraṉ is a gatekeeper-watchman—first of Pŏmmiyammāḷ, in his father's stead; then in the employ of the rulers of Tiruccirāppaḷḷi and Maturai; finally, of the goddess Mīnākṣī, at whose feet he stands today. Maturaivīraṉ is worshiped at the threshold of many Tamil shrines. But the full force of his ambivalence is expressed in his actions: he seduces and steals the woman he is supposed to be guarding; and, as a disembodied spirit at the entrance to the Mīnākṣī shrine, he preys upon the citizens of Maturai in order to extort offerings from them. This is a guardian who is innately dangerous; one is never sure on which side of the boundary he stands—in the realm of order or of disorder, as protector or plunderer. His identity includes both roles, which seem to alternate unpredictably. It appears that he can be held in place, so to speak, only by constant appeasement and worship, that is, by voluntarily giving up to him the offerings (women, gold, food, honor) that he would otherwise forcibly appropriate. By definition a boundary figure, he knows no real boundary himself, although he does succumb to a paralyzing consciousness of his own transgressions when he is apprehended with the ravished dancing-girl at the gate of the Mīnākṣī temple. All in all, he recalls the symbolism of his Kaḷḷar opponents and rivals, with whom Mīnākṣī's gatekeepers understandably confuse him.

Second, the link between divinity and outrageous heroism is again apparent. Maturaivīraṉ is a quintessential Tamil hero (*vīraṉ*, Skt. *vīra*) endowed with a perilous plenitude of power that cannot but spill over the paltry limits set by society. Violence, freedom of action, a contempt for risks and dangerous consequences, a certain hardness of character, the abrogation of boundaries (including, in particular, sexual restrictions)—all these are part of the hero's nature. They also appear to justify his claim to popular admiration and, ultimately, to divinity. As Kampaṉ says in another context (describing the enormous power of Rāma's opponent and victim, Vālin), "Who does not love a hero (*vīrar*)?"[67] Maturaivīraṉ draws on these connotations of heroism in making the transition from human "bandit" to ambivalent god.[68] In his case, as with other "deified" heroes in this culture, divinity resides already in the initial outrages he perpetrates—indeed, the more outrageous, the more divine. As Grottanelli has shown in his analysis of the trickster-type, figures such as Maturaivīraṉ achieve their unique power not simply through their conventional *association* with boundaries—their liminal aspect—but through their dynamic breach of the boundary:

> Having crossed the boundary, the trickster is impure, but having had access to, having taken, what is across the boundaries, he is a giver of riches and, having had the courage to cross them, he is powerful. Power and impurity, pollution and salvation, go together because they are all products of the same daring gesture.[69]

The "redemptive" aspect that Grottanelli notes is essentially missing from our story—this is a point to which we will return—but in other respects his characterization admirably suits the Maturai hero. A strikingly similar case is that of the famous Kārtavīrya-Arjuna, the king punished by Paraśurāma for making off with his father Jamadagni's cow: Kārtavīrya, an outstanding example of the predatory robber-king, is eventually worshiped as a guardian deity who offers protection against thieves.[70] Although some texts seek to show Kārtavīrya in a more positive light, as a righteous ruler and partial avatar of Viṣṇu, his emergence as a deity seems more closely related to his inherent ambivalence as a hero and thief.

Third, there is another side to Maturaivīraṉ's divinity. It is not altogether simple to ignore the breaking of a moral barrier, not even for the superhuman hero, not even in a society which insists that banditry is divine. A moralistic note creeps into the dénouement of our poem: Maturaivīraṉ sees the evil of his ways and accepts his punishment in silence, even reimposes a punishment upon himself after his miraculous cure. But this theme clearly goes much deeper.

[67] *Irāmāvatāram* 4.7.67.

[68] Cf. the cult of hero-stones mentioned earlier. Many of the Teyyam stories recorded by Kurup (1973) follow a similar pattern (pp. 59-60, 66-67, 71-72, etc.).

[69] Grottanelli (1983), p. 137.

[70] See above, III.3; *MBh* 3.116-17; discussion by Tripathi (1979), and sources cited there; cf. *Takkayākapparaṇi*, commentary to verse 417; *Kārtavīryavijayaprabandha*. Biardeau, who has studied the Kārtavīrya myths extensively (see above, III.3 n. 45), has suggested that the name of this king may underlie that of the Tamil bandit-deity Kāttavarāyaṉ.

The hero's final translation to divinity requires his death in a spectacularly self-sacrificing fashion. Indeed, the entire episode of the king's intervention with the goddess and her response to his prayers (to restore Maturaivīraṉ to health and wholeness) seems designed to allow Maturaivīraṉ the possibility of a total, consciously willed renunciation and death. Such self-sacrifice has a double edge to it: on the one hand, it aligns the bandit-hero with other "renunciatory" figures (such as the king, whose interest in the transcendent, legitimating potential of renunciation has been remarked upon above); on the other hand, it functions as yet another power ploy, a kind of last-ditch trump card in the hands of the antinomian tragic hero. For the act of self-sacrifice creates a controlled imbalance in the cosmic reckoning; it demands recompense on a higher level, in the form of a more permanent power to extract goods or worship. Like any sacrifice, it opens up a gap that must be filled from the other side—in the case of Maturaivīraṉ, through the cooperation of the goddess Mīnākṣī and her people. In this way, by choosing his death and dramatically achieving it, the hero realizes the divine potential that inheres in his *human* role. Death and the subsequent attainment of divine status thus essentially confirm the "divine" characteristics latent in the hero's life.

There is also a convergence here with the idea, widespread in South Indian village cults, that injustice—especially an injust or premature death—can create the conditions for the worship of the now divinely powerful victim.[71] This theme, which may be called the "tragic apotheosis," deserves a closer look. In its simpler forms, it embodies a protest, an angry refusal to make peace with tragic loss or injustice, and at the same time, an oddly persistent faith in the accountability of the ordered world. Human tragedy is thus somehow recompensed by the victim's translation to divinity; the painful sacrifice now borders on meaningfulness and expresses the positive action of a logical causality. But in the case of Maturaivīraṉ, the pattern is considerably more complex, for the question of the hero's responsibility is raised in connection with his fate. The hero, in fact, is engaged from the moment of his birth in an ambiguous relation to his personal destiny or fate (inevitably a tragic one)—recall the serpent's prophecy over the abandoned baby in the forest.[72] The prophecy is certain to be fulfilled,

[71] See the discussion by Brubaker (1978), pp. 86-90, 99-124; and see above, III.3, on the apotheosis of Reṇukā at Kāñcipuram.

[72] This "prophetic" motif is often far more explicit about the tragic end in store for the hero: thus with Pāpaḍu (Richards and Rao, 1980, p. 110) and Bālacandruḍu in Palnāḍu (Roghair, 1982, pp. 243-52). On fate in the epic, see John Smith (1980). Again, one cannot help but recall Oedipus.

yet the hero remains responsible for his actions: does not Maturaivīraṉ singlehandedly bring about the disaster—his abduction of Vĕḷḷaiyammāḷ—that leads directly to his death? Of course the Tamil hero, unlike Oedipus (another "fated" victim of his own actions), can hardly be said to combine a subjective innocence with objective guilt;[73] nor, perhaps for that very reason, can he provide for his society the saving power of future blessing and hope that the Greek tragic heroes sometimes do.[74] There is nothing very innocent about Maturaivīraṉ, at any stage of his career. Alive or dead, he requires propitiation; all he can offer to others is the power—equally protective and destructive—with which he was born. But in exercising that power, he acquires something of the paradoxical responsibility of the hero who is driven toward tragedy. This is the background to his self-sacrifice and consequent apotheosis: he brings coherence and a measure of vindication to his life by simultaneously accepting his fate and overcoming it.[75]

Fourth, let us note in passing the role of the woman as a source of conflict and a symbol of the bandit's inner nature. The abduction of Pŏmmiyammāḷ leads to the battle between Pŏmmaṇaṉ and Maturaivīraṉ and to the death of the former. The attempted rape of Vĕḷḷaiyammāḷ brings about Maturaivīraṉ's punishment and eventual death. The erotic adventures of the hero both symbolize his freedom and pave the way to his ruin. In this respect the bandit-hero is marked off from the king, whose romantic recklessness is held in check by a countervailing attribute of severe control, as we saw in the previous chapter. For the hero, sexual abandon is the rule, with physical violence its usual corollary.[76] The major theme of forbidden sexual union (between Untouchable and high-caste female)—here softened by the admission of the hero's royal birth—recurs in the Kāttavarāyaṉ story and in many village myths.[77] Here is disorder in its supreme affective

[73] See Grene and Lattimore (1959), pp. 3-7.

[74] For example, Philoctetes and Oedipus. See Grottanelli's remarks on the trickster, above, n. 69.

[75] Richards and Rao (1980), p. 116, offer a somewhat different perspective: "In folk mythology, destiny plays the supreme role in the development of a hero. His birth, or the beginning of his heroic activities, is related to a higher power manifesting itself. . . . In the same way his death also becomes an act of destiny. A hero does not die because he is killed or for other such normal reasons. He dies because his role has come to an end."

[76] Similarly, Pāpaḍu makes a habit of ravishing high-caste married women.

[77] Brubaker (1978), pp. 89-94, 331-59; *Kāttavarāya cuvāmi katai, passim.* Kāttavarāyaṉ lusts for Āriyamālai, the daughter of a Brahmin temple priest; his mother, the seductive goddess Kāmākṣī, sets trials for her son before allowing him to win the girl. Like Maturaivīraṉ, Kāttavarāyaṉ undergoes a self-sacrificing death and becomes a gatekeeper figure. Cf. Oppert (1893), pp. 482-83.

symbol: the violation of the virgin by an Untouchable male, at the height of her impurity (first menses). Small wonder that the hero must pay with his life. The prominence of this theme fits well with the dominant role of the goddess in the Maturaivīraṉ cult; he now guards the shrine that he violated by abducting the dancing-girl of Mīnākṣī.[78]

At the same time, however, the goddess is a source and guarantor of a transformation toward a higher unity or resolution. Mīnākṣī—or her human representative (*pattiṉi*), stolen by the hero—accepts his self-sacrifice and thereby effects his transition from the bandit-servant of the king to a divinity worshiped by the king. In other words, the conflict centered on the woman is also in some sense resolved or mediated by the woman, with the help, of course, of the main male figures (the king and Maturaivīraṉ). Dennis Hudson has written cogently of this role of the woman in Tamil myths as the focal point of a unity or balance that is riddled with tension, antagonism, and rivalry.[79] It is this underlying structure of intimate conflict and tense affinity that we must now explore through the relations of the bandit-hero and the king.

Fifth, this relationship is central to the unfolding of our story. Maturaivīraṉ is royal by birth, but he is raised by Untouchables, while his career closely resembles that of a Kaḷḷar watchman-thief. Much depends here on the interpretation one gives to the theme of the exiled prince. To begin with, this is, of course, a common folklore motif (the prince brought up in humble surroundings, usually in ignorance of his true birth).[80] The theme has even been adopted by Indian philosophical schools as a metaphor for the original, forgotten divinity of the soul: like the king's son (*rājaputravat*) exiled from the capital and brought up among wild tribes and outcasts, the *puruṣa* lives in the exile of *saṃsāra* and is unaware of its true nature.[81] There are other possibilities for interpreting the theme: Blackburn sees here a process of "puranization" by which an original Untouchable hero, popular among lower castes and expressing their protest, was made palatable to the Brahmins.[82] Maturaivīraṉ's royal birth would then be a later addition grafted on to the original story and legitimizing it in the eyes of the higher castes, the central motif of the illicit sexual union having in this way been neatly emptied of its horror. Blackburn points out

[78] These stories also fit the pattern in which the shattering of the goddess's protective enclosure costs the male intruder his life; see Shulman (1980b), pp. 192-211.

[79] Hudson (1978). Cf. Heesterman (1971), pp. 12-15.

[80] Thompson (1955-1958), motifs P.31, P.35, H.41.5.

[81] See Zimmer (1969), pp. 308-309.

[82] Blackburn (1978), pp. 143-44.

other "puranic" features of the text and cites parallel instances of popular texts "revised" according to high-caste pressures. Nevertheless, the relation that is established by our text through the use of this theme—the king's son who acts for all the world like the Untouchables who reared him—is by no means devoid of meaning. Rather, we seem to have here a structural relation no less "loaded" with significance than the celebrated conjunction of Brahmins and Untouchables;[83] and we may, perhaps, recall the other tales of Untouchable kings discussed above in relation to the king's "exilic" phase.[84]

Without seeking to be deliberately paradoxical, I suggest that we may formulate the relation King-Untouchable/bandit under three headings: opposition, identity, and complementarity. Let us take them one by one.

Opposition is much the easiest and requires little comment. In India as in the West, the king opposes bandits as order struggles against disorder. Even if, as we have seen, the bandit has a recognized place in the social scheme, the king will attempt to contain him. Thus in our text we find the contest between the Kaḷḷar raiders and the forces of order embodied in Maturaivīraṉ as representative of the rulers of Tiruccirāppaḷḷi and Maturai. On the other hand, Maturaivīraṉ is himself the bandit who attempts to steal a woman and is punished accordingly by the king. In caste terms, the king is high, the bandit low (even an Outcaste); there is a clear polarization between them.

Identity simultaneously permeates their relationship. One can observe this in many ways: the royal birth of the bandit-hero; the royal titles that the text constantly gives him; the attributes he shares with the king, notably the role of protection, which is the central task of the ruler,[85] and the basic reliance on brute force. Let us recall the comparison of kings and robbers as stated by Coranātha-Viṣṇu in Śrīvaikuṇṭam: both take money by force.[86] Kings and bandits share the use, and the misuse, of power. It is in this light that we see Maturaivīraṉ high-handedly exacting tribute from the "poligars" south of Tiruccirāppaḷḷi; theoretically, he represents that city's king, but in reality he seems to be acting for himself. Is he king or bandit here? Both, it would seem, for the two are intertwined. There is something royal in the bandit, as one learns from the tradition of royal descent kept alive by the Kaḷḷar, Maṟavar, and Akampaṭiyar. There

[83] Above, III.1. Note that even *after* Maturaivīran's death, he takes the form of an Untouchable when he appears in Tirumalai Nāyakkar's dream.

[84] See V.2-3.

[85] *Yājñavalkya* 1.119; *Manusmṛti* 7.3; above, I.3 and II.1.

[86] See section 2 above at notes 13-14; and cf. *Cīvakacintāmaṇi* 741, and discussion of this verse by Cāminātaiyar (1953), pp. 106-13.

is also a great deal of the bandit in the king. We might say that the bandit gives expression to the real ambivalence of power; he "lives through" the latent violence, the spontaneity and instability, the recurring impurity that theory attempts to deny the ideal king. Divinity also lurks in both figures: we have seen how it is attached to the bandit, whereas the king claims it by virtue of his role, regardless of his original caste—*nāviṣṇuḥ pṛthivīpatiḥ*, there is no king who is not divine.[87]

If so much is shared, in what ways are the two figures distinct? The relations of opposition and identity contribute to the construction of ultimately *complementary* symbolic roles. On a superficial level, one can see this complementarity in the professed relation of hierarchy and service: Maturaivīraṉ claims to be the servant of the king (Pŏmmaṇaṉ, Vijayaraṅkacŏkkaliṅkam, Tirumalai Nāyakkar), from whom he derives his authority; the king, for his part, receives the benefits of service (suppression of the Kaḷḷar; a share in the tribute exacted from local landlords). Yet we have seen how readily the servant merges with the rival; the hero's subordination to the king is always problematic, always in danger of dissolving into equality and opposition. Complementarity is nevertheless affirmed in subtler ways. Each partner to this relation needs the other: the king depends upon the bandit's power (thus Tirumalai Nāyakkar petitions the goddess to save Maturaivīraṉ); the bandit seeks to cloak himself in the king's delegated legitimacy. Each lays claim to a semi-autonomous sphere that the other longs for. We might formulate this relation as expressive of two distinct notions of transcendence that reveal the higher and lower limits of the society. The king, who is so closely identified with the community that his freedom of action is seriously impaired,[88] desperately seeks a transcendent source for his authority; he finds it, on the one hand, in his relation with the Brahmins, and, on the other, in imitating the renunciatory aspects of the Brahmin inheritance himself. (We should note that this aspect of the king has an echo in Maturaivīraṉ's self-sacrificing death, which is even framed by the language of *māyā* and *mokṣa*; again the king and bandit have coalesced.) The bandit, however, generally represents the transcendence associated with disorder and impurity, with the breaking of limits. His true home is the dangerous wilderness that threatens to engulf the settled world of city and village, but that also imparts vitality to that world. The difficulty here is that these two kinds of transcendence tend to merge with one another, as we have seen with reference to the Brahmin gatekeepers;

[87] See above, II.4 at n. 64.

[88] Heesterman (1978), pp. 5-7.

the upper and lower limits are uncannily close.[89] The freedom and wholeness of release are theoretically opposed to but in reality not far removed from the wild breaking down of barriers associated with the disorderly thief or bandit.

The relation we are describing could also be described in the language of Indian symbols as the classic tension between the center and the remnant or remainder. The center, basically pure, linked by the axis mundi (the throne) with the transcendent worlds above and below, integrates the scattered segments into a unified but dissonant whole; the center contains the totality by holding conflicting forces in balanced suspension. In Hindu myth, as we have noted, this concept is often linked to the god Viṣṇu. The remnant, on the other hand, is impure and dynamic; as leavings, it can only be dangerously impure, yet it constitutes the seed of a new birth. Śiva, or his antecedent Rudra, is the god of the remnant and of the outsiders (be they Brahmins or bandits). Center and remnant stand apart, opposed, yet each partakes of the other's nature—the center is also, in a sense, left over or set apart from all other points, whereas the remnant has the essential wholeness of the center, the possibility of generating an entire universe. Each can easily become the other.

Similarly with bandit and king: the king is identified with the center, the balancing point of conflict and tension; the bandit is the remnant that is both excluded and somehow incorporated, even sought after and worshiped as divine. Both identities, moreover, interpenetrate and merge. And it is this interpenetration that we see in the South Indian political structure—the theoretical balance of the center is, in reality, a structural imbalance; "excluded" disorder infuses the ordered sphere with a necessary vitality and power; the king knows himself, as others know him, to be a bandit who has "made good," and who may yet easily revert to his former role. A large portion of his energies, and of his resources, is invested in maintaining the tenuous distinction between his royal pretensions and his ruffian's credentials. Let us now examine this process of self-definition by which a man—prince or commoner, bandit and/or hero—can become (and remain) a South Indian king.

5. From Bandit to King

There are many stories that describe just such a transition—not simply the symbolic affinities between bandits and kings, but an actual grad-

[89] Above, III.1 and III.3-4.

uation from one category to another.[90] In some cases the barrier is not quite bridged: thus the outrageous Telugu folk hero Sarvāyi Pāpaḍu acquires, in the course of his gruesome career, a number of kingly signs—a twelve-hooded cobra that shades him from the sun; twelve mistresses (from various castes, including high-caste brides whom he ravishes on their wedding day); a regal palanquin; an army and a series of forts; and, at the end, a royal funeral—and yet he is never fully assimilated to the category of proper kings.[91] What is it that stands between the bandit-hero, so kinglike in many ways, and a complete royal identity? How can the transition be successfully accomplished? What brings an erstwhile bandit recognition as a legitimate ruler?

There is a verse in a medieval Telugu classic that indirectly addresses these questions. Nandi Timmana was one of the court poets of King Kṛṣṇadevarāya;[92] in the introduction to his *Pārijātāpaharaṇamu*, he praises his king as an avatar of the god Kṛṣṇa, and even explains why Kṛṣṇa felt it necessary to take this form:

> Because as a cowherd he could not sit upon a throne,
> he came again, to ascend *this* brilliant throne;
> because he had flirted with the cowherds' wives,
> he wished to act now as a brother
> to the wives of other men;
> because he had surrendered Mathurā to Jarāsandha,
> he now would conquer with his power
> all his enemies' forts;
> because he had coveted the *pārijāta* tree, and stolen it,
> he would atone by lavish gifts of charity:
>
> to remove these faults of his in his former birth as Kṛṣṇa,
> he came down, willingly, playfully, to be Kṛṣṇa again
> as the illustrious son of Narasa the king,
> Kṛṣṇarāya, husband of the Earth.[93]

The god has traveled the path from wild, antinomian, unpredictable *gŏlla* (a cowherd-shepherd) to a great ruler of the Vijayanagar state; each of the defects enumerated for his earlier, *gŏlla* avatar has a corresponding, compensating royal virtue. Let us take them one by one.

[90] See de Casparis (1979); Derrett (1957), p. 15; Toshikazu Arai (1978), pp. 87-88.

[91] Richards and Rao (1980).

[92] Kṛṣṇadevarāya is the familiar victim of Tĕnāli Rāma's jokes: above, IV.4.

[93] *pīṭhika*, v. 17: *yādavatvamuna simhāsanasthūḍu kāmi simhāsanasthūḍai cĕnnu mĕraya/ gŏllayillāṇḍratō godigiñcuṭā jesi parakāminīsahodaratā cūpa/ maṟi jarāsutunakai mathura ḍiñcuṭā jesi paravargadurgamul balimī gŏnāgā/ bārijātamun āsapaḍi paṭṭi tĕccuṭan audāryamuna dānin aḍuguvuṟupā/ gori tolumenā danakaina kŏduvalĕlla/ mārcukŏna vacci bhuvanaikamānyalīlan/ avatariñcina kṛṣṇuḍ' aun' anāga miñcĕn/ narasavibhukṛṣṇarāyabhūnāyakuṇḍu.*

The cowherd is naturally without a throne; the king reigns upon his throne, surrounded by all the powerful symbols and insignia of kingship. This is, apparently, the first requirement: to be a king one must look like a king; the aspirant to kingship must display himself, with the conspicuous ornamentation and conventional signs of royal status (not merely a throne but also the fly whisk, parasol, peacock-feather fan, gilded palanquin, the elephant and horse, royal banner, and assorted weapons).[94] Symbolic display, as we have seen, is fundamental to South Indian kingship. Second, there is the matter of women: the *gŏlla* has a banditlike obsession with forbidden women (other men's wives); the king must stand in relation to other women—*all* women—but this relation is governed by the usual bars and restrictions (and, as noted earlier, by a generalized frustration). Kṛṣṇarāya is thus a chastely restrained and protective "brother" to others' wives (*parakāminīsahodaratā jūpa*). He has, however, his share of violent physical prowess—the *gŏlla* failed to protect Mathurā, but Kṛṣṇarāya successively attacks his enemies' fortresses and, presumably, incorporates them in his kingdom. In this respect—the possession of violent power—the king and the cowherd/hero seem most closely allied, but the final item shatters this closeness and makes a definitive distinction: Kṛṣṇa was, we must remember, wholeheartedly a thief; among his many thefts, the poet chooses to recall that of the *pārijāta* tree from Indra's heaven (the subject of his poem!). But the king must now atone for this propensity of his earlier incarnation, and he does so in the classic manner of the South Indian monarch in his compulsive struggle with evil—by distributing gifts. The bandit takes, the king both takes and gives. One sure sign of royalty is a profligate generosity that denudes the king of his resources even as it legitimizes his position.

Does Timmana's verse lay down a program of self-improvement for the aspiring bandit? His list is clearly not exhaustive, but it does point to four important criteria for assessing kingship, along with four corresponding nonkingly failings. One wonders, too, if the list comprises an ascending series: anyone, perhaps, can build a throne and a parasol, but the remaining items are increasingly severe: chaste forbearance in sexual matters; the steady strength to fight and overcome external threats; and, above all, the capability for lavish charitable expenditure. Taken together, the four criteria may suggest a minimal definition of kingship. Note, however, that the king's link with his "heroic" *gŏlla* past is by no means severed; indeed, Kṛṣṇa has come down, as the king, "to be Kṛṣṇa again" (*kṛṣṇūḍ' aun' anāga*)—not only

[94] See discussion of these signs by Frykenberg and Deyell (1982).

in name, one imagines, but in a deeper penetration of the royal personality. The king holds within him the latent antinomian powers of the *gŏlla* trickster-thief. The propriety he now assumes is still, as the poet says, a volitional guise, and a form of play.

Timmana's depiction of Kṛṣṇadevarāya belongs with what we have called the "iconic" vision of kingship, and, like other iconic images we have studied, it points beyond itself to the ambiguous realities of kingship. It speaks of transformation, and of subtle continuities with an "anti-iconic" past. In general, it would seem, the iconic king is uneasily situated between anti-iconic reality (his bandit nature) and the inner forces of dissolution and disintegration that are operative even within a normative kingship. These forces, which we have studied largely in relation to the king's clownish transformations, also stand, paradoxically, between the king and the bandit. The bandit has nothing of his own to decompose; he is all power in its tragic fullness, sealed into the integral wholeness of the border; but when this power is brought into the "central" structure of the state—as it invariably must be—it acts as a solvent, threatening that structure with collapse. But this center is, in addition, already engaged in processes of self-corrosion and decomposition under the guidance of the king. Insofar as the latter retains his link with the bandit and the bandit's power, he remains tied to tragedy and heroic sacrifice; but in dissociating himself from the bandit, he must undergo an endless kenosis of power and wealth, whether through simple display, through conspicuous renunciation of one kind or another (gifts to Brahmins and others; yogic control of his senses, and thus an impassivity in eroticism; or an actual retreat to the forest, or at least the threat of taking this step), or through a devotional madness. Only through such a kenosis can the king demonstrate his authority; he can, in other words, use the power that he must have only by dispersing it, by emptying out his world, or by opening it to the transformations that take it apart from within.

There are several distinct levels to this process. In terms of social economics, it entails the diffusion of power and resources, a constant radiation from the center outward with relatively little accumulation in the palace; in addition, there is a cycle of breakdown and explosion outward, in plunder and war.[95] On the level of the metaphysics of statehood, we find both a fundamental questioning of the premises of the cultural order and a Brahminical monopoly on ultimate authority, which is removed from the center. The only legitimate Hindu ruler

[95] Above, I.4 and V.7.

is one who recognizes his essential illegitimacy. On the symbolic level, there is the spectrum of kingly images in their dynamic transformations—icon to anti-icon to comic shadow-self; satirical inversions[96] and tragi-comic combinations (Harlequinesque divisions into black-and-white kings).[97] This spectrum is a symbolic statement of a set of conceptual principles—the transcendence of tragedy through constant transformation; the fluidity of form; the primacy of feeling over static ideals of perfection; comic indeterminacy; a playful open-endedness; "integration" through disintegration and dissonance—which inform the life of the state. On the ontological plane, there is the strong sense of the insufficiency of perceived facts, indeed of all that is rigidly condemned to be "real." The epistemology of this kingdom is one in which ambiguity and paradox are central; its aesthetics favor irony and other reflexive modes. Spatially, its ordered center is permeated by the outer wilderness—in other words, by its own antithesis, a creative disorder.

Indeed, we can now see that the king, the hub of this unbalanced kingdom, is associated with two different kinds of disorder. He is subject to the passionate, *pravṛtti*-oriented disorder of the bandit, for he is reckless in loving and in war, given to violent, uncontrolled excesses; his power and sensuality victimize him, although the overflow may serve to energize his kingdom.[98] He is thus, in a sense, both the protector of his people and an embodiment of the threat from which they need to be protected. But he also undergoes the *nivṛtti*-disorder of exile, with its *dīkṣā*-like reversals, its saturation with the experiences of anxiety and the loss of self; here he is victimized not by power but by impotence, whereas he brings to his kingdom the liberated emotion and the creative restructuring of the clown. The *nivṛtti* aspect separates him from the bandit as surely as do his idealized attributes of control and lavish endowment. Yet the king remains at once bandit and clown as well as an iconic paragon of order, hovering above these two personae and partially veiling them from sight. Perhaps, in the light of this conclusion, we can extend Timmana's minimal definition of the king to a more comprehensive statement of the role: we find the ruler endowed with the reckless imbalance of the bandit, and something of his power, which he tempers with a designated powerlessness; he is also bound in specific, complex relations with women, with the Brahmins, and with the god of his devotion; he

[96] Such as Anayasindhu: above, II.5.

[97] As with Pṛthu-Vena: above, II.4 and V.8.

[98] Joanne Waghorne (1980) focuses on this aspect of kingship, with its links to fertility and regeneration.

must carry through the spectacular dramas of public ceremony and conspicuous ornamentation and consumption, not least of which is the profuse display of generosity; he thus disperses wealth even as he deliberately renounces elements of power, and the fantasy of powerful wholeness and mastery; he both safeguards and endangers the social fabric; he is vulnerable to madness, indeed to all intense emotion, and to romantic illusion; he provides, by his own radical transformations, a symbolic focus for the transformative processes of the kingdom as a whole and for the ludic decomposition that largely accounts for its continuity and coherence. To summarize these traits under simple rubrics: the king is defined in relation to 1) display, 2) women, 3) Brahmins, 4) gifts, 5) physical force, 6) formal impotence, 7) "madness" (devotion, the god), and 8) passionate play. He symbolizes and absorbs the forces of order and disorder, excess and abstinence, power and powerlessness, tragedy and comedy, stasis and transformation. He fuses the ambiguity of the clown and the ambivalence of the bandit with the elusive, self-transcending ideal.

This unstable set of characteristics is, it seems, what legitimacy and centricity are about in South India. A legitimate center expands the ordered sphere of social and political life to include the ambiguity and dynamism of disorder, without relinquishing the ideals of orderly separation and control. The center is by nature inclusive, relatively elastic, and consciously perceived as limited, hence as demanding transcendence. How different are the relations of legitimacy and power in, let us say, medieval Europe (in other ways, so reminiscent of medieval India)! There a stable, neatly bounded cosmology—the earthly realm clearly separated from heaven and from God—allows for a far more stable vision of social order and of the state; control of power and resources is a legitimate goal for both king and Church, and there is, therefore, a long historical struggle between these two powers to seize control, to demarcate their respective jurisdictions, to resolve the contradiction in their rival claims to authority, and ultimately to stabilize their relations. The original interpenetration of "secular" and "sacred" authority—with the consequent interweaving of their symbols (so that the king rules for Christ, while the Church is an imperium)[99]—has eventually to be disentangled, the two spheres rendered quite distinct; in terms of power in the real world, only one side can truly win. The South Indian king, in contrast, never even approaches enduring stability, since his authority, such as it is, proceeds out of a creative imbalance, an impulsive emotionalism, a play-

[99] See Kantorowicz (1957); Duby (1979); Leyser (1979).

ing with power and identity, a recognition of his limitations in the light of transcendent forces that eat away at the polity. He faces no institutional challenge like that of the Church, but rather the frustrating, ambiguous, localized, diffuse authority of the Brahmin, who is himself deeply implicated in power and yet ambivalent toward its use. A theoretical separation of spheres—king in politics and power, Brahmin freed of power and its impurities—exists in the context of their incessant intermingling; while the king, to be king, must concede the Brahmin's radical premise that political order as such is a rather dubious phenomenon.

Seen from a slightly different perspective, Brahmin, king, and bandit present us with three responses to the disruption of the ancient, holistic sacrificial universe. The primeval sacrifice produced renewed life and power out of destruction, in an unending, cyclical process; but the Brahmin, as we have seen, rejected the destructive aspect of the cycle and retreated to the cultural boundary, the site of his own, deathless sacrifice. As a result, already by Pallava times the integrity of the heroic kingly order was shattered and royal power itself exposed to the Brahmin's authoritative doubts. In the symbolic world of medieval kingship, brute power in its simplest, most immediate manifestations now belongs with the bandit. The Brahmin's relation to power remains highly ambivalent; in theory, he will devote himself to symbolic surrogate sacrifices, independently of the king. The latter, cut off from ultimate authority, is left with a series of masks that hide the vacuity of the royal center. Moreover, this division has implications for the symbolic composition of each of the figures. If the Brahmin is basically divided into two related, tensely oscillating halves, the bandit remains essentially homogeneous, wearing no mask, at home in the real world with its inevitable violence—and ultimately destroyed by it. But the king now becomes a malleable, mutating figure with a horror of becoming trapped in any wholly defined or delimited guise. He is acutely sensitive to context: the effort to preserve a precarious balance requires him to adapt *himself* to each changing constellation; but if his chameleonlike parade of identities is temporarily halted—if, that is, like Mucukunda, Triśaṅku, or Nahuṣa, he becomes stuck—he will seek to escape through an act of involution, by rearranging his internal composition. Lacking the Brahmin's whole-hearted support, he can never give himself wholly to power—only the bandit has that option—but must content himself with playing with it, dissipating it, emptying himself. In his innermost being, he is nothing but a mélange of self-substitutes. He lives a kingly illusion: that of a potential, if always elusive, equilibrium and order. But he is not the only one to be deluded: the Brahmin subscribes to *his* peculiar fiction—that his reconstituted microcosm can determine the macrocosm—while the bandit, for his part, is seduced by the fantasy that there really *is* something to kingship, an integrated face behind the mask.

The interaction of these three types also reveals the underlying fragmentation of the political universe: power adheres naturally to the least legitimate figure, who can only use it to achieve his own limited, tragic transfiguration, not to impinge upon the center; the most authoritative figure, the Brahmin, is largely paralyzed by self-exclusion; the center itself, or what is left of it, discharges its power and resources through the king's public consumption (*bhoga*), distribution (*dāna, tyāga*), and, above all, his self-subversive games (*līlā*).

6. *Nŏṇṭināṭakam*: The Bandit as Clown

The bandit is an outer force assimilated to the center; the clown is the center emptied out. The two coalesce in the figure of the king. But we cannot take leave of our bandit-heroes without looking briefly at a late genre, mentioned several times in these chapters, that also unites the two categories of bandit and clown in conscious satire of the former and, perhaps, unconscious parody of the king. This is the picaresque genre of the *nŏṇṭināṭakam*, "dramas about a cripple," which emerges from out of a folk-poetic milieu during the late seventeenth and early eighteenth centuries (perhaps roughly the time when the *Maturaivīracuvāmikatai* was composed). Like the Maturaivīraṉ story, the Tamil *nŏṇṭināṭakam* reflects the political order of the "poligars"—a time of great political fragmentation, of "little kings" and bandit heroes; it is thus greatly removed from the cultural atmosphere of Chola times and from the Chola structures of power. Nevertheless, the *nŏṇṭināṭakam* develops ancient themes: the physical deformity of the clown (here a roguish hero transformed); the hero's relation to women, and to the *bhakti* god; the contest between bandit and king. It also offers us a peculiar type of Tamil folk-hero, the tragic trickster saved from his own tricks.

We shall follow, at least in outline, the adventures of Matappuli ("Furious Tiger"), the hero of the *Tiruccĕntūr nŏṇṭināṭakam* by Kantacāmippulavar, a well-known poet of the early eighteenth century.[100] Our hero is a Kaḷḷar, born at Tirupati. As a young boy, he learns all

[100] He is also known as the author of the *Tiruvāppaṉūrppurāṇam*. For his date and career, see the remarks by Ta. A. Aruṇācalam Piḷḷai in his introduction to the text. On *nŏṇṭināṭakam* generally, see Zvelebil (1974), p. 224. As Zvelebil states, works of this genre are a particularly rich source for the social history of this neglected period.

the inherited wisdom of his caste—the wisdom of this Kali Age, stained with "gambling, lies, and theft" (verse 32). With this expertise in hand and wanderlust in his heart, Matappuli, now come of age, heads south. His first stop is Citamparam, home of the dancing Śiva, whom he worships along with Viṣṇu/Kovintarāyaṉ; he is overcome by joyful feeling. Suddenly all is lost—he catches sight of a *devadāsī* (*tevaṭiyāḷ*) called Citampararatnam. He is transfixed; he studies her movements, follows her home. She is by no means indifferent to his attention; after the briefest of introductions, she leads him into the house:

> I followed her into her home. At once
> she hurried to tell her mother,
> "This is our lucky day—
> the ship of our good fortune
> has put into port." (44)

The *devadāsī*'s mother is the traditional caricatured figure of the *veśyāmātṛ*, an unscrupulous old harlot who works her daughters without mercy. Citampararatnam, no doubt under her instructions, now sets about seducing our innocent hero. The scene is described in lingering, sardonic detail, from the first kiss to the moment when

> I caressed her firm breast,
> embraced that woman
>   with long eyes reaching to her ears.
> Sipping the sweetness of her lips,
> I gave way
>   to the ecstasy
> of two bodies
>   becoming one. (53)

Soon Matappuli's beloved finds it necessary to feed him a love-potion made up of various exotic items (tiger's milk, the right eye of an owl, bile from a frog, a bear's hair, bones of a bird, a variety of roots and leaves, and, finally, milk from her breasts—the recipe is given in an exhaustive description, for the benefit of anyone who might wish to try it out). And it works: Matappuli is wholly bound to the girl, who mulcts him of all his hoard of golden coins. His purse grows lighter day by day, until he is wholly destitute—at which point the heartless mother throws him out of the house and bolts the door. Still pervaded by desire, he hides on the pyal-porch in front of her house. After some days in this state, one night he creeps into the house of a wealthy citizen (*tillai nampiyār*) and carries off a box of treasure. The Kaḷḷar has emerged in his professional guise.

He takes the box straight to Citampararatnam:

> First she saw the box, and then
> she saw my face—
> suddenly
> she was eight times more passionate
> than before. (79)

But our hero's happiness is short-lived; the harlot (or her mother) has fully understood her victim. Having appropriated the treasure, Citampararatnam explains, politely, affectionately, to her lover that she can be released from her vow to the god, Naṭarāja, only if another young girl is found or purchased to take her place. Matappuli sadly promises to find money for this purpose. There is a touching farewell—"Come back soon," the lady says—and our hero once again heads south, pulled backwards by his desire and impelled forward by his *karma* (86).

He goes to Cīkāḻi, then to Tiruvārūr. There, one day, he sees a wedding celebration in the merchants' quarter. Surreptitiously, he joins the crowd and, after the festive meal, when everyone has gone to sleep, he steals into the bridal chamber, casts a magic powder over the sleeping bride and groom, and makes off with their rich ornaments. Still exhausted by his experiences with the harlot in Citamparam, he goes to Tanjore to rest and recover his strength.

While he is there, a war breaks out: the king of Maturai, Vicaiyaraṅkatirumalaicŏkkanātaṉ, sends an army of Muslims, Vaṉṉiyar, Maṟavar, Pŏntiliyar, Telugu warriors, and others to besiege Tanjore (then ruled by the Maratha king Cākoci). The Maturai army, under the command of Kumārattaḷavāy, sets up camp in Tirukkāṭṭuppaḷḷi; meanwhile, the citizens of Tanjore panic and desert the city. This gives our robber hero a perfect opportunity to ransack their houses. But he is not content with the loot he accumulates in this way; he needs yet more gold for his beloved dancing-girl. And he has a plan: he will make his way into the enemy camp at Tirukkāṭṭuppaḷḷi and steal one of their horses, to sell for gold.

He disguises himself as an ascetic. Wearing a tiger's skin, covered with sacred ash, with long matted hair, *rudrākṣa* beads, long earrings, a red cloth, a three-pronged staff, he enters the camp; freely distributing sacred ash to the gatekeepers, who bow to him, he goes to the tent of Irāyat Tŏṇṭaimāṉ, one of Maturai's allies in this campaign. This little king receives him as if he were his family deity: he prostrates himself before the disguised ascetic, accepts sacred ash from his hands, seats him beside himself, and has him fed royally. Several days pass in this fashion; Matappuli becomes a familiar sight around the camp, respected and worshiped by all, the honored guest of Tŏṇṭaimāṉ. He shows a particular interest in the stables, where he spends hours with the grooms and stable boys, learning about horses. Then, one black night, he decides that the moment has come. Discarding his disguise, he blackens his body with ink and enters the stable. All are asleep, "like painted pictures." He chooses a fine horse and, "with the help of Murukaṉ's great mercy" (175), manages to bridle it and to lead it away. So far so good—until our hero tries to mount the horse, which neighs loudly and arouses the whole camp. At once the search is on: the Paṟaiya guards kindle torches, night is turned to day; the theft is discovered, and a great hullabaloo erupts on all sides. Matappuli dives into a large barrel. But the guards approach: he exchanges this hiding place for another, a pile of cut fodder. There, covered by the dry grass, his body contracted into a small ball, he is attacked by scorpions and vicious red centipedes (*cĕyyāṉ*); an ant creeps into his ear. In short,

> The throbbing and the burning in my body
> kept getting worse;
> like a stone, unmoving,
> I huddled in the grass
> like a dog with a broken hip;
> how can I tell you
> of that piteous state? (188)

Worst of all is the ant's tormenting movement through his ear: is this some trial set by the god? Or the fruit of some evil action in his former birth (190-91)? But soon a greater danger looms: the armed soldiers decide to set the pile of fodder alight. In the cloud of smoke that rises up, the thief crawls out, unobserved, his skin torn by sharp thorns, blood pouring from his wounds. A new refuge presents itself; he plunges into a cesspool filled with the urine of horses and other animals. Urine pours into his mouth, his nose, his eyes, and—at last! relief from the hated ant—his ears (197). But he has been seen; they cluster around the pit, crying, "Has the Kaḷḷaṉ lost his wits?" (198). Holding their noses, they haul him to the surface, clean him off—and, to their surprise, recognize the famous *sannyāsin*, reduced to a common horse thief.

His punishment is swift. He is hauled ignominiously before his former patron, Tŏṇṭaimāṉ, who mourns over him—"Is this not the master who gave me sacred ash? Even if he steals a thousand times,

I cannot punish him" (222)—and sends him on to the commander-in-chief, Kumārattaḷavāy. The latter interrogates him, and Matappuli tells the truth: "Your highness, I am a Kaḷḷaṉ. . . ." He speaks of his caste, his birthplace, and his history. Note the hero's utter lack of contrition: he has, after all, only been living up to the *dharma* of his caste. Yet he must be punished; the general inquires of the Brahmins as to the suitable ruling, and they inform him that, according to the laws of Manu, the hands and feet of a thief are to be cut off. This ruling is confirmed, and the order is swiftly carried out. Matappuli is left to die in pain, lamenting the fact that he had ever left Tirupati, and conscious only that fate (*ūḻviti*) cannot be overcome (238-39).

From this point on, the poem loses its satirical overlay and becomes a tale of piety miraculously rewarded. There is, first, a pious intervention by a passing landowner/little king, Anantapaṟpanāpaṉ of Nallūr (who, we may be sure, was one of the patrons of the author!). This kind lord takes pity on the dying thief, sends for doctors who heal his open wounds, and encourages him: if, when he is healed, he makes his way to the shrine of Lord Murukaṉ at Tiruccĕntūr, the god will restore his lost limbs. The remainder of the poem describes the maimed hero's progress toward this shrine. The comic-reflexive character of the work is not wholly lost: among the many places Matappuli visits on his journey southward is Muttālaṅkuṟicci, where

> I saw Kantacāmi, immortal
> king of poets, and drank in
> his marvelous poetry with my ears,
> just as I swallowed the tasty feast for my belly
> that this glorious man prepared. (265-66)

The author has worked his way into his own poem as a minor character who entertains the wayward hero! But Muttālaṅkuṟicci is only one of many stations on this sacred journey; Matappuli worships at most of the famous shrines of the southern Tamil country and eventually arrives at his goal, Tiruccĕntūr. He crawls painfully into the main shrine of the god Murukaṉ and collapses there on the floor. In his dream he hears the god speak: "Arise, O thief—we have given back your feet and hands; they will grow full by themselves (*taṟcĕyalāka*, 324)." He wakes up, restored, and walks away. The temple trustees, seeing this miracle of the Kali Age, give him a new name—"Provider of the Sacred Service to Ṣaṇmukha"—and charge him with adorning the god with his golden ornaments and jewels. Matappuli remains, with his family, at Tiruccĕntūr, have been finally converted, it would seem, to a new way of life.

The hero of the *nŏṇṭināṭakam* might qualify for Grottanelli's definition of the trickster—"a breaker of rules who is funny because he is lowly"—though he lacks the trickster's usual versatility.[101] Matappuli is a low-caste Kaḷḷaṉ, a professional bandit-thief whose escapades are, at least through the first half of the poem, both scandalous and amusing. Indeed, the genre as a whole builds its ironic perspective out of a kind of outrageous innocence. The hero who, for his own good reasons, as the natural result of his background and training, violates the social norm is himself the butt of bitter satire; he is duped and ridiculed by his beloved harlot, and even his lame attempt at a professional coup—the theft of a royal horse—lands him in a cesspool, like the victim of a slapstick farce. (Indeed, this entire episode reads like a parody of the Jain parable of the pit[102] or of the famous scene where Gautama Buddha parts from his faithful horse.[103]) The comic spirit of the work is immediately evident in its language, a rich, incongruous amalgam of pompous diction, poetic clichés, colloquial directness, and popular vocabulary, with a sprinkling of occasional obscenities—in short, a racy blend that nicely conveys the low-caste hero's pretentious attempt at an *apologia pro vita sua*. In addition, the picaresque adventures of the rogue-as-hero eventually culminate in a physical deformity only a step beyond that of the clown—or, for that matter, of the crippled king.[104]

Yet, by the time this punishment is brought down upon the hero, the tone of the work is no longer comic; it has turned to the tragic or the pathetic, as prelude to the serious devotional conclusion. The text reverts to the more common tragic aspect of South Indian bandit lore. With this reversion, the comic trickster-hero also loses any redemptive quality he might have; unlike Hermes, unlike the Winnebago trickster, Matappuli can no longer transgress and get away with it,[105] nor can he effect by his own powers the transmutation of evil or impurity into blessing. Rather, he has to be rescued from his own bungling foolishness and error, which have left him a helpless invalid-cripple; only his inner transformation will persuade the god to intervene and cure him. This is no magic regeneration, no carnivalesque turning-the-tables on death, even if the hero ends up whole once more. It is not *his* doing that he is saved. Matappuli is thus a tragic or, considering the whole of his career, a tragi-comic trickster whose

[101] Grottanelli (1983), p. 120.
[102] Basham (1958), pp. 56-58, quoting *Samarādityakathā* 2.55-80.
[103] See, e.g., *Buddhacarita* 6.53-55.
[104] See above, IV.2 (on the Vidūṣaka); II.5, for the impaired or crippled king.
[105] See Grottanelli (1983), pp. 137-39.

attacks upon order have no real impact upon it, and who is himself eventually reformed. But he knows nothing of the bandit's tragic apotheosis: such a possibility is precluded by the original comic coloring of the story, by Matappuli's merely half-hearted roguishness and general failure as a hero. Were he a little wiser and more self-deprecating, we could see him as a shlemiel.[106] In some ways, despite his Kaḷḷar caste, he seems even closer to the king than to a bandit. His story, in fact, takes place on the edges of kingship: note the connection with the *devadāsī*/prostitute; the *sannyāsin*'s disguise (like the Pāṇḍavas' Brahmin disguises at Draupadī's *svayaṃvara*, among many other instances);[107] the symbolic focus on the royal horse, a major emblem of kingship; the humble, dependent relation to the god who saves him; the grotesque physical deformity, and the tragi-comic combination of dynamic power (exceeding the social limits) and abject powerlessness. Many of the criteria mentioned in the last section as defining the king could be applied to Matappuli; what is clearly lacking is any regal pretension with its concomitant symbolic display.

The *nŏṇṭināṭakam* is the product of a period when little kings were moving ever closer to bandit-heroes; Matappuli, who mimics both these figures, deepens their symbolic affinity by imparting to the bandit's role something of the king's reflexive self-parody. The result is a new kind of hero no doubt suited to the fragmented, small-scale polities of this time—the tragic trickster who ridicules the solemn social order, its most powerful individuals, its ritualized poetic language, and, above all, himself. But he remains, in the end, too closely linked to the burlesque, to the satirical and the risqué, to be given a crown, just as the more conventional bandit-heroes are too deeply enmeshed in tragedy. For the South Indian king, as we have seen, must mingle these two modes in a manner that allows the self-limiting cultural order to transcend those same limits; a manner that both maintains and erodes the integrity of the socio-cultural ideals. This highly charged combination of disparate modes has both structural and semantic implications for the dynamics of power and the state. To conclude this chapter, and with it the main body of this essay, we turn now to a final consideration of the semantics of kingship, with reference to another negative example—that of a hero who chooses a heroic death over kingship and its inevitable compromises or, worse still, its evasion of meaning.

[106] Wisse (1971).

[107] See above, III.3 at n. 40.

7. The Man Who Would Not Be King: Karṇa's Tragedy and the Karunic Clown

There is, perhaps, no more popular hero in India's classical literature than Karṇa, the "hidden" eldest brother to the five Pāṇḍava heroes of the *Mahābhārata*. Pampa, the author of the classical Kannada version of the epic, exhorts his audience: "If you remember anyone among the heroes, let it be Karṇa!"[108] South Indian folk traditions glorify Karṇa in various ways: he is said to have been reborn as Ciṟuttŏṇṭar, the famous "Little Devotee" who served his own son as the main course of a meal for Śiva, at the latter's request;[109] and one finds many hints of a clandestine love between Karṇa and Draupadī, the common wife of his five Pāṇḍava brothers.[110] As we shall see, there are good reasons for Karṇa's popularity; he is, indeed, a peculiarly attractive character both in his own right and in comparison with the rogue's gallery that surrounds him—the deeply flawed epic heroes from *both* sides of the battle, as well as the deceitful and murderous deity who uses them for his designs.

Moreover, ever since Western scholars proclaimed that Indian literature is devoid of tragedy, in the Greek sense, a defensive minority opinion has rebutted this charge by citing Karṇa.[111] And, it is true, Karṇa does have the makings of a tragic hero even by the criteria of Western tragedy: his story undoubtedly arouses the "tragic emotions" of terror and "ruth" (*phobos* and *eleos*)[112] as well as rage, sorrow, pathos; he demonstrates the essential nobility of his nature in the face of personal disaster, for which he is himself partly, paradoxically, responsible;[113] his personal tragedy is, however, also mysteriously related to the obscure workings of *dharma*, of fate (*daiva*—both personal and cosmic), of *karma*, and of the god's will: a rich blend of forces which, seen together, are not unlike the complex moral universe in which the Greek hero must act; within this interplay of ambiguous forces, there is room, indeed need, for Karṇa to achieve a moment of understanding, an *anagnorisis*—even for a general revelation to take

[108] *Pampabhāratam (Vikramārjuna vijayam)* 12.217. I am grateful to G. H. Nayak for this reference.

[109] *Ciṟuttŏṇṭapattaṉ katai*, p. 3.

[110] See Hiltebeitel (1980), p. 110 n. 24; *idem* (1976), p. 226.

[111] See Sreekantaiya (1980), pp. 32-53; Ingalls (1965), pp. 16-17.

[112] To adopt the Aristotelian perspective. (Kaufmann, 1968a, p. 46, suggests "ruth" for *eleos*.) The Sanskrit poeticians would no doubt speak of *karuṇarasa* and its *sthāyibhāva*, *śoka*.

[113] Cf. Orwell (1962), p. 108.

place; and the whole tragic tale is laden with bitter irony, "tragedy's regular accomplice."[114] But our concern here is not with fitting Karṇa into a Western model of tragedy but rather with understanding the problems he raises for his own cultural setting and, specifically, his contrasting links with kingship. Here it should be stressed that Karṇa's career is one of the central narrative reliefs of the *Mahābhārata*, and one of the most sensitively drawn; he is the main champion in the Kaurava army and thus the main threat to the Pāṇḍavas—above all, to Arjuna, his true rival. Indeed, this conflict between the two brothers is itself a particularly expressive component of the epic's world, for both Karṇa and Arjuna represent a specific range of vision and feeling. The two stand on opposite sides of the divide between heroism and kingship. We shall pursue this problem further; let us first, however, briefly review Karṇa's story as it appears in the Sanskrit *Mahābhārata* before we turn to its climactic episode in Villiputtūrār's Tamil account.

Karṇa was the first-born son of Kuntī, mother to the Pāṇḍavas. He was born to his mother when she was still a virgin: as a young girl she had served the sage Durvāsas during his visit to her father's kingdom, and he had bestowed upon her the boon of calling any god to her side by means of a secret *mantra*. With the reckless curiosity of a teenage girl, Kuntī tried out the *mantra* by calling the sun god, Sūrya, who appeared to her while she was in her menstrual impurity, and left her pregnant with his child. Kuntī hid the pregnancy, and when her son, Karṇa, was born—a divine child, with congenital armor and magic earrings—she placed him in a golden box and sent him off upon the river.

The foundling was eventually discovered and adopted by the low-caste Sūta, Adhiratha—the only father the boy would really know. Adhiratha brought him up and, when the time was ripe, sent him to learn the arts of war from the greatest master of his generation, Droṇa, the teacher of the Pāṇḍavas and their Kaurava cousins. From this point onward, we can trace the developing tragedy of Karṇa's life, a tragedy that follows largely upon his close friendship with Duryodhana, his benefactor and protector. Karṇa's loyalty (*bhakti*) to his rather unworthy friend is a major factor in his life, a focal point of his attempt to give meaning and nobility to a painful and problematic career.

There are four major turning points in Karṇa's life. The first occurs during Karṇa's dramatic entry onto the epic stage, at the tournament of arms that marks the end of the heroes' period of training. Karṇa steps forward as Duryodhana's champion against Arjuna, successfully

[114] Nevo (1972), p. 24.

repeats all of Arjuna's stunning feats, and challenges Arjuna himself to combat, when an objection is voiced—how can Arjuna fight against someone whose family and background are unknown? Duryodhana at once proposes a solution: there are three sources, he says, of kingly identity: royal birth; heroism; and the command of an army. If Arjuna refuses to fight Karṇa because the latter was not born a Kṣatriya, then he, Duryodhana, will grant Karṇa a kingdom. Now Brahmins are hastily called in to consecrate Karṇa as the king of the small country of Aṅga, within Duryodhana's domains; Karṇa is at once "joined to Śrī" (*śriyā yukto*) and given a regal parasol and chowrie. He is, we must assume, somewhat shocked by this sudden transformation; how, he asks, can he ever repay Duryodhana? "By limitless friendship (*atyantaṃ sakhyam*)," Duryodhana replies, thereby binding Karṇa to him forever in the tragic bond of faithfulness. And now we witness the first of the sudden reversals—almost an Aristotelian *peripeteia*—that haunt Karṇa throughout his life. With his head still wet from the water of his consecration, he suddenly sees his aged foster father, Adhiratha, come limping into the arena; and, as a pious son, the newly crowned king of Aṅga bows to his father's feet, thus revealing to everyone his "true," low origins. It is almost sunset (always a crucial time for Karṇa, the solar hero),[115] and the duel between Karṇa and Arjuna is postponed, the issue of Kṣatriya propriety still basically unresolved. Indeed, Karṇa will never fully resolve the tantalizing issues bound up with his identity, although the attempt to do so is a recurrent part of his struggles.[116] Already in this early scene we can observe his attempt to create and to maintain an identity as a noble Kṣatriya fighter (more precisely, to recapture the noble identity which is his by birth, but of which he is ignorant); we also see how he nevertheless remains trapped by his personal history. The past is always rising up to confront him, to drive him back to his unhappy fate.[117]

The second turning point reveals Karṇa's famed quality of generous giving—a conventional royal trait, as we know. Indra wishes to protect his son, Arjuna, in the war which is soon to come, and he sees Karṇa as the basic danger; but as long as Karṇa retains his native armor and divine earrings, he cannot be defeated. Indra therefore disguises himself as a Brahmin beggar and appears before Karṇa to ask him for the gift of his armor and earrings. Karṇa sees through the disguise—he has been forewarned in a dream by his true father, Sūrya—but he

[115] On the solar symbolism in Karṇa's story, see Dumézil (1968), pp. 125-44; Hiltebeitel (1980); Biardeau (1978), pp. 171-75.

[116] This theme is perceptively treated by Karve (1974), pp. 122-40.

[117] The episode of the tournament appears in *MBh* 1.126-27.

is still unable to refuse the request. Is he not the most generous of donors? Before the eyes of the suppliant god, he peels his armor off his body—a painful act of self-mutilation—and gives it to Indra together with the earrings (*MBh* 3.285-294).[118] We shall find the essential features of this episode recurring, in a new form and context, in Villiputtūrār's *Pāratam*.

But the truly pivotal moment in Karṇa's life—the moment of his conscious tragic choice—occurs during the period immediately preceding the outbreak of war, the period of negotiation and preparation described in the *Udyogaparvan*. Kṛṣṇa, the support of the Pāṇḍavas, attempts to "turn" Karṇa to their side by informing him in secret of the real circumstances of his birth. In this way Karṇa discovers that he is, in fact, the eldest son of Kuntī, and that the enemies he has been so eager to fight are none other than his brothers. Moreover, this revelation is accompanied by an enticing offer: if Karṇa will only change sides, he will, as the eldest, become king; Kṛṣṇa himself will perform the coronation ceremony. The wily god paints a splendid picture of Karṇa's future glory: Yudhiṣṭhira will hold his white fan, Bhīma his parasol; Arjuna will drive him in a great chariot drawn by white horses; and the future king will take his place as Draupadī's sixth husband. Indeed, Kṛṣṇa argues, Karṇa has little choice, and certainly no reason to hesitate—*dharma* itself "constrains" him to become king (*nigrahād dharmaśāstrāṇām ehi rājā bhaviṣyasi*, 5.138.9). But Karṇa disagrees; in his reply he makes it clear that he does have a choice, and that the whole force of his personality and his life up to this point impels him to reject Kṛṣṇa's temptation. He has given his word to Duryodhana; nothing—not the whole earth, not heaps of gold, not joy or fear—could make him retract it.[119] Even if his own death in battle were a certainty (as Karṇa now thinks it is), he could not bring himself to betray his friend. Moreover, Karṇa is tied, not by birth but through the far stronger bonds of love, to his Sūta foster parents and to his low-caste wives and children; his foster mother Rādhā cared for him, cleaned him when he was a baby, nourished him—is he to leave her, and the life she gave him, for the sake of the "real" mother who abandoned him? It is altogether a moving reply, this speech of Karṇa's to the god; one can see the hero's preference for universalistic values (loyalty, truthfulness, love) over the unsatisfactory, entangling claims of family and dharmic propriety. But there

[118] "Bhāsa's" *Karṇabhāra* beautifully expands upon this episode.

[119] *na pṛthivyā sakalayā na suvarṇasya raśmibhiḥ/ harṣād bhayād vā govinda anṛtaṃ vaktum utsahe//* (5.139.12).

is a further dimension to Karṇa's stand at this point, as we learn from the next few verses; Karṇa now launches into the classic statement of the epic's central metaphor, that of the "sacrifice of arms" (*śastrayajña*) that is in store for the heroes and their world. The war that is soon to come will be a holocaust in which all the heroes will find their deaths, and in which they will attain a glory that will never pass from the earth. Each moment of this battle has its metaphoric ritual equivalent; "when you see me felled by Arjuna, that will be the repiling (*punaściti*) of the sacrifice" (5.139.46). Kṛṣṇa laughs—a sure sign that some horror is in the offing—and agrees with this gruesome vision, which he seems to relish. But Karṇa hardly needs this confirmation; he has had a dream (actually a nightmare), in which he saw Yudhiṣṭhira and his brothers ascend into a palace of a thousand pillars after Kṛṣṇa had covered the earth, reeking of blood, with entrails. It is all quite clear and unavoidable; for Karṇa the only question is how, given this certainty, his death can carry through the values by which he has lived his life. It is in this light that he has made his decision. He also utters another famous sentence: the Pāṇḍavas' victory will be the victory of *dharma (yato dharmas tato jayaḥ)*. But this cannot affect his choice, which has its own integrity, its consistent rationale. He wonders only why Kṛṣṇa, who must know all this quite well, has tried to deceive him by his offer, as if the war *could* be avoided. This prompts another of Kṛṣṇa's smiles: the destruction is, indeed, now certain (remarks the god), since Kṛṣṇa's words have failed to touch Karṇa's heart.

Karṇa, then, has insisted on his freedom—the freedom to choose a meaningful death—within a situation that he perceives as wholly determined. The drive toward tragedy is irresistible. But Karṇa still must face another test, a pathetic repetition of the god's temptation. This time it is his mother, Kuntī, who comes to him and pleads with him not to fight against his own brothers. A voice from the skies, the voice of his true father, the sun, reinforces Kuntī's plea. Karṇa thus stands before his parents for the first time in his life; but he shows no hesitation whatsoever about refusing their desperate request. He is both sure of himself and deeply embittered. What kind of a mother were you, he taunts Kuntī: "You had no compassion on me *then*; not even my enemy could have done me a greater evil than you did when you cast me off (5.144.5-6)." And, once more, he sings a paean to loyalty and to truth; he will not abandon his friends in their hour of need. His goal is "to persevere in the humane conduct that becomes a decent man."[120] Yet, suddenly, surprisingly—perhaps as part of that

[120] Van Buitenen's insightful translation (*ānṛśaṃsyam atho vṛttaṃ rakṣan satpuruṣocitam*).

same human decency he holds dear—Karṇa makes a promise to his mother: he will not kill any of his brothers in battle except for his destined rival, Arjuna; whatever happens, Kuntī will be left with five—and only five—sons. The mother embraces her son (for the first time since she had sent him away as an infant) and voices her despair: the Kurus will be destroyed; fate (*daiva*) is stronger than she.

And this divine fate, with which Karṇa has been so intimately associated ever since his birth,[121] does, of course, take its disastrous course. Arjuna's combat with Karṇa occupies a central place in the epic's eighth book, the *Karṇaparvan*. Its conclusion, like most of the Pāṇḍava victories,[122] involves the Pāṇḍava side (with their divine protector) in a shocking violation of the rules of fairness and honor. When Karṇa shoots his miraculous arrow, the *nāgāstra*,[123] Kṛṣṇa, serving as Arjuna's charioteer, lowers his chariot slightly into the ground; the weapon misses its mark, only knocking away Arjuna's crown. Now one of the wheels of Karṇa's chariot sinks into the earth. This is too much for the embittered hero, who has put his trust in fate; all the unfair burdens of his sorrowful life must weigh upon his consciousness at this moment, for he pours out his anger in a curse against *dharma* (as does Yudhiṣṭhira in a similarly bitter moment).[124] As he leaps from his chariot to extricate the wheel, he calls out to Arjuna to be mindful of *dharma*—in other words, not to shoot at an unarmed, helplessly exposed opponent. One wonders what Arjuna might have done had it not been for Kṛṣṇa's intervention at this point with a harsh verbal attack upon Karṇa: "How very nice that you should remember *dharma* just now. Scoundrels usually blame fate (*daiva*) when they are in trouble, rather than their own evil actions" (8.67.1). Kṛṣṇa goes on to list Karṇa's various misdeeds (his implication in the humiliation of Draupadī in the *sabhā*, in the loaded dice game with Śakuni, and so on). By now Arjuna is enraged and, again at Kṛṣṇa's urging, he shoots at his defenseless foe and slays him.

Karṇa thus dies resentful, angry, and alone. His lonely death is the natural culmination of a lonely, tragic life, the life of a stranger (even in the court of Duryodhana, his patron) always struggling with the questions of his identity and his fate. Like the Tamil bandit heroes, he is an outsider, a symbolic embodiment of the "remnant"—cast off,

[121] Cf. *MBh* 3.292.27, where *daiva* accompanies the infant Karṇa as he is sent away in his golden box by Kuntī.

[122] Hiltebeitel (1976), pp. 244-86.

[123] Note Karṇa's association with the serpent. In Villiputtūrār's *MBh*, Karṇa has promised Kuntī that he will use this deadly weapon only once.

[124] *MBh* 18.2.49-50. For Karṇa's curse, see 8.66.43-44.

impure,[125] but at the same time endowed with the first-born hero's wholeness and power. He is both of the Pāṇḍavas (as their brother) and against them, remnant interwoven with and yet opposed to center—a classic Indian opposition. He is also symbolically linked to the serpent, a primary representative of the remnant[126]—recall the way he peels off his congenital armor, like a snake emerging from its worn skin—and to the earth, the serpent's home (he is, in fact, identified with the demon Narakāsura, son of the Earth goddess).[127] By the same logic, he has an intimate tie to sacrifice, the ritual enactment of the earth's processes of life-through-death; it is not by chance that Karṇa serves as the voice of the central epic metaphor, that of the *śastrayajña*, the sacrifice of arms. This sacrificial idiom is the metaphysical expression of his "earthiness" (in itself no doubt a factor in Karṇa's undying popularity); he sees the world with a kind of simple directness, with a "tragic" clarity that freezes it into a sacrificial arena. The world is, in Karṇa's eyes, an altar, a meeting point of life and death; the true hero, like Karṇa himself, is a sacrificer, an archetypal Vedic *yajamāna*,[128] and also a potential victim at this rite. His death is a meaningful part of the sacrificial framework, within which there is also room for the human values of nobility, loyalty, generosity, love. Life, in short, makes sense, despite—actually because of—its tragic coloring. Essential to this vision is the hero's willful submission to his "fate"; like Maturaivīraṉ, Karṇa chooses his death—in effect, freely choosing not to be free. But while the bandit hero is usually suggestive of a violent disorder, Karṇa represents an equally violent order, a coherent semantics of sacrificial fate. In the interests of this coherent perception, which safeguards the validity of universalistic human ideals and thereby ennobles the hero's willed self-sacrifice, Karṇa distances himself from the kingship that is proffered by the god. He prefers the

[125] Recall his conception at the time of Kuntī's menstrual impurity.

[126] Shulman (1980b), pp. 119-23. The cosmic serpent Ādiśeṣa embodies this conception. One wonders if Karṇa's congenital earrings do not contribute to this symbolic linkage; cf. *MBh* 1.3 (the story of Utaṅka); 2.9.15; Kuiper (1979), p. 90. In effect, there are *three* ophidian heroes on the Kaurava side (whose serpentine characteristics stand out more clearly as the battle draws toward its close): Karṇa; Aśvatthāman, who bears the serpent's forehead jewel (see above, III.4); and Duryodhana, whose banner is the serpent, and who is compared to a serpent when he goes into hiding in the pool (9.31.33).

[127] *MBh* 3.240.19,32. Karṇa is the only figure in the epic identified with both a demon (Narakāsura) and a god (Sūrya). Note the symmetry of Arjuna-Nara's positioning alongside Nārāyaṇa, the god, and opposite Karṇa-Narakāsura, the "demon." Cf. Biardeau (1975-1976), p. 174.

[128] This may throw new light on Karṇa's role as generous patron, the author of lavish gifts.

heroic stance over a kingship antithetical to his ideals, even if these ideals cost him his life. Is it his history of bitter personal struggle that makes Karṇa so intent upon the universalistic values which may justify his life? In any case, it is interesting to find the myth of the Tripura demons told in conjunction with Arjuna's final battle with Karṇa (8.24.3-125). In some sense Karṇa may be assimilated to the gods' demonic—and, in the later versions of this myth that we have discussed above, their paradoxically idealistic—foes.[129] And, here as there, the "good demon" pays the price of a particular brand of innocence. For the heart of Karṇa's tragedy lies not so much in his own tragic perception of the universe as in the disappointment that the world forces upon him. *Daiva* has let him down; he dies in anger, cursing *dharma*, at war with the world. Let us listen again to Kṛṣṇa's "lesson" administered to Karṇa as he falls: "Scoundrels usually blame fate when they are in trouble, rather than their own evil actions." Karṇa, it seems, was freer than he knew. He falls victim to his own innocent faith in fate, in sacrificial order, in a universe infused with the possibility of meaning. Perhaps the world is not only a sacrificial arena; perhaps things do not really mean what, in their conventionally ordered perception, they are felt to mean.

There is much more to be said about Karṇa in the Sanskrit *Mahābhārata*, but our interest must now be focused on the Tamil transformation of his story. Here, too, we find a tragic vision, though of a rather different cast. Villiputtūrār is, perhaps above all, a devotee; Karṇa therefore interests him because of his relation to the god Kṛṣṇa, whose responsibility for the hero's fate is now made entirely clear. This relationship is expressed in a striking and innovative version of Karṇa's death scene—a passage that is undoubtedly one of the high points of Villiputtūrār's long poem. We shall limit our discussion to this passage, noting only by way of introduction that Villiputtūrār has, in general, "reformed" Karṇa's image to some extent: thus Karṇa has no real part to play in the humiliation of Draupadī in the *sabhā*;[130] his nobility and generosity are consistently stressed; the richly ambivalent confrontation between Karṇa and his charioteer, Śalya, is reduced to a single verse in the Tamil text, in which Śalya acquires the entire blame;[131] and, most striking of all, Karṇa's violent attack upon *dharma* during his final battle with Arjuna has simply disap-

[129] See above, III.2.

[130] Villiputtūrār 2.2.232-43. Karṇa's role passes here to Duḥśāsana, who insults Draupadī, calling her a prostitute.

[131] 8.2.40. See Hiltebeitel (1982) on this incident. Villiputtūrār does, however, describe a more violent conclusion to Śalya's quarrel with Karṇa: both men draw their swords, and only Duryodhana's intervention prevents them from coming to blows.

peared—there is no curse, no sarcastic reply by the god. Instead, the hero and the god are given an even more dramatic opportunity to explain themselves to one another.

At first, Villiputtūrār adheres quite closely to the Sanskrit original in describing the final battle between Arjuna and Karṇa. Here, too, Karṇa's *nāgāstra* misses its target because of Kṛṣṇa's hasty action; and the wheels of Karṇa's chariot sink into the earth, and Karṇa must climb down to free them (8.2.232-3).[132] But Kṛṣṇa does *not* urge Arjuna to shoot at his exposed enemy; Karṇa simply gets into another chariot and continues the fight. He is, however, becoming exhausted, as Kṛṣṇa observes to his protégé; Arjuna immediately sends a barrage of arrows that find their mark:

> Incomparable
>   was that hero
> in giving,
>   in the gift that brings
>   both victory and its joys:
>
> now his body opened up
> and blood poured out
>   like the rays of the setting sun.
>
> His garland of budding flowers,
> his crown,
> his armor and earrings—
> all lost their proper shape,
> and yet his hands—
>
>   those hands could not forget
>   their task
>   but went on bending back the bow,
>   releasing deadly arrows. (236)

Karṇa has thus been wounded—mortally wounded, as we shall see. The drama is nearly over. And it is at this point that Villiputtūrār—apparently drawing upon a widespread folk tradition[133]—introduces a new element into the story. If Kṛṣṇa is not to be accused, in this version, of bringing about Karṇa's death by his habitual deceitful

[132] Villiputtūrār adds another detail: when Paraśurāma's curse—that at the critical moment Karṇa would forget whatever he had learned from this teacher—comes true at this time, Karṇa turns in desperate prayer to his *guru*—and resumes the fight (233).

[133] See John Smith (1982). In the Rajasthani folk *MBh*, Karṇa gives Kṛṣṇa his *teeth* at the time of his death.

means, the Tamil poet is still not prepared to ignore the deity's essential responsibility, or its implications. Thus Kṛṣṇa must now put Karṇa to one last trial, a test that will reveal both Karṇa's true nobility and the god's utter lack of any such quality. It is sunset—the proper moment for the solar hero to die, and the perfect time for the god's last masquerade:

Two bow-shot lengths beneath the Sunset Hill
the burning sun sank down
as Kṛṣṇa watched—
  the First,
  primordial offshoot of the Vedic tree,
  root cause of liberation
    for all who are freed.

He turned to Vijaya,[134] whose hands
  still grasped his painted bow,
and ordered him to stop the battle.
Leaving him there on his chariot,
he took the form of an ascetic Brahmin
and approached the sun's
  own son. (237)

"I have heard," he said,
that on this earth surrounded
  by the dark sea's surging waves,
you will give whatever is asked of you
  to those who are in need.
Long have I practiced *tapas* on Mount Meru's slopes;
now I wander in the distress
  of painful poverty.
Give me but one, proper thing,
hero born by the gift of that Light
  who drives his chariot with his swift horses
  through the skies." (238)

So spoke that Brahmin,
and his words were a sweet elixir
in Karṇa's ears
  as he lay fallen upon his chariot,
  his body broken by the victorious
                arrows of Vijaya.

[134] = Arjuna.

"Good," he said, and smiled; "tell me
what it is you wish from me."

Obsequious,
the beggar pleaded:
"Give me all
  the merit
that is yours"—

and Karṇa's heart rejoiced. (239)

Let us pause to note the bitter irony of this request: the god, Villiputtūrāra's chosen deity and the true subject of the entire work (as the author states in his introduction),[135] is in truth a poor beggar who could use the hero's gift of merit. By any normal *human* standard, the god must surely be heavily burdened by evil—evil that is, in fact, infinite in scope and consequence, the direct and necessary result of the god's creation of the imperfect world as the arena for his cruel amusements—and he quite naturally looks to man, his potential devotee, for help in lightening this load. Karṇa's accumulated merit (*puṇṇiyam*) is thus in some ways a fitting gift to the god who has injured him consistently throughout his life. But the request is nevertheless astonishingly severe, a total—and a totally unfair—demand: Karṇa is being asked to renounce the fruits of his faithfulness, his devotion to Duryodhana, his generosity—all, in short, that has given meaning to his struggles, and that has held out the promise of some ultimate compensation for his griefs. Such totalistic demands are by no means unusual in the moral universe of South Indian devotional religion; the god often springs them, as a test, upon his devotees, and the latter inevitably respond by surrender. But in this case Karṇa has still not penetrated the god's disguise, and he thus remains unaware of the true nature of the request.[136] For all that, he cannot, of course, refuse without undermining a central value in the ongoing construction of his identity; without, that is, denying the coherence of his past. This, clearly, he will not do; indeed, the beggar's demand has, instead, the effect of sweetening his final, terrible hour:

"My spirit is shaken from its proper place.
I know not if it is still within my body
  or outside it.

[135] *tar̲cir̲appuppāyiram* 8.

[136] In this respect this episode is clearly different from that in which Karṇa gives his armor and his earrings to the disguised Indra (*MBh* 3.294)—for there Karṇa is aware from the beginning of the god's true identity.

You did not come at the time when I,
evil that I am,
gave everything that was asked
  to whoever came to me.
Yet I give you now, unstintingly,
all the merit I have acquired.
Take it! It is yours.
Not even Brahmā on his lotus
  could equal you; and is my merit
any greater
          than the merit
of letting go?" (240)

So he spoke
with his hands joined in worship
  and entreaty.
The god who is like a thunderbolt
  to foes who fail to pay him worship
looked joyfully at Karṇa
and said: "Seal your promise
  with the water sign."[137]

The hero poured out his blood
  issuing from the arrow's wound
  in his heart,
and the god—who had once, long ago,
received water from the demon,[138] and then
stole his three worlds—
now, with the same outstretched hand,
accepted *this* gift. (241)

Villiputtūrār, like other Tamil poets, searches for the most striking concrete images with which to clothe a moral statement; here the pouring of water, traditional sign of the gift, has become an offering of blood to a bloodthirsty god. The poet deliberately evokes the parallel myth of Bali and Trivikrama-Viṣṇu (the deceitful dwarf who deprives a noble demon-king of sovereignty): like Bali, Karṇa is an enemy to the side of *dharma*, and must therefore be defeated; but this defeat takes the form of an unfair, unworthy attack upon a morally superior, beloved figure whose very nobility constitutes a threat to

[137] The conventional symbolic act accompanying a gift in South India is the pouring of water.

[138] Bali.

normative order. Moreover, in both cases the result is an epiphany, replete with elements of horror, and offered solely to the "good" demon hero and foe.

Clearly, Karṇa has passed the test. Kṛṣṇa has played his part to the end, learned whatever he apparently needed to know, or to experience. But he is still disguised; his unmasking awaits a final demonstration of Karṇa's spirit.

Exulting, the sage turned
to the king adorned with a rich garland:
  "Tell me the boons you desire,
  and I shall grant them."
Said the great son of the sun:
  "If, through cruel *karma*, the source of misery,
  I must be born again
  in whatever kind of birth,[139]
  then let me have a heart
  that never says 'no'
  to anyone who says he has nothing." (242)

When the lord heard these words of truth
uttered by his cousin,[140]
his heart blossomed into joy;
with his hands, delicate as flowers,
he embraced him, drew him near,
and bathed him in the tears of mercy
  flowing from his lotus eyes.

Said the One who appears as Three:
"However often you will be reborn,
in each birth you will have
both generosity and splendid wealth,
and, in the end, you will attain
release." (243)

This is a moment of transition, one of the most powerful and poignant in all of Tamil *bhakti* poetry—the moment when the all-powerful god moves to embrace his human victim and to bathe with compassionate tears (*karuṇai nīr*) the wounds that he, the god, has caused. The notion of divine compassion or mercy, *karuṇai* (Skt. *karuṇā*), is central to this scene; subsequent verses emphasize it again and explore its meaning.

[139] Literally, "in one of the seven kinds of birth" (or: in 7 x 7 births).
[140] Kuntī, Karṇa's mother, was the sister of Vasudeva, Kṛṣṇa's father.

We should hesitate to see it as primarily ironic, although deep irony is surely part of what the poet is describing. Rather, Kṛṣṇa's *karuṇā* is both ironic and sincere; rooted in an acknowledged reality of suffering, it transcends tragedy through a free acceptance of the evident contradiction—that of a compassionate love working through, or along with, the infliction of pain—even as it supersedes the tragic insistence upon meaningfulness and order. The god's *karuṇā* is real, open-ended, unpredictable, and without any easily intelligible, rational aim or meaning. Its transporting presence is accompanied by a vision: Kṛṣṇa can now remove his disguise and appear to the dying hero in his "cosmic" form, with his dark body, his weapons, his conventional iconic attributes. Witnessing this revelation, Karṇa feels an overriding joy:

> "Now, as I give up my life,
> felled on the battlefield by Dhanañjaya's arrow,[141]
> I have been blessed with a vision of flawless
>   Nārāyaṇa, of the red lotus eyes.
>
> I have performed many fiery sacrifices,
> bathed in the holy Ganges and other sacred rivers,
> burned in the fire of yoga,
> worshiped the gods with flowers,
> and seen you, the omnipresent,
>   firmly established in my heart.
> I have disciplined myself with heavy penances
>   that no one else could do,
> kept apart from all pleasures—
>
> but the great reward
> which could not be won
>   by any of these actions
> has now, through your mercy (*tiruvaruḷ*),
> become mine." (245-46)

Does this vision—the ultimate reward that the hero can seek in his life—diminish his terror and his pain? Karṇa will die happy, but only after reaffirming the tragic consistency of his fate in the face of the unsettling *anagnorisis* pressed upon him by the god. Like the Shakespearean tragic hero, Karṇa sees, in his final moments, the sorrowful events of his life pass before his eyes:

[141] Dhanañjaya = Arjuna.

I fought in battle against Dharma's son
  and against his beloved brothers.
In the violent struggle of arms,
I repaid my debt to my friend, dear to me
  as my life;
I gave my superb armor and my earrings
  to the king of the gods,
and to *you* I have given
  all the good deeds I accomplished—

to you, red-eyed Māl,
who long ago crawled between the Marutu trees:[142]

this is how I lived my life,
in penance,
all alone. (248)

Indeed, Karṇa has been alone most of his life, as he strove to fashion an identity for himself from the heroic values of loyalty and sacrifice; and he has just witnessed the shattering of this system of values by the god's obviously nonheroic stance. Kṛṣṇa will soon drive home this point by a confession. But note the way in which Karṇa clings still to the sense of his life's integrity, and to its pain. Has his loneliness finally been breached by the god's revelation? If so, Karṇa is still caught up in pathos and in irony. The joy he now feels must be brought into relation with an awareness of Kṛṣṇa's awesome and incomprehensible misdeeds. Let us listen to the final words of the two partners to this confrontation, as Karṇa speaks:

"These boons have I won:
  the boon of worshiping the fragrant feet
    washed by the heavenly river;[143]
  the boon of being honored by that great heart
    which gave birth to the moon;
  the boon of being touched,
    caressed,
    by your arms,
    being held to your breast adorned with sandal
    and honey-soaked *tulasī*;
  the boon of uttering your name
    in awareness, as I lay fallen, slain
    by the arrow that tore through my flesh;

[142] Kṛṣṇa's boyhood feat of crawling between two Marutu trees while tied to a mortar.
[143] The heavenly Ganges pours over Viṣṇu's feet.

who among all who are born to live on the wide earth
has struggled and attained greater fortune
than is mine?" (249)

So spoke the sun's son as he worshiped
in his delight,
in joy.
Now Kṛṣṇa addressed him,
the god who had followed in the wake of the cattle
in the fertile meadowlands,
who had flung a calf at the demon in the *viḷā* tree,[144]
and he said to Karṇa: "It was I
who sent the lord of the gods to take from you
your armor and your earrings
that day;
I was the one who used Kuntī to extort your promise
that you would shoot the serpent-weapon
only one, single time;
it was I who told you the truth about your birth,
and I who diverted that serpent-weapon, Takṣaka's child,[145]
so that it failed to strike Dhanañjaya—

it was all my doing,
for your sake,
out of true compassion (*mĕykkaruṇai*)—"

and with these words he turned back
and became again Vijaya's charioteer—

that god who is all the oceans, all the hills,
all the worlds, all gods and men,
and who stole from the dark-eyed young *gopīs*
their fine clothes, their shyness,
their colorful bangles, and all the innocence
of their hearts. (250-51)

Nietzsche would have understood Karṇa's joy, which clearly arises "not in order to be liberated from terror and pity, not in order to purge oneself of a dangerous affect by its vehement discharge—Aristotle understood it that way—but in order to be *oneself* the eternal joy of becoming, beyond all terror and pity—that joy which included

[144] Another boyhood feat of Kṛṣṇa's, according to Tamil tradition.
[145] Aśvasena, the son of the serpent Takṣaka, inhabited the *nāgāstra* used by Karṇa.

even joy in destroying."[146] But what about Kṛṣṇa? How does *he* understand it? And what about the Tamil poet who tells the story?

It is still a question of *karuṇā*, as the god himself states. Kṛṣṇa reviews the critical points in Karṇa's life and takes total responsibility for each of them in turn. This is his last message to Karṇa, the clinching confession that rounds off his *anagnorisis*. There is no room for any doubts; the god seems almost to be boasting of his crimes. To add insult to injury, Kṛṣṇa ends by asserting that it was all done for the victim's own good, and out of *karuṇā*. So much for Karṇa's claims of consistent nobility and coherent goals; so much for his ideals. Look what he was up against! A trickster-god who loaded the dice against him; who is quite prepared to admit his responsibility for the hero's disastrous life; who has "used" Karṇa, embittered his experience, and has now killed him after putting him through a final, bitter trial. In these circumstances, tragedy alone will not do: the tragic hero confronts a capricious, admittedly brutal, and yet by his own account compassionate clown. Let us add him to our collection—Kṛṣṇa in this episode is the karunic clown linked with tragedy, with a "painful" contradiction,[147] and with their transcendence through the playful abrogation of the premises of tragic order. He is beyond the Nietzschean affirmation, beyond, too, the sheer seductiveness of meaning and closure which lures the hero into tragedy. There is no real attempt to justify Karṇa's fate; the clown scoffs at such efforts. Kṛṣṇa has acted through the series of painful events that comprise Karṇa's experience as if to create a medium of cumulative relatedness and revelation, culminating in the battlefield epiphany; viewed in this light, the series becomes, perhaps, somewhat more bearable, at least in the consciousness of the dying hero. But his terrible struggles, his noble choices, above all his self-sacrifice no longer matter much in themselves; ultimately, they were all, quite literally, for nothing. Or, from another, divine perspective, for the play—note Villiputtūrār's description of the god, at the end of his confession, as the prankster who made off with the *gopīs*' clothes "and all the innocence of their hearts." We are again in the presence of the divine bandit/thief, the beloved, and loving, exemplar of disorder.

[146] Nietzsche (1930, pp. 181-82; trans. Kaufmann, 1968, pp. 562-63): "Nicht um von Schrecken und Mitleiden loszukommen, nicht um sich von einem gefährlichen Affekt durch dessen vehemente Entladung zu reinigen—so verstand es Aristoteles—: sondern um, über Schrecken und Mitleid hinaus, die ewige Lust des Werdens selbst zu sein,—jene Lust, die auch noch die Lust am Vernichten in sich schliesst. . . ."

[147] *Pace* Aristotle and Kierkegaard (above, V.8 n. 191), but not, perhaps, so far removed from Dante's understanding of *commedia*.

On one level, however—perhaps that of the poet who sang this passage—the tragic vision survives. This is no longer the somewhat primitive tragedy of a bandit-hero such as Maturaivīraṉ, with the emphasis upon fame, self-sacrifice, and apotheosis—a pattern that may approximate the heroic tragedy of the *Iliad*; by now we are closer to an Aeschylean mode, in which the guiding powers of the universe are deeply implicated in evil. Kṛṣṇa cannot escape his devotees' righteous anger. The tragic emotions continue to predominate in the aftermath of Karṇa's death, as one sees from another innovation of Villiputtūrār's. According to the Tamil text, Karṇa had made a request to his mother in their last interview, before the battle: if he were to die in the war, she must then come to him and offer him the milk she had denied him when he was an infant.[148] This is what we now see: no sooner is Karṇa slain—by one final shot from Arjuna's bow—than a disembodied voice announces the death; Kuntī hears it and, weeping, her hair disheveled, striking herself in grief, picks her way among the corpses on the battlefield until she arrives at the side of her first-born son. She laments his tragic life, recalls her own heartlessness in abandoning him, and concludes with the terrible cry:

> "By the power of fate,
> or by the *māyā* of the gods,
> unrewarded,
>   you have passed on—
>
> alas, my son!"
>
> Thus she mourned over him, and all the kings
>   standing on the battlefield heard her,
>   and were amazed:
>
> with love, she took him gently to her breast
> and fed him the milk that came flowing from her nipples,
>
> while she suffered, like a cow, grieving, bewildered,
> for her calf
> that has died at the very moment
> of its birth. (256-57)

Kuntī takes her place among the Tamil warrior-mothers depicted in Caṅkam poetry, where the nursing on the battlefield is a well-known

[148] 5.4.260. This is also Karṇa's major request from Kṛṣṇa—that Kuntī nurse him after his fall—according to the Tamil folk-ballad about Karṇa's death: *Karṇamakārājaṉ caṇṭai*, pp. 40-41.

topos.[149] But even this dramatic scene cannot conclude the tragic narrative of Karṇa's death. For now, for the first time, the Pāṇḍavas have learned of Karṇa's true identity from their mother's action; and they are furious at her for concealing the fact that he was their brother[150]—furious, too, at the wily god who has engineered this debacle. Sahadeva, the wisest of the brothers, angrily lists Kṛṣṇa's various acts of cruelty: he killed the demon Hiraṇyakaśipu by means of his, the demon's, son; he used Vibhīṣaṇa, Rāvaṇa's brother, to destroy Rāvaṇa; now he has caused Karṇa's death in battle with *his* brother, Arjuna. "Who can fathom the gods' cunning ways?" (*viraku*, 268). This mood continues through the opening of the *Śalyaparvan*, which is devoted to the laments for Karṇa's death. To cite but one more example:

> The goddess Shadow[151] was filled with hatred,
> and the Earth goddess felt even stronger hate
> because Arjuna, conqueror of demons, had fought and killed
> the son of the sun, without knowing they were brothers.
> And the young king himself (Arjuna), Bhīma's brother,
> hated Kṛṣṇa, who causes hate
>   by his deceitful tricks;
> hated his hard-hearted mother;
> and, finally, he hated
> fate. (9.12)

Karṇa's death is not to be passed over lightly, whatever the god might say. And has not the poet projected his own basic feeling onto Arjuna, heroic instrument of the god's nefarious "design?"

Arjuna is the "young king"; Karṇa chooses not to be king. The two belong on opposite sides of a symbolic and semantic divide. There is a rich symbolic significance in the fact that Karṇa's true rival, who eventually defeats him with the help of the trickster-deity, is none other than Arjuna, the androgynous clown of the Virāṭa episodes and, in general, a figure of tranformation and ambiguity. Arjuna is heroic, yet capable of doubt and reflection—as in the crisis that prompts the god to utter the *Bhagavadgītā*. Karṇa, on the other hand, has no hesitation about the coming battle, no doubts as to its necessity and its link to enduring values; he is quite prepared to die a hero's death that will confirm the integrity of those values; ultimately, he accepts the

[149] For example, *Puṛan*. 295 (and cf. 278).

[150] Thus Yudhiṣṭhira says (8.2.264): "How true it is (as they say) that strangers are better than one's own mother."

[151] Chāyā, the sun's second wife, here seen as Karṇa's second mother. Cf. Dumézil (1968), pp. 126-30.

world and the sacrificial process which rules it. Not so Arjuna: his triumph is, in large measure, the victory of the clown, or of the boundary, now deeply internalized, rationalized through devotion, yet still corrosive of the very order that he fights to preserve. Karṇa can never be king—even Kṛṣṇa seems to know this when he offers Karṇa the kingship, at the cost of Karṇa's betrayal of Duryodhana—for he is wholly identified with the ethos of the hero, with the hero's self-sacrificing path to fame and his devotion to principles and to an unchanging vision of what is right. His world is closed, relatively static, locked into meaning. No doubt it is always easier to live in such a world, despite its inevitable pain, its affinity with sacrifice and heroic death—this is the subtle allure of tragedy, which provides an ordered universe in which to die. The tragic hero, part victim, part creator of his fate, gives voice to a profound affirmation at the end. But it is precisely this vision that the king must renounce. In his heroic guise, the king is still like Karṇa—a pathetic but illustrious plaything of a brutal yet compassionate god; the king almost always begins this way, and always retains something of the hero's tragic determinacy. But insofar as this heroic identity is subsumed within the larger and inherently more ambiguous sphere of kingship, the royal hero loses both pathos and consistency until he approximates the god as another clown, another despoiler of meaning.

This is the vision that pervades South Indian kingship and the state: not a stable harmony, not static closure, not the meaningfulness of universal ideals, not consistency and continuity with a personal and communal past, not the nobility of holding fast in the face of suffering, not tragic yearning and the orderliness of a world of separation—though all of this is also present within the South Indian semantic universe—but the divine clown's savage mercies, his disastrous playing with the world. This is a game that undermines every mortal construction; that scatters pain on a universal scale and then mocks the paltry human effort to find significance in suffering. Yet it is also truly *karuṇā*—an act of love. It is the unencumbered, literally aim-less playing of the creative clown, and it brings its own coherence to a deeply riven world. Tragedy starts with an unacknowledged presupposition of harmony and meaningfulness and proceeds to find this premise torn away in the face of irreparable, total conflict; the clown's premise, if one can use such a word for him, is playful and irreverent decomposition, the obvious insufficiency of "meaning"—and his effect is cohesive, an integration by way of disorder and collapse. The dynamism and dissonance that characterize the South Indian state can thus be correlated to a specific, antitragic semantic range. Note the distinction, for example, from ancient Greek kingship, which marks the king with an enduring nobility and an ever-present potential for tragedy; the Hindu king, by way of contrast, is always likely to abandon his tenuous dignity, then to mimic, as a clownish antiking and antihero, his former iconic self. Tragedy inheres in his heroic beginning and in his periodic restorations; his comic propensities usually preclude—at least in the mature medieval state—the symbolic domination of his kingship by the seductive tragic mode.[152]

Medieval South Indian kingship, in sum, is an institution that must accommodate conflicting drives: toward life, and away from it; toward the clarity of tragedy, and beyond it. It is suspicious of determinate meaning and of propriety, suspicious even (or especially) of the god who has initiated its unfolding. It takes the hero's power as a necessary starting point and then disperses it, plays with it, renounces it, uses it to engender movement—not the linear movement of "progress" and construction, but an unsteady spiral around a dark and empty center which, like Kṛṣṇa, like the Vidūṣaka and the other clowns who symbolize it, continually devours power, meaning, and all merely human order.

[152] Again it should be noted that the "heroic" Caṅkam kingship cannot be characterized in this way; it tends rather to the tragic, as the *puṟam* poems suggest. It is also of interest that Karṇa is claimed as an ancestor by the Veḷāḷas, the landed caste that offers crucial support to kingship and the state, but that is not properly "royal" in itself.

· VIII ·

Postscript: In the Absence of the King of Kings

> No doubt the world is entirely an imaginary world, but it is only once removed from the true world.[1]

> "And even I can remember
> A day when the historians left blanks
> in their writings,
> I mean for the things they didn't know,
> But that time seems to be passing."[2]

In the twenty-fifth year of his reign (1009-1010), some five years before his death, the great Chola ruler Rājarāja I completed the consecration of his outstanding monument, the Bṛhadīśvara temple in Tanjore, with the gift of a gold-covered finial for the top of the central *vimāna*—a huge edifice towering over 200 feet, containing the shrine of the god Śiva within it. As its name implies—Bṛhadīśvara is the "Great Lord"—this temple is a rhapsody to size, to the power that sheer mass and height hold for the imagination. Everything here—the *liṅga* in the central shrine, the *vimāna* above it, the eighty-ton stone crowning the latter, the immense, monolithic Nandin in front of it—is of colossal dimensions. Indeed, so the story goes, things might have gone even further in this direction: when the Nandin was first carved, it kept on swelling and growing until a nail was driven into its back. This local myth nicely encapsulates the notion of a dynamic, restless power at work in the construction of this most famous Chola shrine.

Still, the name that its architect preferred for this temple seems to have been not "Bṛhadīśvara" but "Rājarājeśvaram-uṭaiyār," after Rājarāja's own title, "King of Kings." This shrine is his statement and his signature. His image, we are told, graced one of the inner chambers;

[1] Isaac Bashevis Singer (1957), p. 23.
[2] Pound (1957), Canto XIII, p. 116.

his portrait appears in the murals surrounding the sanctum; the long inscriptions that cover the plinth make constant reference to his names and epithets; indeed, it has all been executed, we learn from these records, "according to his word."[3] Yet what we hear, of course, are not Rājarāja's words but the *śilpin*-engraver's pompous formulas: this is the king "who took to heart his rightful possession of the Earth-Lady, even as he possessed Śrī" (*tirumakaḷ polap pĕrunilaccĕlviyun taṉa-kkey urimai pūṇṭamai manakkŏḷ* . . .)—a glorious, conquering king, in other words, who could issue commands and somehow orchestrate the astonishing effort that must have gone into building this monument. But is he really here? Can we sense his vital presence behind the formulaic façade, or, for that matter, within the stone walls of this temple that bears his name? When one looks for him, he is gone. As always, his real voice is silent. What is left is simply this Tamil Tower of Babel and the hints it embodies of a certain vision, a frozen cry.

Was the king aware of the approach of death when he lavished on this shrine the vast quantities of gold and silver treasure looted during his campaigns?[4] What was in his mind? The work was, of course, begun long before his twenty-fifth regnal year; but one feels that his attention became more and more focused on this site, as the ongoing inscriptional record would suggest. Rājarāja may well have been indifferent to the idea of leaving behind him some enduring monument to his fame—one does not usually build temples for this purpose in South India[5]—but he might have wished to celebrate again, in a final, culminating display, those forces that had guided his life and his kingship. These forces were obviously not limited to the volitional field of a single man. By all accounts, the building of the Bṛhadīśvara was an act of "integration"; the channeling of resources, the labor, the technical accomplishment of a shared conception—all expressed the oddly fragmented unity of this medieval state. Like the stones of the *vimāna*, held together without mortar, the community demonstrated its seemingly miraculous coherence in creating the god's new home. If kingship was at the center of the endeavor, it could nevertheless be carried out only by virtue of the wider process of aggregation around this center—a process we have not examined in this book, the process which takes us from kingship to the state. This is the subject for

[3] *ippaṭi uṭaiyār śrīrājarājadevar tiruvāy mŏḻint' aruḷiṉa paṭi*: SII 2, no. 66 (first section, p. 261).

[4] *Ibid.*, nos. 1, 91, 93.

[5] Although the building of a temple is sometimes listed as one of the seven *santānas*; e.g. *Manucaritramu* of Pĕddana, 1.14.

another study; but the above chapters surely indicate that the king fulfils a crucial role as symbol, articulating the most dynamic aspects of statehood and delimiting a specific range of feeling and of meaning. He is, in fact, rather like the temple itself—another symbol, another "center," another point of transition. Is the act of building this shrine then a tribute to his power—or to its dispersal in the royal dramas of kenosis? The Bṛhadīśvara is, like many other shrines, a site where the royal patron puts forward his claims by divesting himself of wealth in relentless, grandiose display. One must agree with George Spencer's careful conclusion: "Such patronage, far from representing the self-glorification of a despotic ruler, was in fact a method adopted by an ambitious ruler to enhance his very uncertain power."[6] And further: a ruler's power can, in general, flourish in this polity only through such acts of highly visible renunciation and diffusion, the center's self-limiting mechanisms for achieving legitimacy and recognition.

We cannot know Rājarāja's thoughts; but we can follow, to some extent, the conceptions that animated his painters, who fashioned the famous murals in the passageway around the inner sanctum. Moreover, in these murals (recovered from under a layer of seventeenth-century Nāyak paintings) we can review for the last time the major themes of this book, as exemplified in several of the stories that were explored in these pages. Let us go in the direction of *pradakṣiṇa*, as any pilgrim of the eleventh century, or of the twentieth, would naturally do. One begins, as is only fitting, with the god: on the south wall we find Śiva seated as Dakṣiṇāmūrti, teacher and master of meditation, with a great banyan tree over his head. Monkeys play in the tree's branches; perhaps one of them will yet become the mad Chola king Mucukunda, half-ape and half-man.[7] Near the tree we behold Śiva again, this time as the unclean Brahminicide Bhairava, with his dog; the Outcaste-deity, boundary become center, is worshiped by a hero, another powerful symbolic figure from the cultural border. We are still at the brink of the Chola vision of kingship.

That vision strikes us with full force when we move on to the western wall. Here we stand before the huge mural depicting the career of Cuntaramūrttināyaṉār, from his beginning in the village of Tirunāvalūr to his final ascent, with the Cera king, to Śiva's heaven. The painters have captured the force of a single movement rushing upward, sweeping the saint through the dramatic events of his life. The panel starts at the lower left with the preparations for Cuntarar's wedding

[6] Spencer (1969), p. 45.

[7] Above, V.4.

in the village, a wedding destined to be interrupted—for the prankster-god Śiva now appears as an old Brahmin, waving in his hand the palm-leaf document which, he claims, proves that the prospective bridegroom is his slave. We see Cuntarar, regally dressed—indeed, this Brahmin boy had been brought up as a king, as Cekkiḻār informs us[8]—staring with some disdain at the unlikely figure of the masquerading god. The bridegroom is surely justified in regarding this interloper as a madman (*pittaṉ*).[9] But it is no use: the panel moves on to show us the erstwhile bridegroom following after his new "master," who has succeeded in proving his outlandish claim before the village court. The god will shortly disappear into the shrine at Tiruvĕṇṇeynallūr—and Cuntarar will thus, at last, recognize his identity; recognize, too, with a shock that will traumatize him for life, that he is, indeed, this person's slave. From this moment on, he will be carried along on a violent current of song, pleading, and argument, much of it angry and bitter, with the god who has possessed him. Further up the wall, we can, indeed, see the saint engaged in worshiping the dancing Śiva at Cidambaram. But the visual focus of the mural as a whole is the majestic scene at the upper right; this is the final ascension and transfiguration in which Cuntarar, mounted on a white elephant, climbs into the heavens, with his friend Ceramāṉ Pĕrumāḷ riding his horse beside him.[10] We recognize our Brahmin clown, always at odds with the social order to which he is also paradoxically committed, with the royal Auguste at his side. The two crazed devotees and friends, whose interaction constitutes the core of medieval kingship, are shown in the moment of their transcendence of its limits; they have left behind them the deeply impaired mundane world of village, court, and temple—the familiar kingdom of clowns oriented in the direction of their ascent. Before them, at the top right, sits the god with his wife, the vanishing center of their devotion and of the kingdom they have deserted.

Was this not also Rājarāja's design, evident in the very structure he has built? The Bṛhadīśvara repeats in its major features the ascension of Śiva's heroic clowns; its form is petrified movement and transformation, a physical assault upon the heavens, a bridging of the painful gap between man and god. Like Ceramāṉ Pĕrumāḷ, like Mucukunda, like Nahuṣa and Triśaṅku,[11] the Chola king thinks in terms of scaling

[8] *PP* 151-52.

[9] As he, in fact, calls him during this scene—hence, according to the tradition, the first word of Cuntarar's *Tevāram, pittā* ("Madman"!).

[10] Above, V.5.

[11] Above, V.2-3.

the skies; we can easily enough imagine the tall *vimāna* he has erected taking off, flying through the air—like the demons' Triple City,[12] or the many South Indian temple-*vimānas* that are said to have come circling through the atmosphere to land at some local shrine. Rājarāja looks not toward an apotheosis—*that* is for the tragic hero—but toward another form of bodily ascent. His vehicle is the shrine's *vimāna*, which articulates the line of communication between cosmic realms; this structure is the *skambha*, the axis mundi, analogous to his throne. And the king, as usual, is thus perched between worlds at the point of precarious intersection and transition. Seen from below, from the vantage point of his subjects, the king's form masks the god's; the two figures, deity and ruler, seem to coalesce, to cast a single shadow. Their nature and attributes, even their interests, appear to be largely shared. But from the king's position, the distance from heaven still seems overwhelming—and a challenge. At this level one is most conscious of the distinction, and of the urge to transcend it: there *is* divinity in kingship—what in South India is not divine?—but the essential relation of king and god is now an analogical one that is always in danger of being taken too literally (as in the case of Vena).[13] Moreover, in normative terms this means that the king's transfiguration will take a devious route; the *vimāna* is, after all, not his but truly the god's, a gift from his abject royal servant. It is this act of devotion, of kenosis, that raises the ruler on high. The king becomes "divine" in his assumed humility, by recognizing the gap that separates him from the god, thus opening himself to "possession" by the deity or his avatar. The ascent he contemplates requires a prior self-abasing descent to the position of the lowest and humblest of the god's devotees.

Thus Rājarāja is repeatedly referred to in the inscriptions as Śivapādaśekhara—he whose crown is Śiva's foot. Elsewhere on the western wall we see him worshiping together with his queens before the lord of Cidambaram. Let us take notice of these Chola queens, at once sensual and demure—the latter quality contrasting with the bold, beckoning power of the dancing-girls scattered at other points in the murals. These dancing-girls, strategically inserted into the design to hold the eye, to give respite from the bewildering, restless movement of the whole, are the counterparts, no doubt, of the 399 *devadāsīs* brought to Tanjore from other shrines by the order of the king.[14] As we know from the literary sources, the royal sphere is suggested and demarcated

[12] Above, III.2.

[13] Above, II.4.

[14] SII 2, no. 66.

by the presence of these female figures—queens *and* dancing-girls, the most conspicuous markers of the king's public identity. They, too, are involved in worship, and in the process of the king's ascent (witnessed by celestial dancers from their place in the clouds). Again we perceive the Chola hallmark of vital energy on display, pulled past the given limits. But the agitated motion of the crowded mural becomes somewhat simpler, more contained, in the iconic vignette painted in the northwest corner of the chamber: here stand Rājarāja and his Brahmin *guru*, Karuvūrttevar, as we saw them at the very outset of our study.[15] One senses a fragile balance: they seem to hold movement within them, barely stilled, as they stare at us with haunted eyes, with dignity, a hint of longing. Observe how they lean toward one another—the Brahmin, naturally, in front, turning his left shoulder *backward* toward the king, toward the world. The king is partly obscured by this Brahminical shadow, his visage less translucent than that of the sage. The Brahmin appears to be teaching, the king hanging on his words—a moment of pregnant, transient harmony. The icon is situated between the ascension of Cuntarar and Ceramāṉ Pĕrumāḷ and the wild Tripurāntaka mural of the northern wall: would one have guessed at the commotion and conflict, the metamorphoses and ceaseless flux, that the idealized images conceal?

We come at last to the northern wall. Śiva, his eyes wide open and staring (in the hero's uncompromising fierceness? in horror at what he is about to do?), is bending back his great bow, formed from the cosmic mountain, to destroy the demons of the Triple City. The latter, for their part, are preparing to die, as their wives clutch at them in terror. Indeed, terror pervades the whole vibrant scene: the figures of the god and his enemies virtually leap out to engulf the spectator, who is no doubt intended to become part of this battle. What part must he play? Surely he cannot help but feel something of the demons' passion as they stand face to face with the violent, consuming god. And let us recall that these demons are, or were, Śiva's own devotees, corrupted through the god's own cruel and cunning plan.[16] Śiva has gone to war against his former servants—reason enough for the terror to become overpowering; reason even to feel rage. We are again beyond order, beyond logic, in the ambiguous boundary zone bearing down on the kingdom's heart—the Brahmin's native realm of rejection and paradoxical connection to a sacrificial world. The Brahmin follows the oscillating, two-way movement of this god, struggling with, or

[15] Above, I.3 at notes 44-45 (Fig. 2).
[16] Above, III.2.

against, his world. He, too, is committed to the violence of sacrifice and to the violent imposition of limits upon an absolute ideal, like the god who is prepared to destroy his devotees; and he is outside, or at the edge, of this process, pointed toward its transcendence, already partly detached from the terror. Like Śiva, the Brahmin affirms through his negation, sacrifices and decries the creation he thus achieves.

The frightening aspect of things is plain; the demons are soon to die. Yet, in the midst of all this horror, there is another, jarring element. There are other spectators for this drama—the gods, of course, cheering on their divine master; but also Śiva's grotesque *gaṇas*, the pudgy dwarfs and other deformed creatures who conventionally accompany this god. If awe has any place in the emotions evoked by this painting, it is also deliberately punctured by the ridiculous, as so often happens with Śaiva icons.[17] The dwarfs seem nearly to mock the seriousness of the mythic event, as does the ungainly Gaṇeśa rushing in on his rat.[18] On the one hand, a savage attack by the most powerful of the deities; on the other, the sheepish, playful grins of his closest companions and witnesses. The myth is framed for us from within. Moreover, Śiva himself is far closer to the *gaṇas* than we might, at first, assume. Tamil versions of this story often say that Śiva shot not an arrow but a smile, or a laugh, at the demon-foes. Thus Cuntarar, our Brahmin clown and royal companion, sings to Śiva in his very first *patikam*:

> You bear the cool
>   crescent moon;
> your body
>   is like fire!
>
> You laughed,
> and fire devoured
> the Triple City of the heedless.[19]

The fiery god simply, literally, laughs his victims to death. The smile or the laughter are still terrifying, ironic, but also genuine—for this destructive deity is also the enduring embodiment of compassion, *karuṇā*, our unpredictable karunic clown playing his murderous games with our lives.

[17] One thinks of Elephanta, where a comic *gaṇa* stands immediately beside the "awesome" Maheśamūrti.

[18] See the remark by Sivaramamurti (1973), p. 20.

[19] Cuntarar *Tevāram* 6 (*patikam* 1.6).

Let us look back, for a moment, at the series as a whole. Beginning with the serious, contemplative Dakṣiṇāmūrti and the outcaste Bhairava, attended by a hero, we have moved on to the vast mural of the two clowns, king and Brahmin—the mad devotees of a mad and shocking god. We have followed them in their wild rush to heaven, their final escape from the world. Close on their heels, but far more reserved, still only dreaming of ascent, came the Chola king with his queens and dancing-girls, dependable emblems of his power. With the Brahmin poet and adviser, the king is held in place—an iconic gesture—between two dynamic, passionately painted scenes: White Clown and Auguste climbing into heaven, Tripurāntaka-Śiva at war with the demons. The latter scene, on the north wall, presents the culminating comedy-and-terror of this visionary landscape of royal symbolism; we end up outside, with the divine karunic clown. The progression takes us through vivid images of power drifting steadily into comedy and serious clowning. And the process does not end here. A later generation would add another series of paintings, around the inner walls of the courtyard surrounding the Bṛhadīśvara shrine—a series depicting each of Śiva's sixty-four "amusements" (*tiruviḷaiyāṭal*) at Maturai, so that the structure as a whole would now be ringed round with comedy.[20] But the Chola paintings that we have been discussing express the mixed outlook of the Chola kingdom—the creative tension and intensity conjoined to, and partially contained by, reflexive comedy; the sensual undercurrent and affect breaking beyond the cultural limits; heroic tragedy—the nobility of the iconic ideal—and its negation through comic transformation and transcendence. Notice that this vision speaks to us from the painted walls of the passageway surrounding the inner sanctum, so that here, too, as in so many of the stories we have studied, kingship is seen at the edge, as the boundary of the real, enclosing and incorporating it, dissolving in it, serving as threshold. The true center is the dark *śivaliṅga* within, encircled by these walls—the *liṅga* which is, as the name originally indicated, simply a "sign," a hint of the god, an ambiguous presence and absence, a suggestion of transition, a movement in stone.

[20] This is the Maratha-period *tiruviḷaiyāṭal* series adorning the *prākāra* wall.

Glossary

Tamil words are marked (T).

abhiṣeka: "anointing"; the consecration of a king; the bathing of a divine image
akam (T): the inner part; in poetics, the poetry of love
amṛta: the ambrosia of the gods, food of immortality
aṉpu (T): love, devotion
apsaras: a nymph or dancing-girl from Indra's heaven
aṟam (T): *dharma*; right conduct
aruḷ (T): mercy, divine compassion or grace
āśrama: a retreat, the dwelling-place of a sage in the forest; also, one of the four stages of life
astra: a weapon
asura: a demon; an enemy of the gods (*devas*)
aśvamedha: the Vedic horse-sacrifice
bhakta: devotee
bhakti: devotion, faithfulness, love
bhoga: "enjoyment"; sensual pleasure; consumption
bhūta: a ghost or spirit
brahmabandhu: a lowly or unworthy Brahmin
brahmadeya: the gift of land to Brahmins, for settlement
daiva: fate
dāna: the act of giving
daṇḍa: "the rod"; by extension, the king's duty to punish
deva: a god; an enemy of the demons (*asuras*)
dharma: the universal order; also, the proper conduct demanded of an individual as a member of society; righteousness
dīkṣā: initiation; ritual preparation, marked by withdrawal and ascetic practices, for a sacrifice
gandharva: a celestial musician
guṇa: one of the three "strands" or qualities comprising the phenomenal world, i.e., *sattva*, *rajas*, and *tamas*
jajmāni: (from Skt. *yajamāna*); the village system of caste-interdependence, by which each caste contributes its occupation and receives in turn a share of the produce
kāma: desire, especially sexual desire
karma: action; by extension, the law by which one's actions determine one's fate
karuṇā: compassion, mercy

kāvya: poetry or ornate prose, embodying language at its most refined; a composition in this style
kolam (T): threshold design made from rice flour; also known as *raṅgoli* and *muggu* (Telugu)
kṣatriya: a warrior; a member of the social category of warriors and kings, ranked beneath the Brahmins in the *varṇa* system
līlā: play; a game or amusement
liṅga: a sign; the phallus, symbol of Śiva
mantra: a sacred formula, prayer, incantation; Vedic verse
maṟam (T): heroism; the hero's violent power and excess; *adharma*—unrighteous action; cruelty
māyā: the divine power to create; magic; deception, fraud, illusion, especially the confusing appearance of the phenomenal world
muni: a sage
nakṣatra: an asterism
nāmam: literally, "name"; the Śrīvaiṣṇava sectarian mark on the forehead
nāyaka: the (usually royal) hero of Sanskrit drama
nivṛtti: "retraction"; involution, dissolution, or quiescence (opposed to *pravṛtti*)
pāpa, pāpman: evil
pitṛs: the ancestors
prākāra: a large wall, such as surrounds a shrine or temple complex
pralaya: the periodic dissolution of the universe
pravṛtti: active engagement in the world; creative activity (opposed to *nivṛtti*)
pūjā: worship
puṟam (T): the outer part (opposed to *akam*); in poetics, the poetry of heroism, war, and panegyric
purāṇa: literally, "old, ancient story"; a text in which myths and other sacred traditions are preserved
purohita: a Brahmin priest
pyal: the raised platform on the entrance porch attached to the traditional South Indian village home
rajas: the second of the three *guṇas*, associated with energy and passion
sabhā: a meeting place; royal court; gambling hall
samādhi: a state of deep meditation
saṃsāra: the cosmic flux characterizing the created world
saṃskāra: refining, giving form, perfecting; a life-cycle ritual (one of a series performed by members of the first three *varṇas*)
sandhi: juncture; rules governing the phonetic changes resulting from the juncture of sounds and words
sannyāsin: a Renouncer, who has left society to achieve truth and liberation
sattva: the first of the three *guṇas*, embodying goodness and pure being
śivaliṅga: see *liṅga*
śrāddha: the offering to the ancestors (*pitṛs*)
śrauta: relating to the sacred books (*śruti*); a public ritual prescribed by *śruti*
śrī: royal splendor; prosperity, success, beauty; the goddess Lakṣmī

tamas: the third of the three *guṇas*, associated with darkness, dullness, ignorance
tapas: literally, "heat"; austerities, penance
tejas: radiance, splendor
tīrtha: a sacred site or shrine; originally, a ford or bathing place
tyāga: renunciation
upanayana: the sacred-thread ceremony
vajra: Indra's thunderbolt
varṇa: one of the four ranked social categories of Brahmin, Kṣatriya, Vaiśya, and Śūdra
veśyā: a courtesan
vimāna: a celestial vehicle; the central tower of Pallava and Chola shrines
viraha: separation
yajamāna: the patron at a sacrifice
yakṣa: a class of semi-divine beings; a nature spirit
yoga: "yoking"; the spiritual discipline of concentration and meditation
yogin (feminine *yoginī*): a practitioner of *yoga*

Bibliography

Tamil and Telugu Texts

Akanāṉūṟu. With commentary by Na. Mu. Veṅkaṭacāmi Nāṭṭār. Madras, 1965.
Aḻakarvarṇippu. Madras, 1950.
Aruṇācalapurāṇam of Ĕllappanayiṉār. Madras, 1920.
Basavapurāṇamu of Pālakuriki Somanātha. Madras, 1952.
Bhojarājīyamu of Anantāmātyuḍu. Hyderabad, 1969.
———. Translated by V.A.K. Ayer. *Untold Stories of King Bhoja*. Bombay, 1975.
Caṅkararācentiracoḻaṉ ulā. Edited by Ki. Vā. Jagannātaṉ. Tiruvāṉmiyūr, 1977.
Cĕyaṅkŏṇṭārvaḷakkam. Edited by T. Chandrasekharan. Madras, 1955.
Cilappatikāram of Iḷankovaṭikaḷ. With Arumpatavurai and the commentary of Aṭiyārkkunallār. Edited by U. Ve. Cāminātaiyar. Madras, 1927.
Ciṟuttŏṇṭapattaṉ katai. Madras, 1975.
Cīvakacintāmaṇi of Tiruttakkatevar. Madras, 1968.
Civavākkiyar pāṭal. Madras, 1974.
Irāmāvatāram of Kampaṉ. Edited by U. Ve. Cāminātaiyar Library. Tiruvāṉmiyūr, 1967.
Kāḷahastīśvaramāhātmyamu of Dhūrjaṭi. Madras, 1960.
Kaliṅkattupparaṇi of Cayaṅkŏṇṭār. With commentary by Puliyūrkkecikaṉ. Madras, 1963.
———. With commentary by Pĕ. Paḻaṉivela Piḷḷai. Madras, 1975.
Kalittŏkai. With commentary of Nacciṉārkkiṉiyar. Madras, 1938.
Kāñcippurāṇam of Civañāṉayokikaḷ. Edited by C. Aruṇai Vaṭivelu Mutaliyār. Kāñcipuram, 1937.
Kantapurāṇam of Kacciyappacivācāriyar. With commentary by Ma. Ti. Pāṉukavi. 2 vols. Madras, 1907.
Karṇamakārājaṉ cantai. Madras, 1974.
Kāttavarāyacuvāmi katai. Madras, 1974.
Kumpecar kuṟavañci nāṭakam of Muttamiḻkkavirājacekarar Pāpanāca Mutaliyār. Madras, 1961.
Kuṟuntŏkai. Edited by U. Ve. Cāminātaiyar. 2nd ed. Madras, 1947.
Maṇimekalai of Cīttalaic cāttaṉār. Edited by Na. Mu. Veṅkaṭacāmi Nāṭṭār and Auvai. Cu. Tuṟaicāmippiḷḷai. 2nd ed. Madras, 1951.
Manucaritramu of Allasāni Pĕddana. Vijayavada, 1968.
Maturaivīracuvāmi katai. Madras, 1972.
Mūvar ulā of Ŏṭṭakkūttar. With commentary by Ti. Caṅkuppulavar. Madras, 1967.

Nālaṭiyār. Edited by G. U. Pope. Oxford, 1893.
Naḷavĕṇpā of Pukaḻentippulavar. Madras, 1960.
Nālāyirativyaprapantam. Edited by Citrakūṭam Kantāṭai Tiruveṅkaṭācāryar. Madras, 1898.
Naṟṟiṇai nāṉūṟu. With commentary by A. Nārāyaṇacāmi Aiyar. Madras, 1956.
Nīlakeci. Edited by A. Chakravarti. N.p., 1936.
Pāmpāṭṭi cittar pāṭal. Madras, 1972.
———. Translated by David C. Buck, *Dance, Snake! Dance!* Calcutta, 1976.
Pārijātāpaharaṇamu of Mukku (Nandi) Timmana. Madras, 1968.
Paripāṭal. With commentary of Parimelaḻakar. Edited by U. Ve. Cāminātaiyar. 3rd ed., Madras, 1948.
———. Translated by François Gros. *Le Paripāṭal.* Pondicherry, 1968.
Pĕriya purāṇam ĕṉṉum tiruttŏṇṭar purāṇam of Cekkiḻār. With commentary by C. K. Cuppiramaṇiya Mutaliyār. Coimbatore, 1975.
Perūrppurāṇam of Kacciyappamuṉivar. Edited by I. Irāmacuvāmippiḷḷai (Ñāṉacampantappiḷḷai). Madras, 1944.
Pŏṉvaṇṇattantāti of Ceramāṉ Pĕrumāḷ Nāyaṉār. Madras, 1970.
Puṟanāṉūṟu. Edited by U. Ve. Cāminātaiyar. 6th ed., Madras, 1963.
Puṟappŏruḷ vĕṇpāmālai of Aiyaṉāritaṉār. With commentary by Puliyūrkkecikaṉ. Madras, 1963.
Sumatiśatakamu. Edited and translated by Velcheru Narayana Rao. Madison, n.d.
Takkayākapparaṇi of Ŏṭṭakkūttar. Edited by U. Ve. Cāminātaiyar. Madras, 1960.
Tamiḻnāvalarcaritai. Edited by Auvai. Cu. Tuṟaicāmippiḷḷai. Madras, 1972.
"Tennālrāmaṉ katai." In *Katācintāmaṇi ĕṉṟu vaḻaṅkukiṟa mariyātairāmaṉ katai.* Madras, 1975.
Tevāram. 7 vols. Tarumapuram, 1953.
Tirimūrttimalaipurāṇavacaṉam of Aruṇācala Kavuṇṭar. Madras, 1936.
Tiruccĕntūr nŏṇṭināṭakam of Muttālaṅkuṟiccik Kantacāmippulavar. Edited by Ta. A. Aruṇācalam Piḷḷai. Tiruccĕntūr, 1948.
Tirukkuṟaḷ of Tiruvaḷḷuvar. Madras, 1972.
Tirukkuṟṟālakkuṟavañci of Tirikūṭarācappakkavirāyar. Madras, 1980.
Tiruvālavāyuṭaiyār tiruviḷaiyāṭaṟpurāṇam of Pĕrumpaṟṟappuliyūrnampi. Edited by U. Ve. Cāminātaiyar. Madras, 1906.
Tiruvāṉaikkāppurāṇam of Kacciyappamuṉivar. Śrīraṅkam, 1909.
Tiruvāṉmiyūr stalapurāṇavacaṉam of Rā. Vicuvanātaṉ. Madras, 1966.
Tiruvārūrppurāṇam of Aḷakai Campantamuṉivar. Edited by Cu. Cuvāminātatecikar. Madras, 1894.
Tiruvatikai talamāṉmiyamum tevāra patikaṅkaḷum of Ka. Rā. Citamparam Mutaliyār, Madras, 1940.
Tiruvāymŏḻi. See *Nālāyirativyaprapantam.*
Tiruviḷaiyāṭaṟpurāṇam of Parañcotimuṉivar. With commentary by Na. Mu. Veṅkaṭacāmi Nāṭṭār. 2 vols. Madras, 1965.
———. *Maturaikkāṇṭam.* Maturai, 1973.

Tiyākarācalīlai of Tiricirapuram Mīṉāṭcicuntaram Piḷḷai. Madras, 1928.
Tŏlkāppiyam. Pŏruḷatikāram. With commentary of Iḷampūraṇar. Madras, 1977.
———. With commentary of Nacciṉārkkiṉiyar. Madras, 1967.
Vikkiramātittaṉ katai. Edited by Pa. Vĕ. Mukammatu Ipuṟākim Cākipu. Madras, 1938.
———. Translated by V.A.K. Aiyer. *Stories of Vikramaditya.* Bombay, 1974.
Villiputtūrār Pāratam. With commentary by Vai. Mu. Kopālakiruṣṇamācāriyar. Madras, 1972.
Vinotaracamañcari of Vīracāmi Cĕṭṭiyār. Madras, n.d.

Sanskrit Texts

Abhijñānaśakuntalā of Kālidāsa. Edited by S. K. Belvalkar. New Delhi, 1965.
———. Bengal Recension. Edited by R. Pischel. Cambridge, Mass., 1922. HOS No. 16.
Adhyātmarāmāyaṇa. Rājamaṇḍri, 1963 (Telugu script).
Agnipurāṇa. Poona, 1957. ASS no. 41.
Aitareya Brāhmaṇa. Calcutta, 1895-1896. Bib. Ind.
Arthaśāstra of Kauṭilya. Edited by J. Jolly. Lahore, 1923. Panjab Sanskrit Series no. 4.
Atharvaveda. Bombay, 1895.
———. Translated by William Dwight Whitney, edited by Charles Lanman. Cambridge, Mass., 1905. HOS nos. 7-8.
Bhagavadajjukaprahasana of Mahendravikramavarman. Edited and translated by Michael Lockwood and A. Vishnu Bhat. Madras, 1978.
Bhāgavatapurāṇa. Gorakhpur, samvat 2022.
Bhāsanāṭakacakra. Plays Ascribed to Bhāsa. Edited by C. R. Devadhar. Poona, 1962.
Brahmāṇḍapurāṇa. Edited by J. L. Shastri. Delhi, 1973.
Brahmapurāṇa. Poona, 1895. ASS no. 28.
Brahmavaivartapurāṇa. Poona, 1935. ASS no. 102.
Bṛhaddevatā attributed to Śaunaka. Edited by A. A. Macdonell. Cambridge, Mass., 1904. HOS no. 5.
Buddhacarita of Aśvaghoṣa. Edited by E. H. Johnston. Calcutta, 1935-1936. Panjab University Oriental Publications, nos. 31-32.
Devībhāgavatapurāṇa. Benares, 1955.
Hālāsyamāhātmya (on Maturai). Maturai, 1870.
Harivaṃśa. Varanasi, 1964.
Hāsyārṇavaprahasana of Jagadīśvara. Edited by Ishwar Prasad Chaturvedi. Varanasi, 1963.
Jaiminīya Brāhmaṇa of the *Sāmaveda.* Edited by Raghu Vira and Lokesh Chandra. Nagpur, 1931. Sarasvati Vihara Series no. 31.
Jātakas. Edited by Viggio Fausbøll. 7 vols. London, 1877-1897.
Karpūramañjarī of Rājaśekhara. Edited by Sten Konow, translated by Charles R. Lanman. Cambridge, Mass., 1901. HOS no. 4.

Kārtavīryavijayaprabandha of Aśvati Tirunāḷ Rāmavarma. Trivandrum, 1947.
Kathāsaritsāgara of Somadeva. Edited by Durgāprasād and Kāśināth Pāndurang Parab. 4th ed., Bombay, 1930.
———. Translated by C. H. Tawney, edited by N. M. Penzer. *The Ocean of Story*. 10 vols. London, 1924-1928.
Kauṣītaki Brāhmaṇa. Edited by E. R. Sreekrishna Sarma. Wiesbaden, 1968.
Kāvyaprakāśa of Mammaṭa. Edited by Sivaprasad Bhattacharyya. Calcutta, 1961.
Kumārasambhava of Kālidāsa. Edited by Suryakanta. New Delhi, 1962.
Kūrmapurāṇa. Edited by A. S. Gupta. Varanasi, 1972.
Liṅgapurāṇa. Bombay, 1906.
Mahābhārata. Edited by Vishnu S. Sukthankar et al. Poona, 1933-1959. 37 fascicules.
———. Southern Recension. Edited by P.P.S. Sastri. Madras, 1931-1933. 18 vols.
———. Translated by J.A.B. van Buitenen. *The Mahābhārata*. Vol. I: Chicago, 1973. Vol. II: Chicago, 1975. Vol. III: Chicago, 1978.
Manusmṛti (Mānavadharmaśāstra). Calcutta, 1932. Bib. Ind.
Mārkaṇḍeyapurāṇa. Calcutta, 1862. Bib. Ind.
Matsyapurāṇa. Poona, 1909. ASS no. 54.
Mṛcchakaṭika of Śūdraka. Edited by M. R. Kale. Bombay, 1962.
———. Translated by J.A.B. van Buitenen. *Two Plays of Ancient India*. 1966; reprinted Delhi, 1971.
Nāgānanda of Śrīharṣa. Benares, 1956. Benares Sanskrit Series no. 87.
Nārāyaṇīya of Meppattūr Nārāyaṇa Bhaṭṭātiri. Madras, 1976.
Nāṭyaśāstra. Benares, 1929.
Padmapurāṇa. Poona, 1894. ASS no. 131.
Pañcatantra (Pūrṇabhadra). Edited by Johannes Hertel. Cambridge, Mass., 1908. HOS no. 11.
Pañcavaradakṣetramāhātmya. See Gros and Nagaswamy.
Priyadarśikā of Śrīharṣa. Srirangam, 1906. Sri Vani Vilas Sanskrit Series no. 3.
Raghuvaṃśa of Kālidāsa. Delhi, 1971.
Rāmāyaṇa of Vālmīki. Madras, 1958.
———. Edited by G. H. Bhatt et al. Baroda, 1960-1975. 7 vols.
Ṛgveda. With the commentary of Sāyaṇa. 6 vols. London, 1849-1864.
Śatapatha Brāhmaṇa of the White Yajurveda. With the commentary of Sāyaṇa. Edited by Albrecht Weber. Calcutta, 1903-1910. Bib. Ind.
Saurapurāṇa. Poona, 1889. ASS no. 18.
Śivapurāṇa. Bombay, 1953.
Śivarahasyakhaṇḍa of the *Śaṅkarasaṃhitā* of the *Skandapurāṇa*. Published as *Śrīskāndamahāpurāṇa*. Edited with Tamil translation by Ceṅkālipuram Aṉantarāma Tīkṣitar. 3 vols. Celam, n.d.
Skandapurāṇa. Bombay, 1867.

Taittirīya Āraṇyaka of the Black Yajurveda. With commentary of Sāyaṇa. Edited by Rajendra Lal Mitra. Calcutta, 1872. Bib. Ind.

Ubhayābhisārikā of Vararuci. Translated by Amiya Rao and B. H. Rao. New Delhi, 1979.

Upaniṣads. Aṣṭādaśa upaniṣadaḥ. (Eighteen Principal Upaniṣads.) Poona, 1958.

Uttararāmacarita of Bhavabhūti. Delhi, 1962.

Vāmanapurāṇa. Edited by A. S. Gupta. Varanasi, 1967.

Varadāmbikāpariṇayacampū of Tirumalāmbā. Edited with translation, notes, and introduction by Suryakanta. Varanasi, 1970. Chowkhamba Sanskrit Series no. 79.

Varāhapurāṇa. Calcutta, 1893. Bib. Ind.

Vāyupurāṇa. Poona, 1905. ASS no. 49.

Viddhaśālabhañjikā of Rājaśekhara. Varanasi, 1965. Vidyabhawan Sanskrit Granthamala no. 125.

Vikramorvaśīya of Kālidāsa. Edited by M. Monier-Williams. 1849, reprinted Delhi and Varanasi, 1976.

Viṣṇupurāṇa. With *Vaiṣṇavakūṭacandrikā* of Ratnagarbha Bhaṭṭācārya. Bombay, 1866.

———. Translated by H. H. Wilson. *The Vishnu Purana, A System of Hindu Mythology and Tradition*. 1840, reprinted with an introduction by R. C. Hazra, Calcutta, 1972.

Other References

Altekar, A. S. *State and Government in Ancient India*. Benares, 1949.

Ananthakrishna Iyer, L. K. See Nanjundayya, H. V.

Anantha Murthy, U. R. *Samskara, A Rite for a Dead Man*. Translated by A. K. Ramanujan. Delhi, 1976.

Anjaneyulu, D. "A Kannada Writer Looks at the Literary Scene." *The Hindu*, August 17, 1980.

Appadurai, Arjun. "Right and Left Hand Castes in South India." IESHR 11 (1974), 216-60.

———. "Kings, Sects, and Temples in South India, 1350-1700 A.D." In Stein (1978a), pp. 47-73. (1978)

———. Comments on Ferro-Luzzi (1980). *Current Anthropology* 21, p. 54.

———. *Worship and Conflict under Colonial Rule*. Cambridge, 1981.

———. "The Puzzling Status of Brahman Temple Priests in Hindu India." *South Asian Anthropologist* (1983), pp. 43-52.

———, and Carol Appadurai Breckenridge. "The South Indian Temple: Authority, Honour, and Redistribution." CIS (n.s.) 10 (1976), 187-211.

Arai, Toshikazu. "Jaina Kingship as viewed in the *Prabandhacintāmaṇi*." In Richards, ed. (1978), pp. 74-114.

Aṟavāṇaṉ, Ka. Pa. *Kaliṅkattupparaṇi: Ŏru matippīṭu*. Madras, 1976.

Arokiaswami, M. *The Kongu Country*. Madras, 1956.

Artola, George T. "Ten Tales from the *Tantropākhyāna.*" *ALB* 29 (1965), 30-73.

Ashton, Martha Bush, and Bruce Christie. *Yakṣagāna, a Dance Drama of India.* New Delhi, 1977.

Asian Puppets, Wall of the World. Los Angeles, 1976.

Auboyer, Jeannine. *Le trône et son symbolisme dans l'Inde ancienne.* Paris, 1949.

Auerbach, E. *Mimesis: The Representation of Reality in Western Literature.* Translated by Willard R. Trask. New York, 1957.

Ayer, V.A.K. See *Bhojarājīyamu* and *Vikkiramātittaṉ katai.*

Babcock, Barbara A., ed. *The Reversible World: Symbolic Inversion in Art and Society.* Ithaca, N.Y., and London, 1978. "Introduction," pp. 13-36.

Bailey, G. M. "Brahmā, Pṛthu, and the Theme of the Earth-Milker in Hindu Mythology." *IIJ* 23 (1981), 105-16.

Baines, Sir Athelstane. *Ethnography (Castes and Tribes).* Strassburg, 1912.

Bakhtin, Mikhail. *Rabelais and his World.* Translated by Helene Iswolsky. Cambridge, Mass., 1968.

———. *The Dialogic Imagination.* Translated by Caryl Emerson and Michael Holquist. Austin, 1981.

Balasubrahmanyam, S. R. *Middle Chola Temples: Rajaraja I to Kulottunga I (A.D. 985-1070).* Faridabad, 1975.

Balasubramanian, C. *A Study of the Literature of the Cera Country (up to 11th Century A.D.).* Madras, 1980.

Basham, A. L. "Jainism and Buddhism." In Wm. Theodore de Bary, ed., *Sources of Indian Tradition.* Vol. I, 37-202. New York, 1958.

Beck, Brenda E. F. "Colour and Heat in South Indian Ritual." *Man* 4 (1969), 553-72.

———. "The Authority of the King: Prerogatives and Dilemmas of Kingship as Portrayed in a Contemporary Oral Epic from South India," in Richards, ed. (1978), pp. 168-91.

———. "The Logical Appropriation of Kinship as a Political Metaphor: An Indian Epic at the Civilizational and Regional Levels." *Anthropologica* 20 (1978), 47-64. (1978a)

———. *The Three Twins: The Telling of a South Indian Folk Epic.* Bloomington, 1982.

Belkin, A. A. *Russkie Skomoroxi.* Moscow, 1975.

Berger, Peter L., and Thomas Luckmann. *The Social Construction of Reality.* Harmondsworth, 1972.

Bergson, Henri. *Laughter* (with George Meredith, *An Essay on Comedy*). New York, 1956.

Bhat, G. K. *The Vidusaka.* Ahmedabad, 1959.

Bialik, Ch. N. "Language, Closing and Disclosing." Translated by Yael Lotan. *Ariel* 50 (1979), 106-14.

Biardeau, Madeleine. "Brahmanes combattants dans un mythe du sud de l'Inde." *ALB* 31-32 (1967-1968), 519-30.

———. "La decapitation de Reṇukā dans le mythe de Paraśurāma." In J. C.

Heesterman, G. H. Schokker, and V. I. Subramoniam, eds., *Pratidānam* (Festschrift Kuiper), pp. 563-72. The Hague, 1968.

———. "The Story of Arjuna Kārtavīrya without Reconstruction." *Purāṇa* 12:2 (1970), 286-303.

———. "Compte-rendu, Conférences de Mlle Madeleine Biardeau." *Annuaire de l'École pratique des Hautes Études*, Section des Sciences Religieuses, 82 (1973-1974), 89-101; 84 (1975-1976), 165-86.

———. "Études de mythologie hindoue (IV)." *BEFEO* 63 (1976), 11-263.

———. "Études de mythologie hindoue (V)." *BEFEO* 65 (1978), 87-238.

———. Review of Kuiper (1979). *IIJ* 23 (1981), 293-300.

———, with Charles Malamoud. *Le sacrifice dans l'Inde ancienne.* Paris, 1976.

Blackburn, Stuart H. "The Folk Hero and Class Interests in Tamil Heroic Ballads." *Asian Folklore Studies* 37 (1978), 131-49.

———. "The Kallars: A Tamil 'Criminal Tribe' Reconsidered." *South Asia*, n.s. 1 (1978), 38-51. (1978a)

Bouissac, Paul. *Circus and Culture: A Semiotic Approach.* Bloomington, 1976.

Breckenridge, Carol Appadurai. "From Protector to Litigant-Changing Relations between Hindu Temples and the Raja of Ramnad." In Stein (1978a), pp. 57-77. (1978)

———. See also Appadurai, Arjun.

Brown, Peter. *The Making of Late Antiquity.* Cambridge, Mass., 1978.

Brown, W. Norman. "The Creation Myth of the Rig Veda." *JAOS* 62 (1942), 85-98.

Brubaker, Richard. "Lustful Woman, Chaste Wife, Ambivalent Goddess: A South Indian Myth." *Anima* 3:2 (1977), 59-62.

———. "The Ambivalent Mistress: A Study of South Indian Village Goddesses and their Religious Meaning." Ph.D. dissertation, University of Chicago, 1978.

Buck, David C. "The Snake in the Song of a Sittar." In Buck and Yocum (1974), pp. 162-83.

———. See also *Pāmpāṭṭi cittar* (1976).

Buck, Harry M., and Glenn E. Yocum, eds. *Structural Approaches to South India Studies.* Chambersburg, Pa., 1974.

Cāminātaiyar, U. Ve. *Niṉaivu mañcari II.* 3rd ed., Madras, 1953.

———. See also *Takkayākapparaṇi.*

Campantam. *Tĕṉālirāmaṉ kataikaḷ.* Madras, 1963.

Castro, Américo. *An Idea of History: Selected Essays of Américo Castro.* Translated and edited by Stephen Gilman and Edmund L. King. Columbus, Ohio, 1977.

Chakravartinayanar, A., and A. N. Upadhye, eds. *Pañcāstikāyasāra, the Building of the Cosmos.* New Delhi, 1975.

———. See *Nīlakeci.*

Champakalakshmi, R. "Peasant State and Society in Medieval South India: A Review Article." *IESHR* 18 (1981), 411-26.

Chandra, Moti. *The World of Courtesans.* Delhi, 1973.

Christie, Bruce. See Ashton, Martha Bush.
Claus, Peter J. "*Cenne* (Mancala) in Tuluva Myth and Cult." MS., 1980.
Cohen, Erik, and Eyal Ben Ari. " 'Hard Choices': The Sociological Analysis of Value Incommensurability." Manuscript, Jerusalem, 1979.
Coomarasamy, Ananda K. *Spiritual Authority and Temporal Power in the Indian Theory of Government*. New Haven, 1942.
Cooper, Lane. *An Aristotelean Theory of Comedy*. New York, 1922.
Coulson, Michael. *Three Sanskrit Plays*. Harmondsworth, 1981.
Das, R. K. *Temples of Tamilnad*. Bombay, 1964.
Das, Veena. *Structure and Cognition: Aspects of Hindu Caste and Ritual*. Delhi, 1977.
Davis, Natalie Zemon. *Society and Culture in Early Modern France*. Stanford, 1975.
de Casparis, J. G. "Van avonturier tot vorst: een belangrijk aspect van de oudere geschiedenis en geschiedschrijving van Zuid- en Zuidoost-Azië." Inaugural lecture, University of Leiden, 1979.
Defourny, Michel. *Le mythe de Yayāti dans la littérature épique et purāṇique*. Paris, 1978.
de Heusch, Luc. *Le roi ivre ou l'origine de l'état*. Paris, 1972.
de Jong, J. W. Review of van Buitenen (1978). *IIJ* 22 (1980), 58-62.
Deleury, G. A. *The Cult of Viṭhobā*. Poona, 1960.
Derrett, J.D.M. *The Hoysalas, a Medieval Indian Royal Family*, Madras, 1957.
———. "Rājadharma." *JAS* 35 (1976), 597-609.
Devasahayam, N. "Puppets in the Collection of the Madras Government Museum." *BMGM*, n.s. 11:1 (1973).
Dickinson, Emily. *The Poems of Emily Dickinson*. Edited by Thomas H. Johnson. Cambridge, Mass., 1955.
Dimock, Edward C., Jr. *The Thief of Love: Bengali Tales from Court and Village*. Chicago, 1963.
———. "Doctrine and Practice among the Vaiṣṇavas of Bengal." In Milton Singer, ed. (1971), pp. 41-63.
——— et al. *The Literatures of India: An Introduction*. Chicago, 1974.
Dirks, Nicholas B. "Political Authority and Structural Change in Early South Indian History." *IESHR* 13 (1976), 125-57.
———. "The Structure and Meaning of Political Relations in a South Indian Little Kingdom." *CIS*, n.s. 13 (1979), 169-206.
———. "The Pasts of a Pāḷaiyakārar: The Ethnohistory of a South Indian Little King," *JAS* 41 (1982), 655-83.
———. "Ritual Kingship and Civilization: The Political Dynamic of Cultural Change in Medieval South Indian History." Manuscript, 1983.
Drekmeier, C. *Kingship and Community in Early India*. Stanford, 1962.
Duby, Georges. *Saint Bernard, l'art cistercien*. Paris, 1979.
Duckworth, George E. *The Nature of Roman Comedy: A Study in Popular Entertainment*. Princeton, 1971.
Dumézil, Georges. *Servius et la Fortune*. Paris, 1943.

———. *Mythe et épopée*. Vol. I: Paris, 1968. Vol. II: Paris, 1971.

———. *The Destiny of the Warrior*. Translated by Alf Hiltebeitel. Chicago, 1969.

Dumont, Louis. *Une sous-caste de l'Inde du sud: organisation sociale et religion des Pramalai Kallar*. Paris, 1957.

———. "A Structural Definition of a Folk Deity of Tamil Nad: Aiyanar, the Lord." *CIS* 3 (1959), 75-87.

———. *Religion/Politics and History in India*. Paris, 1970.

———. *Homo Hierarchicus*. London, 1972.

Durga, S.A.K. *The Opera in South India*. Delhi, 1979.

Eaton, Richard. *Sufis of Bijapur, 1300-1700*. Princeton, 1978.

Eck, Diana. "India's *Tīrthas*: 'Crossings' in Sacred Geography." *HR* 20 (1981), 323-44.

Egnor, Margaret Trawick. "The Sacred Spell and Other Conceptions of Life in Tamil Culture." Ph.D. dissertation, University of Chicago, 1978.

Eisenstadt, S. N. "Comparative Analysis of State Formation in Historical Contexts." *International Social Science Journal* 32 (1980), 624-54.

———. "The Paradox of the Construction of Other-Worldly Civilizations—Some Reflections in the Wake of Max Weber's Analysis of Hinduism and Buddhism." Manuscript (1983), published as "Die Paradoxie von Zivilisationen mit ausserweltlichen Orientierungen. Überlegungen zu Max Webers Studie über Hinduismus und Buddhismus," in Wolfgang Schluchter, ed., *Max Webers Studie über Hinduismus und Buddhismus: Interpretation und Kritik*, 333-60. Frankfurt, 1984.

Falk, Nancy E. "Wilderness and Kingship in Ancient South Asia." *HR* 13 (1974), 1-15.

Fellini, Federico. *Fellini on Fellini*. London, 1976.

Ferro-Luzzi, Gabriella Eichinger. "The Female *lingam*: Interchangeable Symbols and Paradoxical Associations of Hindu Gods and Goddesses." *Current Anthropology* 21 (1980), 45-54.

Florentin, Marie-Claude. See Gaignebet, Claude.

Foucault, Michel. *The Order of Things*. New York, 1970.

Fox, Richard G. *King, Clan, Raja and Rule: State-Hinterland Relations in Pre-Industrial India*. Berkeley and Los Angeles, 1971.

———, ed. *Realm and Region in Traditional India*. New Delhi, 1977.

Francis, W. *South Arcot District Gazeteer*. Madras, 1906.

Frykenberg, R. E. "Traditional Processes of Power in South India: An Historical Analysis of Local Influence." *IESHR* 1 (1963), 122-42.

———, and John S. Deyell. "Sovereignty and the '*Sikka*' under Company Raj: Minting Prerogative and Imperial Legitimacy in India." *IESHR* 19 (1982), 1-25.

Fussell, Paul. *The Great War and Modern Memory*. New York, 1975.

Gaignebet, Claude, and Marie-Claude Florentin. *Le carnaval, essais de mythologie populaire*. Paris, 1974.

Gail, Adalbert. *Paraśurāma, Brahmane und Krieger*. Wiesbaden, 1977.

Geary, Patrick. *Furta Sacra: Thefts of Relics in the Central Middle Ages*. Princeton, 1978.

Geertz, Clifford. *Negara, the Theatre State in Nineteenth-Century Bali*. Princeton, 1980.

Gehrts, Heino. *Mahabharata, Das Geschehen und seine Bedeutung*. Bonn, 1975.

Gerow, Edwin. *A Glossary of Indian Figures of Speech*. The Hague, 1971.

Ghoshal, U. N. *A History of Indian Political Ideas*. Bombay, 1959.

Gluckman, Max. *Politics, Law and Ritual in Tribal Society*. Chicago, 1965.

GoldbergBelle, Jonathan R. "The Ramayana in the Leather Puppet Theatre of Andhra Pradesh." Paper presented at the Conference on Oral Epics in India, Madison, June 1982.

Goldman, Robert. *Gods, Priests, and Warriors: The Bhṛgus of the Mahābhārata*. New York, 1976.

Goldmann, Lucien. *Le Dieu caché: Étude sur la vision tragique dans les Pensées de Pascal et dans le théâtre de Racine*. Paris, 1955.

Goldsmith, Robert Hillis. *Wise Fools in Shakespeare*. East Lansing, 1955.

Gonda, Jan. *Ancient Indian Kingship from the Religious Point of View*. Leiden, 1969.

———. "Ascetics and Courtesans." Reprinted in *Selected Studies*, Vol. IV, pp. 223-47. Leiden, 1975.

Grene, David. *Reality and the Heroic Pattern*. Chicago, 1967.

———, and Richard Lattimore, eds. *The Complete Greek Tragedies: Sophocles*, Vol. II. Chicago, 1959.

Gros, François, and R. Nagaswamy. *Uttaramērūr: Légendes, histoire, monuments*. Pondicherry, 1970.

Grottanelli, Cristiano. "Tricksters, Scapegoats, Champions, Saviors." *HR* 23 (1983), 117-39.

Halbfass, Wilhelm. "Karma, *apūrva*, and 'Natural' Causes: Observations on the Growth and Limits of the Theory of Saṃsāra." In O'Flaherty (1980a), pp. 268-302 (1980).

Hall, Kenneth R. *Trade and Statescraft in the Age of the Cōḻas*. New Delhi, 1980.

———. Peasant State and Society in Chola Times: A View from the Tiruvidaimarudur Urban Complex." *IESHR* 18 (1981), 393-410.

Hamori, Andras. *On the Art of Medieval Arabic Literature*. Princeton, 1975.

Handelman, Don. "The Ritual-Clown: Attributes and Affinities." *Anthropos* 76 (1981), 321-70.

Hara, Minoru. "The King as Husband of the Earth (*mahī-pati*)." *Asiatische Studien* 27 (1973), 97-114.

Hardy, Friedhelm E. "Emotional Kṛṣṇa Bhakti." D. Phil. dissertation, Oxford University, 1976.

———. "Ideology and Cultural Contexts of the Śrīvaiṣṇava Temple." In Stein (1978a), pp. 119-51. (1978)

———. "The Tamil Veda of a Śūdra Saint (The Śrīvaiṣṇava Interpretation of Nammāḻvār)." *Contributions to South Asian Studies* 1, edited by Gopal Krishna, pp. 29-87. Oxford, 1979.

———. "Some Reflections on Indian Spirituality, III: Commuting within One World." *King's Theological Review* 4:1 (1981), 7-15.

Hart, George L., III. "Some Aspects of Kinship in Ancient Tamil Literature." In T. Trautmann, ed., *Kinship and History in South Asia*, pp. 29-60. Ann Arbor, 1974.

———. *The Poems of Ancient Tamil*. Berkeley, 1975.

———. *The Relation between Tamil and Classical Sanskrit Literature*. In J. Gonda, ed., *A History of Indian Literature*, Vol. X, fasc. 2, pp. 317-52. Wiesbaden, 1976.

———. *Poets of the Tamil Anthologies*. Princeton, 1979.

———. "The Theory of Reincarnation among the Tamils." In O'Flaherty (1980a), pp. 116-33. (1980)

Hastrup, Kirsten, and Jan Ovesen. "The Joker's Cycle." *Journal of the Anthropological Society of Oxford* 7:1 (1976), 11-26.

Hawley, John Stratton. "Thief of Butter, Thief of Love." *HR* 18 (1979), pp. 203-20.

———. *Krishna, the Butter Thief*. Princeton, 1983.

Heesterman, Jan. *The Ancient Indian Royal Consecration: The Rājasūya Described According to the Yajus Texts and Annotated*. The Hague, 1957.

———. "Vrātya and Sacrifice." *IIJ* 6 (1962), 1-37.

———. "Brahmin, Ritual and Renouncer." *WZKSO* 8 (1964), 1-31.

———. "The Case of the Severed Head." *WZKSO* 11 (1967), 22-43.

———. "On the Origin of the Nāstika." *WZKSO* 12-13 (1968-1969), 171-85.

———. "Kauṭalya and the Ancient Indian State." *WZKSO* 15 (1971), 5-22.

———. "The Conundrum of the King's Authority." In Richards, ed. (1978), pp. 1-27.

———. "Veda and Dharma." In Wendy Doniger O'Flaherty and J. Duncan M. Derrett, eds., *The Concept of Duty in South Asia*, pp. 80-95. Delhi, 1978. (1978a)

———. "Power and Authority in Indian Tradition." In R. J. Moore, ed., *Tradition and Politics in South Asia*, pp. 60-85. New Delhi, 1979.

———. "Veda and Society. Some Remarks à propos of the Film, 'Altar of Fire.' " *Studia Orientalia* (Finnish Oriental Society) 50 (1981), 51-64.

Held, Gerrit Jan. *The Mahābhārata, an Ethnological Study*. Amsterdam, 1935.

Hiltebeitel, Alf. *The Ritual of Battle*. Ithaca and London, 1976.

———. "Nahuṣa in the Skies: A Human King of Heaven." *HR* 16 (1977), 329-50.

———. Review of Gehrts (1975). *Erasmus* 29 (1977), 86-91. (1977a)

———. "The Indus Valley 'Proto-Śiva,' Reexamined through Reflections on the Goddess, the Buffalo, and the Symbolism of the *vāhanas*." *Anthropos* 73 (1978), pp. 767-97.

———. "Draupadī's Garments." *IIJ* 22 (1980), pp. 98-112.

———. "Śiva, the Goddess, and the Disguises of the Pāṇḍavas and Draupadī." *HR* 20 (1980), pp. 147-74. (1980a)

Hiltebeitel, Alf. "Draupadī's Hair." *Puraṣārtha* 5 (1981), 179-214.

———. "Sītā *Vibhūṣitā*: The Jewels for her Journey." *Indologica Taurinensia* 8-9 (1980-1981), 193-200. (1981a)

———. "Brothers, Friends, and Charioteers: Parallel Episodes in the Irish and Indian Epics." *Journal of Indo-European Studies*, Monograph Series no. 3 (Homage to Georges Dumézil), 1982, pp. 85-112.

Hobsbawm, E. J. *Bandits*, London, 1969.

Hocart, A. M. *Kingship*, Oxford, 1927 (reprinted 1969).

Holtzmann, Adolf. "Indra nach den Vorstellungen des *Mahābhārata*." *Zeitschrift der Deutschen Morgenländischen Gesellschaft* 32 (1878), pp. 290-340.

Hudson, Dennis. "Śiva, Mīnākṣī, Viṣṇu—Reflections on a Popular Myth in Madurai." In Stein (1978a), pp. 107-18. (1978)

———. "Two Citrā Festivals in Madurai." In G. R. Welbon and G. E. Yocum, eds., *Religious Festivals in South India and Sri Lanka*, pp. 101-56. New Delhi, 1982.

Huizinga, Johan. *The Waning of the Middle Ages*. 1924, reprinted Harmondsworth, 1972.

———. *Erasmus of Rotterdam*. London, 1952.

———. *Homo Ludens. A Study of the Play Element in Culture*. London, 1971.

Inden, Ronald. *Marriage and Rank in Bengali Culture: Caste and Clan in Middle Period Bengal*. Berkeley and Los Angeles, 1976.

———. "Ritual, Authority and Cyclic Time in Hindu Kingship." In Richards, ed. (1978), pp. 28-73.

Ingalls, D.H.H., trans. *An Anthology of Sanskrit Court Poetry: Vidyākara's Subhāṣitaratnakoṣa*. Cambridge, Mass., 1965. HOS no. 44.

Irākavaiyaṅkār, Mu. *Kaliṅkattupparaṇi ārāycci*. Maturai, 1925.

Irāmacāmi, Mu. "Tamiḻakat toṟpāvai niḻaṟkūttu." Ph.D. dissertation, University of Maturai, 1978.

Irāmacāmippulavar, Cu. A. *Meṟkoḷviḷakkak katai akaravaricai*. 2 vols. Madras, 1963.

Irāmakiruṣṇaṉ, Ĕs. *Kampaṉ kaṇṭa araciyal*. Maturai, 1959.

Jagannātaṉ, Ki. Vā. *Nāṭoṭi ilakkiyam*. Madras, 1967.

———. See *Caṅkararācentiracoḻaṉ ulā*.

Janaki, S. S. "Le piu recenti composizioni teatrali di tipo *bhāṇa*." *Atti della Accademia delle Scienze di Torino. II Classe di Scienze morali, storiche e filologiche* 107 (1973), 459-90.

Jefferds, Keith N. "Vidūṣaka versus Fool: A Functional Analysis." *Journal of South Asian Literature* 16 (1981), pp. 61-73.

Jellinek, Adolph, ed. *Beit Hamidrash*, 3rd ed. Jerusalem, 1967.

Jesudasan, C., and Hephzibah Jesudasan. *A History of Tamil Literature*. Calcutta, 1961.

Johnston, David B. "Bandit, *Nakleng*, and Peasant in Rural Thai Society." *Contributions to Asian Studies* 15 (1980), 90-101.

Kaelbar, Walter O. "The 'Dramatic' Element in Brāhamaṇic Initiation: Symbols of Death, Danger, and Difficult Passage." *HR* 18 (1978), 54-76.

Kailasapathy, K. *Tamil Heroic Poetry*, Oxford, 1968.
———. *Ŏppiyal ilakkiyam*. Madras, 1969.
Kāḷahastirājeśvara Rao. *Tĕnālirāmaliṅguni kathalu*. Rājamaṇḍri, 1967.
Kantorowicz, E. H. *The King's Two Bodies: A Study in Medieval Political Theology*. Princeton, 1957.
Karve, Iravati. *Yuganta, the End of an Epoch*. New Delhi, 1974.
Kaufmann, Walter, ed. and trans. *The Portable Nietzsche*. New York, 1968.
———. *Tragedy and Philosophy*. New York, 1968. (1968a)
Kersenboom, Saskia C. "Nityasumaṅgalī: Towards the Semiosis of the Devadāsī Tradition of South India." Ph.D. dissertation, University of Utrecht, 1984.
Kierkegaard, Søren. *Concluding Unscientific Postscript*. Translated by David F. Swenson and Walter Lowrie. Princeton, 1941 (reprinted 1960).
Kramrisch, Stella. *The Hindu Temple*. Calcutta, 1946.
———. "Two: Its Significance in the Ṛgveda." In E. Bender, ed., *Indological Studies in Honor of W. Norman Brown*, pp. 109-36. New Haven, 1962.
———. *The Presence of Śiva*. Princeton, 1981.
Krishnaswami, T. B. *South Arcot in Sacred Song*. Madras, 1937.
Kuiper, F.B.J. "The Basic Concept of Vedic Religion." *HR* 15 (1975), 107-20.
———. *Varuṇa and Vidūṣaka: On the Origin of the Sanskrit Drama*. Amsterdam, 1979.
Kulke, Hermann. *Cidambaramāhātmya*. Wiesbaden, 1970.
———. "Kshatriyaization and Social Change: A Study in Orissa Setting." In S. Devadas Pillai, ed., *Aspects of Changing India: Studies in Honour of Professor G. S. Ghurye*, pp. 398-409. Bombay, 1976.
———. "Royal Temple Policy and the Structure of Medieval Hindu Kingdoms." In A. Eschmann, H. Kulke, and G. C. Tripathi, eds., *The Cult of Jagannath and the Regional Tradition of Orissa*, pp. 125-38. Delhi, 1978.
———. *Jagannātha-Kult und Gajapati-Königtum*. Wiesbaden, 1979.
———. "Fragmentation and Segmentation versus Integration? Reflections on the Concept of Indian Feudalism and the Segmentary State in Indian History." *Studies in History* (New Delhi) 4 (1982), 237-63.
Kunjunni Raja, K. *Indian Theories of Meaning*. Madras, 1969.
———. "Kootiyattam (A General Survey)." *Quarterly Journal, National Center for the Performing Arts* 3:2 (1974), 1-12.
Kurup, K.K.N. *The Cult of Teyyam and Hero Worship in Kerala*. Calcutta, 1973.
Layard, John. "Labyrinth Ritual in South India: Threshold and Tattoo Designs." *Folklore* 48 (1937), 115-82.
Le Goff, Jacques. *Pour un autre moyen âge: Temps, travail et culture en occident*. Paris, 1977.
Lévi, Sylvain. *Le théâtre indien*. 1890, reprinted Paris, 1963.
Levin, Richard. *The Multiple Plot in English Renaissance Drama*. Chicago, 1971.

Leyser, K. J. *Rule and Conflict in Early Medieval Society: Ottonian Saxony*. London, 1979.

Lincoln, Bruce. "The Indo-European Cattle-Raiding Myth." *HR* 16 (1976), 42-55.

Lingat, Robert. "Time and the Dharma, on Manu 1.85-6." *CIS* 6 (1962), 7-16 (originally published as "Dharma et temps," 1961).

———. *The Classical Law of India*. Translated by J.D.M. Derrett. Berkeley and Los Angeles, 1973.

Long, Bruce. "Life out of Death: A Structural Analysis of the Myth of the Churning of the Ocean of Milk." In Bardwell Smith, ed., *Hinduism: New Essays in the History of Religion*. Supplements to *Numen* 33 (Leiden, 1976), pp. 171-207.

Lotman, Yu. M. and A. M. Piatigorsky. "Text and Function." *New Literary History* 9 (1978), 231-44.

Luckmann, Thomas. See Berger, Peter.

Ludden, David Ellsworth. "Agrarian Organization in Tinnevelly District: 800-1900 A.D." Ph.D. dissertation, University of Pennsylvania, 1978.

Mahalingam, T. V. *South Indian Polity*. 2nd ed. Madras, 1967.

Malamoud, Charles. "Terminer le sacrifice: Remarques sur les honaires rituels dans le brahmanisme." In Biardeau and Malamoud (1976), pp. 155-204.

———. "Conférence (Compte-rendu)." *Annuaire de l'École Française des Hautes Études, V^e section—Sciences Religieuses* 85 (1976-1977), 177-87.

Mandelstam, Osip. *Kamen'*. Petrograd, 1916.

Marglin, Fréderique Apffel. "Power, Purity, and Pollution: Aspects of the Caste System Reconsidered." *CIS* n.s. 11 (1977), 246-69.

———. "Wives of the God-King: The Rituals of Hindu Temple Courtesans." Ph.D. dissertation, Brandeis University, 1980.

Marr, J. R. "The *Pĕriya purāṇam* Frieze at Tārācuram: Episodes in the Lives of the Tamil Śaiva Saints." *BSOAS* 42 (1979), 268-89.

Marriott, McKim. "Hindu Transactions: Diversity without Dualism." In B. Kapferer, ed., *Transaction and Meaning: Directions in the Anthropology of Exchange and Symbolic Behavior*, pp. 109-42. Philadelphia, 1976.

Meenakshisundaram, T. P. "The Paraṇi Poetry." *Proceedings of the First International Conference Seminar of Tamil Studies*, Vol. II. Kuala Lumpur, 1969.

Miller, D. A. "Royauté et ambiguïté sexuelle." *Annales: Économies, sociétés, civilisations* 26 (1971), 639-52.

Mojumder, Atindra. *The Caryāpadas*. 2nd revised ed. Calcutta, 1973.

Moss, David. "Bandits and Boundaries in Sardinia." *Man* 14 (1978), 477-96.

"Muttamiḻmaṇi." *Tĕṉālirāmaṉ*. Madras, 1951.

Muttuccaṇmukaṉ and Nirmalā Mokaṉ. *Kuṟavañci*. Maturai, 1977.

Nagaswamy, R. *Studies in Ancient Tamil Law and Society*. Madras, 1978.

———. *Thiruttani and Velanjeri Copper Plates*. Madras, 1979.

———. "Tamil Painting." In *Splendours of Tamil Nadu*, pp. 103-24. Bombay, 1980.

———. *Tantric Cult of South India*. Delhi, 1982.

———. See also Gros, François.

Nanjundayya, H. V., and L. K. Ananthakrishna Iyer. *The Mysore Castes and Tribes*. 4 vols. Mysore, 1931-1935.

Narayan, R. K. *Gods, Demons, and Others*. Mysore, 1973.

———. *The Dark Room*. Chicago, 1981.

Narayanan, M.G.S. *Re-Interpretations in South Indian History*. Trivandrum, 1977.

Narrainsawmy, W. M. *Select Tamil Tales*. Madras, 1839.

Natesa Sastri, S. M. *Indian Folk-Tales*. Madras, 1908.

Neevel, Walter G. *Yāmuna's Vedānta and Pāñcarātra: Integrating the Classical and the Popular*. Missoula, Montana, 1977.

Neogi, Dwijendra Nath. *Sacred Tales of India*. London, 1916.

Nevo, Ruth. *Tragic Forms in Shakespeare*. Princeton, 1972.

———. *Comic Transformations in Shakespeare*. London, 1980.

Nicoll, Allardyce. *Masks, Mimes, and Miracles: Studies in the Popular Theatre*. 1931, reprinted New York, 1963.

Nietzsche, F. *Götzendämmerung. Der Antichrist. Gedichte*. Leipzig, 1930.

Nilakanta Sastri, K. A. *Foreign Notices of South India from Megasthenes to Ma Huan*. Madras, 1939.

———. *The Cholas*. 2nd revised ed. Madras, 1955.

Oertel, Hans. "Contributions from the Jāiminīya Brāhmaṇa to the History of the Brāhmaṇa Literature." *JAOS* 26 (1905), 176-96.

O'Flaherty, Wendy Doniger. "The Origin of Heresy in Hindu Mythology." *HR* 10 (1971), 271-333.

———. *Asceticism and Eroticism in the Mythology of Śiva*. Oxford, 1973.

———. *Hindu Myths*. Harmondsworth, 1975.

———. *The Origins of Evil in Hindu Mythology*. Berkeley and Los Angeles, 1976.

———. *Women, Androgynes, and Other Mythical Beasts*. Chicago, 1980.

———, ed. *Karma and Rebirth in Classical Indian Traditions*. Berkeley and Los Angeles, 1980. (1980a)

———. *The Rig Veda*. Harmondsworth, 1981.

———. *Dreams, Illusion, and Other Realities*. Chicago, 1984.

Ogibenin, B. L. *Structure d'un mythe védique: le mythe cosmogonique dans le Ṛgveda*. The Hague, 1973.

Ohnuki-Tierney, Emiko. *Illness and Healing among the Sakhalin Ainu: A Symbolic Interpretation*. Cambridge, 1981.

Oppert, Gustav. *On the Original Inhabitants of Bharatavarṣa or India*. Westminster, 1893.

Oreglia, Giacomo. *The Commedia dell'arte*. London, 1968.

Orwell, George. *Inside the Whale and Other Essays*. Harmondsworth, 1962.

Östör, Ákos. *The Play of the Gods: Locality, Ideology, Structure, and Time in the Festivals of a Bengali Town*. Chicago, 1980.

Ovesen, Jan. See Hastrup, Kirsten.

Panchapakesa Ayyar. *Tenali Rama*. Madras, 1947.

Parikh, J. T. *The Vidusaka: Theory and Practice*. Surat, 1953.

Parry, Jonathan. "Ghosts, Greed and Sin: The Occupational Identity of the Benares Funeral Priests." *Man* n.s. 15 (1980), 88-111.

Pāskarat Tŏṇṭaimāṉ, Tŏ. Mu. *Veṅkaṭam mutal kumari varai. IV: Pŏrunait tuṟaiyile*. Tirunĕlveli, 1971.

Peacock, James L. "Symbolic Reversal and Social History: Transvestites and Clowns of Java." In Babcock, ed. (1978), pp. 209-224.

Periyakaruppan, Rm. *Tradition and Talent in Cankam Poetry*. Maturai, 1976.

Piatigorsky, A. M. See Lotman, Yu. M.

Pillai, K. K. "Were the Pallavas Brahmins?" *Annals of Oriental Research, Madras*. Silver Jubilee Volume, 1975, pp. 222-45.

Pocock, D. F. *Mind, Body, and Wealth: A Study of Belief and Practice in an Indian Village*. Oxford, 1973.

Pope, G. U. *Tamil Heroic Poems*. Madras, 1973.

Pound, Ezra. *Selected Poems*. New York, 1957.

Price, Pamela Gwynne. "Raja-dharma in Nineteenth-century South India: Land, Litigation and Largess in Ramnad Zamindari," *CIS* n.s. 13 (1979), 207-39.

———. "Resources and Rule in Zamindari South India, 1802-1903: Sivagangai and Ramnad as Kingdoms under the Raj." Ph.D. dissertation, University of Wisconsin, 1979. (1979a)

Rabelais, François. *Gargantua and Pantagruel*. Translated by J. M. Cohen. Harmondsworth, 1979.

Radha Krishna, K. N., ed. *Thirumalirunjolaimalai (Sri Alagar Kovil) Stala Purana* (= *Vṛṣabhādrimāhātmya*). Maturai, 1942.

Raghavan, V. "Variety and Integration in the Pattern of Indian Culture. *FEQ* 15 (1965), 497-505.

———. "Kālidāsa in Tamil." In *Kālidāsa and South Indian Literature*, pp. 37-40. Madras, 1973.

———. *Bhoja's Śṛṅgāra Prakāśa*. 3rd ed. Madras, 1978.

Rajaruthnam Pillai, T. A. *Kambar Charitram (sic)*. Madras, 1909.

Rama the Jester. An Original and Up-to-date Version of the Stories of Tenali Rama, or Tales of Indian Wit and Humour. Author unknown. Coimbatore, n.d.

Ramacandra Rao, S. K. *The Indian Temple—Its Meaning*. Bangalore, 1979.

Ramanujan, A. K. *Speaking of Śiva*. Harmondsworth, 1973.

———. *Hymns for the Drowning*. Princeton, 1981.

———. "The Relevance of Folklore." In press.

———. See also Anantha Murthy (1976).

Ramaswamy, M. See Irāmacāmi, Mu.

Ramesan, N. *Temples and Legends of Andhra Pradesh*. Bombay, 1962.

Rao, V. Narayana, ed. and trans. *Sumatiśatakamu*. Madison, n.d.

———. See also Richards, J. F.

———, and Hank Heifetz. *Kāḷahastīśvaraśatakamu*. Translated with Introduction. In press.

Rau, W. *Staat und Gesellschaft im alten Indien.* Wiesbaden, 1957.
Reiniche, Marie-Louise. "La notion de jajmānī: Qualification abusive ou principe d'intégration?" *Puruṣārtha* 3 (1977), 71-108.
———. *Les Dieux et les hommes. Étude des cultes d'un village du Tirunelveli, Inde du Sud.* Paris, The Hague, and New York, 1979.
Rĕṭṭiyār, Na. Cuppu. *Paraṇi pŏḻivukaḷ.* Tirupati, 1972.
Richards, J. F., ed. *Kingship and Authority in South Asia.* Madison, 1978.
———, and V. N. Rao. "Banditry in Mughal India: Historical and Folk Perceptions." *IESHR* 17 (1980), 95-120.
Richman, Paula. "Religious Rhetoric in Maṇimekalai." Ph.D. dissertation, University of Chicago, 1982.
Robinson, Edward Jewitt. *Tales and Poems of South India.* London, 1885.
Roghair, Gene J. *The Epic of Palnāḍu: A Study and Translation of Palnāṭi Virula Katha.* Oxford, 1982.
Rosenfield, John M. *The Dynastic Arts of the Kushans.* Berkeley and Los Angeles, 1967.
Rossetti, Carlo Giuseppe. "The Ideology of Banditry." *Man* n.s. 17 (1982), 158-60.
Ruben, Walter. *Kālidāsa, Die menschliche Bedeutung seiner Werke.* Berlin, 1956.
Sachs, Arieh. *Sheqiyat haletz (The Prankster's Decline).* Jerusalem, 1978.
Sandall-Forgue, Stella. *Le gītāgovinda: Tradition et innovation dans le kāvya.* Stockholm, 1977.
Sathyanatha Aiyar. *History of the Nayaks of Madurai.* Madras, 1924.
Schuyler, M., Jr. "The Origin of the Vidūṣaka and the Employment of this Character in the Plays of Harṣadeva." *JAOS* 20 (1899), 338-40.
Scott-Kemball, J. *Javanese Shadow Puppets.* London, 1970.
Seltmann, Friedrich. "Schattenspiel in Mysore und Andhra Pradeś." *BKI* 127 (1971), 428-89.
———. "The Religious Functions of the Bhāgavata in the Shadow-play of South India (Karnataka-Orissa-Kerala) and of the Dalang in Indonesia and South-East Asia." Paper delivered at the conference on Asian Puppet Theatre, School of Oriental and African Studies, London, 1979.
Sheik Ali, B. "Ideal of Kingship in the Hoysala Period." In B. Sheik Ali, ed., *The Hoysala Dynasty*, pp. 20-27. Mysore, 1972.
Shulman, David. "The Cliché as Ritual and Instrument: Iconic Puns in Kampaṉ's Irāmāvatāram." *Numen* 25 (1978), 135-55.
———. "On the Prehistory of Tyāgarāja-Śiva at Tiruvārūr." *Art and Archaeology Research Papers* 13 (1978), 55-58. (1978a)
———. "The Serpent and the Sacrifice: An Anthill Myth from Tiruvārūr." *HR* 18 (1978), 107-37. (1978b)
———. "Divine Order and Divine Evil in the Tamil Tale of Rāma." *JAS* 38 (1979), 651-69.
———. Murukaṉ, the Mango, and Ekāmbareśvara-Śiva: Fragments of a Tamil Creation Myth?" *IIJ* 21 (1979), 27-40. (1979a)

Shulman, David. "Sītā and Śatakaṇṭharāvaṇa in a Tamil Folk Narrative." *Journal of Indian Folkloristics* 2 (1979), 1-26. (1979b)

———. "Mirrors and Metaphors in a Medieval Tamil Classic." *Hebrew University Studies in Literature* 8 (1980), 195-237.

———. "On South Indian Bandits and Kings." *IESHR* 17 (1980), 283-306. (1980a)

———. *Tamil Temple Myths: Sacrifice and Divine Marriage in the South Indian Śaiva Tradition.* Princeton, 1980. (1980b)

———. "The Green Goddess of Tirumullaivāyil." *East and West* 30 (1980), 117-31. (1980c)

———. "The Crossing of the Wilderness: Landscape and Myth in the Tamil Story of Rāma." *Acta Orientalia* 42 (1981), 21-54.

———. "The Enemy Within: Idealism and Dissent in South Indian Hinduism." In S. N. Eisenstadt, R. Kahane, and D. Shulman, eds., *Orthodoxy, Heterodoxy and Dissent in India*, pp. 11-55. Berlin, New York, and Amsterdam, 1984.

———. "Muslim Popular Literature in Tamil: The *Tamīmaṉcāri mālai*." In Yohanan Friedmann, ed., *Islam in Asia*. Vol. I: *South Asia*, pp. 174-207. Jerusalem, 1984. (1984a)

Siegel, Lee. *Fires of Love/Waters of Peace: Passion and Renunciation in Indian Culture*. Honolulu, 1983.

Singer, Isaac Bashevis. *Gimpel the Fool*. New York, 1957.

Singer, Milton, ed. *Krishna: Myths, Rites and Attitudes*. 1966, reprinted Chicago, 1971.

Sivaramamurti, C. *The Chola Temples Thañjāvūr, Gaṅgaikoṇḍacholapuram, and Dārāsuram*. New Delhi, 1973.

Smith, Brian K. "Thoughts on the Vedic Sacrifice: Ritual Structure and Its Meanings." Manuscript, 1979.

Smith, John D. "The Two Sanskrit Epics." In A. T. Hatto, ed., *Traditions of Heroic and Epic Poetry*. Vol. I, pp. 48-78. London, 1980.

———. "The Rajasthani Folk-Mahābhārata." Paper delivered at the conference on Oral Epics in India, Madison, June 1982.

Somasundaram Pillai, J. M. *The Great Temple at Tanjore*. 2nd ed. Tanjore, 1958.

Sontheimer, Günther-Dietz. *Birobā, Mhaskobā und Khaṇḍobā: Ursprung, Geschichte und Umwelt von Pastoralen Gottheiten in Mahārāṣṭra*. Wiesbaden, 1976.

South Indian Inscriptions. Madras, 1890—.

Speaight, George. *Punch and Judy, A History*. Boston, 1970.

Spencer, George W. "Religious Networks and Royal Influence in Eleventh-Century South India." *JESHO* 12 (1969), 42-56.

———. "Royal Initiative under Rajaraja I." *IESHR* 7 (1970), 431-42.

———. "The Politics of Plunder: The Cholas in Eleventh-Century Ceylon." *JAS* 35 (1976), 405-19.

———. "Sons of the Sun: The Solar Genealogy of a Chola King." *Asian Profile* 10 (1982), 81-95.

———. *The Politics of Expansion: The Chola Conquest of Sri Lanka and Sri Vijaya*. Madras, 1983.

Sreekantaiya, T. N. *"Imagination" in Indian Poetics and other Literary Studies.* Mysore, 1980.

Staal, F. "Über die Idee der Toleranz im Hinduismus." *Kairos* 1 (1959), 215-18.

Stein, Burton. "The Economic Function of a Medieval Hindu Temple." *JAS* 19 (1960), 163-76.

———. "Medieval Coromandel Trade," in John Parker, ed., *Merchants and Scholars*, pp. 49-62. Minneapolis, 1965.

———. "Integration of the Agrarian System of South India." In R. E. Frykenberg, ed., *Land Control and Social Structure in Indian History*, pp. 175-216. Madison, 1969.

———. "The State and the Agrarian Order in Medieval South India: A Historiographical Critique." In Burton Stein, ed., *Essays on South India*, pp. 64-91. Delhi, 1975.

———. "The Segmentary State in South Indian History." In Fox, ed. (1977), pp. 3-51.

———. "Circulation and the Historical Geography of Tamil Country." *JAS* 37 (1977), 7-26. (1977a)

———. "All the King's *Mana*: Perspectives on Kingship in Medieval South India." In Richards, ed. (1978), pp. 115-67.

———, ed. *South Indian Temples: An Analytical Reconsideration*. New Delhi, 1978. (1978a)

———. *Peasant, State and Society in Medieval South India*. Delhi, 1980.

Steiner, George. Review of Bakhtin (1981). *Times Literary Supplement*, July 17, 1981, p. 799.

Stern, Henri. "Power in Traditional India: Territory, Caste and Kinship in Rajasthan." In Fox, ed. (1977), pp. 52-78.

Sternbach, Ludwik. *Gaṇikā-vṛtta-saṅgraha. Texts on Courtezans in Classical Sanskrit*. Hoshiarpur, 1953.

Subrahmanya Aiyar, K. V., ed. *Travancore Archaeological Series*. Vol. III. Trivandrum, 1921.

Subramania Aiyar, A. V. *Tamil Studies, First Series*. Tirunelveli, 1969.

Subramanian, M. V. *Vyasa and Variations*. Madras, 1967.

Swain, Barbara. *Fools and Folly during the Middle Ages and the Renaissance*. New York, 1932.

Swami Sivananda. *Ten Upanisads with Notes and Commentary*. Shivanandanagar, 1973.

Syrkin, Alexander Y. "On the Behavior of the Fool for Christ's Sake." *HR* 22 (1982), 150-71.

Tambiah, S. J. *World Conqueror and World Renouncer*. Cambridge, 1976.

Tamil Lexicon. 7 vols. Madras, 1926-1939.

Taṇṭapāṇi Tecikar, Ca. *Tiruvārūr*. Tarumapuram, 1949.

Tapper, Bruce Elliot. "Andhra Shadow-Play Jesters: Meaning, Iconography, and History." Paper delivered at the conference on Asian Puppet Theatre, School of Oriental and African Studies, London, 1979.

Tarlekar, Ganesh Hari. *Studies in the Nāṭyaśāstra, with Special Reference to the Sanskrit Drama in Performance*. Delhi, 1975.

Tawney, C. H. See *Kathāsaritsāgara*.

Thapar, Romila. *Ancient Indian Social History: Some Interpretations*. New Delhi, 1978.

———. "State Formation in Early India." *International Social Science Journal* 32 (1980), 655-69.

Thompson, Stith. *Motif-Index of Folk Literature*. Revised edition. 6 vols. Bloomington, Indiana, 1955-1958.

Thurston, E. *Castes and Tribes of Southern India*. 7 vols. Madras, 1909.

Torrance, Robert M. *The Comic Hero*. Cambridge, Mass., 1978.

Trautmann, Thomas R. *Dravidian Kinship*. Cambridge, 1981.

Tripathi, Gaya Charan. "Nalakalevara: The Unique Ceremony of the 'Birth' and the 'Death' of the 'Lord of the World.' " In A. Eschmann, H. Kulke, and G. C. Tripathi, eds., *The Cult of Jagannath and the Regional Tradition of Orissa*, pp. 125-38. Delhi, 1978.

———. "The Worship of Kārtavīrya-Arjuna: On the Deification of a Royal Personage in India." *JRAS*, 1979, pp. 37-52.

Turner, Victor. *Dramas, Fields, and Metaphors*. Ithaca, 1974.

———. "Comments and Conclusions." In Babcock (1978), pp. 276-96.

———. *From Ritual to Theatre: The Human Seriousness of Play*. New York, 1982.

Ulanov, Ann, and Barry Ulanov. "The Clown Archetype." *Quadrant* 13 (1980), 4-27.

Unni, N. P. *Sanskrit Dramas of Kulasékhara: A Study*. Trivandrum, 1977.

van Buitenen, J.A.B. "On the Archaism of the Bhāgavata Purāṇa." In Milton Singer, ed. (1971), pp. 23-40.

———. See also *Mahābhārata* (1973-1978) and *Mṛcchakaṭika* (1971).

van den Hoek, A. W. "The Goddess of the Northern Gate: Cellattamman as the 'Divine Kṣatriya' of Madurai." *Asie du sud, traditions et changements*, p. 1-10. Sixth European Conference on Modern South Asian Studies, Paris, 1978.

Vaudevile, Ch. "Paṇḍharpūr—The City of Saints." In Buck and Yocum, eds. (1974), pp. 137-61.

Venkataraman, B. *Temple Art under the Chola Queens*. Faridabad, 1976.

von Stietencron, Heinrich. *Indische Sonnenpriester: Sāmba und die Śākadvīpīya-Brāhmaṇa*. Wiesbaden, 1966.

Waghorne, Joanne. "Sacral Kingship on the Borders of Orthodox India." Manuscript, 1980.

Walcot, Peter. "Cattle Raiding, Heroic Tradition, and Ritual: Greek Evidence," *HR* 18 (1979), 326-51.

Weber, Max. *The Religion of India*. Translated by Hans H. Gerth and Don Martindale. New York, 1958.

Welbon, G. R. See Hudson, Dennis.

Wells, Henry W. *The Classical Drama of India*. London, 1963.

Welsford, Enid. *The Fool, His Social and Literary History*. London, 1935.

Whitehead, Henry. *The Village Gods of South India*. 2nd ed. Calcutta, 1921.

Willeford, William. *The Fool and His Sceptre*. Evanston, Illinois, 1969.

Wilson, H. H. See *Viṣṇupurāṇa*.

Winther, Paul Christian. "Chambel River Dacoity: A Study of Banditry in North Central India." Ph.D. dissertation, Cornell University, 1972.

Wisse, Ruth R. *The Schlemiel as Modern Hero*. Chicago, 1971.

Yamaguchi, Masao. "Kingship as a System of Myth: An Essay in Synthesis." *Diogenes* 77 (1972), 43-70.

Yocum, Glenn, E. See Buck, Harry M. and Hudson, Dennis.

Zaehner, R. C. *Hinduism*. London, 1962.

Zimmer, H. *Kunstform und Yoga im indischen Kultbild*. Berlin, 1926.

———, translated by Gerard Chapple and James B. Lawson with J. Michael McKnight. *Artistic Form and Yoga in the Sacred Images of India*. Princeton, 1984.

———. Review of Śūlapāṇi's *Caturaṅgadīpikā*. *Polski Biuletyn Orientalistyczny* (Warsaw) 1 (1937), 90-92.

———. *Hindu Medicine*. Baltimore, 1948.

———. *Philosophies of India*. 1951, reprinted Princeton, 1969.

Zvelebil, Kamil Veith. *The Poets of the Powers*. London, 1973.

———. *The Smile of Murugan, on Tamil Literature of South India*. Leiden, 1973. (1973a)

———. *Tamil Literature*. Wiesbaden, 1974. In J. Gonda, ed., *A History of Indian Literature*.

———. *Tamil Literature*. Leiden, 1975. Handbuch der Orientalistik.

Index

Library of Congress Cataloging in Publication Data

Shulman, David Dean, 1949-
The king and the clown in South Indian myth and poetry.

Bibliography: p.
Includes index.
1. India, South—Politics and government.
2. India, South—Kings and rulers—Mythology.
3. Clowns—India, South—Mythology. 4. Mythology, Hindu. 5. Indic literature—History and criticism.
6. Kings and rulers in literature. 7. Clowns in literature. I. Title.
JQ200.Z9S657 1985 954'.8 85-42706
ISBN 0-691-05457-6